The Global Resistance Reader

In Genoa, riot police sent in to quell demonstrations against a summit of the G8 end up killing a young Italian activist; the Zapatistas organize resistance to the exploitation of their communities in Mexico; in Seattle, thousands take to the streets against the World Trade Organization and provide a huge shock to our global rulers; worldwide activism ensures that Third World debt becomes a key issue on the international stage; a former World Bank economist writes a best-selling critique of globalization; there are riots in the sleepy Swiss town of Geneva; a group of artists satirize images of global financial transactions; an anti-corporate analysis by a Canadian journalist becomes a surprise worldwide bestseller called *No Logo*. Something is happening...

The Global Resistance Reader provides the first comprehensive collection of work on the phenomenal rise of transnational social movements and resistance politics: from the visible struggles against the financial, economic and political authority of large international organizations such as the World Trade Organization, World Bank and International Monetary Fund, to the much less visible acts of resistance in everyday life. The conceptual debates, substantive themes and case studies have been selected to open up the idea of global resistance to interrogation and discussion by students and to provide a one-stop orientation for researchers, journalists, policymakers and activists.

Contributors include James Scott, Naomi Klein, Stephen Gill, Arundhati Roy and Saskia Sassen.

Louise Amoore is Lecturer in International Politics at the University of Newcastle. Her previous publications include *Globalization Contested: An International Political Economy of Work* (Manchester University Press, 2002). She is one of the series editors for the Routledge/RIPE Series in Global Political Economy.

The Global Resistance Reader

Edited by
Louise Amoore

Routledge
Taylor & Francis Group

LONDON AND NEW YORK

First published 2005
by Routledge
2 Park Square, Milton Park, Abingdon, Oxon OX14 4RN

Simultaneously published in the USA and Canada
by Routledge
270 Madison Ave, New York, NY 10016

Routledge is an imprint of the Taylor & Francis Group

British Library Cataloguing in Publication Data
A catalogue record for this book is available from the British Library

Library of Congress Cataloging in Publication Data
A catalog record for this book has been requested

ISBN 0–415–33583–3 (hbk)
ISBN 0–415–33584–1 (pbk)

This book is dedicated to my daughter Grace, who brings hope for a better future

Contents

Preface

This *Reader* should not be taken to be the definitive set of writings on global resistance. No such text could claim to be exhaustive in the sense of including all the key contributions that have been made to such an enduring and interdisciplinary debate. After all, where would we draw the parameters around the chosen texts? How would we justify the exclusion of alternative perspectives and examples? Instead, *The Global Resistance Reader* offers a range of avenues of inquiry that may be taken in opening up our understanding of the nature and sources of global resistance. Rather than offering a singular understanding of global resistance, then, the emphasis is placed on competing approaches and interpretations of global resistance. Perhaps inevitably, this has tended to foreground academic debates surrounding global resistance, though the assumed boundaries between academics, activists and citizens are called into question throughout.

The selection of texts for a reader, then, is a problematic process and one that can in no real sense claim to produce some form of representative sample of readings. In many ways the selected texts reflect my own interests in the relationship between globalization and the concept and practices of resistance, and in the interplay between the overt resistances we may see in the news media and the less visible everyday acts of dissent that are all around us. Of course, my own interest in global resistance is itself subject to ongoing interaction with other approaches. The discussions that have taken place in my under- and postgraduate classes on the politics of globalization and resistance have challenged and shaped the selection of texts for this *Reader*. Likewise, the formal and informal review processes for the *Reader* have stimulated questions that are now reflected in the chosen texts. Overall, the final texts have been selected on the grounds that they both reflect and stimulate an ongoing dialogue and debate about the theoretical understandings and practical political possibilities of global resistance. It is hoped that the *Reader* will be read and discussed by students in a similar spirit – one that emphasizes their own perceptions and experiences of global resistance.

Though those who have shaped the *Reader* in a broad sense are too numerous to mention by name, I am indebted to those who have offered advice and encouragement, and to a number of individuals who have read and commented specifically on the contents and commentaries. Colleagues and friends have responded to my requests for their 'favourite' resistance readings with good humour. My thanks to Randall Germain, Rorden Wilkinson, Marieke de Goede and Paul Langley. The comments of the anonymous academic referees used by Routledge have been invaluable in shaping and revising the *Reader*. I hope that I have done some justice to the thoughtful and incisive comment that was made at the proposal and draft stages. A special thanks to the contributors who have so generously supported this project by consenting to the inclusion of their texts in the volume, and by shaping its direction and content. Many of the contributors offered much more than their work, making suggestions and generally supporting the progress of the project. Many thanks to James Mittelman, Stephen Gill and Robin Balliger, whose enthusiasm for the project gave me renewed energy during the drafting, and to Janine Brodie and Marieke de Goede who contributed original works to the book. The enthusiasm and efficiency of the commissioning editor, Craig Fowlie, who first persuaded me of the need for this project, has been unwavering. Many thanks to all at Taylor and Francis/Routledge for their patience and dedication to the project. All reasonable steps were taken to secure permissions from copyright holders. In the rare cases where this was not practicable, we offer our apologies.

Finally, the research for the *Reader* could not have been completed without the love and support of my husband Paul. Thank you for reading drafts in the small hours, for suspending banners from bridges, and reminding me of who the subjects of global resistance really are.

Acknowledgements

The publishers would like to thank the following for permission to reproduce their work: Princeton University Press for James H. Mittelman and Christine B. N. Chin 'Conceptualizing Resistance to Globalization', in James H. Mittelman, *The Globalization Syndrome: Transformation and Resistance* (2000); Lawrence & Wishart for Antonio Gramsci, 'State and Civil Society', *The Prison Notebooks*, Quentin Hoare and Geoffrey Nowell Smith (eds and trans) (1971); Cambridge University Press for Robert W. Cox, 'Gramsci, Hegemony and International Relations: An Essay in Method' in Stephen Gill (ed.) *Gramsci, Historical Materialism and International Relations* (1993), originally published by *Millennium*; Henry Holt and Co. for Karl Polanyi, *The Great Transformation: The Political and Economic Origins of Our Time* (1957), excerpts from 'The Self-Regulating Market and the Fictitious Commodities'; Zed Books for Stephen Gill, 'Theorizing the Interregnum: The Double Movement and Global Politics in the 1990s', in Björn Hettne (ed.) *International Political Economy: Understanding Global Disorder* (1995); Yale University Press for James C. Scott, 'The Infrapolitics of Subordinate Groups', in *Domination and the Arts of Resistance: Hidden Transcripts* (1990); Cambridge University Press for Fantu Cheru, 'The Silent Revolution and the Weapons of the Weak: Transformation and Innovation from Below', in Stephen Gill and James H. Mittelman (eds) *Innovation and Transformation in International Studies* (1997); Penguin & Georges Borchardt Inc. for Michel Foucault, 'Method', in his *The Will to Knowledge: The History of Sexuality Volume 1* (1976/1998); Cambridge University Press for Roland Bleiker, 'Writing Human Agency After the Death of God' in *Popular Dissent, Human Agency and Global Politics* (2000); Cambridge University Press for Robert W. Cox, 'Civil Society at the Turn of the Millennium: Prospects for an Alternative World Order', *Review of International Studies*, 25: 1 (1999); Taylor & Francis for Richard Falk, 'Global Civil Society: Perspectives, Initiatives, Movements', *Oxford Development Studies*, 26: 1 (1998), http://www.tandf.co.uk/journals/carfax/13600818.html; *Millennium* for R. B. J. Walker, 'Social Movements/World Politics', *Millennium: Journal of International Studies*, 23: 3 (1994); *Millennium* for Stephen Gill, 'Toward a Postmodern Prince? The Battle in Seattle as a Moment in the New Politics of Globalisation', *Millennium: Journal of International Studies*, 29: 1 (2000); The Merlin Press for Naomi Klein, 'Farewell to the 'End of History': Organization and Vision in Anti-Corporate Movements', *Socialist Register 2002*; The Merlin Press for André C. Drainville 'Québec City 2001 and the Making of Transnational Subjects', *Socialist Register 2002*; Verso for Michael Hardt, 'Porto Alegre: Today's Bandung?', *New Left Review* 14 (2002); Routledge for Mark Rupert, 'The New World Order: Passive Revolution or Transformative Process', *Ideologies of Globalization: Contending Visions of a New World Order* (2000), excerpts from 'Passive Revolution or Transformative Process'; University of South Carolina Press for

Marianne H. Marchand, 'Some Theoretical "Musings" about Gender and Resistance', in R. Teske and M. A. Tétreault (eds) *Feminist Approaches to Social Movements, Community, and Power* (2000); The Perseus Books Group for V. Spike Peterson and Anne Sisson Runyan, *Global Gender Issues* (1993), excerpts from 'The Politics of Resistance: Women as Nonstate, Antistate, and Transstate Actors'; Verso for Kim Moody, *Workers in a Lean World* (1997), excerpts from 'Toward an International Social-Movement Unionism; The Merlin Press for Beverly J. Silver and Giovanni Arrighi, 'Workers North and South', *Socialist Register* (2001); Routledge for Kamala Kempadoo, 'Globalizing Sex Workers' Rights', in Kamala Kempadoo and Jo Doezema (eds) *Global Sex Workers: Rights, Resistance, and Redefinition* (1998); Perseus Press for Arturo Escobar, 'Culture, Economics, and Politics in Latin American Social Movements: Theory and Research', in Arturo Escobar and Sonia Alvarez (eds) *The Making of Social Movements in Latin America* (1992); *New Left Review* for Ann Pettifor 'The Economic Bondage of Debt – and the Birth of a New Movement', *New Left Review* 230 (1998); Palgrave for Cyril I. Obi, 'Globalization and Local Resistance: The Case of Shell versus the Ogoni', in Barry K. Gills (ed.) *Globalization and the Politics of Resistance* (2000); HarperCollins Publishers for Arundhati Roy, 'Power Politics', in *The Algebra of Infinite Justice* (2002); Routledge for Paul Ekins, *A New World Order: Grassroots Movements for Global Change*, excerpts from 'Environmental Regeneration' (1992); State University of New York Press for Paul Wapner, 'Environmental Activism and World Civic Politics', in *Environmental Activism and World Civic Politics* (1996); *The Guardian* for George Monbiot, 'Stronger than Ever', *The Guardian*, January 28, 2003; Bellwether Publishing for Manuel Castells, 'Grassrooting the Space of Flows', *Urban Geography* 20: 4 (1999); Sage Publications for Saskia Sassen, 'Digital Networks and the State: Some Governance Questions', *Theory, Culture and Society*, 17: 4 (2000); Yale University Press for James C. Scott, 'Beyond the War of Words: Cautious Resistance and Calculated Conformity', in *Weapons of the Weak: Everyday Forms of Peasant Resistance* (1985); Cambridge University Press for Roland Bleiker, *Popular Dissent, Human Agency and Global Politics*, excerpts from 'Political Boundaries, Poetic Transgressions' (2000); Autonomedia: http://www. autonomedia.org for Robin Balliger, 'Sounds of Resistance', in Ron Sakolsky and Fred Wei-han Ho (eds), *Sounding Off: Music as Subversion/Resistance/Revolution* (1995); HarperCollins Publishers for Naomi Klein, *No Logo* excerpts from 'Culture Jamming: Ads Under Attack' (2000).

Every effort has been made to contact authors and copyright holders of works reprinted in *The Global Resistance Reader*, but this has not been possible in every case. Please contact the publisher if you have information regarding the copyright position of such material and this will be remedied in future editions.

Introduction

Global resistance – global politics

Louise Amoore

Only a few decades ago, a collection such as this, with a focus on the global nature of resistances, would have been problematic to compile. Not because social protest, dissent and social movements were not highly significant in the past, but because attempts to understand resistances tended not to attend to the intricate connections between situated struggles. By contrast, in recent times the images, slogans and practices of global resistance have become almost commonplace, perhaps even accepted as an integral part of the intensified processes of globalization. The lines of 'Robocop-style' police protecting the entrance to Niketown in downtown Seattle in December 1999; the coining of the slogan 'another world is possible' at the inaugural meeting of the World Social Forum at Porto Alegre in January 2001; or Jonah Peretti's globally circulated e-mail correspondence with Nike on his request to have 'sweatshop' stitched into his Nike 'I-D' trainers in February 2001.[1] These are just some of the more visible faces of global resistance – the instances that we all recognize as somehow representing a rebuttal to the prevailing logics of globalization. We tend now to clearly identify street demonstrations, protests and internet activists' websites, for example, with a form of trans-border 'anti-globalization'. Yet, resistances may not be quite so easily classified in this way. Much less visible have been the ordinary and commonplace acts of resistance that may blend into peoples' everyday lives so that they become almost indistinguishable from coping strategies, compliance, co-option or acceptance. Perhaps, the first question to ask in our studies of global resistance is 'how do we know global resistance when we see it?' This *Reader* has been put together precisely to facilitate a questioning of what we think we know about global resistance, and to encourage thought about what we do not see and why our prevailing knowledge may leave aspects of global resistance in deep shadow.

In the spirit of the *Reader* as a whole, then, I will begin by introducing a number of questions and problematics which arise at various points in the texts that follow. As with most research themes in social science, global resistance does not simply appear to us as a neat and ready-made parcel of ideas and practices with clear boundaries. Rather, the parameters are always drawn and re-drawn according to what we understand to be happening in the world, how we choose to look at it, and the surfacing of new challenges to our thinking. Rather than set solid boundaries, I prefer to outline parameters that remain permeable, taking the form of open questions that may provoke a range of responses. Put simply, the introduction will explore the 'what', 'why', 'who' and 'how' of global resistances.

Each question opens up a number of possible avenues of inquiry and further questions for discussion:

1   What is global resistance?
    • Why are there multiple definitions and meanings associated with global resistance?
    • In what ways do theories of power and politics shape competing understandings of the scope, sources and effects of resistances?
    • In what ways do resistances challenge our efforts to understand them as they emerge in new contexts?
2   Why study global resistance?
    • How should we understand the relationship between globalization(s) and resistance(s)?
    • How have past approaches to understanding resistances been reinterpreted to speak to contemporary themes?
    • What are the concrete resistances emerging around, for example, the expansion of financial globalization, the intensification of global production networks and the globalization of cultural flows?
3   Who speaks?
    • To whom do we refer when we discuss the politics of global resistance?
    • Can global resistances be effectively captured by terms such as a global civil society or an international public sphere?
    • Can we firmly fix the agency of global resistances with a particular group or named actor? What are the implications of this for marginalized voices?
4   How is resistance expressed?
    • How do we recognize resistances as they are expressed in social and political life? Do we acknowledge some forms of resistance more readily than others?
    • Is it possible to make clear distinctions between, for example, practices of resistance and compliance, or between apparently global or local sites of resistance?
    • In what ways are everyday forms of global resistance expressed?

What is global resistance?

Theorizing global resistance confronts the difficulty that, as a concept and a set of practices, it does itself resist being singularly defined or pinned down. While for some, the incorporation and subordination of people within global capitalism has produced the possibility for 'transnational democratizing projects' (Rupert, 2000: 92), for others, resistances are beset by the difficulties of 'forging private troubles into public issues' in an increasingly individualized world (Bauman, 1999: 7). Understandings of the meanings of global resistance, together with perceptions of the scope and possibility for concrete resistances, are shaped by competing views of the world. Global resistance is, by its nature, an ambiguous, amorphous concept that derives its multiple meanings from concrete contexts – from peoples, places, images, sounds and voices. Indeed, it is common to find an animate metaphor used to depict the mobile and organic quality of the social movements that appear as constitutive of global resistances. Rob Walker describes social movements as 'but mosquitos on the evening breeze, irritants to those who claim maturity and legitimacy at the centres of political life' (see Walker in Part 2), and Fantu Cheru depicts 'an army of termites eating away the wooden structure of a house inch by inch' (see Cheru in Part 1). The effect is to give the impression of an organic body made up of smaller individuals whose barely perceptible actions are nonetheless damaging. We can see here echoes of Rudyard Kipling's portrayal of resistance in *A Pict Song*:

We are the worm in the wood!
We are the rot at the root!
We are the taint in the blood!
We are the thorn in the foot!

Mistletoe killing an oak-
Rats knawing cables in two-
Moths making holes in a cloak-
How they must love what they do!

Yet, at the same time as resistances have been depicted as having a mobile and organic quality, specific forms of global resistance have also been defined instrumentally by a constituency of non-governmental organizations (NGOs), governments and international organizations. The World Bank, for example, outlines its guidelines for consulting with civil society organizations, describing this process as an 'arena in which people come together to pursue the interests they hold in common – not for profit or the exercise of political power, but because they care enough about something to take political action' (2000: 5). Here, global resistance takes on a very specific and benign meaning in the form of a potential global civil society that can be usefully invited to 'counterbalance' the neoliberal institutions of global governance. Similarly, in his presentation to the World Trade Organization (WTO), European Trade Commissioner Pascal Lamy argued that: 'we need a broad public debate about the way in which the global trading system should develop, and NGOs obviously have a contribution to make to this debate' (WTO, 2001: 1). So, while in practice global resistances continually challenge our efforts to understand and explain them as they emerge in new contexts, they are simultaneously being reincorporated into a global governance agenda. On the one hand, then, we have a politicized sense of global resistance as constituted through ever-changing political and social practices. On the other, we find a somewhat neutralized or depoliticized sense of global resistance as identifiable with specific groups that can be incorporated in order to 'give globalization a human face' (Rupert in Part 2).

The contested nature of global resistances means that there is a need to consider the meanings we attribute to global resistance always in relation to power and to politics. As Part 1 of the *Reader* reveals, competing accounts of global resistance tend to have their differences located in specific understandings of what power means, how it is exercised, and what is the nature of politics and political life. In reading and discussing these texts a key question to raise is this: how are power and politics understood by this commentator? In what ways does this shape their view of the scope, sources and effects of resistances? Of course, theories of power and politics are themselves always situated in real lived experiences, observations and interpretations. The texts in this *Reader* have been chosen so as to illustrate the importance of the relationship between theories and practices of global resistance. In this sense, the theoretical consideration of global resistance should never appear as 'abstract' but always as situated in the world we see around us. As Thompson once put it: 'The real is not "out there" and thought within the quiet lecture theatre of our heads "inside here" ' (1978: 211). Indeed, even where the *Reader* draws upon traditions of thought about resistance, the emphasis is on how and why these texts are being reinterpreted to shed light on contemporary resistances, and on what is revealed in terms of actual political practices of resistance.

Why study global resistance?

The concept of globalization has, for some considerable time now, established a grip on the social sciences and on wider societal perceptions of dynamics of restructuring and change. The literature on the processes and problematics of globalization is truly vast and I do not propose to rehearse the debates here.[2] However, though the idea of globalization received much attention in academic and media circles from the 1980s, there was initially relatively little written on what we might call its 'discontents' – the struggles and tensions that also seemed to take on a trans-border quality (Sassen, 1998; Stiglitz, 2002). From around the mid-1990s, a series of apparently disparate and localized resistances and protests – from the MOSOP struggle in Nigeria (Obi in Part 3), to the Zapatistas of the Chiapas, from Seattle, Washington DC, Genoa and Quebec City, to the coping strategies of those gripped by the 1997 financial crises – began to be observed and studied as though they were some-how intimately interconnected. It is not that these instances of resistance mark some funda-mental watershed in world politics, nor that they are necessarily a direct product of globalization, nor indeed that dissent from prevailing sources of power has not been evident throughout human history. Rather, the politics of these resistances has come to be floodlit by a broader set of connections to globalization and the oft-cited neoliberal restructuring strategies of states, multinational corporations and international organizations. A further question to foreground in our discussion, then, is why it is that contemporary times draw our eye to the ideas and practices of resistance. In what ways do contemporary patterns of resis-tance either confound or reaffirm historical themes seen in, for example, the suffragette move-ment or the civil rights movement? Why study something we might call *global* resistance?

The nature of the relationship between globalization and resistance is, of course, a further source of dispute and debate. As I discuss in Part 1, theorists draw on a number of traditions in seeking to explain the interplay between globalization and resistance. For those who draw on the tradition established by Karl Polanyi, for example, we are witnessing a necessary 'counter movement' as societies seek to protect themselves from the global extension of the market economy into their lives (Mendell and Salée, 1991; cf. Bernard, 1997; Birchfield, 1999; Lacher, 1999). In a similar framing of the relationship, those who draw on Gramsci's writings understand globalization in terms of the hegemony of neoliberalism that has provoked a series of crises and a counter-hegemonic movement that seeks redress (Gill and Cox in Part 2; cf. Arrighi, 1993; Hoogvelt, 2001). By contrast, many feminists tend to see a very different relationship between globalization and resistance. They emphasize the particular experiences of women in the global restructuring of states, firms and societies. As public spaces are privatized, as welfare systems are retrenched, as production moves to the 'offshore' sites of export processing zones (EPZs), and as the effects of structural adjustment begin to bite in the developing world, it may be more localized practices of resistance that are of most signifi-cance (Marchand in Part 3). Indeed, for those drawing on a Foucauldian reading of resis-tance, practices of resistance cannot be readily ascribed to spatial locations such as the 'national', 'global' or 'local'. As Roland Bleiker describes it, struggles 'are not limited to established spheres of sovereignty. They are neither domestic nor international' (2000: 7).

Defining the extent and nature of the globalization–resistance relation, then, is both controversial and contested. The themes that run through this debate are clearly numerous, readers will be able to think of many more in their own discussions, nevertheless I will discuss some that have become central. First, processes of financial globalization have extended banking and financial discipline into many aspects of social life around the world (Leyshon and Thrift, 1997). The controversies surrounding these processes have exposed a number of sites of struggle and resistance. The institutions of the World Bank and IMF, for example, have become the focus for those seeking to draw attention to the inequalities and exclusions of global finance (Rupert in Part 2). Indeed, former chief economist at the World Bank, Joseph Stiglitz, and legendary speculator George Soros became leading critics and commentators on the unstable and inequitable forces of global financial markets (Soros, 1998; Stiglitz, 2002). As the implications of the growth of third world debt and a series of financial crises began to unfold in the late 1990s, movements such as Jubilee 2000 and ATTAC, for example, sought to challenge the global financial system, campaigning for policy reforms (Pettifor in Part 3). But it is not only in opposition to global financial institutions and the casino-like qualities of the financial system that we find the stirrings of resistance. The exclusionary effects of the contemporary financial markets have led social groups to develop alternative systems of financial exchange. Local exchange trading systems (LETS), for example, operate outside the formal economy, usually on the basis of an exchange in skills and tasks between people within a local community. There has been much debate as to whether these alternative economies, along with others such as credit unions or microcredit, can be considered instances of resistance to the global economy (Douthwaite, 1996; Pacione, 1997). The issue of whether daily coping strategies can also constitute resistances is considered in depth in Part 4.

Closely related to the tensions surrounding the extension of global financial markets into the fabric of societies, is the second theme I wish to draw out for discussion – the globalization of production. There is perhaps no sphere of globalization so fiercely contested as the trans-border power now exercised by multinational corporations (Klein, 2000; Sklair, 2001). The global explosion of production networks and supply chains, and the reliance of economies and societies on attracting foreign direct investment, have led to struggles surrounding the environment (Roy in Part 3), labour and work (Moody in Part 3), and development (Obi in Part 3). Widespread opposition to the OECD's Multilateral Agreement on Investment (MAI), and to the WTO's General Agreement on Trade in Services (GATS), for example, illustrate the tensions surrounding the exercise of private corporate authority over states and societies. Movements such as Corporatewatch focus their campaigns on the actions of specific MNCs, particularly where they find the use of child labour or other unprotected workers. They also participate in campaigns with a wider constituency, such as the pressure exerted on the pharmaceutical companies to relinquish their intellectual property rights over HIV/AIDS drugs supplied to developing countries.[3] But it is not only the large scale campaigns that constitute sources of resistance within global production. The experiences of women, for example, suggest that the implications of trans-border production have a wider resonance – in, for example, the growth of the global sex industry (Kempadoo in Part 3) and the globalized garment sector (Hale and Shaw, 2001). Though, as you will see from Part 3, many of the resistances in these spheres tend to be localized and everyday, they also make up elements of a wider set of resistances, such as those represented by as the Self-Employed Women's Association (SEWA) and Homenet.[4]

Finally, in this discussion of the relationship between globalization and resistance I raise the themes of technology and culture. Communications and transportation technologies and the media, in particular, have become significant sites of struggle in the global political economy. For some commentators the globalization, or indeed Americanization, of culture has become an inexorable force transforming all societies and cultures in its path (Barber, 1996; cf. Ritzer, 1996). Others, however, identify a process of cultural hybridization in which indigenous or ethnic or religious identities resist the onslaught of global brands, images and lifestyles (Appadurai, 1996). In this understanding of cultural globalization there are numerous contradictions that open up spaces for the affirmation of identity or the expression of alternative ideas and ways of living. This may take the form of, for example, poetry or music that challenges dominant ideas (Bleiker and Balliger in Part 4), or indeed the translation of advertising images into political statements as in 'adbusting' (Klein in Part 4). Of course resistance in this sphere displays many faces. On the one hand, for example, campaigns such as No Borders seek to support the identities and human rights of migrants and displaced peoples.[5] On the other hand, we are simultaneously seeing a resurgence of xenophobic nationalism and neo-facist groups who seek to resist perceived threats to their identity or nationality. Here we find another key question that will no doubt resurface in your studies and discussions. Is it possible to unambiguously identify and distinguish between emancipatory or positive resistances on the one hand, and discriminatory or negative resistances on the other?

Who speaks?

A central question addressed by the *Reader* is to whom we refer when talking about the politics of resistance. There are many phrases coined to capture the human agents of resistance. The term 'global civil society', for example, has become a shorthand means of depicting 'a supranational sphere of social and political participation' (Anheier *et al.*, 2001).[6] Similarly, both academic commentators and international organizations tend to name particular organizations or movements in order to explain a form of civil collective agency. The Commission on Global Governance, for example, identifies 'women's groups, trade unions, chambers of commerce, farming or housing cooperatives, religion-based organizations, and so on' (1995: 32). Scholar of globalization, Jan Aart Scholte includes:

> academic institutes, community-based organisations, consumer protection bodies, criminal syndicates, development cooperation groups, environmental campaigns, ethnic lobbies, charitable foundations, farmers' groups, human rights advocates, labour unions, relief organisations, peace activists, professional bodies, religious institutions, women's networks, youth campaigns and more.
>
> (2000: 277)

It seems that to give a name to a specific group or movement is a means of locating a particular struggle or campaign with a bounded agent or group of interests. Though studies of global resistance and social movements have done much to transcend traditional state-centred approaches to international relations, the remnants of this tradition continue to influence our understanding. There remains a tendency to look for identifiable and atomized agents, and to place resistance politics in opposition to a sovereign state or fixed world order. 'The capacity to wield power as a resource over other agents', writes David Campbell, becomes 'an important proviso of agency' (1996: 11). The problem, of course, is that matters are rarely so clear-cut in the concrete practices of movements and resistances.

When studying and discussing global resistances, then, we should ask ourselves whether agency can be unequivocally ascribed to a named group or movement. Arjun Appadurai cautions against looking for fixed forms of agency in resistance politics, arguing that they 'do not capture the mobility and malleability of those creative forms of social life that are localized transit points for mobile forms of civic and civil life' (2001: 4). To explore an example, trade union resistances have begun to be explained through the rubric of 'global social movement unionism', suggesting that institutionalized labour groups now speak for a wider constituency (Moody in Part 3). Indeed, the Director General of the International Labor Organization, Juan Somavia, offers transnational union networks as 'the most organised actors and the most articulate voices in society' (1999: 6). Though there is little doubt that cooperation with NGOs has broadened the agenda of trade union politics, we should perhaps ask whether this also serves to fix worker resistances within an exclusive frame. As you can see from the contributions to the *Reader* by Kempadoo and Brodie, it is not always the case that marginalized voices can be heard within this frame. There is always difficulty, then, in identifying and claiming a 'we' in global resistance politics. Who is speaking and on whose behalf do they claim to speak? Can collective agencies be mapped onto class solidarities, or do they more closely mirror ethnic, gendered or racial identities? I am not offering a solution to these conundrums here, but rather suggesting why it may be that we recognize some resistances more readily than others.

How is resistance expressed?

If, as I have suggested, global resistances are more transient and elusive than we might first acknowledge, then a central question must be how we recognize resistances as they are expressed in social and political life. The problem is put clearly by James Scott:

> For a social science attuned to the relatively open politics of liberal democracies and to loud, headline-grabbing protests, demonstrations and rebellions, the circumspect struggle waged daily by subordinate groups is, like infrared rays, beyond the visible end of the spectrum.
>
> (1990: 183, see Part 1 of the *Reader*)

The suggestion is that we tend to recognize resistances to take a particular form, and that in doing this we increase the visibility of these modes of politics whilst simultaneously rendering other modes invisible. Put simply, 'politics' becomes synonymous with the instrumental actions of sovereign individuals or states, and thus becomes narrowly delimited and far removed from the messy and contingent practices of everyday life. Conventionally, political and social thought has functioned around a series of binaries: state/non-state; global/local; resistance/compliance; individual/collective, for example. These oppositions have dominated understandings of the politics of resistance, with the effect that resistance is either understood to be 'non-state', often in opposition to state power, or clearly fixed in a spatial location of the 'global' or the 'local'. The texts in this *Reader* have been selected so as to open up some discussion around the ways in which concrete resistances transcend many of the binaries that are often used to explain them.

Though resistance is characteristically understood to be expressed through the politics of protest, demonstration, public statement or declaration, then, the more mundane gestures of everyday life reveal significant sites of political struggle. James Scott refers to these gestures as the 'hidden transcripts', the 'offstage discourse of the powerless' that should not be seen as poor substitutes for 'real resistance' (Scott in Part 1). Similarly, Cynthia Enloe (1990) adapts the feminist slogan of the 1970s that 'the personal is political' to argue that 'the personal is international', that ordinary and everyday lives are no way distinct from a sphere we choose to call 'global' or 'international'. The texts in Part 4 are selected precisely to explore the expression of resistance through, for example, language and communication, music and poetry, images and artwork. Manuel Castells' discussion of the use of the Internet, for example, illustrates the problem with ascribing a clear global or local spatiality to resistances. He explores how the relatively invisible politics of Mexican women's groups concretely informed the Zapatistas' use of the Internet to communicate their struggle. While the Zapatistas have become emblematic of a politics that we call 'global' resistance, the politics of the women's groups are viewed as occupying the margins of resistance politics (Castells in Part 4).

If the more covert politics discussed in Part 4 have a mode of resistance in common, it is perhaps that they seek to expose and chip away at the dominant ways of thinking about the order of social and political life. They may, for example, make comedy of a particular system or order, ridiculing its practices and opening up the space to see things differently. In her essay on music as resistance, Robin Balliger argues that music can be 'a threat to hegemonic forms of discourse', in particular a challenge to capitalist consumerism that seeks to commodify pleasure (Balliger in Part 4). In her discussion of the performance art that has become 'adbusting', Naomi Klein makes the similar point that a successful 'culture jam' provokes reflection on the concealed politics of the original advertising campaign. Rather than offering a directly opposing image or message, it reveals 'what is hiding beneath the layers of advertising euphemisms' (Klein in Part 4). The assumed boundary between resistance and compliance, then, is revealed to be insecure and contradictory. Music can simultaneously offer a vehicle for the making of compliant global consumers, while also opening a space for dissent and alternatives to global consumerism. The use of advertising billboards and slogans to express resistance ultimately uses and reinforces corporate styles and symbols at the same time as it challenges them. Indeed, many global corporations have reappropriated adbuster symbolism for their own campaigns so that the boundaries become ever more unclear. Nike, for example, used the slogan 'our most offensive boot to date' to advertise a football boot, giving the offensive position on a football field an ambiguous meaning that could have been given by their critics.

James Scott summarizes the problem of how resistance is expessed when he says that 'open collective protest is rare' (see Part 4). His study of peasant resistances reveals how arson, petty theft, poaching, sabotage and boycotts are the 'garden variety resistances' seen in everyday life. Where we do see the instances of open collective protest or the loud headline-grabbing demonstrations, these are but the ripples on the surface of a deeper and more diffuse pattern of struggles that may often be about getting by or coping. In this sense, the less visible practices of resistance are not meaningfully separable from the overt expressions, but rather they may form the language, structures and meanings that make the grand gestures possible. While the *Reader* provides texts on the more overt 'hand to hand' resistances that we have come to know shorthand as 'Seattle' or 'Porto Alegre', it also attends to the whispered dissent of more 'behind the hand' resistances.

Using the *Reader*

The overall point of my introductory comments is that global resistance is not simply an uncontested term used to describe the activities of groups who, for a variety of reasons, seek to challenge globalization. A central guiding objective of this *Reader* is to emphasize the contested and contradictory nature of the concept, while not undermining its political importance or contemporary significance. The questions that I have raised here are in no sense intended to enclose or limit the discussions and themes that may arise from the texts that follow. The parameters that I have outlined provide one possible route into the study of global resistances, but it should be remembered that this is a debate that is in constant flux. Any attempt to freeze the debate on the politics of global resistance, even momentarily, suffers from the problem that it may underplay the transience of resistance practices. The sections that follow are thus organized so as to open up the questions I have outlined to further debate and discussion.

This *Reader* is divided into four parts, each of which broadly maps onto one of the questions discussed above. Part 1 addresses the *what* question by exploring the conceptualization of resistance. The section introduces the concept through a series of classic texts on the nature of dissent and resistance. These classic texts are paired with contemporary writings that employ the concept of resistance in a contemporary global context. Taken together, the readings in Part 1 provide the theoretical and conceptual grounding for the volume.

Part 2 then provides an overview of debates as to the sources of contemporary global resistance. In many ways it opens up the question of *why* we study resistance in a global context. The major themes include: the potential political power of social movements; the role of movements in contesting aspects of the world order; the situated resistances of Seattle, Porto Alegre and Québec City; and the attempt by international organizations to 'humanize' globalization in response. As a whole, the section will enable the reader to explore competing interpretations of the so-called 'anti-globalization' movements.

Part 3 explores *who* is represented by specific instances of global resistance. The emphasis is on actual case studies of the practices and politics of resistance in four spheres: gender and women's movements; work and labour; debt and development; and environment. The readings have been selected to encourage thought about the dynamics of constructing solidarities among diverse social groups and distinctive identities.

The final part of this *Reader* explores the expression of globalized practices through the ordinary acts of everyday life. In many ways this section responds to the question of *how* resistance is expressed by focusing on less clearly visible acts of resistance. The readings cover the technologies of resistance, focusing on the Internet; resistance in the context of ridicule and carnival; rural and peasant resistances; and the use of music and performance art as an expression of dissent.

In my experience students push this debate further, challenge it through their own critical reflections, and indeed through their own experiences of resistance. Global resistance is constantly changing shape, not only on the streets, on the websites, or in academic fora, but also in the classroom (see Amoore and Langley, 2002; Drainville, 2003). During the writing of this *Reader* my own students have produced, among many examples, diaries of a summer of environmental activism in Canada; photographs of Thai women organizing against MNCs commodifying Jasmine rice; and accounts of interviews with Clean Clothes Campaign activists. It is hoped that the *Reader* has been left sufficiently open for the debate to continue to be shaped by our own engagements with the changing faces of global resistance politics.

Notes

1 For further details on these examples, *The Guardian* has an online archive of articles on the so-called 'Battle in Seattle', see a selection at www.guardian.co.uk/wto/article/0,2763,195956,00.html. For an overview of a recent World Social Forum meeting see www.portoalegre2003.org. The Clean Clothes Campaign provide a good illustrated account of Jonah Peretti's exchange with Nike at www.cleanclothes.org/companies/nike01-02-16htm

2 For a range of different approaches to the globalization debate, see Appadurai (2001); Inda and Rosaldo (2002); Scholte (2000) and Beck (2000).

3 See www.corporatewatch.org for further details of campaigns.
4 See www.sewa.org and www.homenetww.org.uk for further details on these organizations representing women working in the informal economy or from home.
5 See www.no-borders.co.uk for further details.
6 See also Pasha and Blaney (1998); Keane (2003) and Cox in Part 2.

References

Amoore, L. and Langley, P. (2002), 'Experiencing Globalization: Active Teaching and Learning in International Political Economy', *International Studies Perspectives*, 2: 1, pp. 15–32.

Anheier, H., Glasius, M. and Kaldor, M. (2001), 'Introducing Global Civil Society', in H. Anheier, M. Glasius and M. Kaldor (eds), *Global Civil Society 2001*, Oxford: Oxford University Press.

Appadurai, A. (1996), *Modernity at Large: Cultural Dimensions of Globalization*, Minneapolis, MN: University of Minnesota Press.

Appadurai, A. (2001), 'Grassroots Globalization and the Research Imagination', in A. Appadurai (ed.), *Globalization*, Durham, NC: Duke University Press.

Arrighi, G. (1993), 'The Three Hegemonies of Historical Capitalism', in S. Gill (ed.), *Gramsci, Historical Materialism and International Relations*, Cambridge: Cambridge University Press.

Barber, B. (1996), *Jihad Versus McWorld*, New York: Ballantine Books.

Bauman, Z. (1999), *In Search of Politics*, Cambridge, UK: Polity.

Beck, U. (2000), *What is Globalization?*, Cambridge: Polity.

Bernard, M. (1997), 'Ecology, Political Economy and the Counter-Movement: Karl Polanyi and the Second Great Transformation', in S. Gill and J. H. Mittelman (eds), *Innovation and Transformation in International Studies*, Cambridge, UK: Cambridge University Press.

Birchfield, V. (1999), 'Contesting the Hegemony of Market Ideology: Gramsci's "Good Sense" and Polanyi's "Double Movement"', *Review of International Political Economy*, 6: 1, pp. 27–54.

Bleiker, R. (2000), *Popular Dissent, Human Agency and Global Politics*, Cambridge, UK: Cambridge University Press.

Campbell, D. (1996), 'Political Prosaics, Transversal Politics, and the Anarchical World', in M. J. Shapiro and H. R. Alker (eds), *Challenging Boundaries: Global Flows, Territorial Identities*, Minneapolis, MN: University of Minnesota Press.

Commission on Global Governance (1995), *Our Global Neighbourhood*, Oxford: Oxford University Press.

Douthwaite, R. (1996), *Short Circuit: Strengthening Local Economies for Security in an Unstable World*, Dublin: Lilliput Press.

Drainville, A. (2003), 'Critical Pedagogy for the Present Moment: Learning from the Avant-Garde to Teach Globalization from Experiences', *International Studies Perspectives*, 4: 3, pp. 231–249.

Enloe, C. (1990), *Bananas, Beaches and Bases: Making Feminist Sense of International Politics*, Berkeley, CA: University of California Press.

Hale, A. and Shaw, L. (2001), 'Women Workers and the Promise of Ethical Trade in the Globalised Garment Industry', *Antipode*, 33: 3, pp. 510–529.

Hoogvelt, A. (2001), *Globalization and the Postcolonial World*, Basingstoke: Macmillan.

Inda, J. X. and Rosaldo, R. (eds) (2002), *The Anthropology of Globalization*, Oxford: Blackwell.

Keane, J. (2003), *Global Civil Society?*, Cambridge: Cambridge University Press.

Klein, N. (2000), *No Logo*, London: Flamingo.

Lacher, H. (1999), 'The Politics of the Market: Re-reading Karl Polanyi', *Global Society*, 13: 3, pp. 313–327.

Leyshon, A. and Thrift, N. (1997), *Money/Space: Geographies of Monetary Transformation*, London: Routledge.

Mendell, M. and Salée, D. (1991), 'Introduction', in M. Mendell and D. Salée (eds), *The Legacy of Karl Polanyi: Market, State and Society at the End of the Twentieth Century*, Basingstoke: Macmillan.

Pacione, M. (1997), 'Local Exchange Trading Systems as a Response to the Globalisation of Capitalism', *Urban Studies*, 34: 8, pp. 1179–1199.

Pasha, M. K. and Blarey, D. L. (1998), 'Elusive Paradise: The Promise and Peril of Global Civil Society', *Alternatives*, 23: 3, pp. 417–450.

Ritzer, G. (1996), *The McDonaldization of Society: An Investigation into the Changing Character of Contemporary Life*, Thousand Oaks, CA: Pine Forge Press.

Rupert, M. (2000), *Ideologies of Globalization: Contending Visions of a New World Order*, London: Routledge.

Sassen, S. (1998), *Globalization and its Discontents*, New York: New Press.

Scholte, J. A. (2000), *Globalization: A Critical Introduction*, Basingstoke: Palgrave.

Sklair, L. (2001), *The Transnational Capitalist Class*, Oxford: Blackwell.

Somavia, J. (1999), 'Trade Unions in the 21st Century', Keynote Speech, Geneva: ILO.

Soros, G. (1998), *The Crisis of Global Capitalism: Open Society Endangered*, New York: Public Affairs.

Stiglitz, J. (2002), *Globalization and its Discontents*, London: Allen Lane.

Thompson, E. P. (1978), *The Poverty of Theory and Other Essays*, London: Merlin Press.

World Bank (2000), *Consultations with Civil Society Organizations: General Guidelines for World Bank Staff*, Washington, DC: World Bank.

World Trade Organization (2001), *Symposium on Issues Confronting the World Trading System*, Geneva: WTO.

Part 1

Conceptualizing resistance
Theories and problematics

Introduction

Though the four parts of this *Reader* address themes that are closely interrelated, it is Part 1 that maps the terrain of the debates that are to follow. We begin with James Mittelman and Christine Chin's analysis of competing conceptualizations of resistance that raises a central question: 'What is the meaning of resistance in the context of globalization?' Though Mittelman and Chin do introduce a series of oppositions or dualisms in their analysis – 'movement from below' against 'globalization from above', the 'hegemonic project of neoliberalism' versus 'liberal democracy' – the broad thrust of their argument is that the concept of resistance is thoroughly ambiguous. They highlight, for example, the 'coexistence of conformity and resistance', suggesting that resistances may be contradictory and may embody highly fragmented identities and interests. The chapter urges caution on those who would seek to ascribe an essential unity and declared purpose to social movements. Instead, they suggest that both 'the conduct and meaning of resistance are culturally embedded', so that our eyes must be open to the theories and practices of global resistance that reflect and are 'constitutive of specific ways of life'.

The contributions that follow provide four conceptual touchstones for thinking about the theory and practice of resistance. Each of these classic texts is paired with a chapter that seeks to reinterpret the theoretical insights so that they speak to contemporary themes. In this way, Part 1 places the concept of resistance in historical context, and explores the possibilities for thinking about resistance under conditions of globalization. In Chapters 2 and 3, the relationships between resistance, power and hegemony are explored in extracts from Antonio Gramsci's *Prison Notebooks*, and in Robert Cox's discussion of how Gramsci's ideas 'may be adapted to the understanding of problems of world order'. Gramsci's understanding of the nature and functioning of power, and specifically his concept of hegemony, inform a distinctive reading of resistance: 'one might say that State = political society + civil society, in other words hegemony protected by the armour of coercion'. In Chapter 2, hegemony rests upon a balance of consent and coercion, where the realm of civil society is, by and large, the source of the former and military power the source of the latter. Resistance, then, as interpreted by Cox for contemporary world conditions, becomes a counter-hegemonic struggle fought in the civil society sphere. While for Gramsci the wars of movement and position were conceived as resistance to state power by revolutionary parties, in Cox's analysis we witness the emergence of a nascent world hegemony and a potential global civil society. A central question in the conceptualization of resistance, then, is the extent to which state-centred framings of resistance á la Gramsci are relevant to understanding transnational or trans-border struggles.

Karl Polanyi's concept of resistance is similarly framed within a specific historical context. Focusing on the industrialization of Britain and France, Polanyi explores the conditions under which an economic system begins to attack the fabric of a society. For him, the creation of a market economy requires the extension of market principles into all areas of social life, to the point that the 'fictitious commodities' of land, labour and capital are bought and sold. Faced with this process of commodification, Polanyi argues, 'no society could stand the effects... unless its human and natural substance was protected against the ravages of this satanic mill'. Perhaps Polanyi's most frequently cited concept, the 'double movement', refers to 'a deep seated movement' that 'sprang into being to resist the pernicious effects of a market-controlled economy'. As Stephen Gill's use of Polanyi illustrates, 'today we relate the metaphor of the "double movement" to those socio-political forces which wish to assert more democratic control over political life'. The globalization of finance and production is understood to intensify the commodification of land (natural resources, environment), labour (the process of work and the use of labour power) and capital (money and systems of credit and exchange). Polanyi's fictitious commodities thus do seem to resonate with our contemporary experience. As with Gramsci's counter-hegemony, however, it can be argued that Polanyi's double movement gives a certain automatic and inevitable quality to resistance, as though it emerges naturally from subordination. We may wish to ask, then, which forms of resistance become visible when viewed through these frames, and which are left invisible.

James Scott's concept of 'infrapolitics' offers an understanding of resistance that not only attends to the everyday struggles that are so often invisible in social science, but also brings fresh insight to visible 'headline-grabbing' protests. For Scott, 'infrapolitics provides much of the cultural and structural underpinning of the more visible political action on which our attention has generally been focused'. In this way, unobtrusive or covert forms of resistance provide the 'building blocks' for 'a more elaborate political action that could not exist without it'. The politics of resistance takes on a more contradictory and ambiguous meaning when viewed in this way. Take, for example, Scott's discussion of the forest crimes of eighteenth- and nineteenth-century France. He suggests that the petty thefts, poaching and taking of grazing access take on multiple meanings for peasant communities. Ultimately, he argues, property laws and state control made direct resistance highly risky, but left open the possibility for practices that challenged the landlords' rights to police his property and established alternative norms that were accepted by the wider community. Drawing on Scott's analysis to explore the everyday resistances of peasant farmers in Ethiopia, Fantu Cheru illustrates how techniques of survival can become forms of resistance that 'require little coordination, avoid direct confrontation with authorities and are not subject to elite manipulation'.

The last two chapters in Part 1 suggest a framing of power and agency that stands in contrast to those we find in many explanations of contemporary resistance. The extract from Michel Foucault's *History of Sexuality I* cautions that we 'must not assume that the sovereignty of the state, the form of the law, or the over-all unity of domination are given at the outset'. Foucault's chapter on power, then, problematizes a clear and unambiguous divide between domination and resistance. His arguments that power is 'exercised' rather than 'seized'; that relations of power are never exterior to other types of social relationships; that there is no 'all-encompassing opposition between rulers and ruled' and that we should not look for the 'headquarters' from which power is rationally exercised have important implications for the conceptualization of resistance. The effect is to frame resistances as multiple, situated, mobile and transitory:

> Points of resistance are present everywhere in the power network. Hence there is no single locus of great Refusal, no soul of revolt, source of all rebellions, or pure law of the revolutionary. Instead there is a plurality of resistances, each of them a special case: resistances that are possible, necessary, improbable; others that are spontaneous, savage, solitary, concerted, rampant, or violent; still others that are quick to compromise, interested, or sacrificial... The points, knots, or focuses of resistance are spread over time and space at varying densities, at times mobilizing groups or individuals in a definitive way, inflaming certain points of the body, certain moments in life, certain types of behavior.

For Foucault, discourse can be simultaneously an instrument of power and a point of resistance or opposition. In this way, discourse 'transmits and produces power' while it also 'renders it fragile and makes it possible to thwart it'. In Roland Bleiker's interpretation of the dissent that led to the collapse of the Berlin Wall, he argues that 'practices of dissent in global politics should be viewed in discursive terms'. His use of Foucault's work allows him to recognize resistances that have 'hitherto been obscured'. Bleiker is interested in the way that media coverage of spectacular revolutions may mask the 'slow transformation of values that preceded them'.

1 Conceptualizing resistance to globalization

James H. Mittelman and Christine B. N. Chin

Source: James H. Mittelman (2000), *The Globalization Syndrome: Transformation and Resistance*, Princeton: Princeton University Press, pp. 165–178

Assessments of resistance to globalization are necessarily influenced by the manner in which one conceptualizes resistance. Too often, this term is used promiscuously, sometimes as a synonym for challenges, protests, intransigence, or even evasions. Hence, we seek to juxtapose alternative explanations of resistance and highlight the complexities of theorizing it. The purpose of this chapter, then, is to explore the question, What is the meaning of resistance in the context of globalization?

One way to approach this issue is with the proposition that a major asymmetry in the globalization trend is between its economic and political levels. Although it would be wrong to concede the neoclassical premise that economics and politics are separable realms, it is clear, at least in analytical terms, that globalization's hegemonic project is neoliberalism and that liberal democracy has not kept pace with its spread. In the space opened by this disjuncture, resistance to globalization is on the rise. But it cannot solely be understood as a political reaction. Rather, in the teeth of globalizing tendencies, resistance movements shape and are constitutive of cultural processes.

There is no dearth of culturally laden manifestations of resistance to globalization. Culminating in the election of a Government of National Unity, led by the African National Congress (ANC) in 1994, the worldwide anti-apartheid movement against a racial monopoly of the means of production is one of the foremost examples of a mobilization against globalization from above. This was *a movement from below against globalization from above* in the sense that South Africa was, and is, the site of substantial foreign investment and where many TNCs have touched down; their role in maintaining the white redoubt was successfully contested by large-scale collective action at home, including armed struggle, in conjunction with a transnational network of support groups. The demise of apartheid may also be understood as a *movement from above against globalization from above* inasmuch as it was facilitated by a split in South African capitalism, in which the modernizers and globalizers abandoned an obsolescent capitalism based on an increasingly less profitable form of racial segregation, Thus in 1985, Gavin W. H. Relly, the retired chairman of the Anglo American Corporation, the largest conglomerate in South Africa, defied official government policy and led a delegation of business leaders to meet privately with the banned ANC in Lusaka, Zambia, where they discussed the transition to a new order. In addition, there are numerous illustrations of more localized resistance, including the Zapatista armed uprising among the Maya Indians against the Mexican government's neoliberal reforms, a struggle in which the rebels quickly turned to modern technologies, including the Internet, to rally transnational support. But it would be facile to conceptualize resistance only as declared organized opposition to institutionalized economic and military power. One must dig deep to excavate the everyday individual and collective activities that fall short of open opposition. To grasp resistance to globalization, one must also examine the subtexts of political and cultural life, the possibilities and potential for structural transformation.

We begin to delve into the constitutive role of power in shaping cultural critiques of economic globalization as well as patterns of struggle by revisiting the works of three master theorists of resistance, even if their writings were not explicitly directed at the contemporary phase of globalization: Antonio Gramsci's concept of counterhegemony, Karl Polanyi's notion of countermovements, and James C. Scott's idea of infrapolitics. For the sake of brevity, our scope is limited to these authors – other conceptualizations would take us too far afield; . . . . We hold that the trilogy of Gramsci-Polanyi-Scott, set forth through a critical evaluation of each author's work in the next three sections of this chapter, offers a sound basis for reconceptualizing resistance. The conclusion then probes the convergence and contrasting emphases within this triad, and also suggests directions for further study and exploratory research.

Resistance as counterhegemony

Ostensibly, Gramsci's analysis of social change as explicated in *Selections from the Prison Notebooks* (1971) could neither have anticipated nor accounted for globalization. The notes were written between 1929 and 1935 while Gramsci, a member of parliament and the general secretary of the Communist Party, was imprisoned by the fascist regime in Italy. In his discussions of state-society relations, Gramsci was concerned particularly with orthodox Marxist and bourgeois liberal theoretical frameworks that privileged economism by reducing transformations in all aspects of social life to economic determinants. His theoretical efforts to transcend economism are applicable to conceptualizing resistance at the turn of the millennium. To replace economism, Gramsci developed the concept of hegemony, which encompasses whole ways of life. For Gramsci, hegemony is a dynamic lived process in which social identities, relations, organizations, and structures based on asymmetrical distributions of power and influence are constituted by the dominant classes. Hegemony, then, is as much economic as it is "ethico-political" in shaping relations of domination and subordination.

The institutions of civil society, such as the church, family, schools, media, and trade unions, give meaning and organization to everyday life so that the need for the application of force is reduced. Hegemony is established when power and control over social life are per-ceived as emanating from "self-government" (i.e., self-government of individuals embedded in communities) as opposed to an external source(s) such as the state or the dominant strata (Gramsci 1971, 268). Since hegemony is a lived process, different historical contexts will produce different forums of hegemony with different sets of actors, such as the nineteenth-century "passive revolution" of the Risorgimento, in which the bourgeoisie in Italy attained power without fundamental restructuring from below, and the early twentieth-century proletarian revolutionary leadership in Russia.

The processes of establishing hegemony, however, can never be complete because a hegemonic project presumes and requires the participation of subordinate groups. While hegemony is being implemented, maintained, and defended, it can be challenged and resisted in the interlocking realms of civil society, political society, and the state. Different forms and dimensions of resistance to hegemony are subsumed under the rubric of coun-terhegemony. Implicit in a counterhegemonic project are "wars of movement" and "wars of position," in which people engage in openly declared collective action against the state. Wars of movement are frontal assaults against the state (e.g., labor strikes or even military action), whereas wars of position can be read as nonviolent resistance, e.g., boycotts that are designed to impede everyday functions of the state (Gramsci 1971, 229–30).[1] The objective of both types of war is to seize control of the state. Wars of movement and position are expressions of counterhegemonic consciousness at the collective level. They represent moments in history when individuals come together in violent and nonviolent confrontations with the state. The question nevertheless arises: Why and how does counterhegemonic consciousness emerge in everyday life, leading to openly declared collective action?

Gramsci's discussion of common sense in the development of counterhegemonic consciousness is crucial to explaining historical and/or contemporary forms of resistance. Common sense that is held and practiced in everyday life is neither linear nor unitary; it is the product of an individual's relationship to and position in a variety of social groups:

> In acquiring one's conception of the world one always belongs to a particular grouping which is that of all the social elements which share the same mode of thinking and acting. We are all conformists of some conformism or other.... *When one's conception of the world is not critical and coherent but disjointed and episodic, one belongs simultaneously to a multiplicity of mass human groups.* ...The starting-point of critical elaboration is the consciousness of what one really is, and is "knowing thyself" as a product of the historical process to date which has deposited in you an infinity of traces, without leaving an inventory.
>
> (Gramsci 1971, 324; emphasis added)

Importantly, the coexistence of conformity and resistance in common sense can give rise to inconsistencies between thought and action, which help explain contradictory behavior on the part of a subaltern group which may embrace its "own conception of the world" while still adopting conceptions borrowed from dominant classes (Gramsci 1971, 326–7). By arguing that individuals and groups possess critical consciousness – albeit "in flashes" – of their subordinate positions in society, Gramsci acknowledged the ambiguity of resistance and dismissed the overly deterministic and unidimensional explanation of false consciousness.

Nevertheless, in the discussion of thought and action, Gramsci was careful not to suggest that submission in the face of domination is the simple product of the subaltern's rational calculation of costs and benefits (in the sense that resistance would be futile at best, or would elicit retaliatory action, at worst). The fragmentation of social identity that characterizes and is characterized by simultaneous membership in different groups means that it is possible, if not probable, that the subaltern can be progressive on certain issues and reactionary on others in the same instance.

A Gramscian reading of resistance would have to explicate the development of counterhegemonic consciousness that informs wars of movement and position, as well as national-popular actions led by organic intellectuals from all walks of life who can meld theory and praxis to construct and embed a new common sense that binds disparate voices and consciousness into a coherent program of change. In his time, Gramsci called for organic intellectuals to infuse common sense with a philosophy of praxis that encourages subaltern groups' critical understanding of their subordination in society. The objective is a "national-popular" movement constituted by alliances between the leaders (in league with their organic intellectuals) and the led (subaltern). Whereas wars of movement and position aim to capture the state, the national-popular movement provides the new basis for whole ways of life.

Gramsci did not offer programmatic ways that a philosophy of praxis could transcend the fragmentation of identity and interests. With contemporary globalization, the interpenetration of forces at the local, national, regional, and world levels implies that different peoples enter into alliances that can be and are ever more contradictory: e.g., low-wage female factory workers in EPZs who also are members or supporters of Islamist movements in Southeast Asia. A new common sense has to address effectively or make coherent women's critical understanding of the tensions, limitations, and opportunities inherent in their identities as daughters or wives in the household, as low-wage workers on the factory floor, as citizens, and as Muslims in the local, national, and transnational Islamic communities.

Moreover, globalization begets openly declared forms of resistance that may or may not have the state as a target. Rotating the holders of state power may not alleviate the problems that ignited resistance in the first place. In a context in which liberal, authoritarian, and ex-communist states-in-transition alike are often becoming facilitators for transnational capital, if and when it occurs, the driving force(s) of openly declared resistance against the state must be analyzed within a larger framework. At issue are the contradictory ways in which state structures and policies assume "educative" functions that nurture a new kind of citizenry and civilization commensurate with the requirements of transnational capital, while trying to maintain the legitimacy with which to govern (Chin 1998). In this connection, one can profitably invoke Gramsci's insights into civil society and resistance, about which he offered many pointers, although they are not always congruent with one another. Additionally, Gramsci's concepts can be pushed beyond the domestic realm to world order, and scholars have begun to extend the framework in this manner (especially Cox 1986, 1987, 1999; Augelli and Murphy 1988, 1997).

Although wars of movement and position may still be discerned, sometimes in nascent form, the compression of time and space has created new venues of and for *collective resistance transcending national borders*. Contemporary social movements simultaneously occupy local, national, transnational, and global space as a result of innovations in, and applications of, technologies such as the Internet, facsimile machines, cellular mobile phones, and globalized media, which produce instantaneous communication across traditional frontiers. The Gramscian framework of resistance thus must be stretched to encompass new actors and spaces from which counterhegemonic consciousness is expressed. In the following section, we discuss the possibility of further considering social movements as a form of resistance.

Resistance as countermovements

A different emphasis in regard to resistance may be found in Polanyi's notion of the double *movement*. To add to what has been said in previous chapters about his notion of how, during the eighteenth and nineteenth centuries, the state-supported drive to install and expand the "self-regulating" market sparked protective measures or countermovements to reassert social control over the market, it is important to bear in mind that Polanyi understood resistance in the form of countermovements as having arisen from, and affecting, different ways of life. Protecting workers from the commodification process implies defending the social relations and institutions of which they are a part:

> *In disposing of a man's labor power the system would, incidently, dispose of the physical, psychological, and moral entity "man" attached to that tag. Robbed of the protective covering of cultural institutions, human beings would perish from the effects of social exposure*; they would die as victims of acute social dislocation through vice, perversion, crime, and starvation.... [N]o society could stand the effects of such a system of crude fictions even for the shortest stretch of time unless its human and natural substance as well as its business organization was protected against the ravages of this satanic mill.
>
> (Polanyi 1957, 73; emphasis added)

The movement-countermovement framework thus allows one to conceptualize contemporary social movements as a form of resistance since the latter are, in the main, defined as "a form of collective action (a) based on solidarity, (b) carrying on a conflict, (c) breaking the limits of the system in which action occurs" (Melucci 1985, 795). The level of analysis would have to be extended from the national to the transnational and/or global since some contemporary social movements, e.g., those that concern environmental destruction, women's rights, and indigenous peoples' rights, appear to go beyond the state in search of transnational or global solutions.

There are two implicit problems in the counter/social movement framework. Collectivity is assumed in the notion "movement" and this has the effect of constructing counter/social movements as united fronts in and of themselves. In the past decade or so, the fragmented nature of the feminist movement is evidenced in the internal conflict and domination generated from differences of race, religion, class, and nationality in spite of, and because of, attempts to address national and global patriarchy (Hooks 1981, 1984; Mohanty, Russo, and Torres 1991).

Also imputed in counter/social movements is the presence of organizational structure. This may be the case with some social movements (e.g., Greenpeace and Friends of the Earth in the environmental realm), but "submerged networks" with no clearly defined organizational structure too have formed in an era of globalization. Participants in submerged networks live their everyday lives mostly without engaging in openly declared contestations: "They question definition of codes, nomination of reality. They don't ask, they offer. They offer by their own existence other ways of defining the meaning of individual and collective action. They act as new media: they enlighten what every system doesn't say of itself, the amount of silence, violence, irrationality which is always hidden in dominant codes" (Melucci 1985, 812).

The presence of submerged networks gives new meaning to resistance. Even though participants can mobilize to protest state policies, open engagement or confrontation with the state or even TNCs is not the immediate, or even ultimate, objective. In the absence of openly declared collective action, resistance has to be read as the ways in which peoples live their everyday lives. Submerged networks affirm that even though resistance can be manifestly political and economic, it is shaped by and shapes ways of life. In advanced industrialized societies, examples of submerged networks are those in which families and their friends make it a point – in their consumption habits – to refuse to buy tuna fish caught using methods that destroy entire dolphin populations, or to purchase consumer products only from companies that actively practice environmental conservationism. Such acts have economic consequences in the corporate world, and political consequences for policy makers. Significantly, submerged networks are sites of emerging alternative values and life styles.

In Egypt, for example, submerged networks exist in the popular quarters and among the common people, known as the *sha'b*.[2] Networks radiate from the family – the basic unit of social organization in the *sha'b* – to include ties that transcend class, occupation, and kin. The "familial ethos" governs the allocation and distribution of material and symbolic resources in the *sha'b*. In the present unspoken pact between the Egyptian state and the *sha'b*, state legitimacy is maintained by the distribution of basic goods and services to the *sha'b* in return for political acquiescence. Participants of the *sha'b* acquiesce to, as much as they engage in, resistance against the state. Members of the Islamist movement, who also are members of the *sha'b*, have been known to and can draw on submerged network ties to smuggle arms and, on occasion, to mobilize and organize mass protests against the state.

The notion of the Polanyian double movement thus has a distinct advantage of neatly encapsulating openly declared demands on the national, transnational, and global levels for protective measures against various dimensions in the implementation and expansion of the self-regulating market. As discussed, however, the movement-countermovement framework neither advances analysis of differences within countermovements nor adequately anticipates undeclared forms of resistance, both of which have emerged and must be addressed in conceptualizing collective resistance to globalization.

Resistance as infrapolitics

In 1990, James C. Scott introduced the idea of "infrapolitics" as everyday forms of resistance conducted singularly and collectively, but which fall short of openly declared contestations. What began as his attempt to understand the conditions for peasant rebellions in Southeast Asia and the absence of openly declared resistance in a village in rapidly industrializing Malaysia gradually led to the conceptualization of infrapolitics: a way to explain the changing meaning of politics and resistance in most forms of day-to-day, dominant-subordinate relations (Scott 1976, 1985, 1990). Scott warned that, in the context of increasingly complex societies, the absence of openly declared contestations should not be mistaken for acquiescence. It is in the realm of informal assemblages such as the parallel market, workplace, household, and local community, when people negotiate resources and values on an everyday basis, that "counterhegemonic consciousness is elaborated" (Scott 1990, 200). These are the sites of infrapolitical activities that range from foot-dragging, squatting, and gossip to the development of dissident subcultures.

Taken at face value, such activities cannot tell us anything about counterhegemonic discourse until we account for the conditions from which they emerge. Infrapolitics is identified by juxtaposing what Scott calls the "public" and "hidden transcripts." Public transcripts are verbal and nonverbal acts carried out by the dominant party or, "to put it crudely, the *self*-portrait of dominant elites as they would have themselves seen" (Scott 1990, 18; emphasis in original). They are the public record of superior-subordinate relations in which the latter appears to acquiesce willingly to the stated and unstated expectations of the former. Hidden transcripts, on the other hand, consist of what subordinate parties say and do beyond the realm of the public transcript or the observation of the dominant. In the context of surveillance structures set up by the dominant class(es) or the state, hidden transcripts record infrapolitical activities that surreptitiously challenge practices of economic, status, and ideological domination.

The study of infrapolitics, we believe, is premised on what sociologists call ontological narratives (Somers 1994). Ontological narrativity does not refer to the mode of representation or the traditional "story-telling" method of historians (i.e., a method of presenting historical knowledge) considered nonexplanatory and atheoretical by mainstream social scientists. Rather, ontological narratives are the stories that social actors tell, and in the process they come to define themselves or to construct their identities and perceive conditions that promote and/or mitigate the possibility for change (see, especially, Butler and Scott 1992; Geertz 1983; Taylor 1989).

Even though hidden transcripts record contestations over material and symbolic resources and values in everyday life, they do not occur in a localized vacuum. Infrapolitical activities are the product of interactions between structure and agency: the ways that real and perceived constraints and opportunities affect the behavior of subordinate groups. Scott's analysis of infrapolitical activities thus falls short of capturing the complexities inherent in undeclared forms of everyday resistance. In his study of landlord-peasant relations in a rural Malay village, Scott asserted that analyses of state structures and policies were important *only* to the extent that they impinged on local class relations (1985, xix). Especially during the 1980s and in the context of national agricultural development policies and fluctuating global prices of commodities, landlord-peasant relations were shaped by impingements on, and interactions among, the rural community, state structures and policies, as well as the transformations marking a globalizing economic system.

Superior-subordinate relations, such as those of the landlord-peasant, manager-worker, husband-wife, and state official-squatter, are embedded in the ways of life, of which state structures and policies play an important part. Take, for instance, policies designed to normalize the patriarchal nuclear family form as most natural in and for the expansion and maintenance of capitalist free markets, and/or that privilege scientific and other technical education at the expense of the humanities. Such policies frame worldviews insofar as they directly and indirectly affect all aspects of social life from the rate of urbanization, housing development, and employment opportunities, to the control and distribution of resources in the household. In increasingly complex social contexts, subalterns do not have an unproblematic unitary identity. Nor can their behavior be explained by implicit reference to the economic model of the self-interested utility maximizer. Put simply, infrapolitical activities are not the mere product of subaltern decisions to conduct undeclared resistance in the face of surveillance structures set up by the dominant strata.

Class is but one important modality of identity in landlord-peasant or other forms of dominant-subordinate relations. The different and possibly conflicting modalities of subaltern identity can be as real, and under certain conditions, as constraining on behavior as the actual or perceived futility and fear of openly declared resistance in the face of domination. By putting a unidimensional face on resistance, Scott inadvertently assigned a similar unidimensional countenance to domination, even though he analytically distinguished economic, status, and ideological domination. In this connection, Gramsci reminded us that subaltern identities are embedded in complex overlapping social networks in which individuals simultaneously assume positions of domination and subordination (perhaps as a husband or wife, an elder or junior, a manager or office clerk, and a donor or recipient of aid). Analysis of the manner in which particular combinations of identity are expressed in the context of structural constraints can help explain why, given systems of surveillance (in which rewards and punishments inhere), some conform while others engage in infrapolitical activities of different types. Conversely, this approach also deepens analysis of the changing nature of domination.

Hidden transcripts have the potential to facilitate understanding of the internal politics of subaltern groups. The phenomenon of "domination within domination" occurs in cases in which contradictory alliances are formed between the dominant and the subordinate that, in turn, dominate others. Although Scott acknowledges this point, his emphasis on class without a sufficiently subtle exploration of the interactions between class and nonclass forces undermines the efficacy of the infrapolitical framework. The immediate focus on class presumes that the development of class consciousness stands apart exclusively from other modalities of identity. It is, indeed, possible to argue that class contests in the context of surveillance can and do lead to infrapolitical activities that are grounded in material life. This argument is made possible *only* after having considered how and why the class dimension comes to be privileged and expressed over other modalities of identity. To do otherwise would reaffirm what Gramsci called "economism," and subsequently relegate noneconomic considerations to the ambit of superstructure.

Infrapolitics is embedded in whole ways of life, part of which is the material dimension. They embody contestations over the processes of grounded identity construction, maintenance, and transformation, of which the symbolic and material dimensions of class are intertwined with other modalities of identity, such as age, gender, race-ethnicity, religion, and nationality. The identification, juxtaposition, and analyses of public and hidden transcripts can highlight the conditions in which certain dimensions of counterhegemonic consciousness develop, and how different or even conflicting perspectives within hidden transcripts are negotiated and/or (not) resolved in everyday life.

Resistance conceptualized as infrapolitical activities offers a possible avenue for generating theoretically grounded studies of everyday responses to globalizing structures and processes. If conducted with sensitivity to the complex interplay between or among multiple identities in the context of structural constraints, the study of public and hidden transcripts may reveal changing notions and practices of work, family, and politics, for example, as peoples seek to negotiate a semblance of social control over the expansion of market forces in diverse spheres of their everyday lives. At the same time, one should not overwork the broad category of infrapolitics by imagining that every sort of reaction to globalizing structures is resistance. Whereas Scott carefully argues that diverse modes of resistance may or may not coalesce into opposition to authority structures, it is important to avoid treating resistance as an omnibus category.

An emerging framework

The conduct and meaning of resistance are culturally embedded. This foundational proposition is no less applicable or relevant in conceptualizing contemporary resistance to globalization, as it was to Gramsci, Polanyi, and Scott's analyses of social change in different historical periods. The three master theorists acknowledged, implicitly and explicitly, that resistance arises from and is constitutive of specific ways of life. From this elemental proposition, however, the theorists diverged in their respective discussions of the forms and dimensions of resistance. Gramsci and Polanyi focused on the collective level, whereas Scott drew attention more to the level of the individual, as well as class, in everyday life. As delineated in Table 1.1, the main targets and modes of resistance differ from one theorist to another: Gramscian wars of movement and position against the state (though not to the neglect of change within civil society short of toppling the state), Polanyian countermovements against market forces, and Scott's infrapolitical activities in the face of everyday domination.

Differences in levels of analysis, main targets, and modes of resistance should not be reasoned only by way of the intellectual proclivities of each theorist per se. Rather, the conceptual tensions among the theorists correspond to, and reflect, the changing conditions of social life: From Gramsci to Polanyi to Scott, as societies became more complex, so too did the targets and modes of resistance. Contemporary transformations in social life in general, and state-society relations in particular, imply that all three major targets and modes of resistance coexist and are modified in globalizing processes.

Table 1.1 Three analyses of resistance

	Main target	*Mode of resistance*
Gramsci	State apparatuses (understood as an instrument of education)	Wars of movement and position
Polanyi	Market forces (and their legitimation)	Countermovements aimed at self-protection
Scott	Ideologies (public transcripts)	Counterdiscourses

This important conversation among the theorists forms a grid that may be profitably fastened to neoliberal globalization. The emerging framework helps to identify possibilities for contesting forms of domination, expanding political space, and opening new venues – hence redefinitions of politics. Seen from the observation points of this triad, a conceptualization of contemporary resistance to globalization sensitizes one to the ontological shift suggested below.

Forms of resistance

As certain dimensions of political and economic power become more diffuse and less institutionalized, so too will forms of resistance. Undeclared forms of resistance conducted individually and collectively in submerged networks parallel openly declared forms of resistance embodied in wars of movement and position, and countermovements. Depending on the context, everyday activities, such as what one wears (e.g., the veil in Muslim societies or the dashiki in the African-American community), buys, or consumes, may qualify as resistance – as much as that of organized strikes, boycotts, and even armed insurgencies against states and TNCs throughout the world. One of the key challenges here is to problematize the absence of openly declared forms of resistance. Doing so can explicate the changing meaning of politics as a result of interactions between forces of change on the local, national, regional, and global levels.

Agents of resistance

In the past, agents of resistance were synonymous mostly with union workers, armed rebels (many of them peasants), and political dissidents, including students and certain intellectuals, as class contestations assumed overt political and, in some cases, military dimensions. At present, agents of resistance are not restricted to such actors. They range from blue-collar and white-collar workers to clerics, homemakers, and middle managers. It is important to note that even state functionaries can resist the wholesale implementation of neoliberal development paths (especially the veneer of liberal democratic politics), such as those who insist on "Asian-style democracy" in the midst of establishing open markets and free trade. It is the complex ways in which symbolic resources and values articulate with the material conditions of life in different societies that produce a variety of organic intellectuals, a more encompassing group in the current phase of globalization. Class contests only partly form the basis of resistance. Instead, agents of resistance emerge from interactions between structure and agency that lead to the contextual privileging of particular intersections of different modes of identity, i.e., class-nationality-gender-race/ethnicity-religion-sexual orientation. Implicit in the designation of diverse peoples as agents of resistance is an expansion of the boundaries associated with the traditional sites of political life.

Sites of resistance

Resistance is localized, regionalized, and globalized at the same time that economic globalization slices across geopolitical borders. What this means, in part, is that the "public-private" dichotomy no longer holds, for most, albeit not all, dimensions of social life are affected in varying and interconnected ways by globalizing forces. Everyday life in the household and the informal market can facilitate, as well as resist, such forces in distinctly material and symbolic ways. Another closely related phenomenon is the development of cyberspace, a site at which resistance finds its instantaneous audience via the Internet or World Wide Web. Counterdiscourse is a mode of globalized resistance in cyberspace. One has to bear in mind, however, that although states in general are incapable of effectively monitoring and censoring cyberspatial counterdiscourse, this particular means of resistance is open only to those who have access to computers, modems, and the Internet.

Strategies of resistance

By strategies, we refer to the actual ways that people, whose modes of existence are threatened by globalization (e.g., through job loss, encroachment on community lands, or undermining of cultural integrity), respond in a sustained manner toward achieving certain objectives. While forms of struggle differ, groups may adopt varied means to contest, and link objectively and subjectively to their counterparts in other countries or regions. Local movements become transnational or global with sustained access to communication technologies that construct and maintain communities of like-minded individuals. For example, community activists and scholars meet at different forums for the exchange of information and plans. An emerging strategy of "borderless solidarity" is to link single issues such as environmental degradation, women's rights, and racism, and to highlight the interconnectedness of varied dimensions of social life. Analyses of this may bring to bear the conditions and methods by which commonality can be achieved in spite of, and because of, the fragmentation of identities and interests while economic and political life is being globalized. Nonetheless, evolving global strategies of resistance do not necessarily sidetrack the state. Under certain circumstances, strategies of resistance can, and do, pit state agencies against one another (e.g., in the case of shipping toxic waste to the developing world, state agencies in charge of environmental protection may join in protests, while their counterparts responsible for industrial development continue to encourage the kind and methods of industrialization that cause environmental damage). Studies of global, transnational, and local resistance must then take into account transformations in state structures, whether or not strategies of resistance manifestly engage the state.

Quite clearly, an ontology of resistance to globalization requires grounding. When contextualized, the elements of *forms*, *agents*, *sites*, and *strategies* may be viewed in terms of their interactions so as to delimit durable patterns and the potential for structural transformation. The Gramsci-Polanyi-Scott triad calls for conceptual frameworks that link different levels of analysis. Integration of the local and the global can bring to the fore the conditions in which diverse forms, agents, sites, and strategies of resistance emerge from the conjunctures and disjunctures in the global political economy, as shown in the following chapters, which are intended to exemplify the intricacy and the variability of *combinations* of resistance from above and below.

Notes

1 Gramsci (1971, 106–20) also linked wars of position to "passive revolution" of the dominant classes – i.e., revolution from above – that sidesteps the need for fundamental restructuring from below.
2 "While the noun, the *sha'b*, refers to a collective people, populace, or folk and has an implicit collective connotation to it, as an adjective *sha'bi* demarcates a wide range of indigenous practices, tastes, and patterns in everyday life" (Singerman 1995, 10–11).

Selected references

Augelli, E. and Murphy, C. (1988), *America's Quest for Supremacy and the Third World*, London: Pinter.
Augelli, E. and Murphy, C. (1997), "Consciousness, Myth and Collective Action: Gramsci, Sorel and the Ethical State," in S. Gill and J. Mittelman (eds), *Innovation and Transformation in International Studies*, Cambridge: Cambridge University Press.

Butler, J. and Scott, J. (eds) (1992), *Feminists Theorize the Political*, London: Routledge.

Chin, C. (1998), *In Service and Servitude: Foreign Female Domestic Workers and the Malaysian "Modernity Project,"* New York: Columbia University Press.

Cox, R. W. (1986), *Production, Power and World Order*, New York: Columbia University Press.

Cox, R. W. (1987), *Production, Power and World Order: Social Forces in the Making of History*, New York: Columbia University Press.

Cox, R. W. (1999), 'Civil Society at the Turn of the Millennium: Prospects for an Alternative World Order', *Review of International Studies*, 25: 1, pp. 3–28.

Geertz, C. (1983), *Local Knowledge: Further Essays in Interpretive Anthropology*, New York: Basic Books.

Gramsci, A. (1971), *Selections from the Prison Notebooks*, translated and edited by Quintin Hoare and Geoffrey Nowell Smith, London: Lawrence and Wishart.

Hooks, B. (1981), *Ain't I Woman? Black Women and Feminism*, Boston: South End Press.

Hooks, B. (1984), *Feminist Theory: From Margin to Center*, Boston: South End Press.

Melucci, A. (1985), "The Symbolic Challenge of Contemporary Social Movements," *Social Research*, 52, p. 795.

Mohanty, C., Russo, A. and Torres, L. (1991), *Third World Women and the Politics of Feminism*, Bloomington: Indiana University Press.

Polanyi, K. (1957), *The Great Transformation: The Political and Economic Origins of Our Time*, London: Beacon Press.

Scott, J. C. (1976), *The Moral Economy of the Peasant: Rebellion and Subsistence in Southeast Asia*, New Haven: Yale University Press.

Scott, J. C. (1985), *Weapons of the Weak: Everyday Forms of Peasant Resistance*, New Haven: Yale University Press.

Scott, J. C. (1990), *Domination and the Arts of Resistance: Hidden Transcripts*, New Haven: Yale University Press.

Singerman, D. (1995), *Avenues of Participation: Families, Politics and Networks in Cairo*, Princeton: Princeton University Press.

Somers, M. R. (1994), "The Narrative Constitution of Identity: A Relational and Network Approach," *Theory and Society*, 23, pp. 605–49.

Taylor, C. (1989), *Sources of the Self: The Making of the Modern Identity*, Cambridge, Mass: Harvard University Press.

2   State and civil society

Antonio Gramsci

Source: Antonio Gramsci (1971), *The Prison Notebooks*, Quentin Hoare and Geoffrey Nowell Smith (eds and trans), London/New York: Lawrence & Wishart, pp. 210–276

[…]

Political struggle and military war

In military war, when the strategic aim – destruction of the enemy's army and occupation of his territory – is achieved, peace comes. It should also be observed that for war to come to an end, it is enough that the strategic aim should simply be achieved potentially: it is enough in other words that there should be no doubt that an army is no longer able to fight, and that the victorious army "could" occupy the enemy's territory. Political struggle is enormously more complex: in a certain sense, it can be compared to colonial wars or to old wars of conquest – in which the victorious army occupies, or proposes to occupy, permanently all or a part of the conquered territory. Then the defeated army is disarmed and dispersed, but the struggle continues on the terrain of politics and of military "preparation".

Thus India's political struggle against the English (and to a certain extent that of Germany against France, or of Hungary against the Little Entente) knows three forms of war: war of movement, war of position, and underground warfare. Gandhi's passive resistance is a war of position, which at certain moments becomes a war of movement, and at others underground warfare. Boycotts are a form of war of position, strikes of war of movement, the secret preparation of weapons and combat troops belongs to underground warfare. A kind of commando tactics[1] is also to be found, but it can only be utilised with great circumspection. If the English believed that a great insurrectional movement was being prepared, destined to annihilate their present strategic superiority (which consists, in a certain sense, in their ability to manœuvre through control of the internal lines of communication, and to concentrate their forces at the "sporadically" most dangerous spot) by mass suffocation – i.e. by compelling them to spread out their forces over a theatre of war which had simultaneously become generalised – then it would suit them to *provoke* a premature outbreak of the Indian fighting forces, in order to identify them and decapitate the general movement. Similarly it would suit France if the German Nationalist Right were to be involved in an adventurist *coup d'état*; for this would oblige the suspected illegal military organisation to show itself prematurely, and so permit an intervention which from the French point of view would be timely. It is thus evident that in these forms of mixed struggle – fundamentally of a military character, but mainly fought on the political plane (though in fact every political struggle always has a military substratum) – the use of commando squads requires an original tactical development, for which the experience of war can only provide a stimulus, and not a model.

[…]

Another point to be kept in mind is that in political struggle one should not ape the methods of the ruling classes, or one will fall into easy ambushes. In the current struggles this phenomenon often occurs. A weakened State structure is like a flagging army; the commandos – i.e. the private armed organisations – enter the field, and they have two tasks: to make use of illegal means, while the State appears to remain within legality, and thus to reorganise the State itself. It is stupid to believe that when one is confronted by illegal private action one can counterpose to it another similar action – in other words, combat commando tactics by means of commando tactics. It means believing that the State remains perpetually inert, which is never the case – quite apart from all the other conditions which differ. The class factor leads to a fundamental difference: a class which has to work fixed hours every day cannot have permanent and specialised assault organisations – as can a class which has ample financial resources and all of whose members are not tied down by fixed work. At any hour of day or night, these by now professional organisations are able to strike decisive blows, and strike them unawares. Commando tactics cannot therefore have the same importance for some classes as for others. For certain classes a war of movement and manœuvre is necessary – because it is the form of war which belongs to them; and this, in the case of political struggle, may include a valuable and perhaps indispensable use of commando tactics. But to fix one's mind on the military model is the mark of a fool: politics, here too, must have priority over its military aspect, and only politics creates the possibility for manœuvre and movement.

[…]

On the subject of parallels between on the one hand the concepts of war of manœuvre and war of position in military science, and on the other the corresponding concepts in political science, Rosa [Luxemburg]'s little book, translated (from French) into Italian in 1919 by C. Alessandri, should be recalled.[2]

In this book, Rosa – a little hastily, and rather superficially too – theorised the historical experiences of 1905. She in fact disregarded the "voluntary" and organisational elements which were far more extensive and important in those events than – thanks to a certain "economistic" and spontaneist prejudice – she tended to believe. All the same, this little book (like others of the same author's essays) is one of the most significant documents theorizing the war of manœuvre in relation to political science. The immediate economic element (crises, etc.) is seen as the field artillery which in war opens a breach in the enemy's defences – a breach sufficient for one's own troops to rush in and obtain a definitive (strategic) victory, or at least an important victory in the context of the strategic line. Naturally the effects of immediate economic factors in historical science are held to be far more complex than the effects of heavy artillery in a war of manœuvre, since they are conceived of as having a double effect: 1. they breach the enemy's defences, after throwing him into disarray and causing him to lose faith in himself, his forces, and his future; 2. in a flash they organise one's own troops and create the necessary cadres – or at least in a flash they put the existing cadres (formed, until that moment, by the general historical process) in positions which enable them to encadre one's scattered forces; 3. in a flash they bring about the necessary ideological concentration on the common objective to be achieved. This view was a form of iron economic determinism, with the aggravating factor that it was conceived of as operating with lightning speed in time and in space. It was thus out and out historical mysticism, the awaiting of a sort of miraculous illumination.

[...]

In wars among the more industrially and socially advanced States, the war of manœuvre must be considered as reduced to more of a tactical than a strategic function; that it must be considered as occupying the same position as siege warfare used to occupy previously in relation to it.

The same reduction must take place in the art and science of politics, at least in the case of the most advanced States, where "civil society" has become a very complex structure and one which is resistant to the catastrophic "incursions" of the immediate economic element (crises, depressions, etc.). The superstructures of civil society are like the trench-systems of modern warfare. In war it would sometimes happen that a fierce artillery attack seemed to have destroyed the enemy's entire defensive system, whereas in fact it had only destroyed the outer perimeter; and at the moment of their advance and attack the the assailants would find themselves confronted by a line of defence which was still effective. The same thing happens in politics, during the great economic crises. A crisis cannot give the attacking forces the ability to organise with lightning speed in time and in space; still less can it endow them with fighting spirit. Similarly, the defenders are not demoralised, nor do they abandon their positions, even among the ruins, nor do they lose faith in their own strength or their own future. Of course, things do not remain exactly as they were; but it is certain that one will not find the element of speed, of accelerated time, of the definitive forward march expected by the strategists of political Cadornism.[3]

[...]

The transition from the war of manœuvre (frontal attack) to the war of position – in the political field as well

This seems to me to be the most important question of political theory that the post-war period has posed, and the most difficult to solve correctly. It is related to the problems raised by Bronstein [Trotsky], who in one way or another can be considered the political theorist of frontal attack in a period in which it only leads to defeats. This transition in political science is only indirectly (mediately) related to that which took place in the military field, although certainly a relation exists and an essential one. The war of position demands enormous sacrifices by infinite masses of people. So an unprecedented concentration of hegemony is necessary, and hence a more "interventionist" government, which will take the offensive more openly against the oppositionists and organise permanently the "impossibility" of internal disintegration – with controls of every kind, political, administrative, etc., reinforcement of the hegemonic "positions" of the dominant group, etc. All this indicates that we have entered a culminating phase in the political-historical situation, since in politics the "war of position", once won, is decisive definitively. In politics, in other words, the war of manœuvre subsists so long as it is a question of winning positions which are not decisive, so that all the resources of the State's hegemony cannot be mobilised. But when, for one reason or another, these positions have lost their value and only the decisive positions are at stake, then one passes over to siege warfare; this is concentrated, difficult, and requires exceptional qualities of patience and inventiveness. In politics, the siege is a reciprocal one, despite all appearances, and the mere fact that the ruler has to muster all his resources demonstrates how seriously he takes his adversary. [1930–32]

"A resistance too long prolonged in a besieged camp is demoralising in itself. It implies suffering, fatigue, loss of rest, illness and the continual presence not of the acute danger which tempers but of the chronic danger which destroys." Karl Marx: Eastern Question. 14 September 1855.

Politics and military science

Tactic of great masses, and immediate tactic of small groups. Belongs to the discussion about war of position and war of movement, in so far as this is reflected in the psychology both of great leaders (strategists) and of their subordinates. It is also (if one can put it like that) the point of connection between strategy and tactics, both in politics and in military science. Individuals (even as components of vast masses) tend to conceive war instinctively as "partisan warfare" or "Garibaldine warfare" (which is a higher form of "partisan warfare"). In politics the error occurs as a result of an inaccurate understanding of what the State (in its integral meaning: dictatorship + hegemony) really is. In war a similar error occurs, transferred to the enemy camp (failure to understand not only one's own State but that of the enemy as well). In both cases, the error is related to individual particularism – of town or region; this leads to an underestimation of the adversary and his fighting organisation. [1930–32]

[…]

Hegemony (civil society) and separation of powers

The separation of powers,[4] together with all the discussion provoked by its realisation and the legal dogmas which its appearance brought into being, is a product of the struggle between civil society and political society in a specific historical period. This period is characterised by a certain unstable equilibrium between the classes, which is a result of the fact that certain categories of intellectuals (in the direct service of the State, especially the civil and military bureaucracy) are still too closely tied to the old dominant classes. In other words, there takes place within the society what Croce calls the "perpetual conflict between Church and State", in which the Church is taken as representing the totality of civil society (whereas in fact it is only an element of diminishing importance within it), and the State as representing every attempt to crystallise permanently a particular stage of development, a particular situation. In this sense, the Church itself may become State, and the conflict may occur between on the one hand secular (and secularising) civil society, and on the other State/Church (when the Church has become an integral part of the State, of political society monopolised by a specific privileged group, which absorbs the Church in order the better to preserve its monopoly with the support of that zone of "civil society" which the Church represents).

Essential importance of the separation of powers for political and economic liberalism; the entire liberal ideology, with its strengths and its weaknesses, can be encapsulated in the principle of the separation of powers, and the source of liberalism's weakness then becomes apparent: it is the bureaucracy – i.e. the crystallisation of the leading personnel – which exercises coercive power, and at a certain point it becomes a caste. Hence the popular demand for making all posts elective – a demand which is extreme liberalism, and at the same time its dissolution (principle of the permanent Constituent Assembly, etc.; in Republics, the election at fixed intervals of the Head of State gives the illusion of satisfying this elementary popular demand).

Unity of the State in the differentiation of powers: Parliament more closely linked to civil society; the judiciary power, between government and Parliament, represents the continuity of the written law (even against the government). Naturally all three powers are also organs of political hegemony, but in different degrees: 1. Legislature; 2. Judiciary; 3. Executive. It is to be noted how lapses in the administration of justice make an especially disastrous impression on the public: the hegemonic apparatus is more sensitive in this sector, to which arbitrary actions on the part of the police and political administration may also be referred. [1930–32]

[...]

If one had to translate the notion "Prince", as used in Machiavelli's work, into modern political language, one would have to make a series of distinctions: the "Prince" could be a Head of State, or the leader of a government, but it could also be a political leader whose aim is to conquer a State, or to found a new type of State; in this sense, "Prince" could be translated in modern terms as "political party". In certain States, the "Head of State" – in other words, the element which balances the various interests struggling against the predominant (but not absolutely exclusivistic) interest – is precisely the "political party". With the difference, however, that in terms of traditional, constitutional law it juridically neither rules nor governs. It has "*de facto* power", and exercises the hegemonic function and hence that of holding the balance between the various interests in "civil society"; the latter, however, is in fact intertwined with political society to such an extent that all the citizens feel that the party on the contrary both rules and governs. It is not possible to create a constitutional law of the traditional type on the basis of this reality, which is in continuous movement; it is only possible to create a system of principles asserting that the State's goal is its own end, its own disappearance, in other words the re-absorption of political society into civil society. [1930]

[...]

It should be remarked that the general notion of State includes elements which need to be referred back to the notion of civil society (in the sense that one might say that State = political society + civil society, in other words hegemony protected by the armour of coercion). In a doctrine of the State which conceives the latter as tendentially capable of withering away and of being subsumed into regulated society, the argument is a fundamental one. It is possible to imagine the coercive element of the State withering away by degrees, as ever-more conspicuous elements of regulated society (or ethical State or civil society) make their appearance.

The expressions "ethical State" or "civil society" would thus mean that this "image" of a State without a State was present to the greatest political and legal thinkers, in so far as they placed themselves on the terrain of pure science (pure utopia, since based on the premise that all men are really equal and hence equally rational and moral, i.e. capable of accepting the law spontaneously, freely, and not through coercion, as imposed by another class, as something external to consciousness).

It must be remembered that the expression "nightwatchman" for the liberal State comes from Lassalle, i.e. from a dogmatic and non-dialectical statalist (look closely at Lassalle's doctrines on this point and on the State in general, in contrast with Marxism). In the doctrine of the State as regulated society, one will have to pass from a phase in which "State" will be equal to "government", and "State" will be identified with "civil society", to a phase of the State as nightwatchman – i.e. of a coercive organisation which will safeguard the development of the continually proliferating elements of regulated society, and which will therefore progressively reduce its own authoritarian and forcible interventions. Nor can this conjure up the idea of a new "liberalism", even though the beginning of an era of organic liberty be imminent. [1930–32]

If it is true that no type of State can avoid passing through a phase of economic-corporate primitivism, it may be deduced that the content of the political hegemony of the new social group which has founded the new type of State must be predominantly of an economic order: what is involved is the reorganisation of the structure and the real relations between men on the one hand and the world of the economy or of production on the other. The superstructural elements will inevitably be few in number, and have a character of foresight and of struggle, but as yet few "planned" elements. Cultural policy will above all be negative, a critique of the past; it will be aimed at erasing from the memory and at destroying. The lines of construction will as yet be "broad lines", sketches, which might (and should) be changed at all times, so as to be consistent with the new structure as it is formed. This precisely did not happen in the period of the mediaeval communes; for culture, which remained a function of the Church, was precisely anti-economic in character (i.e. against the nascent capitalist economy); it was not directed towards giving hegemony to the new class, but rather to preventing the latter from acquiring it. Hence Humanism and the Renaissance were reactionary, because they signalled the defeat of the new class, the negation of the economic world which was proper to it, etc. [1931–32]

Another element to examine is that of the organic relations between the domestic and foreign policies of a State. Is it domestic policies which determine foreign policy, or vice versa? In this case too, it will be necessary to distinguish: between great powers, with relative international autonomy, and other powers; also, between different forms of government (a government like that of Napoleon III had two policies, apparently – reactionary internally, and liberal abroad).

Conditions in a State before and after a war. It is obvious that, in an alliance, what counts are the conditions in which a State finds itself at the moment of peace. Therefore it may happen that whoever has exercised hegemony during the war ends up by losing it as a result of the enfeeblement suffered in the course of the struggle, and is forced to see a "subordinate" who has been more skilful or "luckier" become hegemonic. This occurs in "world wars" when the geographic situation compels a State to throw all its resources into the crucible: it wins through its alliances, but victory finds it prostrate, etc. This is why in the concept of "great power" it is necessary to take many elements into account, and especially those which are "permanent" – i.e. especially "economic and financial potential" and population. [1932–32]

Notes

1 "*Arditismo.*" During the First World War, the "*arditi*" were volunteer commando squads in the Italian army. The term was adopted by d'Annunzio for his nationalist volunteer "legions", and was also used by the "*arditi del popolo*", formed to combat the fascist squads in the summer of 1921. This latter organisation emerged outside the left parties, but the mass of its local leaders and members were communist or socialist. The PSI (who signed a "concilation pact" with the fascists at this time) condemned the organisation; they advocated a policy of non-resistance. The PCI also condemned the organisation, for sectarian reasons, preferring to concentrate on its own, purely communist, defence squads. Gramsci had written and published articles welcoming the organisation before the official condemnation, and even afterwards did so obliquely, by criticising the PSI's attitude. However, as his comments later in this note indicate, he did not feel that working-class "*arditi*" could in fact hope to stand up to the fascist squads, who enjoyed the connivance of the State. It was only *mass* as opposed to *volunteer* action which could provide a viable response.

2 Rosa Luxemburg: *The General Strike – The Party and the Unions*. The Italian edition was published by *Società Editrice "Avanti!"* in Milan, 1919.

3 Luigi Cadorna (1850–1928) was commander-in-chief of the Italian armed forces until the defeat at Caporetto in 1917, for which he was held responsible. Cadorna was taken by Gramsci as the symbol of the authoritarian leader who makes no attempt to win the "consent" of those he is leading. See note 29 on p. 145.

4 The doctrine developed by Montesquieu in his *Esprit des Lois* – on the basis of the contemporary bourgeois political system in England as he saw it – whereby executive, legislative and judiciary functions are exercised independently of each other. The principle inspired the American Constitution and others modelled on it.

3 Gramsci, hegemony and international relations

An essay in method

Robert W. Cox

Source: Stephen Gill (ed.) (1993), *Gramsci, Historical Materialism and International Relations*, Cambridge: Cambridge University Press, pp. 49–66

Some time ago I began reading Gramsci's *Prison Notebooks*. In these fragments, written in a fascist prison between 1929 and 1935, the former leader of the Italian Communist Party was concerned with the problem of understanding capitalist societies in the 1920s and 1930s, and particularly with the meaning of fascism and the possibilities of building an alternative form of state and society based on the working class. What he had to say centred upon the state, upon the relationship of civil society to the state, and upon the relationship of politics, ethics and ideology to production. Not surprisingly, Gramsci did not have very much to say directly about international relations. Nevertheless, I found that Gramsci's thinking was helpful in understanding the meaning of international organisation with which I was then principally concerned. Particularly valuable was his concept of hegemony, but valuable also were several related concepts which he had worked out for himself or developed from others. This essay sets forth my understanding of what Gramsci meant by hegemony and these related concepts, and suggests how I think they may be adapted, retaining his essential meaning, to the understanding of problems of world order. It does not purport to be a critical study of Gramsci's political theory but merely a derivation from it of some ideas useful for a revision of current international relations theory.[1]

Gramsci and hegemony

Gramsci's concepts were all derived from history – both from his own reflections upon those periods of history which he thought helped to throw an explanatory light upon the present, and from his personal experience of political and social struggle. These included the workers' councils movement of the early 1920s, his participation in the Third International and his opposition to fascism. Gramsci's ideas have always to be related to his own historical context. More than that, he was constantly adjusting his concepts to specific historical circumstances. The concepts cannot usefully be considered in abstraction from their applications, for when they are so abstracted different usages of the same concept appear to contain contradictions or ambiguities.[2] A concept, in Gramsci's thought, is loose and elastic and attains precision only when brought into contact with a particular situation which it helps to explain – a contact which also develops the meaning of the concept. This is the strength of Gramsci's historicism and therein lies its explanatory power. The term 'historicism' is however, frequently misunderstood and criticised by those who seek a more abstract, systematic, universalistic and non-historical form of knowledge.[3]

Gramsci geared his thought consistently to the practical purpose of political action. In his prison writings, he always referred to Marxism as 'the philosophy of praxis'.[4] Partly at least, one may surmise, it must have been to underline the practical revolutionary purpose of philosophy. Partly too, it would have been to indicate his intention to contribute to a lively developing current of thought, given impetus by Marx but not forever circumscribed by Marx's work. Nothing could be further from his mind than a Marxism which consists in an exegesis of the sacred texts for the purpose of refining a timeless set of categories and concepts.

Origins of the concept of hegemony

There are two main strands leading to the Gramscian idea of hegemony. The first ran from the debates within the Third International concerning the strategy of the Bolshevik Revolution and the creation of a Soviet socialist state; the second from the writings of Machiavelli. In tracing the first strand, some commentators have sought to contrast Gramsci's thought with Lenin's by aligning Gramsci with the idea of a hegemony of the proletariat and Lenin with a dictatorship of the proletariat. Other commentators have underlined their basic agreement.[5] What is important is that Lenin referred to the Russian proletariat as both a dominant and a directing class; dominance implying dictatorship and direction implying leadership with the consent of allied classes (notably the peasantry). Gramsci, in effect, took over an idea that was current in the circles of the Third International: the workers exercised hegemony over the allied classes and dictatorship over enemy classes. Yet this idea was applied by the Third International only to the working class and expressed the role of the working class in leading an alliance of workers, peasants and perhaps some other groups potentially supportive of revolutionary change.[6]

Gramsci's originality lies in his giving a twist to this first strand: he began to apply it to the bourgeoisie, to the apparatus or mechanisms of hegemony of the dominant class.[7] This made it possible for him to distinguish cases in which the bourgeoisie had attained a hegemonic position of leadership over other classes from those in which it had not. In northern Europe, in the countries where capitalism had first become established, bourgeois hegemony was most complete. It necessarily involved concessions to subordinate classes in return for acquiescence in bourgeois leadership, concessions which could lead ultimately to forms of social democracy which preserve capitalism while making it more acceptable to workers and the petty bourgeois. Because their hegemony was firmly entrenched in civil society, the bourgeoisie often did not need to run the state themselves. Landed aristocrats in England, Junkers in Prussia, or a renegade pretender to the mantle of Napoleon I in France, could do it for them so long as these rulers recognised the hegemonic structures of civil society as the basic limits of their political action.

This perception of hegemony led Gramsci to enlarge his definition of the state. When the administrative, executive and coercive apparatus of government was in effect constrained by the hegemony of the leading class of a whole social formation, it became meaningless to limit the definition of the state to those elements of government. To be meaningful, the notion of the state would also have to include the underpinnings of the political structure in civil society. Gramsci thought of these in concrete historical terms – the church, the educational system, the press, all the institutions which helped to create in people certain modes of behaviour and expectations consistent with the hegemonic social order. For example, Gramsci argued that the Masonic lodges in Italy were a bond amongst the government officials who entered into the state machinery after the unification of Italy, and therefore must be considered as part of the state for the purpose of assessing its broader political structure. The hegemony of a dominant class thus bridged the conventional categories of state and civil society, categories which retained a certain analytical usefulness but ceased to correspond to separable entities in reality.

As noted above, the second strand leading to the Gramscian idea of hegemony came all the way from Machiavelli and helps to broaden even further the potential scope of application of the concept. Gramsci had pondered what Machiavelli had written, especially in *The Prince*, concerning the problem of founding a new state. Machiavelli, in the fifteenth century, was concerned with finding the leadership and the supporting social basis for a united Italy; Gramsci, in the twentieth century, with the leadership and supportive basis for an alternative to fascism. Where Machiavelli looked to the individual Prince, Gramsci looked to the Modern Prince: the revolutionary party engaged in a continuing and developing dialogue with its own base of support. Gramsci took over from Machiavelli the image of power as a centaur: half man, half beast, a necessary combination of consent and coercion.[8] To the extent that the consensual aspect of power is in the forefront, hegemony prevails. Coercion is always latent but is only applied in marginal, deviant cases. Hegemony is enough to ensure conformity of behaviour in most people most of the time. The Machiavellian connection frees the concept of power (and of hegemony as one form of power) from a tie to historically specific social classes and gives it a wider applicability to relations of dominance and subordination, including, as shall be suggested below, relations of world order. It does not, however, sever power relations from their social basis (i.e., in the case of world order relations by making them into relations among states narrowly conceived) but directs attention towards deepening an awareness of this social basis.

War of movement and war of position

In thinking through the first strand of his concept of hegemony, Gramsci reflected upon the experience of the Bolshevik Revolution and sought to determine what lessons might be drawn from it for the task of revolution in Western Europe.[9] He came to the conclusion that the circumstances in Western Europe differed greatly from those in Russia. To illustrate the differences in circumstances, and the consequent differences in strategies required, he had recourse to the military analogy of wars of movement and wars of position. The basic difference between Russia and Western Europe was in the relative strengths of state and civil society. In Russia, the administrative and coercive apparatus of the state was formidable but proved to be vulnerable, while civil society was undeveloped. A relatively small working class led by a disciplined avant-garde was able to overwhelm the state in a war of movement and met no effective resistance from the rest of civil society. The vanguard party could set about founding a new state through a combination of applying coercion against recalcitrant elements and building consent among others. (This analysis was partly apposite to the period of the New Economic Policy before coercion began to be applied on a larger scale against the rural population.)

In Western Europe, by contrast, civil society, under bourgeois hegemony, was much more fully developed and took manifold forms. A war of movement might conceivably, in conditions of exceptional upheaval, enable a revolutionary vanguard to seize control of the state apparatus; but because of the resiliency of civil society such an exploit would in the long run be doomed to failure. Gramsci described the state in Western Europe (by which we should read state in the limited sense of administrative, governmental and coercive apparatus and not the enlarged concept of the state mentioned above) as 'an outer ditch, behind which there stands a powerful system of fortresses and earthworks'.

> In Russia, the State was everything, civil society was primordial and gelatinous; in the West, there was a proper relation between State and civil society, and when the State trembled a sturdy structure of civil society was at once revealed.
>
> (Gramsci, 1971: 238)

Accordingly, Gramsci argued that the war of movement could not be effective against the hegemonic state-societies of Western Europe. The alternative strategy is the war of position which slowly builds up the strength of the social foundations of a new state. In Western Europe, the struggle had to be won in civil society before an assault on the state could achieve success. Premature attack on the state by a war of movement would only reveal the weakness of the opposition and lead to a reimposition of bourgeois dominance as the institutions of civil society reasserted control.

The strategic implications of this analysis are clear but fraught with difficulties. To build up the basis of an alternative state and society upon the leadership of the working class means creating alternative institutions and alternative intellectual resources within existing society and building bridges between workers and other subordinate classes. It means actively building a counter-hegemony within an established hegemony while resisting the pressures and temptations to relapse into pursuit of incremental gains for subaltern groups within the framework of bourgeois hegemony. This is the line between war of position as a long-range revolutionary strategy and social democracy as a policy of making gains within the established order.

Passive revolution

Not all Western European societies were bourgeois hegemonies. Gramsci distinguished between two kinds of society. One kind had undergone a thorough social revolution and worked out fully its consequences in new modes of production and social relations. England and France were cases that had gone further than most others in this respect. The other kind were societies which had so to speak imported or had thrust upon them aspects of a new order created abroad, without the old order having been displaced. These last were caught up in a dialectic of revolution-restoration which tended to become blocked as neither the new forces nor the old could triumph. In these societies, the new industrial bourgeoisie failed to achieve hegemony. The resulting stalemate with the traditionally dominant social classes created the conditions that Gramsci called 'passive revolution', the introduction of changes which did not involve any arousal of popular forces.[10]

One typical accompaniment to passive revolution in Gramsci's analysis is caesarism: a strong man intervenes to resolve the stalemate between equal and opposed social forces. Gramsci allowed that there were both progressive and reactionary forms of caesarism: progressive when strong rule presides over a more orderly development of a new state, reactionary when it stabilises existing power. Napoleon I was a case of progressive caesarism, but Napoleon III, the exemplar of reactionary caesarism, was more representative of the kind likely to arise in the course of passive revolution. Gramsci's analysis here is virtually identical with that of Marx in *The Eighteenth Brumaire of Louis Bonaparte*: the French bourgeoisie, unable to rule directly through their own political parties, were content to develop capitalism under a political regime which had its social basis in the peasantry, an inarticulate and unorganised class whose virtual representative Bonaparte could claim to be.

In late nineteenth-century Italy, the northern industrial bourgeoisie, the class with the most to gain from the unification of Italy, was unable to dominate the peninsula. The basis for the new state became an alliance between the industrial bourgeoisie of the north and the landowners of the south – an alliance which also provided benefits for petty bourgeois clients (especially from the south) who staffed the new state bureaucracy and political parties and became the intermediaries between the various population groups and the state. The lack of any sustained and widespread popular participation in the unification movement explained the 'passive revolution' character of its outcome. In the aftermath of the First World War, worker and peasant occupations of factories and land demonstrated a strength which was considerable enough to threaten yet insufficient to dislodge the existing state. There took place then what Gramsci called a 'displacement of the basis of the state'[11] towards the petty bourgeoisie, the only class of nation-wide extent, which became the anchor of fascist power. Fascism continued the passive revolution, sustaining the position of the old owner classes yet unable to attract the support of worker or peasant subaltern groups.

Apart from caesarism, the second major feature of passive revolution in Italy Gramsci called *trasformismo*. It was exemplified in Italian politics by Giovanni Giolitti who sought to bring about the widest possible coalition of interests and who dominated the political scene in the years preceding fascism. For example, he aimed to bring northern industrial workers into a common front with industrialists through a protectionist policy. *Trasformismo* worked to co-opt potential leaders of subaltern social groups. By extension *trasformismo* can serve as a strategy of assimilating and domesticating potentially dangerous ideas by adjusting them to the policies of the dominant coalition and can thereby obstruct the formation of class-based organised opposition to established social and political power. Fascism continued *trasformismo*. Gramsci interprets the fascist state corporatism as an unsuccessful attempt to introduce some of the more advanced industrial practices of American capitalism under the aegis of the old Italian management.

The concept of passive revolution is a counterpart to the concept of hegemony in that it describes the condition of a non-hegemonic society – one in which no dominant class has been able to establish a hegemony in Gramsci's sense of the term. Today this notion of passive revolution, together with its components, caesarism and *trasformismo*, is particularly apposite to industrialising Third World countries.

Historic bloc (*blocco storico*)

Gramsci attributed the source of his notion of the historic bloc (*blocco storico*) to Georges Sorel, though Sorel never used the term or any other in precisely the sense Gramsci gave to it.[12] Sorel did, however, interpret revolutionary action in terms of social myths through which people engaged in action perceived a confrontation of totalities – in which they saw a new order challenging an established order. In the course of a cataclysmic event, the old order would be overthrown as a whole and the new be freed to unfold.[13] While Gramsci did not share the subjectivism of this vision, he did share the view that state and society together constituted a solid structure and that revolution implied the development within it of another structure strong enough to replace the first. Echoing Marx, he thought this could come about only when the first had exhausted its full potential. Whether dominant or emergent, such a structure is what Gramsci called an historic bloc.

For Sorel, social myth, a powerful form of collective subjectivity, would obstruct reformist tendencies. These might otherwise attract workers away from revolutionary syndicalism into incrementalist trade unionism or reformist party politics. The myth was a weapon in struggle as well as a tool for analysis. For Gramsci, the historic bloc similarly had a revolutionary orientation through its stress on the unity and coherence of socio-political orders. It was an intellectual defence against co-optation by *trasformismo*.

The historic bloc is a dialectical concept in the sense that its interacting elements create a larger unity. Gramsci expressed these interacting elements sometimes as the subjective and the objective, sometimes as superstructure and structure.

> Structures and superstructures from an 'historic bloc'. That is to say the complex contradictory and discordant *ensemble* of the superstructures is the reflection of the *ensemble* of the social relations of production.
>
> (Gramsci, 1971: 366)

The juxtaposition and reciprocal relationships of the political, ethical and ideological spheres of activity with the economic sphere avoids reductionism. It avoids reducing everything either to economics (economism) or to ideas (idealism). In Gramsci's historical materialism (which he was careful to distinguish from what he called 'historical economism' or a narrowly economic interpretation of history), ideas and material conditions are always bound together, mutually influencing one another, and not reducible one to the other. Ideas have to be understood in relation to material circumstances. Material circumstances include both the social relations and the physical means of production. Superstructures of ideology and political organisation shape the development of both aspects of production and are shaped by them.

An historic bloc cannot exist without a hegemonic social class. Where the hegemonic class is the dominant class in a country or social formation, the state (in Gramsci's enlarged concept) maintains cohesion and identity within the bloc through the propagation of a common culture. A new bloc is formed when a subordinate class (e.g., the workers) establishes its hegemony over other subordinate groups (e.g., small farmers, marginals). This process requires intensive dialogue between leaders and followers within the would-be hegemonic class. Gramsci may have concurred in the Leninist idea of an avant-garde party which takes upon itself the responsibility for leading an immature working class, but only as an aspect of a war of movement. Because a war of position strategy was required in the western countries, as he saw it, the role of the party should be to lead, intensify and develop dialogue within the working class and between the working class and other subordinate classes which could be brought into alliance with it. The 'mass line' as a mobilisation technique developed by the Chinese Communist Party is consistent with Gramsci's thinking in this respect.

Intellectuals play a key role in the building of an historic bloc. Intellectuals are not a distinct and relatively classless social stratum. Gramsci saw them as organically connected with a social class. They perform the function of developing and sustaining the mental images, technologies and organisations which bind together the members of a class and of an historic bloc into a common identity. Bourgeois intellectuals did this for a whole society in which the bourgeoisie was hegemonic. The organic intellectuals of the working class would perform a similar role in the creation of a new historic bloc under working class hegemony within that society. To do this they would have to evolve clearly distinctive culture, organisation and technique and do so in constant interaction with the members of the emergent block. Everyone, for Gramsci, is in some part an intellectual, although only some perform full-time the social function of an intellectual. In this task, the party was, in his conception, a 'collective intellectual'.

In the movement towards hegemony and the creation of an historic bloc, Gramsci distinguished three levels of consciousness: the economico-corporative, which is aware of the specific interests of a particular group; the solidarity or class consciousness, which extends to a whole social class but remains at a purely economic level; and the hegemonic, which brings the interests of the leading class into harmony with those of subordinate classes and incorporates these other interests into an ideology expressed in universal terms (Gramsci, 1971: 180–95). The movement towards hegemony, Gramsci says, is a 'passage from the structure to the sphere of the complex superstructures', by which he means passing from the specific interests of a group or class to the building of institutions and elaboration of ideologies. If they reflect a hegemony, these institutions and ideologies will be universal in form i.e., they will not appear as those of a particular class, and will give some satisfaction to the subordinate groups while not undermining the leadership or vital interests of the hegemonic class.

Hegemony and international relations

We can now make the transition from what Gramsci said about hegemony and related concepts to the implications of these concepts for international relations. First, however, it is useful to look at what little Gramsci himself had to say about international relations. Let us begin with this passage:

> Do international relations precede or follow (logically) fundamental social relations? There can be no doubt that they follow. Any organic innovation in the social structure, through its technical-military expressions, modifies organically absolute and relative relations in the international field too.
>
> (Gramsci, 1971: 176)

By 'organic' Gramsci meant that which is structural, long-term or relatively permanent, as opposed to the short-term or 'conjunctural'. He was saying that basic changes in international power relations or world order, which are observed as changes in the military-strategic and geo-political balance, can be traced to fundamental changes in social relations.

Gramsci did not in any way by-pass the state or diminish its importance. The state remained for him the basic entity in international relations and the place where social conflicts take place – the place also, therefore, where hegemonies of social classes can be built. In these hegemonies of social classes, the particular characteristics of nations combine in unique and original ways. The working class, which might be considered to be international in an abstract sense, nationalises itself in the process of building its hegemony. The emergence of new worker-led blocs at the national level would, in this line of reasoning, precede any basic restructuring of international relations. However, the state, which remains the primary focus of social struggle and the basic entity of international relations, is the enlarged state which includes its own social basis. This view sets aside a narrow or superficial view of the state which reduces it, for instance, to the foreign policy bureaucracy or the state's military capabilities.

From his Italian perspective, Gramsci had a keen sense of what we would now call dependency. What happened in Italy he knew was markedly influenced by external powers.

At the purely foreign policy level, great powers have relative freedom to determine their foreign policies in response to domestic interests; smaller powers have less autonomy (Gramsci, 1971: 264). The economic life of subordinate nations is penetrated by and intertwined with that of powerful nations. This is further complicated by the existence within countries of structurally diverse regions which have distinctive patterns of relationship to external forces (Gramsci, 1971: 182).

At an even deeper level, those states which are powerful are precisely those which have undergone a profound social and economic revolution and have most fully worked out the consequences of this revolution in the form of state and of social relations. The French Revolution was the case Gramsci reflected upon, but we can think of the development of US and Soviet power in the same way. These were all nation-based developments which spilled over national boundaries to become internationally expansive phenomena. Other countries have received the impact of these developments in a more passive way, an instance of what Gramsci described at the national level as a passive revolution. This effect comes when the impetus to change does not arise out of 'a vast local economic development... but is instead the reflection of international developments which transmit their ideological currents to the periphery' (Gramsci, 1971: 116).

The group which is the bearer of the new ideas, in such circumstances, is not an indigenous social group which is actively engaged in building a new economic base with a new structure of social relations. It is an intellectual stratum which picks up ideas originating from a prior foreign economic and social revolution. Consequently, the thought of this group takes an idealistic shape ungrounded in a domestic economic development; and its conception of the state takes the form of 'a rational absolute' (Gramsci, 1971: 117). Gramsci criticised the thought of Benedetto Croce, the dominant figure of the Italian intellectual establishment of his own time, for expressing this kind of distortion.

Hegemony and world order

Is the Gramscian concept of hegemony applicable at the international or world level? Before attempting to suggest how this might be done, it is well to rule out some usages of the term which are common in international relations studies. Very often 'hegemony' is used to mean the dominance of one country over others, thereby tying the usage to a relationship strictly among states. Sometimes 'hegemony' is used as a euphemism for imperialism. When Chinese political leaders accuse the Soviet Union of 'hegemonism' they seem to have in mind some combination of these two. These meanings differ so much from the Gramscian sense of the term that it is better, for purposes of clarity in this paper, to use the term 'dominance' to replace them.

In applying the concept of hegemony to world order, it becomes important to determine when a period of hegemony begins and when it ends. A period in which a world hegemony has been established can be called hegemonic and one in which dominance of a non-hegemonic kind prevails, non-hegemonic. To illustrate, let us consider the past century and a half as falling into four distinguishable periods, roughly, 1845–75, 1875–1945, 1945–65 and 1965 to the present.[14]

The first period (1845–75) was hegemonic: there was a world economy with Britain as its centre. Economic doctrines consistent with British supremacy but universal in form – comparative advantage, free trade and the gold standard – spread gradually outward from Britain. Coercive strength underwrote this order. Britain held the balance of power in Europe, thereby preventing any challenge to hegemony from a land-based power. Britain ruled supreme at sea and had the capacity to enforce obedience by peripheral countries to the rules of the market.

In the second period (1875–1945), all these features were reversed. Other countries challenged British supremacy. The balance of power in Europe became destabilised, leading to two world wars. Free trade was superseded by protectionism; the Gold Standard was ultimately abandoned; and the world economy fragmented into economic blocs. This was a non-hegemonic period.

In the third period, following the Second World War (1945–65), the United States founded a new hegemonic world order similar in basic structure to that dominated by Britain in mid nineteenth century but with institutions and doctrines adjusted to a more complex world economy and to national societies more sensitive to the political repercussions of economic crises.

Sometime from the later 1960s through the early 1970s it became evident that this US-based world order was no longer working well. During the uncertain times which followed, three possibilities of structural transformation of world order opened up: a reconstruction of hegemony with a broadening of political management on the lines envisaged by the Trilateral Commission; increased fragmentation of the world economy around big-power-centred economic spheres; and the possible assertion of a Third-World-based counter-hegemony with the concerted demand for the New International Economic Order as a forerunner.

On the basis of this tentative notation, it would appear that, historically, to become hegemonic, a state would have to found and protect a world order which was universal in conception, i.e., not an order in which one state directly exploits others but an order which most other states (or at least those within reach of the hegemony) could find compatible with their interests. Such an order would hardly be conceived in inter-state terms alone, for this would likely bring to the fore oppositions of state interests. It would most likely give prominence to opportunities for the forces of civil society to operate on the world scale (or on the scale of the sphere within which hegemony prevails). The hegemonic concept of world order is founded not only upon the regulation of inter-state conflict but also upon a globally-conceived civil society, i.e., a mode of production of global extent which brings about links among social classes of the countries encompassed by it.

Historically, hegemonies of this kind are founded by powerful states which have undergone a thorough social and economic revolution. The revolution not only modifies the internal economic and political structures of the state in question but also unleashes energies which expand beyond the state's boundaries. A world hegemony is thus in its beginnings an outward expansion of the internal (national) hegemony established by a dominant social class. The economic and social institutions, the culture, the technology associated with this national hegemony become patterns for emulation abroad. Such an expansive hegemony impinges on the more peripheral countries as a passive revolution. These countries have not undergone the same thorough social revolution, nor have their economies developed in the same way, but they try to incorporate elements from the hegemonic model without disturbing old power structures. While peripheral countries may adopt some economic and cultural aspects of the hegemonic core, they are less well able to adopt its political models. Just as fascism became the form of passive revolution in the Italy of the inter-war period, so various forms of military-bureaucratic regime supervise passive revolution in today's peripheries. In the world-hegemonic model, hegemony is more intense and consistent at the core and more laden with contradictions at the periphery.

Hegemony at the international level is thus not merely an order among states. It is an order within a world economy with a dominant mode of production which penetrates into all countries and links into other subordinate modes of production. It is also a complex of international social relationships which connect the social classes of the different countries. World hegemony is describable as a social structure, an economic structure, and a political structure; and it cannot be simply one of these things but must be all three. World hegemony, furthermore, is expressed in universal norms, institutions and mechanisms which lay down general rules of behaviour for states and for those forces of civil society that act across national boundaries – rules which support the dominant mode of production.

The mechanisms of hegemony: international organisations

One mechanism through which the universal norms of a world hegemony are expressed is the international organisation. Indeed, international organisation functions as the process through which the institutions of hegemony and its ideology are developed. Among the features of international organisation which express its hegemonic role are the following: (1) they embody the rules which facilitate the expansion of hegemonic world orders; (2) they are themselves the product of the hegemonic world order; (3) they ideologically legitimate the norms of the world order; (4) they co-opt the elites from peripheral countries and (5) they absorb counter-hegemonic ideas.

International institutions embody rules which facilitate the expansion of the dominant economic and social forces but which at the same time permit adjustments to be made by subordinated interests with a minimum of pain. The rules governing world monetary and trade relations are particularly significant. They are framed primarily to promote economic expansion. At the same time they allow for exceptions and derogations to take care of problem situations. They can be revised in the light of changed circumstances. The Bretton Woods institutions provided more safeguards for domestic social concerns like unemployment than did the Gold Standard, on condition that national policies were consistent with the goal of a liberal world economy. The current system of floating exchange rates also gives scope for national actions while maintaining the principle of a prior commitment to harmonise national policies in the interests of a liberal world economy.

International institutions and rules are generally initiated by the state which establishes the hegemony. At the very least they must have that state's support. The dominant state takes care to secure the acquiescence of other states according to a hierarchy of powers within the inter-state structure of hegemony. Some second-rank countries are consulted first and their support is secured. The consent of at least some of the more peripheral countries is solicited. Formal participation may be weighted in favour of the dominant powers as in the International Monetary Fund and World Bank, or it may be on a one-state-one-vote basis as in most other major international institutions. There is an informal structure of influence reflecting the different levels of real political and economic power which underlies the formal procedures for decisions.

International institutions perform an ideological role as well. They help define policy guidelines for states and to legitimate certain institutions and practices at the national level. They reflect orientations favourable to the dominant social and economic forces. The OECD, in recommending monetarism, endorsed a dominant consensus of policy thinking in the core countries and strengthened those who were determined to combat inflation this way against others who were more concerned about unemployment. The ILO, by advocating tripartism, legitimates the social relations evolved in the core countries as the desirable model for emulation.

Elite talent from peripheral countries is co-opted into international institutions in the manner of *trasformismo*. Individuals from peripheral countries, though they may come to international institutions with the idea of working from within to change the system, are condemned to work within the structures of passive revolution. At best they will help transfer elements of 'modernisation' to the peripheries but only as these are consistent with the interests of established local powers. Hegemony is like a pillow: it absorbs blows and sooner or later the would-be assailant will find it comfortable to rest upon. Only where representation in international institutions is firmly based upon an articulate social and political challenge to hegemony – upon a nascent historic bloc and counter-hegemony – could participation pose a real threat. The co-optation of outstanding individuals from the peripheries renders this less likely.

Trasformismo also absorbs potentially counter-hegemonic ideas and makes these ideas consistent with hegemonic doctrine. The notion of self-reliance, for example, began as a challenge to the world economy by advocating endogenously determined autonomous development. The term has now been transformed to mean support by the agencies of the world economy for do-it-yourself welfare programmes in the peripheral countries. These programmes aim to enable the rural populations to achieve self-sufficiency, to stem the rural exodus to the cities, and to achieve thereby a greater degree of social and political stability amongst populations which the world economy is incapable of integrating. Self-reliance in its transformed meaning becomes complementary to and supportive of hegemonic goals for the world economy.

Thus, one tactic for bringing about change in the structure of world order can be ruled out as a total illusion. There is very little likelihood of a war of movement at the international level through which radicals would seize control of the superstructure of international institutions. Daniel Patrick Moynihan notwithstanding, Third World radicals do not control international institutions. Even if they did, they could achieve nothing by it. These superstructures are inadequately connected with any popular political base. They are connected with the national hegemonic classes in the core countries and, through the intermediacy of these classes, have a broader base in these countries. In the peripheries, they connect only with the passive revolution.

The prospects for counter-hegemony

World orders – to return to Gramsci's statement cited earlier in this essay – are grounded in social relations. A significant structural change in world order is, accordingly, likely to be traceable to some fundamental change in social relations and in the national political orders which correspond to national structures of social relations. In Gramsci's thinking, this would come about with the emergence of a new historic bloc.

We must shift the problem of changing world order back from international institutions to national societies. Gramsci's analysis of Italy is even more valid when applied to the world order: only a war of position can, in the long run, bring about structural changes, and a war of position involves building up the socio-political base for change through the creation of new historic blocs. The national context remains the only place where an historic bloc can be founded, although world-economy and world-political conditions materially influence the prospects for such an enterprise.

The prolonged crisis in the world economy (the beginning of which can be traced to the late 1960s and early 1970s) is propitious for some developments which could lead to a counter-hegemonic challenge. In the core countries, those policies which cut into transfer payments to deprived social groups and generate high unemployment open the prospects of a broad alliance of the disadvantaged against the sectors of capital and labour which find common ground in international production and the monopoly-liberal world order. The policy basis for this alliance would most likely be post-Keynesian and neomercantilist. In peripheral countries, some states are vulnerable to revolutionary action, as events from Iran to Central America suggest. Political preparation of the population in sufficient depth may not, however, be able to keep pace with revolutionary opportunity and this diminishes the prospect for a new historic bloc. An effective political organisation (Gramsci's Modern Prince) would be required in order to rally the new working classes generated by international production and build a bridge to peasants and urban marginals. Without this, we can only envisage a process where local political elites, even some which are the product of abortively revolutionary upheavels, would entrench their power within a monopoly-liberal world order. A reconstructed monopoly-liberal hegemony would be quite capable of practising *trasformismo* by adjusting to many varieties of national institutions and practices, including nationalisation of industries. The rhetoric of nationalism and socialism could then be brought into line with the restoration of passive revolution under new guise in the periphery.

In short, the task of changing world order begins with the long, laborious effort to build new historic blocs within national boundaries.

Notes

1 This essay was originally published in *Millennium* (1983), 12(2): 162–75. I refer in citation to Gramsci (1971), herafter cited as *Selections*. The full critical edition is Gramsci (1975), hereafter cited as *Quaderni*.

2 This seems to be the problem underlying Anderson (1976–77) which purports to find inconsistencies in Gramsci's concepts.

3 On this point see Thompson (1978), which contrasts a historicist position analogous to Gramsci's with the abstract philosophical structuralism of Althusser. See 'Marxism is not Historicism', in Althusser and Balibar (1979).

4 It is said that this was to avoid confiscation of his notes by the prison censor who, if this is true, must have been particularly slow-witted.

5 Buci-Glucksmann (1982) places Gramsci squarely in the Leninist tradition. Buci-Glucksmann's work seems to me to be more fully thought through. See also Mouffe (1979) and Showstack-Sassoon (1982).

6 This notion fitted well with Gramsci's assessment of the situation in Italy in the early 1920s; the working class was by itself too weak to carry the full burden of revolution and could only bring about the founding of a new state by an alliance with the peasantry and some petty bourgeoise elements. In fact, Gramsci considered the workers' council movement as a school for leadership of such a coalition and his efforts prior to his imprisonment were directed toward building this coalition.

7 See Buci-Glucksmann (1975: 63).

8 Gramsci (1971: 169–90).

9 The term 'Western Europe' refers here to the Britain, France, Germany and Italy of the 1920s and 1930s.

10 Gramsci borrowed the term 'passive revolution' from the Neapolitan historian Vincenzo Cuocco (1770–1823) who was active in the early stages of the Risorgimento. In Cuocco's interpretation, Napoleon's armies had brought passive revolution to Italy.

11 Buci-Glucksmann (1975: 121).

12 Gramsci, *Quaderni* (1975: 2,632).

13 See Sorel's discussion of myth and the 'Napoleonic battle' in the letter to Daniel Halevy.

14 The dating is tentative and would have to be refined by enquiry into the structural features proper to each period as well as into factors deemed to constitute the breaking points between one period and another. These are offered here as mere notations for a revision of historical scholarship to raise some questions about hegemony and its attendant structures and mechanisms.

Imperialism, which has taken different forms in these periods, is a closely related question. In the first, *Pax Britannica*, although some territories were directly administered, control of colonies seems to have been incidental rather than necessary to economic expansion. Argentina, a formally independent country, had essentially the same relationship to the British economy as Canada, a former colony. This, as George Lichtheim noted, may be called the phase of 'liberal imperialism'. In the second period, the so-called 'new imperialism' brought more emphasis on direct political controls. It also saw the growth of capital exports and of the finance capital identified by Lenin as the very essence of imperialism. In the third period, which might be called that of the neo-liberal or monopoly-liberal imperialism, the internationalising of production emerged as the pre-eminent form, supported also by new forms of finance capital (multinational banks and consortia). There seems little point in trying to define some unchanging essense of imperialism but it would be more useful to describe the structural characteristics of the imperialisms which correspond to successive hegemonic and non-hegemonic world orders. For a further discussion of this as regards *Pax Britannica* and *Pax Americana*, see Cox (1983).

References

Althusser, L. and Blaibar, E. (1979), *Reading Capital*, London: Verso.

Buci-Glucksmann, C. (1982), 'Hegemony and Consent: A Political Strategy', in Sassoon, A. S. (ed.) *Approaches to Gramsci*, London: Writers and Readers Publishing Cooperative.

Cox, R. W. (1983), 'Gramsci, Hegemony and International Relations: An Essay in Method', *Millennium* 12, 162–75.

Gramsci, A. (1971), *Selections from the Prison Notebooks of Antonio Gramsci*, translated by Q. Hoare and G. Nowell Smith, London: Lawrence and Wishart.

Gramsci, A. (1975), *Quaderni del Carcere*, Torino: Einaudi.

Mouffe, C. (ed.) (1979), *Gramsci and Marxist Theory*, London: Routledge.

Sassoon, A. S. (1982), 'Hegemony, War of Position and Political Intervention', in Sassoon, A. S. (ed.) *Approaches to Gramsci*, London: Writers and Readers Publishing Cooperative.

Thompson, E. P. (1978), 'The Poverty of Theory', in Thompson, E. P. (ed.) *The Poverty of Theory and Other Essays*, New York: Monthly Review.

4 The self-regulating market and the fictitious commodities

Labor, land, and money

Karl Polanyi

Source: Karl Polanyi (1957), *The Great Transformation: The Political and Economic Origins of Our Time*, Boston, MA: Beacon Press, pp. 68–76

This cursory outline of the economic system and markets, taken separately, shows that never before our own time were markets more than accessories of economic life. As a rule, the economic system was absorbed in the social system, and whatever principle of behavior predominated in the economy, the presence of the market pattern was found to be compatible with it. The principle of barter or exchange, which underlies this pattern, revealed no tendency to expand at the expense of the rest. Where markets were most highly developed, as under the mercantile system, they throve under the control of a centralized administration which fostered autarchy both in the households of the peasantry and in respect to national life. Regulation and markets, in effect, grew up together. The self-regulating market was unknown; indeed the emergence of the idea of self-regulation was a complete reversal of the trend of development. It is in the light of these facts that the extraordinary assumptions underlying a market economy can alone be fully comprehended.

A market economy is an economic system controlled, regulated, and directed by markets alone; order in the production and distribution of goods is entrusted to this self-regulating mechanism. An economy of this kind derives from the expectation that human beings behave in such a way as to achieve maximum money gains. It assumes markets in which the supply of goods (including services) available at a definite price will equal the demand at that price. It assumes the presence of money, which functions as purchasing power in the hands of its owners. Production will then be controlled by prices, for the profits of those who direct production will depend upon them; the distribution of the goods also will depend upon prices, for prices form incomes, and it is with the help of these incomes that the goods produced are distributed amongst the members of society. Under these assumptions order in the production and distribution of goods is ensured by prices alone.

Self-regulation implies that all production is for, sale on the market and that all incomes derive from such sales. Accordingly, there are markets for all elements of industry, not only for goods (always including services) but also for labor, land, and money, their prices being called respectively commodity prices, wages, rent, and interest. The very terms indicate that prices form incomes: interest is the price for the use of money and forms the income of those who are in the position to provide it; rent is the price for the use of land and forms the income of those who supply it; wages are the price for the use of labor power, and form the income of those who sell it; commodity prices, finally, contribute to the incomes of those who sell their entrepreneurial services, the income called profit being actually the difference between two sets of prices, the price of the goods produced and their costs, *i.e.*, the price of the goods necessary to produce them. If these conditions are fulfilled, all incomes will derive from sales on the market, and incomes will be just sufficient to buy all the goods produced.

A further group of assumptions follows in respect to the state and its policy. Nothing must be allowed to inhibit the formation of markets, nor must incomes be permitted to be formed otherwise than through sales. Neither must there be any interference with the adjustment of prices to changed market conditions – whether the prices are those of goods, labor, land, or money. Hence there must not only be markets for all elements of industry,[1] but no measure or policy must be countenanced that would influence the action of these markets. Neither price, nor supply, nor demand must be fixed or regulated; only such policies and measures are in order which help to ensure the self-regulation of the market by creating conditions which make the market the only organizing power in the economic sphere.

To realize fully what this means, let us return for a moment to the mercantile system and the national markets which it did so much to develop. Under feudalism and the gild system land and labor formed part of the social organization itself (money had yet hardly developed into a major element of industry). Land, the pivotal element in the feudal order, was the basis of the military, judicial, administrative, and political system; its status and function were determined by legal and customary rules. Whether its possession was transferable or not, and if so, to whom and under what restrictions; what the rights of property entailed; to what uses some types of land might be put – all these questions were removed from the organization of buying and selling, and subjected to an entirely different set of institutional regulations.

The same was true of the organization of labor. Under the gild system, as under every other economic system in previous history, the motives and circumstances of productive activities were embedded in the general organization of society. The relations of master, journeyman, and apprentice; the terms of the craft; the number of apprentices; the wages of the workers were all regulated by the custom and rule of the gild and the town. What the mercantile system did was merely to unify these conditions either through statute as in England, or through the "nationalization" of the gilds as in France. As to land, its feudal status was abolished only in so far as it was linked with provincial privileges; for the rest, land remained *extra commercium*, in England as in France. Up to the time of the Great Revolution of 1789, landed estate remained the source of social privilege in France, and even after that time in England Common Law on land was essentially medieval. Mercantilism, with all its tendency towards commercialization, never attacked the safeguards which protected these two basic elements of production – labor and land – from becoming the objects of commerce. In England the "nationalization" of labor legislation through the Statute of Artificers (1563) and the Poor Law (1601), removed labor from the danger zone, and the anti-enclosure policy of the Tudors and early Stuarts was one consistent protest against the principle of the gainful use of landed property.

That mercantilism, however emphatically it insisted on commercialization as a national policy, thought of markets in a way exactly contrary to market economy, is best shown by its vast extension of state intervention in industry. On this point there was no difference between mercantilists and feudalists, between crowned planners and vested interests, between centralizing bureaucrats and conservative particularists. They disagreed only on the methods of regulation: gilds, towns, and provinces appealed to the force of custom and tradition, while the new state authority favored statute and ordinance. But they were all equally averse to the idea of commercializing labor and land – the precondition of market economy. Craft gilds and feudal privileges were abolished in France only in 1790; in England the Statute of Artificers was repealed only in 1813–14, the Elizabethan Poor Law in 1834. Not before the last decade of the eighteenth century was, in either country, the establishment of a free labor market even discussed; and the idea of the self-regulation of economic life was utterly beyond the horizon of the age. The mercantilist was concerned with the development of the resources of the country, including full employment, through trade and commerce; the traditional organization of land and labor he took for granted. He was in this respect as far removed from modern concepts as he was in the realm of politics, where his belief in the absolute powers of an enlightened despot was tempered by no intimations of democracy. And just as the transition to a democratic system and representative politics involved a complete reversal of the trend of the age, the change from regulated to self-regulating markets at the end of the eighteenth century represented a complete transformation in the structure of society.

A self-regulating market demands nothing less than the institutional separation of society into an economic and political sphere. Such a dichotomy is, in effect, merely the restatement, from the point of view of society as a whole, of the existence of a self-regulating market. It might be argued that the separateness of the two spheres obtains in every type of society at all times. Such an inference, however, would be based on a fallacy. True, no society can exist without a system of some kind which ensures order in the production and distribution of goods. But that does not imply the existence of separate economic institutions; *normally, the economic order is merely a function of the social, in which it is contained.* Neither under tribal, nor feudal, nor mercantile conditions was there, as we have shown, a separate economic system in society. Nineteenth century society, in which economic activity was isolated and imputed to a distinctive economic motive, was, indeed, a singular departure.

Such an institutional pattern could not function unless society was somehow subordinated to its requirements. A market economy can exist only in a market society. We reached this conclusion on general grounds in our analysis of the market pattern. We can now specify the reasons for this assertion. A market economy must comprise all elements of industry, including labor, land, and money. (In a market economy the last also is an essential element of industrial life and its inclusion in the market mechanism has, as we will see, far-reaching institutional consequences.) But labor and land are no other than the human beings themselves of which every society consists and the natural surroundings in which it exists. To include them in the market mechanism means to subordinate the substance of society itself to the laws of the market.

We are now in the position to develop in a more concrete form the institutional nature of a market economy, and the perils to society which it involves. We will, first, describe the methods by which the market mechanism is enabled to control and direct the actual elements of industrial life; second, we will try to gauge the nature of the effects of such a mechanism on the society which is subjected to its action.

It is with the help of the commodity concept that the mechanism of the market is geared to the various elements of industrial life. Commodities are here empirically defined as objects produced for sale on the market; markets, again, are empirically defined as actual contacts between buyers and sellers. Accordingly, every element of industry is regarded as having been produced for sale, as then and then only will it be subject to the supply-and-demand mechanism interacting with price. In practice this means that there must be markets for every element of industry; that in these markets each of these elements is organized into a supply and a demand group; and that each element has a price which interacts with demand and supply. These markets – and they are numberless – are interconnected and form One Big Market.[2]

The crucial point is this: labor, land, and money are essential elements of industry; they also must be organized in markets; in fact, these markets form an absolutely vital part of the economic system. But labor, land, and money are obviously *not* commodities; the postulate that anything that is bought and sold must have been produced for sale is emphatically untrue in regard to them. In other words, according to the empirical definition of a commodity they are not commodities. Labor is only another name for a human activity which goes with life itself, which in its turn is not produced for sale but for entirely different reasons, nor can that activity be detached from the rest of life, be stored or mobilized; land is only another name for nature, which is not produced by man; actual money, finally, is merely a token of purchasing power which, as a rule, is not produced at all, but comes into being through the mechanism of banking or state finance. None of them is produced for sale. The commodity description of labor, land, and money is entirely fictitious.

Nevertheless, it is with the help of this fiction that the actual markets for labor, land, and money are organized;[3] they are being actually bought and sold on the market; their demand and supply are real magnitudes; and any measures or policies that would inhibit the formation of such markets would *ipso facto* endanger the self-regulation of the system. The commodity fiction, therefore, supplies a vital organizing principle in regard to the whole of society affecting almost all its institutions in the most varied way, namely, the principle according to which no arrangement or behavior should be allowed to exist that might prevent the actual functioning of the market mechanism on the lines of the commodity fiction.

Now, in regard to labor, land, and money such a postulate cannot be upheld. To allow the market mechanism to be sole director of the fate of human beings and their natural environment, indeed, even of the amount and use of purchasing power, would result in the demolition of society. For the alleged commodity "labor power" cannot be shoved about, used indiscriminately, or even left unused, without affecting also the human individual who happens to be the bearer of this peculiar commodity. In disposing of a man's labor power the system would, incidentally, dispose of the physical, psychological, and moral entity "man" attached to that tag. Robbed of the protective covering of cultural institutions, human beings would perish from the effects of social exposure; they would die as the victims of acute social dislocation through vice, perversion, crime, and starvation. Nature would be reduced to its elements, neighborhoods and landscapes defiled, rivers polluted, military safety jeopardized, the power to produce food and raw materials destroyed. Finally, the market administration of purchasing power would periodically liquidate business enterprise, for shortages and surfeits of money would prove as disastrous to business as floods and droughts in primitive society. Undoubtedly, labor, land, and money markets *are* essential to a market economy. But no society could stand the effects of such a system of crude fictions even for the shortest stretch of time unless its human and natural substance as well as its business organization was protected against the ravages of this satanic mill.

The extreme artificiality of market economy is rooted in the fact that the process of production itself is here organized in the form of buying and selling.[4] No other way of organizing production for the market is possible in a commercial society. During the late Middle Ages industrial production for export was organized by wealthy burgesses, and carried on under their direct supervision in the home town. Later, in the mercantile society, production was organized by merchants and was not restricted any more to the towns; this was the age of "putting out" when domestic industry was provided with raw materials by the merchant capitalist, who controlled the process of production as a purely commercial enterprise. It was then that industrial production was definitely and on a large scale put under the organizing leadership of the merchant. He knew the market, the volume as well as the quality of the demand; and he could vouch also for the supplies which, incidentally, consisted merely of wool, woad, and, sometimes, the looms or the knitting frames used by the cottage industry. If supplies failed it was the cottager who was worst hit, for his employment was gone for the time; but no expensive plant was involved and the merchant incurred no serious risk in shouldering the responsibility for production. For centuries this system grew in power and scope until in a country like England the wool industry, the national staple, covered large sectors of the country where production was organized by the clothier. He who bought and sold, incidentally, provided for production – no separate motive was required. The creation of goods involved neither the reciprocating attitudes of mutual aid; nor the concern of the householder for those whose needs are left to his care; nor the craftsman's pride in the exercise of his trade; nor the satisfaction of public praise – nothing but the plain motive of gain so familiar to the man whose profession is buying and selling. Up to the end of the eighteenth century, industrial production in Western Europe was a mere accessory to commerce.

As long as the machine was an inexpensive and unspecific tool there was no change in this position. The mere fact that the cottager could produce larger amounts than before within the same time might induce him to use machines to increase earnings, but this fact in itself did not necessarily affect the organization of production. Whether the cheap machinery was owned by the worker or by the merchant made some difference in the social position of the parties and almost certainly made a difference in the earnings of the worker, who was better off as long as he owned his tools; but it did not force the merchant to become an industrial capitalist, or to restrict himself to lending his money to such persons as were. The vent of goods rarely gave out; the greater difficulty continued to be on the side of supply of raw materials, which was sometimes unavoidably interrupted. But, even in such cases, the loss to the merchant who owned the machines was not substantial. It was not the coming of the machine as such but the invention of elaborate and therefore specific machinery and plant which completely changed the relationship of the merchant to production. Although the new productive organization was introduced by the merchant – a fact which determined the whole course of the transformation – the use of elaborate machinery and plant involved the development of the factory system and therewith a decisive shift in the relative importance of commerce and industry in favor of the latter. Industrial production ceased to be an accessory of commerce organized by the merchant as a buying and selling proposition; it now involved long-term investment with corresponding risks. Unless the continuance of production was reasonably assured, such a risk was not bearable.

But the more complicated industrial production became, the more numerous were the elements of industry the supply of which had to be safeguarded. Three of these, of course, were of outstanding importance: labor, land, and money. In a commercial society their supply could be organized in one way only: by being made available for purchase. Hence, they would have to be organized for sale on the market – in other words, as commodities. The extension of the market mechanism to the elements of industry – labor, land, and money – was the inevitable consequence of the introduction of the factory system in a commercial society. The elements of industry had to be on sale.

This was synonymous with the demand for a market system. We know that profits are ensured under such a system only if self-regulation is safeguarded through interdependent competitive markets. As the development of the factory system had been organized as part of a process of buying and selling, therefore labor, land, and money had to be transformed into commodities in order to keep production going. They could, of course, not be really transformed into commodities, as actually they were not produced for sale on the market. But the fiction of their being so produced became the organizing principle of society. Of the three, one stands out: labor is the technical term used for human beings, in so far as they are not employers but employed; it follows that henceforth the organization of labor would change concurrently with the organization of the market system. But as the organization of labor is only another word for the forms of life of the common people, this means that the development of the market system would be accompanied by a change in the organization of society itself. All along the line, human society had become an accessory of the economic system.

We recall our parallel between the ravages of the enclosures in English history and the social catastrophe which followed the Industrial Revolution. Improvements, we said, are, as a rule, bought at the price of social dislocation. If the rate of dislocation is too great, the community must succumb in the process. The Tudors and early Stuarts saved England from the fate of Spain by regulating the course of change so that it became bearable and its effects could be canalized into less destructive avenues. But nothing saved the common people of England from the impact of the Industrial Revolution. A blind faith in spontaneous progress had taken hold of people's minds, and with the fanaticism of sectarians the most enlightened pressed forward for boundless and unregulated change in society. The effects on the lives of the people were awful beyond description. Indeed, human society would have been annihilated but for protective countermoves which blunted the action of this self-destructive mechanism.

Social history in the nineteenth century was thus the result of a double movement: the extension of the market organization in respect to genuine commodities was accompanied by its restriction in respect to fictitious ones. While on the one hand markets spread all over the face of the globe and the amount of goods involved grew to unbelievable proportions, on the other hand a network of measures and policies was integrated into powerful institutions designed to check the action of the market relative to labor, land, and money. While the organization of world commodity markets, world capital markets, and world currency markets under the aegis of the gold standard gave an unparalleled momentum to the mechanism of markets, a deep-seated movement sprang into being to resist the pernicious effects of a market-controlled economy. Society protected itself against the perils inherent in a self-regulating market system – this was the one comprehensive feature in the history of the age.

Notes

1 Henderson, H. D., *Supply and Demand*, 1922. The practice of the market is twofold: the apportionment of factors between different uses, and the organizing of the forces influencing aggregate supplies of factors.
2 Hawtrey, G. R., *op. cit.* Its function is seen by Hawtrey in making "the relative market values of all commodities mutually consistent."
3 Marx's assertion of the fetish character of the value of commodities refers to the exchange value of genuine commodities and has nothing in common with the fictitious commodities mentioned in the text.
4 Cunningham, W., "Economic Change," *Cambridge Modern History*, Vol. I.

5 Theorizing the interregnum

The double movement and global politics in the 1990s

Stephen Gill

Source: Björn Hettne (ed.) (1995), *International Political Economy: Understanding Global Disorder*, London: Zed Books, pp. 65–99

[...]

One might argue that what is emerging in world politics in the 1990s is something akin to the 'double movement' outlined by Karl Polanyi in *The Great Transformation* (1957). By this Polanyi – in some ways reminiscent of Gramsci – referred to the historical countermovements which attempted, in disparate but interrelated ways, to reassert social control over the movement towards the unfettered power of capital in determining the possibilities for social choice. Polanyi's two cases of this were in the late nineteenth century, and again in the interwar period, after the attempts to restore a liberal world economic order under Anglo-American dominance in the 1920s. Today we can relate the metaphor of the 'double movement' to those sociopolitical forces which wish to assert more democratic control over political life, and to harness the productive aspects of world society to achieve broad social purposes on an inclusionary basis, across and within different types of civilization. This involves a critique of the moral bankruptcy and social consequences of the narrow application of a crass consumerist materialism which lies at the heart of the neo-liberal discourse.

With these highly political issues in mind, the purpose of this chapter is to sketch a historical materialist conceptualization of selected aspects of the political economy of the emerging world order, so as to probe its limits and contradictions. In normative terms, my purpose is to develop a form of understanding which can contribute to the construction of alternatives to the present world order configuration, one based upon the principles of democratization and diffusion of power, greater social equity and human autonomy, moderation, and where possible non-violence in dealing with conflict. All of this means collective action – at local and global levels. This is necessary to countervail repressive, morbid and dehumanizing forces (for example, the orthodox deflationary policies of the *rentier* liberals on the one hand, and the forces of authoritarianism and fascism on the other) in the emerging world order.

Conceptualizing world orders

To make sense of the vast complexity of the emerging world order, our conceptualization should involve the social forces of ideas (including ideologies, ethics, intersubjective meanings), institutions (such as state, and market, international organizations) as well as material aspects of social life (production broadly defined, including the means of destruction). We need to analyse the nature of this order at the levels of production, state and civil society, and world order (Cox, 1987). We need to do so with a sense of responsibility and thus combine political economy and ethico-political analysis. We can then analyse changes in world order in terms of the dialectic between forms of state, structures of production and ethico-political life. This requires an integrated form of political economy analysis which is open to conceptual and theoretical innovation. In this chapter, 'order' is understood as how things actually are, in a particular historical period, not as a normatively desirable or stable condition. To synthesize both Cox (1987) and Braudel (1981), a world order consists of a relatively persistent pattern of ideas, institutions and material forces which form historical structures over time, where structures can transcend particular societies or civilizational forms, in both space and time. Historical structures and the nature of political consciousness together configure the 'limits of the possible' for different groups, classes and nations.

The type of structural analysis I have in mind draws on the idea of historical structures, or patterns of behaviour which take on a particular character over time. Collective actions of human beings form historical structures with particular temporal duration. Since these structures are historically specific they cannot be adequately explained by using transhistorical generalizations, such as those associated with cyclical theories of history (for example, those which theorize the rise and decline of nations, hegemonies and empires). Rather, social scientific innovation is related to a 'second-order reality' which is not fully knowable (it involves the consciousness and intersubjectivities of human beings who can change the course of their actions). Thus social scientific generalizations must be limited and require a conditional vocabulary (Gunnell, 1968). At the same time, human action can change these structures. One should seek to analyse clearly the realities of our current situation. In this context we should outline the nature of, and potential for changes in, the 'limits of the possible' (Braudel, 1981). This is especially important for those groups who seek to democratize and to humanize global society.

[...]

Since the 1970s, there has been a shift towards a neo-liberal, disciplinary world order, although this is now in the process of being countervailed and constrained. I will discuss this in more detail later. One aspect of neo-liberal dominance is the growing structural power of capital, relative to labour, and relative to states. This neo-liberal shift involves, then, the growing strength and positional power of neo-liberal ideas (for example, my comments about heresy and the economics priesthood, above), their application in the practices and organizational forms of key social institutions (for example, state, market, international organization), and the reconfiguration of material power relations and a redistribution of wealth (with the growth in the power of capital, relative to labour). Instead of discipline being exercised authoritatively (for example, through social institutions such as the state, the family, churches), increasingly this discipline is market-based, and both direct (for example, capital's superior bargaining power over labour, or relative to states which bid for investment against one another) and indirect (for example, discipline exercised on firms, their workers, or on governments in the financial – especially stock and bond – markets). At the same time, the trends of the 1970s have gone with a deterioration in the material position of women, especially in the Third World and the former communist states.

Of course, there are many differences between the interwar period and the 1990s. Much of the world in the 1990s experiences what can be called – for want of a better expression – a form of not only market discipline, but of organized chaos (Vieille, 1988). By this I mean it is systematic in form, linked to the spread of *laissez faire* ideas and practices, and is sustained politically by a relatively affluent, politically active minority of the world's population (this minority is larger than that in the 1930s, partly because of the widening of political participation and economic growth). It is chaotic in the sense that the integration of the world into a single market also involves the disintegration of existing sets of social arrangements and state forms – such that social provision of many basic public goods becomes unsustainable. Most fundamentally, such organized and institutionalized chaos stems from the increasingly liberalized economic structures of contemporary capitalism. Often this chaos worsens because of the actions of instrumental, irresponsible, unaccountable or corrupt political elites or ruling classes. In this context, a relentless social Darwinism is tending to increase the level of socioeconomic inequality and political marginalization in much of the world, and, dialectically, to generate a growing disillusion with conventional organized politics.

Whilst a minority of the world's population enjoys relatively affluent and secure conditions in 'islands' of 'contentment', a substantial proportion of the world's population lives in vast 'seas' of poverty, and in situations characterized by insecurity, economic deprivation, ecological degradation and violence. The maxim of distributive justice of this system, to paraphrase the Book of Matthew is, 'to him that hath shall be given, from him that hath not shall be taken away'. Thus, although one could argue that the recent extension and deepening of the power of capital is equivalent to the latest phase of the bourgeois revolution, we are witnessing more generally a crisis of development of global proportions. Indeed, there is a revolution of the powerful against the weak. Nevertheless, the powerful are not omnipotent, and it is possible to speak of the power of the powerless, in the sense of the everyday forms of resistance to oppression and to commodification of life (Scott, 1993). At the same time, the failure of political orthodoxies in the context of economic depression and the collapse of communism are giving rise to new forms of right-wing authoritarianism and fascism.

In other words, since the onset of global economic crisis in the early 1970s, at least at the global level, a particular model of capitalist development – Anglo-American neo-liberalism – has tended to prevail. This model, in turn, is based on a set of institutions and practices which tend to promote a Social Darwinist reconfiguration of priorities, policies and outcomes. The most pervasive – and perverse – consequence of this shift has been a rapid deepening of social inequality within particular states and social formations, and between nations. It is reflected in the observations of many – from disillusioned former Thatcherites to religious and civic leaders, including the Pope – that capitalism has moved into a brutalizing and criminal phase, especially in parts of the Third World and the former Soviet Union. Bound up with this tendency is the intensification of (international) competition, and not only between firms. It involves also a competition between state forms, both in the sense of their ability to attract and retain flows of mobile capital and investment, and in terms of the appropriateness of their social structures of accumulation for social cohesion and economic growth – for example, the debate concerning competing capitalisms (Michel Albert's (1993) book on Anglo-American versus 'Rhineland' capitalisms, with its critique of the contradictions of the US obsession with short-term profit).

Thus, whilst neo-liberal discourse characterizes much Anglo-American thinking in matters of economics, and is practised in a variety of important contexts – for example, in the conditionality attached to loans from the World Bank and International Monetary Fund – different models of capitalist development characterize the political economies of East Asia and parts of Western Europe. Nevertheless, the Anglo-American neo-liberal model – and the social forces it seeks to promote and to protect – form the centrepiece of structural adjustment programmes for both the Third World and the former communist states.

[...]

Global political economy in the 1990s

Explaining the transition from a relatively integral and hegemonic order to a post-hegemonic one is complex and cannot be done here (on this, see Gill, 1990). Thus my explanation of the new forces and dynamics in the political economy of world order will necessarily be an oversimplified and schematic one because of constraints of space. However, an initial way to explain the developments in the 1980s is with reference to the restructuring and strengthening of the power of capital on a world scale, in the context of increased levels of competition and innovation (Gill and Law, 1989). In Toffler's phrase, the world became more clearly divided between the 'fast' and the 'slow' (Toffler, 1990). Toffler argues in effect that, inevitably, in the restructuring of the global political economy, the fast succeed and the slow fail or are marginalized. At the same time, in the deep recession of the early 1990s, many of the 'fast' went to the wall economically, destroying millions of businesses: a social Darwinism which afflicted the affluent as well as the poor.

Nevertheless, the global economy is dominated by, concentrated in, and organized from, a number of mega-sized urbanized regions or world cities (and their contiguous hinterlands) which form the major centres of production and consumption, and which house the vast bulk of corporate headquarters. These privileged 'islands' of production and consumption are organized hierarchically, and are both internally and externally policed and thus defended and protected from the encroachment of the marginalized people of world society.

Several elements in this complex process of the restructuring of the global may be highlighted. I start with the most general 'material forces', and then discuss new discourses of power and mutations in forms of state, and the intensified commodification of social relations. It is beyond the scope of a short chapter to discuss other aspects of the political economy of world order – for example, strategic realignments and militarization – crucial though they are.

The restructuring of production and finance

The restructuring of global production since the early 1970s (and the late 1960s in Japan as it turned to more information- and capital-intensive production) was intimately connected to both the onset of a third industrial–technological revolution and the growing power of transnational capital. This occurred in the context of greater international competition and intensified innovation in a period of slower growth, punctuated by recessions of increasing severity. Restructuring accelerated in the 1980s (especially during and following the 1979–82 recession, the most severe since the 1930s). These conditions entailed growing pressures on states and economic agents (individuals, firms, unions, governments), speeding up the necessary response time for economic (and political) survival.

There was an accelerating shift away from Fordism to post-Fordism in the OECD region. Fordism here denotes the system of accumulation based on mass production and mass consumption which originated in the USA in the 1920s and which spread globally in the post-World War II period. The auto and consumer electronics industries are exemplary here, in that both required semi-automated mass production and a mass market based upon rising real wages, in a demand-led system which was pump-primed by government policies. Economic policy was primarily Keynesian in complexion and reflected a great deal of confidence among economists and planners that the business cycle could be fine-tuned and that the scourge of capitalist depression had been finally eradicated. However, the conditions of the 1950s and 1960s were especially propitious for Keynesianism and Fordism, since surging demand was fuelled by postwar reconstruction, a regime of cheap energy, and a number of other conjunctural factors which all began to change by the early 1970s. At this time, production became less mass based, more specialized and 'flexible' (involving more part-time, often female, workers, and less security of employment for virtually all), and the golden age of postwar welfarism and corporatism – the political counterparts of Fordism – began to draw to an end.

In some senses much of the restructuring in the 1980s was 'ultra-Fordist': it entailed longer work hours, more control over labour, increased work intensity, increased use of machines, and so on, and an associated secular decline in the power of traditional forms of organized labour. Labour discipline tightened and increasing numbers of workers were subordinated more comprehensively in the workplace and the home to the rhythms and dictates of the new organizational systems and forms of surveillance.

National systems of financial regulation and control – a centrepiece of Keynesian planning and macroeconomic management – were displaced by an integrated, and much less regulated, 24-hour global financial system, which some commentators, following John Maynard Keynes's *General Theory* (1936), have suggested resembled a casino. A casino is in reality a structured environment where the gambling odds are significantly weighted in favour of the 'bank'. Not only was the new global financial system outside the control of any single government (except perhaps that of the US); it operated systematically in favour of financial interests, as opposed to those associated with productive manufacturing or with government planning. Access to credit became organized not only on a global scale but also in a much more discriminatory and hierarchical manner, and in ways which emphasized the short-term over the longer-term. This meant a type of law of the jungle, with only the fittest able to survive. Other aspects of the Keynesian metaphor are significant. A short-term speculative mentality came to prevail in the relatively deregulated financial markets. Indeed, Susan Strange (1986), like Keynes in the 1930s, suggested that this type of development is inimical not only to production, but also to the ethico-political legitimacy of liberal democracy.

These developments, then, helped to give rise to a more competitive, social Darwinist struggle of the survival of the fittest, and a growth in social inequality within and between nations. Indeed, the already massive gap in income and wealth between the richest 10 per cent and the poorest 10 per cent of the people on the planet increased almost tenfold during the 1980s, according to United Nations statistics. Nevertheless, by the late 1980s economic globalization approached levels which approximated those immediately prior to 1914, often considered to be the high-water mark of capitalist economic internationalism. At the same time, it is important to remember that the areas and populations who are the beneficiaries of the global political economy still represent a small proportion of the world's population. In this context there is a simultaneous and interlinked process of incorporation and/or marginalization into/from the global political economy. This process can be illuminated with reference to the wrenching transitions – involving town and country, agriculture and industry – occurring in much of the Third World.

Those who are completely marginalized from the production and consumption aspects of the global political economy are, for example, subsistence farmers in Africa. However, many peasants are forced off the land and often go to the cities and may be incorporated into production for the global economy, such as the peasant women who work as cheap, 'dextrous and docile' workers in the factories in the Maquiladoras in Mexico. For the rest of the world, the processes of incorporation/marginalization which I have mentioned have continued, often with devastating consequences as in Africa and Latin America, where real incomes fell precipitately in the 1980s. These processes are, albeit in different ways, mirrored within the OECD countries, where a growing underclass is increasingly visible, even in wealthy societies with apparently low unemployment such as in Japan.

New constitutionalism and mutations in forms of state

In other essays (for example, Gill, 1992a and 1992b) I have linked the new discourses of power which have emerged in the OECD countries – in the context of the neo-conservative 'revolution' of the 1970s and 1980s – to the idea of a 'new constitutionalism'. This can be understood as a term intended to describe the varied and complex efforts, especially by the forces of the political right and those of neo-classical economists and financial capital, to develop a politico-legal framework for the reconstitution of capital on a world scale, and thus for the intensification of market forms of discipline. That is, one way to interpret the latest phase in the worldwide bourgeois revolution is in terms of a new level of globalization of capitalist production and competition, with the need for institutional and political inno-vation as a counterpart – ideology is not enough to secure the property rights and political prerogatives of capital on a world scale.

This discourse serves to protect the privileges of the dominant agents in the new forms of oligopolistic competition in the 1980s, and to restrain future governments from intervening to undermine such privileges. This is also linked to attempts to privilege business and business-oriented ideas in parts of the public sector (which may be difficult to privatize, such as health care and education), whilst decreasing the accountability of parts of the public sector. Both of the above relate, then, to the broader purpose of extending and deepening the power of capital, in both the 'public' and 'private' sectors.

The new constitutionalism seeks to reinforce a process whereby government policies are increasingly accountable to (international) capital, and thus to market forces (especially those exercised in and from the financial markets). Sovereignties, political associations and forms of state are redefined to reflect this new categorical imperative. State policies thus become more attuned to the imperatives of global economic forces, in the context of the new ide-ologies of competitiveness and 'human capital'. Increasingly governments in the OECD countries – and worldwide – seek to strengthen political discipline, in part to provide a more hospitable investment climate to attract production. Credibility with the financial markets is, for governments, becoming perhaps more important than credibility with voters.

[...]

The 'local' level

The first of these changes involves a 'domestic' shift from the welfare-nationalist state, a state form which was redistributive and which constrained the inherent tendency in capitalist economies towards deepening social inequality, and which organized the authoritative (that is, non-market) provision of a wide range of public goods. This state form characterized many of the OECD countries after World War II (and allowed for substantial state capitalism, domes-tic protection and social-welfare provision). We can now see a movement towards the 'compe-tition' state (premised on relative success in the world market and on attracting mobile capital for investment and finance through, for example, competitive deregulation and tax breaks to foreign investors). In parts of the Third World, the counterpart to this change is a shift from various types of state capitalism towards variants of a neo-liberal form of state.

As Polanyi noted, in the case of Britain, the creation of a self-regulating market society was not only an unprecedented and revolutionary development, it was also premissed upon a strong state which was able to implement and enforce the measures which created the market society: '*laissez faire* itself was enforced by the state [and involved] an enormous increase in the administrative functions of the state, which was now endowed with a central bureaucracy able to fulfil the tasks set by the adherents of liberalism' (Polanyi, 1957: 139). Today, the trend (or at least the announced aim of liberal policy) is towards downsizing this bureaucracy and making its operations more 'economical' or efficient, and imbued with market values.

[...]

The 'global' level

The second, 'global' dimension of changes in prevailing forms of state is a redefinition of external sovereignty and practice: a shift from the traditional mercantilist and developmental state towards more globalized neo-liberal state structures, consistent, for example, with IMF and World Bank structural adjustment programmes (SAPs). In this sense, the internal purposes and public goals of the state are increasingly subordinated to external (economic) considerations, and the domestic and the international are increasingly articulated through the interplay of international capital based on more global structures of production, finance and exchange.

[...]

The restructuring of state and capital on a world stage towards a more globally integrated and competitive market-driven system is the process we can call the 'globalization' of the state. It involves the transformation of the state so as to give greater freedom to the private aspects of capital accumulation in the extended state at the local, national and transnational levels. These changes involve the growth in the power of capital at both the 'domestic' and 'international' levels in a transnational process of class formation. In this sense, a key characteristic of global politics in the last decades of the twentieth century is a redefinition of the role and purpose of government in the emerging world order. This has been a transnational process, involving both key elements in the state structures of the most powerful members of the G7 (Canada, Britain, France, Germany, Italy, Japan, the USA and the EC) and drawn from private banks, corporations, think-tanks, universities, the media, and conservative and liberal political parties, as well as influential private international-relations councils such as the Trilateral Commission and the World Economic Forum. In Gramscian terms, this is a transnational historic bloc of forces (combining internationally oriented elements of the states and civil societies of many nations, but anchored in the leading positions of the G7 countries, especially the USA). We will, for the sake of shorthand, call this transnational historic bloc 'the G7 nexus'.

[...]

Commodification and insecurity

Partly because of the developments noted above, the commodification of social relations within modern capitalism has deepened: this is a sociological counterpart to the growth in the power of capital relative to states and to labour. By commodification I mean the propensity of capitalist society to define and to quantify social life in market terms. Thus elements which were previously integrated into the fabric of society before the rise of modern capitalism now become subject increasingly to the laws of the marketplace. Thus land (nature), labour (lived time) and productive capacity (the construction of society, living space and the capacity to provide for human needs) become commodities which are bought and sold. Money becomes the principal medium of social exchange, and future production is in large part premissed upon the provision of credit, allocated in the capital markets.

Of course, this aspect of socioeconomic and cultural change in the 1980s has a long lineage. In this sense, the current phase of transformation – a deepening of commodification, especially since the early 1970s – can be related to Braudel's concept of *longue durée*. In this sense, the structure and language of social relations is more systematically conditioned by market forces and practices. This means that capitalist norms and practices increasingly pervade the *gestes répétés* of everyday life: in sports, in leisure, in play, in the process of consumption more generally. At the same time, the process of commodification is increasingly monitored, aggregated and controlled by the use of surveillance technologies. The process of consumption is massaged and channelled by mass communications, especially television. Privileged (that is, wealthier) consumers can be de-massified, according to market segments, and thus can be targeted more accurately. Potential consumers are identified and 'constructed', on the basis of very detailed and sophisticated information about their income, lifestyles, credit rating, health and criminal history, and so on. The use of these technologies is related to the spread of money and credit structures into more and more aspects of everyday life; that is, into not only the home, but also the workplace, such that in the USA it is increasingly difficult to obtain a job unless one has a good credit rating and health record. The basis for these information structures is to a large extent everyday transactional activity in the marketplace (Gandy, 1993).

[...]

The contradictions of neo-liberalism and counterhegemony

The policies which have gone with new constitutionalist neo-liberal discourse are even queried by those interests which tend to benefit most from deflationary policies: financial and creditor interests more generally. This is because policies imbued with this type of orthodoxy have been globally deflationary, and have tended not only to accelerate the restructuring of production but also to increase mass unemployment and social unrest. In its most developed form, in western Europe, then, it is associated with protracted economic slump. Thus whereas politicians are able to press for deregulation and market discipline on grounds of greater efficiency, they do so in the context of what economists call the 'fallacy of composition': namely, if all deflate depression ensues. Moreover, politicians move towards new constitutionalist policies in ways which not only undermine the economic sovereignty of their nations; they also tie their own hands politically and deny themselves flexibility in reacting to economic conditions.

Thus a fully neo-liberal world will never emerge, because of the very contradictions and moral bankruptcy of neo-liberalism itself. We can expect increasing struggle taking place between *laissez faire*, social Darwinist conceptions of the appropriate form of state and other models of capitalist social structures of accumulation and industrial organization – for example, the 'Rhineland model' and that of East Asian bureaucratic authoritarian capitalisms, both of which have a more planned, long-term and more productivist orientation than Anglo-American capitalisms (Albert, 1993). It may be no coincidence that the more neo-liberal forces win the struggle over the appropriate political form for capital accumulation, the more social inequality – including gender inequality – tends to deepen and political conflict intensifies. The broader social Darwinism intersects here with questions concerning the political, social and ecological sustainability of the current situation.

In eastern Europe, the reintroduction of neo-liberal marketization is generating a combination of widespread disillusionment and resentment, sentiments which are to a certain extent reflected in the resurgence of populism, racism, fascism and gangsterism. In present-day Russia, for example, the concept of 'marketization' is increasingly associated with desperation, a massive upsurge in crime and violence, as nuclear power stations begin to decay and collapse, and as state arsenals are plundered of weapons by armed gangs. The 'market' is being reintroduced in the context of a general collapse of law and order.

Structural adjustment in Latin America and Africa, and now in the former USSR, is atomizing many state capacities and is generating new social movements and political parties which may in time come to challenge the thrust of neo-liberal orthodoxies. Some of these forces will be ecologists, women's movements and traditional workers' organizations and trade unions. Not all of these movements and parties will represent beneficent trends in world politics: some, such as the far right in Russia, will be malignant elements.

When this is related more broadly to the turmoil in the Third World it gives grounds for considering whether the emerging world order is socially and ethically sustainable. Yet the world is increasingly interdependent both economically and ecologically. Political turbulence and growing disparities in living conditions are driving unstoppable waves of migration. The governments defending the regions of privilege will be hard pressed to cope with or to contain such pressures. To stem such migration requires a more just and egalitarian economic and political structure to the emerging world order.

Thus, whilst there has been some democratization in the 1980s and early 1990s (for example, in some of the bureaucratic authoritarian nations referred to as the newly industrializing countries (NICs), such as South Korea and to a lesser extent Taiwan), at the same time there has been a worldwide growth in authoritarianism and populism, and a resurgence of fundamentalism (with negative implications for women) of both metaphysical and social types; in this sense, the 1930s and the 1990s are in some ways comparable. Part of the reason for this is that in much of the Third World the processes of urbanization and economic decline have gone with social chaos, anomie and nihilism (Vieille, 1988), although in the NICs they have gone with rapid economic growth and the creation of a civil society which can begin to countervail the unfettered power of the state and the monopolistic producers. China, of course, with its massive and rapid economic growth since the late 1970s is a case of a country in which many of the contradictions associated with commodification and democratization have begun to surface, and where the economic situation seems on the verge of spinning completely out of control.

Elsewhere in the Third World, new types of politics are developing, some relatively invisible and outside traditional conceptions of political action, in a silent revolution of the apparently powerless against those who oppress them. And their oppressors are not just in the G7 countries; they are mainly at home – those urban elites, cadres and ruling classes who are, as I have mentioned, the principal beneficiaries of loans from the World Bank and aid projects from the richer countries.

Whereas the leaders of the G7 countries appear unable to contain the rise of new right-wing forces which challenge the status quo within their own territories and to reverse the widespread disillusionment and alienation with 'normal politics', many in the Third

World – and not just women – are taking responsibility for their own survival and beginning to exercise social choices which reflect their own interests. It is in this sense that Yoshikazu Sakamoto (1995) speaks of the 'powerlessness of the powerful' and the 'power of the powerless'. In this process, then, the poor are not powerless: they have the capacity not only to disrupt the privileged islands of production and consumption, but also to practise 'everyday forms of resistance' to totalizing forces and political and social domination (Scott, 1993).[1] Another indicator of the power of the apparently poor and powerless is the new forms of multilateralism which have begun to emerge among the 'poor' and 'marginalized', to challenge the multilateralism of the powerful (for example, the indigenous peoples of Latin America), as well as myriad forms of local cooperatives, associations and programmes. It is important to link both these local and transnational initiatives in a global political process which also involves progressive social movements and parties from the wealthier nations.

By contrast, the formal multilateralism of the G7 nexus has gone with a politics of deflation, mass unemployment and social polarization, and in so doing has all but relinquished the legitimacy to govern in the name of world society. In this sense, the old Cold War categories of left and right, and the organized political parties and forms of state which corresponded to this period, appear to look increasingly obsolete as the world enters a new type of world order.

Some of the issues I have raised in this chapter thus relate to the problematic of politics for the 1990s, and the way that we might begin to conceptualize the 'limits of the possible' and consequently forms of transnational political mobilization of a progressive kind. A certain pessimism is necessary to see how the global crisis will develop and open up 'windows of opportunity'. The 'organic intellectuals' of counterhegemonic forces can help, therefore, to prepare the ground for more constructive, rather than destructive, forms of change. Whereas Schumpeter, following Marx, characterized the process of capitalist development as one of 'creative destruction', it is incumbent on the intellectuals not to dream of impossible utopias but to think creatively and constructively on the basis of an analysis of real historical forces, in order to begin to contain and transcend the destructive forces and impulses of our age. I do not think I am being too pessimistic when I conclude that not all the symptoms during the interregnum are entirely morbid ones.

Acknowledgements

I would like to thank David Law for detailed comments, and the participants in the United Nations symposium in Oslo on 15–16 August 1993 for their reaction to and reflections on some of the ideas contained in this chapter. I would also like to thank Professor Björn Hettne for arranging the opportunity to deliver some of these thoughts to the inaugural meeting of the Nordic International Studies Association on 17 August 1993.

Note

1 Indeed, Scott cites the example of the Chinese peasantry whose collective resistance to the power of the state and the mass starvation associated with Mao's 'Great Leap Forward' effectively forced the post-Maoist leaders to institute reforms which included the dismantling of the ruinous collectivization of agriculture. The market reforms which ensued provided one of the pillars of the 'Four Modernizations' policy of Deng. This example shows that the problem is not the market *per se*, but the conditions of its introduction. Today's new China – 'one nation, two systems' – shows, at least in the coastal regions, the tendency which is built into market society: to commodify increasingly virtually all aspects of human life. This appears to be happening in a virtually unregulated and uncontrolled manner.

References

Albert, M. (1993) *Capitalism vs. Capitalism*, Four Wall Eight Windows, New York.

Braudel, F. (1981) *The Structures of Everyday Life: The Limits of the Possible*. Vol. I of *Civilisation and Capitalism, 15th–18th Centuries*, trans. S. Reynolds, Harper & Row, New York.

Cox, R. W. (1987) *Production, Power and World Order*, Columbia University Press, New York.

Gandy, O. H. Jr. (1993) *The Panoptic Sort: A Political Economy of Personal Information*, Westview Press, Boulder, CO.

Gill, S. (1990) *American Hegemony and the Trilateral Commission*, Cambridge University Press, Cambridge.

—— (1992a) 'The Emerging World Order and European Change: The Political Economy of European Economic Union', in R. Miliband and L. Panitch, eds, *The New World Order: Socialist Register, 1992*, Merlin Press, London, pp. 157–96.

—— (1992b) 'Economic Globalization and the Internationalization of Authority: Limits and Contradictions', *Geoforum* 23, pp. 269–83.

Gill, S. and D. Law (1989) 'Global Hegemony and the Structural Power of Capital', *International Studies Quarterly* 33, pp. 475–99.

Gunnell, J. G. (1968) 'Social Science and Political Reality: The Problem of Explanation', *Social Research* 35, pp. 159–201.

Polanyi, K. (1957) *The Great Transformation* [1944], Beacon Press, Boston, MA.

Sakamoto, Y. (1995) 'Democratization, Social Movements and World Order', in B. Hettne, ed., *International Political Economy: Understanding Global Disorder*, Halifax, Fenwood.

Scott, J. C. (1993) 'Everyday Forms of Resistance', *PRIME: Occasional Papers Series*, No. 15, International Peace Research Institute Meigaku, Yokohama.

Strange, S. (1986) *Casino Capitalism*, Basil Blackwell, Oxford.

Toffler, A. (1990) *Power Shift: Knowledge, Wealth, and Violence at the Edge of the 21st Century*, Bantam Books, New York.

Vieille, P. (1988) 'The World's Chaos and the New Paradigms of the Social Movement', in Lelio Basso Foundation, eds, *Theory and Practice of Liberation at the End of the Twentieth Century*, Bruylant, Brussels.

6 The infrapolitics of subordinate groups

James C. Scott

Source: James C. Scott (1990), *Domination and the Arts of Resistance: Hidden Transcripts*, New Haven, CT: Yale University Press, pp. 183–201

> The cultural forms may not say what they know, nor know what they say, but they mean what they do – at least in the logic of their praxis.
>
> (Paul Willis, *Learning to Labour*)

> [The supervision of gleaning] exasperated morale to the limit; but there is such a void between the class which was angered and the class that was threatened, that words never made it across; one only knew what happened from the results; [the peasants] worked underground the way moles do.
>
> (Balzac, *Les Paysans*)

In a social science already rife – some might say crawling – with neologisms, one hesitates to contribute another. The term *infrapolitics*, however, seems an appropriate shorthand to convey the idea that we are dealing with an unobtrusive realm of political struggle. For a social science attuned to the relatively open politics of liberal democracies and to loud, headline-grabbing protests, demonstrations, and rebellions, the circumspect struggle waged daily by subordinate groups is, like infrared rays, beyond the visible end of the spectrum. That it should be invisible, as we have seen, is in large part by design – a tactical choice born of a prudent awareness of the balance of power. The claim made here is similar to the claim made by Leo Strauss about how the reality of persecution must affect our reading of classical political philosophy: "Persecution cannot prevent even public expression of the heterodox truth, for a man of independent thought can utter his views in public and remain unharmed, provided he moves with circumspection. He can even utter them in print without incurring any danger, provided he is capable of *writing between the lines*."[1] The text we are interpreting in this case is not Plato's *Symposium* but rather the veiled cultural struggle and political expression of subordinate groups who have ample reason to fear venturing their unguarded opinion. The meaning of the text, in either case, is rarely straightforward; it is often meant to communicate one thing to those in the know and another to outsiders and authorities. If we have access to the hidden transcript (analogous to the secret notes or conversations of the philosopher) or to a more reckless expression of opinion (analogous to subsequent texts produced under freer conditions) the task of interpretation is somewhat easier. Without these comparative texts, we are obliged to search for noninnocent meanings using our cultural knowledge – much in the way an experienced censor might!

The term *infrapolitics* is, I think, appropriate in still another way. When we speak of the infrastructure for commerce we have in mind the facilities that make such commerce possible: for example, transport, banking, currency, property and contract law. In the same fashion, I mean to suggest that the infrapolitics we have examined provides much of the cultural and structural underpinning of the more visible political action on which our attention has generally been focused. The bulk of this chapter is devoted to sustaining this claim.

First, I return briefly to the widely held position that the offstage discourse of the powerless is either empty posturing or, worse, a substitute for real resistance. After noting some of the logical difficulties with this line of reasoning, I try to show how material and symbolic resistance are part of the same set of mutually sustaining practices. This requires reemphasizing that the relationship between dominant elites and subordinates is, whatever else it might be, very much of a material struggle in which both sides are continually probing for weaknesses and exploiting small advantages. By way of recapitulating some of the argument, I finally try to show how each realm of open resistance to domination is shadowed by an infrapolitical twin sister who aims at the same strategic goals but whose low profile is better adapted to resisting an opponent who could probably win any open confrontation.

The hidden transcript as posing?

A skeptic might very well accept much of the argument thus far and yet minimize its significance for political life. Isn't much of what is called the hidden transcript, even when it is insinuated into the public transcript, a matter of hollow posing that is rarely acted out in earnest? This view of the safe expression of aggression against a dominant figure is that it serves as a substitute – albeit a second-best substitute – for the real thing: direct aggression. At best, it is of little or no consequence; at worst it is an evasion. The prisoners who spend their time dreaming about life on the outside might instead be digging a tunnel; the slaves who sing of liberation and freedom might instead take to their heels. As Barrington Moore writes, "Even fantasies of liberation and revenge can help to preserve domination through dissipating collective energies in relatively harmless rhetoric and ritual." [2]

The case for the hydraulic interpretation of fighting words in a safe place is, as we have noted, perhaps strongest when those fighting words seem largely orchestrated or stage-managed by dominant groups. Carnival and other ritualized and, hence, ordinarily contained rites of reversal are the most obvious examples. Until recently, the dominant interpretation of ritualized aggression or reversal was that, by acting to relieve the tensions engendered by hierarchical social relations, it served to reinforce the status quo. Figures as diverse as Hegel and Trotsky saw such ceremonies as conservative forces. The influential analyses of Max Gluckman and Victor Turner argue that because they underline an essential, if brief, equality among all members of a society and because they illustrate, if only ritually, the dangers of disorder and anarchy, their function is to emphasize the necessity of institutionalized order. [3] For Ranajit Guha the order-serving effects of rituals of reversal lie precisely in the fact that they are authorized and prescribed from above. [4] Allowing subordinate groups to play at rebellion within specified rules and times helps prevent more dangerous forms of aggression.

In his description of holiday festivities among slaves in the antebellum U.S. South, Frederick Douglass, himself a slave, resorts to the same metaphor. His reasoning, however, is slightly different:

> Before the holidays, there are pleasures in prospect; after the holidays, they become pleasures of memory, and they serve to keep out thoughts and wishes of a more dangerous character... these holidays are conductors or safety-valves to carry off the explosive elements inseparable from the human mind, when reduced to the condition

of slavery. But for those, the rigors and bondage would become too severe for endurance, and the slave would be forced to dangerous desperation.[5]

Douglass's claim here is not that some ersatz rebellion takes the place of the real thing but simply that the respite and indulgence of a holiday provide just enough pleasure to blunt the edge of incipient rebellion. It is as if the masters have calculated the degree of pressure that will engender desperate acts and have carefully adjusted their repression to stop just short of the flashpoint.

Perhaps the most interesting thing about the safety-valve theories in their many guises is the most easily overlooked. They all begin with the common assumption that systematic subordination generates pressure of some kind from below. They assume further that, if nothing is done to relieve this pressure, it builds up and eventually produces an explosion of some kind. Precisely how this pressure is generated and what it consists of is rarely specified. For those who live such subordination, whether Frederick Douglass or the fictional Mrs. Poyser, the pressure is a taken-for-granted consequence of the frustration and anger of being unable to strike back (physically or verbally) against a powerful oppressor. That pressure generated by a perceived but unrequited injustice finds expression, we have argued, in the hidden transcript – its size, its virulence, its symbolic luxuriance. In other words, the safety-valve view implicitly accepts some key elements of our larger argument about the hidden transcript: that systematic subordination elicits a reaction and that this reaction involves a desire to strike or speak back to the dominant. Where they differ is in supposing that this desire can be substantially satisfied, whether in backstage talk, in supervised rituals of reversal, or in festivities that occasionally cool the fires of resentment.

The logic of the safety-valve perspective depends on the social psychological proposition that the safe expression of aggression in joint fantasy, rituals, or folktales yields as much, or nearly as much, satisfaction (hence, a reduction in pressure) as direct aggression against the object of frustration. Evidence on this point from social psychology is not altogether conclusive but the preponderance of findings does not support this logic. Instead, such findings suggest that experimental subjects who are thwarted unjustly experience little or no reduction in the level of their frustration and anger unless they are able to directly injure the frustrating agent.[6] Such findings are hardly astonishing. One would expect retaliation that actually affected the agent of injustice to provide far more in the way of catharsis than forms of aggression that left the source of anger untouched. And, of course, there is much experimental evidence that aggressive play and fantasy increase rather than decrease the likelihood of actual aggression. Mrs. Poyser felt greatly relieved when she vented her spleen directly to the squire but presumably was not relieved – or not sufficiently – by her rehearsed speeches and the oaths sworn behind his back. There is, then, as much, if not more, reason to consider Mrs. Poyser's offstage anger as a preparation for her eventual outburst than to see it as a satisfactory alternative.

If the social-psychological evidence provides little or no support for catharsis through displacement, the historical case for such an argument has yet to be made. Would it be possible to show that, other things equal, dominant elites who provided or allowed more outlets for comparatively harmless aggression against themselves were thereby less liable to violence and rebellion from a subordinate group? If such a comparison were undertaken, its first task would be to distinguish between the effect of displaced aggression per se and the rather more material concessions of food, drink, charity, and relief from work and discipline embedded in such festivities. In other words, the "bread and circuses" that, on good evidence, are often political concessions *won* by subordinate classes may have an ameliorating effect on oppression quite apart from ritualized aggression.[7] An argument along these lines would also have to explain an important anomaly. If, in fact, ritualized aggression displaces real aggression from its obvious target, why then have so many revolts by slaves, peasants, and serfs begun precisely during such seasonal rituals (for example, the carnival in Romans described by Le Roy Ladurie) designed to prevent their occurrence?[8]

The hidden transcript as practice

The greatest shortcoming of the safety-valve position is that it embodies a fundamental idealist fallacy. The argument that offstage or veiled forms of aggression offer a harmless catharsis that helps preserve the status quo assumes that we are examining a rather abstract debate in which one side is handicapped rather than a concrete, material struggle. But relations between masters and slaves, between Brahmins and untouchables are not simply a clash of ideas about dignity and the right to rule; they are a process of subordination firmly anchored in material practices. Virtually every instance of personal domination is intimately connected with a process of appropriation. Dominant elites extract material taxes in the form of labor, grain, cash, and service in addition to extracting symbolic taxes in the form of deference, demeanor, posture, verbal formulas, and acts of humility. In actual practice, of course, the two are joined inasmuch as every public act of appropriation is, figuratively, a ritual of subordination.

The bond between domination and appropriation means that it is impossible to separate the ideas and symbolism of subordination from a process of material exploitation. In exactly the same fashion, it is impossible to separate veiled symbolic resistance to the ideas of domination from the practical struggles to thwart or mitigate exploitation. Resistance, like domination, fights a war on two fronts. The hidden transcript is not just behind-the-scenes griping and grumbling; it is enacted in a host of down-to-earth, low-profile stratagems designed to minimize appropriation. In the case of slaves, for example, these stratagems have typically included theft, pilfering, feigned ignorance, shirking or careless labor, foot-dragging, secret trade and production for sale, sabotage of crops, livestock, and machinery, arson, flight, and so on. In the case of peasants, poaching, squatting, illegal gleaning, delivery of inferior rents in kind, clearing clandestine fields, and defaults on feudal dues have been common stratagems.

[...]

A penetrating study of forest poaching in early eighteenth-century England and the draconian death penalties enacted to curb it reveals the same link between a sense of popular justice that cannot be openly claimed and a host of practices devised to exercise those rights in clandestine ways.[9] In this period, the titled owners of estates and the Crown began in earnest to restrict local customary rights to forest pasturage, hunting, trapping, fishing, turf and heath cutting, fuel wood gathering, thatch cutting, lime burning, and quarrying on what they now insisted was exclusively their property. That yeomen, cottagers, and laborers considered this breach of customary law to be an injustice is abundantly clear. Thompson can thus write of yeomen with a "tenacious tradition of memories as to rights and customs ... and a sense that they and not the rich interlopers, owned the forest."[10] The term *outlaws* as applied to those who continued to exercise these now-proscribed rights has a strange ring when we recall that they were certainly acting within the norms and hence with the support of most of their community.

And yet, we have no direct access to the hidden transcript of cottagers as they prepared their traps or shared a rabbit stew. And of course there were no public protests and open declarations of ancient forest rights in a political environment in which all the cards were stacked against the villagers in any sustained, open confrontation. At this level we encounter almost total silence – the plebeian voice is mute. Where it does speak, however, is in every-day forms of resistance in the increasingly massive and aggressive assertion of these rights, often at night and in disguise. Since a legal or political confrontation over property rights in the forest would avail them little and risk much, they chose instead to exercise their rights piecemeal and quietly – to take in fact the property rights they were denied in law. The con-trast between public quiescence and clandestine defiance was not lost on contemporary authorities, one of whom, Bishop Trelawny, spoke of "a pestilent pernicious people…such as take oaths to the government, but underhand labor its subversion."[11]

Popular poaching on such a vast scale could hardly be mounted without a lively backstage transcript of values, understandings, and popular outrage to sustain it. But that hidden tran-script must largely be inferred from practice – a quiet practice at that. Once in a while an event indicates something of what might lie beneath the surface of public discourse, for example, a threatening anonymous letter to a gameskeeper when he continued to abridge popular custom or the fact that the prosecution couldn't find anyone with a radius of five miles to testify against a local blacksmith accused of breaking down a dam recently built to create a fish pond. More rarely still, when there was nothing further to lose by a public declaration of rights, the normative content of the hidden transcript might spring to view. Thus two convicted "deer-stealers," shortly to be hanged, ventured to claim that "deer were wild beasts, and that the poor, as well as the rich, might lawfully use them."[12]

The point of this brief discussion of poaching is that any argument which assumes that disguised ideological dissent or aggression operates as a safety-valve to weaken "real" resis-tance ignores the paramount fact that such ideological dissent is virtually always expressed in practices that aim at an unobtrusive renegotiation of power relations. The yeomen and cottagers in question were not simply making an abstract, emotionally satisfying, backstage case for what they took to be their property rights; they were out in the forests day after day exercising those rights as best they could. There is an important dialectic here between the hidden transcript and practical resistance.[13] The hidden transcript of customary rights and outrage *is* a source of popular poaching providing that we realize, at the same time, that the practical struggle in the forests is also the source for a backstage discourse of customs, hero-ism, revenge, and justice. If the backstage talk is a source of satisfaction, it is so in large part owing to practical gains in the daily conflict over the forests. Any other formulation would entail an inadmissible wall between what people think and say, on the one hand, and what they do, on the other.

Far from being a relief-valve taking the place of actual resistance, the discursive practices offstage sustain resistance in the same way in which the informal peer pressure of factory workers discourages any individual worker from exceeding work norms and becoming a rate-buster. The subordinate moves back and forth, as it were, between two worlds: the world of the master and the offstage world of subordinates. Both of these worlds have sanctioning power. While subordinates normally can monitor the public transcript performance of other subordinates, the dominant can rarely monitor fully the hidden transcript. This means that any subordinate who seeks privilege by ingratiating himself to his superior will have to answer for that conduct once he returns to the world of his peers. In situations of systematic subordination such sanctions may go well beyond scolding and insult to physical coercion, as in the beating of an informer by prisoners. Social pressure among peers, however, is by itself a powerful weapon of subordinates. Industrial sociologists discovered very early that the censure of workmates often prevailed over the desire for greater income or promotion. We can, in this respect, view the social side of the hidden transcript as a political domain striving to enforce, against great odds, certain forms of conduct and resistance in relations with the dominant. *It would be more accurate, in short, to think of the hidden transcript as a condition of practical resistance rather than a substitute for it.*

One might argue perhaps that even such practical resistance, like the discourse it reflects and that sustains it, amounts to nothing more than trivial coping mechanisms that cannot materially affect the overall situation of domination. This is no more real resistance, the argument might go, than veiled symbolic opposition is real ideological dissent. At one level this is perfectly true but irrelevant since our point is that these are the forms that political struggle takes when frontal assaults are precluded by the realities of power. At another level it is well to recall that the aggregation of thousands upon thousands of such "petty" acts of resistance have dramatic economic and political effects. In production, whether on the factory floor or on the plantation, it can result in performances that are not bad enough to provoke punishment but not good enough to allow the enterprise to succeed. Repeated on a massive scale, such conduct allowed Djilas to write that "slow, unproductive work of disinterested millions ... is the calculable, invisible, and gigantic waste which no communist regime has been able to avoid."[14] Poaching and squatting on a large scale can restructure the control of property. Peasant tax evasion on a large scale has brought about crises of appropriation that threaten the state. Massive desertion by serf or peasant conscripts has helped bring down more than one ancient regime. Under the appropriate conditions, the accumulation of petty acts can, rather like snowflakes on a steep mountainside, set off an avalanche.[15]

[...]

Resistance below the line

We are now in a position to summarize a portion of the argument. Until quite recently, much of the active political life of subordinate groups has been ignored because it takes place at a level we rarely recognize as political. To emphasize the enormity of what has been, by and large, disregarded, I want to distinguish between the open, declared forms of resistance, which attract most attention, and the disguised, low-profile, undeclared resistance that constitutes the domain of infrapolitics (see Table 6.1). For contemporary liberal democracies in the West, an exclusive concern for open political action *will* capture much that is significant in political life. The historic achievement of political liberties of speech and association has appreciably lowered the risks and difficulty of open political expression. Not so long ago in the West, however, and, even today, for many of the least privileged minorities and marginalized poor, open political action will hardly capture the bulk of political action. Nor will an exclusive attention to declared resistance help us understand the process by which new political forces and demands germinate before they burst on the scene. How, for example, could we understand the open break represented by the civil rights movement or the black power movement in the 1960s without understanding the offstage discourse among black students, clergymen, and their parishioners?

Taking a long historical view, one sees that the luxury of relatively safe, open political opposition is both rare and recent. The vast majority of people have been and continue to

Table 6.1 Domination and resistance

	Material domination	*Status domination*	*Ideological domination*
Practices of domination	Appropriation of grain, taxes, labor, etc.	Humiliation, disprivilege, insults, assaults on dignity	Justification by ruling groups for slavery, serfdom, caste, privilege
Forms of public declared resistant	Petitions, demonstrations, boycotts, strikes, land invasions, and open revolts	Public assertion of worth by gesture, dress, speech, and/or open desecration of status symbols of the dominant	Public counter-ideologies propagating equality, revolution, or negating the ruling ideology
Forms of disguised, low profile, undisclosed resistance, INFRA-POLITICS	Everyday forms of resistance, e.g. poaching, squatting, desertion, evasion, foot-dragging Direct Resistance by Disguised Resisters, e.g. masked appropriations, threats, anonymous threats	Hidden transcript of anger, aggression, and disguised discourses of dignity e.g. rituals of aggression, tales of revenge, use of carnival symbolism, gossip, rumor, creation of autonomous social space for assertion of dignity	Development of dissident subcultures e.g. millennial religions, slave "hush-arbors," folk religion, myths of social banditry and class heroes, world-upside-down imagery, myths of the "good" king or the time before the "Norman Yoke"

be not citizens, but subjects. So long as we confine our conception of *the political* to activity that is openly declared we are driven to conclude that subordinate groups essentially lack a political life or that what political life they do have is restricted to those exceptional moments of popular explosion. To do so is to miss the immense political terrain that lies between quiescence and revolt and that, for better or worse, is the political environment of subject classes. It is to focus on the visible coastline of politics and miss the continent that lies beyond.

Each of the forms of disguised resistance, of infrapolitics, is the silent partner of a loud form of public resistance. Thus, piecemeal squatting is the infrapolitical equivalent of an open land invasion: both are aimed at resisting the appropriation of land. The former cannot openly avow its goals and is a strategy well suited to subjects who have no political rights. Thus, rumor and folktales of revenge are the infrapolitical equivalent of open gestures of contempt and desecration: both are aimed at resisting the denial of standing or dignity to subordinate groups. The former cannot act directly and affirm its intention and is thus a symbolic strategy also well suited to subjects with no political rights. Finally, millennial imagery and the symbolic reversals of folk religion are the infrapolitical equivalents of public, radical, counterideologies: both are aimed at negating the public symbolism of ideological domination. Infrapolitics, then, is essentially the strategic form that the resistance of subjects must assume under conditions of great peril.

The strategic imperatives of infrapolitics make it not simply different in degree from the open politics of modern democracies; they impose a fundamentally different logic of political action. No public claims are made, no open symbolic lines are drawn. All political action takes forms that are designed to obscure their intentions or to take cover behind an apparent meaning. Virtually no one acts in his own name for avowed purposes, for that would be self-defeating. Precisely because such political action is studiously designed to be anonymous or to disclaim its purpose, infrapolitics requires more than a little interpretation. Things are not exactly as they seem.

The logic of disguise followed by infrapolitics extends to its organization as well as to its substance. Again, the form of organization is as much a product of political necessity as of political choice. Because open political activity is all but precluded, resistance is confined to the informal networks of kin, neighbors, friends, and community rather than formal organization. Just as the symbolic resistance found in forms of folk culture has a possibly innocent meaning, so do the elementary organizational units of infrapolitics have an alternative, innocent existence. The informal assemblages of market, neighbors, family, and community thus provide both a structure and a cover for resistance. Since resistance is conducted in small groups, individually, and, if on a larger scale, makes use of the anonymity of folk culture or actual disguises, it is well adapted to thwart surveillance. There are no leaders to round up, no membership lists to investigate, no manifestos to denounce, no public activities to draw attention. These are, one might say, the elementary forms of political life on which more elaborate, open, institutional forms may be built and on which they are likely to depend for their vitality. Such elementary forms also help explain why infrapolitics so often escapes notice. If formal political organization is the realm of elites (for example, lawyers, politicians, revolutionaries, political bosses), of written records (for example, resolutions, declarations, news stories, petitions, lawsuits), and of public action, infrapolitics is, by contrast, the realm of informal leadership and nonelites, of conversation and oral discourse, and of surreptitious resistance. The logic of infrapolitics is to leave few traces in the wake of its passage. By covering its tracks it not only minimizes the risks its practitioners run but it also eliminates much of the documentary evidence that might convince social scientists and historians that real politics was taking place.

Infrapolitics is, to be sure, real politics. In many respects it is conducted in more earnest, for higher stakes, and against greater odds than political life in liberal democracies. Real ground is lost and gained. Armies are undone and revolutions facilitated by the desertions of infrapolitics. De facto property rights are established and challenged. States confront fiscal crises or crises of appropriation when the cumulative petty stratagems of its subjects deny them labor and taxes. Resistant subcultures of dignity and vengeful dreams are created and nurtured. Counterhegemonic discourse is elaborated. Thus infrapolitics is, as emphasized earlier, always pressing, testing, probing the boundaries of the permissible. Any relaxation in surveillance and punishment and foot-dragging threatens to become a declared strike, folktales of oblique aggression threaten to become face-to-face defiant contempt, millennial dreams threaten to become revolutionary politics. From this vantage point infrapolitics may be thought of as the elementary – in the sense of foundational – form of politics. It is the building block for the more elaborate institutionalized political action that could not exist without it. Under the conditions of tyranny and persecution in which most historical subjects live, it *is* political life. And when the rare civilities of open political life are curtailed or destroyed, as they so often are, the elementary forms of infrapolitics remain as a defense in depth of the powerless.

Notes

1 Strauss, L. (1952), *Persecution and the Art of Writing*, New York: Free Press, 24. It should be abundantly clear that my analysis is fundamentally at cross purposes with much else of what passes as "Straussianism" in contemporary philosophy and political analysis (e.g. its unwarranted claim of

privileged access to the true interpretation of the classics, its disdain for the "vulgar multitude" as well as for dim-witted tyrants). The attitude of Straussians toward nonphilosophers strikes me as comparable to Lenin's attitude toward the working class in *What is to Be Done*. What I do find instructive, however, is the premise that the political environment in which Western political philosophy was written seldom permits a transparency in meaning.

2 Moore, B. (1987), *Injustice: The Social Bases of Obedience and Revolt*, New York: ME Sharpe, 459n.

3 Max Gluckman (1954), *Rituals of Rebellion in South-East Africa*, Manchester: Manchester University press; and Turner, V. (1969), *The Ritual Process: Structure and Anti-Structure*, Chicago: Aldine, esp. chap. 2.

4 Guha, R. (1983), *Elementary Aspects of Peasant Insurgency*, Delhi: Oxford University Press, pp. 18–76. "It is precisely in order to prevent such inversions from occurring in real life that the dominant culture in all traditional societies *allows* these to be simulated at regular calendric intervals," 30, emphasis added.

5 Douglass, F. (1987), *My Bondage and My Freedom*, edited and with an introduction by William L. Andrews, Urbana: University of Illinois Press, p. 156.

6 Berkowitz, L. (1962), *Aggression: A Social Psychological Analysis*, New York: McGraw Hill, pp. 204–27. In one experiment, for example, two groups of subjects were insulted by a powerful figure in identical ways. Some of the "victims" were then allowed to give an electric shock to their victimizer, while others were not. Those who struck back then felt less hostile toward their victimizer and also experienced a decline in blood pressure. Those who were not permitted to strike back, even though they could fully voice their aggressive fantasies indirectly in interpreting a thematic apperception test, experienced no decline in blood pressure. Indirect aggression, then, seems a poor substitute for direct retaliation.

7 This perspective is suggested by the monumental work of Veyne, P. (1984), *Le pain et le cirque*, Bologna: IL Mulino. Veyne treats the bread and circuses of classical Rome as something as much *wrung* from elites as conferred by them to neutralize anger. As he claims, "The government does not provide the circus to the people to depoliticize them but, certainly, they would be politicized against the government if it refused them the circus" (94).

8 The coincidence by itself does not, of course, prove that such rituals, as rituals, were a provocation to revolt. Here one would have to distinguish between the effects of ritual symbolism on the one hand, and the mass assembly of subordinates on the other.

9 Thompson, E. P. (1975), *Whigs and Hunters: The Origin of the Black Act*, New york: Pantheon.

10 Ibid., 108.

11 Ibid., 124.

12 Ibid., 162.

13 A comparable dialectic, moreover, joins the practices of domination to the hidden transcript. The predations of game wardens, arrests and prosecutions, new laws and warnings, the losses of subsistence resources would continually find their way into the normative discourse of those whose earlier rights to the forest were being curtailed.

14 Djilas, M. (1983), *The New Class: An analysis of the Communist System*, New York: Praeger.

15 This argument is made at much greater length in Scott, J. C. (1985), *Weapons of the Weak: Everyday Forms of Peasant Resistance*, New Haven: Yale University Press.

7 The silent revolution and the weapons of the weak

Transformation and innovation from below

Fantu Cheru

Source: Stephen Gill and James H. Mittelman (eds) (1997), *Innovation and Transformation in International Studies*, Cambridge: Cambridge University Press, pp. 153–169

In the arcane and isolated world of academia, the 'everyday forms of resistance' of ordinary poor people across the globe rarely attract the attention of researchers or funding agencies until these local level struggles break out into spasms of violence that could threaten the *status quo*.[1] The conventional view is that everyday resistance represents trivial coping mechanisms that are non-political and these merit no serious investigation. This view completely misses the point. The consequences of such silent resistance on the policy decisions of governments may not always be visible on the surface and one must carefully search for their long-term effects. Nevertheless, like an army of termites eating away the wooden structure of a house inch by inch, silent resistance by millions of poor peasants can have the same result, eroding the foundations of a political system – perhaps even making for a 'silent revolution'.

Thus this chapter highlights various forms of resistance with reference to a number of African cases. Indeed, I hope to provide an account of both innovation and transformation 'from below' as seen and practised by marginalised groups in rural Africa. Although peasants in Africa have had no formal training in International Relations, they understand from experience how historical forces are constituted and how the prevailing global strategy of the Group of Seven nations and the dominant international financial institutions (e.g., World Bank and IMF) is based on the cold-blooded abandonment of large numbers of humanity. Peasants also understand how such forces might be changed, that is, by relying on 'hidden' forms of everyday resistance. In this context, peasants are raising innovative issues of moral or ethical political economy.

Indeed these forms of resistance, independent of traditional political parties, and outside the state, appear related to a critical theory approach to social transformation. Indeed it is vital that the agenda for study in International Relations focuses on a wider range of dimensions of transformation and innovation, including those that come from 'below', from subordinate positions in the global social hierarchy. This agenda should also involve the development of institutions which can express grass-roots democratic concerns and deal with the kinds of community and global problems that can no longer be ignored.

A peasant perspective on myths of development

It is a well-known fact that the post-independence history of Africa is replete with examples of broken promises and unfulfilled dreams. The policies of both colonial and post-independence governments have had disastrous effects on the silent majority of African peasants and landless labourers (Leys, 1974; Watts, 1983; Palmer and Parsons, 1977; Beckman, 1981).

Peasants, by and large, have been treated with less respect than that accorded to cattle. The granting of formal political independence to African countries brought neither participation nor accountability to local structures (Hyden, 1983; Coulson, 1980).

The post-independence development model has, in more ways, been very similar to the colonial development model which stifled peasant autonomy and production. Rural development policy has, by and large, been geared towards the production of primary commodities for the export market to pay for prestige development projects. Like their forebears in the colonial era, peasants are expected to provide the bulk of resources required for national development through increased taxes and by engaging themselves in primary resource production (Andrea and Beckman, 1987). Far from being a war against poverty, development has turned out to be a war against the poor and the natural resource base that sustains them.

In some African countries, the forced removal of peasants and pastoralists from fertile areas to marginal lands to make way for export plantations and game parks has been justified by the authorities on the grounds of advancing the 'national interest' (Cheru, 1992; Rosenblum and Williamson, 1987; Timberlake, 1986). In northern Nigeria, for example, the World Bank funded Talak-Mafara irrigation project near the Sokoto River resulted in the displacement of 60,000 peasants in a three-year period. In Ethiopia, the Awash Valley Development Authority irrigation projects, largely funded by donors, resulted in the eviction of thousands of nomadic Afars from their traditional pasture land in the Awash Valley (Zerihun, 1983). These projects also attracted absentee landowners and merchants to engage in extensive mechanisation in the adjacent areas which resulted in excessive land speculation, further compounding the problems of the local people. Similar strategies are still being followed faithfully in many countries at the expense of self-reliance, social justice, political autonomy and ecological harmony.

Independence has largely meant more power and privileges to the urban elites while the rural poor were left to fend for themselves. Elite bureaucrats and party loyalists, far removed from the reality of rural life, continue to dictate what peasants can and cannot produce, to whom they can sell and at what price (Bates, 1981; World Bank, 1989). What the peasants and the urban poor know and what they might need are of no concern to them (Chambers, 1989; Rahmato, 1989). This situation is compounded by insecure tenure systems, inadequate marketing, storage facilities and weak extension services in rural areas. The onset of subsequent droughts has simply compounded their vulnerable condition. Millions perish needlessly in far-away scattered villages through 'silent genocide' of hunger, lack of clean water and basic health services.

The peasants could demand neither better prices for their goods nor a fair distribution of land and other productive resources since they are effectively shut off from the decision-making process. Those who migrated to urban areas in search of scarce jobs live in slums under a constant threat of eviction, and they face daily harassment by the police when they try to sell their fruits and vegetables at street corners. This explains why ordinary people see governments as their number one enemy and try to avoid them altogether.

Does poor people's knowledge matter?

Paradoxically, the present African economic crisis, painful as it may be in the short term, could provide the poor for the first time with a real chance to experiment with alternative strategies of their own. As a person of peasant roots and twenty-five years of work in the field of social justice, I have come to the conclusion that those in a position of power and privilege not only ignore the demands of the poor for fundamental change, but they actually hate the poor. The peasantry, on the other hand, regard elite-initiated development as a threat to their existence. In an environment of mutual suspicion, the poor take matters in their own hands since they know from experience that 'the oppressors never make change; only the oppressed do' (Freire, 1971).

Let us now explore how far and in what ways the delegitimation of the post-colonial state has opened up room for individual and collective defensive action, and more recently, for the elaboration of new civil-society relations as a moment of political innovation. The first example I discuss involves organising around subsistence both at the household and community level (Taylor and Mackenzie, 1992). The second concerns mass political mobilisation to challenge oppressive systems of government.

Individual/household level struggles for subsistence

The peasant sector

Peasants and the urban poor in Africa experience similar problems on a daily basis: poverty, hunger, unemployment, landlessness, intimidation and down-right scorn and disdain from those who govern 'from above'. At the same time, I am humbled by the capacity of the poor to laugh at their own misery and, more importantly, the tenacity that appears to propel even the poorest of the poor to make a living out of thin air, to fight for their dignity.

After many years of being treated like donkeys, the peasants in Africa have realised their powerless situation within the context of orthodox politics, and have drawn conclusions: it is better to avoid the state altogether and withdraw within their local communities on a subsistence basis and to engage in collective action to find solutions to common problems. In some communities, peasants have switched from growing export crops to food production for local consumption. Where quota delivery of grain to marketing boards is mandatory, as was the case in Ethiopia between 1980 and 1989, peasants traded a small portion of their high grade maize or wheat for large sums of low quality grain which they delivered to the marketing board. I have documented a similar experience in Kenya where mandatory delivery of milk by peasant farmers to Kenyan Creamers at state-determined prices had forced farmers to dilute the milk with water, thus making a sizeable profit on the undiluted portion which they with-held to sell privately. Such actions are logical because, for peasants and the urban poor, the future is not necessarily more predictable and thus they prefer security and subsistence to uncertain conceptions of 'progress'.

Indeed, for a peasantry living in acute destitution and imminent danger, survival considerations are always paramount, and every peasant learns the techniques of survival as part of his/her everyday experience. These techniques may be crude or ingenious, depending on the perceptions of the people and the stock of accumulated knowledge having to do with production and survival, the resources of the community, and the social relations and communal values existing at a given time. Everyday forms of resistance are not simply spur of the moment reactions by the marginalised to the problems they confront daily. Rather, the desire to resist is based on a rational calculation of both risks and gains by the participants. Such resistance requires little co-ordination, avoids direct confrontation with authorities and is not subject to elite manipulation (Scott, 1993; Cheru, 1989). I will illustrate this with reference to the Ethiopian case.

Growing up in rural Ethiopia, I had the privilege of being both a participant in and a witness to everyday forms of peasant resistance. Starting with the feudal rule of Emperor Haile Selassie and the military socialist regime that governed the country from 1974 until May 1991, the Ethiopian peasantry had fought hard, first to keep body and soul together and then to liberate themselves from oppressive regimes (Pausewang *et al.*, 1990; Rahmato, 1993). Although the struggle for democracy and sustainable development remains elusive, Ethiopian peasants have demonstrated that undemocratic governments could be brought to their knees. The sudden collapse of the entire military and socialist apparatus of the regime of Colonel Mengistu Haile Mariam in May 1991 was due largely to the prolonged resistance of the peasantry rather than to the military strength of the largely Tigrean-led Ethiopian Peoples Revolutionary Defence Forces (EPRDF) which came into power in 1991.

Throughout the feudal rule of Emperor Haile Selassie, peasant agriculture stagnated partly due to the parasitic nature of the feudal lords and the land tenure system, but more so because of bad economic policies of the regime. The imperial regime continued to starve peasant agriculture of capital investment, technical services and extension support until the early 1970s when an experimental green revolution package called Minimum Package Programme was introduced in easily accessible parts of high potential areas to help improve the performance of peasant production. This minimal programme was initiated after prodding by the donors, not in response to the needs of the peasantry (Aredo, 1990).

The condition of the peasantry deteriorated further by the absence of any channel of communication to air their grievances to the highest authorities. The emperor had made it a policy that no major mass organisation be formed without his approval. The Office of Association in the Ministry of Interior was granted broad authority to judge the registration application to be 'unlawful or immoral' or 'against the national unity or interest' (Clapham, 1969). In practice, the ministry used its authority under the Association's Registration Regulation of 1966 to outlaw all organisations posing a potential threat to the interest of the regime. Similar control measures exist in many parts of Africa in an attempt to suffocate civil society.

In the absence of any democratic opening, peasants had no choice but to resort to innovation, that is, to ingenious forms of resistance. In my own family, such resistance took many forms: underreporting of crop output to the tax collectors, illegal cutting of trees from a state forest designed to supply fuel wood for urban residents, and illegal grazing in government owned land. From the point of view of the peasantry, repeated encroachment on government owned lands was a justifiable act. The land, which used to be communally owned, was the only grazing area available for the entire village before it was forcefully taken away by the government.

When the traditional water sources that sustained my village and the surrounding community were diverted towards a government owned irrigation project that was growing carnation flowers for export, the peasants in the community disrupted production for a prolonged period by cutting down several big pylons that carried electricity to the power transmission station at the project site, while other peasants chipped away sections of the dike in the cover of darkness, allowing water to escape in the direction of the village and the surrounding farms. With operating costs running high, the government had no choice but to accommodate the demands of the community by allowing the peasants in my village to have water for their farms at scheduled hours. Call it tax evasion, bootlegging or stealing, these activities represent a defence of self and community.[2]

[...]

The urban informal sector

The struggle for dignity by the urban poor must be viewed as being part and parcel of the broader rural struggle. Urban poverty and unemployment are structurally linked to the decay of rural society. Again parallels with the period of enclosures and industrialisation in Britain could easily be made.

In urban areas, the portrait of official joblessness does not reflect the work taking place in the informal sector that keeps thousands of families from starving. Millions are engaged in trades of every description, from back-alley foreign exchange houses, road-side restaurants, curb-side automobile and small appliance maintenance shops, to production and distribution of farm equipment made out of scrap metals, often at much cheaper prices than imported ones. In countries where the supply of medicine is hampered either by the lack of foreign exchange or by official corruption, imaginative individuals who can barely read and write, have stepped in to fill the void and are providing valuable service to the population by opening up their own underground pharmacies, stocked with medicine brought into the country by middle-men who make their living at cross-border trade.

Let me illustrate my point clearly. In a recent trip to western Kenya, I wanted to make an urgent telephone call to the capital. When I inquired at the front desk of my hotel for assistance, the attendant informed me that the line had not been working for many months. All the copper wiring connecting the town to the capital had been stolen by ingenious individuals who supply the Nairobi blacksmith who makes and sells beautiful bracelets to foreign tourists. Although this attitude of 'eat or be eaten' may appear irrational for a Western observer, copper smuggling represents the main source of income for poor citizens who feel forgotten by their own government. The smugglers do not experience a crisis of conscience for taking down government property since they neither have a telephone nor could they expect in the future any type of public employment programme in their region if they behave differently.

Although the driving force for self-help and improvisation is survival, the millions of poor Africans operating outside of the official market are in fact providing vital services where governments have failed to carry out their responsibilities. Instead of castigating the poor and characterising their professions as 'criminal' or 'illegal', we should celebrate them for elevating the human spirit, for fighting to preserve their dignity, and for allowing the rest of us to find our own humanity. The revenge of the poor against oppressive systems could open the way for a far more fundamental transformation of society, for equal justice, liberty and the pursuit of happiness. This is what I call the 'silent revolution' of the poor.

Organised struggles for subsistence

As the state has become increasingly irrelevant in the eyes of ordinary peasants, traditional institutions have assumed greater responsibility in mobilising and facilitating the creative adaptation of the poor. Communities pull their resources together to raise income and family nutrition, to build their own schools, mobilise savings and informal credit to help their members start a business, or push back the desert by planting crops that hold the soil together, and reclaim the self-reliance that was theirs until the advent of the modern nation-state. In the process, peasants and the urban poor in Africa are educating themselves in organisational dynamics and self-government. Several cases are worth mentioning.

The detrimental effects of marketing boards in Africa have been noted. In many parts of Africa, peasants now market their produce and livestock through their own channels, disregarding political boundaries and marketing boards. For example, in the Kaolack region of Senegal, peasants have formed a federation called the Peasant Association of Kaolack (ADAK), which established barter agreements with farmer groups. They exchange millet and salt for palm oil, dried fish and honey, thereby avoiding the market, taxes and government boards (Pradervand, 1989). In eastern Senegal, the Federation of Sarakolle Village has successfully resisted efforts by the state agricultural agency and the United States Agency for International Development (USAID) to promote rice production via large-scale irrigation schemes and centralised control over production and marketing (Adams, 1981). The federation's persistence has forced changes in the state marketing board's approach in other areas where it operates.

Like the colonial system, the post-colonial state has lost its role as an instrument of development and ordinary citizens do not expect anything from the state. Instead, they are determining their own development. In Burkina Faso, for example, thousands of innovative village development groups have been transforming their communities. The most visible institution has been the Naam, the traditional Burkinable village co-operative. These groups grew spontaneously in the early 1970s in response to the rapid and far-reaching environmental and economic crises facing their communities. Using the traditional concept of self-help, the Naam groups organised themselves at the village level and began constructing dams and dikes, reforesting, opening new roads, digging wells and undertaking soil conservation projects. The groups also introduced basic literacy, improved cooking stoves, and constructed cereal banks, grain mills and village pharmacies (Cheru and Bayili, 1991; Pradervand, 1989). Six S, another indigenous organisation, provides the funding for local communities. Six S is organised so that it can respond to local needs without intimidation.

In Kenya, the Green Belt movement, headed by Wangari Maathai, assists Kenyan women in planting trees in their homesteads and in other activities such as job creation for the handicapped and the promotion of sound nutrition. The movement has established more than 1,000 nurseries, producing over 10,000 seedlings per year and involving more than 50,000 households, comprising half a million villagers (Maathai, 1985; Topouzis, 1990). But when the group publicly challenged President Moi's plan to build a 67-storey skyscraper for $250 million at the centre of a popular Nairobi city park, arguing that the money could best be spent to alleviate poverty and ecological degradation in the country, Maathai and the movement were publicly condemned by the parliament and the group lost its limited funding from the government. Still others, such as the Semi-Arid Land Use movement in Kenya, are organised on a co-operative basis to develop land that had been given up as unreclaimable.

[...]

From silent to overt resistance: limits and contradictions

The second form of resistance, growing out of the first, is the challenge to the nation-state and the demand for substantive democratisation, as evidenced in the growth of democracy movements over the past five years. As ordinary citizens have become more and more aware of what they want and how they might attain it, they have entered into political action and organisations to demand an accounting from those who govern. Flag-bearers of this new renaissance are social movements based in the church, informal sector, human rights, environment and development communities that have sprung up all across Africa in the last decade to articulate alternative visions of survival and democratic governance (Cheru, 1996). Popular protests and movements have challenged not only the policies but even the character of the regimes. The concerns of these movements have been economic (unemployment, declining real wages), social (cuts in welfare services), and political (repression, lack of human rights) – all a testimony to the misdirection of resources and accountability.

It would be a great mistake, however, to attribute the growth of democracy movements strictly to the mobilisation efforts of elite-led parties that have sprung up in recent years.

Rather, the movement owes its success to the debilitating economic impact of the 'silent revolution' of ordinary peasants on the capacity of African governments to provide even the most basic services to previously protected groups (teachers, civil servants, doctors, etc.). This process dates back to the mid-1970s when peasants began to drop out in large numbers from the formal economy to demonstrate their anger at the perceived hostility of the state towards them.

The demand for fundamental change has been born of a decade of painful economic decline and disenchantment with autocratic rule. The crucial factor which provided the impetus for mass political mobilisation in the decade of the 1980s has been the resistance to externally imposed structural adjustment programmes (SAPs), which have had a disastrous impact on peasants and the urban poor as well as previously protected (or privileged) groups, such as the urban elites and the middle classes. As many people began to draw a direct connection between their economic plight and the paucity of basic liberties, local grievances very quickly escalated into popular challenges to the established systems of governments that are seen domestically as predatory and corrupt and internationally, servile executors of the economic agenda of the ruling classes of the major OECD nations.

Yet, the euphoria over multiparty democracy has been short lived for many reasons. Incumbent regimes were able to use resources at their disposal to splinter civil society either through more repression or co-optation. But, more importantly, opposition parties lacked vision, organisation and leadership. Ethnicity, elitism and corruption further undermined their credibility. The creation of new parties has not directly involved many citizens from outside of extant political elites, and particularly not on the basis of pre-existing grass-roots organisations and interest groups in rural areas. In country after country, the new opposition leaders are often none other than people who served the single party long and faithfully without any great sign of a crisis of conscience.

This did not come as a surprise to the peasantry who are suspicious of elite-led initiatives. As elections in Kenya and Zambia had demonstrated, multiparty systems could lead to new forms of old hierarchies. Although USAID proudly advertises that many countries in Africa had made the transition from military or autocratic rule to democracy in the past ten years, the collapse of one-party states is rarely accompanied by a substantial reorientation of power relations between urban and rural areas. Many citizens, particularly those in the rural areas, have been excluded and broad based programmes of economic and social reforms have rarely been pursued.

Given these facts, peasants have been reluctant to participate in formal political parties or pin their hopes on democracy. Rather, they view the democratisation drive as another ideology of domination, an attempt to turn them into destitutes just the way agrarian socialism did. They particularly find the decisions of newly elected governments to impose austerity measures, requiring them to make more sacrifice, to be harsh and unacceptable. In response, peasants seek to secure greater autonomy from the state through disengagement just as they had done before (Beckman, 1992). In short, democratisation in Africa has little chance of success if it cannot revive economic fortunes.

International Relations in an age of marginalisation: problems and prospects

With the so-called end of the Cold War, the abstractions of free elections and free markets have assumed greater importance in the foreign policies of Western powers and in the programmes of both multilateral and bilateral aid agencies. The shift in the rhetoric and to an extent the practice of official Western policy is in response to the rapid growth of popular movements (environmental, women, indigenous groups and human rights groups) giving voice to the poor and disenfranchised throughout the Third World, challenging not only the character of regimes, but also the basic assumptions of conventional development strategies. Innovation from below, in this sense, involves some marginal political innovation from above so as to transform popular pressures into a co-opted frame of reference – what Gramsci (1971) called *trasformismo*.

When closely scrutinised, therefore, the new foreign policy of 'democracy and free markets' is inconsistent with the views of popular movements in Africa. The USAID Democracy Initiative, for example, states that 'democracy is complementary to and supportive of the transition to market-oriented economies and sustainable, broadly-based economic development'. This same view is expressed by the World Bank, which defines its new mission to be the rapid transformation of developing countries to market-oriented principles (World Bank, 1989). In this context, democracy simply means multiparty elections and implementation of market-oriented economic policies: it is democracy in form but does not contain the substance of participation and popular control over people's everyday lives.

In other words, while multiparty elections and universal suffrage are important formal criteria, they are by no means sufficient to judge the democratic qualities of a society. Northern interpretations of democracy suffer from the same flaw as did their interpretation of development, that is, that democratisation is not a process but a product that the North imposes upon the South. As André Gunder Frank (1992) succinctly put it, 'freedom of the market does not equal democratic freedom', because, in the market, it is one dollar, one vote; so that many dollars mean many votes and no dollar no vote. In a free market system of 'one dollar, one vote', there will not be a place for small farmers and poor people in general unless they increase their leverage to exert influence over decisions. Only then can markets be structured to ensure the allocation of resources to small farmers.

In contrast, most discussions of democratisation in the South stress the need to loosen the links between indigenous governments and national elites with Western governments, and the empowerment of the people so that they can define and steer a democratic development process. While the connections between economics and democratisation are clearly made, the assumptions behind this linkage differ sharply from the common Northern assumption that democratisation and free-market economic policies go hand-in-hand. For example, SAPs that have introduced or reinforced free-market policies across much of the South are widely considered to be anti-democratic. The formulation of these policies does not reflect a democratic, participatory process and the impact of SAPs is not spread evenly across societies. The cost of adjustment has been borne by the poor, particularly women and children in urban areas – a new urbanisation that forms part of what Karl Polanyi (1957) called the 'stark utopia' of the self-regulating market society that the West seems now to be attempting to foster in post-colonial Africa.

In addition to the above, the notions of accountability, decentralisation, civil society and popular participation mean different things to Northern policy makers and Southern activists. In the North, accountability primarily refers to financial accountability and the need to challenge corruption; in the Southern context, the term is used more broadly to include financial, economic as well as political accountability. Similarly, decentralisation in the North is used in reference to the decentralisation of authority from the level of the state to the local government and on to the people. In the Arusha Charter, decentralisation begins in the North and includes decentralisation from the state to local government to popular levels (UNECA, 1990).

The notion of civil society may or may not be innovatory or emancipatory. Civil society in the North has traditionally referred not necessarily to the grass-roots organisations, but to professional associations such as lawyers, public interest groups, political parties, business associations, churches, the media and universities; usage in the South needs further specification but commonly refers to grass-roots and popular organisations – it is in some ways a more democratic conception. Similarly, popular participation, when used in the North tends to refer to participation at the project or programme level in Third World development; Southern development activists expand the notion of popular participation to include policy formulation at national, regional and international levels (Melin, 1995).

The fashionable notion of 'transnational civil society' also masks many contradictions. While Northern and Southern non-governmental organisations (NGOs) are collaborating together to lobby governments through the United Nations system on issues of human rights, ecology, poverty and other social issues of global dimensions, or in cofinancing of community development projects, their strength and capacity to conduct human-centred transnational foreign policy, independent of states, are exaggerated (Korten, 1990; Ekins, 1992). NGOs are no substitute for governments. Not only are their activities governed by official laws, but their success is partly attributed to the support they receive from host governments in the form of exemptions from tax, import duties, etc. Furthermore, the relationships between Northern and Southern NGOs are characterised by unequal power and influence. It is not uncommon to hear complaints from African partners that Northern NGOs are spreading clientelism, thus undermining collective action. In this sense transnational civil society is antithetical to notions of grass-roots innovation and emancipation.

To a significant degree, the transition to democracy, and equitable and environmentally sustainable development is one that the people of Africa can undertake themselves. However, the current fad of multiparty elections and economic reforms, largely crafted in the North, will only help perpetuate the present economic and political crisis. Indeed, it may be easy for outsiders to teach Africans how to speak the English language; but they cannot teach Africans how to govern themselves. That is a task that Africans themselves must figure out on their own, innovating in their own ways and transforming the circumstances that they face. Although both the World Bank and USAID claim that democracy cannot be exported, they both proceed to define the components of democratic governance for the South.

Conclusion

With few exceptions, International Relations has largely been dominated by pro-establishment scholars, more concerned with the protection of privileges, and less about the creation of a more just, sustainable, non-sexist, and non-racial world order. Some of these commentators have gone even further to proclaim the collapse of communism and the triumph of Western liberalism as 'the end of history' (Fukuyama, 1989). Yet, the end of the Cold War has not translated into the end of domination, exploitation and marginalisation of Third World countries. The growing gap between the North and the South is compounded further by the process of globalisation, which has both integrating and disintegrating tendencies, deepening the existing inequalities in incomes and power at various levels of our society (Mittelman, 1996). This is the study of International Relations 'from above'. It is incomplete unless it is joined with a perspective on the world 'from below'.

In practical terms, peace and security will not be achieved unless International Relations is extended to deal with the threats that stem from failures in development, environmental degradation, lack of progress towards democracy and the challenges posed by the process of economic globalisation. It is here that critical theory is needed to understand historical structures, which contain contradictions, conflict and coherence, and to propose the necessary changes.

This implies that International Relations as a field must embark on a new research agenda aimed at developing alternative sources of innovative knowledge and understanding which will help identify the forces of opposition to the new global conditions of the 1990s. Seen 'from below', the following research questions are apposite in the African context: how can we create a new balance between the interests of a transnational economy and the real needs of local communities in the face of diminishing state power? How would the poverty-induced migration of millions of destitute people affect relations between states and among those people who see themselves as losing out or as threatened? At the same time, we are witnessing a growing trend in core-periphery social co-operation as exemplified in the global environmental and human rights and other solidarity movements. Are these transnational social movements potential agents of transformation? If so, in what ways? In what ways are they not? Research in these and other areas will foster collective awareness, promote cross-cultural understanding, and eventually come closer to constructing a just and more humane world society in which human innovation and emancipation become the 'order' of the day.

Notes

1   In the title of this chapter, the phrase, 'silent revolution' is from Cheru (1989); 'the weapons of the weak' is taken from James C. Scott (1985). In some ways, this essay is a personal testimony based on my own experience growing up in a peasant household, and as a professional who has lived and worked in poor communities in many parts of Africa. While my accounts of the deplorable condition of the poor peasants and their everyday struggles for fundamental change may not fit neatly into predetermined categories of social theory, and thus by extension be labelled as unscientific, poor peoples' knowledge and their experienced reality counts, for they alone can change their situation for the better.

2   Editor's note (by Stephen Gill). The responses of peasants in Africa outlined by Fantu Cheru are similar to those noted by E. P. Thompson (1980) in his account of the peasantry and urban poor in the period of intensified enclosure of land and expropriation of the commons and the development of industrialisation in eighteenth- and nineteenth-century Britain. Thompson's work showed how poaching (one of the most common 'crimes' of that period) was a relatively spontaneous survival mechanism. However, this crime was widely perceived as legitimate action by the bulk of the population under conditions of expropriation. Access to the commons had been denied and such access was perceived as a threat to both moral economy and the means of existence by the mass of the population. It was thus the subject of intense and protracted political struggle (see also Polanyi, 1957 on this point). Similarly, James C. Scott (1993) discusses how the silent and apparently uncoordinated and unplanned resistance of the Chinese peasantry was in direct response to the disastrous collectivisation of agriculture in Mao's ill-fated Great Leap Forward, a leap which produced mass starvation. The subsequent 'Four Modernisations' policy of Deng is only comprehensible in terms of the limits that such structural resistance – akin to a broad-based class force – posed for the state's agricultural policies. Deng's policies merely recognised and ratified what had already become the reality in the political economy of rural China.

Selected references

Adams, A. (1981), 'The Senegal River Valley', in J. Heyer (ed.), *Rural Development in Tropical Africa*, New York: St Martins.

Andrea, G. and Beckman, B. (1987), *The Wheat Trap: Bread and Underdevelopment in Nigeria*, London: Zed Books.

Aredo, D. (1990), 'The Evolution of Rural Development Policies in Ethiopia', in S. Pausewang, F. Cheru, S. Brune, and E. Chole (eds), *Ethiopia: Rural Development Options*, London: Zed.

Bates, R. H. (1981), *Markets and States in Tropical Africa: The Political Basis of Agricultural Policies*, Berkeley, CA: University of California Press.

Beckman, B. (1981), 'Ghana, 1951–78: The Agrarian Basis of the Post-Colonial State', in J. Heyer (ed.), *Rural Development in Tropical Africa*, New York: St Martins.

Beckman, B. (1992), 'Empowerment or Repression?: The World Bank and the Politics of African Adjustment', in P. Gibbon, Y. Bangura and A. Ofstad (eds), *Authoritarianism, Democracy and Adjustment*, Uppsala: Scandinavian Institute of African Studies, pp. 83–105.

Chambers, R. (1989), *The State and Rural Development: Ideologies and an Agenda for the 1990s*, IDS Paper, University of Sussex.

Cheru, F. (1989), *The Silent Revolution in Africa: Debt, Development and Democracy*, London: Zed Books.

—— (1992), 'Structural Adjustment, Primary Resource Trade, and Sustainable Development in Sub-Saharan Africa', *World Development*, 20: 4, pp. 497–512.

—— (1996), 'New Social Movements: Democratic Struggles and Human Rights in Africa', in J. Mittelman (ed.), *Globalization: Critical Reflections*, Boulder, CO: Lynne Rienner.

Cheru, F. and Bayili, J. (1991), *Burkina Faso: Assessment of Micro-Economic Policy and its Impact on Grassroots and Non-Governmental Organizations*, Washington, DC: African Development Foundation.

Clapham, C. (1969), *Haile Selassie's Government*, London: Longman.

Coulson, A. (ed.) (1980), *African Socialism in Practice: The Tanzanian Experience*, London: Spokesman Books.

Ekins, P. (1992), *A New World Order: Grassroots Movements for Global Change*, London: Routledge.

Frank, A. G. (1992), 'No Escape from the Laws of World Economics', *Review of African Political Economy*, 50, pp. 20–31.

Freire, P. (1971), *Pedagogy of the Oppressed*, New York: Herder and Herder.

Fukuyama, F. (1989), 'The End of History?', *National Interest*, 16, pp. 3–18.

Gramsci, A. (1971), *Selections from the Prison Notebooks of Antonio Gramsci*, translated by Q. Hoare and G. Nowell Smith, London: Lawrence and Wishart.

Hyden, G. (1983), *No Shortcuts to Progress: African Development Management in Perspective*, London: Heinemann.

Korten, D. (1990), *Getting to the 21st Century*, West Hartford: Kumarian.

Leys, C. (1974), *Underdevelopment in Kenya*, Berkeley, CA: University of California Press.

Maathai, W. (1985), 'Kenya: The Green Belt Movement', *IFDA Dossier*, 49, pp. 4–12.

Mittelman, J. (1996), *Globalization: Critical Reflections*, Boulder, CO: Lynne Rienner.

Nyoni, S. (1995), 'Is Democracy Possible? The Role of Grassroots Movements', in M. Merlin (ed.), *Democracy in Africa: On Whose Terms?*, Stockholm: Forum.

Palmer, R. and Parsons, N. (eds) (1977), *The Roots of Rural Poverty in Central and Southern Africa*, Berkeley, CA: University of California Press.

Polanyi, K. (1957), *The Great Transformation: Political and Economic Origins of Our Time*, Boston: Beacon Press.

Pausewang, S. *et al.* (eds) (1990), *Ethiopia: Rural Development Options*, London: Zed Books.

Pradervand, P. (1989), *Listening to Africa: Developing Africa from the Grassroots*, New York: Praeger.

Rahmato, D. (1989), 'Rural Resettlement in Post Revolution Ethiopia', paper prepared for Conference on Population Issues, ONCCP, Addis Ababa.

Rahmato, D. (1993), 'Agrarian Change and Agrarian Crisis: State and Peasantry in Post-Revolution Ethiopia', *Africa*, 63: 1, pp. 66–75.

Rosenblum, M. and Williamson, D. (1987), *Squandering Eden: Africa at the Edge*, New York: Harcourt Brace.

Scott. J. C. (1985), *Weapons of the Weak*, New Haven, CT: Yale University Press.

Scott, J. C. (1993), *Everyday Forms of Resistance*, International Peace Research Institute, Meigaku. Occasional Paper Series no. 15. Yokahama.

Taylor, D. F. and Mackenzie, F. (1992), *Development from Within*, London: Routledge.

Thompson, E. P. (1980), *The Making of the English Working Class*, Harmondsworth: Penguin.

Timberlake, L. (1986), *Africa in Crisis*, London: Earthscan.

Topouzis, D. (1990), 'Kenya Women Fight Deforestation', *Africa Recovery*, 4, October, pp. 43–45.

UNECA (1990), *African Charter for Popular Participation in Development and Transformation*, Addis Ababa: ECA.

Watts, M. (1983), *Silent Violence: Food, Famine and Peasantry in Northern Nigeria*, Berkeley, CA: University of California Press.

World Bank (1989), *Sub-Saharan Africa: From Crisis to Sustainable Growth*, Washington, DC: World Bank.

Zerihun, T. (1983), *Rural Settlement Schemes*, MSc thesis, Uppsala: Swedish University of Agricultural Sciences.

8 Method

Michel Foucault

Source: Michel Foucault (1976/1998), *The Will to Knowledge: The History of Sexuality Volume 1*, London: Penguin, pp. 92–97

[...] The word *power* is apt to lead to a number of misunderstandings – misunderstandings with respect to its nature, its form, and its unity. By power, I do not mean "Power" as a group of institutions and mechanisms that ensure the subservience of the citizens of a given state. By power, I do not mean, either, a mode of subjugation which, in contrast to violence, has the form of the rule. Finally, I do not have in mind a general system of domination exerted by one group over another, a system whose effects, through successive derivations, pervade the entire social body. The analysis, made in terms of power, must not assume that the sovereignty of the state, the form of the law, or the over-all unity of a domination are given at the outset; rather, these are only the terminal forms power takes. It seems to me that power must be understood in the first instance as the multiplicity of force relations immanent in the sphere in which they operate and which constitute their own organization; as the process which, through ceaseless struggles and confrontations, transforms, strengthens, or reverses them; as the support which these force relations find in one another, thus forming a chain or a system, or on the contrary, the disjunctions and contradictions which isolate them from one another; and lastly, as the strategies in which they take effect, whose general design or institutional crystallization is embodied in the state apparatus, in the formulation of the law, in the various social hegemonies. Power's condition of possibility, or in any case the viewpoint which permits one to understand its exercise, even in its more "peripheral" effects, and which also makes it possible to use its mechanisms as a grid of intelligibility of the social order, must not be sought in the primary existence of a central point, in a unique source of sovereignty from which secondary and descendent forms would emanate; it is the moving substrate of force relations which, by virtue of their inequality, constantly engender states of power, but the latter are always local and unstable. The omnipresence of power: not because it has the privilege of consolidating everything under its invincible unity, but because it is produced from one moment to the next, at every point, or rather in every relation from one point to another. Power is everywhere; not because it embraces everything, but because it comes from everywhere. And "Power," insofar as it is permanent, repetitious, inert, and self-reproducing, is simply the over-all effect that emerges from all these mobilities, the concatenation that rests on each of them and seeks in turn to arrest their movement. One needs to be nominalistic, no doubt: power is not an institution, and not a structure; neither is it a certain strength we are endowed with; it is the name that one attributes to a complex strategical situation in a particular society.

Should we turn the expression around, then, and say that politics is war pursued by other means? If we still wish to maintain a separation between war and politics, perhaps we should postulate rather that this multiplicity of force relations can be coded – in part but never totally – either in the form of "war," or in the form of "politics"; this would imply two different strategies (but the one always liable to switch into the other) for integrating these unbalanced, heterogeneous, unstable, and tense force relations.

Continuing this line of discussion, we can advance a certain number of propositions:

- Power is not something that is acquired, seized, or shared, something that one holds on to or allows to slip away; power is exercised from innumerable points, in the interplay of nonegalitarian and mobile relations.

- Relations of power are not in a position of exteriority with respect to other types of relationships (economic processes, knowledge relationships, sexual relations), but are immanent in the latter; they are the immediate effects of the divisions, inequalities, and disequilibriums which occur in the latter, and conversely they are the internal conditions of these differentiations; relations of power are not in superstructural positions, with merely a role of prohibition or accompaniment; they have a directly productive role, wherever they come into play.

- Power comes from below; that is, there is no binary and all-encompassing opposition between rulers and ruled at the root of power relations, and serving as a general matrix – no such duality extending from the top down and reacting on more and more limited groups to the very depths of the social body. One must suppose rather that the manifold relationships of force that take shape and come into play in the machinery of production, in families, limited groups, and institutions, are the basis for wide-ranging effects of cleavage that run through the social body as a whole. These then form a general line of force that traverses the local oppositions and links them together; to be sure, they also bring about redistributions, realignments, homogenizations, serial arrangements, and convergences of the force relations. Major dominations are the hegemonic effects that are sustained by all these confrontations.

- Power relations are both intentional and nonsubjective. If in fact they are intelligible, this is not because they are the effect of another instance that "explains" them, but rather because they are imbued, through and through, with calculation: there is no power that is exercised without a series of aims and objectives. But this does not mean that it results from the choice or decision of an individual subject; let us not look for the headquarters that presides over its rationality; neither the caste which governs, nor the groups which control the state apparatus, nor those who make the most important economic decisions direct the entire network of power that functions in a society (and makes *it* function); the rationality of power is characterized by tactics that are often quite explicit at the restricted level where they are inscribed (the local cynicism of power), tactics which, becoming connected to one another, attracting and propagating one another, but finding their base of support and their condition elsewhere, end by forming comprehensive systems: the logic is perfectly clear, the aims decipherable, and yet it is often the case that no one is there to have invented them, and few who can be said to have formulated them: an implicit characteristic of the great anonymous, almost unspoken strategies which coordinate the loquacious tactics whose "inventors" or decision-makers are often without hypocrisy.

- Where there is power, there is resistance, and yet, or rather consequently, this resistance is never in a position of exteriority in relation to power. Should it be said that one is always "inside" power, there is no "escaping" it, there is no absolute outside where it is concerned, because one is subject to the law in any case? Or that, history being the ruse of reason, power is the ruse of history, always emerging the winner? This would be to misunderstand the strictly relational character of power relationships. Their existence depends on a multiplicity of points of resistance: these play the role of adversary, target, support, or handle in power relations. These points of resistance are present everywhere in the power network. Hence there is no single locus of great Refusal, no soul of revolt, source of all rebellions, or pure law of the revolutionary. Instead there is a plurality of resistances, each of them a special case: resistances that are possible, necessary, improbable; others that are spontaneous, savage, solitary, concerted, rampant, or violent; still others that are quick to compromise, interested, or sacrificial; by definition, they can only exist in the strategic field of power relations. But this does not mean that they are only a reaction or rebound, forming with respect to the basic domination an underside that is in the end always passive, doomed to perpetual defeat. Resistances do not derive from a few heterogeneous principles; but neither are they a lure or a promise that is of necessity betrayed. They are the odd term in relations of power; they are inscribed in the latter as an irreducible opposite. Hence they too are distributed in irregular fashion: the points, knots, or focuses of resistance are spread over time and space at varying densities, at times mobilizing groups or individuals in a definitive way, inflaming certain points of the body, certain moments in life, certain types of behavior. Are there no great radical ruptures, massive binary divisions, then? Occasionally, yes. But more often one is dealing with mobile and transitory points of resistance, producing cleavages in a society that shift about, fracturing unities and effecting regroupings, furrowing across individuals themselves, cutting them up and remolding them, marking off irreducible regions in them, in their bodies and minds. Just as the network of power relations ends by forming a dense web that passes through apparatuses and institutions, without being exactly localized in them, so too the swarm of points of resistance traverses social stratifications and individual unities. And it is doubtless the strategic codification of these points of resistance that makes a revolution possible, somewhat similar to the way in which the state relies on the institutional integration of power relationships.

It is in this sphere of force relations that we must try to analyze the mechanisms of power. In this way we will escape from the system of Law-and-Sovereign which has captivated political thought for such a long time. And if it is true that Machiavelli was among the few – and this no doubt was the scandal of his "cynicism" – who conceived the power of the Prince in terms of force relationships, perhaps we need to go one step further, do without the persona of the Prince, and decipher power mechanisms on the basis of a strategy that is immanent in force relationships.

To return to sex and the discourses of truth that have taken charge of it, the question that we must address, then, is not: Given a specific state structure, how and why is it that power needs to establish a knowledge of sex? Neither is the question: What over-all domination was served by the concern, evidenced since the eighteenth century, to produce true discourses on sex? Nor is it: What law presided over both the regularity of sexual behavior and the conformity of what was said about it? It is rather: In a specific type of discourse on sex, in a specific form of extortion of truth, appearing historically and in specific places (around the child's body, apropos of women's sex, in connection with practices restricting births, and so on), what were the most immediate, the most local power relations at work? How did they make possible these kinds of discourses, and conversely, how were these discourses used to support power relations? How was the action of these power relations modified by their very exercise, entailing a strengthening of some terms and a weakening of others, with effects of resistance and counterinvestments, so that there has never existed one type of stable subjugation, given once and for all? How were these power relations linked to one another according to the logic of a great strategy, which in retrospect takes on the aspect of a unitary and voluntarist politics of sex? In general terms: rather than referring all the infinitesimal violences that are exerted on sex, all the anxious gazes that are directed at it, and all the hiding places whose discovery is made into an impossible task, to the unique form of a great Power, we must immerse the expanding production of discourses on sex in the field of multiple and mobile power relations.

Which leads us to advance, in a preliminary way, four rules to follow. But these are not intended as methodological imperatives; at most they are cautionary prescriptions.

Rule of immanence

One must not suppose that there exists a certain sphere of sexuality that would be the legitimate concern of a free and disinterested scientific inquiry were it not the object of mechanisms of prohibition brought to bear by the economic or ideological requirements of power. If sexuality was constituted as an area of investigation, this was only because relations of power had established it as a possible object; and conversely, if power was able to take it as a target, this was because techniques of knowledge and procedures of discourse were capable of investing it. Between techniques of knowledge and strategies of power, there is no exteriority, even if they have specific roles and are linked together on the basis of their difference. We will start, therefore, from what might be called "local centers" of power-knowledge: for example, the relations that obtain between penitents and confessors, or the faithful and their directors of conscience. Here, guided by the theme of the "flesh" that must be mastered, different forms of discourse – self-examination, questionings, admissions, interpretations, interviews – were the vehicle of a kind of incessant back-and-forth movement of forms of subjugation and schemas of knowledge. Similarly, the body of the child, under surveillance, surrounded in his cradle, his bed, or his room by an entire watch-crew of parents, nurses, servants, educators, and doctors, all attentive to the least manifestations of his sex, has constituted, particularly since the eighteenth century, another "local center" of power-knowledge.

Rules of continual variations

We must not look for who has the power in the order of sexuality (men, adults, parents, doctors) and who is deprived of it (women, adolescents, children, patients); nor for who has the right to know and who is forced to remain ignorant. We must seek rather the pattern of the modifications which the relationships of force imply by the very nature of their process. The "distributions of power" and the "appropriations of knowledge" never represent only instantaneous slices taken from processes involving, for example, a cumulative reinforcement of the strongest factor, or a reversal of relationship, or again, a simultaneous increase of two terms. Relations of power-knowledge are not static forms of distribution, they are "matrices of transformations." The nineteenth-century grouping made up of the father, the mother, the educator, and the doctor, around the child and his sex, was subjected to constant modifications, continual shifts. One of the more spectacular results of the latter was a strange reversal: whereas to begin with the child's sexuality had been problematized within the relationship established between doctor and parents (in the form of advice, or recommendations to keep the child under observation, or warnings of future dangers), ultimately it was in the relationship of the psychiatrist to the child that the sexuality of adults themselves was called into question.

Rule of double conditioning

No "local center," no "pattern of transformation" could function if, through a series of sequences, it did not eventually enter into an over-all strategy. And inversely, no strategy could achieve comprehensive effects if did not gain support from precise and tenuous relations serving, not as its point of application or final outcome, but as its prop and anchor point. There is no discontinuity between them, as if one were dealing with two different levels (one microscopic and the other macroscopic); but neither is there homogeneity (as if the one were only the enlarged projection or the miniaturization of the other); rather, one must conceive of the double conditioning of a strategy by the specificity of possible tactics, and of tactics by the strategic envelope that makes them work. Thus the father in the family is not the "representative" of the sovereign or the state; and the latter are not projections of the father on a different scale. The family does not duplicate society, just as society does not imitate the family. But the family organization, precisely to the extent that it was insular and heteromorphous with respect to the other power mechanisms, was used to support the great "maneuvers" employed for the Malthusian control of the birthrate, for the populationist incitements, for the medicalization of sex and the psychiatrization of its nongenital forms.

Rule of the tactical polyvalence of discourses

What is said about sex must not be analyzed simply as the surface of projection of these power mechanisms. Indeed, it is in discourse that power and knowledge are joined together. And for this very reason, we must conceive discourse as a series of discontinuous segments whose tactical function is neither uniform nor stable. To be more precise, we must not imagine a world of discourse divided between accepted discourse and excluded discourse, or between the dominant discourse and the dominated one; but as a multiplicity of discursive elements that can come into play in various strategies. It is this distribution that we must reconstruct, with the things said and those concealed, the enunciations required and those forbidden, that it comprises; with the variants and different effects – according to who is speaking, his position of power, the institutional context in which he happens to be situated – that it implies; and with the shifts and reutilizations of identical formulas for contrary objectives that it also includes. Discourses are not once and for all subservient to power or raised up against it, any more than silences are. We must make allowance for the complex and unstable process whereby discourse can be both an instrument and an effect of power, but also a hindrance, a stumbling-block, a point of resistance and a starting point for an opposing strategy. Discourse transmits and produces power; it reinforces it, but also undermines and exposes it renders it fragile and makes it possible to thwart it. In like manner, silence and secrecy are a shelter for power, anchoring its prohibitions; but they also loosen its holds and provide for relatively obscure areas of tolerance. Consider for example the history of what was once "the" great sin against nature. The extreme discretion of the texts dealing with sodomy – that utterly confused category – and the nearly universal reticence in talking about it made possible a twofold operation: on the one hand, there was an extreme severity (punishment by fire was meted out well into the eighteenth century, without there being any substantial protest expressed before the middle of the century), and on the other hand, a tolerance that must have been widespread (which one can deduce indirectly from the infrequency of judicial sentences, and which one glimpses more directly through certain statements concerning societies of men that were thought to exist in the army or in the courts). There is no question that the appearance in nineteenth-century psychiatry, jurisprudence, and literature of a whole series of discourses on the species and subspecies of homosexuality, inversion, pederasty, and "psychic hermaphrodism" made possible a strong advance of social controls into this area of "perversity"; but it also made possible the formation of a "reverse" discourse: homosexuality began to speak in its own behalf, to demand that its legitimacy or "naturality" be acknowledged, often in the same vocabulary, using the same categories by which it was medically disqualified. There is not, on the one side, a discourse of power, and opposite it, another discourse that runs counter to it. Discourses are tactical elements or blocks operating in the field of force relations; there can exist different and even contradictory discourses within the same strategy; they can, on the contrary, circulate without changing their form from one strategy to another, opposing strategy. We must not expect the discourses on sex to tell us, above all, what strategy they derive from, or what moral divisions they accompany, or what ideology – dominant or dominated – they represent; rather we must question them on the two levels of their tactical productivity (what reciprocal effects of power and knowledge they ensure) and their strategical integration (what conjunction and what force relationship make their utilization necessary in a given episode of the various confrontations that occur).

In short, it is a question of orienting ourselves to a conception of power which replaces the privilege of the law with the viewpoint of the objective, the privilege of prohibition with the viewpoint of tactical efficacy, the privilege of sovereignty with the analysis of a multiple and mobile field of force relations, wherein far-reaching, but never completely stable, effects of domination are produced. The strategical model, rather than the model based on law. And this, not out of a speculative choice or theoretical preference, but because in fact it is one of the essential traits of Western societies that the force relationships which for a long time had found expression in war, in every form of warfare, gradually became invested in the order of political power.

9 Writing human agency after the death of God

Roland Bleiker

Source: Roland Bleiker (2000), *Popular Dissent, Human Agency and Global Politics*, Cambridge: Cambridge University Press, pp. 23–50

> God is dead; but given the way people are, there may still be caves for thousands of years in which his shadow will be shown. – And we – we still have to vanquish his shadow, too.[1]

The concept of human agency occupies a central position in the history of Western thought. From Aristotle onwards countless leading minds have philosophised how people may or may not be able to influence their social environment. Do our actions, intentional or not, bear upon our destiny? Or are we simply creatures of habit, blind followers of cultural and linguistic orders too large and too powerful to be swayed?

Today, the echoes of these questions resonate more than ever. Can there be human agency in an increasingly globalised and transversal world, an epoque of rapid change and blurring boundaries between nations, cultures, knowledges, realities? Who or what shapes the course of social dynamics at a moment when new communicative technologies constantly redefine time, space and the ways in which people relate to each other? Can shifting social designs and their designers be discerned at all?

These are difficult theoretical questions and they must be posed in an investigation that seeks to understand the role of transversal dissent in global politics. Human agency, this book argues, is a concept and a field of inquiry that should be retained despite the existence of a number of serious obstacles. But outlining the long and sometimes crooked path that leads to this position is far more intricate than merely presenting its affirmative endpoint. It requires a fundamental rethinking of what human agency is and how we could possibly understand it without imposing our preconceived ideas upon far more complex social phenomena. The present introductory chapter provides a rough map of the journey that emerged from this premise. [...]

The task of a genealogy of popular dissent

[...]

What, then, can a genealogy of dissent tell us about human agency in contemporary global politics? A great deal, for questions of agency are above all questions of power relations. And power relations are best understood, Michel Foucault argues convincingly, by examining specific attempts that are made to uproot them.[2] Dissent thus becomes a field of inquiry that has the potential to reveal far more about power and agency than one may think initially. The process of undermining authority says as much, for instance, about the values and functioning of the existing social and political order as it does about the urge to break out of it.

The first part of this book thus engages in a genealogical inquiry that seeks to understand how we have come to think about dissident practices such as street demonstrations and civil disobedience campaigns. In keeping with the principles of a disruptive reading that is essential to a genealogy, the analysis does not begin with historical texts or practices that are normally recognised as lying at the origin of dissent or current international politics. Instead, it commences with a relatively unfamiliar Renaissance treatise, Étienne de la Boétie's *Discourse of Voluntary Servitude*,[3] known also under its alternative and perhaps more adequate title of *Contr'un*, or *Anti-One*.[4] La Boétie claimed, in 1552, that any form of rule is dependent upon popular consent. In the context of its articulation, sixteenth-century France, this was a radical claim. But the idea that people hold the key to social change, which is implied in la Boétie's treatise, was also part of a larger humanist movement that started to challenge the prevalent medieval order. In this sense, the *Anti-One* symbolised the re-emergence of the concept of human agency, which had been celebrated in ancient Greece, but was largely pushed into obscurity during the Middle Ages.

Although la Boétie's *Anti-One* is a relatively unknown text today, it played a significant role in shaping practices of popular dissent during some of the preceding centuries.[5] Comparable to Niccolò Machiavelli's humanist texts, which became catalysts for the burgeoning literature on international relations and the art of governing the state,[6] la Boétie's more obscure *Anti-One* gave rise to a body of literature that deals with radical resistance to existing forms of authority.

[...]

The la Boétiean tradition, which developed at times in a close relationship with anarchist thought, is of course not the only story about popular dissent in the modern period. Countless other and often better-known stories could be narrated too. There are influential liberal and Marxist narratives of resistance and social change. There are structural and functional approaches to revolutionary upheavals, psychological analyses of the crowd or, more recently, inquiries into social movements.[7] There are even more investigations into the nature of human agency. Virtually every philosopher and theorist has dealt with this issue in one way or another. Ensuing ruminations range from questions of intentionality, causality and responsibility to reflections about the evaluation of desire or the moral dimensions of human action. All of these different stories are part of how we have come to perceive dissent and human agency today. Rather than trying to synthesise all of them in a sweeping intellectual *tour de force* – a task that would be doomed from the start – a genealogy must aim at appreciating the complexities and multiplicities of our past. Its power lies in telling different stories about our world, in making room for voices that have been silenced by conventional historiography. In this sense a genealogy reveals, as Michael Shapiro notes, the arbitrariness of the constitution of meaning 'by producing unfamiliar representations of persons, collectivities, places, and things, and by isolating the moments in which the more familiar representations have merged'.[8]

The la Boétiean story is one of many that have been laid to rest in the graveyards of our collective memory. It is a story about dissent that is worth unearthing, worth being retold in a different light – not to be exhaustive, not to be true or even representative, but to problematise what has been constituted as unproblematic, to illustrate the framing of dominant narratives, to scrutinise how and with what consequences we have come to think about popular dissent today.

[...]

Postmodern discontinuities: transversal dissent and processes of globalisation

While displaying a strikingly consistent attachment to key modern themes, the practice of popular dissent is also characterised by strong discontinuities. What began as a rhetorical idea in Renaissance France and later became a series of localised forms of resistance eventually turned into a tradition of dissent that acquired global dimensions. The writings of Thoreau, Tolstoy and Gandhi, in particular, have contributed to an ever-more widespread application of la Boétiean principles of resistance. By the twentieth century, popular dissent began to play an important role in virtually all parts of the world, from independence struggles in South Africa and India to the civil rights movements in the United States or the velvet revolutions in East-Central Europe.

But the practice of popular dissent has not only spread beyond national boundaries, it has also changed in nature. Processes of globalisation have radically transformed the manner in which dissent engenders human agency.

Globalisation is an important and much debated contemporary phenomenon. At the minimum it signifies 'a coalescence of varied transnational processes and domestic structures, allowing the economy, politics, culture, and ideology of one country to penetrate another'.[9] For some commentators, though, globalisation has far greater implications. It is a process that has fundamentally reorganised the relationship between space and time.[10] Advances in economic, technological and informational domains have led to what could be called a 'deterritorialisation' of the world – a series of transformations that are characterised, according to Gearóid Ó Tuathail, by the diminishing power of states.[11] Deterritorialisation is particularly far-reaching in the domains of finance and production, but it is perhaps with regard to the flow of information that processes of globalisation most evidently transgress the boundaries of the territorial state system:

> [G]lobal political space is skimmed twenty-four hours a day and produced as a stream of televisual images featuring a terrorist attack here, a currency crisis there, and a natural disaster elsewhere. Global space becomes political space. Being there live is everything. The local is instantly global, the distant immediately close. Place-specific political struggles become global televisual experiences, experiences structured by an entertainmentized gaze in search of the dramatic and the immediate.[12]

There is considerable debate about the nature of these phenomena and the extent to which they have led to a qualitative transformation of global politics. Indisputable, though, is the fact that processes of globalisation have substantially altered the functioning of popular dissent.

As remarked at the outset of this book, dissident practices no longer take place in a purely local context. The presence of global media networks now provide a protest march or a civil disobedience campaign with the potential of an immediate worldwide audience. Dissent has become transversal in nature, for it now has the ability to transgress the political and mental boundaries erected by existing practices of international relations. The local, in Ó Tuathail's words, is instantly global. The ensuing dynamics, of course, call into question the very spatial organisation of the interstate system, that is, the key pillars of 'state sovereignty, territorial integrity and community identity'.[13]

Once one has recognised the transversal nature of contemporary global politics a number of questions immediately arise. The most obvious one is whether or not a long tradition of modern thought can still adequately account for political dynamics that are unfolding in a fundamentally transformed global space. More specifically, does the la Boétiean vision of human agency, which is based on an ahistoric and spatial understanding of relationships between ruler and ruled, remain adequate to assess the changing nature of dissent in a media-infused contemporary world?

An instance of transversal dissent: reading and rereading the collapse of the Berlin Wall

[...]

The massive street demonstrations that preceded the collapse of the Berlin Wall were undoubtedly key manifestations of popular dissent. They may, at least at first sight, also be read as endorsements of the la Boétiean image of human agency. During the autumn of 1989, after decades of harsh authoritarian rule, hundreds of thousands of East Germans took to the streets and demanded political reform. Day after day, their monophonic battle cry 'we are the people' echoed throughout the country, in East Berlin, Dresden, Leipzig, Karl-Marx-Stadt and many other cities. These protests attracted immediate world-wide attention and triggered a series of discursive maelstroms that defied the political logic of national boundaries. The effects were startling: one of the most repressive regimes in East-Central Europe collapsed like a house of cards. Jürgen Habermas, one of Germany's best known philosophers and political commentators, remarked that 'the presence of large masses gathering in squares and mobilizing on the streets managed, astonishingly, to disempower a regime that was armed to the teeth'.[14] The scenes of common citizens walking through the Berlin Wall remain one of the key images – televised around the world – that symbolised the end of the Cold War and the transition into a new era of international politics. A sense of optimism was in the air. It was a time of crumbling walls and falling dictators. It was a time of turmoil and change. It was a time when dissent not only transgressed, but also uprooted the spatial constitution of global politics. Decades of entrenched political structures were swept away by popular resistance. The romantic subject re-emerged, inflated with unbounded confidence. History was once more open to be shaped by human agency.

But was all this really the result of popular dissent? Can the East German revolution be explained, for instance, by the la Boétiean proposition that any form of rule, no matter how authoritarian, crumbles as soon as people withdraw their consent? Does human agency work so directly and so consensually? Can it be understood in the context of spatial and relational linkages between ruler and ruled?

A critical look at the events in East Germany reveals a much more complex picture. A whole range of transversal factors – political maelstroms that unravelled in-between local, domestic and international spheres – contributed to the fall of the regime. The political contexts within which the events unfolded were far too intricate to be assessed by a parsimonious model of power relations, yet alone by a grand theory of popular dissent or a rigid spatial separation into different levels of analysis. The events that led to the fall of the Berlin Wall are best characterised as a series of diverse but interconnected occurrences that transgressed the spatial and political givenness of both East German and Cold War international politics. This reading is, of course, consistent with an already widespread Foucauldian position that views power as working in a diffused and stratified way, constantly intersecting with the production and diffusion of knowledge.[15] What, then, are the consequences that emerge from such a transversal interpretation?

At first sight, the East German revolution seems to vindicate a well-known image of popular dissent: a spectacular unfolding of social change through great events. But such events are often far less potent than their dramatic appearance suggests. This is not to say that the East German revolution was ineffective. It did, after all, uproot a dictatorial regime, tear down the Iron Curtain and redraw the boundaries of Cold War geopolitics. But in doing so it also entrenched more subtle and persistent forms of domination that are embedded in discursive practices. A second, gender-oriented reading of the events of 1989 reveals a different picture. Despite their unusually active participation in the protest movement, East German women suffered disproportionately from the subsequent process of unification. For them the democratic dawn ushered in drastic setbacks in such realms as reproductive rights, access to day care or employment opportunities. A revived civil society, which identifies men with the public and women with the private sphere, further increased the masculinist character of post-Wall German politics. Whether or not other emerging benefits for women will outweigh these setbacks in the long run remains to be seen. At this point, however, the East German revolution underlines that patriarchy is a discursively embedded system of exclusion that cannot simply be overthrown by popular dissent.

A transversal interpretation of the East German revolution suggests that we must understand issues of dissent, agency and social change from a variety of different perspectives. The collapse of the Berlin Wall can be read from yet another vantage point – one that focuses not on the role of spectacular popular dissent, but on the slow transformation of values that preceded them. Transversal dynamics now become particularly evident, for one notices how a porous Iron Curtain permitted a constant cross-border flow of information, and how the ensuing presence of international media sources influenced the thoughts and actions of the East German populace. Such a discourse-oriented approach to power and social change creates various possibilities to rethink human agency. It not only recasts agency as a transversal process of interfering with the constitution of social and spatial practices, but also resists the temptation of subsuming unique features into a universalised and foundationalist narrative. But as soon as this thinking space is ripped open, new puzzles and dilemmas start to flood through its gaping doors.

The problem of grounding an understanding of human agency: the usefulness of the concept of discourse

A transversal interpretation of the collapse of the Berlin Wall implies that practices of dissent in global politics should be viewed in discursive terms. This is to say that dissent exerts human agency not primarily through localised spatial dynamics, but through a transformation of values that takes place across a variety of political territories. Viewing dissent in discursive terms opens up possibilities to recognise practices of resistance that have hitherto been obscured. The third and last part of this study explores their potential and limits. But before such a task can begin, a number of difficult conceptual questions must be confronted. How to lift a concept of human agency out of a genealogical critique? How to ground thought, critique, action, norms, transversal life itself, if there are no universal values that can enable such a process of grounding? How to retain a positive approach to the problem of agency without having to anchor one's position in stable foundations?

Evoking the notion of discourse as a way of investigating the framing of global politics often elicits suspicion. Is discourse not merely a faddish term, destined to wax and wane with fleeting intellectual trends of the postmodern and poststructural kind? Does the concept of discourse, as many fear, reduce the world to playful interactions of texts and meanings that are void of any relevance to the so-called 'real', the concrete daily aspects of our lives?

These questions are being posed very often today, and they must be taken seriously. The prologue has already shown how many international relations theorists are sceptical of authors who employ the concept of discourse. They fear that such an approach cannot but lead, in Robert Keohane's representative words, to 'an intellectual and moral disaster'.[16] This scepticism goes far beyond the domain of international relations. Critics of so-called postmodern scholarship often draw attention to the pitfalls of discursive approaches, particularly their alleged inability to speak of agents and agency. Seyla Benhabib represents many concerned scholars when arguing that a postmodern position mistakenly dissolves the subject into chains of signification that lie beyond human influence.[17] We would find ourselves in a conceptual order dominated by overarching discursive systems. People would be reduced to mere bystanders, passive, impotent, irrelevant. Crushed into oblivion. But is this elusive spectre called postmodernism really so menacing that it must be warded off at any cost? Is it leading us into an apocalyptic world in which 'man would be erased', as a famous Foucauldian passage speculates, 'like a face drawn in the sand at the edge of the sea'?[18]

Taking on these important critiques of postmodern theory is a tall order. There are no easy answers to the above questions, and there are certainly no ready-made solutions. [...] At this stage a short illustration, taken from a rather unexpected source, must suffice to underline the usefulness of discourse theory. Consider how no other than Plato works with an implied concept of discourse, even though his search for an ahistoric form of truth is often taken to counter Nietzschean and Foucauldian elaborations on the power-knowledge nexus. Consider the strategy through which Plato dismisses his chief philosophical rivals, the Sophists. *The Republic* is divided into ten so-called books, all of which revolve around dialogues. Peculiar about this structure is that only book I, in which Plato refutes his Sophist rival Thrasymachus, is set against a larger public. In all of the remaining books Glaucon and Adeimantus are the only respondents. Cornelius Castoriadis argues that this crucial difference is to be explained by Plato's inability to dismiss the Sophists through rational argumentation.[19] Thrasymachus' claim that 'justice is the interest of the stronger' cannot be dismissed on objective grounds by Plato's position that 'justice is goodness'.[20] Hence Plato needed a cheering public to support his critique, he needed a discursive context that rendered his position rational. Thrasymachus is portrayed as wild, noisy, offensive, irrational. Plato then strengthened his position in the dialogues by discursive reinforcements from the gallery, like 'Glaucon and the others backed up my request' or 'it was clear to everyone that his [Thrasymachus] definition of justice had been reversed'.[21] Once the discursive order and its corresponding power relations were established, at the end of book I, there was no more need for a gallery. Plato could go on and dismiss on newly established rational grounds what was left of the Sophist challenge.

Discursive dynamics in the realm of global politics function not unlike those in Plato's rhetorical dialogues. Foreign policy decisions, for instance, are not taken based on purely objective grounds, they are formed, articulated and justified in relation to a set of transversally recognised values that render these decisions rational – or irrational, depending on the issue and the perspective.

Transversal forms of dissent are the thoughts and actions that interfere with these rationalisations. They are discursive in nature, but they do not necessarily operate in a void of values. Discursive interventions do not preclude formulations of critique or advancements of specific political positions. A discursive understanding of transversal struggles does, however, engender the need for a more differentiated approach to the problem of anchoring thought and justifying action.

Notes

1 Friedrich Nietzsche, *The Gay Science*, tr. W. Kaufmann (New York: Vintage Books, 1974/1882), § 108, p. 167 (translation altered).

2 Foucault, 'The Subject and Power', in H. L. Dreyfus and P. Rabinow (eds.), *Michel Foucault: Beyond Structuralism and Hermeneutics* (New York: Harvester Wheatsheaf, 1982), pp. 210–11.

3 Étienne de la Boétie, *Discours de la Servitude Volontaire*, in P. Bonnefon (ed.), *Oeuvres Complètes* (Genève: Slatkine Reprints, 1967/1552).

4 La Boétie's supporter, the famous essayist Michel de Montaigne, said about his friend's text that 'it is a discourse that he named *Voluntary Servitude*, but those who have not known him have since renamed it properly *Anti-one*'. This practice has largely remained intact until today. Montaigne, *Essais* (Paris: Gallimard, 1950), book I, chapter 28, p. 219.

5 La Boétie still featured prominently in Pierre Mesnard's path-breaking work on early modern thought, *L'Essor de la Philosophie Politique au XVIe Siècle* (Paris: J. Vrin, 1951/1935), pp. 389–406. By contrast, many contemporary historians of political thought do not deal with the influence of la Boétie. His work barely warrants a mention, for instance, in Quentin Skinner's influential *The Foundations of Modern Political Thought* (Cambridge: Cambridge University Press, 1978).

6 See Michel Foucault, 'Governmentality', in G. Burchell *et al.* (eds), *The Foucault Effect: Studies in Governmentality* (London: Harvester Wheatsheaf, 1991/1978), pp. 87–104.

7 For key contributions to the sociology of action see Talcott Parsons, *The Structure of Social Action* (Glencoe, IL: The Free Press, 1949/1937); Alain Touraine, *Sociologie de l'Action* (Paris: Éditions du Seuil, 1965); Jürgen Habermas, *Theorie des kommunikativen Handelns* (Frankfurt: Suhrkamp, 1988). For analysis of the psychological and social impact unleashed by the gathering of large crowds see Elias Canetti, *Masse und Macht* (Frankfurt: Fischer, 1994/1980); Gustave le Bon, *Psychologie des Foules* (Paris: Félix Alcan, 1911) and George Rude, *The Crowd in History* (London: Lawrence and Wishart, 1981). Among the many works that deal with collective action and new social movements are Alberto Melucci, *Nomads of the Present* (London: Hutchinson Radius, 1989); Mancur Olson, *The Logic of Collective Action* (Cambridge, MA: Harvard University Press, 1965); Sidney Tarrow, *Power in Movement: Social Movements, Collective Action and Politics* (New York: Cambridge University Press, 1994); Charles Tilly, *From Mobilization to Revolution* (Reading, MA: Addison-Wesley, 1978) and Alain Touraine, *La Voix et le Regard* (Paris: Seuil, 1978).

8 Michael J. Shapiro, *Reading the Postmodern Polity: Political Theory as Textual Practice* (Minneapolis: University of Minnesota Press, 1992), p. 2.

9 James H. Mittelman, 'The Dynamics of Globalization', in Mittelman (ed.), *Globalization: Critical Reflections* (Boulder, CO: Lynne Rienner, 1996), p. 3.

10 See, for instance, Paul Virilio, *Vitesse et Politique* (Paris: Éditions Galilée, 1977); David Harvey, *The Condition of Postmodernity* (Oxford/Cambridge, MA: Blackwell, 1989).

11 Gearóid Ó Tuathail, *Critical Geopolitics: The Politics of Writing Global Space* (London: Routledge, 1996), pp. 228–9.

12 Ibid., pp. 250, 228–9.

13 Ibid., p. 230.

14 Jürgen Habermas, 'The Rectifying Revolution and the Need for New Thinking on the Left', in *New Left Review*, 183, 1990, p. 7.

15 See Michel Foucault, *Power/Knowledge: Selected Interviews and Other Writings 1972–1977*, (ed.) Colin Gordon (New York: Pantheon, 1980).

16 Robert O. Keohane, 'International Relations Theory: Contributions of a Feminist Standpoint', *Millennium*, 18, 2, 1989, p. 89.

17 Seyla Benhabib, 'Feminism and Postmodernism', in *Feminist Contentions* (New York: Routledge, 1995), p. 20.

18 Michel Foucault, *Les Mots et les Choses* (Paris: Gallimard, 1966), p. 398.

19 Cornelius Castoriadis, 'Ontologie et Anthropologie', seminar presented at the École Normale Supérieure, Paris, 26 October 1995.

20 Plato, *The Republic*, tr. D. Lee (London: Penguin, 1987/1955), pp. 90, 95.

21 Ibid., pp. 74–84.

Part 2

Situating resistance

What's in a movement?

Introduction

The chapters in Part 2 represent a slice through the debates as to the sources of contemporary global resistance. All too often we are convinced that we will know global resistance when we see it, that is to say that the sites and situations of global resistance are very familiar to us. But, can we take the names of Seattle, Porto Alegre, Québec City, and so on, as clear and given locations of resistance? What role do the so-called new social movements have in contesting the logics of globalization? On whose behalf do movements claim to speak, and whose interests and experiences do they represent? The chapters in this part, when read together, have been chosen so as to engage discussion around questions such as these. The chapters by Cox, Falk and Walker discuss, from different perspectives, the prospects for, and limitations of, an emergent global civil society sphere. The remaining five chapters then explore resistances as they are situated in particular places and at particular moments.

For both Robert Cox and Richard Falk, the emergence of a transnational public sphere – we might call 'global civil society' – has come about as a backlash to 'economic globalization'. The influence of Gramsci's counter-hegemony and Polanyi's double movement is strong in both these concepts. In Cox's interpretation, the nascent global civil society represents a sphere of voluntary association that is 'distinct from both corporate power and the state', and that embraces 'autonomous' social groups. In both Cox and Falk we find reference to civil society 'from below' or 'bottom-up' as a counterweight to neoliberal globalization 'from above' or 'top-down'. We also find a clear distinction between 'positive' or 'emancipatory' civil society struggles on the one hand, and 'negative' or 'backlash' politics on the other. Indeed, for both authors the central challenge facing social movements is to find a 'unifying ideology capable of mobilizing disparate social forces' (Falk), or a 'strong spirit of solidarity' (Cox). In effect, these chapters offer a blueprint of what a global civil society might look like – a blueprint that can perhaps only be critically explored through the concrete examples of resistances in the texts that follow. As starting points for studying the themes of social movements and global resistance, the two concepts leave a number of questions unanswered:

- Can the politics of resistance be clearly positioned 'outside' the politics of states and corporate power, and, by extension, 'inside' the realm of a global civil society?
- Does neoliberal globalization represent the common foe against which all struggles, however diverse or fragmented, are fought?

- Is it possible to draw a clear distinction between positive or emancipatory resistance, and negative resistance or backlash politics?
- Are social movements best understood, for example, in terms of unifying ideologies, shared interests or a leadership structure?

R. B. J. Walker's chapter serves as a critical intervention in the debates about the nature of civil society and social movements, and a possible route into responding to the questions outlined earlier. Walker writes:

> Social movements are, to the modern political imagination, most easily fixed within a sphere of social life that is distinguished from and even counterposed to the sphere of politics – within the so-called civil society that has been so carefully, though problematically, distinguished from the explicitly political affairs of the modern state.

This fixing of social movements within the familiar and state-centred practices of modern politics, he argues, fails to attend to the ways in which these movements actually challenge and confound conventional boundaries. Movements, for Walker, 'are precisely *movements*. They will not stand still'. To deny this constant mobility and transience and 'invoke a unitary identity', he suggests, is to assume, for example, that 'gender', 'environment' or 'peace' are unproblematic categories. His study of the Indian Swadhyaya movement reveals the uncertainty and cultural specificity of their political practices, leading him to suggest that 'a politics of connection is not necessarily a politics of a united front or a counterhegemonic strategy'. So, while some commentators respond to the question 'what's in a movement' by looking for a united front or definitive solidarity, others urge that social movements cannot be understood in these terms. It is perhaps only through empirical readings of situated resistances that we can grapple with this conundrum.

When we explore concrete and situated practices of resistance, then, do we recognize movements in terms of their having a unifying ideology or common purpose? In Stephen Gill's study of the Seattle protests, though he sees a 'very diverse range of organisations and political tendencies', he finds a unity of purpose by identifying a common foe. For him, the movements share a common belief that 'there is centralisation and concentration of power under corporate control in neoliberal globalization, with much of the policy agenda for this project orchestrated by international organizations such as the WTO, the IMF, and the World Bank'. For Gill, then, it is possible to locate a common foe in what he calls the 'new constitutionalism of disciplinary neoliberalism', and to personify the source of this enemy in named international organizations, governments, corporations or institutions. Much of the criticism of the so-called anti-globalization movement, though, has centred on their identity being rooted in what they are against, rather than what they offer as an alternative. Naomi Klein's response has been to consistently assert the importance of a movement having a mobile agenda. In her reading of the World Social Forum (WSF) in Porto Alegre she is critical of the WSF's billing as 'an opportunity for an emerging movement to stop screaming about what it is against and start articulating what it is for', or 'to whip the chaos on the streets into a structured shape'. For Klein, it is not a single movement that is emerging, but rather multiple movements with diverse identities, connected like the 'hotlinks' on their websites in a network-like form.

Like Gill, then, Klein observes diversity in the essence of social movements but wants to find some common ground in 'battling the same forces'. In some senses, both authors go some way to addressing Walker's point that social movements defy the expected and normalized structures of modern politics. Gill's Seattle is 'a party of movement that cannot easily be decapitated', a place where conventional requests by the media for interviews with, or images of, 'the leaders' have to go unobserved. The contributions by Klein, Gill, Rupert, Hardt and Drainville contain many examples of the politics of movements residing precisely in their leaderless, network-like and mobile dynamics. As Michael Hardt neatly puts it, 'no-one speaks for a network. How do you argue with a network?'

However, where for Klein and Gill the politics of social movements are fairly unambiguously 'anti-corporate' or 'anti-neoliberal', for André Drainville the relationship is more ambiguous. Drainville's analysis reveals that at least some elements of the politics of resistance in Quebec City were fixed within the framework of institutionalized world politics. Rather than oppose a civil society sphere to the sphere of government, governance and world markets, Drainville explores the complexity of social movements' relationship to networks of power and government. In Part 1, Foucault's insights on the intractability and mutuality of power and resistance suggested that domination and dissent cannot be singularly opposed. For Drainville, the study of global resistances should begin from 'concrete, contingent practices, in specific locations', studying the shaping of mentalities that goes into the 'making of transnational subjects'. Put simply, Drainville understands the People's Summit in Québec City as a means of legitimating the decisions and authority of the Summit of the Americas. 'The attempt to create a responsible hemispheric civil society and the People's move from "Resisting" to "Proposing" should be seen as "twinned enterprises"'. The delineation of a sphere of 'civil' resistance distinct from state, corporation or international organization, then, may be rather more problematic than it first appears in Cox and Falk. Both Drainville and Mark Rupert refer to the attempts by international organizations to 'humanize global capitalism' (Drainville) and to 'give globalization a human face' (Rupert). In this *Reading*, at least some forms of resistance have been amenable to compliance in return for an invitation to the table.

It is not that Drainville, Hardt and Rupert, in their very different ways, do not see spaces for emerging resistances. However, their studies of situated social movements reveal the contested and contradictory nature of contemporary resistances. To draw out just one example, Drainville exposes some of the tensions and competing world views present on the streets of Seattle:

> Medea Benjamin and her colleagues from the San Francisco-based Global Exchange, which had waged a four year campaign against Nike, stood on the steps of Nike Town and other sweatshop outlets in downtown Seattle to defend them against anarchists and other trouble-makers, calling on the police to identify and arrest them.

A sense of shared purpose and collective solidarity then, can perhaps not be seen to emerge spontaneously from the onward march of neoliberal globalization. The readings in this section should spark some discussion of how the identities of social movements are forged, and how they transform and adapt. When we ask ourselves 'what's in a movement', we should perhaps consider Michael Hardt's comment on Porto Alegre, that 'the Forum was unknowable, chaotic, dispersive', and reflect on whether this, rather than a unified force and single manifesto, might actually be the essence and the strength of contemporary social movements.

10 Civil society at the turn of the millennium

Prospects for an alternative world order

Robert W. Cox

Source: Robert W. Cox (1999), 'Civil Society at the Turn of the Millennium: Prospects for an Alternative World Order', *Review of International Studies*, 25: 1, pp. 3–28

Eric Hobsbawm has written that '[t]he world at the end of the Short Twentieth Century [1914–1991] is in a state of social breakdown rather than revolutionary crisis...'[1]. The conclusion is hard to avoid. 'Real socialism' has collapsed; the anti-imperialist struggle in the former colonial world has resolved itself into a series of new states seeking a *modus vivendi* in subordination to global capitalism; the Left in Europe is searching uncertainly for an alternative to neoliberal globalization while in the main adapting to it; even the Islamic revolution in Iran is hesitatingly moving towards an adjustment to dominant world economic forces. There is much violence – in the Balkans, central Africa, Algeria, and Ulster – but none of it could be called revolutionary in the sense of promising a transformation of society. Global finance has lurched from the Mexican peso crisis in the 1980s to the Asian crisis in the 1990s, leaving a marginalized Africa almost unnoticed; but while finance dominates and constrains all governments' policies, there is no concerted means of global financial management.

If world politics is in such a condition of turbulent stasis, with little hope of calm but no prospect of fundamental change, the polarization of rich people and poor people is becoming increasingly accentuated throughout the world. There is also evidence that people have become disenchanted with existing forms of politics. In these circumstances, many activists and theorists have looked to civil society as the source from which alternative, more equitable forms of society might arise. Is civil society in the late 20th century the surrogate for a revolution that seems unlikely to happen? There is a debate on the Left about this and that is the question behind the revival of interest in civil society.

The concept of civil society has a long history in European and American thought. From that source, it has been exported around the world. In order to explore the transformatory potential of civil society in our time, it is useful to consult some of that history. Antonio Gramsci, drawing upon that tradition, constructed a view of civil society particularly pertinent to the present debate; and he did so at a time when revolutionary transformation still seemed a possibility. I propose to examine the changing meanings of the term 'civil society' over the years, placing these meanings in their historical and contemporary contexts, and then to reflect upon Gramsci's thought as an approach to understanding society and politics that took form in the specific historical context of Italy in the 1920s and 1930s but still has fruitful applicability in the changed world-wide context of the late twentieth century.

Gramsci was not concerned as an abstract theorist with building a system of political analysis that would stand the test of time. He was concerned with changing his world. Any development of his thinking should keep that goal to the fore and should thus both arise from reflection on the condition of the world as it is, and serve as a guide to action designed to change the world so as to improve the lot of humanity in social equity.

Civil society, in Gramsci's thinking, is the realm in which the existing social order is grounded; and it can also be the realm in which a new social order can be founded. His concern with civil society was, first, to understand the strength of the *status quo*, and then to devise a strategy for its transformation. The emancipatory potential of civil society was the object of his thinking. In the *Prison Notebooks*,[2] civil society is an elastic concept, having different connotations in different passages. Often civil society appears as a function of the state as in the frequently quoted equation: 'State = political society + civil society, in other words hegemony protected by the armour of coercion' (PN, p. 263). Gramsci honed much of his thought against the philosophy of Benedetto Croce. Croce saw the state, following Hegel, in idealistic terms as the embodiment of ethics.[3] Gramsci, in an historical materialist perspective, understood ethics as emanating from the social and cultural practices that enable historically conditioned human communities to cope with their environment. Croce's ethical state, for Gramsci, becomes ethical through the instrumentality of civil society. There is a dialectic inherent in civil society. In one aspect, the educational and ideological agencies that are sustained ultimately by the state's coercive apparatus shape morals and culture. Yet in another aspect civil society appears to have autonomy and to be more fundamental than the state, indeed to be the basis upon which a state can be founded. Civil society is both shaper and shaped, an agent of stabilization and reproduction, and a potential agent of transformation.

There is little point in trying to establish a fixed definition of Gramsci's concepts from exegesis of his text. That would negate Gramsci's way of thinking. He thought historically and dialectically, that is to say, his concepts are derived from his perceptions of reality and they serve not only to seize the momentary essence of a changing reality but also to become intellectual tools for fomenting change. Certain basic guidelines are essential in order to discern what Fernand Braudel later called the limits of the possible, the starting point from which strategic planning for social transformation has to begin. The first of these is to know accurately the prevailing relations of social forces. These have material, organizational, and ideological components, together constituting the configuration of an historic bloc.

Yet Gramsci was less concerned with the historic bloc as a stable entity than he was with historical mutations and transformations, and with the emancipatory potential for human agency in history. The concept of civil society in this emancipatory sense designates the combination of forces upon which the support for a new state and a new order can be built. These forces operate in a political and social space, a terrain occupied by different conflicting forces as historical change proceeds – a terrain which is narrowed when there is a close identity between people and their political and social institutions (in Gramsci's terms, when hegemony prevails) but which is widened when this identity is weak.

Any fixed definition of the content of the concept 'civil society' would just freeze a particular moment in history and privilege the relations of social forces then prevailing. Rather than look for clearer definitions, we should try to understand the historical variations that have altered the meanings of the concept in the ongoing dialectic of concept and reality. We should not stop with the world of the 1930s which Gramsci knew but carry on the process into the late 20th century. To continue and develop Gramsci's way of thinking is more true to his purpose than to mummify his text.

The changing meanings of 'civil society'

Writing in the last decade of the 20th century, we must recognize that the European tradition of political thought will now be seen as that of a particular civilization coexisting with others. It can no longer make an uncontested claim to universality, even though the concepts evolved in western discourse have penetrated into all parts of the world through the era of Western dominance. Thus, Western terms may cover realities that are different. To Westerners these terms may obscure these differences by assimilating them to familiar Western meanings. This must be borne in mind in using a term like 'civil society'. We must be alert not only to the surface appearance but also to a non-Western meaning that may be deeply buried. Nevertheless, it is necessary to retrace the concept of civil society to its European roots in the Enlightenment.

Civil society in Enlightenment thought was understood as the realm of particular interests, which in practice then meant the realm of the bourgeoisie. The state ideally embodied universality, the rule of law. The monarch was to be the first servant of the state, bound by and applying the rule of law. An intellectual problem for the Enlightenment was how to explain the necessary compatibility of the two, of the realm of particular interests and the realm of universality. If the state were to embody universality, then civil society must generate universal principles in the ethicojuridical sphere; civil society must be seen as creating the basis of common welfare out of the pursuit of particular interests. Both Hegel and Adam Smith thought they had achieved this reconciliation by in effect refurbishing the Christian doctrine of Providence, in Smith's case as the 'invisible hand' and in Hegel's as the 'ruse of reason'.[4] In its European origins, civil society and the bourgeoisie were synonymous. Civil society signified the self-conscious social group whose influence, if not necessarily its executive power, was expanding.

Karl Marx was, of course, sceptical about the emergence of common good from the pursuit of individual interests. He saw rather that civil society was generating a force within itself that would ultimately destroy or change it: the proletariat. He also cast his regard beyond Europe to sketch an outline of an 'Asiatic mode of production' in which rural villages reproduced themselves *ad infinitum*; and in his analysis of French society of the mid-19th century he discerned a social structure more complex than the bourgeois/proletarian dualism of his capitalist mode of production. If the bourgeoisie was the starting point for civil society, the 19th century opened up the concept to embrace a variety of conflicting social groups and interests.

A particularly significant 19th century addition to the complexity of the concept came from Alexis de Tocqueville's work on American democracy.[5] What impressed Tocqueville was the flourishing of associations, spontaneously formed by people for the achievement of common purposes outside of the state. In the context of American politics, Tocqueville saw this proliferation of associations as a guarantee against a tyranny of the majority that might result from an electoral sweep in an era of populist politics. He drew an analogy to the stabilizing influence he saw in European societies as arising from the existence of secondary bodies inherited from medieval times which acted as a restraint upon monarchic power.

The spirit of voluntary association thus became a significant aspect of the concept of civil society. Civil society is no longer identified with capitalism and the bourgeoisie but now takes on the meaning of a mobilized participant citizenry juxtaposed to dominant economic and state power. For Gramsci, who was concerned with the problem of mobilizing the working class for action in combination with other potential class allies, there was never a pure spontaneity in the construction of social organization but always a combination of leadership and movement from below. His sense of the optimum relationship was to 'stimulate the formation of homogeneous, compact social blocs, which will give birth to their own intellectuals, their own commandos, their own vanguard – who will in turn react upon those blocs in order to develop them...' (PN, pp. 204–5). Gramsci's historical context was very different from that in which Tocqueville discovered the spirit of association in a society of farmers, artisans, and merchants untrammelled by the class and status inheritance of European societies. To counter the fascist politics of the 1930s, he rejected both 'spontaneity' or 'voluntarism', on one side, and the notion of a revolutionary elite manipulating the masses, on the other.

As counterpoint to the flourishing in America of autonomous voluntary associations outside of the state, 19th century Europe experienced the merger of civil society with the state in the form of corporatism. State leaders, perceiving the disruptive potential of class struggle in industrializing societies, sought to bring employers and organized workers into a consensual relationship with the state for the management of the economy and the support of state political and military goals. Corporatism left those who are relatively powerless in society out of account; but being powerless and unorganized they could hardly be considered part of civil society. The corporatist era began in mid-century with conservative leaders like Disraeli and Bismark and extended into the post-World War II decades in the form of the welfare state. This era is well encapsulated in Gramsci's equation: State = political society + civil society.

The French Revolution left another legacy with implications for civil society: the rejection of anything that would intervene between the state and the citizen. Conceived as a means of liquidating medieval corporations, the principle as embodied in the Le Chapelier law of 1791 was in the early 19th century turned against the formation of trade unions. The same principle was reasserted by the Bolsheviks in the 20th century revolutionary Russian context: all allowable associations under 'real socialism' would have to be part of an all-embracing Party-state. Civil society was denied existence.

Gramsci recognized the weakness inherent in this situation in his juxtaposition of the war of manoeuvre with the war of position when he referred to conditions at the onset of the Bolshevik revolution:

> In Russia the state was everything, civil society was primordial and gelatinous; in the West, there was a proper relation between State and civil society, and when the State trembled a sturdy structure of civil society was at once revealed. The State was only on outer ditch, behind which there stood a powerful system of fortresses and earthworks; more or less numerous from one State to the next, it goes without saying – but this precisely necessitated an accurate reconnaissance of each individual country.
>
> (PN, p. 238)

The 'proper relation between State and civil society' suggests that the State should rest upon the support of an active, self-conscious and variegated civil society and should, in turn, sustain and promote the development of the constructive forces in that society. The organic intellectual was, for Gramsci, the key link in this process.

This brief review of the use of the term 'civil society' in European and American thought yields broadly two juxtaposed meanings. One shows a 'top-down' process in which the dominant economic forces of capitalism form an intellectual and cultural hegemony which secures acquiescence in the capitalist order among the bulk of the population. The other envisages a 'bottom-up' process led by those strata of the population which are disadvantaged and deprived under the capitalist order who build a counterhegemony that aspires to acquire sufficient acceptance among the population so as to displace the erstwhile hegemonic order. With regard to the latter, Gramsci insisted that the revolution must occur (in civil society) prior to the revolution (in the form of the state).[6]

Civil society in the late 20th century

Since Gramsci made his analysis, there have been significant changes affecting the relationship of state to civil society and in the development of civil society in different parts of the world. The world crisis of capitalism of the 1970s brought about a reversal of corporatism. Business persuaded governments that recovery of investment and growth from a situation of 'stagflation' required an attack on the power of trade unions and a reduction of state expenditures on social welfare, together with deregulation of capital, goods, and financial markets. As governments acquiesced in this business analysis, trade unions and social-democratic forces were weakened in most economically advanced countries. Protection for the more vulnerable elements in society was cut back; and these elements were implicitly challenged to organize independently of the state both to protest the loss of state support and to compensate for this loss by voluntary initiative and self-help. The collapse of 'real socialism' in the late 1980s seemed to herald a possible rebirth of civil society in those countries where civil society had been eradicated by the Party-state. New independent organizations of protest grew into the political space that was opened by the disruption and uncertainty of political authority. In both cases, the political and social space in which civil society could develop was expanded. Whether or not the opportunity would be realized was a challenge to human agency.

The restructuring of society by economic globalization

The globalization of production is restructuring the world labour force in ways that challenge 19th and early 20th century notions of class structure. Gramsci's keen sense of the strategic importance of building class alliances into a counterhegemonic bloc which could ultimately displace the bourgeoisie – he advocated linking peasantry and petty bourgeois elements with the working class – remains pertinent in today's world. What is relevant today is the strategy of class alliance rather than Gramsci's particular form of alliance derived from his understanding of the class structure of Italy in the 1920s and 1930s. It is problematic today whether the proletariat can still be considered to be a 'fundamental' universal class. Indeed, the very notion of a proletariat as a single class juxtaposed to the bourgeoisie has lost substance in reality even if its ideological persuasiveness retains some impetus.

International production is dividing the world's producers into broadly three categories:

- At the top is a core workforce of highly skilled people *integrated* into the management process. These people take the decisions about what is produced and where and by whom. They carry on research and development; they maintain the productive apparatus; and they staff the administrative frameworks and propagate the ideology of globalization.
- At a second level, this integrated core is flanked by a larger number of supporting workers whose numbers vary with levels of demand for products. Their lesser levels of skill make them more easily disposable and replaceable. These are the *precarious* workers. They are located where business is offered the lowest labour costs, the greatest flexibility in the use of labour, i.e. the least protection of workers' rights in jobs; and the weakest environmental controls. These workers are segmented by ethnicity, religion, gender, and geography, and thus are not easily organized collectively to confront management in a united manner. Transnationalized production has accentuated social fragmentation and environmental degradation.

• The third level comprises those people who are *excluded* from international production. They include the unemployed and many small low-technology enterprises in the richer countries and a large part of the marginalized population in poor countries.

The proportions in this three-fold hierarchical structure (integrated, precarious, and excluded) vary from country to country, but the categories cut across territorial boundaries and the ability of governments to alter the proportions is severely limited by their dependence upon global finance. Precarious employment and exclusion were accentuated by the decline in social expenditures that followed from the capitalist crisis of the 1970s. Economic orthodoxy now focuses on state budget deficits and urges states to further reduce social expenditures.

These tendencies give a new configuration to the material basis of civil society. People who speak of civil society today do not usually have in mind the realm of economic interests as did Hegel and Adam Smith. The distinction common today is between dominant power over society shared by corporations and states, on the one side, and popular forces on the other. 'Civil society' is now usually understood to refer to the realm of autonomous group action distinct from both corporate power and the state. The concept has been appropriated by those who foresee an emancipatory role for civil society. There is thus a marked distinction between the meaning of 'civil society' in the work of 18th and 19th century theorists and the way that term is commonly understood today. In the earlier meaning, civil society is another term for the social power relations deriving from the economy. Gramsci's usage stemmed from that of Hegel and Marx. It differed from Marx's, as Norberto Bobbio has shown, by including the ethical and ideological superstructure and not just the economic base.[7]

The current widely understood usage which excludes dominant power in the state and corporations from the concept of civil society received impetus from the movements of opposition to Stalinist rule in Eastern Europe. They were characterized as a 'rebirth of civil society'.[8] Similarly, movements of opposition to authoritarian rule and capitalist dominance in Asian and Latin American countries are commonly perceived as emanations of civil society. So 'civil society' has become the comprehensive term for various ways in which people express collective wills independently of (and often in opposition to) established power, both economic and political.

This current usage has more affinity to Tocqueville than to Hegel, Adam Smith or Marx. But it also has affinity to Gramsci's usage, since Gramsci regarded civil society not only as the realm of hegemony supportive of the capitalist *status quo*, but also as the realm in which cultural change takes place, in which the counter-hegemony of emancipatory forces can be constituted. Civil society is not just an assemblage of actors, i.e. autonomous social groups. It is also the realm of contesting ideas in which the intersubjective meanings upon which people's sense of 'reality' are based can become transformed and new concepts of the natural order of society can emerge.

There is little point in arguing that one usage of the term 'civil society' is correct and the other is wrong. Let us take current identification of civil society with autonomous social forces as a basis for discussion and examine its implications. Even conceived in this more limited way, i.e. without including the powerful economic forces, civil society in the late 20th century, though generally viewed as potentially emancipatory and transformative of the social order, can be seen to reflect the dominance of state and corporate economic power.

In a 'bottom-up' sense, civil society is the realm in which those who are disadvantaged by globalization of the world economy can mount their protests and seek alternatives. This can happen through local community groups that reflect diversity of cultures and evolving social practices world wide. Looking beyond local grass roots initiatives is the project of a 'civic state', a new form of political authority based upon a participatory democracy.[9] More ambitious still is the vision of a 'global civil society' in which these social movements together constitute a basis for an alternative world order.[10]

In a 'top-down' sense, however, states and corporate interests influence the development of this current version of civil society towards making it an agency for stabilizing the social and political *status quo*. The dominant hegemonic forces penetrate and coopt elements of popular movements. State subsidies to non-governmental organizations (NGOs) incline the latter's objectives towards conformity with established order and thus enhance the legitimacy of the prevailing order. This concords with a concern on the part of many people for survival in existing conditions rather than for transformation of the social order. For many people, clientelism may seem preferable to revolutionary commitment, especially when backed by the force of state and economic power. Moreover, the basic conflicts between rich and poor, powerful and powerless, are reproduced within the sphere of voluntary organizations, whether trade unions or the new social movements.[11]

Global governance

Gramsci's sense that national situations are specific still has validity but now these distinct national situations are much more dependent upon the global economy.[12] The territorial distinctness of national economies and societies is penetrated by global and transnational forces. The problem of hegemony is posed at the level of the global political economy as well as at regional, national and local levels. As many analysts of world affairs have suggested, we seem to be moving towards a 'new medievalism' with multiple layers of authority and multiple loyalties.[13]

At the top, there is no identifiable regime of dominance. The new popularity of the term 'global governance' suggests control and orientation in the absence of formally legitimated coercive power. There is something that could be called a nascent global historic bloc consisting of the most powerful corporate economic forces, their allies in government, and the variety of networks that evolve policy guidelines and propagate the ideology of globalization. States now by and large play the role of agencies of the global economy, with the task of adjusting national economic policies and practices to the perceived exigencies of global economic liberalism. This structure of power is sustained from outside the state through a global policy consensus and the influence of global finance over state policy, and from inside the state from those social forces that benefit from globalization (the segment of society that is integrated into the world economy).[14] Competitiveness in the world market has become the ultimate criterion of state policy which justifies the gradual removal of the measures of social protection built up in the era of the welfare state. Neo-liberalism is hegemonic ideologically and in terms of policy. Where ideological and policy hegemony is not sufficient to protect the structure of global governance, then military force is available. The Gulf War was an object lesson in how military force intervenes when a regional power tries to ignore the global hegemony.[15]

This global hegemony has profound consequences for the relationship of political society to civil society. As the state retreats from service and social protection to the public, the public loses confidence in the integrity and competency of the political class. Political corruption is inherent in the transformation of public goods into marketable commodities; a political favour acquires a market value. The loyalty of people to their political institutions becomes more questionable as scepticism and cynicism about the motives and abilities of politicians grows. These tendencies vary among countries. Americans honour the symbols of flag and constitution, but about half of them do not bother to vote and most seem to have low expectations of their politicians. Corruption scandals are rife in Europe and Japan, and public hopes for salvation through politics are equally low. Throughout most of the rest of the world, in Asia, Africa and Latin America, people have endured government more than they have felt themselves to be a part of it. At the end of this century, there is a world-wide problem of repairing or building political societies, of constructing a sense of identity between people and political authorities. There is a wide political space between constituted authority and the practical life of people.

Revival of civil society as a response to globalization?

Civil society would be the base upon which a new or reconstructed political authority would have to rest. This was Machiavelli's insight when he advocated the replacement of merce-naries by a citizen militia. There is some evidence of growth in civil society coming about as a reaction to the impact of globalization. In the French strikes of late 1995 and the strikes in South Korea in early 1997, reaction has come through trade union movements, in the French case with broad public support. In Japan and some other Asian countries, there has been a growth of many non-governmental organizations, often of a local self-help kind, and often actively building linkages and mutual help relationships with similar organizations in other countries. In some poor countries of Africa and southeast Asia, community organiza-tions, often led by women, endeavour to meet basic needs on a local level, turning their backs upon states and international economic organizations that are perceived as acting against the people. In central America, the Mayan people have recovered historical initiative through armed revolt in the Mexican state of Chiapas, and the indigenous people of Guatemala have fought a civil war to the point of gaining recognition of their claims. These various instances are indicative of something moving in different societies across the globe towards a new vitality of 'bottom-up' movement in civil society as a counterweight to the hegemonic power structure and ideology. This movement is, however, still relatively weak and uncoordinated. It may contain some of the elements but has certainly not attained the status of a counterhegemonic alliance of forces on the world scale.

Exclusionary populism and the covert world

There is a gap between the retreat of the state and the still small development of civil society. This space, this void, attracts other forces. One is exclusionary populism: various forms of extreme right political movements and xenophobic racism. Social anomie is also a propitious recruiting ground for hermetic religious cults. Another set of forces can be called the covert world, a complex congeries of underground activities, some carried out secretly in the name of states, some criminal.

Exclusionary populism has an ambiguous relationship to established power. Extreme right-wing movements in some European countries (France, Italy, Austria, Belgium, Norway) have captured fifteen per cent or more of the popular vote in the 1990s, and challenge the conventional right to legitimize them by accepting their support.[16] In the United States, the far right perceives a global conspiracy against the basic principles of American life – especially private property, freedom from government control, and the right to have guns – in which the federal government is collusive.[17] Cults like *Aum Shinrikyo* in Japan, or the Solar Temple in Canada, France and Switzerland, and Heaven's Gate in the United States, pose a nihilistic threat to society; they attract well educated people, an indicator of the extent of alienation, and mobilize them in the service of a doomsday scenario.[18]

The covert world comprises intelligence services, organized crime, terrorist groups, the arms trade, money-laundering banks, and secret societies. There is a certain overlap between right wing extremism and the covert world and also between doomsday cults and the covert world. Right wing terrorists have been suspected of collusion with intelligence services in Italy in several bombings. *Aum Shinrikyo* furthered its doomsday plans, including the sarin gas attack in the Tokyo subway in March 1995, with the help of transnational arms dealers.

The various elements of the covert world have usually been studied one by one. Their activities have often been treated as *faits divers*, the material for spy novels and crime fiction. They have not been considered in their interrelationships as constituting a particular sphere of politics existing between visible government and the people. Yet there are many instances of cooperation as well as of conflict among its component elements.

The covert world penetrates the visible authorities in government and corporations. Its expansion was encouraged by the Cold War when, for instance, *mafia* in Italy and *Yakuza* in Japan acquired a supportive relationship with the political party formations that constituted the bulwark against internal opposition to United States Cold War strategy. Money for electoral politics was channelled through covert agencies to sustain anti-Communist coalitions and to influence electoral outcomes. Covert forces assume a functional relationship with neo-liberal deregulated economies. Covert power substitutes for legitimate authority in a totally unregulated market – contracts are enforced by goons with guns.[19] The high cost of electoral politics encourages clandestine political financing which opens the door to covert influences in national politics.

The political space between constituted authority and the people is the terrain on which civil society can be built. A weak and stunted civil society allows free rein to exclusionary politics and covert powers. An expansive participant civil society makes political authority more accountable and reduces the scope for exclusionary politics and covert activity.

[…]

Variations in prospects for civil society

The restructuring of production is experienced world-wide in generating the threefold hierarchy of social relations referred to above: integrated, precarious, and excluded. The proportions, however, differ from society to society. The balance between top-down and bottom-up forces in civil society, and the relative importance of right-wing populism and the covert world, result in distinct types of state/society configurations with different implications for civil society. Tentatively, four different patterns may serve to illustrate the range of conditions and prospects of civil society in the world today. These patterns or types are not intended to be exhaustive in covering the whole world, but they do illustrate some of the significantly different situations and prospects for civil society at the present time.

Evolved capitalism in Europe and America

Evolved capitalism in North America and western Europe constituted the point of impetus for economic globalization. Its influence penetrates to the rest of the world, the impact varying according to the level of material development and the resistance of persisting cultural practices in other regions. Production is being restructured in the form of post-Fordism which brings about the pattern of integrated core workers flanked by precariously linked supporting workers. Global finance exerts a continuing pressure on state budgets to reduce the social expenditures built up during the era of Fordism which gave social legitimacy to capital.

There is an implicit contradiction here between production and finance. Production and the 'real economy' that provides goods and services requires time to develop (research and development and the training of a committed labour force); finance has a synchronic space-oriented perspective directed to short-term returns which can often ignore the time dimension and undermine not only the social legitimacy of capital but also the productive apparatus itself (for example, through predatory buy-outs and asset stripping). In the late 20th century, it is global finance rather than production and the 'real economy' that focuses people's attention on the frailties of the economic order.

Another contradiction is between the real economy and the biosphere. Expansion of consumer demand is the driving force of the global economy. World-wide emulation of the consumption model of North America and western Europe would, however, through resource depletion and environmental destruction, bring ruin to the biosphere – the ultimate feed-back mechanism. To escape this disaster would require shifting the use of labour which is surplus to that required to satisfy the basic needs of society (the labour resource currently employed in arousing and in gratifying the superfluity of consumerism) to investment in social and human services (education, health, care of children and the aged, protection of the environment, and conviviality in social life). This would imply a fundamental change in economic organization and values – a revolution in social practices and in the structure of social power.

A further contradiction is in social relations. A large proportion of jobs are in the precarious category. Downgraded skilled workers in this category are often resentful of immigrants and women who are the other significant groups among the precariously employed. Youth and minorities are prominent among the more or less permanently excluded, a volatile and potentially destabilizing group. There is no longer any such formation as the 'working class' of the early 20th century. A privileged part of that former working class has been absorbed into the integrated category. Other elements are in both precarious and excluded categories; and their material conditions can easily be perceived as generating adversarial relationships between downgraded manual workers, immigrants and women workers. The fragmentation of the old working class, a consequence of post-Fordism reinforced by pressures of global finance towards dismantling of the Fordist-era social safety net, has strengthened capital and weakened and divided labour.

The problem for the organic intellectuals of the Left is how to envisage a strategy that could build from this fragmented situation of subordinate social groups a coherent alternative to economic globalization that would transcend (*Aufhebung* in Hegel's meaning) the contradictions just referred to. These organic intellectuals are now themselves a fragmented lot: trade union leaders, environmentalists, social activists on behalf of the poor and homeless and the unemployed, and promoters of self-help community organizations. They compete for potential clientele with right-wing populists, anti-immigrant racists, and religious cults. All of these various movements are meanwhile developing transnational linkages and organizations.

The covert world (organized crime, the drug trade, and intelligence services) occupies a political space that has, if anything, been enlarged by public disillusionment with conventional politics. The high cost of electoral politics sustains hypocrisy in the political class, who ostensibly respond to public support for campaign finance reform while continuing to rely on occult financial contributions, thus remaining open to occult influences. This, in turn, further erodes public confidence in political leadership.

In Europe, evolved capitalism has two variants. One is the 'pure' hyperliberal form which espouses removal of state intervention in the economy by deregulation and privatization and makes competitiveness in the global market its ultimate criterion. This is the dominant variant. The other is the European tradition of social market or social democratic capitalism which sees the viability and legitimacy of an economy as dependent upon its being embedded in social relations recognized as equitable by the general population.[20] The issue between the two forms of capitalism is being fought out at the level of the European Union in the debate over 'social Europe' and the filling of the 'democratic deficit' in European institutions.

In very general terms, we can think of three constellations of forces: first, the dominant forces in states and markets (corporate management and the political class, surreptitiously sustained by the covert world); second, a heterogeneous category of groups commonly identified as constituting civil society in the emancipatory sense (trade unions and 'new social movements'); and third, right-wing and populist movements and religious cults that compete with the preceding groups for support among the unorganized mass of the people.

In attempts to construct a 'bottom-up' social force, the question arises of compatibility between trade unions and the new social movements, e.g. environmentalism, feminism, anti-poverty movements, and peace movements. The new social movements have often been suspicious of organized labour, fearing domination by labour's tighter and more hierarchical organization which might not respect the social movements' far more loosely structured and more participatory forms of organization. Moreover, the new movements arise more frequently from problems related to consumption, e.g. poverty and homelessness, rather than, as for unions, from the realm of production. On the other hand, organized labour can sometimes, despite its weakened condition in evolved capitalism, be a catalyst for a more broadly based social movement to confront the established powers in state and corporations. Furthermore, a sustained concertation of social forces, i.e. one that would outlast a particular event or crisis, is hard to achieve among groups with the loose and participatory character of the new movements. Coherence and durability over time would be a necessary condition for having a sustained impact on political parties and thus on the state.

Asian capitalism and the cultural dimension

Japanese capitalism is the prototype of another form of capitalism with a different social context.[21] In its origins, the pre-capitalist social and cultural form provided a foundation for imported Western technology and state sponsorship of industrialization. The result was a Japanese form of corporatism in which the state worked closely with business, and the firm developed on the concept of an extended, if bureaucratized, patriarchal family. Group loyalty contributed to organizational strength; but workers were divided between those integrated with the firm and others with a more casual or remote link to the central production organization (contract or out-sourcing workers). The lifetime employment of the first category corresponded to the impermanence of the second. In this manner, Japanese practice prefigured the pattern that globalization has projected on to the world scale.

This initial Asian pattern coincided with authoritarian political structures. The rapid growth of economies, first in Japan during the post-World War II years, and subsequently in several of the newly industrializing Asian economies (Hong Kong, South Korea, Taiwan and Singapore, followed by the Philippines, Thailand, Indonesia and Malaysia), brought into existence both a large middle class oriented towards consumerism and a more combative working class. In some of these countries, pressures from both of these social forces has resulted in attenuation of authoritarianism.

Japan's political structures show continuity in many respects with pre-war patterns. Democratization was introduced under the auspices of the American occupation authorities. Domestic forces in Japan, reacting against the militaristic state that had brought war and ruin, supported the democratic innovations. These forces continued to urge further democratization when US policy shifted ground to bring Japan into the anti-communist Cold War alliance. Other domestic elements, including those associated with the wartime regime, rallied to the new US anti-communist line.[22] Japan's post-war condition is a case of passive revolution in Gramsci's sense. The revolution/restoration balance remains non-catastrophic because the economic growth priority of Japanese governments during the later Cold War period achieved, at least temporarily, a high degree of depoliticization. The democratizing forces of the post-war years were to a large extent demobilized by the general preoccupation with economic growth.

Japanese society has sufficient cohesion on its own, sustained by the long period of economic growth, so that it has in practice made slight demands upon the state. Whether this would continue through a prolonged period of economic stagnation or recession is an open question. Moreover, some Japanese are concerned that the formerly strong cohesion of family and community may be dissolving as a consequence of modernization leading to more emphasis on individualism as well as consumerism and to a lesser commitment to work and organizational loyalties.[23] The covert world, particularly in the forms of organized crime and political corruption, thrives in Japan as it does also in South Korea and other Asian countries.

Asian scholars point to a distinction among three spheres: state, market, and civil society.[24] They see civil society in Asia as a late and still, relatively to Europe, weak development which has focused on democratization, environmentalism, human rights, the peace movement, and various mutual self-help and internationalist goals. In these respects, civil society has made gains in Japan, South Korea, Taiwan and the Philippines. Private groups (including organized crime) contributed spontaneously and effectively to relief after the Kobe earthquake disaster of 1995, when the state's response proved to be disorganized and ineffective. Indeed, the current emphasis on civil society in Asia could be seen; in its emancipatory aspect, as the transnationalizing of the democratizing and people-based forces of Japan and their effort to atone for Japan's war guilt by building cooperative arrangements with communities in other parts of Asia. There is also a movement towards 'Asianization', or the imagining of a regional Asia-wide community of which Japan is a part, which reflects both the consumerist material values of middle-class economic success and a right-wing aesthetic rejection of 'the West'.[25] Authoritarianism has impeded the democratization movement in Singapore, Malaysia and Indonesia, although many local non-governmental organizations exist in these countries. It is difficult to speak of civil society in China so long as the authoritarianism of the Party-state limits the expression of aggrieved elements, although rapid economic growth and social polarization in coastal China is generating stresses that may be hard to contain.

Recent events in South Korea have thrown new light on the condition of civil society. The challenge here has come from the effort of the large South Korean corporations, the *chaebols*, to compete as multinational corporations in the global market. Towards this end they persuaded the government to revert to earlier authoritarian practices by restricting labour rights recently acquired so as to give the *chaebols* more flexibility in hiring and firing. At the same time, the government sought to increase the powers of the intelligence services

(Korean CIA). This attempt to revert to authoritarianism and to enlarge the sphere of the covert world provoked a general strike in which the labour movement became united and gained support from students, teachers, and religious organizations. The protest was a direct reaction to globalization.[26]

As in the case of the French strikes of December 1995, the trade unions in South Korea provided the impetus for a response by civil society to state authoritarianism. Change in South Korea may be more authentic than passive, but it does not seem to be oriented towards radical structural transformation, but rather to a more liberal legitimation of political authority. In Japan, trade unions have not been identified with a 'bottom-up' transformation of civil society. They have been more aligned with corporations and the jobs they provide. During the 1970s, environmental protests that resulted in political changes at municipal and regional levels in Japan were led by citizens apart from unions. Union members identified their jobs with corporate interests in maintaining production, while their wives might feel freer to participate in the environmentalist revolt.

Thus in some Asian countries capitalist development has generated the class basis for a development of civil society which is weaker than that of Europe in the face of state and corporate authoritarianism but which has nevertheless made some significant progress in recent years. The social forces involved in this emergent civil society are both middle class (including students, environmentalists, peace activists and feminists) and organized workers. The coherence between middle class and worker elements is problematic. Asia gives a mixed picture of authentic and passive structural change in societies.

State breakdown and predatory capitalism

The prototype for this category is the breakdown of the Soviet Union; but instances of the phenomenon are not limited to the former Soviet bloc. Similar situations have arisen in countries of Latin America affected by the debt crisis. In broad outline, the circumstances leading to this situation are: an economic crisis generated by both internal and external causes leaves an authoritarian state unable to carry out the functions it has assumed; external pressures, welcomed by a politically aware stratum of the population, lead to the establishment of a liberal democratic regime based on electoral politics, but civil society is insufficiently developed to provide a firm basis for the new regime; external pressures then succeed in reducing state powers over the economy in favour of an expansion of market forces; the weakness of institutions to regulate the market and the collapse of state authority open the way for organized crime and political corruption to gain control in both state and market spheres; the general population, struggling for personal survival, becomes politically apathetic and non-participant, while some elements nourish a nostalgic hope for salvation by a charismatic leader. The weakness of civil society is the critical element in this catastrophic cycle.

The domestic cause of the collapse of the Soviet regime stemmed from its failure to make the transition from extensive development, i.e. the addition of more productive capacity of the same kind, to intensive development, i.e. innovating production technology with higher productivity. This was exacerbated by the external pressure to accelerate the arms race which placed an intolerable burden on the economy, preventing the state from maintaining the social services it had instituted as basic citizen rights.[27]

In the eastern and central European countries of the bloc, where the arms burden was less than in the Soviet Union, opposition movements developed openly. In Poland, *Solidarnošc* as a trade union became a rallying point for a broad based opposition to the communist regime; and the Catholic Church had long stood as an alternate pole of loyalty to the state. In East Germany, *Neues Forum* mobilized people into the streets to demonstrate against the authoritarian regime. As noted above, the current scholarly interest in civil society very largely originated in observation of the popular movements in Poland, Czechoslovakia, Hungary and the German Democratic Republic which toppled the communist regimes in these countries after the Soviet Union had signalled it would not or could not support them.

These movements crumbled later after they had achieved their initial purpose of overthrowing established state power. In retrospect, in Gramsci's terms, they may seem more like the phenomena of a war of manoeuvre than of a war of position. Liberal democratic regimes were then established in these countries, encouraged by western politicians and media and welcomed by local citizens. These were cases of passive revolution. In the Soviet Union, change came from the top. In Eastern and Central Europe, civil society played a bigger role. But after the collapse of the communist regimes, those who led the popular revolt did not for long remain as major political forces; and the bureaucratic elites of the former regime became the typical private market elites of post-communism. The solidity and durability of civil society remains questionable.

External support for the new regimes came more in the form of exhortations and technical advice urging 'democracy and market reform' than in large-scale investment and access for trade. It was clear that market reform in the ex-communist sphere had priority in western policy and that democracy was perceived as instrumental towards market economics.

When the erosion of state authority and the absence of effective regulation of the market led to a dramatic growth of mafia control over economic activity, corrupt penetration of the state, and the forging of international criminal links, apologists for liberal economics showed their preference for crime over state regulation. They could view it with equanimity as a probably necessary stage of primitive capital accumulation.[28] The collapse of state authority also unleashed sub-national forces of ethnic nationalism which became vehicles for garnering the residues of economic and political power.

Several Latin American countries also fit the model – Mexico and Columbia, for example. The decline of state authority is associated with the imposition of 'structural adjustment' policies advocated with financial leverage by the International Monetary Fund and backed by US pressure. Initially, US policy looked to authoritarian solutions to introduce economic liberalism in Latin America, in the manner of the Pinochet coup in Chile. Subsequently, US policy began to advocate liberal democratic forms of state as being more able to sustain the continuity of a liberal economic regime while allowing for changes of government, making the economy less vulnerable to political coup.[29] This, again, implied passive revolution.

In these societies various forms of popular movements have taken root – trade unions, left wing political parties, and the 'new social movements', as well as the episodic manifestations of 'people power' such as toppled the Marcos regime in the Philippines or 'IMF riots' provoked by rising food and transport prices. There is some evidence that, under the impact of structural adjustment, unions and social action movements have pulled together despite their mutual suspicions of earlier years and have worked to support left wing political parties.[30] However, groups led by social activists have focused more on local demands often obtained by the old patterns of clientelism and compromise with authorities than on the broader aims of change in social and economic structures which are the concern of left wing political parties. These left wing parties have, in turn, been weakened nationally by the hegemony of globalization ideology. Furthermore, promotion of civil society has been coopted by forces behind the propagation of neo-liberal economics as a way of defusing and channelling potential protest.[31] Consequently, civil society, in its dual form of class-based organizations and social activism, has a latent but not very fully realized potential for social and political transformation. The covert world, in the form of organized crime, drug cartels and political corruption, is rife in these countries. The decline of state authority is not matched by a development of civil society.

The most open challenge to the impact of globalization on social and political structures has come from a new type of revolutionary movement, the *Zapatista* rebellion of the Mayan Indians in the southern Mexican state of Chiapas that broke out on New Year's day 1994. This was the day on which the North American Free Trade Area came into effect, which symbolized the anti-globalization message of the revolt. Indigenous peoples in different parts of the world have proclaimed their distinctness as social formations demanding control of their ancestral lands. The *Zapatistas* have gone beyond this to cultivate international support and attempt to change the Mexican political system. They have sought to transcend both the hierarchical military character of the rebellion in its initial phase and its ethnic base of support in order to become a rallying force in civil society of all forces for democratic change, in other words to create the beginnings of a counterhegemonic bloc.[32]

Africa: civil society versus the state

In Africa there are even more extreme cases of state breakdown and of alienation of people from the state. State structures inherited from colonial regimes had no close relationship to local populations to begin with; yet the state controlled access to any economic activity more substantial than peasant agriculture and petty trading. The political struggle for control of the state was thus a struggle for a share of the economic product of the country, a product divided between foreign investors and the power holders in the state. There has been a history of resistance to this pattern. Some social revolutionary movements and attempts at social democratic experiments have endeavoured to create political authorities that were based on African community life – movements led by Amilcar Cabral in Guinea-Bissau, Samora Machel in Mozambique, and Julius Nyerere in Tanzania, for example. However, obstacles, mainly external in origin, impeded the success of these struggles for a more participant polity.[33] The Cold War came to dominate African politics as both the United States and the Soviet Union chose allies among the power-holders in African states and armed them. This strengthened the tendency towards military rule and towards African states taking the form of kleptocracies – dictators with armed bands that served both as praetorian guards and as gangs who pillaged the population. Mobutu's Zaire was a prime example.

In these circumstances, it is not to be wondered that African people did not readily identify with their rulers. Furthermore, foreign capital proved to be equally hostile to people's welfare. Foreign investors, with the connivance of African states, have damaged the ecology upon which local people depend for their livelihood. The international financial agencies (IMF and World Bank) impose structural adjustment policies that have placed heavy burdens on the populations of these countries. In consequence, many Africans have come to see the state and the international institutions as their enemies and have organized in a variety of self-help community groups to confront the daily problems of life, shunning any link to the state. Women have been prominent as initiators and leaders in this movement. An Ethiopian economist has called it 'the silent revolution in Africa'.[34] Similar movements exist in some other poor countries.

This is a form of incipient civil society that has turned its back on the state. The question remains open whether it could develop into a force that would engage with the state to alter the state's character and become the foundation for a new participant form of democracy.[35]

Conclusions

The nature and condition of civil society is very diverse, looked at on a world scale. It is, nevertheless, tempting to look at this diversity through the analytic lens of Gramsci's conceptualization of relations of forces (PN, pp. 180–5). Civil society is itself a field of power relations; and forces in civil society relate, in support or opposition, to powers in state and market.

The first level in Gramsci's relation of forces, is the 'relation of social forces' by which he meant objective relations independent of human will brought about by the level of development of the material forces of production. Through the effect of economic globalization and the passage from Fordism to post-Fordism in the present day world, this has brought about a basic cleavage between, on the one hand, the beneficiaries of globalization or those people who are integrated into the world economy, and on the other hand, those who are disadvantaged within or excluded from the world economy. The latter would include some who, in a precarious way, may become intermittent adjuncts to the world economy and whose interests may thus waver between hope for more stable affiliation and outright antagonism in despair of achieving it.

This cleavage does not yield anything so clear as the Marxian cleavage along property lines between bourgeoisie and proletariat. The proletariat is divided now between some beneficiaries of globalization and many disadvantaged. The petty bourgeoisie is also divided between some who would identify with the world economy and others who are disadvantaged or excluded in relation to it. Many people would need to be understood more in their relationship to consumption (or the inability to consume adequately) rather than to production – the more or less permanently unemployed, the inhabitants of shanty towns, welfare recipients, and students. The old production-related categories are not entirely superseded; but the scheme of categories of people relevant to the problematic of social change needs to be rethought.

Gramsci's second level, which he called the relation of political forces, addresses the question of consciousness. In today's context, the challenge is to bridge the differences among the variety of groups disadvantaged by globalization so as to bring about a common understanding of the nature and consequences of globalization, and to devise a common strategy towards subordinating the world economy to a regime of social equity. This means building a counterhegemonic historic bloc that could confront the hegemonic formation of globalization in a long term war of position.

Gramsci's strategic concepts are pertinent here, including particularly the role of organic intellectuals. Their task now is to be able to work simultaneously on local, regional and world levels. The obstacles are considerable in that the active or potential opposition to globalization is divided on many issues. There is opposition between manual workers protecting their jobs in environmentally destructive and polluting industries and environmentalists working to stop these industrial practices. Other conflicts arise between manual workers in mature industrial countries who face downgrading through global competition and workers in recently industrializing countries or immigrant workers from poor countries who are perceived to be taking away their jobs. Still other conflicts arise from the claims by indigenous peoples for lands and control of resources that conflict with the aims of mining and forestry corporations and their workers. Also there is the issue between the claims of women's movements for equity in employment and the fears of precariously employed male workers. Organic intellectuals linked to these various groups face a difficult task of transcending the immediate corporative instincts of these groups and the oppositions they engender to other disadvantaged or excluded groups, in order to achieve a commonly shared vision of a desirable and feasible alternative future and a strategy for joint action. They must at the same time do battle with the right wing forces of anti-immigrant racist nationalism, neo-fascism, authoritarian populism, and nihilistic religious cults, which compete for the allegiance of people where social bonds have disintegrated and apathy and alienation has become the norm.

Gramsci's third level in the relation of forces was the relation of military forces, which he divided into two parts: one, the technical military function which we may read as control of the repressive apparatus of a state; and the other, the politico-military, refers to the morale of a population, to the degree of coherence or disintegration among people. In the absence of high morale, struggle against a dominant power over people, whether foreign or domestic, would be improbable. The condition that sustains an oppressive regime, Gramsci wrote, is a 'state of social disintegration of the...people, and the passivity of the majority among them' (PN, p. 183). This, in varying degrees, is the situation characteristic of the populations engulfed by globalization today. To overcome this social disintegration and passivity will require the creation of a vibrant civil society inspired by a strong spirit of solidarity at the community level and, by linkage with other strong communities in other countries, at the transnational or global level. Upon such a basis of participatory democracy new political authorities may in the long run be constructed at national, regional and world levels.

One aspect in developing a vision and strategy is to shift from a predominantly space-oriented and synchronic mode of thinking to a predominantly time-oriented and diachronic or dialectical mode of thinking: Oppositions that are apparently objective in the immediate may be overcome through attacking the structures that ensure the persistence of these oppositions. First among these is the doctrine subscribed to by corporate capital and most governments, and propagated by the intellectuals and media of the status quo, that competitiveness in the world economy is the ultimate criterion of policy. This is the primary form of alienation in the world today – the imagining of a force created by people that stands over them proclaiming that 'there is no alternative'. This contemporary deity will have to be deconstructed to make way for an alternative vision of a world economy regulated in the interest of social equity and non-violent resolution of conflict.

The other important aspect of creating a counterhegemonic bloc is revival of a spirit of solidarity. The crisis of capitalism in the mid 1970s and the subsequent supremacy of the globalization dynamic has not only weakened psychological bonds between people and states but also the level of trust among people themselves and their disposition for collective action. The result is an increase in cynicism, apathy and non-participation of people in politics and social action.[36] Increasingly politics are not about choices concerning the future of society but rather about choices among competing sets of would-be managers of the status quo, many of whom are tainted by corruption and most of whom are professedly incompetent to think of, let alone pursue, an alternative.[37] The political space abandoned by people has been readily taken up by the covert world, which has become functional to the financing of established political systems and is involved in a substantial part of world markets.

Civil society has become the crucial battleground for recovering citizen control of public life. It seems that very little can be accomplished towards fundamental change through the state system as it now exists. That system might be reconstructed on the basis of a rein-vigorated civil society which could only come about through a long term war of position. Meanwhile, a two-track strategy for the Left seems appropriate: first, continued participa-tion in electoral politics and industrial action as a means of defensive resistance against the further onslaught of globalization; and secondly, but ultimately more importantly, pursuit of the primary goal of resurrecting a spirit of association in civil society together with a continuing effort by the organic intellectuals of social forces to think through and act towards an alternative social order at local, regional and global levels.

Acknowledgements

The original version of this article was a paper presented to the Conference on Gramsci, Modernity, and the Twentieth Century, convened by the Fundazione Istituto Gramsci, Rome, in Cagliari, 15–18 April 1997. In revising it, I am most grateful for comments by Yoshikazu Sakamoto, James Mittelman, Masaharu Takashima, Michael Schechter, Timothy Sinclair, Michael Cox and two anonymous readers for the *Review of International Studies*. I am especially indebted to Yoshikazu Sakamoto for directing my attention to the question of civil society in our times. I, of course, alone bear responsibility for the text as it appears here.

Notes

1 Eric Hobsbawm, *The Age of Extremes. A History of the World, 1914–1991* (New York: Pantheon, 1994) p. 459.
2 References in the text to the *Prison Notebooks* are taken from Antonio Gramsci, *Selections from the Prison Notebooks* edited and translated by Quintin Hoare and Geoffrey Nowell Smith (New York: International Publishers, 1971), subsequently referred to as PN.
3 See, e.g., Benedetto Croce, *Politics and Morals* (New York: Philosophical Library, 1945) pp. 22–32, where he described the state as 'the incarnation of the human ethos'.
4 Carl Becker, *The Heavenly City of the Eighteenth Century Philosophers* (New Haven, CT: Yale University Press, 1932).
5 Alexis de Tocqueville, *De la Démocratie en Amérique* 2 vols (Paris: Gallimard, 1951).
6 There is a current of 'political Marxism' expressed by Ellen Meiskins Wood, *Democracy Against Capitalism. Renewing Historical Materialism* (Cambridge: Cambridge University Press, 1995), which is very critical of the hopes of some people on the Left that civil society will play an emancipatory role. In her view, civil society retains its original identity with the bourgeois order. This originated with the conceptual distinction made in bourgeois ideology between politics and economics, creating the illusion that economics, the realm of civil society, was not an arena of politics, that is to say, of power relations. This mystification of private power has made possible the acceptance and reproduction of the bourgeois social order. She writes: 'It is certainly true that in capitalist society, with its separation of "political" and "economic" spheres, or the state and civil society, coercive public power is centralized and concentrated to a greater degree than ever before, but this simply means that one of the principal functions of "public" coercion by the state is to sustain "private" power in civil society.' (p. 255) Her charge against the current appeal to civil society by the 'new social movements' and postmodernism is that it occludes the reality of class domination and fragments the opposition to the bourgeois order into a variety of distinct struggles for 'identity', thereby perpetuating capitalist domination.
   Justin Rosenberg, *The Empire of Civil Society. A Critique of the Realist Theory of International Relations* (London: Verso, 1994) transposes Ellen Wood's reasoning to international relations, arguing that the classical Westphalian concept of state sovereignty and the balance of power mystify the reality of power in the capitalist world order. The 'public' sphere of the state system is paralleled by the 'private' sphere of the global economy; and the state system functions to sustain 'private' power in the latter, the 'empire of civil society'.
   'Political Marxism' provides a cogent argument with regard to the 'top-down' meaning of civil society, and in its critique of a postmodernism that indiscriminate deference to identities implies a fragmentation and therefore weakening of opposition to the dominant order. The argument is more questionable in its apparent rejection of the Gramscian 'war of position' as a counterhegemonic strategy for the conquest of civil society and for the transformation of civil society in an emancipatory direction. Two key points in the 'political Marxist' thesis that bear reexamination are: (1) the positing of capitalism as a monolithic 'totalizing' force which excludes the possibility of historicizing capitalism so as to perceive that it is subject to historical change and can take different

forms; and (2) the freezing of the concept of 'class' in a 19th and early 20th century form with a two class model juxtaposing bourgeoisie and proletariat which obscures the ways in which changes in production have restructured social relations, especially during recent decades. Both points are discussed below.

7 Norberto Bobbio, 'Gramsci and the concept of civil society', in John Keane (ed.), *Civil Society and the State. New European Perspectives* (London and New York: Verso, 1988). The essay was originally published in *Gramsci e la cultura contemporarea: Atti del Convengno Internazionale di Studi Gramsciani*, Rome 1968.

8 Adam Przeworski, 'Democratic socialism in Poland?', *Studies in Political Economy* 5 (Spring 1981), pp. 29–54, esp. pp. 37–41.

9 I take the term 'civic state' from Yoshikazu Sakamoto, in personal correspondence. See also his article 'Civil society and democratic world order', in Stephen Gill and James H. Mittelman (eds), *Innovation and Transformation in International Studies* (Cambridge: Cambridge University Press, 1997) pp. 207–19.

10 See, e.g., David Held, *Democracy and the Global Order. From the Modern State to Cosmopolitan Governance* (Stanford: Stanford University Press, 1995). Michael G. Schechter, 'Globalization and civil society', paper presented to the annual meeting of the Academic Council on the United Nations System (ACUNS), San Jose, Costa Rica, June 1997, contains a critical review of literature on 'global civil society'. Even the most optimistic writers regard 'global civic society' in the emancipatory sense as something to be achieved, not as something that already exists. In the 'top-down' hegemonic sense, by contrast, Rosenberg (see note 6) refers to the 'empire of civil society' as control by global capitalism. In the same sense, but without the Marxist theoretical framework, Susan Strange has written about a 'non-territorial empire' ('Toward a theory of transnational empire', in E.-O. Czempiel and James N. Rosenau (eds), *Global Changes and Theoretical Challenges. Approaches to World Politics for the 1990s*, Lexington, MA: Lexington Books, 1989).

11 Laura Macdonald, *Supporting Civil Society. The Political Role of Non-Governmental Organizations in Central America* (Basingstoke: Macmillan, 1997) gives a useful classification of 'ideal types' of NGOs according to their consequences for maintenance or transformation of social and political order. She suggests three types: neo-conservative, liberal-pluralist, and post-Marxist (or Gramscian) (pp. 15–23). With regard to opposition between dominant and subordinate groups within the labour movement, see Robert W. Cox, 'Labor and hegemony' and 'Labor and hegemony: a reply', in Cox with Timothy J. Sinclair (eds), *Approaches to World Order* (Cambridge: Cambridge University Press, 1996).

12 Bernadette Madeuf and Charles-Albert Michalet, 'A new approach to international economics', *International Social Science Journal* 30: 2 (1978), pp. 253–83, made the distinction between the international economy (understood as flows of goods, payments, and investments across frontiers) and an emerging form of economy in which production was being organized on an integrated basis among entities located in a number of countries. In the English translation of their article, which was written in French, the emerging economy was called the 'world economy', which accords with the French term applied to the process generating it, *mondialisation*. The term 'global economy' is commonly used now in English to designate the organization of production and finance on a world scale and 'globalization' as the process generating it. Of course, much of the world's economic activity still goes on outside this global economy, albeit increasingly constrained by and subordinated to the global economy. I reserve the term 'world economy' for the totality of economic activities of which the global economy is the dominant part. The impact of the globalization process on power relations among social forces and states, and in the formation of institutions designed to entrench the global economy or in stimulating resistance to it is the realm of 'global political economy'.

13 See, for example, Hedley Bull, *The Anarchical Society. A Study of Order in World Politics* (New York: Columbia University Press, 1977) esp. pp. 254–5; also Susan Strange, *The Retreat of the State. The Diffusion of Power in the World Economy* (Cambridge: Cambridge University Press, 1996); and Bertrand Badie and Marie-Claude Smouts, *Le retournement du monde. Sociologie de la scène internationale* (Paris: Presses de la Fondation Nationale des Sciences Politiques & Dalloz, 1992). On this theme of the increasing complexity of world politics and the obsolescence of conventional boundaries and distinctions, see also James N. Rosenau, *Along the Domestic-Foreign Frontier. Exploring Governance in a Turbulent World* (Cambridge: Cambridge University Press, 1997).

14 See Leo Panitch, 'Rethinking the role of the state', in James H. Mittelman (ed.), *Globalization: Critical Reflections* (Boulder, CO: Lynne Rienner, 1996).

15 Robert W. Cox, 'Production and security', in Cox with Timothy J. Sinclair (eds), *Approaches to World Order* (Cambridge: Cambridge University Press, 1996) pp. 276–95.

16 Ignacio Ramonet, 'Néofascisme', *Le Monde diplomatique* (April 1998).

17 Mark Rupert, 'Globalisation and contested common sense in the United States', in Stephen Gill and James H. Mittelman (eds), *Innovation and Transformation in International Studies* (Cambridge: Cambridge University Press, 1997). The most extreme manifestation of this tendency is withdrawal from American political society with the formation of private militias and perpetration of terrorist acts like the Oklahoma City bombing.

18 Yumiko Iida, 'Virtual kingdom and dreams of apocalypse; contemporary Japan mirrored in *Aum Shinrikyo*', paper presented at the 10th annual conference of the Japan Studies Association of Canada, Toronto, October 1997.

19 The most obvious case today is the role of *mafias* in the Russian economy; but an anecdotal instance relates to Argentina where deregulation has led to increased polarization of rich and poor and former members of the naval intelligence service, notorious torturers during the 'dirty war', have been reemployed by private corporations as 'security' staff. Amaranta Wright, 'Argentine killers find new line of work', *The Globe and Mail* (Toronto), 28 February 1997.

20 Michel Albert, *Capitalisme Contre Capitalisme* (Paris: Seuil, 1991).

21 See Shigeto Tsuru, *Japan's Capitalism* (Cambridge: Cambridge University Press, 1993); Chalmers Johnson, *MITI and the Japanese Miracle* (Stanford: Stanford University Press, 1982); and James Fallows, *Looking at the Sun: The Rise of the New East Asian Economic and Political System* (New York: Pantheon, 1994).

22 Yoshikazu Sakamoto, 'The international context of the occupation of Japan', in Robert E. Ward and Yoshikazu Sakamoto (eds), *Democratizing Japan: The Allied Occupation* (Honolulu, HI: University of Hawaii Press, 1987); also Yoshikazu Sakamoto, 'Fifty years of the two Japans', typescript, 1995.

23 Professor Tamotsu Aoki, a cultural anthropologist, Research Center for Advanced Science and Technology, University of Tokyo, at a symposium convened jointly by the International House of Japan and the Friedrich-Ebert-Stiftung, Tokyo, September 26 1996.

24 Yoshikazu Sakamoto, Professor emeritus of International Relations, Tokyo University and Young-Ho Kim, Professor at Kyungpook National University, South Korea, at a symposium on Prospects for Civil Society in Asia, International House of Japan, Tokyo, September 24 1996.

25 The 'Asianization' idea is presented in Yoichi Funabashi, 'The Asianization of Asia', *Foreign Affairs* 72: 5 (1993). The notion of a regional civil society is discussed in Mitchell Bernard, 'Regions in the global political economy: beyond the local-global divide in the formation of the eastern Asian region', *New Political Economy* 1: 3 (November 1996). For a critical assessment, see Yumiko Iida, 'Fleeing the West, making Asia home: transpositions of otherness in Japanese pan-Asianism, 1905–1930', *Alternatives* 22 (1997), pp. 409–32.

26 A series of articles by Philippe Pons in *Le Monde*, 3 January, 15 January, and 16 January, 1997; and by Laurent Carroué, *Le Monde diplomatique*, February 1997.

27 See various writings of János Kornai, including *Economics of Shortage* (Amsterdam: North-Holland, 1980; and 'Dilemmas of a socialist economy', *Cambridge Journal of Economics*, 4: 2 (1980); also Wlodzimierz Brus and Tadeus Kowalik, 'Socialism and development', *Cambridge Journal of Economics*, 7 (1983); and Robert W. Cox, '"Real socialism" in historical perspective', in Ralph Miliband and Leo Panitch (eds), *Socialist Register 1991* (London: Merlin Press, 1991).

28 László Andor, 'Economic transformation and political stability in East Central Europe', *Security Dialogue*, 27: 2 (June 1996).

29 See William I. Robinson, *Promoting Polyarchy. Globalization, US Intervention, and Hegemony* (Cambridge: Cambridge University Press, 1996) which contains case studies of the Philippines, Chile, Nicaragua, Haiti, South Africa, and the former Soviet bloc; also William I. Robinson, 'Globalization, the world system, and "democracy promotion" in US foreign policy', *Theory and Society*, 25 (1996), pp. 615–65.

30 Judith Adler Hellman, 'The riddle of new social movements: who they are and what they do', in Sandor Halebsky and Richard L. Harris (eds), *Capital, Power, and Inequality in Latin America* (Boulder, CO: Westview Press, 1995).

31 Laura Macdonald, *Supporting Civil Society* (see note 11).

32 Maurice Najman, 'Le grand virage des zapatistes', in *Le Monde diplomatique*, January 1997. A sketch of the world view of the Zapatistas is to be found in Sous-commandant Marcos, 'La 4e guerre mondiale a commencé', *Le Monde diplomatique*, August 1997.

33 Amilcar Cabral was a particularly articulate leader who expounded in theory and practice, the position that popular participation in revolutionary action and cultural change were essential for African peoples to raise themselves out of imperialist domination. Although the momentum of his movement stalled, following Cabral's assassination by agents of Portuguese colonialism, the historian Basil Davidson thinks that Cabral's success in mobilizing Africans to make their own history has left its impact and example to inspire a renewed movement. See Basil Davidson, *The Search for Africa. History, Culture, Politics* (New York: Random House, 1994) esp. pp. 217–43; and *Unity and Struggle. Speeches and Writings of Amilcar Cabral* (New York and London: Monthly Review, 1979). Cabral's speeches and writing have striking similarity to Gramsci's thought.

34 Fantu Cheru, *The Silent Revolution in Africa: Debt, Development and Democracy* (Harare and London: Zed/Anvil Press, 1989). Basil Davidson, *The Search for Africa* (see note 33) has also referred to this phenomenon: 'One finds [in Africa] the striving of countless individuals and collectives towards new types of self-organization – perhaps one should say self-defense – aimed in one way or another at operating outside the bureaucratic centralism of the neocolonial state' (p. 290).

35 Basil Davidson, 'Africa: the politics of failure', in Ralph Miliband and Leo Panitch (eds), *Socialist Register 1992* (London: Merlin Press, 1992), envisaged the possibility that more participatory politics in Africa might develop within the framework of market economics, but concluded rather pessimistically: 'How far the developed world of multinational concentrations of power will bring itself to tolerate this devolutionary politics of participation, and its democratic implications, is [a] question to which, at present, we do not have an answer' (p. 225). The fall of the Mobutu regime in Zaire and its replacement by the Democratic Republic of the Congo under Laurent-Désiré Kabila did not really test Davidson's proposition. Kabila's victory was achieved by military means with considerable support from Ugandan and Rwandan military forces. The struggle seemed to take place over the heads of the vast majority of Zaire's population which has evolved techniques of survival in communities that have avoided involvement with the state and the formal economy. Although these elements of autonomous civil society do exist, they have not yet been able to evolve a real politics of participation that could be the foundation for a new state. See, e.g., Colette Braeckman, 'Comment le Zaïre fut libéré', *Le Monde diplomatique*, July 1997. In other works, Davidson seems more optimistic about the long range potential for the development of civil society and 'the elaboration of a culture capable of drawing the civilization of the Africans out of the fetters into which it has fallen, and of giving that civilization, in its multitudinous aspects and varieties, a life and meaning appropriate to its present tasks and destiny.' (Basil Davidson, *The Search for Africa*, pp. 261–2 (see note 33)).

36 The American sociologist Robert D. Putnam has suggested that civil society in the United States has lost much of the spirit of association once noted by de Tocqueville as its salient characteristic. He sees this as being replaced by non-participation in group activities and a privatizing or individualizing of leisure time. He calls this a decline of 'social capital' which refers to networks, norms, and social trust that facilitate coordination and cooperation for mutual benefit. See Putnam, 'Bowling alone: America's declining social capital', *Journal of Democracy*, 6: 1 (January 1995). The same author has made a study about social capital in Italy: Putnam with Robert Leonardi and Raffaella Y. Nanetti, *Making Democracy Work. Civic Traditions in Modern Italy* (Princeton: Princeton University Press, 1993).

37 See, for example, the brilliant essay by Jean-Marie Guéhenno, *La fin de la démocratie* (Paris: Flammarion, 1993).

11 Global civil society

Perspectives, initiatives, movements

Richard Falk

Source: Richard Falk (1998), 'Global Civil Society: Perspectives, Initiatives, Movements', *Oxford Development Studies*, 26: 1, pp. 99–110

Note on terminology

The emphasis of this article is upon social forces that respond to the patterns of behavior associated with the phenomena of economic globalization. As a consequence, it seems preferable on balance to frame such activity by reference to "global civil society" rather than to "transnational civil society". Even so the word "society" is definitely problematic at this stage of global social and political evolution, due to absence of boundaries and weakness of social bonds transcending nation, race and gender. Such a difficulty exists whether the reference is to "transnational civil society" or to "global civil society". But the transnational referent tends to root the identity of the actors in the subsoil of national consciousness to an extent that neglects the degree to which the orientation is not one of crossing borders, but of inhabiting and constructing a polity appropriate for the global village. Such a nascent global polity is already partly extant, yet remains mostly emergent. (For helpful conceptual discussion of these issues of conceptual framing, see Wapner, 1996.)

A similar issue arises with respect to the terminology useful in aggregating the actors. It seems convenient to retain the term non-governmental organizations (NGOs) to designate those actors associated with global civil society because it is accurate and convenient, being so widely used and thus easily recognizable. But it is also somewhat misleading in relation to the fundamental hypothesis of a diminishing ordering capability by the sovereign state and states system. To contrast the actors and action of global civil society with the governments of states, as is done by calling them NGOs, is to confer a derivative status and to imply the persistence of a superordinate Westphalian world of sovereign states as the only effective constituents of contemporary world order. Until recently this hierarchical dualism was justifiable because the preeminence of the state was an empirical reality, reinforced by the absence of any other significant international actors capable of autonomous action.

To overcome this difficulty of relying upon this somewhat anachronistic statist rhetoric, James Rosenau has proposed an alternative terminology to that of NGOs by calling such entities "sovereignty free actors" (Rosenau, 1990). Besides being obscure, such a substitute terminology is still operating in a Westphalian shadowland in which actor identities are exclusively derived from sovereign actors, namely, states. A comparable problem exists if the reference is to "transnational social forces", although the sense of "transnational" is more flexible and autonomous than "sovereignty free". Another possibility was proposed some years ago by Marc Nerfin (1986), in the form of a framework that recognized the social reality of "the third system" (the first sector being that of states, the second of market forces), from which issued forth civil initiatives of motivated citizens supportive of the global public good.

There is by now a wide and growing literature on "global civil society", especially as related to environmental politics on a global level. (For concise overview see Wapner, 1996; Lipschutz, 1996.) For the purposes of this article global civil society refers to the field of action and thought occupied by individual and collective citizen initiatives of a voluntary, non-profit character both within states and transnationally. These initiatives proceed from a global orientation and are responses, in part at least, to certain globalizing tendencies that are perceived to be partially or totally adverse. At present, most of the global provocation is associated directly or indirectly with market forces and the discipline of regional and global capital. As will be made clear, such a critical stance toward economic globalization does not entail an overall repudiation of these developments, but it does seek to regulate adverse effects and correct social injustices.

To focus inquiry further, I also propose to rely upon a distinction that I have used previously: drawing a basic dividing-line between global market forces identified as "globalization-from-above" and a set of oppositional responses in the third system of social activism that is identified as "globalization-from-below" (Falk, 1993, 1995). This distinction may seem unduly polarizing and hierarchical, apparently constructing a dualistic world of good and evil. My intention is neither hierarchical nor moralistic, and there is no illusion that the social forces emanating from the third system are inherently benevolent, while those from the first and second systems are necessarily malevolent. Far from it. One of the arguments of the article is that there are dangerous chauvinistic and extremist societal energies being released by one series of responses to globalization-from-above that are threatening the achievements of the modern secular world that had been based on the normative side of the evolution of an anarchic society of states in the cumulative direction of humane governance. (This normative potential of statism has been most influentially articulated by Hedley Bull, 1977.) To situate the argument, it is important to acknowledge that there are strong positive effects and potentialities arising from the various aspects of globalization-from-above. At the same time, the historic role of globalization-from-below is to challenge and transform the negative features of globalization-from-above, both by providing alternative ideological and political space to that currently occupied by market-oriented and statist outlooks and by offering resistances to the excesses and distortions that can be properly attributed to globalization in its current phase. That is, globalization-from-below is not dogmatically opposed to globalization-from-above, but addresses itself to the avoidance of adverse effects and to providing an overall counterweight to the essentially unchecked influence currently exerted by business and finance on the process of decision at the level of the state and beyond.

Deforming historical circumstances

The distinctive challenges posed by globalization-from-above have been accentuated by certain defining historical circumstances. Above all, the ending of the Cold War generated an ideological atmosphere in the North supportive of an abandonment of Keynesian approaches to economic policy, and its replacement by a strong version of neo-liberal reliance on private sector autonomy and an economistic approach to social policy, that is, eroding the social compromises between labor and business by way of achieving fiscal austerity, efficient allocation of resources, privatization and international competitiveness. There were other pressures to move in these directions, including a pendulum swing in societal attitudes against "the welfare state" in many states, a generalized distrust of government and public sector approaches to problem-solving, the steadily declining political leverage of organized labor, the waning of industrialism and the waxing of electronics and informatics, an overall disenchantment with ameliorative rhetoric and proposals, and, above all, pressures to neutralize the alleged competitive advantages of countries in the South, especially those in the Asia/Pacific region.

These alleged competitive advantages are associated with the political and economic unevenness of states, and refer especially to cheap skilled labor, minimal regulation and high profit margins that have been supposedly draining jobs and capital away from the North. These differentials have ethically ambiguous consequences, reinforcing neo-liberal rationalizations for harsher economic policy and contributing to chauvinistic backlash politics in the North, while liberating many of the most populous countries in the South from centuries of acute poverty and massive human suffering.

In effect, the material and technological foundation of globalization, based on the possibilities for profitable expansion of business operations without regard to state boundaries, did not necessarily have to be linked to an ideological abandonment of the social agenda and downsizing pressures on public goods, including a disturbing decline in support for mechanisms to protect the global commons and the global public good. Neo-liberal approaches and ideological justifications have been latent in market economies ever since the birth of capitalism during the industrial revolution, but somewhat surprisingly the nastiest features of early capitalism were moderated to varying degrees in the 19th and 20th Centuries in response to the rise of "the dangerous classes", the labor movement, the ordeal of business cycles culminating in The Great Depression, and the adjustments promoted by different versions of "social democracy", and what came to be known in the USA as "liberalism".

Indeed, the recent change in ideological atmosphere can be rapidly understood by the delegitimation of liberalism in the USA since the 1980s, making even those political perspectives of the most socially sensitive leaders in the Democratic Party unwilling any longer to use or accept the liberalism as a label of what came to be derisively called "the L word". What has emerged in this first stage of globalization after the end of the Cold War is a neo-liberal consensus among political élites in the world, powerfully disseminated by a business-oriented and consumerist global media, a power shift that helps explain the economistic orientation of most governments. (For a more historically grounded view of globalization, see Clark, 1997.) In the North, this consensus tends to be justified by reference to the discipline of global capital, or simply by reference to "competitiveness", the struggle for market shares and the virtues of free trade. Such an ideological setting is often merged with globalization to make the one indistinguishable from the other.

The evolving perspective of those social forces associated with globalization-from-below is that it remains possible and essential to promote the social agenda while retaining most of the benefits of globalization-from-above (Hirst and Thompson, 1996, 1 17, 170–194). In effect, globalization can be enacted in a variety of governance and fiscal scenarios, including some that are more people-oriented and supportive of global public goods and the goals of the social agenda. The ideological infrastructure of globalization is rather structural, and its reformulation is at the core of the convergent perspectives implied by the emergence of global civil society as the bearer of alternative visions of a more sustainable and compassionate future world order (Falk, 1995). Often this normative convergence is concealed beneath the more particularized banners of human rights, environmental protection, feminism and social justice that have been unfurled within global civil society by issue-oriented social movements that have been transnationally active during the last several decades.

It is also important to acknowledge the limited undertaking of globalization-from-below. It is not able to challenge globalization as such, only to alter the guiding ideas that are shaping enactment. Globalization is too widely accepted and embedded to be reversible in its essential integrative impact. Recent global trends establish the unchallengeable dominance of markets and their integration. In Jeffrey Sachs' words, "…capitalism has now spread to nearly 90% of the world's population, since nearly all parts of the world are now linked through open trade, convertible currencies, flows of foreign investment, and political commitments to private ownership as the engine of economic growth" (Sachs, 1997, 11). Sachs points out that only 20 years earlier such conditions pertained to only 20% of the world's population, the rest of humanity being subjected either to command socialist economies or to clumsy Third World efforts to combine capitalism and socialism. Such a shift in so short a time, of course, inevitably produces a fundamental reshaping of the ideas and practices constitutive of world order.

It is this process of economic restructuring according to the logic of markets that establishes the context for globalization-from-below. The strategic question is how can these forces effectively challenge the uneven adverse effects of globalization-from-above as it is currently evolving. These adverse consequences include insufficient attention to environmental protection and resource conservation, failures to offset severe vulnerabilities of social segments, countries and regions that are not currently able to gain sufficient access to the market, and a generalized lack of support for the social agenda and global public goods, including the United Nations (UN), especially in its efforts to coordinate and promote moves to overcome world poverty and to close the gaps that separate rich from poor.

Responding to economic globalization

There have been varied failed responses to economic globalization, conceived of as the capitalist portion of the world economy. Without entering into an assessment of these failures, it is worth noticing that both Soviet-style socialism and Maoism, especially during the period of the Cultural Revolution, were dramatic efforts to oppose economic globalization that ended in disaster. By contrast, despite the difficulties, the subsequent embrace of the market by China under the rubric of "modernization" and even by Russia (and the former members of the Soviet empire) in the form of the capitalist path have been spectacularly successful. The same is true for many Third World countries that had forged a middle path between socialism and capitalism that made the state a major player in the economy, particularly with respect to public utilities and energy; for most of these countries, as well, the change from a defensive hostility toward the world market to a position of unconditional receptivity has been generally treated as a blessing.

The learning experience at the level of the state has been one of submission to the discipline of global capital as it pertains to the specific conditions of each country. Fashionable ideas of "delinking" and "self-reliance" are in a shambles, perhaps most easily appreciated by the inability of North Korea to feed its population, while its capitalist sibling in South Korea is scaling the peaks of affluence. In effect, the geopolitical managers of the world economy use such policies as a punishment for supposedly deviant states, seeking to legitimize the exclusion under the rubric of "sanctions", a policy often widely criticized in this period because of its cruel effects on the civilian population of the target society. Even Castro's Cuba, for so long an impressive holdout, is relying on standard capitalist approaches to attract foreign investment and open its economy to market forces. Fukuyama's notorious theme about the end of history is partially correct, at least for now, if understood as limited in its application to economic aspects of policy, and not extended to political life (Fukuyama, 1992).

Another direction of response to economic globalization has been negative in the form of backlash politics that looks either at some pre-modern traditional framework as viable and virtuous (as with religious extremists of varying identity, or of indigenous peoples) or ultra-territorialists that seek to keep capital at home and exclude foreigners to the extent possible. These responses, aside from those of indigenous peoples, have a rightist flavor because of their emphasis on the sacred religious or nationalist community of the saved that is at war with an evil "other", being either secularist or outsider. To the extent that such movements have gained control of the state, as in Iran since the Islamic Revolution, or even threatened to do so, as in Algeria since 1992, the results have been dismal: economic deterioration, political repression, and widespread civil strife. Specific causes of these backlash phenomena are related to the failures of globalization and its related secularist outlook, but the correctives proposed have yet to exhibit a capacity to generate an alternative that is capable of either successful economic performance or able to win genuine democratic consent from relevant political communities.

Related to this predominance of market forces is a series of attempts by civil society to avoid the adverse effects of economic globalization. The most effective of these responses have been issue-oriented, often involving local campaigns against a specific project. One notable attempt to enter the domain of transformative politics more generally was made by the green parties in Europe during the 1980s. This green movement often exhibited tactical brilliance in its moves to expose the deficiencies of globalizing trends, especially their dangers to the environment. Its political success was less its ability to mobilize large numbers in support of its causes and programmes, but the extent to which its challenge influenced the whole center of the political spectrum to put the environmental challenge high on its policy agenda. But the green movement's attempt to generalize its identity to provide an alternative leadership for the entire society across the full range of governance or to transnationalize its activities to promote global reform met with frustration and internal controversy that fractured green unity, most vividly in Germany, but elsewhere as well. Those who argued for a new radicalism beyond established political parties within a green framework were dismissed as Utopian dreamers while those who opted for influence within the existing framework were often scorned as victims of co-optation or derided as opportunists. The green movement and its political parties have persisted in the 1990s, but as a voice on the margins with neither a credible alternative world view to that provided by globalization nor a sufficiently loyal constituency to pose a threat to the mainstream.

Localism has been another type of response directed at the siting of a nuclear power reactor or dam, mobilizing residents of the area facing displacement and loss of traditional livelihood, and sometimes involving others from the society and beyond, who identify with the poor or nature. These struggles have had some notable successes (Shiva, 1987; Rich, 1994). But these are reactions to symptomatic disorders associated with globalization, and do little more than influence entrepreneurial forces to be more prudent or to make more public relations efforts.

More relevant have been attempts by elements of global civil society to protect the global commons against the more predatory dimensions of globalization. Here Greenpeace has a distinguished record of activist successes, exhibiting an imaginative and courageous willingness to challenge entrenched military and commercial forces by direct action that has had an impact: helping to discourage whaling, protesting against the effort of Shell Oil to dispose of the oil rig Brent Spar in the North Sea, supporting a 50 year moratorium on mineral development in

Antarctica and, most memorably, resisting for many years nuclear testing in the Pacific. Rachel Carson's lyrical environmentalism and Jacques Cousteau's extraordinarily intense dedication to saving the oceans suggest the extent to which even single, gifted individuals can exert powerful counter-tendencies to the most destructive sides of an insufficiently regulated market. But these efforts, although plugging some of the holes in the dikes, are not based on either a coherent critique or alternative ideology, and thus operate only at the level of the symptom, while neglecting the disorders embedded in the dynamics of globalization.

Some other efforts to awaken responses have arisen from global civil society on the basis of a more generalized assessment. One of the earliest such initiatives was that promoted by the Club of Rome, a transnational association of individuals prominent in business, science and society that led to the famous study *The Limits to Growth* (Meadows *et al.*, 1972). The argument, tied closely to a sophisticated computer program that was measuring trends in population growth, pollution, resource scarcity and food supply concluded that industrialism as being practised was not sustainable, but was tending toward imminent catastrophe. Around the same time a group of distinguished scientists from various countries working with the British journal, *The Ecologist*, issued their own warning call under the title *Blueprint for Survival* (Goldsmith, 1972). These alarms provoked a debate and led to some adjustments, but the resilience of the world capitalist system was such that no fundamental changes occurred, and the warnings issued as signals soon faded into the cultural noise. Neither a sense of alternative nor a movement of protest and opposition took hold.

The World Order Models Project (WOMP) is illustrative of a somewhat more remote effort to challenge the existing order and find alternatives, through the medium of diagnosis and prescription by a transnational group of independent academicians. The efforts of this group have been confined to the margins of academic reflection on world conditions. Also, until recently, the policy focus and animating preoccupation was centered on war, and then broadened somewhat later to include environmental danger. Although WOMP did produce overall assessments, its background and participants made it less sensitive to the distinctive challenges and contributions of economic globalization (Falk, 1995, 1996, 1997a). As such, its emphasis on war and the war-making sovereign state did not come to terms with either the durability of the state or the need to avoid its *instrumentalization* by global market forces. That is, the principal world order danger is no longer the absolute security claims of the sovereign state, but rather the inability of the state to protect its own citizenry, especially those who are most vulnerable, in relation to the workings of the world economy.

A better connected effort to address overall global issues was attempted by the Commission on Global Governance, as expressed in its main report, *Our Global Neighborhood* (Commission, 1995). This initiative, claiming authority and credibility on the basis of the eminence of its membership drawn from the leading ranks of society, and stressing past or present government service at leadership or ministerial levels, seemed too farsighted for existing power structures and too timid to engage the imagination of the more activist and militant actors in civil society. The Commission report failed to arouse any widespread or sustained interest despite the comprehensiveness and thoughtfulness of its proposals. As an intellectual tool it is also disappointing, failing to clarify the challenge of globalization and the troublesome character of Bretton Woods approaches to world economic policy. As a result, its efforts to anchor an argument for global reform around an argument for "global governance" seemed more likely to consolidate globalization-from-above than to promote a creative equilibrium relying on the balancing contribution of globalization-from-below. In part, this Commission report was unlucky, beginning its efforts in the aftermath of the Gulf War when attention and hopes were centered on the future of the UN and finishing its work at a time when the world organization was widely, if somewhat unfairly, discredited as a result of the outcomes in Somalia, Bosnia and Rwanda. But this was not the fundamental problem, which was more a failure of nerve to address the adverse consequence of globalization, a focus that would have put such a commission on a collision course with adherents of the neo-liberal economistic world picture. Given the claims of "eminence" and "independent funding" that characterize such a commission, it is not to be expected that it would be willing or able to address the structural and ideological deficiencies attributable to the prevailing world order framework. This means that its best efforts confirm pessimism about finding an alternative world picture to that provided by the neo-liberal prism on globalization.

What is being argued, then, is that the challenges posed by economic globalization have not as yet engendered a sufficient response in two connected respects: first, the absence of an ideological posture that is comparably coherent to that being provided by various renditions of neo-liberalism, and that could provide the social forces associated with globalization-from-below with a common theoretical framework, political language and programme; secondly, a clear expression of a critique of globalization-from-above that cuts deeply enough to address the most basic normative challenges associated with poverty, social marginalization and environmental decay, while accepting the emancipatory contributions being made, as well as the unchallengeable persistence of state and market; the political goals of globalization-from-below are thus at once both drastic and reformist.

It is central to realize that the world order outcomes arising from the impact of economic globalization are far from settled, and in no sense pre-determined. The forces of globalization-from-above have taken control of globalization and are pushing it in an economistic direction that considerably instrumentalizes the state on behalf of a set of attitudes and policies: privatization, free trade, fiscal austerity and competitiveness. But there are other options: "sustainable development", "global welfare", "cybernetic libertarianism". The eventual shape of globalization will reflect the play of these diverse perspectives and priorities. The perspectives and priorities of globalization-from-above are being challenged in various ways, but mainly piecemeal. The effort of the final section is to encourage a mobilization of the now disparate forces of globalization-from-below in the direction of greater solidity and political weight. It is my conviction that such mobilization is most likely to occur beneath the banner of democracy, but democracy reformulated in relation to the basic aspirations of peoples everywhere to participate in the processes that are shaping their lives.

The purpose of the next section is mainly to clarify what is meant by "democracy" in relation to the analysis of globalization.

Toward coherence: the theory and practice of normative democracy

To introduce the idea of "normative democracy" is to offer a proposal for a unifying ideology capable of mobilizing and unifying the disparate social forces that constitute global civil society, and provide the political energy that is associated with globalization-from-below. The specification of normative democracy is influenced strongly by David Held's work on democratic theory and practice, particularly his formulations of "cosmopolitan democracy", but it offers a slightly different terminology so as to emphasize the agency role of global civil society with its range of engagements that go from the local and grassroots to the most encompassing arenas of decision (Archibugi *et al.*, 1995; Held, 1995). Normative democracy also draws upon Walden Bello's call for "substantive democracy", set forth as a more progressive movement alternative to the more limited embrace of constitutional democracy

(Bello, 1997). I prefer normative to substantive democracy because of its highlighting of ethical and legal norms, thereby reconnecting politics with moral purpose and values, which calls attention to the moral emptiness of neo-liberalism, consumerism and most forms of secularism. There is also a practical reason: to weaken the political appeal of resurgent organized religion while at the same time acknowledging the relevance of moral purpose and spiritual concerns to the renewal of progressive politics.

Contrary to widespread claims in the West, there is no empirical basis for the argument that economic performance is necessarily tied to constitutional democracy and human rights. Several countries in the Asia/Pacific region, most significantly China, have combined an outstanding macroeconomic record with harsh authoritarian rule. Globalization-from-above is not an assured vehicle for the achievement of Western style constitutional democracy, including the protection of individual and group rights. But democracy, as such, is of the essence of a meaningful form of political action on the part of global civil society, especially to the extent that such action even when revolutionary refrains from and repudiates violent means. In this regard, there is an emergent, as yet implicit, convergence of ends and means on the part of several distinct tendencies in civil society issue-oriented movements; non-violent democracy movements; governments that minimize their links to geopolitical structures. This convergence presents several intriguing opportunities for coalition-building, and greater ideological coherence in the outlook associated with globalization-from-below. Against this background, normative democracy seems like an attractive umbrella for theorizing, not dogmatically, but to exhibit affinities.

Normative democracy adopts comprehensive views of fundamental ideas associated with the secular modern state: security is conceived as extending to environmental protection and to the defense of economic viability (e.g. Mahathir complains about George Soros' financial speculations as jeopardizing Malaysian development successes; *Turkish Daily News*, 1997); human rights are conceived as extending to social and economic rights, as well as to such collective rights as the right to development, the right to peace, the right of self-determination; democracy is conceived as extending beyond constitutional and free, periodic elections to include an array of other assurances that governance is oriented toward human well-being and ecological sustainability, and that citizens have access to arenas of decision.

The elements of normative democracy can be enumerated, but their content and behavioral applications will require much amplification in varied specific settings. This enumeration reflects the dominant orientations and outlook of the political actors that make up the constructivist category of "globalization-from-below". It is thus not an enumeration that is a wishlist, but intends to be descriptive and explanatory of an embedded consensus. The elements of this consensus are as follows:

1　Consent of citizenry: some periodic indication that the permanent population of the relevant community is represented by the institutions of governance, and confers legitimacy through the expression of consent. Elections are the established modalities for territorial communities to confer legitimacy on government, but referenda and rights of petition and recall may be more appropriate for other types of political community, especially those of regional or global scope, while direct democracy may be most meaningful for local political activity; the idea is to be flexible and adaptive.

2　Rule of law: all modes of governance subject to the discipline of law as a way of imposing effective limits on authority and of assuring some form of checks and balances as between legislative, executive, judicial and administrative processes; also, sensitivity to the normative claims of civil initiatives associated with codes of conduct, conference declarations, societal institutions (for instance, Permanent Peoples Tribunal in Rome).

3   Human rights: taking account of differing cultural, economic and political settings and priorities, the establishment of mechanisms for the impartial and effective implementation of human rights deriving from global, regional, state and transnational civil sources of authority; human rights are comprehensively conceived as encompassing economic, social and cultural rights, as well as civil and political rights, with a concern for both individual and collective conceptions of rights, emphasizing tolerance toward difference and fundamental community sentiments.

4   Participation: effective and meaningful modes of participation in the political life of the society, centered upon the processes of government, but extending to all forms of social governance, including workplace and home; participation may be direct or indirect, that is, representational, but it enables the expression of views and influence upon the processes of decision on the basis of an ideal of equality of access; creativity is needed to find methods other than elections by which to ensure progress toward full participation.

5   Accountability: suitable mechanisms for challenging the exercise of authority by those occupying official positions at the level of the state, but also with respect to the functioning of the market and of international institutions; the ideal of an international criminal court is one mechanism for assuring accountability by those in powerful positions that have been traditionally treated as exempt from the Rule of Law.

6   Public goods: a restored social agenda that corrects the growing imbalance, varying in seriousness from country to country, between private and public goods in relation to the persistence of poverty amid affluence, pertaining to health, education, housing and basic human needs, but also in relation to support for environmental protection, regulation of economic globalization, innovative cultural activity, infrastructural development for governance at the regional and global levels. In these regards, a gradual depoliticalization of funding either by reliance on a use or transaction tax imposed on financial flows, global air travel, or some form of reliable and equitable means to fund public goods of local, national, regional, and global scope.

7   Transparency: an openness with respect to knowledge and information that builds trust between institutions of governance and the citizenry at various levels of social interaction, in effect, establishing the right to know as an aspect of constitutionalism, including a strong bias against public sector secrecy and covert operations, and criminalizes government lies of the sort recently revealed where for years to protect air force spy missions the CIA lied about alleged "UFO sightings"; internationally, transparency is particularly important in relation to military expenditures and arms transfers.

8   Non-violence: underpinning globalization-from-below and the promotion of substantive democracy is a conditional commitment to non-violent politics and conflict resolution. Such a commitment does not nullify rights of self-defense as protected in international law, strictly and narrowly construed, nor does it necessarily invalidate limited recourse to violence by oppressed peoples; such an ethos of non-violence clearly imposes on governments an obligation to renounce weaponry of mass destruction and the negotiation of phased disarmament arrangements, but also maximum commitments to demilitarizing approaches to peace and security at all levels of social interaction, including peace and security at the level of city and neighborhood; such commitments suggest the rejection of capital punishment as an option of government.

Globalization-from-below and the state: a decisive battle

Without entering into detailed discussion, it seems that different versions of neo-liberal ideology have exerted a defining influence upon the orientation of political élites governing sovereign states. Of course, there are many variations reflecting conditions and personalities in each particular state and region, but the generalization holds without important exception (Sakamoto, 1994; Falk, 1997b). Even China, despite adherence to the ideology of state socialism, has implemented by state decree, with impressive results, a market-oriented approach to economic policy. The state can remain authoritarian in relation to its citizenry without necessarily jeopardizing its economic performance so long as it adheres, more or less, to the discipline of global capital, thereby achieving competitiveness by reference to costs of production, savings and attraction of capital. In these respects, neo-liberalism as a *global* ideology is purely economistic in character, and does not imply a commitment to democratic governance in even the minimal sense of periodic fair elections.

Globalization-from-below, in addition to a multitude of local struggles, is also a vehicle for the transnational promotion of substantive democracy as a counterweight to neo-liberalism. It provides an alternative, or series of convergent alternatives, that has not yet been posited as a coherent body of theory and practice, but remains the inarticulate common ground of emergent global civil society. Substantive democracy, unlike backlash politics that closes off borders and identities, seeks a politics of reconciliation that maintains much of the openness and dynamism associated with globalization-from-above, while countering its pressures to privatize and marketize the production of public goods. In effect, the quest of substantive democracy is to establish a social equilibrium that takes full account of the realities of globalization in its various aspects. Such a process cannot succeed on a country-by-country basis as the rollback of welfare in Scandinavia suggests, but must proceed within regional and global settings. The state remains the instrument of policy and decision most affecting the lives of peoples, and the primary link to regional and global institutions. The state has been instrumentalized to a considerable degree by the ideology and influences associated with globalization-from-above, resulting in declining support for public goods in an atmosphere of strong sustained economic growth and in polarization of results with incredible wealth for the winners and acute suffering for the losers. An immediate goal of those disparate social forces that constitute globalization-from-below is to reinstrumentalize the state to the extent that it redefines its role as mediating between the logic of capital and the priorities of its peoples, including their short-term and longer term goals.

Evidence of this instrumentalization of the state is present in relation to global conferences on broad policy issues that had been organized under UN auspices, and were making an impact on public consciousness and behavioral standards in the 1990s. These UN conferences increasingly attracted an array of social forces associated with global civil society, and gave rise to a variety of coalitions and oppositions between state, market and militant citizens organized to promote substantive goals (e.g. human rights, environmental protection, economic equity and development). These UN conferences became arenas of political participation that were operating outside the confines of state control, and were regarded as threatening by the established order based on a core coalition between market forces and geopolitical leaders. One effect is to withdraw support for such UN activities, pushing the organization to the sidelines on global policy issues as part of a process of recovering control over its agenda and orientation. Such a reaction represents a setback for globalization-from-below, but it also shows that the social forces that are associated with the promotion of normative democracy can be formidable adversaries.

Such a process of reinstrumentalization could also influence the future role and identity of regional and global mechanisms of governance, especially to the extent of increasing the regulatory mandate directed toward market forces and the normative mandate with respect to the protection of the global commons, the promotion of demilitarization and the overall support for public good.

Conclusion

In this paper it is argued that the positive prospects for global civil society depend very much on two interrelated developments: achieving consensus on "normative democracy" as the foundation of coherent theory and practice, and waging a struggle for the outlook and orientation of institutions of governance with respect to the framing of globalization. The state remains the critical focus of this latter struggle, although it is not, even now, a matter of intrinsic opposition between the state as instrument of globalization-from-above and social movements as instrument of globalization-from-below. In many specific settings, coalitions between states and social movements are emergent, as is evident in relation to many questions of environment, development and human rights. It may even come to pass that transnational corporations and banks adopt a longer term view of their own interests, and move to alter the policy content of globalization-from-above to soften the contrast with the preferences of globalization-from-below. It is helpful to remember that such an unanticipated convergence of previously opposed social forces led to the sort of consensus that produced "social democracy" and "the welfare state" over the course of the 19th and 20th centuries. There is evident reason to preclude such convergencies on regional and global levels as a way of resolving some of the tensions being caused by the manner in which globalization is *currently* being enacted.

References

Archibugi, D. and Held, D. (eds) (1995) *Cosmopolitan Democracy: An Agenda for a New World Order* (Cambridge, Polity).

Bello, W. (1977) Talk at Bangkok Conference on Alternative Security Systems in the Asia-Pacific, *Focus Asia*, March, pp. 27–30.

Bull, H. (1977) *The Anarchical Society: A Study of Order in World Politics* (New York, Columbia University Press).

Clark, I. (1997) *Globalization and Fragmentation: International Relations in the Twentieth Century* (Oxford, Oxford University Press).

Commission on Global Governance (eds) (1995) *Our Global Neighbourhood* (Oxford, Oxford University Press).

Falk, R. (1993) The making of global citizenship, in J. Brecher, J. B. Childs and J. Cutler (eds) *Global Visions: Beyond the New World Order* (Boston, MA, South End Press).

Falk, R. (1995) *On Humane Governance: Toward a New Global Politics* (Cambridge, Polity).

Falk, R. (1996) An inquiry into the political economy of world order, *New Political Economy*, 1, pp. 13–26.

Falk, R. (1997a) Resisting "Globalization-from-above" through "Globalisation-from-below", *New Political Economy*, 2, pp. 17–24.

Falk, R. (1997b) State of siege: will globalization win out?, *International Affairs*, 73, pp. 123–136.

Fukuyama, F. (1992) *The End of History and the Last Man* (New York, Free Press).

Goldsmith, E., Allen, R., Allaby, M., Davoll, J. and Laurence, S. (1972) *Blueprint for Survival* (Boston, MA, Houghton Mifflin).

Held, D. (1995) *Democracy and the Global Order: From the Modern State to Cosmopolitan Governance* (Cambridge, Polity).

Hirst, P. and Thompson, G. (1996) *Globalization in Question* (Cambridge, Polity).

Lipschutz, R. D. (1996) *Global Civil Society and Global Environmental Governance* (Albany, NY, State University of New York Press).

Turkish Daily News (1997) Malaysia PM Mulls Action Against Speculators, 29 July.

Meadows, D. H., Meadows, D. L. and Randers, J. (1972) *The Limits to Growth* (New York, Universe Books).

Nerfin, M. (1986) Neither prince nor merchant: citizen – an introduction to the third system, *IFDA Dossier 56*, Nov./Dec., pp. 3–29.

Rich, B. (1994) *Mortgaging the Earth: The World Bank Environmental Impoverishment and the Crisis of Development* (Boston, MA, Beacon Press).

Rosenau, J. N. (1990) *Turbulence in World Politics: A Theory of Change and Continuity* (Princeton, NJ, Princeton University Press).

Sachs, J. (1997) New members please apply, *TIME*, 7 July, pp. 11–12.

Sakamoto, Y. (ed.) (1994) *Global Transformation: Challenges to the State System* (Tokyo, United Nations University Press).

Shiva, V. (eds) (1987) People's ecology: the Chipko movement, in R. B. J. Walker and S. H. Mendlovitz *Towards a Just World Peace: Perspectives from Social Movements* (London, Butterworths).

Wapner, P. (1996) The social construction of global governance, *American Political Science Association Annual Meeting*, 28–31 August.

12 Social movements/world politics

R. B. J. Walker

Source: R. B. J. Walker (1994), 'Social Movements/World Politics',
Millennium: Journal of International Studies, 23: 3, pp. 669–700

Discursive economies of scale

To place the two terms 'social movements' and 'world politics' into conjunction is to invite serious conceptual trouble. On the face of it, the elusive transience of the one is no match for the monolithic presence of the other, fables of David and Goliath notwithstanding. Two initial considerations are especially important in this respect.

To begin with, there are the apparently obvious disparities of scale. Judged from the regal heights of statecraft, social movements are but mosquitos on the evening breeze, irritants to those who claim maturity and legitimacy at the centres of political life. Some mosquitos, of course, can have deadly effects. Some movements, it can be claimed, have had tremendous impact on states, societies, economies and cultures. But even large movements are difficult to take seriously once compared to the might and reach of a properly world politics. Whatever world politics is taken to be, it is difficult to imagine it as somehow smaller or weaker than those ephemeral groups of people struggling for this and that in particular places. Little David's big victory only serves to confirm the general expectation of inevitable victories by giants, by the big fish who supposedly feed on small fish. Despite occasional claims that small is beautiful, miniaturisation profitable, the explosion of little atoms traumatic, or the predations of guerilla bands frustratingly effective, greater size is difficult to dissociate from images of strength, virility, and importance. Contemporary political life still draws on discursive economies of scale that inform our understanding of what and where power is. These economies, these productions, reproductions and distributions across the multiple sites of modern political life, still largely determine the contours of contemporary political judgement, still constrain our capacity to distinguish the significant from the insignificant, and even the political from the apolitical. The analysis of social movements is especially susceptible to the illusion that bigger is always better.

More crucially, difficulties arise from the apparent disjunction between the realms in which social movements and world politics are usually said to exist. Whether as a simple synonym for 'international relations' or as a label affixed to some more complex array of forces, 'world politics' seems to refer not only to some grand – and therefore presumably determining – structure, but more significantly to things going on 'out there', to processes that occur in realms somewhere 'beyond' society. Social movements are supposed to be precisely *social* movements, phenomena that occur within a society; and societies in turn, the conventions insist, can only exist within those political structures that allegedly make them possible, namely the state and the states system. Social movements and world politics are supposed to be understood as expressions of two distinct ontological realms, the inner and the outer. Moreover, even within the inner realm of society, social movements are, to the modern political imagination, most easily fixed within a sphere of social life that is distinguished from and even counterposed to the sphere of politics – within the so-called civil society that has been so carefully, though problematically, distinguished from the explicitly political affairs of the modern state. To make contact, social movements and world politics require some kind of mediating agent. First, the social has to find some expression within the explicitly political practices of the state. Then the state has to mediate with other states. To show how social movements might be relevant to the emergence of some kind of world politics is therefore to confront the double exclusion that is sustained by the prevailing codes of modern political discourse. Or rather, it is to confront the double exclusion that is sustained by one specific reading of those codes, the one that affirms the priority of the principle of state sovereignty over all other claims to political possibility.

The ontological disjunction between what goes on inside and what goes on outside the modern state that is so crucial to a statist reading of modern politics makes the apparent incongruity of scale between social movements and world politics even more compelling. The merely domestic must obviously submit before the demands of the international or global. Moreover, both the incongruity and the disjunction are affirmed in what is arguably the most profound, but only sporadically acknowledged, reification of modern political discourse: the seemingly innocuous classification of all ontological possibilities that has found its dim and epiphenomenal expression among modern theorists of international relations as the so-called 'levels of analysis' schema.[1] It is striking that much if not most of modern social and political analysis can be understood as an exercise in classification of some kind, and yet the literature on the practices of classification is, to say the least, rather spartan.[2] The scarcity of literature commenting on what is achieved by taking this particular classification for granted is especially telling. As an expression of the inbred common sense of modern political discourse, this schema hides most of its ontological significance under a chaste appeal for analytical clarity and explanatory parsimony. Yet categories that manage to frame an account of the horizontal territorialities of the modern state as a hierarchical arrangement of inclusions and exclusions are neither modest nor simply analytical in their accomplishments, and parsimony often comes at the high cost of conceptual oversimplification and ideological conceit.

Freezing the contingent and horizontal relations between territorial states into a natural hierarchy, the levels of analysis schema affirms the eternal legitimacy of the modern state. The dangerous line between inside and outside is turned into a series of apparently secure distinctions between above and below, big and small, universalising and particularising, strong and weak. A merely contingent point of transitions, transgressions, comings and goings is rendered as an ontological absolute. As a specifically *modern* reconciliation between the old theological categories of heaven and earth and the secular categories of here and there or self and other, this classification is both aesthetically elegant and rhetorically persuasive. As a specifically *liberal* account of a world of individuals, states and anarchies, it renders all other political categories – of class, race, gender, capitalism, modernity, and so on – entirely superfluous. As in many other contexts, the theorists of international relations deserve credit for making explicit what the political theorists have usually assumed but rarely spoken or even acknowledged. They deserve much less credit for affirming the assumptions of the political theorists as the way things are and must be.

The categorial expression of an historically entrenched common sense provides a dubious ground on which to pitch the tents of empirical method. Accounts of political life, within states or between them, that take the ontological densities of this classification for granted are explicitly normative and explicitly ideological. They affirm a specifically modern articulation of spatiotemporal relations and a specifically liberal account of political identity. The modern self-identical subject is assigned its proper place in the universe and told what its fate must be. Framed in this context especially, the conjunction of social movements with world politics offers a clear case of ontological impossibility. Small cannot compete with large, and lower/inner cannot impinge on higher/outer. On both grounds, social movements and world politics can have only the most tenuous of connections. This sense of disjunction is produced, reproduced and exchanged throughout the political discourses of modern societies. Consequently, it is usually very difficult to see how things are, once were, or still could be otherwise.

Even so, the obvious judgement informed by this discursive economy begs two rather important questions. These questions have become more pressing as evidence accumulates that the world is not – and perhaps has never been – the way modern translations of spatial exclusions into hierarchical necessities suggest it must be.

One question concerns the assumed scale on which disparities of size and power can be measured, for it is not clear that political life has yet been completely organised in relation to some universal standard of measurement in the way that most economists believe it possible to use money as the universal arbitration of all differences. Political life tends to thrive on contradictions, contingencies and unintended consequences. Things are rarely quite what they seem to be, let alone what they are supposed to be. The mysteries of power and authority have not yet been revealed either from on high or by the instrumental calculus of collective choice. Abundant traces of this insight can be found in many of the classic texts of international relations theory, but it is an insight that has been largely occluded by the prior assumption that contingency and determination can be reconciled at the boundaries or inner and outer or lower and higher. Even the most 'Machiavellian' of 'political realists' have found it difficult to resist the great divides between truth and illusion or time and eternity that are so elegantly but firmly inscribed on the spatial boundaries of the modern state.

The other question concerns the ontological categories through which disparities of scale are represented as expressions of different realms of political life. The juxtaposition of claims about social movements with claims about world politics invites serious conceptual trouble in that the obvious way of framing their relationship rests upon prior categories of analysis, and prior conceptions of what and where politics must be, that are arguably being challenged both by processes that are usually described as world politics and by some of the explicit practices evoked under the label of social movements. Even on a superficial glance, the practices of social movements do not always conform to the codes of inner and outer, to the account of spatiotemporal relations that informs the normative horizons of modern politics. Indeed, they would hardly be very interesting if they did.

If social movements are to be taken seriously in relation to claims about world politics, at least some attention will have to be paid to ways in which they do, or do not, challenge the constitutive practices of modern politics. It is futile to try to gauge the importance of social movements without considering the possibility that it is precisely the criteria of significance by which they are to be judged that may be in contention. The criteria that seem to me to be especially significant in this context concern the extent to which *some* social movements, in *some* situations, implicitly or explicitly challenge the normative/ideological order reified by the levels of analysis schema and its constitutive modern articulation of spatiotemporal relations, both as the way things are and as the way things must and should be. This is not least because whatever they are, and what they are is far from clear to anyone, social movements are usually designated precisely as social *movements*, as phenomena that are explicitly at odds with the spatial framing of all ontological possibilities, of greater and lesser, higher and lower, inner and outer, that have made it so difficult to envisage any form of politics other than that associated with the modern state and its self-identical subjects.[3]

Yet if the discursive economies of scale and disparities between inner and outer imply serious conceptual trouble for any attempt to place 'social movements' and 'world politics' into conjunction, there always seem to be other – more cosmopolitan or universalist – readings of the codes of modern politics waiting to suggest an easy way out. The Stoics and Immanuel Kant are often invoked in this context, despite the extent to which Stoic and Kantian philosophies have either been appropriated by (in the case of the former) or explicitly framed in relation to (in the case of the latter) the particularistic discourses of the modern state. More generally, it is possible to appeal to some supposedly already existing world politics or universal ethics, as if the grungy skin of modern statist politics can be cast off to reveal some essential or potential humanity beneath. Such appeals are scattered freely in the contemporary literature.[4] Social movements can then be read as agents of this revelation, and world politics can be read as the communion of the humanity thus revealed. More interestingly, perhaps, it is possible to appeal to a rather less abstract and apparently more politically engaged account of an emerging global civil society. Indeed, much of the recent literature attempting to make sense of social movements/world politics has begun to draw quite heavily on the notion of a global civil society, not least so as to avoid falling back on some pre-political or even antipolitical claim about an already existing ethics or world politics through which social movements can act without confronting the limits of modern politics in the modern state.

Yet, I will suggest, the notion of a global civil society, though often suggestive, and though offering an apparently easy but still politically engaged way out of the impasse of modern statist discourse, is the site of some especially serious conceptual trouble. Many of the difficulties of analysing social movements in relation to world politics arise less from the categories of inclusion and exclusion that insist that the task is impossible in principle than from readings of those same categories that make the conjunction between them seem so easy and even entirely unproblematic. Claims about an emerging global civil society, I will argue, usually reveal the reproductive powers of statist discourse more than they do the capacity of social movements to challenge that discourse.

I will develop this argument, first, by making a few brief comments about the analysis of social movements in general; second, by emphasising a crucial and exemplary contradiction expressed in the neo-Habermasian account of social movements offered by Jean Cohen and Andrew Arato; third, by shifting attention to some related puzzles posed by one social movement currently active in parts of India; fourth by trying, and largely failing, to find an entry into the political practices of social movements in some of the recent literature in international relations that begins with some kind of counter-sovereignty discourse, especially in relation to claims about a global civil society; and fifth, by insisting that it is because social movements are precisely *movements*, and because they do not always conform to the prevailing discourses of sovereignty or a simple counter-sovereignty, that they can be read as interesting forms of *political* practice.

What is at stake here, I believe, is the need to recast questions that are conventionally posed in the analysis of social movements in a manner that does not automatically reproduce the expectations of modern statist discourse. Considerable empirical research needs to be done in this field, but it is unlikely to add very much to our existing knowledge without a more sustained interrogation of the theoretical assumptions that inform the procedures of empirical enquiry in this context. The following comments are thus intended to explore the possibility of understanding the conjunction of social movements and world politics without mimicking the usual statist critiques of the modern state or lapsing into a romantic strategy of 'listening to the movements'. The conjunction of social movements and world politics is interesting for my purposes here for what it tells us about the conditions under which we are now able, or unable, to engage in an analysis of world politics. The conclusion to which I am drawn is that it is less interesting to ask how powerful or influential social movements are, or how they fulfil established expectations of what they must be and must become, than how they contribute to the reconfiguration of the political under contemporary conditions.

Merely social, always moving

Most of the literature suggesting that a conjunction between social movements and world politics might be a serious focus for research and analysis tends towards description and affirmation rather than theoretical elaboration. There are many social movements that act across established political boundaries, it is often suggested, and their significance in relation to some of the crucial issues of contemporary politics is frequently affirmed. Think of any of the grand issues of our time, of peace, environment, gender, development, or identity, and the depiction of some kind of social movement seems to follow automatically. Think of who or what is being affirmed as the relevant political subject, and the citizens of particular states are not the only possibility that come to mind.

To act in relation to 'the environment', for example, is to act explicitly in the name of allegedly 'natural' forces and interests that refuse to acknowledge the merely historical boundaries of states; nevertheless, exactly what it means to speak of the environment, or act in the name of nature, or how the relationship between the supposedly natural and the supposedly historical should now be mediated, or who has the authority to act in the name of rainforests and dolphins, is more difficult to specify. To speak in the name of 'women', or to complain about the constitution and dangers of 'masculinity', is again to refer to identities claimed across territorial boundaries, to speak against the convergence of gendered privilege and sovereign authorities; yet what it means to speak on behalf of all women, or even what it means to invoke any unitary identity around the category of gender, are matters of considerable complexity and dispute. Similarly, to speak of 'peace' or 'development' is presumably to be sceptical of the binary inscriptions of peace and war or developed and developing upon the territorial delineations of us and them; yet the meanings of peace or development certainly do not become any clearer with the recognition that violence and injustices legitimised through the reification of others as Other are intolerable. To suggest that the modern categories of citizen and subject cannot possibly exhaust the dynamics of contemporary identity politics does little to indicate how identities are now being reconstituted or how they might enter into forms of political life that do not gamble everything in the casinos of the modern state. To suggest that rights inhere in something that is somehow 'human', or that capitalism is becoming organised globally rather than internationally, is perhaps to recognise the limits of statist modes of reconciling all contradictions; but these suggestions say relatively little about what it might mean to refer to the human or the global given the continuing hold of modern citizenship and modern subjectivities on the contemporary political imagination. Like it or not, modern political discourse still largely equates all political identities, whether of class, race, gender, religion, humanity or planet, with citizenship, with the fusion of universality and particularity in the legitimate authority of the sovereign state. The account of political necessity expressed as a typology of levels is neither arbitrary nor a mere methodological convenience. Its normative and ideological roots are very firmly entrenched.

That many forms of contemporary political practice appeal to and act on the basis of forms of identity and solidarity that are not constrained by statist territorialities is hardly controversial. The migration of birds, the flows of capital, the solidarities of women, and the streets of Miami, Los Angeles and Leicester all offer compelling images that are often sharply at odds with the official story. The precise significance of what it means to act across established political boundaries, on the other hand, most certainly is controversial. Contemporary political life is increasingly strung between two narratives that have both achieved the status of the obvious and banal. One, the official story, affirms the territorial state as the only place in which meaningful political life can occur. The other, usually framed as a universalising negation of the official story, affirms the relative triviality of the state in relation to the flows of technology, imagery, values and people. Each narrative has spawned considerable literature that are more or less oblivious of the other. When these narratives do come into collision, under the banner of an international political economy, for example, doctrinal heat often overwhelms theoretical light. In any case, and perhaps understandably, the difficulties of rethinking the *political* in this context have taken a back seat to attempts to make sense of rearticulations of the *economic*.[5] Not surprisingly, the criteria upon which the significance or insignificance of political practices that cross borders are to be judged are widely understood to be sharply contested. Description is one thing, but coming to terms with the theoretical problems posed by such descriptions is quite another.

Even literature that do seek to develop sophisticated analyses of social movements find it easier to pose questions about criteria of significance in relation to claims about the novelty or otherwise of the so-called 'new social movements', than about the tendency for some kinds of movement to spill out of the official boundaries of political life. To speak about the 'new' social movements is at least to do so in relation to presumptions about what the 'old' ones were like. It is to measure their achievements against other familiar political practices and institutions. There may well be considerable uncertainty about how a movement is to be distinguished from an interest group or political party. There may be ongoing disputes, for example, about the continuities and discontinuities to be discerned between, on the one hand, the movements of women, environmentalists, peace activists and so on that began to emerge in the wealthier parts of the world about thirty years ago and, on the other, the paradigms associated with the labour movements of an earlier era. There may even be a growing consensus that those new social movements have succumbed to cooptation, degenerated into special interest groups among the most privileged. But at least there is some kind of (idealised) analytical base from which to evaluate similarity and difference, continuity or discontinuity, radical potential or cynical capitulation. According to the established conventions, social movements have had a profound effect only by mutating into something else: into *mass* movements, coalitions, organised institutions of interest articulation, revitalisation of the institutions of civil society, or political parties capable of taking on maturity and legitimacy where it really counts, in relation to the state.

There are other, perhaps more serious problems provoked by the notoriously slippery game of evaluating the significance of social movements in contemporary political life. To begin with, movements are precisely *movements*. They will not stand still. Look carefully, be wary of the tendency to reify human energies into inert institutions, and movements proliferate. Look more carefully still and everything moves. What, the frustrated sceptic might ask, is not a social movement? They come and go, rise and decline, provoke a fuss and wither on the vine. They take the familiar path from charisma to regularised routine, from inventiveness and passion to bureaucracy, hierarchy and instrumental reason. Or, alternatively, they fracture, mutate, dissipate, gather no moss. To be in motion is to be at odds with many of the criteria on which serious politics has come to be judged. Like rivers that cannot be stepped into twice, social *movements* cannot be pinned down, cannot keep their powers in place. According to those stereotypes that are captured so effectively in Weber's typology of legitimate authority, the authenticity, energy and dynamism of movements in the making *must* give way to institutions that take root in the structures of society. Movements that *remain* movements may register protest, mobilise resources, articulate interests and identities, but cannot become really serious or important. They must remain, according to categories that still retain their capacity to mesmerise, merely social and not political. The discursive economy of scale is matched by a discursive economy of relative movement in which a premium is assigned to stasis and longevity. As the canonical traditions of modern political theory have kept insisting, a serious politics requires that temporality and movement must be tamed upon the certain ground of spatial form. As Warren Magnusson's analysis reminds us, for example, it now takes considerable effort to recapture Marx's account of capitalism as a movement.[6] In political analysis, it is almost impossible to think except in terms set by Hobbes' paradigmatically frozen architectures.

It is thus not surprising that so much of the literature on social movements is caught in a definitional vortex. To seek a definition of a social movement, let alone a judgement as to whether any particular movement is progressive or emancipatory, is to work along the slippery edges of prevailing political categories, to demand clear distinctions where the social and the political, the transitory and the static, the particular and the general cling together as well as slide asunder.

Nor is it surprising that the study of social movements has remained largely the preserve of sociologists rather than students of politics. This is a division of labour that cuts both ways. Sociologists have undoubtedly offered the richest descriptive and even theoretical analyses of social movements.[7] They have to some extent evaded the narrow readings of what counts as political practice prevalent among students of politics and international relations. But this has not often translated into accounts of social movements precisely as challenges to established accounts of where and what politics must be. On the one hand, the singular statist community often remains the tacit ground on which the advantages of, say, resource mobilisation or identity articulation theories are developed. On the other, attempts to understand social movements in relation to a broader world system of historical capitalism have more to say about such movements in relation to universalising categories of class than to categories of political life constituted in relation to the legitimate authority of sovereign states.[8]

Both the definitional vortex and the tendency in much of the literature to either tacitly and uncritically assume the presence of the singular state or subordinate the state to the constitutive monologic of global capitalism are symptomatic of the difficulty of thinking about politics on other than statist terms. The sociologists are certainly right in thinking that statist categories offer only limited assistance in understanding many social movements, or that the politics of the modern state must to some extent be framed in relation to the historical and structural dynamics of a universalising capitalism. But whatever the global articulations of capitalist economies, it is the state that has captured and reproduced a particularistic account of political possibility, an account that cannot simply be shed like a tattered overcoat, no matter how threadbare the discourses of the modern state have become.

This is precisely why claims about the importance of some kinds of movements in relation to structures and practices that exceed the limits of the official political boundaries must be taken seriously. Such movements may, or may not, be successful on their own terms. They may, or may not, influence states, international organisations, policies, programmes, levels of violence or forms of injustice in particular places. They may, or may not, be judged to be powerful or influential in relation to the established understandings of power and influence. But there is a reason why those who affirm the significance of such movements are wary of theoretical exploration, and why those who invoke theory tend to shy away from a direct encounter with the international or global dimensions of so many social movements. This reason is simply that once one crosses the official boundaries of the established conceptions of politics, the boundaries of the modern state, it becomes very difficult to speak about any kind of politics at all. In the end, it must be the capacity of some social movements to speak to the poverty of the contemporary political imagination that gives them significance beyond their immediate demands, achievements, and even failures.

[...]

Immanent revivals

There are obvious, though still curiously neglected dangers in taking the experiences of those social movements that have recently been thriving in modern European and North American societies as paradigmatic of all social movements. As analysts of international relations/world politics ought to recognise more clearly than most, Europe and North America are not the world, and the experiences of the so-called new social movements or attempts to revitalise the civil societies of modern states do not always translate easily into accounts of what are taken to be social movements elsewhere. To the difficulties of being mis-led by inappropriate discourses of scale, level, relative movement and the relation between the social and the political, it is necessary to add the danger of insensitivity to the diversity of experiences and practices that could plausibly depict the contemporary convergence between social movements and world politics.

Consider, as only one example, a reading of a movement in western India that has recently drawn the attention of scholars concerned with the possibilities of what is still called 'development' in what used to be called the Third World. It is an example that poses many of the same problems associated with Habermasian readings of the 'new social movements', though in perhaps an even sharper manner. Though in no way to be considered a typical example of movements in this context, especially given the continuing hold of nationalist projects in so many places, it does place the question of the cultural and situational speci-ficity of social movements, and the claims of universality they inspire, into rather bold relief.

The *Swadhyaya* movement has a substantial and rapidly growing presence in hundreds of fishing and farming communities of the states of Gujarat and Maharashtra, especially, but also in the city of Bombay. Although active for about forty years, it has neither sought nor received much publicity. And although it has yet to receive much in the way of sustained scholarly analysis, it has certainly caught the attention of many of India's leading students of development movements in general, some of whom regard it as the most interesting social movement to have emerged in the country since independence.[9] On the ground, it is difficult to ignore either the scale or the effectiveness of its achievements. Conservative esti-mates suggest that active participants in the movement number several hundred thousand, and that they have had a major impact on well over one million and perhaps up to four mil-lion people. By the standards of most development movements, and indeed by any standard one would want to apply to attempts to improve the life circumstances of poor peasant and fishing societies, the *Swadhyaya* have been able to transform the social, cultural, economic and – crucially – the spiritual life of communities in ways that attract enormous admiration from observers who come into contact with them. In its present phase, at least, this movement presents an uplifting success story, though the precise reasons for its success are not always easy to unravel.

It is especially difficult to separate the more practical aspects of its success – the revitalisation of communities, the adoption of appropriate technologies, the sharp decline in domestic violence, and so on – from the fact that this is essentially a spiritual movement; one of a familiar cycle of Hindu revival movements, perhaps, but certainly one that presents a sharp contrast with the secular movements that have become so paradigmatic in other contexts. It has been generated largely through a highly creative reworking of spiritual (Vedic) traditions that have very deep roots in the region. Even though the movement is characterised by an extensively articulated political economy that marks it off from most other Hindu revival movements, or even from the Gandhian movements that arose out of the same general region, it is a movement that is probably unimaginable in purely secular terms. Moreover, this is a movement (the terms 'family' and 'stream' are preferred) that is rooted in a specifically immanent account of divinity. God is assumed to be within us and with us all. Notions of the brotherhood of man notwithstanding, it is an account that is not going to find an immediate resonance with cultures informed by theologies of transcendence, whether Christian or Islamic, let alone with cultures that affirm themselves against theologies of any kind.

The term *swadhyaya* refers to self-knowledge, and the central characteristic of this movement is that its practices are grounded in the cultivation of self-respect. This self is construed as potentially open to 'higher' values, to action informed by the laws of *dharma*. The achievement of self-respect is in turn assumed to generate a sense of command over one's destiny, a sense of justice in a larger order, and thus a sense of participation in a broader community. This notion of self within an immanent cosmic order provides the primary basis for an extensive practical programme of community building rooted in a 'divine brotherhood'. The rule of *dharma*, for example, has been recast as the notion of one's 'efficiency', of the skills and potentials that can be contributed to the common good of the community for so many days a year (the two days in every lunar month conventionally reserved for devotion, but now directed to helping others to realise their divine but untapped capacities). This notion of efficiency has in turn been extended into an account of 'impersonal wealth', wealth that is not quite collective in the sense of the familiar traditions of secular socialism but in the sense of being devoted to the God who is in us all.

A proper consideration of a movement like this would require a more extensive elaboration than is possible here, but a number of themes are especially pertinent in the present context. On the one hand, it is possible to compare *Swadhyaya* with other development movements elsewhere and to conclude that it affirms many of the patterns that are often said to characterise such movements. On the other, many of the characteristics of this movement are so specific to its locale, and especially to its roots in Vedic cosmologies, that the possibilities of comparative generalisation, let alone claims about universalisation, are bound to be highly contentious.

The possibilities of comparison are especially apparent if one thinks about the kinds of problems a sizable movement like this is likely to experience as it gets bigger. As a grassroots movement, for example, one whose energies are most dynamic within the rural communities of Gujarat, one would expect it eventually to become attracted to a different kind of 'efficiency', to the instrumental reason of modern 'systems'. This is especially so insofar as much of the recent energy in the movement has been directed by activists among the ex-patriot communities in North America and Europe (among the large Gujarati community in Leicester, for example), most of whom are quite successful businessmen. The attractions of grassroots movements in the villages back home are presumably considerable, and for many reasons, but the principles of organisation on the scale encompassed by a growing international network of affluent activists are at the very least going to be in some tension with those which have become so effective in the villages. A sense of 'efficiency' derived from the law of *dharma* is not easily reconciled with a sense of efficiency derived from the principles of instrumental reason and the supposedly immutable laws of bureaucracy, though it may well be that the capacity to effect such a reconciliation could turn out to be one of this movement's greater achievements.

Similarly, one would expect problems to arise from the transition from the charismatic authority of the movement's founder – Pandurang Shastri Athavale, also known as *Dadaji* or elder brother – to a more routinised form of organisation, from the teachings of the *guru* to the construction of a more formal doctrine and program of action. Indeed, one would especially expect this to become a problem in that Athavale is a remarkably self-effacing *guru*, one who consistently encourages his followers to come to terms with the God in themselves and who seems systematically to refrain from telling anyone what they ought to do. In a frequently invoked metaphor, the emphasis is on the fertiliser and not the seed, on the realisation and cultivation of one's divine potential. In ways that are perhaps comparable with some modern liberal accounts of self, of a Kantian autonomy rewritten in immanent mode, perhaps, (if such a possibility is conceivable) or a Jungian account of self-realisation, this movement's focus on self-respect is intrinsically at odds with the rational codification of any substantive program of action. To this observer, at least, much of the success of this movement seems to depend on a fairly radical reworking of traditional Vedic concepts, and on a degree of openness and tolerance that would be severely compromised by any attempt to construct the kind of doctrinal package that would be useful for mass-mobilisation. Nevertheless, some forms of mass mobilisation are certainly at work here, not least in the prolific use of the new video technologies that add an unmistakably post-modern aura to a reconstituted tradition. Precisely how the emphasis on self-respect and self-initiative will be reconciled with the demands of a systematic doctrine remains to be seen. Perhaps the underlying Vedic traditions will sustain a sufficient degree of coherence. Perhaps post-modern forms of knowledge and communication make the tension less fraught than the Weberian conventions would suggest. Perhaps the notion of a self construed in relation to an immanent cosmology will prove to be especially attractive elsewhere given the widely acknowledged frailty of modern notions of the self framed through a cosmology of transcendence.

This movement poses many other uncertainties that are also typical of movements elsewhere. Its relations with established forms of government, for example, are quite ambiguous. The movement itself explicitly avoids what it calls politics, that is the conventional politics of parties and government, though as with so many other movements this form of antipolitics is part of the key to its own politics. In effect, it has managed to set up parallel forms of social organisation in particular communities. Even so, some activists do have positions within the secular bureaucracies. Conversely, it is not difficult to see how the established political authorities might be drawn to take a benevolently instrumental view of the movement given its impressive organisational and community building capacities. Something like the interface between state and civil society appears to be developing here, though the parallels are potentially misleading, and as an interface between secular and sacred forms of organisation and authority, it could well become at least as explosive a site of political tensions and contradictions as anything associated with the development of modern secular states.

[...] Four considerations seem to me to be especially important here.

First, questions may be raised about the extent to which the success of this movement is grounded in conditions that are quite specific to the region. It has grown most determinedly in an area that has experienced serious dislocations in relation to the world economy and has had a fairly extensive history of similar movements. It might be argued that conditions even in, say, Bihar, are unlikely to prove as hospitable as those in Gujarat. Furthermore, despite its spread to the city of Bombay, it might be argued that as a movement that has had its greatest successes among the villages, it will find distinct limits in those cities that are becoming most fully integrated in new patterns of global capitalism.

Second, there is the cultural specificity of the notion of self that informs the entire movement. This self is not separable from notions of the 'divine'. It is not the quasi-Kantian self assumed by Habermas, which retains the distinct imprint of a thoroughly transcendentalist culture. It is not the modern self caught mid-way between time and eternity, the finite and infinite, the ego and the other. It might be possible to make sense of this movement by imposing on it a claim that, say, the personal is the political, or that a politics of emancipation demands autonomy and reason, but it would clearly be a sense attained only by imposition. Hindu conceptions of the self are after all one of the great Others against which modern conceptions of the self have been constituted, even though it occasionally may have been attractive to some modern or post-modern thinkers who have been rather sceptical about the plausibility of a conception of personal autonomy and rationality that rests upon a radical alienation of self and world.[10]

Third, although many of the achievements of this movement could be read as an attempt at a revitalisation of civil society, the civil society in question is not strictly comparable with the phenomenon invoked by Habermas or Cohen and Arato. Given the centrality of the spiritual impulse here, public life cannot be reduced to civic life. Perhaps the appropriate comparative imagery would be provided less by the idealised coffee shops and democratic theorists of eighteenth century Britain, as for Habermas, than the early-modern radical Protestant sects, or even the contemporary Mormons. In this context, public life is infused with religious idealism, not with secular rationalism. Arguably, and contrary to many of the entrenched dogmas of Indian nationalism, public life in this particular context must be infused with spiritual idealism in order to generate any kind of civic order, an assumption that would certainly generate considerable controversy elsewhere.

Fourth, no matter how much they may have been reconstructed by the movement's founder, or how much they have been adapted in order to generate a plausible political economy of appropriate development, the Vedic premises that inform this movement are rooted in claims about an immanent divinity. These premises do not always travel well. As far as modern or Western cultures are concerned, God may have been dead for a long time, certainly for much longer than Nietzsche's belated reminder a century ago, but the effects of modern secularisations of Christian dualism are still omnipresent. Its trancendentalisms, quite as much as its capitalist commodifications, render Hindu immanence as mere exotica. In any case, if God is immanent, the world is immanent as well. While there are undoubtedly a few participants in *Swadhyaya* who are given to a universalising proselytisation, the integrity of the movement would seem to depend more on finding God and the world in the particular locale, within the grassroots communities, for example, than in trying to spread the word 'out there'. Like Habermas, and the culture he has somehow come to symbolise, this movement is not shy about professing a certain universality. But it is by no means the same universality. The more ecumenical among us might be drawn to underline the universality hiding in all claims to universality. Others will remember that the great divisions of the modern world, the divisions drawn in the territorial conventions of Westphalia and the not-always-territorial delineations of Civilisation and Other, have been constructed precisely around competing claims to universality.

[...]

Nomadic connections

Fine lines often delineate very dense practices. They can both trace and erase the scars of trauma. Historical ruptures and civilisational confrontations disappear beneath legal scripts and cartographic cleanliness. Problematics are put under sedation and the arbitrary becomes symmetrical. The fine lines between 'social movements' and 'world politics', I have argued, have become especially elegant, and especially seductive to the modern political imagination. The brutal chasm between inside and outside is too easily rewritten as an inclusive metaphysics of above and below. It makes intuitive sense to countenance the spatial extension of a movement here to a movement there, to envisage a convergence of progressive forces acting across those merely artificial boundaries that offend planetary integrity and species identity. Similarities and connections are all too readily translated into grand philosophies of history that point upwards to the projected vision of a global civil society, a global governance, and a properly *world* politics.

A politics of connections is, I believe, absolutely crucial. Movements do connect, converse, learn from each other, and sometimes develop partial solidarities. But a politics of connection is not necessarily a politics of a united front or a counterhegemonic strategy. Exactly what a politics of connection would look like is not clear. Whatever the rhetorical and tactical appeal of a women's movement, or an environmental movement, in the singular, it is an appeal that cannot disguise the differences and even intolerances among such movements. Whatever it might come to mean to establish a politics of connections, however, it is unlikely to look like the politics of inclusions and exclusions, of the reconciliation of identities and differences, expressed by the modern territorial state.

A politics of movement is crucial also. For the great strength of social movements is that they are capable of expressing a politics of temporality, a politics that always looks like weakness to those who believe that states, for example, really are unchanging structures, to those whose view of politics affirms the truthfulness of space against the apparent illusions of time. As Machiavelli understood much better than most, this conception of illusions is an especially dangerous illusion. It is necessary to ask how it has become so easy to forget that capitalism is a movement, that states are always in motion, that histories cannot always be captured by territorial form. It is necessary to ask how it has become so easy to believe that movements act 'down there' among the locales, among those forms of life that are contained within the grander structures 'above'. Social movements that work entirely within the modern reification of spatiotemporal relations simply affirm the limits of their ambition.

The limits of this ambition are conventionally framed in relation to the eternal identity of the modern self-identical subject. This is the identity inscribed both by the modern state and by projections of the modern state onto the world as a whole. It is also the identity that informs the categories through which alternatives to the state come to be framed as projections of the state. These are the categories, I have argued, that tell us about what social movements are *supposed* to be. Even though most literatures seeking to explore the conjunction of social movements and world politics tend more towards the descriptive and the affirmative, they tend to express the normative codes of modern politics.

An empirical exploration of this conjunction would more usefully begin by examining whether particular movements do or do not express these codes, in their explicit aspirations or their collective practices. It would ask about the articulations of identity and difference, self and other, space and time that constrain and inform their capacity to rearticulate their understanding of the political under contemporary conditions. It would ask about the connections between such rearticulations in different structural locations.

A politics of movement cannot be grasped through categories of containment. A politics of connections cannot be grasped through a metaphysics of inclusions and exclusion, whether of insides and outsides or aboves and belows. A politics that encompasses 'the world' cannot be envisaged on the assumption that that world already exists along with the categories through which it must be known. An empirical analysis of social movements, and an interpretation of their significance for what a world politics might become, does not have to be bound by the prejudices of modernity. On the contrary, these prejudices can only ensure that the fine lines separating us from them can never be transgressed. An empirical reading of social movements might show that these fine lines are being transgressed all the time.

Notes

1 The classic, and archetypically uncritical articulation of the typology of supposed 'levels' in the analysis of international relations is Kenneth Waltz's, *Man, the State and War* (New York, NY: Columbia University Press, 1959). For an account of attempts to work through the analytical difficulties that ensue once an ontology of such levels is accepted, see Barry Buzan, 'The Level of Analysis Problem in International Relations Reconsidered', in Ken Booth and Steve Smith (eds), *International Relations Theory Today* (Cambridge: Polity, 1995), pp. 198–216. For critical commentary on the ontological assumptions affirmed by this literature see R. B. J. Walker, *Inside/Outside: International Relations as Political Theory* (Cambridge: Cambridge University Press, 1993), pp. 125–40, and Nicholas Onuf, 'Levels', *European Journal of International Relations* (Vol. 1, No. 1, 1995).

2 The practices of classification stand in especially sharp contrast to the attention given to the much rarer practices of explanation, empirical confirmation, theory construction, and so on. For two especially instructive meditations on the politics of classification see, Nicolo Machiavelli, *The Prince* (Cambridge: Cambridge University Press, 1988), especially Chapter 1, and Michel Foucault, *The Order of Things* (London: Tavistock, 1970). For a range of relevant discussions, see Alasdair MacIntyre, 'Is a Science of Comparative Politics Possible?', in his *Against the Self-Image of the Age* (London: Duckworth, 1971), pp. 260–79; David Collier, 'The Comparative Method', in Ada Finifter (ed.), *Political Science: The State of the Discipline II* (Washington, DC: American Political Science Association, 1993), pp. 105–19; Jack Goody, *The Domestication of the Savage Mind* (Cambridge: Cambridge University Press, 1977), especially Chapters 4 and 5; Pierre Bourdieu, *Distinction: A Social Critique of the Judgement of Taste* (Cambridge, MA: Harvard University Press, 1984), especially the Conclusion; Ian Hacking, 'Making Up People', in Thomas C. Weller, Morton Sosna and David E. Wellbeg (eds), *Reconstructing Individualism* (Stanford, CA: Stanford University Press, 1986), pp. 222–36; Zygmunt Bauman, *Modernity and Ambivalence* (Ithaca, NY: Cornell University Press, 1991), especially the Introduction and Chapters 1, 2 and 3; William Connolly, *The Terms of Political Discourse*, Second Edition (Oxford: Robertson, 1983); and Linda Nicholson (ed.), *Feminism/Postmodernism* (New York, NY: Routledge, 1990), especially Part 3.

3 For a brief synoptic account of this general theme, see R. B. J. Walker, 'International Relations and the Concept of the Political', in Booth and Smith (eds), *loc.cit.*, in note 1, pp. 306–27.

4 It is perhaps appropriate to emphasise two points in this context. First, my concern with the way claims about ethics and an already existing world politics are so often used to avoid questions about the political is not to suggest that the discourses of the modern state provide the only context in

which the concerns of this paper might be framed or that ethical concerns are unimportant. On the contrary, claims about world politics make the problems of ethics even more difficult than they are in relation to the modern state, not least because they put into question accounts of the modern subject that have become the common point of departure of the canonical accounts of modern ethical traditions, whether individualist or communitarian. Second, my concern with the categories of *modern* politics is not to be taken either as an affirmation of the priority of those categories or as a straightforward defence of some supposed post-modern position. The continued resort to binary categories – modern/post-modern, critical/post-structural, ethical/political, objectivist/relativist and so on – in so many recent commentaries about post-modern or post-structuralist literatures in this field is, to me, simply puzzling, especially given the extent to which the politics of such categories have been addressed by such literatures. The distinction between critical and dogmatic, on the other hand, still seems to me to have a lot of useful life in it in this context, despite the varieties and difficulties of the critical option. The correlation between deployments of a simple distinction between modernity and post-modernity, the rallying cry against 'relativism', and the appeal to an 'ethics' that appeals to the appealer, remains far too high for comfort.

5 For a brief but helpful discussion of the conceptual issues at stake here, see Stephen J. Rosow, 'On the Political Theory of Political Economy: Conceptual Ambiguity and the Global Economy', *Review of International Political Economy* (Vol. 1, No. 3, Autumn 1994), pp. 465–88. See also Rosow, Naeem Inayatullah and Mark Rupert (eds.), *The Global Economy as Political Space* (Boulder, CO: Lynne Rienner, 1994); and Ronen P. Palen and Barry Gills (eds.), *Transcending the State-Global Divide* (Boulder, CO: Lynne Rienner, 1994).

6 Warren Magnusson, 'Social Movements and the Global City', *Millennium: Journal of International Studies* (Vol. 23, No. 3, 1994), pp. 621–45.

7 See, for example, Alberto Melucci, *Nomads of the Present: Social Movements and Individual Needs in Contemporary Society* (Philadelphia, PA: Temple University Press, 1989) and William K. Carroll (ed.), *Organizing Dissent: Contemporary Social Movements in Theory and Practice* (Toronto, ON: Garamond, 1992).

8 See, for example, Giovanni Arrighi, Terrence K. Hopkins and Immanuel Wallerstein, *Dilemmas of Antisystemic Movements* (London: Verso, 1989).

9 The following comments, which give only a superficial sketch of a complex phenomenon for purposes of a more general argument, are informed by my own brief observations of various *Swadhyaya* communities in December 1994 as well as by extensive discussions with, and in some cases as yet unpublished papers by, several experienced analysts of such movements; I am especially grateful to Dhirubhai Sheth, Ashis Nandy, Imtiaz Ahmed, Madhu Kishwar, Bharat Wariavwalla, R. K. Shrivastava, N. R. Sheth, Majid Rahnema, Marc Nerfin, Christian de Laat, Bjorn Hettne, Mats Frieberg and Daniel Gold, as well as to innumerable *swadhyaya* for their openness and hospitality. For a general account see Ramashray Roy, '*Swadhyaya*: Values and Message', in Ponna Wignaraja (ed.), *New Social Movements in the South* (New Delhi: Vistaar Publications, 1993).

10 On the politics of self-construction in post-colonial contexts see the extensive writings of Ashis Nandy, especially *The Intimate Enemy: Loss and Recovery of Self Under Colonialism* (Delhi: Oxford University Press, 1993); *Traditions, Tyranny and Utopias: Essays in the Politics of Awareness* (Delhi: Oxford University Press, 1987); and *The Illegitimacy of Nationalism: Rabrindrinath Tagore and the Politics of Self* (Delhi: Oxford University Press, 1994).

13 Toward a postmodern prince?

The battle in Seattle as a moment in the new politics of globalisation

Stephen Gill

Source: Stephen Gill (2000), 'Toward a Postmodern Prince? The Battle in Seattle as a Moment in the New Politics of Globalisation', *Millennium: Journal of International Studies*, 29: 1, pp. 131–141

> The modern prince, the myth-prince, cannot be a real person, a concrete individual. It can only be an organism, a complex element of society in which a collective will, which has already been recognised and has to some extent asserted itself in action, begins to take concrete form.[1]

This essay analyses recent protests against aspects of neoliberal globalisation, as for example at the World Trade Organisation (WTO) Ministerial Meeting in Seattle in late 1999 and in Washington, DC in spring 2000 to coincide with the IMF and World Bank Annual Meetings. I first examine the reasons for the failure of the Seattle talks, and secondly, evaluate the protests and their political significance. Finally, I analyse some emerging forms of political agency associated with struggles over the nature and direction of globalisation that I call the 'the postmodern Prince'. This concept is elaborated in the final section of this essay. It is important to stress at the outset, however, that in this essay the term 'postmodern' does not refer, as it often does, to a discursive or aesthetic moment. In my usage, 'postmodern' refers to a set of conditions, particularly political, material, and ecological that are giving rise to new forms of political agency whose defining myths are associated with the quest to ensure human and intergenerational security on and for the planet, as well as democratic human development and human rights. As such, the multiple and diverse political forces that form the postmodern Prince combine both defensive and forward-looking strategies. Rather than engaging in deconstruction, they seek to develop a global and universal politics of radical (re)construction.

The battle in Seattle took place both inside and outside the conference centre in which the meetings took place; the collapse of the discussions was partly caused by the greater visibility of trade issues in the everyday lives of citizens and the increasing concern over how international trade and investment agreements are undermining important aspects of national sovereignty and policy autonomy, especially in ways that strengthen corporate power. These concerns – expressed through various forms of political mobilization – have put pressure upon political leaders throughout the world to re-examine some of the premises and contradictions of neoliberal globalisation.

Why the talks failed

Why specifically did the Seattle talks fail? The first and most obvious reason was US intransigence, principally in defence of the status quo against demands for reform by other nations concerned at the repercussions of the liberalisation framework (the built-in agenda) put in place by the GATT Uruguay Round.[2] The GATT Uruguay Round was a 'Single Undertaking', a generic all-or-nothing type of agreement that meant signatories had to agree to all its commitments and disciplines, as well as to the institutionalisation of the WTO. The wider juridical-political framework for locking in such commitments can be called the new constitutionalism of disciplinary neoliberalism. This encompasses not only trade and investment, but also private property rights more generally (and not just intellectual property rights). It also involves macroeconomic policies and institutions (for example independent central banks and balanced budget amendments) in ways that minimise, or even 'lock out' democratic controls over key economic institutions and policy frameworks in the long-term.[3]

In this context, the US mainly wanted to sustain commitments to existing protections for intellectual property rights and investment and stop any attempts to weaken the capacity of existing agreements to open new markets for American corporations. The US position was based on intelligence work by government agencies, academics, and corporate strategists co-ordinated by the CIA.[4]

So it would be easy to say that protests outside the Seattle Convention Centre and confronted by the Seattle riot police, the FBI, and the CIA had little or no effect on the failure of the talks, other than the fact that many delegates could not get into the building because of the disruptions outside. However, this would be to misunderstand the link between public concern and the negotiating positions of states in the WTO. Indeed, it is becoming clear that the central reasons for the failure of the Seattle Ministerial were linked to the fact that the establishment of the WTO has gone well beyond the traditional role of the GATT in ways that have begun not only increasingly to encroach on crucial domestic policy areas and national sovereignty, but which also have repercussions for international law. In addition, key areas of concern to the public such as food safety, biotechnology, the environment, labour standards, and broader questions of economic development add to the popular disquiet and mobilisation over cultural, social, and ethical questions linked to the globalisation project.

In this regard – and this is very relevant to the concerns of the protesters as well as many governments – the new services negotiations that will occur in Geneva as a result of the Single Undertaking have a wide mandate and the new trade disciplines will have potentially vast impact across major social institutions and programs, such as health, education, social services, and cultural issues. This will allow for wider privatisation and commercialisation of the public sector and indirectly, of the public sphere itself, for example in social programs and education.[5] The logic of the negotiations will likely inhibit many government programs that could be justified as being in the public interest, unless governments are able to convince WTO panels that these programs are not substantially in restraint of trade and investment on the part of private enterprise. Indeed, because the built-in agenda will proceed in Geneva, many divisions among governments, especially between North and South, are emerging. The North-South divisions also revolve around dissatisfaction on the South's part at concessions made in the earlier GATT Uruguay Round, coupled with their frustration in failing to open Northern markets for their manufactured and agricultural exports.

With this agenda in mind, the protesters – although drawn from a very diverse range of organisations and political tendencies – believe there is centralisation and concentration of power under corporate control in neoliberal globalisation, with much of the policy agenda for this project orchestrated by international organisations such as the WTO, the IMF, and the World Bank. Thus, it was not surprising that the battle in Seattle moved to Washington, DC in mid-April where the same set of progressive and environmental activists and organisations, including trade unions, protested the role of the IMF, World Bank, and the G-7.

What is significant here is that the new counter-movements seek to preserve ecological and cultural diversity against what they see as the encroachment of political, social, and ecological mono-cultures associated with the supremacy of corporate rule. At the time of writing, the protests were set to move on to lay siege to the headquarters of Citicorp, the world's biggest financial conglomerate.

The contradictions of neoliberal globalisation and the Seattle protests

Implicitly or explicitly, the failure of the talks and indeed much of the backlash against neoliberal globalisation is linked to the way that people in diverse contexts are experiencing the problems and contradictions linked to the power of capital and more specifically the projects of disciplinary neoliberalism and new constitutionalism. So what are these contradictions and how do they relate to the Seattle protests?

The first is the contradiction between big capital and democracy. Central here is the extension of binding legal mechanisms of trade and investment agreements, such as the GATT Uruguay Round and regional agreements, such as NAFTA. A counterexample, which pointed the way towards Seattle in terms of much of its counter-hegemonic political form was the failed OECD effort to create a Multilateral Agreement on Investment. The MAI was also partly undermined by grass-root mobilisation against corporate globalisation, as well as by more conventional political concerns about sovereignty. The protesters viewed agreements such as NAFTA and organisations such as the WTO as seeking to institution-alise ever-more extensive charters of rights and freedoms for corporations, allowing for greater freedom of enterprise and world-wide protection for private property rights. The protesters perceived that deregulation, privatisation, and liberalisation are a means to strengthen a particular set of class interests, principally the power of private investors and large shareholders. They are opposed to greater legal and market constraints on democracy.

Put differently, the issue was therefore how far and in what ways trade and investment agreements 'lock in' commitments to liberalisation, whilst 'locking out' popular-democratic and parliamentary forces from control over crucial economic, social, and ecological policies.

The second set of contradictions are both economic and social. Disciplinary neoliberalism proceeds with an intensification of discipline on labour and a rising rate of exploitation, partly reflected in booming stock markets during the past decade, whilst at the same time per-sistent economic and financial crises have impoverished many millions of people and caused significant economic dislocations. This explains the growing role of organised labour – for example American based trade unions such as the Teamsters – in the protests, as well as organisations representing feminists, other workers, peasants, and smaller producers world-wide. In this regard, the numbers do not lie: despite what has been the longest boom in the history of Western capitalism, the real incomes of average people have been falling. So if this happens in a boom, what happens in a bust? This question has been answered already in the East Asia crisis when millions were impoverished.

Third, for a number of years now, discipline of capital has become linked to the intensi-fication of a crisis of social reproduction. Feminist political economy has shown how a disproportionate burden of (structural) adjustment to the harsher more competitive circum-stances over the past twenty years has fallen on the shoulders of the less well-paid, on women and children, and the weaker members of society, the old and the disabled. In an era of fiscal stringency, in many states social welfare, health, and educational provisions have been reduced and the socialisation of risk has been reduced for a growing proportion of the world's population. This has generated a crisis of social reproduction as burdens of adjustment are displaced into families and communities that are already under pressure to simply survive in economic terms and risk becomes privatised, redistributed, and generalised in new forms.[6]

The final set of contradictions are linked to how socio-cultural and biological diversity are being replaced by a social and biological mono-culture under corporate domination, and how this is linked to a loss of food security and new forms of generalised health risks. Thus, the protesters argued that if parts of the Seattle draft agenda were ratified, it would allow for a liberalisation of trade in genetically modified crops, provisions to allow world water supplies to be privatised, and the patenting of virtually all forms of life including genetic material that had been widely used across cultures for thousands of years. The protesters also felt particularly strongly about the patenting of seeds and bio-engineering by companies like Novartis and Enron, and other firms seen to be trying to monopolise control over food and undermine local livelihood and food security.[7]

Hence protesters opposed the control of the global food order by corporate interests linked to new constitutionalism. These interests have begun to institutionalise their right 'to source food and food inputs, to prospect for genetic patents, and to gain access to local and national food markets' established through the GATT Uruguay Round and WTO.[8] Transnational corporations have managed to redefine food security in terms of the reduction of national barriers to agricultural trade, ensuring market rule in the global food order. The effect is the intensification of the centralisation of control by 'agri-food capital via global sourcing and global trading', in ways that intensify world food production and consumption relations through

> unsustainable monocultures, terminator genes, and class-based diets [in ways] premised on the elimination of the diversity of natural resources, farm cultures and food cultures, and the decline of local food self-sufficiency and food security mechanisms.[9]

Together, these contradictions contribute to what might be called a global or 'organic crisis' that links together diverse forces across and within nations, specifically to oppose the ideas, institutions, and material power of disciplinary neoliberalism. Much of the opposition to corporate globalisation was summed up by AFL-CIO President John Sweeney, who alongside President Clinton, was addressing the heads of the 1,000 biggest transnational corporations at the annual meeting of the self-appointed and unelected World Economic Forum in Davos in February 2000. Sweeney stated that the protests from North and South represented 'a call for new global rules, democratically developed' to constrain 'growing inequality, environmental destruction, and a race to the bottom for working people', warning that if such rules were not forthcoming 'it will generate an increasingly volatile reaction that will make Seattle look tame'.[10] Indeed Clinton's remarks made at Davos

> seemed designed as a reminder that these fears – even expressed in unwelcome and sometimes violent ways, as they were in Seattle – have a legitimacy that deserves attention in the world's executive suites and government ministries.[11]

We know by now, of course, that the violence in Seattle was almost completely carried out by the heavily armed police militias who took the battle to the protesters. In Washington in April 2000, police pre-emptively arrested hundreds of demonstrators, in actions justified by the local police chief as a matter of prudence. Another example of this was the repression of peaceful protests at the Asia-Pacific Economic Co-operation meeting in Vancouver in 1998. The protests focused on the contradiction of separating free trade from political democracy, dramatised by the presence of the Indonesian dictator, President Suharto. In sum, state authorities will quickly act to restrict basic political rights and freedoms of opposition by alternative members of civil society – rights supposedly underpinned by the rule of law in a liberal constitutional framework – when business interests are threatened. At Seattle, the anonymous, unaccountable, and intimidating police actions seemed almost absurd in light of the fact that the protests involved children dressed as turtles, peaceful activists for social justice, union members, faith groups, accompanied by teachers, scientists, and assorted 'tree huggers' all of whom were non-violent. Indeed, with the possible exception of a small number of anarchists, virtually none of the protesters was in any way violent. In Washington, the police protected the meetings wearing heavy armour from behind metal barricades, in face of protesters carrying puppets and signs that read 'spank the Bank'. Moments such as these, however, illustrate not only a comedy of the absurd but also the broader dialectic between a supremacist set of forces and an ethico-political alternative involved in a new inclusive politics of diversity.

Indeed, since the Seattle debacle the protesters have been able to extend their critique of what they see as the political mono-culture by showing how one of its key components, the 'quality press' and TV media, reported what occurred. In the US, for example, the mainstream media found it impossible to represent the violence as being caused by the authorities in order to provoke and discredit the opposition as being Luddite, anti-science, and unlawful. Seen from the vantage point of the protesters, 'the *Washington Post* and the *New York Times* are the keepers of "official reality," and in official reality it is always the protesters who are violent'.[12]

Toward a postmodern prince?

In conclusion, I advance the following hypothesis: the protests form part of a world-wide movement that can perhaps be understood in terms of new potentials and forms of global political agency. And following Machiavelli and Gramsci, I call this set of potentials 'the postmodern Prince' which I understand as something plural and differentiated, although linked to universalism and the construction of a new form of globalism, and of course, something that needs to be understood as a set of social and political forces in movement.

Let us place this hypothesis in some theoretical context. Machiavelli's *The Prince* addressed the problem of the ethics of rule from the viewpoint of both the prince (the *palazzo*, the palace) and the people (the *piazza*, the town square). Machiavelli sought to theorise how to construct a form of rule that combined both *virtù* (ethics, responsibility, and consent) and fear (coercion) under conditions of *fortuna* (circumstances). *The Prince* was written in Florence, in the context of the political upheavals of Renaissance Italy. Both Machiavelli and later Gramsci linked their analyses and propositions to the reality of concrete historical circumstances as well as to potential for transformation. These included pressing contemporary issues associated with the problems of Italian unification, and the subordinate place of Italy in the structures of international relations. And it was in a similar national and international context that Gramsci's *The Modern Prince* was written in a Fascist prison, a text that dealt with a central problem of politics: the constitution of power, authority, rule, rights, and responsibilities in the creation of an ethical political community. Nevertheless, what Gramsci saw in *The Prince* was that it was 'not a systematic treatment, but a "live" work, in which political ideology and political science are fused in the dramatic form of a "myth" '.[13] The myth for Machiavelli was that of the *condottiere*, who represents the collective will. By contrast, for

Gramsci *The Modern Prince* proposed the myth of the democratic modern mass political party – the communist party – charged with the construction of a new form of state and society, and a new world order.

In the new strategic context (*fortuna*) of disciplinary neoliberalism and globalisation, then a central problem of political theory is how to imagine and to theorise the new forms of collective political identity and agency that might lead to the creation of new, ethical, and democratic political institutions and forms of practice (*virtù*). So in this context, let me again be clear that by 'postmodern Prince' I do *not* mean a form of political agency that is based on postmodern philosophy and the radical relativism it often entails. What I am intending to communicate is a shift in the forms of political agency that are going beyond earlier modernist political projects. So the 'postmodern Prince' involves tendencies that have begun to challenge some of the myths and the disciplines of modernist practices, and specifically resisting those that seek to consolidate the project of globalisation under the rule of capital.

Thus, the battles in Seattle may link to new patterns of political agency and a movement that goes well beyond the politics of identity and difference: it has gender, race, and class aspects. It is connected to issues of ecological and social reproduction, and of course, to the question of democracy. This is why more than 700 organisations and between 40,000 and 60,000 people – principally human rights activists, labour activists, indigenous people, representatives of churches, industrial workers, small farmers, forest activists, environmentalists, social justice workers, students, and teachers – all took part collectively in the protests against the WTO's Third Ministerial on 30 November 1999. The protesters seem aware of the nature and dynamics of their movement and have theorised a series of political links between different events so that they will become more than what James Rosenau called 'distant proximities' or simply isolated moments of resistance against globalisation.[14]

In sum, these movements are beginning to form what Gramsci called 'an organism, a complex element of society' that is beginning to point towards the realisation of a 'collective will'. This will is coming to be 'recognised and has to some extent asserted itself in action'. It is beginning to 'take concrete form'.[15] Indeed the diverse organisations that are connected to the protests seek to go further to organise something akin to a postmodern transnational political party, that is one with no clear leadership structure as such. It is a party of movement that cannot be easily decapitated. This element puzzled mainstream press reporters at Seattle since they were unable to find, and thus to photograph or interview the 'leaders' of the protests. However, this emerging political form is not a signal of an end to universalism in politics as such, since many of the forces it entails are linked to democratisation and a search for collective solutions to common problems. It seeks to combine diversity with new forms of collective identity and solidarity in and across civil societies. Thus the organisers of the April 2000 Washington demonstrations stated that 'Sweeney's prediction' made at Davos was in fact a description of events that were going on right now, but that are largely ignored by the media:

> The Zapatista uprising in Mexico, the recent coup in Ecuador, the civil war in the Congo, the turmoil in Indonesia, and the threat of the U'Wa people to commit mass suicide, are all expressions of the social explosion that has arisen from the desperation caused by the policies of the World Bank, IMF, and their corporate directors… Fundamental change does not mean renaming their programs or other public relations scams. Fundamental reform means rules that empower the people of the world to make the decisions about how they live their lives – not the transnational CEO's or their purchased political leaders.[16]

In this regard, the effectiveness of the protest movements may well lie in a new confidence gained as particular struggles come to be understood in terms of a more general set of inter-connections between problems and movements world-wide. For instance, the Cartagena Protocol on Biosafety on genetically modified life forms was signed in late January 2000 in Montreal by representatives from 133 governments pursuant to the 1992 UN Convention on Biological Diversity for the trade and regulation of living modified organisms (LMOs). The draft Protocol ensures that sovereign governments have rights to decide on imports of LMOs provided this is based on environmental and health risk assessment data. The Protocol is founded on the 'precautionary principle', in effect meaning that where scientific uncertainty exists, governments can refuse or delay authorisation of trade in LMOs. Apart from pressure from NGOs, the negotiations were strongly influenced by scientists concerned at genetic and biological risks posed by the path of innovation. The process finally produced a protocol with significant controls over the freedoms of biotechnology and life sciences companies. Indeed, linkages and contradictions between environmental and trade and investment regulations and laws are becoming better understood by activists world-wide, for instance how the Biosafety Protocol and the rules and procedures of the WTO may be in conflict.

Nevertheless, it must be emphasised that, although they may represent a large proportion of the population of the world in terms of their concerns, in organised political terms the protest groups are only a relatively small part of an emerging global civil society that includes not only NGOs but also the activities of political parties, churches, media communications corporations, scientific and political associations, some progressive, others reactionary. Transnational civil society also involves activities of both transnational corporations, and also governments that are active in shaping a political terrain that is directly and indirectly outside the formal juridical purview of states. Indeed, as the UN Rio conference on the environment and its aftermath illustrated, corporate environmentalism is a crucial aspect of the emerging global civil society and it is linked to what Gramsci called *trasformismo* or co-optation of opposition. For example, 'sustainable development' is primarily defined in public policy as compatible with market forces and freedom of enterprise. When the global environmental movement was perceived as a real threat to corporate interests, companies changed tack from suggesting the environmentalists were either crackpots or misguided to accepting a real problem existed and a compromise was necessary. Of course a compromise acceptable to capital was not one that would fundamentally challenge the dominant patterns of accumulation.

I have not used the term postmodern in its usual sense. Rather, I apply it to indicate a set of conditions and contradictions that give rise to novel forms of political agency that go beyond and are more complex than those imagined by Machiavelli's *The Prince* or Gramsci's *The Modern Prince*. Global democratic collective action today cannot, in my view, be understood as a singular form of collective agency, for example a single party with a single form of identity. It is more plural and differentiated, as well as being democratic and inclusive. The new forms of collective action contain innovative conceptions of social justice and solidarity, of social possibility, of knowledge, emancipation, and freedom. The content of their mobilising myths includes diversity, oneness of the planet and nature, democracy, and equity. What we are discussing is, therefore, a political party as well as an educational form and a cultural movement. However, it does not act in the old sense of an institutionalised and centralised structure of representation. Indeed this 'party' is not institutionalised as such, since it has a multiple and capillary form. Moreover, whilst many of the moments and movements of resistance noted above are at first glance 'local' in nature, there is broad recognition that local problems may require global solutions. Global networks and other mobilising capabilities are facilitated with new technologies of communication.

A new 'postmodern Prince' may prove to be the most effective political form for giving coherence to an open-ended, plural, inclusive, and flexible form of politics and thus create alternatives to neoliberal globalisation. So, whilst one can be pessimistic about globalisation in its current form, this is perhaps where some of the optimism for the future may lie: a new set of democratic identities that are global, but based on diversity and rooted in local conditions, problems, and opportunities.

Acknowledgements

I would like to thank Cemal Acikgoz, Isabella Bakker, Adam Harmes, and Ahmed Hashi for their comments and help in preparing this essay.

Notes

1 Antonio Gramsci, *Selections from the Prison Notebooks of Antonio Gramsci*, trans. Quintin Hoare and Geoffrey Nowell Smith (New York: International Publishers, 1971), 129.
2 Scott Sinclair, 'The WTO: What Happened in Seattle? What's Next in Geneva?', *Briefing Paper Series: Trade and Investment* 1, no. 2 (Ottawa: Canadian Centre for Policy Alternatives, 2000), 6.
3 Stephen Gill, 'Globalisation, Market Civilisation, and Disciplinary Neoliberalism', *Millennium Journal of International Studies* 23, no. 3 (1994): 399–423.
4 See 'CIA Spies Swap Cold War for Trade Wars', *Financial Times*, 14 August 1999, 1.
5 Editorial, 'New Trade Rules Target Education', *Canadian Association of University Teachers Bulletin*, 7 September 1999, 1. The *Bulletin* added that Educational International representing 294 educational unions and associations world wide expressed great concern about how WTO initiatives would undermine public education.
6 See the essays in Isabella Bakker, ed., *The Strategic Silence: Gender and Economic Policy* (London: Zed Books, 1994).
7 Paul Hawken, 'The WTO: Inside, Outside, All Around The World', [http://www.co-intelligence.org/WTOHawken.html] (26 April 2000).
8 Philip McMichael, 'The Crisis of Market Rule in the Global Food Order' (paper presented at the British International Studies Association Annual Meeting, Manchester, 20–22 December 1999).
9 Ibid., 2.
10 John Sweeney, 'Remember Seattle', *Washington Post*, 30 January 2000, B7.
11 Ann Swardson, 'Clinton Appeals for Compassion in Global Trade; World Forum Told Don't Leave "Little Guys" Out', *Washington Post*, 30 January 2000, A18.
12 Posted on [http://www.peoples@post4.tele.dk] (26 April 2000) on behalf of the NGO network 'Mobilization for Global Justice' that organised the Washington protests. Their website [http://www.a16.org] passed 250,000 visitors at the time of the protests.
13 Gramsci, *Selections from the Prison Notebooks*, 125.
14 James Rosenau, 'Imposing Global Order: A Synthesised Ontology for a Turbulent Era', in *Innovation and Transformation in International Studies*, Stephen Gill and James H. Mittelman (eds) (Cambridge: Cambridge University Press, 1997), 220–35.
15 Gramsci, *Selections from the Prison Notebooks*, 129.
16 Posted again by the NGO network 'Mobilization for Global Justice' on [http://www.peoples@post4.tele.dk] (26 April 2000).

14 Farewell to the 'end of history'

Organization and vision in anti-corporate movements

Naomi Klein

Source: Naomi Klein (2002), 'Farewell to the End of History: Organization and Vision in Anti-Corporate Movements', *Socialist Register 2002*, pp. 1–13

'We are here to show the world that another world is possible!' the man on stage said, and a crowd of more than 10,000 roared its approval.[1] What was strange was that we weren't cheering for a specific other world, just the possibility of one. We were cheering for the idea that another world could, in theory, exist.

For the past thirty years, a select group of CEOs and world leaders have met during the last week in January on a mountaintop in Switzerland to do what they presumed they were the only ones entitled to do, or capable of doing: determine how the global economy should be governed. We were cheering because it was, in fact, the last week of January, and this wasn't the World Economic Forum in Davos, Switzerland. It was the first annual World Social Forum in Porto Alegre, Brazil. And even though we weren't CEOs or world leaders, we were still going to spend the week talking about how the global economy should be governed.

Many people said that they felt history being made in that room. What I felt was something more intangible: the end of The End of History. Fittingly, 'Another World Is Possible' was the event's official slogan. After a year and a half of global protests against the World Trade Organization, the World Bank, the International Monetary Fund, the Word Economic Forum, both major US political parties, and Britain's Labour Party – to name just a few – the World Social Forum was billed as an opportunity for an emerging movement to stop screaming about what it is against and start articulating what it is for.

The particular site was chosen because Brazil's Workers Party (Partido dos Trabalhadores, the PT) is in power in the city of Porto Alegre, as well as in the state of Rio Grande do Sul and has become known world-wide for its innovations in participatory democracy. The conference was organized by a network of Brazilian unions and NGOs, as well as ATTAC France. The PT made sure that no expense was spared; state-of-the-art conference facilities, a star-studded roster of speakers and international musicians, delegates greeted by officials from the local tourism department, as well as by friendly police officers – quite a culture shock for a group of people growing accustomed to being met by authorities with clouds of pepper spray, border strip searches and 'no-protest' zones. If Seattle was, for many people, the coming-out party of a resistance movement, then, according to Soren Ambrose, policy analyst with 50 Years Is Enough, 'Porto Alegre is the coming-out party for the existence of serious thinking about alternatives'.

The charge that this movement lacks alternatives – or at least a coherent focus – has become something of a mantra since the Battle in Seattle in November 1999, a criticism summed up by an article on 'The New Radicals' in Newsweek: 'One thing that seems to be lacking today is a mission statement, a credo, that gives the movement, such as it is, some focus'.[2]

There is no doubt that in the absence of such media-friendly packaging, critics have had free reign to portray young activists as everything from tree-wearing, drum-beating bubble brains, to violent thugs bent only on destruction.

Addressing this perceived vision deficit was the *raison d'être* of the World Social Forum: the organizers clearly saw the conference as an opportunity to whip the chaos on the streets into some kind of structured shape. And in 60 lectures and 450 workshops, there were indeed plenty of ideas flying around – about new systems of taxation, like the Tobin Tax, co-operative, organic farming, participatory budgets and free software, to name just a few. But I found myself asking a question that often pops up at similar, smaller-scale events. Even if we did manage to come up with a ten-point plan – brilliant in its clarity, elegant in its coherence, unified in its outlook – to whom, exactly, would we hand down these command-ments? Put another way: who are the leaders of this movement – or are there any?

Last April, after a portion of the protests against the Free Trade Area of the Americas turned violent, the press and the police engaged in a game that might be described as 'Find the Leader'. Mark Steyn, a columnist with Conrad Black's *National Post*, pointed at Maude Barlow, chair of the Council of Canadians (one of the world's largest and most committed anti-free trade NGOs), insistently referring to a group of 50,000 people as 'Maude's Mob' and even going so far as to threaten retaliation against Barlow herself. 'The next time a member of Maude's Mob throws a rock at me, I intend to take it home, and chuck it through her window', he wrote.[3]

The police, for their part, claimed that Jaggi Singh, one of the organizers of the Anti-Capitalist Convergence, ordered his minions to attack the fence that surrounded much of Quebec City. The main weapon the police cited was a theatrical catapult that lobbed teddy bears and other stuffed animals over the fence. Singh had nothing to do with the catapult, nor did he do anything at the protest but give speeches about state violence. Yet the justifi-cation for his arrest, and for later being denied bail, was that he was a kind of protest pup-pet master, allegedly pulling the strings behind the actions of others. The story has been similar at other protests. During the demonstrations against the Republican National Convention in Philadelphia in August 2000, John Sellers, one of the founders of the Ruckus Society, had his bail posted at $1 million. Two months earlier, David Solnit, one of the founders of the puppet-making political theatre group Art and Revolution, also faced a pre-emptive arrest, this time in Windsor, Ontario during a meeting of the Organization of American States.

The systematic police targeting of protest 'leaders' goes a long way towards explaining the deep suspicion of traditional hierarchies that exists in this new movement. Indeed, the figure that comes closest to a bona fide 'leader' is Subcomandante Marcos, a man in the mountains of Chiapas who hides his real identity and covers his face with a mask. Marcos, the quintessential anti-leader, insists that his black mask is a mirror, so that 'Marcos is gay in San Francisco, black in South Africa, an Asian in Europe, a Chicano in San Ysidro, an anar-chist in Spain, a Palestinian in Israel, a Mayan Indian in the streets of San Cristobal, a Jew in Germany, a Gypsy in Poland, a Mohawk in Quebec, a pacifist in Bosnia, a single woman on the Metro at 10 p.m., a peasant without land, a gang member in the slums, an unem-ployed worker, an unhappy student and, of course, a Zapatista in the mountains'.[4] In other words, he is simply us: we are the leader we've been looking for.

This critique of hierarchies goes far beyond charismatic leadership. Many of the partici-pants in the anti-corporate protest movements are equally suspicious of one-size-fits-all ideologies, political parties, indeed of any group that would centralize power and organize the parts of this movement into subordinate cells and locals. So while the intellectuals and organizers up on stage at the World Social Forum may help shape the ideas of the people on the streets, they most emphatically do not have the power or even the mechanisms to lead this street movement. In this amorphous context, the ideas and plans being hatched at the World Social Forum weren't irrelevant exactly, they just weren't important in the way they clearly hoped to be. They were destined to be swept up and tossed around in the tidal wave of information – web diaries, NGO manifestos, academic papers, home-made videos, *cris de coeur* – that the global anti-corporate network produces and consumes each and every day.

To those searching for replicas of more traditional anti-capitalist politics, this absence of clear structure makes the anti-corporate movement appear infuriatingly impassive: Evidently, these people are so disorganized they can't even get it together to respond positively to those who offer to organize them. Sure they've got guts when it comes to protesting, but these are MTV-weaned activists, you can practically hear the old guard saying: scattered, non-linear, no focus.

Only maybe it's not quite so simple. Maybe the protests, from Seattle to Quebec City, look unfocused because they are not demonstrations of one movement at all but rather convergences of many smaller ones, each with its sights trained on a specific multinational corporation (like Nike), a particular industry (like agribusiness) or a new trade initiative (like the Free Trade Area of the Americas), or in defence of indigenous self-determination (like the Zapatistas).

Look a little closer and it's clear that these smaller, targeted movements are indeed battling the same forces, forces perhaps best outlined by the Zapatista National Liberation Army when it began its uprising on January 1, 1994 (the day the North American Free Trade Agreement came into law). The strategic victory of the Zapatistas was to insist that what was going on in Chiapas could not be written off as a narrow 'ethnic' or 'local' struggle – that it was universal. They did this by identifying their enemy not only as the Mexican state but as 'neoliberalism'. The Zapatistas insisted that the poverty and desperation in Chiapas was simply a more advanced version of something happening all around the world, and which began with the first acts of colonialism. Their 500 year head start graces the indigenous people of Chiapas' place at the political vanguard now. In his communiqués, Marcos pointed to the huge numbers of people being left behind by prosperity, whose land, and work, made that prosperity possible. 'The new distribution of the world excludes "minorities." The indigenous, youth, women, homosexuals, lesbians, people of colour, immigrants, workers, peasants; the majority who make up the world basements are presented, for power, as disposable. The distribution of the world excludes the majorities.'[5]

If neoliberalism is the common target there is also an emerging consensus that participatory democracy at the local level – whether through unions, neighbourhoods, farms, villages, anarchist collectives or aboriginal self-government – is where to start building alternatives to it. The common theme is an overarching commitment to self-determination and diversity: cultural diversity, biodiversity, and, yes, political diversity. The Zapatistas call this a movement of 'one "no" and many "yeses" ', a description that defies the characterization that this is one movement at all, and challenges the assumption that it should be.[6]

Rather than a single movement, what is emerging is thousands of movements intricately linked to one another, much as 'hotlinks' connect their websites on the Internet. This analogy is more than coincidental and is in fact key to understanding the changing nature of political organizing. Although many have observed that the recent mass protests would have been impossible without the Internet, what has been overlooked is how the communication technology that facilitates these campaigns is shaping the movement in its own image.

Thanks to the Net, mobilizations are able to unfold with sparse bureaucracy and minimal hierarchy; forced consensus and laboured manifestos are fading into the background, replaced instead by a culture of constant, loosely structured and sometimes compulsive information-swapping.

Despite media descriptions that portrayed the events in Quebec City as two protests – one a 'peaceful' labour march, the other a 'violent' anarchist riot, there were, in fact, hundreds of protests over the course of the weekend. One was organized by a mother and daughter from Montreal. Another by a vanload of grad students from Edmonton. Another by three friends from Toronto who aren't members of anything but their health clubs. Yet another by a couple of waiters from a local café on their lunch break. Sure there were well-organized groups in Quebec City: the unions had buses, matching placards and a parade route; the 'black bloc' of anarchists had gas masks and radio links. But for days the streets were also filled with people who simply said to a friend, 'Let's go to Quebec', and with Quebec City residents who said, 'Let's go outside'.

In the four years before Seattle, similar convergences had taken place outside WTO, G-7 and Asia Pacific Economic Cooperation summits in Auckland, Vancouver, Manila, Birmingham, London, Geneva, Kuala Lumpur and Cologne. What is emerging is an activist model that mirrors the organic, decentralized, interlinked pathways of the Internet – the Internet come to life. Interestingly, the Washington-based research centre TeleGeography has taken it upon itself to map out the architecture of the Internet as if it were the solar system. Last year, TeleGeography pronounced that the Internet is not one giant web but a network of 'hubs and spokes'.[7] The hubs are the centres of activity, the spokes the links to other centres which are autonomous but interconnected.

It seems like a perfect description of the so-called anti-globalization protests. These mass convergences are activist hubs, made up of hundreds, possibly thousands, of autonomous spokes. During the demonstrations the spokes take the form of 'affinity groups' of between two and twenty protesters, each of which elects a spokesperson to represent them at regular 'spokes council' meetings. At some rallies, activists carry actual cloth webs. When it's time for a meeting, they lay the web on the ground, call out 'all spokes on the web' and the structure becomes a street-level boardroom.

The affinity groups agree to loosely coordinate their actions, and, at some events, to abide by a set of non-violence principles (at the very least, they agree not to endanger one another by engaging in violence during a portion of a protest that is planned as non-violent). Apart from that, however, the affinity groups function as discrete units, with the power to make their own strategic decisions – a model of coordinated decentralization that is entirely lost on those looking for leaders and puppet masters. For instance, at the spokes council meetings before the anti-FTAA protests in Quebec City, Jaggi Singh acted only as facilitator – a glorified note-taker, keeping track of all the autonomous actions planned: one group announced they would form a marching band, another planned to wrap the security fence in toilet paper, another planned to throw hundreds of paper air planes through the chain link, another – a group of Harvard grad students – planned to read Foucault to the police. Those with more confrontational plans stayed silent and met only in the relative safety of their own affinity groups.

On the ground, the results of these miniature protests converging is either frighteningly chaotic or inspiringly poetic – or both. Rather than presenting a unified front, small units of activists surround their target from all directions. And rather than build elaborate national or international bureaucracies, temporary structures are thrown up instead: empty buildings are hastily turned into 'convergence centres', and independent media producers assemble impromptu activist news centres. The ad hoc coalitions behind these demonstrations are frequently named after the date of the planned event – J18, N30, A16, S11, S26 – and when the date is passed, they leave virtually no trace behind, save for an archived website.

The hubs and spokes model is more than a tactic used at protests; the protests are themselves made up of 'coalitions of coalitions', to borrow a phrase from Kevin Danaher of Global Exchange. Each anti-corporate campaign is comprised of many groups, mostly NGOs, labour unions, students and anarchists. They use the Internet and regular international conference calls, as well as face-to-face meetings, to do everything from cataloguing the latest transgressions of the World Bank to bombarding Shell Oil with faxes and e-mails to distributing ready-to-download anti-sweatshop leaflets for protests at Nike Town. The groups remain autonomous, but their international coordination is deft and, to their targets, frequently devastating.

The charge that the anti-corporate movement lacks 'vision' falls apart when looked at in the context of these campaigns. It's true that, to a casual observer, the mass protests in Seattle, Washington, DC, Prague and Quebec City can, in their hodgepodge of slogans and causes, seem simply like colourful parades of complaints. But in trying to find coherence in these large-scale shows of strength, observers may be confusing the outward demonstrations of the movement with the thing itself – missing the forest for the people dressed as trees. This movement *is* its spokes, and in the spokes there is no shortage of vision.

The student anti-sweatshop movement, for instance, has rapidly moved from simply criticizing companies and campus administrators to drafting alternate codes of conduct and building its own quasi-regulatory body, the Worker Rights Consortium. More significantly, campus labour activists have been expanding their focus to include targets much closer to home: the caretakers and catering staff on their campuses, as well as the migrant farm workers supplying their cafeterias. The movement against genetically engineered and modified foods has leapt from one policy victory to the next, first getting many GM foods removed from the shelves of British supermarkets, then getting labelling laws passed in Europe, then making enormous strides with the Montreal Protocol on Biosafety. Meanwhile, opponents of the World Bank's and IMF's export-led development models have produced bookshelves' worth of resources on community-based development models, debt relief and reparations, as well as self-government principles.

Critics of the oil and mining industries are similarly overflowing with ideas for sustainable energy and responsible resource extraction – though they rarely get the chance to put their visions into practice. The growing movement against Big Pharma has plenty of ideas about how to get affordable AIDS drugs to those living with the disease, it's just that they keep getting dragged into trade court for their trouble. The Zapatistas, meanwhile, have gone from saying 'Ya Basta' to Nafta, to being at the forefront of a movement for radical democratic reform within Mexico, playing a major role in toppling the corrupt seventy-one-year reign of the Institutional Revolutionary Party, and placing indigenous rights at the centre of the Mexican political agenda.

The fact that these campaigns are decentralized is not a source of incoherence and fragmentation. Rather, it is a reasonable, even ingenious adaptation both to pre-existing fragmentation within progressive networks and to changes in the broader culture. The traditional institutions that once organized citizens into neat, structured groups are all in decline: unions, religions, political parties. Yet something is propelling tens of thousands of individuals onto the streets anyway – an intuition, a gut instinct, perhaps just the profoundly human desire to be part of something larger than oneself. What but this web could catch them all?

The structure of the movement is also a by-product of the explosion of NGOs, which, since the Rio Summit in 1992, have been gaining power and prominence. There are so many NGOs involved in anti-corporate campaigns that nothing but the hubs and spokes model could possibly accommodate all their different styles, tactics and goals. Like the Internet itself, both the NGO and the affinity group networks are indefinitely expandable systems. If somebody doesn't feel like they quite fit in to one of the 30,000 or so NGOs or thousands of affinity groups out there, they can just start their own and link up.

For some, this surfer's appeal to activism is an abomination. But whether or not one agrees with the model, there is no doubt that one of its great strengths is that it has proven extraordinarily difficult to control, largely because it is so different from the organizing principles of the institutions and corporations it targets. It responds to corporate concentration with a maze of fragmentation, to centralization with its own kind of localization, to power consolidation with radical power dispersal.

Once again, this strategy has been employed most deftly by the Zapatistas. Rather than barricading themselves, from the first communiqué they flung open the doors and invited the world 'to watch over and regulate our battles'.[8] The summer after the uprising, the Zapatistas hosted a National Democratic Convention in the jungle; 6,000 people attended, most from Mexico. In 1996, they hosted the first Encuentro For Humanity And Against Neo-Liberalism. Some 3,000 activists travelled to Chiapas to meet with others from around the world. These networks, many of them informal, made the Zapatista struggle impossible to contain.

Joshua Karliner of the Transnational Resource and Action Center calls this web-like system 'an unintentionally brilliant response to globalization'. And because it was unintentional, we still lack even the vocabulary to describe it, which may be why a rather amusing metaphor industry has evolved to fill the gap. I'm throwing my lot in with 'hubs and spokes', but Maude Barlow of the Council of Canadians says, '[w]e are up against a boulder. We can't remove it so we try to go underneath it, to go around it and over it.' Britain's John Jordan, one of the founders of Reclaim the Streets, puts it this way: 'transnationals are like giant tankers, and we are like a school of fish. We can respond quickly; they can't.' The US-based Free Burma Coalition talks of a network of 'spiders', spinning a web strong enough to tie down the most powerful multinationals.

At almost all the global protests, this non-strategy baffled even the most outrageously over-prepared security forces: not only did it delay the opening of the World Trade Organization in Seattle, but a similar strategy saw protesters dressed as 'pink fairies' dancing on the walls of the convention centre during the World Bank/IMF meeting in Prague and saw large portions of the security fence taken down during the Summit of the Americas in Quebec City. Charles Ramsey, Washington DC's police chief, explains what the web looks like from a security point of view. 'You have to experience it to fully appreciate just how well organized they are, how many different ways they can come at you', he said on the second day of the World Bank protests in his city, sounding a little like General Custer describing the wily tactics of the Sioux in 1876.[9]

Fittingly, it's a US military report about the Zapatista uprising that provides the most comprehensive take on these 'network wars'. According to a study produced by RAND, the Zapatistas waged 'a war of the flea' that, thanks to the Internet, the *encuentros*, and the global NGO network, turned into a 'war of the swarm'.[10]

The military challenge of a war of the swarm, the researchers noted, is that it has no 'central leadership or command structure; it is multiheaded, impossible to decapitate'.[11]

Of course, this multiheaded system has its weaknesses too, and they were on full display on the streets of Washington during the anti-World Bank/IMF protests. At around noon on April 16, the day of the largest protest, a spokes council meeting was convened for the affinity groups that were in the midst of blocking all the street intersections surrounding the headquarters of the World Bank and the IMF. The intersections had been blocked since 6 a.m., but the meeting delegates, the protesters had just learned, had slipped inside the police barricades before 5 a.m.

Given this new information, most of the spokespeople felt it was time to give up the intersections and join the official march at the Ellipse. The problem was that not everyone agreed: a handful of affinity groups wanted to see if they could block the delegates on their way out of their meetings. The compromise the council came up with was telling. 'OK, everybody listen up', Kevin Danaher shouted into a megaphone. 'Each intersection has autonomy. If the intersection wants to stay locked down, that's cool. If it wants to come to the Ellipse, that's cool too. It's up to you.' This was impeccably fair and democratic, but there was just one problem – it made absolutely no sense. Sealing off the access points had been a coordinated action. If some intersections now opened up and other, rebel-camp intersections stayed occupied, delegates on their way out of the meeting could just hang a right instead of a left, and they would be home free. Which, of course, is precisely what happened.

As I watched clusters of protesters get up and wander off while others stayed seated, defiantly guarding – well, nothing – it struck me as an apt metaphor for the strengths and weaknesses of this nascent activist network. There is no question that the communication culture that reigns on the Net is better at speed and volume than at synthesis. It is capable of getting tens of thousands of people to meet on the same street corner, placards in hand, but is far less adept at helping those same people to agree on what they are really asking for before they get to the barricades – or after they leave. Perhaps that's why a certain repetitive quality has set in at these large demonstrations: from smashed McDonald's windows to giant puppets, they can begin to look a little like McProtests. The Net made them possible, but it's not proving particularly helpful in taking them to a deeper stage.

For this reason and others, many in the movement have become increasingly critical of 'summit hopping', and generally agree that there needs to be more structure between mass protests. Clearly, far too much expectation is being placed on these large demonstrations: the organizers of the Washington DC demo, for instance, announced they would literally 'shut down' two $30 billion transnational institutions, at the same time as they attempted to convey sophisticated ideas about the fallacies of neoliberal economics to the stock-happy public. They simply couldn't do it; no single demo could, and it's only getting harder. Seattle's direct-action tactics worked as well as they did because they took the police by surprise. Now the police have subscribed to all the e-mail lists and have used the supposed threat posed by anarchists as giant fundraising schemes, allowing them to buy up all manner of new toys, from surveillance equipment to water cannons. More substantively, it was clear that by the time the protests in Prague rolled around in September 2000, the movement, no matter how decentralized, was in grave danger of seeming remote, cut off from the issues that affect people's day to day lives.

So the question is, if there is to be more structure, what kind should it be? An international political party that pushes to democratize world government? New national parties? How about a network of city and town councils each committed to introducing participatory democracy? Should it exist entirely outside of electoral politics and concentrate exclusively on creating counter-powers to the state?

These questions are more than tactical, they are strategic and often philosophical. Fundamentally, they hinge on how one defines that most slippery of terms: globalization. Is the problem with globalization simply that a good idea has been grabbed by the wrong hands, and the situation could be righted if only international institutions like the WTO were made democratic and accountable; if there were tough global rules protecting the environment, taxing financial transactions, and upholding labour standards? Or is globalization, at its core, a crisis of representative democracy in which power and decision-making are delegated to points further and further away from the places where the effects of those decisions are felt – until representative democracy means voting for politicians every few years who use that mandate to transfer national powers to the WTO and the IMF? Is this a movement trying to impose its own, more humane brand of globalization, or is it a movement against centralization and the delegation of power *on principle*, one as critical of left-wing, one-size-fits-all ideology as of the neoliberal recipe for McGovernment?

While there is near consensus on the need to sit down and start sorting through these questions, there is precious little on the next set of obvious questions: at whose table? And who gets to decide? The World Social Forum was by the far the most ambitious attempt so far to get this process under way, drawing a remarkable 10,000 delegates. Few of them, however, seemed to know what to expect: a model UN? A giant teach-in? A mock parliament? A party? It turned out that the organizational structure of the forum was so opaque that it was nearly impossible to figure out how decisions were made or to find ways to question those decisions. There were no open plenaries and no chance to vote on the structure of future events.

Though the Forum was billed as a break in the protests, by the third day frustrated delegates began to do what they do best: they protested. There were marches and manifestos – a half-dozen at least. Beleaguered forum organizers found themselves charged with everything from reformism to sexism, not to mention ignoring the African continent. The Anti-Capitalist Youth contingent accused them of ignoring the important role direct action played in building the movement. Their manifesto condemned the conference as 'a ruse' using the mushy language of democracy to avoid a more divisive discussion of class. The PSTU, a breakaway faction of the Workers Party, began interrupting speeches about the possibility of another world with loud chants of: 'Another world is not possible, unless you smash capitalism and bring in socialism!' (It sounded much better in Portuguese.)

Some of this criticism was unfair. The forum accommodated an extraordinary range of views, and it was precisely this diversity that made conflicts inevitable. But much of the criticism was legitimate and has implications that reach far beyond a one-week conference. How *are* decisions made in this movement of movements? On the anarchist side, all the talk of radical decentralization often conceals a very real hierarchy based on who owns, understands and controls the computer networks linking the activists to one another – what Jesse Hirsh, one of the founders of the anarchist computer network Tao Communications, calls 'a geek adhocracy'. And on the NGO side, who decides which 'civil society representatives' go behind the fence in Davos or Quebec City – while protesters outside are held back with water cannons and tear gas? There is no consensus among protest organizers about participating in these negotiations, and, more to the point, there is no truly representative process in place to make these decisions: no mechanism to select acceptable members of an activist delegation and no agreed-upon set of goals by which to measure the benefits and pitfalls of taking part.

And yet with a sweeping new round of WTO negotiations set for the fall of 2001, and the Free Trade Area of the Americas negotiation on-going, these questions about process were and are urgent. How do we determine whether the goal is to push for 'social clauses' on labour and environmental issues in international agreements, or to take whole sections – like food safety and agriculture – out of the agreements, or to try to shoot these agreements down altogether?

There are serious debates to be had over strategy and process, but it's difficult to see how they will unfold without bogging down a movement whose greatest strength so far has been its agility. Part of the problem is structural. Among most anarchists, who are doing a great deal of the grassroots organizing, direct democracy, transparency and community self-determination are not lofty political goals, they are fundamental tenets governing their own organizations. But although fanatical about process, anarchists tend to resist efforts to structure or centralize the movement. In contrast, many of the key NGOs, though they may share the anarchists' ideas about democracy in theory, are themselves organized as traditional hierarchies. They are run by charismatic leaders and executive boards, while their members send them money and cheer from the sidelines. The International Forum on Globalization – the brain trust of the North American side of the movement – lacks transparency in its decision-making and isn't accountable to a broad membership. Meanwhile, traditional membership-based structures like political parties and unions have been reduced to bit players in these wide webs of activism.

Perhaps the real lesson of Porto Alegre is that democracy and accountability need to be worked out first on more manageable scales – within local communities and coalitions and inside individual organizations, then broadened out. Without this foundation, there's not much hope for a satisfying democratic process when 10,000 activists from wildly different backgrounds are thrown in a room together.

For a model of how to extract coherence from a movement whose greatest tactical strength so far has been its similarity to a swarm of mosquitoes, it's useful to turn, once again, to the closest thing this movement has to a leader: a mask, two eyes and a pipe – a.k.a. Subcomandante Marcos. Marcos's own story is of a man who came to his leadership not through swaggering certainty, but by coming to terms with political uncertainty, by learning to follow. Though there is no confirmation of Marcos's real identity, the most repeated legend that surrounds him goes like this: an urban Marxist intellectual and activist, Marcos was wanted by the state and was no longer safe in the cities. He fled to the mountains of Chiapas in southeast Mexico filled with revolutionary rhetoric and certainty, there to convert the poor indigenous masses to the cause of armed proletarian revolution against the bourgeoisie. He said the workers of the world must unite, and the Mayans just stared at him. They said they weren't workers and, besides, land wasn't property but the heart of their communities. Having failed as a Marxist missionary, Marcos immersed himself in Mayan culture. The more he learned, the less he knew.

Out of this process, a new kind of army emerged, the EZLN defined itself in terms of not being controlled by an elite of guerrilla commanders but by the communities themselves, through clandestine councils and open assemblies. 'Our army', says Marcos, 'became scandalously Indian.'[12] That meant that he wasn't a commander barking orders, but a subcomandante, a conduit for the will of the councils. His first words said in the new persona were: '[t]hrough me speaks the will of the Zapatista National Liberation Army.'[13]

It's tempting to dismiss the Zapatista model as only being applicable to Indigenous struggles, but that is to miss the point entirely. The reason why there are now 45,000 Zapatista-related websites, why Marcos's communiqués are available in at least fourteen languages, and why twenty-two Zapatista books have been written and twelve documentaries made, is that there is something about the theory of Zapatismo that reaches far beyond Chiapas. It has to do, I think, with the very definition of revolution – and where power should truly rest. A few years ago, the idea of the Zapatista command travelling to Mexico City to address the congress would have been impossible to imagine. The prospect of masked guerrillas (even masked guerrillas who have left their arms at home) entering a hall of political power signals one thing: revolution. But when the Zapatistas travelled to Mexico City in March 2001, they weren't interested in overthrowing the state or naming their leader as president. In fact, when they finally gained entrance to the Congress, they left Marcos outside.

If anything, in their demands for control over land, direct political representation, and the right to protect their language and culture, the Zapatistas are demanding *less* state power over their lives, not more. What sets the Zapatistas apart from typical Marxist guerrilla insurgents is that their goal is not to win control, but to seize and build autonomous spaces where 'democracy, liberty and justice' can thrive. This is intimately linked with an organizing model that doesn't compartmentalize communities into workers, warriors, farmers and students, but instead seeks to organize communities whole, across sectors and across generations, creating genuine 'social movements'. For the Zapatistas, creating these autonomous zones isn't a recipe for dropping out of the capitalist economy, but a base from which to confront it. Marcos is convinced that these free spaces, created from reclaimed land, communal agriculture and resistance to privatization, will eventually create counter-powers to the state.

This organizing model has spread throughout Latin America, and the world. You can see it in the anarchist squats of Italy (called 'social centres') and in the Landless Peasants' Movement of Brazil, which seizes tracts of unused farmland and uses them for sustainable agriculture, markets and schools under the slogan 'Ocupar, Resistir, Producir' (Occupy, Resist, Produce). These same ideas were forcefully expressed by the students of the National Autonomous University of Mexico during the long and militant occupation of their campus. Zapata once said the land belongs to those who work it, their banners blared, WE SAY THAT THE UNIVERSITY BELONGS TO THOSE WHO STUDY IN IT.

What seemed to be emerging organically is not a movement for a single global government but a vision for an increasingly connected international network of very local initiatives, each built on direct democracy.

When critics say that the protesters lack vision, what they are really saying is that they lack an overarching revolutionary philosophy – like Marxism, deep ecology or social anarchy – on which they all agree. That is absolutely true, and for this we should be extraordinarily thankful. At the moment, the anti-corporate street activists are ringed by would-be leaders, anxious for the opportunity to enlist them as foot soldiers. At one end there is the Socialist Workers Party, waiting to welcome all that inchoate energy in Seattle and Washington inside its own sectarian, evangelical framework. On the other, there is John Zerzan in Eugene, Oregon, who sees the rioting and property destruction as the first step toward the collapse of industrialization and a return to pre-lapsarian 'anarcho-primitivism' – a kind of hunter-gatherer utopia.

It is to this young movement's credit that it has as yet fended off all of these agendas and has rejected everyone's generously donated manifesto, holding out for an acceptably democratic, representative process to take its resistance to the next stage. Will it be a ten-point plan? A new political doctrine? Maybe not. Maybe out of the chaotic network of hubs and spokes, something else will emerge: not a blueprint for some utopian new world, but a plan to protect the possibility of many worlds – 'a world', as the Zapatistas say, 'with many worlds in it'.[14]

Maybe instead of meeting the proponents of neoliberalism head on, this movement of movements will surround them from all directions.

Notes

Portions of this essay first appeared in *The Nation*, *The Guardian* and *The Globe and Mail*.

1 In cases where no specific source is referred to, quotations and information are based on personal observation or communication.
2 *Newsweek*, 13 December 1999, p. 36.
3 Mark Steyn, 'Zealots' Only Concrete Argument: They Grasp Their Projectiles; Less So Their Principles', *National Post*, 23 April 2001.
4 Subcomandante Marcos quoted in Robert Collier, 'Commander Marcos Identifies With All', *San Francisco Chronicle*, 13 June 1994.
5 Subcomandante Marcos, *First Declaration of La Realidad For Humanity Against Neoliberalism*, by the Clandestine Indigenous Revolutionary Committee General Command of the Zapatista Army of National Liberation, Mexico, January 1996. Available at http://www.ezln.org/documentos/1996/19960130.en.htm
6 Subcomandante Marcos, 'Dying in Order to Live', in Juana Ponce de Leon, ed., *Our Word Is Our Weapon*, Toronto: Seven Stories Press, 2001.
7 TeleGeography Inc, *Hubs and Spokes: A TeleGeography Internet Reader*, Washington, DC: TeleGeography, 2000, p. 9.
8 Subcomandante Marcos, *EZLN's Declaration of War: Today We Say Enough Is Enough (Ya Basta!)*, General command of the EZLN, 1993.
9 Charles H. Ramsey during a press conference, Washington, DC, 17 April 2000. Bob Dart and Alec Schultz report Ramsey to have said that '[t]hey are very very organized' ('Protests Shut Parts of Capital: Meetings Go On; Bankers Vow Reform', *The Palm Beach Post*, 17 April 2000).
10 David F. Ronfeldt, John Arquilla, Graham E. Fuller, Melissa Fuller, *The Zapatista Social Netwar in Mexico*, Los Angeles, CA: Rand, 1998, p. 50.
11 Ibid., p. 119.
12 Marcos, in Ponce de Leon, ed., *Our Word Is Our Weapon*.
13 Ibid.
14 For the quote 'a world made of many worlds', see Zapatista Army of National Liberation (read by Subcomandante Marcos), *Second Declaration of La Realidad* at the closing act of the First Intercontinental Encounter for Humanity and Against Neoliberalism, August 1996.

15 Québec City 2001 and the making of transnational subjects

André C. Drainville

Source: André C. Drainville (2002), 'Québec City 2001 and the Making of Transnational Subjects', *Socialist Register 2002*, pp. 15–42

In the last two decades, the organizations which are dedicated to managing the world economy, and the social forces wanting to reform or revolutionize it, have both made global politics seem a cosmopolitan affair. Borrowing the inclusive language of city-builders, the World Bank *et al.* have invited selected NGOs and other would-be representatives of 'global civil society' to gather together, think civic thoughts and define the conditions of global civility. In tune, transnational social forces have defined themselves with reference to cosmopolitan *proxies* ('global civil society' here too, 'humanity', 'the peoples of the earth', 'the women – or the workers, or the poor – of the world') and have let themselves be drawn into a variety of scenarios (ranging from the civic schemes of the World Bank to reformist plans for a 'Tobin Tax' or a people's UN assembly, to ideas for global social contracts) that all end with the settling of global social relations.[1]

Though these scenarios may look like radical strategies for bringing transnational capital under social control – and thus seem like important breaches in the global order of things – they actually underestimate what might be born of the global meeting of social forces. Puffed up and ensconced in reverent absolutes, the peoples (or the women, or the workers, or the poor) of the world will not struggle for themselves or establish and sustain positions against transnational power. Cut off from any real social context, these cosmopolitan ghosts are fated to settle for a mollifying consensus from which might – perhaps – be found ways to humanize global capitalism, but nothing to challenge or revolutionize it. We need to reason from concrete, contingent, practices, in specific locations, at critical moments when broad political considerations – always the stuff of cosmopolitan planning – get turned into questions of strategy.[2] Rather than take cosmopolitan subjects for granted, we need to inquire into their making. Only thus can we look beyond ways to humanize global capitalism, and think about ways to revolutionize it.

In Québec City, where this article was written, the 'Summit of the Americas' was held between 20 April and 22 April 2001. A polycentric gathering of would-be hemispheric actors – from globalizing elites intent on making a 'Free Trade Area of the Americas' (FTAA), to sundry 'Peoples of the Americas' collected in a parallel summit, to a saturnalia of protests at the periphery of both events – it was a privileged occasion on which to think critically about the political construction of transnational subjects. This essay begins with a brief survey of the places where the events related to the Summit of the Americas were held. In the second part, these places and what was made in them are related to broader processes of order and change in the world economy.

Québec City 2001

The Summit of the Americas

At the centre of happenings in Québec City was the 'Summit of the Americas', hosted by the 'Bureau of the Summit of the Americas', a concern of Canada's Department of Foreign Affairs and International Trade (DFAIT). After Miami (1994) and Santiago (1998), this was the third official gathering of heads of states of the hemisphere since George Bush launched the 'Enterprise for the Americas Initiative' (EAI, 1991) to 'unify the Americas from Anchorage to Tierra Del Fuego in the world's biggest free trade pact'.[3]

Housed in the *Centre des Congrès*, on René Lévesque Boulevard, near the provincial parliament, shielded behind a 3.5 kilometres long, three-metres high fence establishing a 'security perimeter' defended by a united front of municipal, provincial and federal police, the Summit was a political enigma cloaked in a security spectacle: inside, thirty-four national delegations – 9,000 delegates – worked for the first time with a complete draft of the FTAA (Free Trade Area of the Americas; in French, Zone de Libre Échange des Amériques, or ZLEA) agreement. Yet, what would be discussed was not made public before the summit, in spite of considerable public pressure; nor was what would be discussed between them and the corporate patrons who sponsored various get-togethers (*inside* the security perimeter).

Also organized by the DFAIT's Bureau were song-and-dance celebrations of hemispheric peoples and cultures. Starting in the fall, *Voix des Amériques* concerts were held at Le Capitole, the permanent venue for *The Elvis Story* (in English on the marquise), a hyper-real revue (a 'real copy' in Umberto Eco's term, a perfect substitute for reality) that draws much of its clientele from the tourist trade and the suburbs, whose producers have spearheaded attempts to commodify *Place d'Youville*, a former market place that serves as a gathering place for youths and, sometimes, a starting point for urban riots.[4] The last concert in the *Voix* series, held days before the Summit, was the *Tropicalia* review, that promised 'all the *joie de vivre*, all the colours of Brazil . . . a trip south through the samba and the bossa nova'. At the end of the Summit, DFAIT sponsored an extravaganza of 600 artists, later televised by the Canadian Broadcasting Corporation, the official broadcaster of the Summit.

Other DFAIT-sponsored events included a Summit school (to encourage young reporters to inquire into 'the realities of the Americas'), a Youth Forum ('Emotion, authenticity and cultural diversity') that produced a 'practical, realistic, report', later circulated amongst official delegations; a picture-drawing contest; a cooking festival ('Savouring the Americas'); a 'Writers of the Americas' Summit; a film festival; and a book fair (the 'Library of the Americas'). An 'Inter-American Cooperation Beyond Free Trade' colloquium focusing on the 'wealth and complexity of interamerican cooperation' was hosted by Laval University's *Institut Québécois des Hautes Études Internationales* (a privileged partner of both DFAIT and Canada's Department of Defense).[5]

Implicating academics, representatives of government-created and sponsored NGOs as well as members of national and global governing agencies, it was a model of partnership between academia and governing institutions. It ended on Friday April 20, as the heads of states' Summit began, by making policy recommendations that were, conveniently, a faithful match for the 'Summit of the Americas Declaration and Plan of Action', released as the Summit ended on Sunday April 22.[6]

The People's Summit

Well removed from the security perimeter – in a tent in the old harbour in Lower Town, beside picturesque old Québec – was the second 'Peoples' Summit of the Americas', that had for its theme: 'Resisting. Proposing. Together.' Organized by the *Réseau Québécois d'intégration continentale* (RQIC), and Common Frontiers – respectively Québec's and Canada's link to the Hemispheric Social Alliance (HSA) – the Peoples' summit was itself largely funded and, literally, *placed* by Canada's DFAIT's and Québec's Ministry of External Affairs.[7]

In keeping with the heads of states' summit, the People's Summit was a mix of the purposeful and the festive. From Monday through Thursday, policy forums – involving, for the most part, duly registered representatives of 'civil society' – dealt with issues outlined in the latest draft of the 'People's Hemispheric Agreement' (PHA) on 'women and globalization', 'education', 'labour', 'agriculture', 'communications', 'human rights', the 'environment', and so on. In the evening, plenary sessions were held to find ways to aggregate demands and reach a consensus that could later be incorporated in the next draft of the PHA. On Friday, teach-ins were organized.

On Saturday, the People's work was done and a People's March was held. A first group – roughly 10,000 – gathered on the Plains of Abraham (in Upper Town, near the security perimeter); another, larger, group – estimates vary from 30,000 to 50,000 – gathered in Lower Town near the People's tent. When they met – at the corner of Charest Boulevard and rue de la Couronne in Lower Town, a short walk away from the security perimeter – they formed the largest crowd ever assembled in Québec history (save for that which heard young Céline Dion sing for Pope John-Paul II). But immediately the march split into two, very unequal, groups. Shepherded by 1,500 marshals from the *Fédération des Travailleurs du Québec*, upwards of sixty thousand marched not towards but away from the perimeter to the Parc de l'exposition, where the People were assembled in a parking lot, between a shopping centre and the Pepsi coliseum, to listen to speeches from their representatives.[8] A much smaller group – perhaps 1,000 – broke away from the People's March and walked back uptown to support direct actions against the security perimeter. When they reached the fence, the *Funk Fighting Unaccountable Naughty Korporations* tried, but failed, to organize a sit-in.

Protests: teach-ins, demonstrations and other carnivalesque happenings

In already tried fashion (although only a few years old, anti-summit protests have already established set ways), the Summit of the Americas also occasioned a saturnalia of protests, teach-ins, direct actions and street theatre, organized for the most part either by *Opération Québec Printemps 2001* (OQP 2001), a broad coalition of local community and student groups, or by the *Comité d'accenil du Sommet des Amériques* (CASA) working with the *Convergence des Luttes Anti-Capitalistes* (CLAC), both anarchist groups, the former from Québec city, the latter from Montréal.[9]

Some teach-ins and conferences were held in what was termed the 'solidarity perimeter', in the Limoilou neighbourhood (further removed than even the People's Summit from the security perimeter). Drawing on militants and experts from such nodes of anti-globalization activity as the International Forum on Globalization, the Third World Network, or *L'observatoire sur la Mondialisation*, they focused on a wide variety of political issues related to globalization in general and to the FTAA in particular: the privatization of water, the clear-cutting of forests, union history, human rights, health care, art and activism, education, the Tobin tax, etc. Workshops on interacting with the media, legal rights, direct actions and ways of conducting civil disobedience were also held inside the 'solidarity perimeter'.

On Friday the 20th, a 'Carnaval anti-capitaliste' was organized by the CASA/CLAC. At 1 p.m., a crowd of some 5,000 gathered at Laval University in the suburbs where people joined either a green bloc (peaceful and festive), a yellow bloc (obstructive and defensive) or a red bloc (intent on disturbance and direct actions). Greens went either to the Ilôt Fleuri (a wasteland in Lower Town underneath a highway, remade into a post-industrial happening place: think Blade Runner meets travellers' festivals), or to the Faubourg Saint-Jean Baptiste uptown where the local *Comité populaire* had organized a peaceful occupation of the neighbourhood.[10]

Yellows and reds, along with a small 'black block' assembled by the *ad hoc* Autonomous Organizing Collective of Anti-Authoritarians from the Mid-West, Northeast, Montréal and Québec, marched to the security perimeter. They arrived in the middle of the afternoon. A catapult brought from the Ottawa region by the *Deconstructionist Institute for Surreal Topology* (self-described *Lanarkists*) tried to launch stuffed toy-animals into the security perimeter, while those who had received training in civil disobedience tried to organized a sit-in. Quickly, both were overtaken by events: a segment of the fence was brought down, police fired tear gas and the already familiar to-and-fro of anti-summit protest began.

Giving colour and context to events were theatre groups – some linked to OQP, others to the *CASA*, or from outside Québec – working to foster what the historical avant-garde (Futurists, Dada, the surrealists, etc.) would have recognized as a radically creative ambiance. The best, most derisive, action was in the Saint-Jean Baptiste neighbourhood, where a section of the fence was decorated with bras and girdles, some inscribed with slogans ('My mother is not for sale'), others with bilingual anti-FTAA/anti-*ZLÉA* slogans (English on one cup, French on the other, with more equanimity than is usually found in the politics of language in Québec).

Feeding mainstream and alternative newspapers and working to facilitate links with other events elsewhere in the hemisphere was the *Centre des Médias Alternatifs-Québec 2001* (the CMAQ), Québec's link to the IndyMedia (independent media) family. Set up in the fall of 2000 by *Alternatives* (a DFAIT-funded NGO), officially launched at parties in Québec City (on 25 January) and in Montréal (on 1 February); the CMAQ was headquartered in the Méduse art complex, on côte d'Abraham, a short walk – but more than a stone's throw – away from the security perimeter, but within range of the policemen's gas. There were also housed medics, who helped those harmed by tear gas and rubber bullets.

Matters of security

The separation between the heads of states' summit and other events was as definite and spectacular as it has ever been in the short history of counter-summit protests. To serve the needs of official delegates and protect their intimacy there were more than 6,000 policemen and women, working for all the police corps with some kind of authority in the region: the Québec City municipal police (circulation, perimeter security), the Sainte-Foy municipal police (airport security), the *Sureté du Québec* (crowd control, criminal activities) and the Royal Canadian Mounted police (internal passports, logistics, perimeter security). They were aided in their work by more than 1,200 soldiers and student volunteers from local police colleges, who were stool-pigeons among the protesters.

Giving weight and significance to the police and soldiers was a spectacle of authority that had been under construction for several months, with the help of police forces from Seattle, Prague, Washington and other sites of anti-summit protests. The first move in the construction of the spectacle of authority – a symbolic move, targeted at what police have come to associate with anti-globalization activities – was the Internet publication in August 2000 of the Canadian Security Intelligence Service's report on 'Anti-Globalization protests'. This was a perfectly banal document that revealed nothing about security arrangements but did signal CSIS's intent to monitor all forms of communication.[11]

In real life, the spectacular build-up of authority started on the first of November, when a press conference was held during which the Québec Minister of Public Security Serge Ménard and Québec city police spokesman Gaétan Labbé, backed up by representatives of other police corps, unveiled what they called security measures 'unprecedented in Canadian history'.[12] Afterward, every detail of security arrangements (the number of hotel rooms and apartments rented by the RCMP, the kind of assault vehicles and plastic bullets the SQ might use, the breadth of the security perimeter and the depth of police infiltration of anti-globalization groups, etc.) were similarly unveiled at press conferences by a row of senior police officers. On February 4th, three CASA protesters who were distributing anti-FTAA leaflets to tourists in town for the Winter Carnival (the most media-saturated event in Québec City) were arrested at lunch-time on the most central intersection in the city. They refused to identify themselves and were later released. Two weeks later, the city of Ste-Foy declared (in a by-law later revoked) that the wearing of scarves and balaclavas would be forbidden between 1 April and 2 May, in order, as they openly put it, not to 'interfere with repressive measures' (a direct echo of what the Philadelphia police did before the Republican convention in July 2000).

The making of transnational subjects

Summit happenings are frequently analyzed in the narrow terms of who stood or fought with whom, did what when, won or lost which battle, or what was won or lost in it, but they also need to be related to broader and more diffused processes of order and change in the post-Bretton Woods world economy. Specifically, they can be understood to be part of the making of new transnational subjects.

Consensus and neoliberal governance

Driving attempts to redefine the terms of global order in the post-Bretton Woods period have been what Stephen Gill has termed globalizing elites, gathering 'at the apex of social hierarchies in the emerging world order', in places increasingly detached from national social formations, working with relatively coherent purpose and ideology.[13] In the immediate wake of the Bretton Woods crisis, globalizing elites either gathered in institutions inherited from the Bretton Woods period (the International Monetary Fund, the World Bank, the Bank for International Settlements (BIS), the Organisation for Economic Cooperation and Development) but made more relevant and autonomous by the context of crisis, or they established new forums (the Trilateral Commission, the World Economic Forum in Davos, G7 summits, etc.).

What was done in these exclusive – indeed almost clandestine – gatherings could sometimes be defined in concrete, immediate, terms. Monetarist targeting, for instance – a key neoliberal 'concept of control' and a central component of neoliberal policies in all advanced capitalist countries in the latter half of the 1970s – was born in the BIS and in still more discreet places, such as the Brunner-Meltzer conferences in Konztanz, the bi-annual Carnegie/Rochester Conferences, or the meetings of the Mont Pélerin Society.[14]

More broadly, meetings of global elites served to nurture what the OECD called the 'collegial management of the developed world's interests' and the G7, a 'sense of common purpose and vision'.[15] Thus they were key to defining the terms of neoliberal regulation, arguably the first mode of regulation born in the world economy itself.

Early in the post-Bretton Woods period, neoliberal concepts of control were impressed – by means of structural adjustment plans and monetarist regulation – on debtor countries that faced monetary or balance-of-payment crises, whether at the centre of the world economy (Britain in 1976) or at the periphery (Chile, Argentina or Peru). Echoing what *haute finance* had dreamed of in the age of the *Pax Britannica*, globalizing elites tried to 'impos[e] upon society...the concept of the self-regulating market'.[16] The attempt to regulate the world economy authoritatively – by domination rather than hegemonic leadership, to borrow a distinction dear to contemporary political economy – has remained an integral part of neoliberal ordering. The Multilateral Agreement on Investment (MAI), which tried to install investors as privileged subjects in international law, was the latest and most explicit example.

Beginning in the 1980s, however, political events (IMF riots in Caracas, Warsaw, Buenos Aires, Abidjan and Libreville, the popular removal from office of neoliberal presidents in Brazil, Venezuela and Guatemala), as well as structural rigidities (Fordist mechanisms at the centre of the world economy, state planning in socialist economies, weak or nonexistent mechanisms of financial surveillance at the periphery) exposed the economic costs and political fragility of global overdetermination.[17]

To increase the efficiency of adjustment and solidify the political foundations of neoliberalism, global, regulatory agencies began to concern themselves with political and social processes beyond crude pressure, and to structure their relationship with NGOs and other would-be representatives of global civil society.[18]

It is this concern that defines 'global governance', the political adjunct to global neoliberalism.

'Global governance' is an attempt to invent a political interlocutor with whom globalizing elites might negotiate sustainable terms for global accumulation: a 'real copy', a perfectly fabricated and perfectly acceptable substitute for global civil society. This absolutely crucial attempt is what sets governance apart from previous modes of global regulation: 'mercantile sponsoring' in the seventeenth and eighteenth century, 'free-trade liberalism' in the nineteenth century, 'embedded liberalism' after the Second World War, 'neoliberalism' after the Bretton Woods crisis. Where these all relied for their political sustenance on a relatively exclusive coalition of globalizing elites working in association with a global patchwork of local and nationally-constituted elites (even 'embedded liberalism' was embedded not in the world economy itself, but in national social formations), 'global governance' tries to assemble a broad-based, possibly sustainable, global constituency to bolster and stabilize global order. This constituency, we can think of as a 'global growth machine': a 'broad coalition of social forces that share an apolitical, ostensibly "value-free" understanding of economic growth', and have moved 'beyond opposition to proposition' to define a consensual path for capitalist growth.[19]

Whether it will succeed in moving global neoliberalism beyond mere domination towards something like hegemony will depend on the outcome of political struggles.

The most spectacular places to see governance's growth machine at work are, precisely, 'global summits'. These are to global governance what universal exhibits were to free-trade internationalism in the age of *Pax Britannica*: idealized representations of order. Where, as Charlotte Brontë put it, universal exhibits gathered a 'unique assemblage of all things' promised by free-trade capitalism, global conferences are gatherings of what appears as a model citizenry, ideally bound to find the best – most efficient, most portable and sustainable – solutions to global problems: of development, at the United Nations Conference on Environment and Development in Rio, June 1992; of human rights, in Vienna a year later: of population growth, in Cairo in September 1994: of social development, in Copenhagen in March 1995: of housing, in Istanbul in June 1996; of variformed challenges to the reform of the United Nations, at the 'We the Peoples' Millennium Forum in New York in May 2000; of the production of wealth, social reproduction and related issues at the 'World Social Forum' in Porto Alegre in January 2001.[20]

Exhibited at global conferences, governance solutions get synthesized into blueprints and forward-looking plans of action – Rio's 'Agenda 21', Cairo's 'Programme of Action', Copenhagen's 'World Social Charter', 'Istanbul's 'Habitat Agenda', New York's 'Declaration and Agenda for Action', Porto Alegre's 'Manifest'. These visible artefacts of a broad division of political labours are made elsewhere and imported into global conferences. To inquire into how and by whom they are made is to begin looking into 'governance' as an attempt to construct transnational subjects.

In the last two decades the regulatory agencies of the world economy have broadened and structured their relationship with would-be representatives of global civil society. At the World Bank, for instance, a concerted effort began in the early 1980s to involve NGOs more closely in policy-making (what is termed the 'mainstreaming' and 'upstreaming' of NGOs): new institutional points of contact were created, new funding windows and lending facilities were opened, and new operational directives were issued that defined the terms of NGO-World Bank collaboration. The proportion of projects involving NGO participation – less than 6 per cent between 1973–88 – grew to almost 50 per cent by the mid-1990s.[21]

In like manner, the OECD made 'a political virtue of the necessity to increase economic efficiency' and started in the early 1980s to mix 'good development policy [with] good politics' by folding development aid into national strategies drawn up in collaboration with representative coalitions of local NGOs and social elites.[22]

Here as well, new funding windows were opened and the relationship with NGOs, GONGOs, GOINGOs, QUANGOs and other would-be representatives of global civil society was further structured.[23] At the World Trade Organization, an NGO ombudsman was put in place and a 'Citizen's Summit' was called for the Seattle Ministerial meeting, that was to serve as a background to the official launch of the *Millennium Round* of negotiations before street protests overtook planned events.[24] Even the World Economic Forum in Davos, a quintessential elite place, has opened itself up somewhat: in 2001, Lori Wallach, Director of Global Tradewatch and a key figure of Seattle protests, addressed delegates at the personal invitation of the Forum's founder Klaus Schwab, who thinks of himself as something of a radical amongst the company he keeps.[25]

At a time when governance agencies are working to 'provide security, prosperity, coherence, order and continuity to the [global] system', Québec's Summit of the Americas can be situated in relation both to the making of neoliberal concepts of control, and to efforts to assemble a global civil society acceptable to globalizing elites.[26] About the importance of the Summit of the Americas in this process little can be said for the moment, except that it was an occasion for hemispheric elites to further define the terms of the 'neo-liberal conditioning framework' in the Americas begun by the North American Free Trade Agreement.[27] In marked contrast to the WTO summit in Seattle – 'the first big negotiation on world trade for over five years' – the Québec summit was not defined in relation to any objectives that might give protesters a measure of their success.[28]

About the making of a global growth machine, it needs be said that this has been an integral part of neoliberal integration in the Americas since its inception. George Bush's 'Enterprise for the Americas' speech made explicit reference to the need to 'strengthen hemispheric democratization', a wish later operationalized by the Miami 'Plan of Action' that explicitly instructed governments to 'review the regulatory framework for non-governmental actors with a view to facilitating their operation and promoting their ability to receive funds', with a view to 'giv[ing] depth and durability to democracy'.[29]

Key here is the Inter-American Development Bank (IDB), which has worked – in tune with other regional affiliates of the World Bank – to foster participatory development and to structure relationships with NGOs, 'stakeholders' and other civic partners of globalizing elites. In 'governance' fashion, there have been grand civic gatherings and new sources of funding. The first notable gatherings were IDB conferences held in September 1994 on 'Strengthening Civil Society' and 'Civic Participation and Socioeconomic Participation'.[30] Also in 1994, the IDB held an hemispheric forum on 'Women in the Americas: Participation and Development' from which was born the Oaxaca Initiative ('A Framework for Equitable and Sustainable Development in the Americas'). At the March 1998 IDB Annual Meeting in Cartageana, Executive Vice-President Nancy Birdsall and Edmundo Jarquin. of the newly-created 'State and Civil Society Division', addressed participants at the 'Social Programs, Poverty and Citizen Involvement' seminar, to tell them about the 'inevitability of citizens' involvement in sustainable development'. The two-day seminar concluded on an indisputable 'governance' note: '[c]*itizen participation, properly channeled, generates savings, mobilized additional financial and human resources, promotes equity and makes a decisive contribution to the strengthening of society and the democratic system*'.[31]

In January 1999 the IDB co-sponsored a 'Global Meeting of Generations', in Washington, DC in collaboration with the 'International Association of Students in Economics and Management', 'Youth for Development and Cooperation', the UNDP and the 'International Development Conference'. There, 'one hundred young social entrepreneurs from around the world' sat with 'global, national and grassroots development organizations', to 'discuss key issues and opportunities facing humanity in the 21st century', and to draw up civic blueprints.

Beyond summitry, the IDB has also worked to broaden and structure its relationship with would-be representatives of civil society. Before 'governance', only the 'Small Project Program' (1979) provided a structured, sustained, link between NGOs and the IDB. Back then, representatives of civil society were only involved with the IDB in exceptional circumstances – and then only in a service-delivery capacity.[32] In the last decade, however, the IDB has conducted what Nancy Birdsall called a 'diagnostic survey of the present status of civil society in the region' and, as a result, it set up a variety of outreach and consultation programs for NGOs.[33]

As well, new funding windows and 'social investment funds' were opened to encourage and structure NGO participation: in 1987, a 'Social Investment Fund' was established that was explicitly demand-driven and aimed at fostering the active involvement of community organizations and NGOs in all stages of the project cycle. In 1991, the Indigenous Peoples Fund (IPF) was set up. To 'promote the long-term and sustainable development of the native peoples of Latin America and the Caribbean', the IPF encouraged consultations of all sorts – from information-sharing to decision-making in project-identification and design – between native leaderships and the IDB. In the same spirit, the Multilateral Investment Fund (1992) has concerned itself with building partnerships between NGOs and private voluntary organizations, particularly those representing people usually left out of the economic mainstream. The three investment 'windows' of the MIF – the 'Technical Cooperation Facility', the 'Human Resources Facility' and the 'Small Enterprise Development Facility' – all provide services to build knowledge, encourage economic empowerment and involve women and youth in the 'enterprise economy'.

The IDB has also worked to 'mainstream' and 'upstream' representatives of hemispheric civil society, and to further participatory development, 'defined in broad terms as the process through which people with a legitimate interest (stakeholders) influence and share control over development initiatives, and the decisions and resources which affect them'. In true 'governance' spirit, the IDB has sought efficiency, both political and economic: '[*p*]*articipation improves project design by reducing the cost of obtaining accurate and site-specific data on environmental, social and cultural factors as well as stakeholders' felt needs and priorities. Also, project managers can get input from all groups, including people often marginalized in the development process*'.[34]

As the political contours of regional integration were taking shape in the early 1990s the IDB set up a 'State and Civil Society Division' and a 'Social Programs and Sustainable Development Department'.[35] As well, a Women in Development (WID) unit was created in 1994 that begat a 'Fund for Women's Leadership and Representation' to direct funds to organizations that promote women's participation and leadership at national, regional, and local levels, in the economic, political and social spheres.[36]

Until very recently, the Organization of American States had played a minor role in the construction of a hemispheric growth machine (though sometimes it did act as a secretariat for hemispheric integration – as it did in Lima in June 1997, when OAS Ministers of Foreign relations set the agenda for the Santiago Summit of the Americas).[37] After Santiago, however, a 'Unit for the Promotion of Democracy' was created that has worked, modestly, through state institutions, 'to consolidate both civic practices and mechanisms of participation in the political process'.[38] In June 1999 a 'Committee on Civil Society Participation' was created 'to establish clear, transparent, modern procedures for interaction between civil society and the political organs of the OAS'.[39] These procedures allowed the Committee to consult with more than 900 organizations and to assemble a stock of policy proposals. At the 'Hemispheric Meeting' (Miami, 18–20 January 2001), these proposals were synthesized into the 'Final Document: Recommendations by Civil Society Organizations' that will, in all likelihood, have been part of what was discussed in Québec City.[40]

As well as the IDB and the OAS, other governing agencies have also worked to define efficient and sustainable terms of hemispheric social relations by hosting meetings with designated representatives of civil society. At their fourth meeting in San José (Costa Rica) in March 1998, trade ministers established the 'Committee of Government representatives on the Participation of Civil Society'. In November, this Committee issued an 'Open Invitation to Civil Society' that detailed both its desire to work with civil society representatives and the terms of collaboration. The Committee met twice in the summer of 1999. On November 4, 1999, during the fifth meeting of the trade ministers of the Americas in Toronto, the Committee's report was made public.[41]

In the spring of 2000 a second 'Open Invitation to Civil Society' was extended, in preparation for Québec's Summit of the Americas, arguably the most important gathering yet of the hemispheric growth machine, both quantitatively and in terms of policy-readiness: never did so many gather with such defined purpose or with, in the background, such a decorous, 'colourful tapestry of cultures, values and traditions'.[42]

Standing at the apex of another transnational hierarchy that has taken shape in the last decade, the People's Summit was the other part of the hemispheric growth machine that met in Québec City. For a decade between the mid-eighties and mid-nineties social forces opposed to neoliberal integration in the Americas organized summits, gatherings and *encuentros*. In North America, the FTA and NAFTA negotiations occasioned a veritable explosion of trans-border summits between the Action Canada Network (ACN), the American Fair Trade Campaign (FTC) and the *Red Mexicana de Acción Frente Libre Comercio* (RMAFLC).[43]

Amongst notable summits were: the ACN-RMLAC *Encuentro* (Mexico, October 1990), the ACN-RMAFLC-FTC summit (Mexico, April 1991), the San Ygnacio *encuentro* of environmental groups (April 1991), the Zacatenas meeting (October 1991), the Trinational Working Women's conference (Valle de Bravo, February 1992) and the tri-national cross-border meeting between representatives of the ACN, the RMAFLC, the CTC and the American Alliance for Responsible Trade (Niagara Falls, October 1993). This was the last trinational summit before the NAFTA came into effect on January 1994. After NAFTA, two *Encuentros per la Humanidad* γ *contra el Neoliberalismo* were organized in Mexico by the *Ejército Zapatista de Liberación National* (EZLN): the first took place in Chiapas in July–August 1996, the second in *Belem do Para*, 6 to 11 December 1999.

In the same period, trans-border summits were also being organized nearer Brazil, another pole of transnational integration. The Sao Paulo Forum was founded in 1990 by Brazil's *Partido Dos Trabalhadores* (PT) and representatives from left organizations and movements, including the Sandinista National Liberation Front of Nicaragua, the Farabundo Marti National Liberation Front of EL Salvador, the Broad Front of Uruguay, Bolivia's Free Bolivar Movement. Peru's United Left and the Cuban Communist Party.[44]

The second meeting of the Sao Paulo Forum was held in Mexico City in June 1991; the third in Managua in July 1992, the fourth in Havana in July 1993 and the last in Montevideo in 1995. A gathering of more than two hundred left movements, parties and organizations, it was hailed by Libya's Mu'ammar al-Qadhafi as the embryo of a 'Popular World Front'.[45]

But fronts born of popular summitry did not hold up. Less than four years after Niagara Falls and two after Montevideo, popular summits were already being folded into the process of hemispheric governance. In 1997, the *Nossa América* popular forum was held in Belo Horizonte, alongside the 'Third Summit Meeting of Ministers for Commerce' and the 'Third Business Forum of the Americas'. In true 'governance' fashion, it both gave birth to a new transnational subject (the 'Hemispheric Social Alliance') and, on its behalf, produced a syncretic, reformist, agenda accepting of what Michel Chossudovsky has called the 'dominant counter-discourse', which presses for the inclusion of environmental, labour and human rights clauses within trade agreements, and pushes for poverty alleviation schemes and institutional reforms.[46]

In April 1998, the First Peoples' Summit, convened by the Hemispheric Social Alliance, was held in Santiago, alongside the second Summit of the Americas.[47] 'Two thousand delegates met in twelve sectoral forums, workshopping ideas for an alternative social and economic model in the hemisphere.' Then was drafted the first People's Hemispheric Agreement (PHA), entitled 'Alternatives for the Americas'. Key to it was the People's acceptance of free trade and foreign investments as privileged 'instruments for achieving just and sustainable development'.[48] The HSA campaign continued in March 1999 in Costa Rica, where a Coordinating Group was chosen – that included Common Frontiers and the RQIC – to pilot the PHA push for inclusion and reform. A further draft of the PHA was prepared at a 'civil society meeting' in Rio in June 1999 (held in parallel with the meeting of heads of states from the European Union, Latin Americas and the Caribbean). And during the 'citizens' forum' held prior to the fourth summit of Trade Ministers of the Hemisphere (Toronto, November 1999) the PHA draft was prepared that was discussed and updated when 'hemispheric civil society' reconvened for the Second People's Summit in Québec city.

Thus was being constructed a 'hemispheric growth machine' that operates mainly as a problem-solving body working to define terms for sustainable accumulation. The heads of states' Summits and the People's Summits, of course, are not reducible to one another. In terms of their political origins, as well as in feeling and intent, they are relatively distinct entities. And if there was nothing more to neoliberalism than concepts of control coercively imposed – what global neoliberalism was before the mid-eighties – then the People's Summit would be a radical event indeed. But in the age of governance, when global regulatory agencies are trying to move neoliberal regulation beyond coercion towards consensus, the attempt to create a responsible hemispheric civil society and the People's' move from 'Resisting' to 'Proposing' should be seen as twinned enterprises, both parts of the making of a 'hemispheric growth machine'.

Protest and resistance

The political dynamics of the post-Bretton Woods period opened room not only for transnational concepts of control and governance-defined civility, but also for forms of oppositional politics. To describe it, some have written of 'new left internationalism', others of 'global contention', of 'global social movements', or of 'global resistance'.[49] By many accounts, what is most distinctive about this new kind of global politics – in relation both to the inherited ways of left internationalism and to 'governance' – is how it creates, at the point of contact with global power (where strategic courses meet) what Michel Foucault would have recognized as 'communities of resistance'.[50]

Lately, the best places to observe transnational communities of resistance in action have been protests against gatherings of globalizing elites. Most famously, fifty thousand met in Seattle on 30 November 1999 to force the closing of the second ministerial conference of the World Trade Organization. On 16 April 2000, eight thousand protested the annual meeting of World Bank and IMF in Washington. In September, fifteen thousand were in Prague to protest the 55th annual WB/IMF summit – the first such event to be held in a former East-block country.[51] A few months later, a few hundred were in Davos to protest the opening of the 31st World Economic Summit.[52] Brought together by organizations with an acute sense of the marvellous and the sensational (the Ruckus Society, the Direct Action Network, Reclaim the Streets, Mobilization for Global Justice, etc.), often coloured wondrously (in Prague, yellows were 'ecolos', pinks reds of all sorts, blues anarchists and anti-fascists), fused by tactical preoccupations readily dramatized by journalistic accounts, their carnivalesque aesthetics and sense of happening contrasting markedly with 'governance's' dutiful greys and decorous fêtes (this year at Davos, Youssou N'Dour sang and danced for the globalizing elites), summit protesters are certainly most spectacular communities of resistance.

Less sensational, but more significant, are the transnational communities of resistance being born in countless campaigns against the ways and consequences of globalization: union busting and gender exploitation in export zones (in Saipan, Mexico's *maquilladoras*, Guatemala, etc.), brand-name exploitation (by GAP, General Electric, Guess, Mitsubishi, Nike, Reebok, Suzuki and others), sexual tourism (in South-East Asia and Europe), the ecological impact of structural reforms, the imprisonment of notable labour leaders or social activists (Ken Saro-Wiwa, Mumia Abu-Jamal, Wei Jingsheng, Wariebi K. Agamene,

A. Aidelomon, Frank O. Kokori and others), undemocratic transnational policies (the Multilateral Agreement on Investment, for instance). Organized by a diffused '*nébuleuse*' of relatively new international organizations, documentation and research centres, these campaigns have brought social forces directly onto the terrain of the world economy, not as a severed and regimented lot of problem-solvers, nor as the obligatory agents of cosmopolitan *proxies*, but as rooted and indefinite communities of struggle. Elsewhere, I have called this the radical, ordinary, new internationalism of social movements:

> not radical because it represents a leap of consciousness, because it proclaims ex cathedra its anti-capitalism, or because it invents new and broader solidarities, but because it is an increasingly ordinary, everyday expression of the deep fellowship of the moved and the shaken of the world economy [and] because it expresses a shared marginalization that is more deeply rooted materially than that projected by cosmopolitan projects of the 19th century or desired by Internationals. This is not the crystalline internationalism of those who share a similar position in the mathematical equations explaining the capitalist accumulation process, but the cloudy internationalism of those who live in a capitalist world economy, and who resist global capitalism as an historically specific and contingent mode of social organization.[53]

Transnational campaigns tend to be tied to particular issues, and are dismissed for their 'economic-corporatist' consciousness and their inability to tell us 'what they are fighting for' and what 'they care about.' Although less political than strategic, and certainly lacking in programmatic coherence, they may nonetheless be having a structuring impact on the world economy as a place of politics.[54] Dragging context and politics with them to the world economy, at once global and radically grounded, transnational communities of resistance may be transforming the world economy into a place where ideas and modes of organizations as well as ways of life and struggle become relatively autonomous from individual agency. Charged by contextualized struggles, the world economy may be becoming a conductor, or even a catalyst. This we may take as a guiding hypothesis, as we turn our attention back to Québec's Summit of the Americas.

Québec City and the making of transnational subjects

The protests in Québec City, of course, neither rose in the sky like the sun at an appointed time, nor were they simply induced by some kind of global ambience (or by what Edward Said has called a 'global oppositional mood'[55]). They were made not by cosmopolitan ghosts but by actually-existing groups. Between June 2000 (when SalAMI's first training camp was held in Val Cartier) and the beginning of the Summit, some fifty *formations* (training courses, from prepared kits) were given near and around the city by *formateurs and formatrices*, to a medley of groups (union locals, community groups, nuns, students and women's groups), on a variety of issues related to neoliberal globalization (and, in the case of CMAQ's *Ateliers de formations*, on the manufacturing and dissemination of dissenting news).[56]

In that period there were also teach-ins and *formations* in Montréal, two CLAC/CASA *consultas* in Québec City (the first, in February, brought together between three and four hundred anarchist sympathizers; the second, in March, was open only to group representatives but still gathered about one hundred people); several meetings of the *Université populaire* and *Alternative*-linked radio shows (on CKIA, *Radio Basse-ville*); truly innumerable conferences on globalization-related issues (organized by such diverse groups as the *Table de concertation contre la pauvreté de Sainte Foy-Sillery*, the Ontario Coalition Against Poverty, *Droit de Parole*, *Communication Basse-ville*, the Shakti women of colour collective, the Immigrant Workers' Centre, etc.); at least one workshop on legal rights (organized by the *Ligue des Droits et Libertés*); as well as numerous anti-capitalist activities and spectacles (in Québec city anti-capitalist music may be becoming a genre of its own). Between mid-January and March, a CASA caravan also reached two dozen cities in the Canadian Maritimes and in the North-East United States. During the protests OQP and CASA committees, in collaboration with others, organized food, housing (the equivalent of 300 hotels were set up in a couple weeks, with volunteer labour, no money, while dealing with police harassment) as well as medical assistance and legal aid for those who were injured or arrested (at the time of writing, OQP and the CASA were working with the *Travailleurs Canadiens de l'Automobile* and others to set up a *Comité Légal de soutien* for prisoners).[57]

The protests in Québec City were also made internationally, sometimes by the very groups and people that had organized counter-summit protests elsewhere. Reasoning like a policeman, looking for a confederacy of anti-globalization forces, we could follow trails of personal and political contacts, some open and institutional, others clandestine, both in 'real' life and on-line. Connecting dots, we could show that, indeed, the making of protests in Québec City was linked to like happenings elsewhere, by specific people and organizations who shape the aesthetics of anti-summit protests (anti-capitalist carnivals too are made, by such groups as the Ruckus Society or Reclaim the Streets), give them their language, tactics (lock-downs, street parties, property destruction, affinity groups, civil disobedience, etc.) and a measure of political coherence.

But beyond what was constructed in the most voluntarist sense of the term, the protests in Québec City were also charged by a more abstract – but no less determining – sense of context. Were references to the works of Louis Althusser not so out of fashion as to have become nearly indecipherable we could write of the making of the protests in Québec as having been 'overdetermined' by the global level.[58] Short of that, we can more modestly suggest that protests were more than what could have been made in a vacuum, and, perhaps, more politically significant than what a policeman could see.

A good measure of the significance of a global sense of place to the making of protests in Québec City is how groups and people involved were 'practically conscious' (to borrow Anthony Giddens' term) of happenings elsewhere on the terrain of the world economy, and how their politics were being defined not just locally, but also in answer to what was done elsewhere, in other circumstances.[59] Especially revealing here is how issues inherited from the very short history of summit protests became structuring concerns in preparation for Québec's Summit of the Americas.[60]

Early summit protests were events unto themselves. Sure of their contrapuntal unity, radically defiant of political intent and instrumental thinking, participants subsumed political differences under strategic concerns: 'how to climb trees, block roads, lock down on doors, eat and shit in extreme situations, scale buildings, deal with cops, minister to the injured, show solidarity and survive in jail', how to 'hold...the space, wait..., [and] make...the point that we have a right to be here.'[61] When the 'Peoples' Global Action Against Free Trade and the World Trade Organisation' (PGA) held what was arguably the first contemporary anti-summit protest in Geneva in May 1998, diversity of politics and tactics reigned, with radically little concern for common programs: '*the people came with the banners of all kinds of struggles against some aspect of globalization: local unions fighting privatizations or austerity, groups of solidarity with the south, squatters, plus many personal banners, musicians, and the caravan tractors towing a huge sound system*'.[62]

A year later in Prague, a simple colour scheme sufficed to articulate different positions, and 'despite tactical and strategic differences between protesters, most agreed that their action had been effective in ... shutting down the summit and bringing the destructive policies of the World Bank and IMF to the attention of the world'.[63] But in Seattle – the first significant anti-globalization protest held in the United States and a crucial moment in many respects – the nature of protest changed. Though there were moments of broad collaboration ('Teamsters and Turtles Together at Last'), the Seattle protests are most remembered – and most significantly by militants involved in making the protests in Québec – for a sharp division between street protests and the orderly politics of trade unions wanting to get 'labour a seat at the table' to make globalization work for workers.[64] Tellingly, twenty city blocks separated union workers gathered in a football stadium at the foot of the Space Needle to hear speeches and wave banners 'under the indulgent eyes of the Seattle constabulary', and the convention centre where 'protesters on the front line were taking their stand'. When the divide could have been closed (as the union crowd left the stadium), 'the marshals for the union march steered the big crowds away from the action'.[65]

In that context, the subjective sense of totality that had prevailed earlier disintegrated into the political settling of scores: *in situ* no more, protests became objectivized and politicized. In what must be one of the more curious moments of anti-summit protest, Medea Benjamin and her colleagues from the San Francisco-based Global Exchange, which had waged a four year campaign against Nike, stood on the steps of Nike Town and other sweatshop outlets in downtown Seattle to defend them against anarchists and other trouble-makers, calling on the police to identify and arrest them.[66]

After Seattle, anti-summit protests became remarkably less about themselves, more reflexive and politically deliberate, and more divided. This was evident, for instance, on 16 April 2000, when eight thousand demonstrators met in Washington for the annual meeting of World Bank and IMF (unsupported by organized labour), and in Nice in December when thousands of activists gathered against the summit of European Union heads of state. In both cases, anti-summit protesters were cut off from local political issues and there were sharp conflicts between political affiliations and tendencies.[67]

More explicitly political than Geneva's PGA or Prague's Initiative Against Economic Globalization (INPERG), Québec's OQP was, from the beginning, a more intent host. While the former groups were lithe organizations that functioned as technical links between movements, rather than centres of political power (more like corresponding societies than the Comintern), the OQP made itself into something that resembled an executive committee and it spent almost the whole year preceding the Summit of the Americas wading through broad ideological debates: are 'we' to define ourselves as 'citizens', 'the people' or 'the proletariat'? Are 'we' against 'capitalism', 'neoliberalism', 'globalization' or 'capital'? Are 'we' for 'reform' or 'revolution'? It also tried to settle on a correct plan of action to match its political aims and to draw up an 'invincible, credible, legitimate' political programme that would be 'understandable by all and absolutely realist'.[68]

Not before its *Manifeste* was finally drawn up in February 2001 did OQP put aside political differences with the CASA/CLAC to coordinate housing and food distribution initiatives.[69] Three weeks before the Summit, the immense task of finding housing for out-of-city militants had barely begun, teach-ins and demonstrations to take place in the 'solidarity perimeter' had not yet been planned, and medical and legal assistance services were still divided along broad political lines. The CMAQ – arguably the most politically committed of all IndyMedia outfits – was still working on ways to reconcile the IndyMedia 'open publishing' tradition with its desire for relevant, properly contextualized and informed reporting.

In the weeks, days and hours before the Summit, amazing energy was expended and protests did emerge from having been nearly buried in globally-reflexive politics. Protesters were fed and housed (some at Laval University or in local colleges, others in private homes), an indisputable sense of place and event was created and, again *in situ*, protesters did create a radical presence that challenged both the will-to-order of the heads of states summit and the apolitical reformism of the People's Summit. But still, so animated were protests by global reflexivity (and by the anticipation of tourists, in the majority everywhere, including among the police) that the patient politics of civil disobedience and the fragile ambience of anti-summit protests were rapidly overtaken by more animated and confrontational ways of politics, especially near the security perimeter. In spite of considerable efforts invested in civil disobedience (by one estimate, a third of the people who participated in Friday's CASA/CLAC march had received some form of legal or political training), protests did not shape up at all as planned (or as they did in the student occupation movement of May 1968 in Paris – the first global anti-systemic movement, a generation ago, before global reflexivity).[70]

Reacting to events from Seattle and elsewhere, dynamized by a globally-inflated sense of predetermination, all those involved were looking for a more definite and quicker resolution than they would have otherwise. Thus did cosmopolitan ghosts come back into the picture, carried by global reflexivity: spectres confronting spectres, everyone in Québec acted with more abandon, fighting what the *Economist* had called – before Seattle – the 'fight for globalization'.[71]

In the end, the police ran out of tear-gas and took to using rubber bullets more offensively than they had planned.[72] Carnivalesque happenings – the most fragile indicators of a sense of place and event – were swept away: the *Funk Fighting Unaccountable Naughty Korporations* were gassed out of their efforts to reclaim the streets, the *Lanarkists* were not given much time to catapult stuffed toy-animals into the security perimeter, the Îlot Fleuri was charged by police and the Saint-Jean Baptiste neighbourhood – a green zone no more, as of Saturday – was inundated with tear-gas. The only puppets seen were on the People's march as it walked away from the security perimeter.

Also significant were local links made in the process of what was, in essence, a globally-situated event. Some years ago, writing about anti-NAFTA campaigns in Canada, Mexico and the United States, I suggested that transnational activism did not just transcend locality but was also constitutive of it.[73] This was seen in the *Red Mexicana de Acción Frente Libre Comercio* socializing the politics of opposition to the PRI; and in the role played by the Action Canada Network in the broadening of what was then being celebrated as 'coalition politics' (a part of which has since moved, gingerly, toward a 'structured movement, something transitional that is more than a coalition and less than a party', intent on 'changing how we think about politics, extending the range of what's possible, and considering a fundamental challenge to capitalism').[74]

In Québec, opposition to free trade with the United States and Mexico in the 1980s did not have a similar impact, largely because of the hegemony of neoliberal nationalism, that defined Free Trade as an opportunity for Québec's bourgeoisie. But popular opposition to the Summit of the Americas did encourage new links between local social movements. In the year that preceded the Summit, two corporatist student bodies (the *Fédération des étudiants(es) Universitaire du Québec* and the *Fédération des étudiants(es) des CEGEPS du Québec*), were openly challenged by the new *Association solidaire pour un syndicalisme étudiant*, remarkably more militant, and intimately involved in anti-Summit politics. In like manner, the regrouping of community and alternative media – under the *Altermédia* banner – was closely linked to the creation of the CMAQ (born at the *Colloque des médias alternatifs québécois* in November 2000 in Drummondville). In the Mercier riding in Montréal – held continuously by the *Parti Québécois* since the radical poet Gérald Godin defeated Liberal Premier Robert Bourassa in 1976 – a provincial by-election was held on 9 April contested by the first united left candidate in Québéc history.[75]

All this entered into the politics of opposition to the Summit of the Americas. Four hundred and sixty people were arrested in Québec city during the Summit of the Americas and charged with the habitual menu of offences against the State: assault against a policeman, unlawful assembly, causing a disturbance, riot. Crimes of presence, they signal the limits of neoliberal civility. A dozen protesters were kept in jail in the week that followed. Most notable was the CLAC's Jaggi Singh, who was, for seventeen days, Québec's Mumia Abu-Jamal. To support him and others the OQP and the CASA (now the *Comité d'adieu au Sommet des Amériques*) organized demonstrations at the Orsainville penitentiary in Charlesbourg and at the Palais de Justice in Lower Town, a short walk from the now-empty site of the People's Summit. On 1 May the CASA organized a support march for political prisoners that started at the Parc de l'Amérique française, near where the security perimeter had been, and ended at the Palais de Justice.

Thus was a community of resistance made in Québec City in the months that preceded the Summit of the Americas. Determinedly about itself, radically unbound by the exigencies of problem-solving politics, entirely *in situ*, evanescent where global civility tends to immanence, this community was markedly different from the twinned summits of the hemispheric growth machine. Were terms of this kind not so out of date, we would raise the hypothesis of a 'revolutionary rupture' with existing forms of power.[76]

Conclusion

For three days in April, Québec city was part of what Saskia Sassen calls the 'world-wide grid of strategic places'.[77] Like other places in that grid, it was a contested terrain.

To raise critical awareness of the kind of politics being made in the post-Bretton Woods world economy, I have emphasized differences between two relatively coherent ensembles: i) a hemispheric growth machine gathered to settle social relations in conformity with neoliberal values and perspectives, and ii) a community of resistance charging the world economy with politics.

What actually happened, of course, did not entirely conform to this distinction. Some groups involved in Summit politics – *Alternatives* and *OQP*, for example – did cross the divide between ghosts and resistants; the People's tent was more open to protestors that had originally been planned, though for a fee, and only after organizers realized that fewer delegates had shown up than had registered; some unionists did join the CASA/CLAC march on Friday: and a few who started Saturday's march away from the security perimeter did double back towards it, to support direct action (in spite of the remarkably police-like efforts of FTQ's marshals). Some attended the People's Summit from Monday to Thursday and then went to the solidarity perimeter, to the Îlot Fleurit, or to protests near the security perimeter on Friday and Saturday. After the Summit, the *Travailleurs Canadiens de l'Automobile*, the Québec branch of the Canadian Auto Workers, did help organize legal support for political prisoners, and some of the People's representatives, most notably Françoise David of the *Fédération des femmes du Québec*, did express sympathy for political prisoners, though all the media, including the CBC, had only run human-interest stories on Jaggi Singh. At the level of tactics, there was not, as Thomas Walkom put it, 'a straightforward fissure between young anarchists who advocate so-called direct action – a phrase that covers everything from sit-ins to rock throwing – and those committed to peaceful protest'.[78]

At the level of discourse and in political programmes, those who gathered in the People's summit and those who occupied places near the security perimeter still had more in common with one another than they did with the globalizing elites on whose part no significant divide-crossing was recorded – though we all saw Summit delegates take their tags off, not to join the protests, but to walk about unfenced parts of the old city.

On the whole, though, groups and popular movements opposed to the ways of neoliberal integration in the Americas were configured as argued above – parties to the hemispheric growth machine on one side, resistants on another – not showing what they had in common and amounting to less than they could have. This, undoubtedly, was a political failure. Had the People's tent been more open from the beginning, then something more political than yet another collection of near-parliamentary briefs could have come out of the People's Summit; had 60,000 people walked to the security perimeter on Saturday, a more meaningful occupation of the place could have been organized; or, alternatively, had direct action resisters marched with the People they would have had a less insignificant afternoon.

Looking toward the future, this raises the crucial question of the articulation between parts of what could be, but is not yet, a global movement against neoliberalism. In their optimism, slogans heard in Québec City during the Summit of the Americas – *'L'Union fail la force'*, *'À qui la rue? À nous'*, *'Pueblo unido, jamas sera vencido'* – gave a misleading sense of the ease with which joint actions can be organized by disparate groups.[79]

But, as Althusser suggested in one of his rare political interventions, only in concrete actions can social movements be fused into more than they are individually, to take advantage of moments of revolutionary rupture.[80] In the present context, gatherings of globalizing elites provide excellent occasions for such concrete actions. Properly constructed, organized protests can then provide, as John Merger wrote of mass demonstrations, necessary 'rehearsals of revolutionary awareness'.[81]

The next Summit of the Americas will be held in Buenos Aires.

Acknowledgements

I would like to thank the following, who generously shared thoughts and information: Pierre Beaudet, Sébastien Bouchard, Sacha Alcide Calixte, Sam Gindin. Robert Jasmin, Michel Lambert, Leo Panitch, Évelyne Pedneault, Véronica Rioux.

Notes

1 André C. Drainville. 'Of Social Spaces, Citizenship, and the Nature of Power in the World Economy', *Alternatives*, 20, Spring 1995; André C. Drainville, 'The Fetishism of Global Civil Society: Global Governance, Transnational Urbanism and Sustainable Capitalism in the World Economy", *Comparative Urban and Community Research*, no. 6, 1999 (1998). On scenarios for settling social relations, see for instance: William P. Kreml and Charles W. Kegley Jr., 'A Global Political Party: The Next Step', *Alternatives*, January–March 1996; Daniele Archibugi and David Held, eds, *Cosmopolitan Democracy: An Agenda for a New World Order*, London: Polity Press, 1995; Richard Falk, *On Humane Governance: Towards a New Global Politics*, University Park, PA: The Pennsylvania State University Press/World Order Models Project, 1995; and Ricardo Petrella, *Écucils de la mondialisation: Urgence d'un nouveau contrat social*, Montréal: Fides, 1997.

2 Robert W. Cox, *Production, Power and World Order: Social Forces in the Making of History*, New York: Columbia University Press, 1987.

3 For the complete text of the EAI announcement, see *Public Papers of the Presidents of the United States, George Bush: January 1 to June 30, 1990*, Washington: United States Government Printing Office, 1991, pp. 873–877.

4 Umberto Eco, 'Travels in Hyperreality', in *Travels in Hyperreality: Essays*, San Diego: Harcourt Brace Jovanovich, 1986, pp. 3–58. Between 1996 and 1997, *Place d'Youville* was the starting point of riots on *St-Jean Baptiste* day, Québec's national holiday.

5 Details of DFAIT events can be found at http://www.holaquebec.ca

6 In the spirit of inter-agency collaboration the *Institut* also served as a DFAIT temp agency, recruiting *agents et agentes de liaison* and other support staff for the Summit of the Americas, and it was host to several Summit officials, including, thrice, Marc Lortie, the Prime Minister's sherpa. A press release detailing the Conclusions of the colloqium can be found at the Institut's web site: http://www.ulaval.ca/scom/Communiques.de.presse/2001/avril/IQHEIzlea

7 Founded in 1994, the RQIC is under the hegemonic guidance of Québec's main union confederations (the *Confédération des Syndicat Nationaux*, the *Centrale des enseignants du Québec* and the *Fédération des travailleurs et travailleuses du Québec*). Its membership also includes another, much smaller, union confederation (the *Centrale des syndicats du Québec*), union-made or union-funded NGOs (most notably the *Centre international de solidarité ouvrière* and *Solidarité populaire Québec*), a professional appendage of the union movement (the *Association canadienne des avocats du mouvement syndical*), two state-funded NGO's (the *Association québécoise des organismes de coopération internationale* and the *Fédération des femmes du Québec*) and two research centres based in Montréal universities that are also close to unions (McGill's *Centre d'études sur les régions en développement* and UQUAM's RQIC).

8 On 'protest pits' and anti-summit movements, see Alexander Cockburn, Jeffrey St. Clair, and Allan Sekula, *5 Days that Shook the World: Seattle and Beyond*, London: Verso, 2000, p. 19.

9 Members of OQP included one neighbourhood committee (the *Comité populaire Saint-Jean Baptiste*), several student associations (the *Comité de mobilisation de l'Association étudiante du CEGEP de F-X Gameau*, the *Comité de mobilisation de l'Association étudiante du CEGEP de Saint-Foy*, the *Coalition de l'Université Laval sur le libre-échange dans les Amériques*), left parties and NGOs (the *Parti pour la Démocratie Socialiste*, *ATTAC*, the Rassemblement pour une Alternative Populaire, the *Parti Communiste du Québec*, *Alternatives*), locally-based unions (the *Syndicat des Employés de la Fonction Publique*, the *Syndicats des professeurs du CEGEP de Saiute-Foy*) as well as solidarity NGOs (*Carrefour Tiers-Monde*, *Casa latino Americaine de Québec*, *Plan Nagua*).

10 N.d., 'Sommet des Amériques: tie nous laissons pas intimider. Occupons notre quartier', *L'Info-bourg*, 1, 2001.

11 Canadian Security Intelligence Service, 'Anti-Globalization – A Spreading Phenomenon', Ottawa: CSIS, 2000.

12 CIEPAC, 'Seattle: The World Mobilization of the Century Against Globalization', Chiapas: Centro de Investigaciones Economicas y politicas de Accion Comunitaria, 1999; Claudette Samson, 'Il faudra 3.8 kms de clôture', *Le Soleil*, 2 November 2000, A–3; Claudette Samson, 'Un sommet de sécurité', *Le Soleil*, 2 November 2000, A–1, A–2.

13 Stephen Gill, 'Structural Change and Global Political Economy: Globalizing Élites and the Emerging World Order', in Yoshikazu Sakamoto, ed., *Global Transformation: Challenges to the State System*, Tokyo: United Nations University Press, 1994. On this, see also Robert W. Cox, *Production, Power and World Order: Social Forces in the Making of History*, New York: Columbia University Press, 1987, pp. 250–65.

14 On the neoliberal concept of control, see Peter Burnham, 'Neo-Gramscian Hegemony and International Order', *Capital and Class*, 45, Fall 1991; Henk Overbeek, *Global Capitalism and National Decline*, London: Unwin Hyman, 1990. About the global construction of monetarism, see André C. Drainville, 'Monetarism in Canada and the World Economy', *Studies in Political Economy*, no. 46, Spring 1995.

15 Peter Hajnal, *The Seven Powers Summit: Documents from the Summits of Industrialized Countries*, New York: Kraus International Publications, 1989. OECD, *Facing the Future: Mastering the Probable and Managing the Unpredictable*, Paris: OECD, 1979, p. 78.

16 Karl Polanyi's *Great Transformation*, cited in Robert W. Cox, 'Structural Issues of Global Governance: Implications for Europe', in Stephen Gill, ed., *Gramsci, Historical Materialism and International Relation*, Cambridge: Cambridge University Press, 1993, p. 261.

17 Rutherford M. Poats, ed., *Twenty-Five Years of Development Co-operation: A Review*, Paris: Organization for Economic Cooperation and Development (Development Assistance Committee), 1985. On

IMF riots and early resistance to neoliberal regulation, see also Didier Digo, 'Contestations populaires et émeutes urbaines; les jeux du politique et de la transnationalité', *Cultures et contacts* numéro spécial sur les émeutes urbaines, 1992; John Walton, 'Urban Protests and the Global Political Economy: The IMF Riots', in Michael Peter Smith and Joe R. Feagin, eds, *The Capitalist City: Global Restructuring and Community Politics*, Oxford: Basil BlackWell, 1987.

18 See Peter B. Kenen, 'The Use of IMF Credit', in Catherine Gwin and Richard Feinberg, eds, *The International Monetary Fund in a Multipolar World: Pulling Together*, Washington: Overseas Development Council, 1989, p. 69. On the changing relationship between the World Bank and developing countries and on the Social Dimensions of Adjustment program, administered by the World Bank in cooperation with the United Nations Development Program, see *Making Adjustment Work for the Poor*, Washington: World Bank, 1990.

19 André C. Drainville, *Ways of Global Politics*, Routledge, forthcoming; Harvey Molotch, 'The City as Growth Machine', *American Journal of Sociology*, 82, no. 2, 1976.

20 Charlotte Brönte cited in Carl Malamud, *A World's Fair for the Global Village*, Cambridge: The MIT Press, 1997. The Porto Alegre 'World Social Forum' was divided into four themes: 'The production of wealth and social reproduction', 'Access to wealth and sustainability', 'Civil society and the public arena' and 'Political Power and ethics in the new society'.

21 Alexandre Marc and Mary Schmidt, *Participation and Social Funds*, ed. Environment Department, vol. 4, *Participation Series*, Washington, DC: The World Bank, 1995.

22 Rutherford M. Poats, 'Crisis-Driven Reform', in Poats, ed., *Twenty-Five Years of Development Co-operation*, Washington, DC: Persephone, pp. 59–64.

23 In their introduction to *NGOs, the UN & Global Governance*, Leon Gordenker and Thomas G. Weiss distinguished between NGOs (Non Governmental Organisations), GONGOs (Government Organized Non-Government Organisations (that belonged principally to the cold war period) and QUANGOs (Quasi-Nongovernmental Organisations such as the International Committee of the Red Cross). In World Bank vernacular CBOs are Community-Based Organizations. GOINGOs are Government Induced Non-Governmental Organizations.

24 Michel Chossudovsky, 'Seattle and Beyond: Disarming the New World order', Transnational Foundation for Peace and Future Research, http://www.transnational.org/forum/meetéseattle.html, 2000.

25 Pierre Hazan, 'Riche Idée', *Libération*, 26 January 2001, p. 56.

26 James N. Rosenau, 'Governance in the Twenty-first Century', *Global Governance*, Winter 1995.

27 Ricardo Grinspun and Maxwell A. Cameron, *The Political Economy of North American Free Trade*, Montréal/Kingston/London: Mc Gill-Queen's University Press, 1993.

28 'The Battle in Seattle', *The Economist*, 27 November 1999, pp. 21–23.

29 The Miami 'Plan of Action' is quoted from Thomas Risse-Kappen, ed., *Bringing Transnational Relations Back In: Non-State Actors, Domestic Structures and International Institutions*, Cambridge: Cambridge University Press, 1995.

30 IDB, 'From Grassroots to Government', *The IDB extra* (*Inter-American Development Bank*), 1994, pp. 8–9.

31 IDB, 'Citizens Participation Increases Efficiency of Development', Washington, DC/Cartagena: Inter-American Development Bank, 1998 (emphasis added).

32 IDB, 'Echoes of Forging Links with NGOs', Washington, DC: Inter-American Development Bank, 1997; Leslie M. Fox, 'Sustaining Civil Society', Washington: Civicus (The International Task Force on Enhancing the Resource Base of Civil Society), 1996.

33 Roger Hamilton, 'Turning Residents into Citizens: Latin America's Reform Bandwagon Needs More Drivers – Lots More', *The IDB* (*Inter-American Development Bank*), November 1994, pp. 6–7.

34 IDB. 'Echoes of Forging Links with NGOs' (emphasis added).

35 The FTA came into effect on January 1, 1989; NAFTA in 1994; Mercosur and the 'Group of Three' accord between Columbia, Mexico and Venezuela in 1995; the Adean Community Pact in 1997.

36 Editors, 'Citizens of the Rain Forest', *The IDB* (*Inter-American Development Bank*), August 1993, p. 3; IDB, 'From Grassroots to Government', *The IDB Extra* (*Inter-American Development Bank*), 1994, pp. 8–9; IDB, 'How we put it All Together', *IDB Extra 'Urban Renaissance'* (*Inter-American Development Bank*), 1997, p. 8; IDB, 'IDB Women', 1996.

37 On the OAS's turn to participatory development, see OAS, *Inter-American Strategy for Public Participation in Environment and Sustainable Development: Decision Making in the Americas*, Washington: Organization of American States, 1996.

38 The Santiago Plan of Action designated the OAS as a privileged forum for 'the exchange of experience and information amongst civil society organizations'. On this, see Organization of American States, *Work Plan of the Unit for the Promotion of Democracy*, cited in Guy Gosselin and Jean-Philippe Thérien, 'The Organization of American States and Hemispheric Regionalism', in Gordon Mace and Luyis Bélanger, eds, *The Americas in Transition: The Contours of Regionalism*, Boulder, co: Lynne Rienner, 1999.

39 See http://www.civil-society.oas.org

40 The document is available at http://www.summmit-americas.org/documents

41 Comité de représentants gouvernementaux sur la participation de la société civile, 'Invitation ouverte à la société civile dans les pays de la ZLÉA', http://www.ftaa-alca.org/spcomm/soc2_f.asp, 2000.

42 Translated from http://www.holaquebec.ca/bienvenue/intro_e.html

43 Thalia Kidder and Mary McGinn, 'In the Wake of NAFTA: Transnational Workers Networks', *Social Policy*, Summer 1995.

44 William I. Robinson, 'The Sao Paulo Forum: Is There a New Latin American Left?', *Monthly Review*, no. 44, December 1992, pp. 1–12. On the Sao Paulo Forum, see also 'Left to Start Work on Alternative: Sao Paulo Forum Offers Few Hints Regarding Content', *Latin America Weekly Report*, 15 June 1995, pp. 258–259; Raul Ronzoni, 'Latin America: The Left Meets to Discuss its Role and Integration', *Inter Press Service*, 25 May 1995.

45 BBC Summary of World Broadcasts, Wednesday, 31 May 1995.

46 Michel Chossudovsky, 'Seattle and Beyond: Disarming the New World order', Transnational Foundation for Peace and Future Research, http://www.transnational.org/forum/meetéseattle.html, 2000. According to Julio Turra, of the United Workers Federation of Brazil, 'the whole idea of incorporating social clauses or social charters into these 'free trade' pacts ... was really projected at the 1995 Social Summit in Copenhagen. The goal of integrating trade unions internationally into the whole apparatus of globalization was made explicit at that summit' ('Leader of the Brazilian United Workers Federation (CUT) describes labour summit organized to respond to the extension of NAFTA throughout the Americas', http://www. igc.apc.org/workers/cut.html)

47 Richard Feinberg and Robin Rosenberg, eds, *Civil Society and the Summit of the Americas: The 1998 Santiago Summit*, Boulder, CO: Lynne Rienner, 1999.

48 Alliance for Responsible Trade *et al.*, 'Alternatives for the Americas: Building a People's Hemispheric Agreement', 1998.

49 Reviews of relevant literature can be found in André C. Drainville, 'Left Internationalism and the Politics of Resistance in the New World Order', in David Smith and Jósef Böröcz, eds, *A New World Order: Global Transformations in the Late Twentieth Century*, Westport, CT: Praeger, 1995; André C. Drainville, *Ways of Global Politics*. See also Jeffrey M. Ayres, *Defying Conventional Wisdom*, Toronto: University of Toronto Press, 1998; Robin Cohen and Shirin M. Rai, eds, *Global Social Movements*, London: Athlone Press, 2000; and Saskia Sassen, *Globalization and Its Discontents*, New York: The New Press, 1998.

50 Michel Foucault, 'Le sujet et le pouvoir', in Michel Foucault, ed., *Dits et écrits (1954–1988)*, Paris: Gallimard, 1994, pp. 227–243. See also C. Gordon, ed., *Power/Knowledge: Michel Foucault*, New York: Pantheon Books, 1980.

51 Robin Hahnel, 'Speaking Truth to Power: Speaking Truth to Ourselves', *Z*, June 2000, pp. 44–51.

52 Nicole Pénicaut and Christian Dutilleux, 'Davos et Potrto Alegre, deux sommets du monde', *Libération*, 26 January 2001; Nicole Pénicaut, 'Combler le fossé', *Libération*, 26 January 2001.

53 Drainville, 'Left Internationalism and the Politics of Resistance'.

54 Cited from *Z* staff, 'This Yawning Emptiness', *Z*, June 2000, pp. 4–5.

55 Edward Said, *Representations of the Intellectual*, New York: Pantheon Books, 1994.

56 At the June 2000 camp, formateurs and formatrices were given a broad general Cahier de formation as well as several thematic kits (on 'éducation et mondialisation', 'écologie et mondialisation', 'programmes sociaux', 'droits de la personne', 'femmes et mondialisation', 'droits du travail', etc.)

57 OQP2001, 'Communiqué de Presse', Opération Québec Printemps 2001.

58 On overdetermination, see Louis Althusser, 'Contradiction et surdetermination', in *Pour Marx*, Foundations, Paris: La Découverte, 1986, pp. 85–129.

59 Anthony Giddens, *The Constitution of Society*, Berkeley, CA: University of California Press, 1984.

60 It is a measure of the shortness of this history that Québec's bid to host the Summit of the Americas was presented to the federal government in April 1999, six months before the Seattle WTO summit. See Robert Fleury, 'L'Allier nuance ses propos', *Le Soleil*, 27 March 2001, A3.

61 Citations are, in order, from Cockburn, St. Clair and Sekula, *5 Days that Shook the World*, and Adam Sternbergh, 'The Dirty Kids who Show up for the Gathering', *This Magazine*, November/December 1998.

62 http://www.agp.org/agp/en/PGAInfos/bulletin2/bulletin2b.html (emphasis added).

63 NEFAC, 'Anti-capitalist Resistance in the Streets of Prague'. *The Northeastern Anarchist*, February 2001; Vittorio de Philippis and Christian Losson, 'Assemblées annuelles du FMI et de la Banque mondiale', *Libération*, 27 September 2000, pp. 26–27.

64 Teamster's leader James Hoffa Jr, cited in Cockburn, St. Clair and Sekula, *5 Days that Shook the World*. On 'the myth of Seattle', see for instance: n.d., 'Sommet des Amériques: construction et impact d'une situation', *Le Maquis*, 2001, pp. 3–4.

65 Cockburn, St. Clair and Sekula, *5 Days that Shook the World*.

66 Alex Cockburn, 'So Who Did Win in Seattle? Liberals Rewrite History', http://www.antenna.nl/~waterman/cockburn.html: Global Solidarity Dialogue, 2000.

67 Robin Hahnel, 'Speaking Truth to Power: Speaking Truth to Ourselves', *Z*, June 2000.

68 SalAMI, 'Mobilisations et résistances civiles contre le Sommet des Amériques et le projet de Zone de libre-échange des Amériques: Plan d'action et propositions de SalAMI', http://www.alternatives.ca/salami/html/zlea.html: SalAMi, 2000.

69 The *Manifeste contre le Sommet des Amériques et la Zone de libre-échange des Amériques* was made public on March 20th, a month before the summit. See Jean-Simon Gagné, 'Sommet des Amériques: Un manifeste percutant contre la ZLÉA', *Le Soleil*, 21 March 2001, A12.

70 Immanuel Wallerstein, '1968: Révolution dans le système mondial', *Les Temps Modernes*, May–June 1989, pp. 514–515.

71 After Seattle, where 'the fight for globalization' had been lost by the WTO, *The Economist* took to accusing protestors of having fomented it. See 'Countdown to ruckus', *The Economist*, 4 December 1999, and 'The Battle in Seattle', *The Economist*, 27 November 1999.

72 The SQ alone fired more than 300 plastic bullets at individuals and 1700 *bombes fumigènes* into the crowd. François Cardinal, 'Pleins Gaz à Québec!', *Le Devoir*, 26 April 2001, A2. At the time of writing, reports from other police corps had not yet been presented.

73 André C. Drainville, 'Social Movements in the Americas: Regionalism from Below', in Gordon Mace and Luyis Bélanger, eds, *The Americas in Transition: The Contours of Regionalism*, Boulder, CO: Lynne Rienner, 1999.

74 On the 'Rebuilding the Left' movement, see Sam Gindin, 'Toward a Structured Anti-Capitalist Movement', *Canadian Dimension*, January/February 2001. On Canadian links between global capitalism, local struggles and the 'new spirit of resistance to global capitalism', see David McNally, 'Rebuilding the Left', *Canadian Dimension*, September/October 2000; Harman Rosenfeld and Jayme Gianola, 'Prospects for a New Left? A Report on the Rebuilding the Left Conference', *Canadian Dimension*, January/February 2001.

75 Running as an Independent, Paul Cliche received a quarter of votes, and finished a close third behind the *Libéral* and *Parti Québécois* candidates (Kathleen Levesque, 'Banc d'essai pour la gauche', *Le Devoir*, 15 March 2001, A1–A8).

76 Althusser, 'Contradiction et surdetermination'.

77 Saskia Sassen, *Globalization and its Discontents*, New York: The New Press, 1998.

78 Thomas Walkom, 'Mélange of Quebec protesters united in rethinking strategy', *The Toronto Star*, 29 April 2001.

79 Malcom Reid, *What I Saw*, Québec: Malcom Reid, 2001.

80 See Althusser, 'Contradiction et surdetermination'.

81 John Berger, 'The Nature of Mass Demonstrations', *New Society*, 23 May 1968, pp. 754–755.

16 Porto Alegre

Today's bandung?

Michael Hardt

Source: Michael Hardt (2002), 'Porto Alegre: Today's Bandung?', *New Left Review* 14, pp. 112–118.

Rather than opposing the World Social Forum in Porto Alegre to the World Economic Forum in New York, it is more revealing to imagine it as the distant offspring of the historic Bandung Conference that took place in Indonesia in 1955. Both were conceived as attempts to counter the dominant world order: colonialism and the oppressive Cold War binary in the case of Bandung, and the rule of capitalist globalization in that of Porto Alegre. The differences, however, are immediately apparent. On one hand the Bandung Conference, which brought together leaders primarily from Asia and Africa, revealed in a dramatic way the racial dimension of the colonial and Cold War world order, which Richard Wright famously described as being divided by the 'colour curtain'. Porto Alegre, in contrast, was a predominantly white event. There were relatively few participants from Asia and Africa, and the racial differences of the Americas were dramatically underrepresented. This points toward a continuing task facing those gathered at Porto Alegre: to globalize further the movements, both within each society and across the world – a project in which the Forum is merely one step. On the other hand, whereas Bandung was conducted by a small group of national political leaders and representatives, Porto Alegre was populated by a swarming multitude and a network of movements. This multitude of protagonists is the great novelty of the World Social Forum, and central to the hope it offers for the future.

The first and dominant impression of the Forum was its overflowing enormity; not so much the number of people there – the organizers say 80,000 participated – but rather the number of events, encounters and happenings. The programme listing all the official conferences, seminars and workshops – most of which took place at the Catholic University – was the size of a tabloid newspaper, but one soon realized that there were innumerable other unofficial meetings taking place all over town, some publicized on posters and leaflets, others by word of mouth. There were also separate gatherings for the different groups participating in the Forum, such as a meeting of the Italian social movements or one for the various national sections of ATTAC. Then there were the demonstrations: both officially planned, such as the opening mass May Day-style parade, and smaller, conflictual demonstrations against, for example, the members of parliament from different countries at the Forum who voted for the present war on terrorism. Finally, another series of events was held at the enormous youth camp by the river, its fields and fields of tents housing 15,000 people in an atmosphere reminiscent of a summer music festival, especially when it rained and everyone tramped through the mud wearing plastic sacks as raincoats. In short, if anyone with obsessive tendencies were to try to understand what was happening at Porto Alegre, the result would certainly have been a complete mental breakdown. The Forum was unknowable, chaotic, dispersive. And that overabundance created an exhilaration in everyone, at being lost in a sea of people from so many parts of the world who are working similarly against the present form of capitalist globalization.

This open encounter was the most important element of Porto Alegre. Even though the Forum was limited in some important respects – socially and geographically, to name two – it was nonetheless an opportunity to globalize further the cycle of struggles that have stretched from Seattle to Genoa, which have been conducted by a network of movements thus far confined, by and large, to the North Atlantic. Dealing with many of the same issues as those who elsewhere contest the present capitalist form of globalization, or specific institutional policies such as those of the IMF, the movements themselves have remained limited. Recognizing the commonality of their projects with those in other parts of the world is the first step toward expanding the network of movements, or linking one network to another. This recognition, indeed, is primarily responsible for the happy, celebratory atmosphere of the Forum.

The encounter should, however, reveal and address not only the common projects and desires, but also the differences of those involved – differences of material conditions and political orientation. The various movements across the globe cannot simply connect to each other as they are, but must rather be transformed by the encounter through a kind of mutual adequation. Those from North America and Europe, for example, cannot but have been struck by the contrast between their experience and that of agricultural labourers and the rural poor in Brazil, represented most strongly by the MST (Landless Movement) – and vice versa. What kind of transformations are necessary for the Euro-American globalization movements and the Latin American movements, not to become the same, or even to unite, but to link together in an expanding common network? The Forum provided an opportunity to recognize such differences and questions for those willing to see them, but it did not provide the conditions for addressing them. In fact, the very same dispersive, overflowing quality of the Forum that created the euphoria of commonality also effectively displaced the terrain on which such differences and conflicts could be confronted.

Anti-capitalism and national sovereignty

The Porto Alegre Forum was in this sense perhaps too happy, too celebratory and not conflictual enough. The most important political difference cutting across the entire Forum concerned the role of national sovereignty. There are indeed two primary positions in the response to today's dominant forces of globalization: either one can work to reinforce the sovereignty of nation-states as a defensive barrier against the control of foreign and global capital, or one can strive towards a nonnational alternative to the present form of globalization that is equally global. The first poses neoliberalism as the primary analytical category, viewing the enemy as unrestricted global capitalist activity with weak state controls; the second is more clearly posed against capital itself, whether state-regulated or not. The first might rightly be called an antiglobalization position, in so far as national sovereignties, even if linked by international solidarity, serve to limit and regulate the forces of capitalist globalization. National liberation thus remains for this position the ultimate goal, as it was for the old anticolonial and anti-imperialist struggles. The second, in contrast, opposes any national solutions and seeks instead a democratic globalization.

The first position occupied the most visible and dominant spaces of the Porto Alegre Forum; it was represented in the large plenary sessions, repeated by the official spokespeople, and reported in the press. A key proponent of this position was the leadership of the Brazilian PT (Workers' Party) – in effect the host of the Forum, since it runs the city and regional government. It was obvious and inevitable that the PT would occupy a central space in the Forum and use the international prestige of the event as part of its campaign strategy for the upcoming elections. The second dominant voice of national sovereignty was the French leadership of ATTAC, which laid the groundwork for the Forum in the pages of *Le Monde Diplomatique*. The leadership of ATTAC is, in this regard, very close to many of the French politicians – most notably Jean-Pierre Chevènement – who advocate strengthening national sovereignty as a solution to the ills of contemporary globalization. These, in any case, are the figures who dominated the representation of the Forum both internally and in the press.

The non-sovereign, alternative globalization position, in contrast, was minoritarian at the Forum – not in quantitative terms but in terms of representation; in fact, the majority of the participants in the Forum may well have occupied this minoritarian position. First, the various movements that have conducted the protests from Seattle to Genoa are generally oriented towards non-national solutions. Indeed, the centralized structure of state sovereignty itself runs counter to the horizontal network-form that the movements have developed. Second, the Argentinian movements that have sprung up in response to the present financial crisis, organized in neighbourhood and city-wide delegate assemblies, are similarly antagonistic to proposals of national sovereignty. Their slogans call for getting rid, not just of one politician, but all of them – *que se vayan todos*: the entire political class. And finally, at the base of the various parties and organizations present at the Forum the sentiment is much more hostile to proposals of national sovereignty than at the top. This may be particularly true of ATTAC, a hybrid organization whose head, especially in France, mingles with traditional politicians, whereas its feet are firmly grounded in the movements.

The division between the sovereignty, anti-globalization position and the non-sovereign, alternative globalization position is therefore not best understood in geographical terms. It does not map the divisions between North and South or First World and Third. The conflict corresponds rather to two different forms of political organization. The traditional parties and centralized campaigns generally occupy the national sovereignty pole, whereas the new movements organized in horizontal networks tend to cluster at the non-sovereign pole. And furthermore, within traditional, centralized organizations, the top tends toward sovereignty and the base away. It is no surprise, perhaps, that those in positions of power would be most interested in state sovereignty and those excluded least. This may help to explain, in any case, how the national sovereignty, antiglobalization position could dominate the representations of the Forum even though the majority of the participants tend rather toward the perspective of a non-national alternative globalization.

As a concrete illustration of this political and ideological difference, one can imagine the responses to the current economic crisis in Argentina that logically follow from each of these positions. Indeed that crisis loomed over the entire Forum, like a threatening premonition of a chain of economic disasters to come. The first position would point to the fact that the Argentinian debacle was caused by the forces of global capital and the policies of the IMF, along with the other supranational institutions that undermine national sovereignty. The logical oppositional response should thus be to reinforce the national sovereignty of Argentina (and other nation-states) against these destabilizing external forces. The second position would identify the same causes of the crisis, but insist that a national solution is neither possible nor desirable. The alternative to the rule of global capital and its institutions will only be found at an equally global level, by a global democratic movement. The practical experiments in democracy taking place today at neighbourhood and city levels in Argentina, for example, pose a necessary continuity between the democratization of Argentina and the democratization of the global system. Of course, neither of these perspectives provides an adequate recipe for an immediate solution to the crisis that would circumvent IMF prescriptions – and I am not convinced that such a solution exists. They rather present different political strategies for action today which seek, in the course of time, to develop real alternatives to the current form of global rule.

Parties vs networks

In a previous period we could have staged an old-style ideological confrontation between the two positions. The first could accuse the second of playing into the hands of neoliberalism, undermining state sovereignty and paving the way for further globalization. Politics, the one could continue, can only be effectively conducted on the national terrain and within the nation-state. And the second could reply that national regimes and other forms of sovereignty, corrupt and oppressive as they are, are merely obstacles to the global democracy that we seek. This kind of confrontation, however, could not take place at Porto Alegre – in part because of the dispersive nature of the event, which tended to displace conflicts, and in part because the sovereignty position so successfully occupied the central representations that no contest was possible.

But the more important reason for a lack of confrontation may have had to do with the organizational forms that correspond to the two positions. The traditional parties and centralized organizations have spokespeople who represent them and conduct their battles, but no one speaks for a network. How do you argue with a network? The movements organized within them do exert their power, but they do not proceed through oppositions. One of the basic characteristics of the network form is that no two nodes face each other in contradiction; rather, they are always triangulated by a third, and then a fourth, and then by an indefinite number of others in the web. This is one of the characteristics of the Seattle events that we have had the most trouble understanding: groups which we thought in objective contradiction to one another – environmentalists and trade unions, church groups and anarchists – were suddenly able to work together, in the context of the network of the multitude. The movements, to take a slightly different perspective, function something like a public sphere, in the sense that they can allow full expression of differences within the common context of open exchange. But that does not mean that networks are passive. They displace contradictions and operate instead a kind of alchemy, or rather a sea change, the flow of the movements transforming the traditional fixed positions; networks imposing their force through a kind of irresistible undertow.

Like the Forum itself, the multitude in the movements is always overflowing, excessive and unknowable. It is certainly important then, on the one hand, to recognize the differences that divide the activists and politicians gathered at Porto Alegre. It would be a mistake, on the other hand, to try to read the division according to the traditional model of ideological conflict between opposing sides. Political struggle in the age of network movements no longer works that way. Despite the apparent strength of those who occupied centre stage and dominated the representations of the Forum, they may ultimately prove to have lost the struggle. Perhaps the representatives of the traditional parties and centralized organizations at Porto Alegre are too much like the old national leaders gathered at Bandung – imagine Lula of the PT in the position of Ahmed Sukarno as host, and Bernard Cassen of ATTAC France as Jawaharlal Nehru, the most honoured guest. The leaders can certainly craft resolutions affirming national sovereignty around a conference table, but they can never grasp the democratic power of the movements. Eventually they too will be swept up in the multitude, which is capable of transforming all fixed and centralized elements into so many more nodes in its indefinitely expansive network.

17 The new world order

Passive revolution or transformative process?

Mark Rupert

Source: Mark Rupert (2000), *Ideologies of Globalization: Contending Visions of a New World Order*, London: Routledge, pp. 132–155

Fear and loathing in reverse: the global power bloc and the new populism

By 1996 there were clear signs that the world's most powerful social forces were getting worried. Why? Their agenda of global economic openness and integration via the free flow of trade and investment has been progressively realized over half a century. Over the post-war period world trade has grown more rapidly than output, and foreign investment has in recent decades expanded still more dramatically. In the early decades of this emerging global order, its architects could justify their project in terms of the manichean categories of Cold War ideology as well as the stories of generalized peace and prosperity associated with the classical liberal tradition. And indeed, American working people (or, at least, a substantial proportion of them) were integrated into a hegemonic global order through access to postwar prosperity and through the stark representations of Cold War politics (Rupert, 1995).

But the Cold War is over and its unambiguous political narrative no longer seems to make sense of the world in ways which are adequate to the realities of life faced by many people in the US and elsewhere. Among those realities has been a major shift in socio-political power at various scales from the local to the global. The "historic bloc" of social forces and ideologies which formed the core of the US-centered hegemonic world order is being recon-structed. American industrial labor is no longer secure in its position as a relatively privileged junior partner in this global power bloc, as prevailing interpretations of liberal ideology have shifted away from a version which had endorsed more activist and growth-oriented state policies and which legitimized collective bargaining by mass industrial unions. In place of the kinder, gentler liberalism which was hegemonic during the postwar decades we now find instead a hard-edged liberalism which strives to focus the violence of market forces directly upon working people through policies which emphasize public fiscal retrenchment, contain-ment of inflation, and "flexible labor markets" in a context of rigorous global competition.

It is in this context that a new populism is emerging to challenge the formerly hegemonic narratives of liberal peace and prosperity. The new populism, stoked in the US by Pat Buchanan and company, is not going unnoticed by the constellation of capitalists, state man-agers and intellectuals who have fostered economic globalization as part of a transnational hegemonic project. Even as Buchanan made himself a symbol of popular discontent a steady stream of critical commentaries appeared in the mainstream press bashing his policy propos-als as atavistic, crude, isolationist, protectionist, and dangerous. Among these was a warning from James Bacchus, American member of the World Trade Organization appeals panel, who characterized Buchananism as a threat to the system of global liberalization painstakingly constructed through postwar decades: "It would be economic suicide to throw it all away now" (quoted in Nordheimer, 1996; see also Friedman, 1996; Hormats, 1996). Evidently, Buchanan's populist nationalism provoked real anxiety among the global power bloc.

Ethan Kapstein, then Director of Studies for the Council on Foreign Relations, has suggested that the new populism increasingly evident across the OECD countries represents a backlash against the combination of intensified global competitive pressures and a political climate dominated by the interests of investors. The growth-oriented "embedded liberalism" compromise has been abandoned in favor of anti-inflationary policies which effectively suppresses the real standard of living of working people while maintaining the long-term profitability of investments. Kapstein warned readers of *Foreign Affairs*: "if the post-World War II social contract with workers – of full employment and comprehensive social welfare – is to be broken, political support for the burgeoning global economy could easily collapse." In the absence of growth-oriented and internationally coordinated measures to ease the plight of those hardest hit by the new global competition – primarily less skilled workers and middle managers – politics in the industrial countries could well take an ugly turn. "Populists and demagogues of various stripes will find 'solutions' to contemporary economic problems in protectionism and xenophobia" (Kapstein, 1996: 16–17). Were that to occur, he suggested, the result would be a loss of the potential aggregate income made available by an extended Smithian division of labor, and the emergence of a zero-sum world in which both peace and prosperity would become more difficult to realize.

And Kapstein was not the only representative of the global power bloc expressing such fears. The World Economic Forum (WEF) has become increasingly preoccupied with the politics of globalization. Evolving out of the European Management Forum which Swiss business professor Klaus Schwab founded in 1971, the WEF has become a membership organization for over one thousand major international firms, each of which pays substantial annual fees to the Forum.[1] The Forum explains in its promotional literature why such shrewd business people see this as money well spent: "As a member of the World Economic Forum, you are part of a real Club, and the foremost business and public-interest network in the world" (World Economic Forum, 1997a: 10). In keeping with its program of promoting "entrepreneurship in the public interest," the WEF brings its members together at the annual Davos extravaganza, which Thomas Freidman calls "the ultimate capitalist convention" (Friedman, 1999a: 268). The Davos meetings offer WEF members "intensive networking in a privileged context allowing for the identification of new business opportunities and new business trends." At Davos, WEF members hobnob with their fellow global capitalists, but also with leaders from political and civil society to whom the Forum refers as "constituents" (to distinguish them from WEF "members"): while corporate "members" are entitled to attend WEF events, heads of state and government ministers, academics and policy experts, media figures, and cultural leaders from around the world may attend by invitation only. Thus the WEF offers its members privileged access to "high-level interaction between political leaders and business leaders on the key issues affecting economic development" on regional and global scales (World Economic Forum, 1997a: 10).

> The key to Forum activities is direct access to strategic decisionmakers, in a framework designed to encourage economic development via private sector involvement. This direct interaction between public and private sector and experts leads to the creation of a partnership committed to improving the state of the world.
>
> (World Economic Forum, 1997b)

Representing itself as being at once a private club and a kind of global public sphere, the Forum is an organization in which the various segments of the global power bloc can come together to construct a unifying political vision, and present to the rest of the world the interests of global capital in the guise of a universal vision – "entrepreneurship in the public interest." In short, it attempts to organize the hegemony of a global ruling class, as Kees van der Pijl has argued (van der Pijl, 1998: 132–5).

At the 1996 Davos conclave, the central theme was "sustaining globalization." As the meetings opened, Forum organizers Klaus Schwab and Claude Smadja published an essay in the *International Herald Tribune* suggesting that the process of economic globalization "has entered a critical phase" in which economic and political relationships, both globally and within countries, are being painfully restructured. Schwab and Smadja acknowledge that these changes are having a devastating impact on large numbers of working people in "the industrial democracies," with heightened mass insecurity resulting in "the rise of a new brand of populist politicians." They fear that in the absence of effective measures to address the social circumstances of working people and the weakened ideological legitimacy of global capitalism, the new populism may continue to gain strength, threaten further progress toward the agenda of globalization, and "test the social fabric of the democracies in an unprecedented way." The social forces leading globalization, then, face "the challenge of demonstrating how the new global capitalism can function to the benefit of the majority and not only for corporate managers and investors" (Schwab and Smadja, 1996). In the spirit of this analysis, Schwab addressed the opening session of the 1996 forum: "Business has become a major stakeholder of globalization and has a direct responsibility to contribute to the stability of our global system" (World Economic Forum, 1996; see also Economist, 1996).

As early as 1995, the World Bank's *World Development Report* had focused its attention on "Workers in an Integrating World." While maintaining its basic commitment to "market-friendly" policies and international openness, and representing such policies in familiar liberal terms as generally beneficial, the Bank conceded that "within the industrial countries there is a small but vocal minority who fear that they will lose from the introduction of new technologies, the growth of international trade, and movements of capital and people across national boundaries" (World Bank, 1995: 4–5, 56). This "vocal minority" the Bank viewed as posing a potential political threat to international openness and the prevalence of "sound" economic policies. "Ensuring that a commitment to open trade remains politically acceptable sometimes requires policy measures to ease the plight of the minority that loses out." The Bank warned that such policies should not foster welfare dependence, but should "encourage workers to upgrade their skills, educate their children, and support the mobility of workers into new jobs," thus making themselves more useful and attractive to transnational capital (1995: 60). Further, to insure that the gains from liberal globalization were seen to spread as widely as possible, governments were warranted to deal with inequality, especially that linked to discrimination based on ethnicity or gender. Betraying the fundamental liberal fear of "special interests," the Bank explicitly declined to link trade and international labor standards (1995: 6, 79), but called upon governments to protect (if not necessarily to encourage) basic worker rights such as the right to form unions for purposes of (enterprise-level) collective bargaining (1995: 71, 79–86).

In these remarkable statements – by representatives of the constellation of social forces whose hegemony acted as midwife to long-term processes of capitalist globalization – the importance of ideological struggle and the potential threat of populism and nationalism to a sustained liberal hegemony are frankly acknowledged. Even before, the 1997–8 financial crises which rocked Asia and the world, and the two-time defeat (in 1997 and then again in 1998) of Presidential Fast Track authority in the US, expressions of popular disaffection had awakened some among the dominant bloc to the fragility of neoliberal globalization and of their continued global social power.

The Asian crisis

Through 1997–8, a series of financial panics swept through several newly industrializing countries (NICs) and, as the confidence of the investor class was shaken, reverberations from the crisis were visible in industrializing economies and major financial markets around the world. Among the countries most seriously affected were Thailand, Indonesia, Malaysia, the Philippines, and South Korea – countries which only a short time before had seemed to be rising stars of the new international division of labor. Massive inflows of foreign investment have fueled rapid growth in these economies, including growth in manufacturing for export but also including a great deal of more speculative and unproductive investment, especially after 1985 when Japanese foreign direct investment was increasingly displaced by international portfolio investment and bank capital. As part of their strategy to attract international capital, several Asian NICs had linked the values of local currencies to the US dollar, but when the dollar appreciated this arrangement put pressure on the trade balances of Asian NICs (whose exports became more expensive as a result). As trade balances deteriorated, business confidence became further clouded by the relative magnitude of unproductive investment (especially speculation in real estate) and fears of a bursting bubble began to spread. Investors increasingly fled these economies, dumping local currencies and assets denominated in those currencies.

Smelling blood in the foreign exchange markets, packs of predatory speculators attacked the Thai baht, Malaysian ringgit, Indonesian ruppiah, and the Philippine peso by "selling short." That is, speculators contracted to deliver at future dates currencies which they did not actually hold at the time, betting that by the contractually specified delivery date the market value of the currency would have deteriorated to such a degree that it could be bought more cheaply than the price specified in their contracts to deliver. Near the delivery date, the speculators would buy the promised quantities of currency and deliver them at the previously contracted price which, if they bet successfully, would be higher than the heavily devalued market price which the speculators actually pay for the currency prior to delivery. With increasing volumes of their currencies being dumped onto foreign exchange markets by fleeing investors and speculators selling short, defense of the dollar-linked currency values became untenable, and governments with depleted foreign exchange reserves were compelled to turn to the International Monetary Fund for help in addressing their balance of payments crises. The price of such help was submission to the IMF's standard policy template, a draconian program of austerity designed to reduce inflation and imports, attract foreign capital and expand exports by raising interest rates, slashing public spending, and suppressing wages and consumption (Bello, 1998; Henwood, 1998a, 1998b; on selling short, see Soros, 1998: 136–7).[2]

As the ramifications of the financial crisis spread around the world, George Soros wrote a series of articles and a book in which he made the remarkable claim that financial markets are inherently unstable, and that free market capitalism constitutes a threat to liberal, pluralist values. Soros attacked the atomistic assumptions upon which economic theory is based, arguing that markets, and especially financial markets, operate not on the basis of pre-given individual preferences but rather "reflexively." By this he meant that the preferences of market actors are shaped by the very markets in which they participate, creating the possibility of self-reinforcing cycles of boom and bust. Soros denounced what he calls "the capitalist threat" which results from conjoint influence of the instability of global markets, the erosion of civic values and resistance to regulation in the public interest which arise from the ideology of "market fundamentalism," and the likelihood of political backlash among those in the "periphery" most dependent upon, and vulnerable to, international capital.

> I can already discern the makings of the final crisis. It will be political in character. Indigenous political movements are likely to arise that will seek to expropriate the multinational corporations and recapture "national" wealth. Some of them may succeed in the manner of the Boxer Rebellion or the Zapatista Revolution. Their success may then shake the confidence of financial markets, engendering a self-reinforcing process on the downside. Whether it will happen on this occasion or the next one is an open question.
>
> (Soros, 1998: 134)

Much like the apostasy of John Gray – the former Thatcherite political philosopher who penned a bitterly critical attack on neoliberal globalization and its corrosive effects upon deeper social bonds and traditional institutions (Gray, 1998) – Soros' critique is remarkable not so much for its originality, but rather for its source. Soros – billionaire, financier, philanthropist, and amateur philosopher – has been a major player in the new world of global finance and was deeply implicated in the currency speculation which contributed to the Asian crisis.

The crisis not only unleashed fears about the instability of globalizing markets, it also called into question the institutional infrastructure of neoliberalism. In particular, a storm of controversy raged around the International Monetary Fund (IMF) and its invariant prescriptions of austerity in the face of crisis (Kristof, 1998; Miller, 1998; Sanger, 1998). The Fund's deflationary measures were originally designed for countries with large public deficits and high inflation, neither of which were characteristic of the Asian NICs. As a result of rigid IMF policies, critics claimed, the Asian NICs were subjected to recessions more severe than they might otherwise have had to endure, deepening economic pessimism and generating worldwide ripple effects. Prominent among these critics were officials of the World Bank, especially its chief economist Joseph Stiglitz and its president James Wolfensohn. The latter went so far as to advocate a Comprehensive Development Framework which would link financial bailouts with integrated programs to maintain employment and facilitate access to healthcare and education. "If we do not have greater equity and social justice," Wolfensohn said, "there will be no political stability, and without political stability no amount of money put together in financial packages will give us financial stability" (quoted in Friedman, 1998).

In the US, both conservatives and progressives attacked the IMF when the issue of further US funding arose in Congress, illustrating once again the ambiguities of populist politics. Conservatives such as Senator Lauch Faircloth (Republican, North Carolina), representative Les Paul (Republican, Texas), and the Heritage Foundation (a prominent right-wing think tank), claimed that IMF bailouts amounted to welfare for Wall Street and distorted the operation of a free market (presumably based on individual responsibility for one's economic endeavors). Progressives, on the other hand, criticized IMF programs as not going far enough. Representative David Bonior (Democrat, Michigan) declared: "The American people are going to be very skeptical of any plan to bail out international speculators and repressive regimes that simply encourages them to repeat the same pattern of abuse and excess all over again. We cannot support a bailout that imposes an economic stranglehold on working people, tramples democratic rights, ignores the underlying causes of instability and then asks the American taxpayer to foot the bill" (quoted in Sanger, 1998). Some progressives called for replacement of the IMF by a new institution which would be funded by a modest tax on all international capital flows, which would dampen short-term speculative flows and make financial aid to investors and governments conditional upon their commitment to encourage long-term productive investment, pay living wages, and respect international labor standards. Others suggested a global equivalent of the Federal Deposit Insurance Corporation, funded by levies upon international banks and investment firms (Borosage, 1998; Miller, 1998).

While the IMF was subjected to extraordinary critical scrutiny, and there was for a time much talk of a "new architecture" for the global financial system, the storm seems largely to have blown over without effecting major change (Sanger, 1988). The administration and its major allies, such as the Business Roundtable, lobbied strenuously for immediate US support for the IMF. In return for IMF promises of greater disclosure of the terms of its bailout loans, and stiffer terms to act as a disincentive for borrowers, Congress agreed to continue funding with billions of dollars (Blustein, 1998).

[...]

Responses to the new populism: "globalization with a human face"

It is not clear to me that the global ruling class is prepared to abandon its hegemonic doctrine of low inflation and fiscal retrenchment, "flexible labor markets," and free flows of goods and capital, all policies which promote the interests of investors and magnify the impact of market forces on working people. Yet it seems safe to say that its confidence has been shaken and that the ideological grip of neoliberalism is weakening, even among those whose political project it has been. It is in this context that some in the global power bloc are beginning to engage critics of neoliberal globalization on the terrain of ideological struggle.

Addressing the World Trade Organization in May, 1998, President Clinton reassured the WTO membership that despite the ongoing battles over Fast Track, the US was not turning away from the project of global liberalization: "we must pursue an ever-more-open global trading system" which, he said, will bring in train increasing economic opportunity, prosperity, freedom, and democracy. But Clinton was clearly impressed by the resistance to liberal globalization, and sought to co-opt some of their central arguments:

> We must do more to make sure that this new economy lifts living standards around the world and that spirited economic competition among nations never becomes a race to the bottom in environmental protections, consumer protections and labor standards. We should level up, not level down. Without such a strategy, we cannot build the necessary public support for the global economy. Working people will only assume the risks of a free international market if they have the confidence that this system will work for them.
>
> (Clinton, 1998)

Clinton called on the WTO to create a forum in which the voices of labor, consumer, and environmental groups might be heard, along with that of business, and he urged the organization to make its deliberations more open and public. In his 1999 State of the Union address, Clinton returned to this theme of legitimating the global economic order. He bemoaned the divisiveness of the trade issue and called for the construction of a new consensus: "Somehow we have to find a common ground. . . . We have got to put a human face on the global economy" (Clinton, quoted in Dionne, 1999).

The first US President to address the International Labor Organization (ILO) in Geneva, in the summer of 1999 Clinton reiterated his "firm belief that open trade is not contrary to the interest of working people" insofar as it brings with it efficiency gains, faster growth, better jobs, and higher incomes. "Unfortunately, working people the world over do not believe this," he lamented, reiterating his call to "put a human face on the global economy." Clinton proposed a three-pronged program. First, he advocated closer cooperation between the ILO and the other major institutions of the global economy, especially the IMF and the WTO, in order to promote more widespread respect for "core labor standards." He called for generalized adoption of the ILO's new *Declaration on Fundamental Principles and Rights at Work* – which he described as "a charter for a truly modern economy" – and for abolition of "the worst forms of child labor." And to assist the world's poorest countries, Clinton prescribed some measure of debt relief (Clinton, 1999).

While some observers saw in these declarations evidence that fundamental changes were afoot in US policy toward the world economy (Dionne, 1998, 1999), others have greeted Clinton's declarations with a healthy measure of skepticism, for Clinton's new global charter is weak beer indeed. In the anticlimactic debate over GATT–WTO in the US, the Clinton administration had purchased the quiescence of Lane Kirkland's AFL-CIO by promising to introduce the issue of labor standards into the deliberations of the WTO. And so they did: in the 1996 Singapore Ministerial Declaration, marking the first ministerial-level conference of WTO members, the ministers rhetorically renewed their commitment to internationally recognized labor standards, but made it absolutely clear that any such commitment would in no way be allowed to impede the agenda of liberalization. The WTO deferred to the ILO any active role in institutionalizing such standards, and flatly declared, "There is currently no work on the subject in the WTO" (World Trade Organization, 1998: 51). No direct connections would be forged between labor rights and access to the global trading system.

The ILO's attempts to implement the conventions defining fundamental labor rights have depended upon the willingness of member states to ratify the conventions and bring national labor laws into conformity with them. And this has been uneven at best. Of the seven "fundamental" ILO conventions, ratification rates range from 44 percent of member states up to 86 percent. The Convention on Freedom of Association and Protection of the Right to Organize (which one might imagine to be the *sine qua non* of membership in such an organization) has been ratified by only 71 percent of ILO members. The United States, ostensibly an advocate of international labor standards, has ratified only one of the seven fundamental conventions – Convention 105 proscribing forced labor.[3]

The approach to international labor standards which Clinton has been pushing, then, does not necessarily build into the global trading order mechanisms for enforcement of the standards, nor does it require adoption of ILO conventions and their inscription into national labor laws. Rather, the President has endorsed the ILO's non-binding *Declaration on Fundamental Principles and Rights at Work*, which makes it possible rhetorically to embrace the seven core labor standards without endowing them with the force of law or backing them with the possibility of trade sanctions. International trade union activists have attacked the new Declaration as "a toothless voluntary accord" made up of "hollow principles and rights at work detached from concrete implementation in national labor legislation" (Open World

Conference of Workers, 1999). On these and other issues, progressive critic Robert Borosage sees a larger strategy at work in the performative contradictions of the President: "the gulf between word and deed . . . is essential to the administration's struggle to contain the growing revolt against corporate-defined globalization at home and abroad" (Borosage, 1999).

In calling for a version of "globalization with a human face," the President is not alone among card-carrying members of the neoliberal bloc. This trope was explicitly invoked as a central theme of the 1999 World Economic Forum. In their annual contribution to the opinion page of the *International Herald Tribune*, highlighting the theme of each year's Davos conclave, Forum president Klaus Schwab and managing director Claude Smadja struck a note of urgency:

> We are confronted with what is becoming an explosive contradiction. At a time when the emphasis is on empowering people, on democracy moving ahead all over the world, on people asserting control over their own lives, globalization has established the supremacy of the market in an unprecedented way. . . . We must demonstrate that globalization is not just a code word for an exclusive focus on shareholder value at the expense of any other consideration; that the free flow of goods and capital does not develop to the detriment of the most vulnerable segments of the population and of some accepted social and human standards. . . . If we do not invent ways to make globalization more inclusive, we have to face the prospect of a resurgence of the acute social confrontations of the past, magnified at the international level.
>
> (Schwab and Smadja, 1999)

As interesting as the acuity of the WEF's diagnosis, however, was the banal infirmity of its prescribed treatment. In his opening address, Schwab exhorted members of the global power bloc to "try to define a responsible globality" based on an ethic of "caring for the neighbors in our global village" (Schwab, 1999). In the absence of global standards enforceable through international economic institutions or ILO Conventions inscribed into national laws, it seems that we are reduced to pleading for niceness from the world's largest and most powerful enterprises and their allies. And indeed, Schwab's call for new corporate values was echoed in UN Secretary-General Kofi Annan's plea to the businessmen and women gathered in Davos: "I call on you – individually through your firms, and collectively through your business associations – to embrace, support and enact a set of core values in the areas of human rights, labor standards, and environmental practices" (Annan, 1999).

The United Nations Development Program has become another major global institution to embrace the metaphor of "globalization with a human face." In the 1999 edition of its annual *Human Development Report*, UNDP notes the dramatic worsening of global inequalities which have been attendant upon neoliberal globalization. By the late 1990s, the fifth of the world's population living in the highest-income countries had 86 percent of world GDP, 82 percent of world market exports, 68 percent of foreign direct investment, and 74 percent of the world's telephone lines; while the poorest fifth had only about 1 percent of each of these (United Nations Development Program, 1999: 3). According to UNDP, these inequalities have been deepening as the neoliberal project has unfolded: the wealthiest 20 percent of the world's people received 74 times as much income as the poorest 20 percent in 1997; up from a ratio of 60 to 1 in 1990, and 30 to 1 in 1960. It is frequently claimed that the current period of economic internationalization is not so different from that around the turn of the last century, but UNDP claims that the income gap in 1870 was 7 to 1, and 11 to 1 in 1913. If these figures are even remotely indicative, it would seem that the inequalities fostered by the current processes of globalization are manifoldly more intense than anything witnessed during its nearest historical analog.[4]

According to UNDP, "poverty is everywhere," with more than one-quarter of the population of developing countries facing conditions of dire poverty, and one-eighth of the people of the richest countries confronting significant effects of poverty. Further, UNDP notes that these inequalities have gendered dimensions. As market-led development increasingly integrates producers into the formal labor market, women are more subject to the double burden of paid work outside the home in addition to unpaid work of caregiving and domestic production within the household. At the same time, fiscal pressures associated with the neoliberal global order result in widespread cutbacks in publicly-provided care services, further aggravating the gendered inequalities of neoliberal globalization. Women are more likely than men to be poor, undereducated or illiterate, and politically underrepresented (United Nations Development Program, 1999: 7, 28, 77–83).

But UNDP is not attacking globalization, which it represents as a process pregnant with opportunities for human progress, producing unprecedented levels of wealth and technology, improving health and education, exposing people everywhere to a rich variety of cultural practices, expanding the scope of individual choice, and offering "enormous potential to eradicate poverty in the 21st century." For this potential to be most fully realized UNDP argues that the current, imbalanced form of globalization must be supplanted by one in which the development of competitive markets is matched by the fostering of communal values and construction of institutions of governance. "When the market goes too far in dominating social and political outcomes, the opportunities and rewards of globalization spread unequally and inequitably – concentrating power and wealth in a select group of people, nations and corporations, marginalizing the others" (United Nations Development Program, 1999: 1, 2). In the dramatically imbalanced globalization of recent decades UNDP explicitly implicates "a global ideological shift" toward liberalization and market-driven development, embodied in the norms and practices of the governing institutions of the global economy. It notes the apparent double standard within global regimes by which state governments are bound to respect the rights of firms, but firms are bound by no norm of social responsibility and public accountability (1999: 29, 34–5).

UNDP prescribes better governance at all levels, emphasizing the values of "human development." National governments should complement market-friendly policies with programs which improve productivity, enhance equity, and shelter the vulnerable. For example, by investing in the education of a broad spectrum of their populations, developing countries will attract more long-term investment from transnational capital, enhance the productivity of their labor force, and thus make it possible to raise wage levels and labor standards without putting upward pressure on unit labor costs or undercutting the competitiveness of exports. Further, processes of governance should be extended and made more inclusive, fostering participation by non-governmental organizations (NGOs), allied with local and national governments and entering into negotiations with multinational firms and foreign investors. These negotiations might take place in the context of regionally established frameworks setting out basic labor and environmental standards. Firms and investors ought also to be subject to a global code of conduct, monitored through a global forum in which NGOs and other actors in civil society (for example, labor unions) would be empowered to participate. And governance of international institutions should be reformed so that voting rights correspond more closely to population than wealth, providing poorer countries with a stronger voice. Finally, UNDP called for major institutional innovations at the global level, including the creation of a global central bank to regulate financial flows and act as lender of last resort during liquidity crises, a global investment trust to insure more equitable long-term capital flows to developing countries, a world environment agency to promote sustainable development, and an expansion of the WTO's mandate to enable closer regulation of the operations of multinational firms (United Nations Development Program, 1999: 97–114).

The trope of "globalization with a human face" is then invoked in a variety of contexts, and is associated with various meanings. For the World Economic Forum, it appears to represent a public relations strategy aimed at making the global dominance of corporate capital more palatable; for the President of the United States, it is a public relations strategy wedded to some very modest institutional reforms; and for the United Nations Development Program, it is associated with a somewhat more ambitious set of proposed reforms aimed at making market-based globalization more socially responsible and equitable. It is in the latter view of globalization that the "human face" most prominently features the public visage of the participatory citizen, the NGO activist, the labor unionist. This signifies to me that global institutions are themselves terrains of ideological struggle in which alternative meanings may be associated with globalization and its "human face."

To the extent that "globalization with a human face" can pre-empt grassroots mobilizations and transnational coalitions aimed at the explicit politicization of the world economy and the democratization of its governance, it will have effected what Antonio Gramsci referred to as a "passive revolution" – social reform initiated from above for the purpose of forestalling popular political mobilization and thereby disabling a potentially transformative, self-empowering social movement. On the other hand, as we have seen, not all versions of this trope are equally anti-democratic. In particular, the vision represented by the UNDP appears to offer some scope for politicizing and democratizing the global economy. Such visions are not in themselves progressive; but they represent openings for progressive global politics. Their progressive potential can be realized by articulation with vigorous and active transnational grassroots movements – embracing NGOs, labor unions, women's groups, and various other populist initiatives enacting a critique of the anti-democratic character of transnational capitalist power. It is these latter, and their ideologies of globalization as an open-ended project of democratization, which represent the potential for a post-liberal, and conceivably post-capitalist, New World Order.

Seattle and beyond

During 1999, there was much talk of a "Millennium Round" of negotiations which might emerge from the WTO ministerial-level conference in Seattle and define the horizons for renewed efforts toward global economic liberalization. Instead, what emerged in Seattle was diplomatic deadlock within the conference, and a high water mark of mass organized resistance without.

Prior to the Seattle events, a "Statement from Members of International Civil Society" had circulated via the internet, collecting (as of 27 November, 1999) 1,400 endorsements from non-governmental organizations located in at least 89 countries, all of whom found common ground in a critique of the undemocratic character of the WTO and the inequalities it promotes:

> In the past five years the WTO has contributed to the concentration of wealth in the hands of the rich few; increasing poverty for the majority of the world's population; and unsustainable patterns of production and consumption. The Uruguay Round

Agreements have functioned principally to prise open markets for the benefit of transnational corporations at the expense of national economies; workers, farmers, and other people; and the environment. In addition, the WTO system, rules and procedures are undemocratic, untransparent and nonaccountable and have operated to marginalize the majority of the world's people.

(Members of International Civil Society, 1999)

Together, these NGOs called for a moratorium on negotiations for further liberalization until a comprehensive review of the WTO and its effects could be concluded – a review which, they insisted, should be "conducted with civil society's full participation."

As trade ministers and their delegations arrived in Seattle from 135 member states, they were met by crowds of demonstrators at least fortythousand strong, many engaging in what the *Washington Post* called "one of the largest acts of mass civil disobedience in recent US history" (Burgess and Pearlstein, 1999). Among the demonstrators were environmentalists, labor unionists, advocates of Third World debt relief, consumer activists, indigenous peoples' groups, farmers, Lesbian Avengers, religious groups, student anti-sweatshop activists, animal rights defenders – a rich stew representing, by some estimates, over 700 various grassroots organizations from many countries (Economist, 1999; Henwood, 1999; Longworth, 1999; Moberg, 1999). Simultaneous protests against the WTO occurred in London and numerous other places around the world.

In Seattle, while some staged marches and rallies, organized groups of protesters successfully interrupted traffic in the city center and for a time precluded access to the convention center. The protests discomfited delegates and forced the cancellation of the conference's opening ceremonies. In response to this loss of control over city streets, and to some relatively isolated acts of violence against property, the city's mayor declared a state of emergency, put downtown under a curfew, and called in state police and National Guard troops. Meanwhile Seattle police unleashed clouds of tear gas, pepper spray, and rubber bullets – along with the more traditional boots and batons – at demonstrators and bystanders. Although protests continued on subsequent days, mass arrests by riot police in gas masks and body armor enabled the delegates to go about their business.

The official business soon bogged down, however, as the US clashed with Europe and Japan over agricultural protection and anti-dumping measures, and developing countries expressed frustration with the heavyhanded domination of the WTO and its agenda by the US and the developed countries (Henwood, 1999; Khor, 1999; Pearlstein, 1999b; Sanger, 1999). Most controversial, however, was the Clinton administration's attempt to place core labor standards on the WTO agenda by proposing a working group to study the relationship between trade and labor, a move which would call into question the "Singapore consensus" that labor issues are outside the ambit of the WTO. While the International Confederation of Free Trade Unions and over 100 labor unions from around the world supported it (Cook, 1999), diplomats from developing countries vociferously opposed any such proposal, seeing it as a cover for protectionism designed to discriminate against their products and maintain the privileges of workers in the US.[5] With evident suspicion the Egyptian trade minister asked "Why all of a sudden, when third world labor has proved to be competitive, why do industrial countries start feeling concerned about our workers?" (quoted in Greenhouse and Kahn, 1999). Business interests breathed a sigh of relief as a Presidential remark envisioning the eventual use of trade sanctions to enforce labor rights was greeted with hostility from developing country governments, and representatives of the European Union made it clear they would not support labor-related sanctions. Deadlocked and beleaguered, the ministerial meetings adjourned with little progress toward an agenda for a new round of liberalization.

As in the debates over NAFTA, GATT, and Fast Track, some commentators aligned themselves closely with neoliberal ideology and adopted a posture of near-papal infallibility, refusing to grant the critics' perspective even a measure of legitimacy. With the epic self-certainty characteristic of his profession, Robert Litan, economist of the Brookings Institution, proclaimed: "However well-intentioned many of the protestors might be, they are on the wrong side of the facts and of world history" (Litan, 1999).[6] Litan feared that the protests might be harbingers of "backsliding toward protectionism." Celebrity economist Paul Krugman ridiculed the WTO's critics by likening them to simple-minded conspiracists: "The WTO has become to leftist mythology what the United Nations is to the militia movement: the center of a global conspiracy against all that is good and decent" (Krugman, 1999). Thomas Friedman – foreign affairs columnist for the *New York Times* and captain of the neoliberal globalization cheerleading squad – could not contain his contempt for the protesters and heaped calumny upon them, calling them "ridiculous," "crazy," "a Noah's ark of flat-earth advocates, protectionist trade unions and yuppies looking for their 1960s fix" who, if they only "stopped yapping" long enough to think, "would realize that they have been duped by knaves like Pat Buchanan" (Friedman, 1999b).[7]

While neoliberal positions such as these clearly dominated the preceding instances of public debate over globalization, in the discussions surrounding the events in Seattle some in the mainstream media seemed to glimpse that what is at issue is precisely the *political* limits imposed by the neoliberal ideology exemplified above. Writing in the *Los Angeles Times* and the *International Herald Tribune*, William Pfaff hit the nail on the head: "The prevailing assumption...has been that trade issues should be dealt with in isolation from social and political context and consequences. This idea has been dealt a blow from which it will not recover" (Pfaff, 1999). This revelation has potentially radical implications: if trade relations are intrinsically political, then they are properly issues of public concern and need not be governed by criteria of private profit or "efficiency." Moreover, the Seattle protests may at last have revealed as a hoary canard the formerly widespread presumption which equated opposition to neoliberal globalization with atavistic tribalism and xenophobia. Thomas Friedman notwithstanding, Pat Buchanan's appearance in Seattle was barely noticed, as the unprecedented coalition of left-progressive forces dominated the agenda of protest (Economist, 1999; Henwood, 1999; Longworth, 1999; Moberg, 1999). After witnessing the transnational coalition of groups protesting the WTO, and their agendas of global scope, a *Newsweek* reporter reflected: "Hitherto, it's been easy to insist that anyone opposed to 'trade' was by definition a protectionist, happy to hide behind the walls of the nationstate. That simple equation no longer holds good; one of the most important lessons of Seattle is that there are now two visions of globalization on offer, one led by commerce, one by social activism" (Elliott, 1999). At stake in these debates, a *Washington Post* correspondent recognized, might be things much more fundamental than trade: "People are now openly discussing how the world's political architecture – up to now built around the sovereignty of the nation-state – may have to be reworked to provide for a more global economic governance system that is open and democratic enough to gain legitimacy in the eyes of voters around the world" (Pearlstein, 1999a). Writing for the *Boston Globe*, Ellen Goodman framed succinctly the central question raised in Seattle: "Whose world is it, anyway?" (Goodman, 1999). Since before NAFTA, progressive activists have struggled to suggest that neoliberal globalization had profound implications for the future of democratic self-government on every scale from the local to the global; the Seattle protests seem finally to have placed this issue on the agenda of public debate.

In a stunning editorial statement, the *Seattle Post-Intelligencer* first apologized to the WTO delegates for the "unfriendly" reception they received, and then proceeded to endorse the major demands of the protesters: institutionalized and effective labor and environmental protections, along with openness and inclusion in the negotiation of trade policies and the settlement of disputes (Editorial Board, 1999). The editors of the nation's two leading papers were less inclined to adopt the agenda of the demonstrators, but acknowledged that the WTO had serious problems of "legitimacy." In order to sustain what the *New York Times* (6 December, 1999) called "the main vehicle of international economic progress," both the *Times* and the *Washington Post* prescribed limited reforms and greater institutional openness at the WTO. But, the *Post* cautioned, "The WTO should not seek to buy legitimacy by taking all criticisms to heart. If it took on as much of the role of protecting labor standards and the environment as its critics want, it would quickly lose focus" (1 December, 1999). For the *Post*, it seems, "loss of focus" is too high a price to pay for democratization, so the WTO should enact strictly limited reforms in order to resolve its legitimacy crisis and move on with the fundamental agenda of global liberalization.

If the more optimistic among the progressives are correct, a passive revolution such as the tepid reform agenda envisioned by the *Times* and the *Post* may not suffice. In the wake of Seattle it may be difficult to sustain a depoliticized global economy. Scholar and labor activist Elaine Bernard argues that the rise of "international advocacy networks" so clearly evident in protests against the WTO are of enormous long-term significance, for they represent "a forum for debating, negotiating and deliberating global solidarity. They are the beginnings of an emerging international civil society" which "provides space for the development of public values, and is the process by which a public self, or citizenry, is created" (Bernard, 1999). The process by which such transnational social spaces are constructed, and the negotiation of explicitly political identities and projects within those sites, is a necessary (if not sufficient) condition of global democratization.

Notes

1 Business is booming for the brokers of the global "public sphere": According to a *Washington Post* report (Swardson, 2000), each of the one thousand WEF members pay a basic membership subscription fee of $12,500 and an additional $6,250 for the privilege of sending their executives to the Davos meeting. At least 27 major firms pay an additional quarter million dollars each for the privilege of being designated as "knowledge partners" or "institutional partners." Two dozen others pay $78,000 to become "annual meeting partners." Partners enjoy a leading role in planning the Davos extravaganza and, not surprisingly, are highly visible participants: "They buy sessions," one former WEF staffer told the *Post*. All this generated $32 million in revenue for the WEF in 1999 – a 57 percent increase over 1995.

2 When thinking about the international financial crises of 1997–8, it is important to keep in mind that a crucial condition of possibility for such financial follies was the enormous expansion over recent decades of liquid capital sloshing about in the world economy (see Chapter 3), and the cash surpluses piling up in the hands of corporations and investors as a result of neoliberal political economy in the advanced capitalist countries (Chapter 2).

3 This information was gleaned from the web site of the International Labor Organization: www.ilo.org/public/english/50normes/whatare/fundam/index.htm

4 The escalating magnitudes of global inequality over the last century or more suggest to me that we are witnessing not a cyclical repetition of discrete episodes of economic internationalization, but a cumulative process producing an increasingly hierarchic world.

5 Skepticism from the Third World regarding US labor's motivation in supporting proposals for trade-linked labor standards is, of course, understandable in light of the AFL–CIO's historical record of complicity in US imperial foreign policy which has secured US privilege at their expense

(Sims, 1992). Whether the new AFL–CIO will indeed commit themselves to effective international solidarity – even if this implies eschewing imperial privilege and cozy relations with the Democratic Party – remains an open question. Nonetheless, to dismiss the issue of trade-labor linkages as nothing more than disingenuous protectionism is to lose sight of the contested character of both unions and the global economy. Supplanting competition with solidarity is a necessary step on the road to any democratizing global project, and trade-linked labor standards would inhibit a race to the bottom on the basis of coercive hyper-exploitation, enforced by competitive market pressures in the world economy (see, for example, Wachtel, 1998; Mayne and LeQuesne, 1999). Finally, it must be noted that the USA has a very poor record regarding adoption and fulfillment of core labor standards (International Confederation of Free Trade Unions, 1999), so that an effective trade-labor regime would hardly be a one-way street.

6 Along with Gary Burtless, Robert Lawrence and Robert Shapiro, Litan is an author of *Globaphobia*, a popular text aimed at debunking putatively *mis*-guided opposition to neoliberal globalization (Burtless *et al.*, 1998).

7 Friedman is the author of what must surely be one of the worst books yet written on globalization. Eschewing evidence and analysis in favor of an accretion of facile metaphors and platitudes, Friedman glibly passes off as absolute truth the common sense of his informants in the global investor class, and seems to view even corporate commercial advertisements as unproblematic sources of wisdom about the contemporary world. So abject is Friedman's submission to the ideology of multinational capital that he refers to hedge fund managers as his "best intellectual sources" and happily describes himself as an information arbitrageur (Friedman, 1999a: 21–2).

Selected references

Annan, K. (1999), "Address to the World Economic Forum in Davos," United Nations website: www.un.org/news/press/docs/1999/199990201.sgsm6881.html

Bello, W. (1998), "The End of a 'Miracle'," *Multinational Monitor*, January–February, www.essential. org/monitor/monitor.html

Bernard, E. (1999), "The Battle in Seattle: What was that All About?," *Washington Post*, 5 December.

Clinton, W. J. (1998), "Address to the World Trade Organization," Geneva: US Mission.

Clinton, W. J. (1999), "Remarks by the President to the International Labor Organization," White House Office of the Press Secretary.

Elliott, M. (1999), "The New Radicals," *Newsweek*, 13 December.

Friedman, A. (1998), "Is Free Market a Casualty of the Economic Crisis?," *International Herald Tribune*, 8 October.

Friedman, M. (1996), "Hong Kong vs. Buchanan," *Wall Street Journal*, 7 March.

Friedman, T. (1999a), *The Lexus and the Olive Tree*, New York: Farrar Strauss Giroux.

Friedman, T. (1999b), "Senseless in Seattle," *New York Times*, 1 December.

Goodman, E. (1999), "Coalition's Woes may Hinder Goals of Christian Right," *New York Times*, 2 August.

Gray, J. (1998), *False Dawn: The Delusions of Global Capitalism*, London: Granta.

Henwood, D. (1998a), "Asia Melts," *Left Business Observer*, 81 (January).

Henwood, D. (1998b), "Crisis Update," *Left Business Observer*, 85 (September).

Kapstein, E. (1996), "Workers and the World Economy," *Foreign Affairs*, May–June, pp. 16–37.

Litan, R. (1999), "The Protestors were Wrong, but Trade Means Compromise," *International Herald Tribune*, 6 December.

Members of International Civil Society (1999), "Statement from Members of International Civil Society Opposing a Millennium Round," UK: Friends of the Earth.

Nordheimer, J. (1996), "Buchanan Threatens Longtime Bipartisan Policy," *New York Times* (25 February).

Pfaff, W. (1999), "So Much for the Notion that Trade can Do Without Politics," *International Herald Tribune*, 29 November.

Rupert, M. (1995), *Producing Hegemony*, Cambridge: Cambridge University Press.

Sanger, D. (1988), "World Finance Meeting Ends with No Grand Strategy but Many Ideas," *New York Times*, 8 October.

Schwab, K. and Smadja, C. (1996), "Start Taking the Backlash against Globalization Seriously," *International Herald Tribune*, 1 February.

Schwab, K. and Smadja, C. (1999), "Globalization Needs a Human Face," *International Herald Tribune*, 28 January.

Soros, G. (1998), *The Crisis of Global Capitalism*, New York: Public Affairs.

United Nations Development Program (1999), *Human Development Report*, New York: UNDP/Oxford University Press.

van der Pijl, K. (1998), *Transnational Classes and International Relations*, London: Routledge.

World Bank (1995), *World Development Report: Workers in an Integrating World*, Oxford: Oxford University Press.

World Economic Forum (1996), "Creative Impatience can Manage Problems of Globalization," www.wefforum.org/frames/press

World Economic Forum (1997a), "Committed to Improving the State of the World," Geneva: World Economic Forum.

World Economic Forum (1997b), "About the World Economic Forum," Geneva: World Economic Forum.

Part 3

Exploring resistances

Peoples, practices, politics

Introduction

In Part 2, the chapters explored the possibilities and limits of a global civil society, raising the question of on whose behalf social movements claim to speak. It was emphasized in the introduction that categories such as 'gender' or 'environment', for example, are in practice often highly contested and may not be ascribed a unitary identity. Indeed, it may only be in the concrete practices of situated struggles that the identities of social movements are formed and transformed. In Part 3 our attention turns to exploring the multiple identities that are constituted in specific spheres of resistance. The chapters have been selected for their capacity to reveal how particular spheres of resistance – gender and women's movements; work and labour; debt and development; and environment – are made and remade according to concrete practices and politics. Of course, in many senses these categories overlap and inter-relate, they are separated here only to facilitate the analysis. Readers will also consider other categories – such as race and racism, nationalism and religion, for example – to have been overlooked here. Their omission does not imply that they are of less significance than the four selected spheres, but only that the limitations of framing the *Reader* enforce the artificial drawing of parameters around the discussion.

Gender

In many ways, relations of gender have been somewhat neutralized and depoliticized in the study of global resistances. For many commentators, gender is synonymous with 'women's issues', these issues effectively being 'dealt with' by packing them into the study of social movements. The chapters by Marchand, Peterson and Sisson Runyan, and Brodie, however, reveal that exploring resistance does not automatically settle the gender question. Instead, our very understandings and practices of resistance are themselves inscribed with gendered relations of power. Making global resistances visible, then, cannot be sufficient to make the gendering of resistances visible.

In each of the three essays on the gender question, concerns are raised that 'the gender(ed) dimensions of resistance may be ignored or marginalised' (Marchand). For Marianne Marchand, women's struggles have only tended to become visible where they can be offered as a 'blueprint' for civil society organizations. In this 'instrumental' reading of gender politics, she argues, the concrete struggles of groups such as SEWA and DAWN become subordinated to the search for institutionalized forms of political representation.

Janine Brodie raises similar concerns that 'good governance agendas' do little to address the fundamental needs of social reproduction or pervasive gender inequalities. For Brodie, the first step in bringing the gender 'g word' to the globalization 'g word' debate must be to reveal how the discourses of globalization and governance conceal and exclude gender-specific consequences.

In V. Spike Peterson and Anne Sisson Runyan's contribution we see something of what is revealed when Marchand's call to 'focus on contradictions, inconsistencies, and specific points of intervention' is taken seriously. In their discussion of anti-war movements, Peterson and Sisson Runyan suggest that sometimes struggles may reinscribe gender dichotomies, 'leaving in place the image of men as aggressive and bellicose life-takers/killers in contrast to women as pacifist life-givers/reproducers/mothers'. At the same time, they argue, women's peace movements have challenged the positioning of war in the public/state sphere, asserting the politicized nature of the private sphere of family and household that makes war possible. Indeed, it is in the very challenging of the dichotomy of public and private spheres that much of the gender politics of resistance resides. After all, if we assert global civil society as a transnational public sphere, and position women in a private realm of family and household that is deemed to be outside of political life, then many aspects of women's struggles are likely to remain invisible.

Work

Just as gender resistances tend to be the least visible in accounts of contemporary global struggles, so the politics of labour and work is commonly taken to be the most self-evident sphere of resistance. As Kim Moody writes, 'the most basic effects of the process of globalization' are confronted 'at the workplace level'. Most commonly, the actions and interests of trade unions are understood to be a direct expression of workers' resistances to the dictates of global capital. The three chapters on the subject of work and labour have been chosen so as to open up many of the dominant assumptions about worker resistances. Each of the essays has a different understanding of what the challenges of globalization are for workers, what the potential for resistance might be, and how these resistances might overcome divisions and inequalities between worker groups. In Moody's account it is the power of multi-national corporations within a globally diffuse production system that has precipitated a 'rebellion', at the centre of which is 'the working class and its most basic organization, the trade union'. 'Most of the struggle against globalization', writes Moody, 'necessarily occurs on a national plane'. Yet, across this nation-based set of resistances, Moody envisages the emergence of an international social movement unionism 'that uses the strongest of society's oppressed and exploited, generally organized workers, to mobilize those who are less able to sustain self-mobilization: the poor, the unemployed, the casualized workers, the neighbourhood organizations'. For Moody, then, not only is it possible to conceive of a unitary identity and agenda for workers worldwide, but it is strategically the only ground on which a struggle against globally mobile capital might succeed.

In Beverly Silver and Giovanni Arrighi's analysis, the inequalities of globalization are fundamentally rooted in the wealth gap between North and South. While they share with Moody an interest in the 'conditions of working class formation', they challenge the view that 'the North–South conflict has been superseded by a fundamental unity of the class interests of Northern and Southern workers'. In contrast to Moody, for Silver and Arrighi it is not primarily the globalization of production that has caused the crisis of world labour, but rather the globalization of finance and, in particular, the intensification of financial networks in the advanced industrialized North. This divide limits the possibilities for workers in different geographical regions to communicate and coordinate their concerns and, indeed, encourages the pursuit of 'particularistic interests in opposition to one another'. In contrast to Moody's vision of the strongest workers speaking on behalf of those at the margins, Silver and Arrighi raise the historical spectre of xenophobia that persists in contemporary struggles: 'Nor should we forget that some of the biggest US strikes of the late nineteenth and early twentieth century has among their targets the exclusion of Chinese workers from the US labour market... Only a complete amnesia of the most basic facts of twentieth-century Chinese and world-labour history can give any credence to the claim that US labour's advocacy of the exclusion of China from the WTO is primarily, if at all, motivated by international workers' solidarity'. The assumption that the categories of labour and workers can be treated as unitary and bounded entities, then, is significantly problematized by Silver and Arrighi's discussion of a racialized polarization of wealth.

Though the vision of social movement union resistance is challenged by the inequalities noted by Silver and Arrighi, other divisions and exclusions within the assumed category of labour are not raised in their analysis. Their sense of a 'worker' remains those producing for MNCs, whether as steelworkers in the North, or export processing zone workers in the South. The contribution by Kamala Kempadoo, by contrast, exposes the difficulty of defining a clear and linear relationship between globalization and workers' resistances. Kempadoo's study of the resistances of sex workers was motivated not by a search for a common agenda or cause, but rather by a number of questions that are specific to particular cases: 'Was it a singular incident spurred by an outsider, or did it reflect a local movement? In this part of the world, were women serious about staying in the sex industry or anxious to have prostitution abolished?' Revealing multiple faces of globalization, from migration and trafficking to sex tourism, Kempadoo is concerned to 'shift the focus from simple hierarchies and dichotomies' to a 'problematization of multiple spaces, seemingly contradictory social locations and plural sites of power'. Rather than assuming the representativeness of particular worker organizations, then, Kempadoo inquires into how the identities of sex workers are constituted in different ways in different parts of the world. And, rather than invoking a global organization to speak on behalf of sex workers, she locates the sources of resistance in the workers' everyday experiences.

Debt and development

The challenge to universalizing discourses of resistance that is represented by Kempadoo's work is a strong theme in writing on development struggles. Arturo Escobar's celebrated research on Latin American social movements asks 'that development not be seen solely as an economic and political project but as an overarching cultural discourse that has had a profound impact on the fabric of the Third World'. For Escobar, any political challenge to the restructuring of global capitalism must reject the search for 'the right adjustment package', and seek instead to expose the development discourses that have 'functioned as powerful instruments for shaping and managing the Third World'. Though Escobar does not underestimate the difficulty of dismantling development discourses, he finds potential spaces of resistance in the 'plural, contradictory, and uneven' nature of Latin American modernities. In the margins and interstices of Latin American capitalism, Escobar observes social groups 'taking space away from capitalism and modernity' and hinting at 'different ways of seeing the relationships between capital, the state, culture and the economy'. It will become clear, then, that Escobar sees the politics of Latin American movements as residing in situated struggles that defy conventional political boundaries. In a statement that echoes the conceptual concerns of James Scott in Part 1 of the *Reader*, Escobar writes: 'Struggles over meanings at the level of daily life are the basis of contemporary social movements'. Understood in this way the battleground of structural adjustment, for example, though we may view it as manifested in protests at World Bank and IMF meetings, is located primarily in the meanings that are articulated between social groups and movements in their daily lives.

In the readings by Ann Pettifor and Cyril Obi, we find examples of situated resistances to global debt (Jubilee 2000) and Shell Oil's presence in Nigeria (the movement for the survival of the Ogoni people or MOSOP). In many ways these readings are located within the culturally embedded approach advocated by Escobar. Pettifor's reading of The People's Summit of 1998 emphasizes the attempt to challenge dominant discourses of debt and development. The IMF and World Bank's disciplinary discourse of debt repayment is, in effect, challenged by the Jubilee Coalition's assertion of debt as enslavement. The human chain formed outside the Birmingham G8 summit, notes Pettifor, represents 'the definition of debt as a form of human bondage, or slavery'. Though Jubilee's campaigns cannot be understood as overt or direct resistances, they function more as discursive struggles, working to undermine the governing relationship between creditor and debtor – which positions the debtor as irresponsible miscreant – and exposing the culpability of 'the elites of the more powerful nations'. By revealing the 'striking parallels between the twentieth-century millstone of debt and the practice of slavery in preceding centuries', Pettifor makes the case that the Jubilee resistances are 'challenging the new dominant ethic' of a global trade in debt.

Though Cyril Obi's contribution focuses more on the overt struggles of the Ogoni people, he does emphasize the need to locate resistance to Shell's interventionism in the Ogoni ecosystem within the specific power relations and ethnic divisions of the locale. Obi's analysis somewhat undermines linear understandings of globalization 'from above' and resistance 'from below', revealing the tensions and contradictions that cut across the Ogoni peoples, the Nigerian state, and the forces of oil capital. Obi explores the concrete strategies that MOSOP pursues in order to 'internationalize its struggle', waging its campaign 'through lecture tours, newspaper articles, and documentary films showing the atrocities being committed against the Ogoni by Shell and the state in Nigeria'. Yet, Obi also reveals that the lines between violent and non-violent resistance are also profoundly complex, with the struggle becoming militarized and bloody.

Environment

The last set of chapters in Part 3 are concerned with the politics of resistance in the environmental sphere. Arundhati Roy takes the Narmada Valley Development Project as her focal point for the discussion of resistances to the commodification of indigenous resources in India. For Roy, the global threat posed by MNCs is personified as Rumpelstiltskin, 'an accretion, a cabal, an assemblage, a malevolent, incorporeal, transnational multi-gnome'. Rumpelstiltskin's ambition, as understood by Roy, 'is not simply the privatization of natural resources and essential infrastructure, but the privatization of policy making itself'. Understood in this way, environmental struggles go beyond the protection of the environment, extending into the heart of political and social life. Roy is concerned to use the case of resistances to the Maheshwar dam as a means to expose the wider injustices of the global political economy. Located within the ancient communities threatened with submergence by flooding, Roy finds a struggle that extends beyond a single localized issue: 'We were not just fighting against a dam. We were fighting for a philosophy. For a world view'. Asked what

India can teach the world, Roy responds by exposing three spaces that intersect globalization and Indian experiences. The first, a call centre college that trains young Indians to provide the service labour for the US and UK; the second, a terrorist training camp 'where the terrible backlash to this enforced abasement is being nurtured and groomed'; and finally, the Narmada valley, 'to witness the ferocious, magical, tenacious and above all non-violent resistance that has grown on the banks of that beautiful river'.

The contributions by Paul Ekins and Paul Wapner enable us to explore the relationship between the apparently localized struggles associated with subsistence survival, on the one hand, and the more conspicuously 'global' campaigns of the environmental NGOs, on the other. On the surface it may appear that Ekins addresses the concrete struggles of specific places, while Wapner is concerned with the headline-grabbing activism of transnational organizations. Yet, read together, these chapters reveal the ways in which concrete and situated resistances that we might call 'local' are interwoven with the large-scale campaigns we tend to recognize as 'global'. Both pieces recognize that environmental politics is not simply a material struggle over scarce resources, but also a resistance to dominant ways of thinking. Ekins' discussion of the German consumer movement's attempt to 'raise children's consciousness of environmental issues', for example, reveal the visual and play-based strategies that are used to challenge ways of thinking about the environment. Wapner's understanding of Greenpeace's campaigns similarly leads him to argue that the organization 'tries to change consciousness...to alter people's minds and actions throughout the world'. Both Ekins and Wapner also place an emphasis on resistance emerging through practices rather than a clear institutionalized agenda. Ekins understands the Chipko movement to be 'the result of hundreds of decentralized and locally autonomous initiatives', while for Wapner the World Wildlife Fund's 'emphasis is on just that, *practices*, not institutional arrangements'. Given their focus on consciousness and practice, these readings may lead us to question whether it is helpful to think in terms of clearly defined 'global' and 'local' resistances. 'There are forms of power associated with norms, rules, and discourses', writes Wapner, 'that actually shape people's desires, conceptions, understandings of the self'. We may be led to ask whether these forms of power and resistance are precisely those that transcend conventional boundaries of global and local politics.

18 Some theoretical 'musings' about gender and resistance

Marianne H. Marchand

Source: R. Teske and M. A. Tétreault (eds) (2000), *Feminist Approaches to Social Movements, Community, and Power*, Columbia: University of South Carolina Press, pp. 56–71

We are currently living in times of profound changes, or, more correctly, this is the prevailing perception of our times. Since the mid-1980s we have not only witnessed the tumbling down of the Berlin Wall but also experienced the impact of globalization on our daily lives. While I am not denying that these profound changes are "real," I am more interested in the ways in which they have influenced the production of knowledge in the field of international relations (IR). One of the most interesting aspects of the need for IR scholars to understand and explain the end of the Cold War and globalization is that it has opened up spaces within IR to raise new issues and themes as well as introduce new ontologies and epistemologies: for instance, the end to the Cold War framing of international politics has provided openings for a discourse that extends the security *problématique* to nonmilitary issues like the environment; similarly, human rights concerns have finally received a more legitimate place on the scholarly IR agenda.[1] Ontologically and epistemologically, IR has been the site of the so-called Third Debate which started because of challenges by various critical theories (including feminist, neoGramscian, poststructuralist, deconstructionist, postcolonial theories) to more traditional IR approaches.[2] And the decentering of the state within globalization discourse(s) has allowed IR scholars to train their collective gaze more seriously on non-state actors, such as social movements and transnational corporations, and speculate about the emergence of a global civil society and the importance of civil society or societies in a "New World Order."[3]

These epistemological issues have also their relevance for activists in social movements. Indeed, the rapidly changing international environment is presenting new challenges to social activists and requires the formulation of new objectives, strategies, alternatives, etc. As many activists realize, the old interpretative frames are not providing them with the necessary tools for developing appropriate responses to globalization. Gita Sen acknowledged as much when she called for a blueprint of globalization in order to develop appropriate responses.[4] In their quest for a reformulation of their interpretative frames, social activists have turned to ideas emanating from the social sciences. Social scientists, in turn, look at the (changing) practices of social movements to gain a better understanding of the emerging global civil society and transnational organizing. Therefore, the epistemological and ontological issues raised in the social sciences, including IR, bear relevance for activists since their interpretative frames may copy some of IR's masculinist biases.

It is against the above-sketched background that we should interpret current discussions among critical theorists, especially those working within a broadly defined neo-Gramscian framework, about globalization. Within these discussions there has been a slight shift in focus: early discussions focused primarily on understanding and explaining the politico-economic dimensions of globalization processes and the rise to hegemony of the so-called neoliberal project; this focus has been expanded to include sociopolitical and cultural dimensions of globalization; most recently, and partially informed by a concern with finding a response or alternative(s) to neoliberalism, the focus has shifted toward locating sites and sources of resistance to globalization that may provide the foundation for a concrete counter-hegemonic project.[5] This shift in attention toward resistance in the global political economy is most clearly exemplified by the special issue of *New Political Economy* (2, 1 [1997]) on "Globalization and the Politics of Resistance."

In this essay I am particularly interested in the way in which the emerging research agenda on resistance(s) in the global political economy is being constructed. As an IR scholar interested in gender issues, feminist theory, and global political economy, I fear that the gender(ed) dimensions of resistance may be ignored or marginalized. Therefore, I will use the remainder of this essay to address some questions that I hope will show why it is important to look at resistance through a gender lens. The focus will be on three related questions: How is resistance conceptualized? Are there gendered forms/practices/strategies of resistance? How can we start conceptualizing resistance from a gender perspective? This essay is not meant to provide an exhaustive gender analysis of resistance; its objective is much more modest in that it tries to raise a few critical gender-related questions concerning resistance. Questions that seem to have to be repeated each time a new issue emerges on the IR horizon.

Conceptualizing the politics of resistance

The silencing of gender?

The recent literature on social movements and the politics of resistance is centered around a few debates. The first issue concerns the power of social movements and their potential to counter globalization and undermine the neoliberal project effectively. Skeptics argue that social movements are too fragmented and (single) issue-oriented to mount a credible opposition. According to Rob Walker this view is prevalent because IR scholars are still prone to the notion that bigger or larger movements are more effective and powerful than smaller ones: "Contemporary political life still draws on discursive economies of scale that inform our understanding of what and where power is. These economies, these productions, reproductions and distributions across the multiple sites of modern political life, still largely determine the contours of contemporary political judgment, still constrain our capacity to distinguish the significant from the insignificant, and even the political from the apolitical. The analysis of social movements is especially susceptible [to the notion] that bigger is always better."[6] Those IR scholars who are taking social movements seriously have countered the "bigger is better" view by arguing that it is exactly the multiplicity of opposition by groups worldwide and the constantly changing venues for voicing opposition that give social movements their power.[7] However, many of these forms of resistance involve local grassroots movements and have gone unnoticed by most IR scholars who, in the past, have tended to focus rather narrowly on interstate relations. In Walker's words,

> More crucially, difficulties arise from the apparent disjunction between the realms in which social movements and world politics are usually said to exist. Whether as a simple synonym for "international relations" or as a label affixed to some more complex array of forces, "world politics" seems to refer not only to some grand – and therefore presumably determining – structure, but more significantly to things going on "out there,"

to processes that occur in realms somewhere "beyond" society. Social movements are supposed to be precisely *social* movements, phenomena that occur within a society; and societies in turn, the conventions insist, can only exist within those political structures that allegedly make them possible, namely states and the states system. Social movements and world politics are supposed to be understood as expressions of two distinct ontological realms, the inner and the outer.[8]

A third area of concern with the politics of resistance has focused primarily on the nature of social movements. This concern has been addressed from various angles. For instance, several authors have distinguished so-called new social movements from the old ones.[9] Others have tried to differentiate social movements in terms of their emancipatory potential and inclusiveness.[10] Latin American scholars in particular also have been interested in the question of whether social movements are pursuing narrow political objectives – i.e., vying for state power – or are interested in gaining relative autonomy from dominant and often repressive forces.[11] Finally, feminist scholars have classified women's movements on the basis of their gender needs or strategies whereby short-term strategies and needs such as improving the immediate living conditions of families and neighborhoods are associated with "feminine" movements, and middle or long-term strategies, directed at changing existing gender roles, are associated with feminist movements.[12]

Most recently scholarly attention has shifted from a direct focus on the activities of social movements toward a concern with the possibilities and potentials for a politics of resistance under the conditions of a globalized political economy.[13] As noted in the introduction, critical theoretical analyses of globalization and the search for alternatives to disciplinary neoliberalism serve as the background for this politics of resistance. As Walker observes,

> The development of a global civil society is read in relation to the structural logic and contradictions of an increasingly globalized capitalism, and not in the least in relation to a "global panopticon" associated with a "disciplinary neoliberalism," on the one hand, and the possibility that counter-hegemonic social movements might be able to challenge these emerging social forces on the other.... The structural analysis of changing forms of state and civil society in relation to the dynamics of global capitalism is more persuasive than the analysis of political possibilities for resistance or reconstruction. And despite the emphasis on the historicity and dynamism of global structures, it is instructive that Gill still tends to frame his analysis in terms of a hierarchy of levels.[14]

While Walker is appreciative of Gill's neo-Gramscian/Braudelian/Foucauldian reading of global capitalism, he finds the latter's critical analysis of resistance still weak. Drainville[15] concurs and actually tries to reclaim neo-Gramscian thought from a narrow structuralist focus in order to allow for a more elaborate and critical reading of resistance. In a recent article entitled "Overturning 'Globalisation': Resisting the Teleogical, Reclaiming the Political," Amoore et al. try to overcome weaknesses in analyzing the politics of resistance and alternatives to neoliberalism by reinserting the state as a site of struggle:

> What then is the future for political resistance against neoliberal globalisation? One thing is clear, the close relationship between the state and economic restructuring means that resistance to globalisation will continue to come predominantly from within national civil society and national social movements, including organised labour. The future success of resistance movements to neoliberal gobalisation may be brought a step

closer if resistance organisations themselves highlight the close relationship between the state and globalisation. Resistance groups should act to break down the myth, which is often perpetuated by governments, that they are helpless in the face of globalisation, and refuse to accept that their own hands are tied by the inevitable onrush of global economic forces.[16]

Amoore et al. do not address or resolve Walker's critique concerning the ontological dichotomy of social movements/world politics. However, they do reassert civil society's *political* (as opposed to social) nature and problematize the state as a site of struggle.

As is clear from Walker's critique, these attempts to frame and theorize resistance remain thus far problematic. However, Walker's own framing of resistance and alternative reconceptualization of social movements is not entirely unproblematic either. Arguing for a "politics of connection" and a "politics of movement," Walker calls for "[a]n empirical exploration of this conjunction [i.e., social movements/world politics that] would more usefully begin by examining whether particular movements do or do not express these codes [of modern politics], in their explicit aspirations and practices. It would ask about the articulations of identity and difference, self and other, space and time, that constrain and inform their capacity to rearticulate their understanding of the political under contemporary conditions. It would ask about the connections between such rearticulations in different structural locations."[17] Although Walker's suggestion that social movements need to be analyzed for their "contribut[ion] to the reconfiguration of the political under contemporary conditions"[18] is very important and should be heeded, it is too narrowly focused. Precisely because his suggestion prioritizes boundary negotiations of the "modern political" over other types of boundary negotiations, it actually disqualifies those social movements that are not just engaged in reconfiguring the political, but also (or primarily) in reconfiguring other realms like the economic, the social, the cultural, etc. In saying this I am not implying that these realms are different, distinct, and exclusive spheres. On the contrary, they are overlapping, contingent, fluid, and porous spheres of interaction and they cannot be entirely reduced to a site or realm called the (modern) "political."

In challenging IR's reading of the "modern political" Walker shows how this is intricately tied to its understanding of a hierarchy of levels. Yet, in his critique he never questions biases other than those connected to IR's *modernist* discourse about the levels-of-analysis *problématique*. In so doing, Walker actually silences IR's masculinist bias which has in the past led to the exclusion of the household in discussions about levels of analyses. I am not arguing here that Walker should provide an exhaustive critique of all the problems connected to the levels-of-analysis *problématique* which still remains such a central feature of IR's disciplinary terrain. But, Walker's framing of the levels-of-analysis problem and, in this context, his nonattention to (and thereby reification of) IR's masculinist bias, make it more difficult to raise gender-related concerns even in conjunction with Walker's own reconceptualization of social movements/world politics. The conclusion that we can draw from this is that a different framing of the politics of resistance is needed in order to be able to discuss the possibility of gendered practices of resistance. The next section will be dedicated to this effort.

Gendering the politics of resistance

At first sight it may seem odd to call for the introduction of a gender perspective into discussions about social movements. To my knowledge there is no area of study in IR where authors so frequently and routinely refer to women. Yet, as feminist scholars have argued repeatedly, references to women may bring about a certain gender-awareness but do not necessarily constitute a gender analysis. To illustrate this I turn to a passage in the article by Amoore et al. in which they use the women's health movement as an example to be copied by other social movements:

> With regards to the future development of global resistance by "new" social movements, the women's health movement may provide us with a useful example. The women's health movement is indeed a global social movement, which has successfully campaigned to make reproductive rights the centrepiece for international population policy in the 21st century. Its success is due to the fact that it spanned both the developed and developing world and mobilised on a local, national, regional and global level to get its views adopted. It has effectively used the technique of lobbying international organisations, such as the UN, and by direct pressure and participation succeeded in changing the political agenda of such organisations. Resistance movements which are opposed to globalisation can follow this lead and become organised and develop alliances and linkages with other resistance movements on the local, national, regional and global level.[19]

Although it is interesting to notice that the women's health movement serves as an example for other resistance movements, it is even more interesting to reflect upon the framing involved. In the paper, the women's health movement is analyzed in terms of its organizing potential and effectiveness while the explicitly gendered nature of the movement – i.e., dealing with reproductive health issues – has been silenced. In other words the authors use women's movements (in this case the women's health movement) in an instrumental way by emphasizing *form*, i.e., mobilizational and lobby strategies, over *content*, namely, issues concerning women's reproductive health. Likewise, the emphasis on form silences possible links or connections between form and content as well. This instrumentalist account results in the implicit denial of the gendered nature as well as the possibly gendered practices of the women's health movement.

Looking at resistance politics from a gender perspective involves more than an instrumental treatment of women's movements. Such a gender analysis takes as its starting point the notion of gender, which can be defined as the social construction of relations between men and women as well as the social construction of masculinity and femininity within a specific spatial and temporal frame. These social constructions are not neutral, but involve the production, (re)assertion and perpetuation of unequal power relations. In general, gender operates at the three interconnected levels of the individual, the social, and the ideational. In other words, individual men and women will adopt masculine or feminine characteristics, while at the collective level gender structures the interactions between men and women in terms of their role expectations. Moreover, gender operates ideationally through representations and valorizations of social interactions, spheres, processes, and practices.[20] In other words, gendered practices, spheres, etc., result in part from their association with notions of masculinity and femininity, through representations as well as the production and assigning of meaning.

To develop a gender analysis of resistance involves taking seriously the different levels at which gender operates. One way in which this could be accomplished is by bringing the concept of "positionality" into discussions about the politics of resistance. This would entail looking at how differential/differentiated positionalities[21] of men and women in the global political economy may inform (gendered) practices of resistance. On the one hand, men's and women's different positionalities are circumscribed by (ascribed) gender roles, class, ethnicity, etc. On the other, they are also affected through the association of different spheres and activities within the global political economy with notions of masculinity and femininity, making these different spheres and practices more accessible to either men or women.[22] Put differently, I suggest that the resistance practices in which men and women engage, are informed by their (perceived) subject positionalities within the global political economy.

It should be clear that this suggestion pertains to men and women alike, as gender analysis encompasses the masculine as well as the feminine. However, for a first exploratory venture in this area, I will focus on women's gendered practices because questions concerning women/the feminine are continuing to be underrepresented in IR. For this exploratory endeavor I will turn to the quite innovative and unique practice of testimonials or giving testimony which has become one of the instruments employed by activists in Latin America.[23]

Latin America constitutes an excellent geographical region to locate "sites of resistance" against the new orthodoxy of neoliberal development policies. Since the early 1970s popular or social movements have entered the political arena throughout Latin America. Several reasons account for the emergence of these movements, but most importantly they embody political responses to the (political) repression of authoritarian regimes and to the neoconservative experiments and structural adjustment policies that emerged during the 1980s. Interestingly, a majority of the movements' participants are poor women (some estimate their participation to be as high as 70 to 80 percent). Moreover, many of these social movements specifically address women's issues and concerns. In sum, Latin American women's involvement in these popular movements allows us to explore the possibility of gendered practices of resistance.

As I have suggested elsewhere, testimonies or life histories represent at least two distinct resistance practices.[24] First, testimonies are an important instrument in the political struggles of Latin American grassroots activists and community organizers, because they provide a medium to get their message out. The importance of this should not be underestimated. The project of modernity in contemporary Latin America has created societies that are increasingly text-oriented and organized around the "written word." Consequently, with the fading of oral traditions, important sites of knowledge production and information sharing are also disappearing.[25] To put it differently, the privileging of the written word in contemporary Latin American societies further marginalizes those already marginalized: it creates yet another obstacle for (functionally) illiterate citizens, many of whom are women, to fully and effectively participate in public debates. For Latin American women, testimonies provide a way to (indirectly) access their privileged text-oriented societies and participate in public debates, to have their voices heard (or read) and gain power of knowledge production about their communities' struggles, and, finally, to transnationalize their struggles by informing and enlisting the support of the international community. The testimonies by Elvia Alvarado, Domitila Barrios de Chungara, and Rigoberta Menchú illustrate this.[26] One of their main concerns is to "get their message out" in order to improve the situation of their families and communities. In Rigoberta Menchú's words: "Therefore, my commitment to our struggle knows no boundaries nor limits. This is why I've travelled to many places where I've had the opportunity to talk about my people. Of course, I'd need a lot of time to tell you all about my people, because it's not easy to understand just like that. And I think I've given some idea of that in my account."[27] In sum, giving one's testimony becomes a (political) act of resistance and should be seen as part of a larger struggle for a more just society.

Second, testimonies can also play a significant role in the resistance practices of (feminist) IR scholars. Through these testimonies feminist IR scholars are able to recover silenced Latin American women's voices on such important international issues as development, neoliberalism, militarization, human rights, and globalization. Together their voices can help to counter and subvert the discipline's dominant, masculinist, statecentric discourses.

However, testimonies should not be used in an instrumental, ahistorical and decontextualized manner – i.e., in support of a narrow objective that results in depoliticization of the document itself and of the larger struggle to which it contributes. Moreover, a note of caution is in order concerning authorship and power relations between the ethnographer and the person giving her testimony. Whereas anthropologists have debated the unequal power relations between ethnographer and interviewee, students of Latin American literature have discussed the question of single or multiple authorship. Yet, despite these pertinent concerns, one should not assume that the women who are interviewed are passive victims without agency. Both Daphne Patai and Ruth Behar reveal that these women often structure their life stories according to their own preferences.[28] Moreover, political activists like Elvia Alvarado, Domitila Barrios de Chungara, and Rigoberta Menchú have kept relatively high profiles after they gave their testimonies. For instance, Domitila Barrios and Rigoberta Menchú have been on lecture tours throughout Latin America, Europe, and the United States. This would have allowed them to publicly counter possible misrepresentations of their communities and themselves and construct their own representations of their communities' struggles. In other words, these women have been active and effective participants in public debates and in the production of knowledge about their societies.

Against this background I would, therefore, argue that it is important for IR scholars to pay attention to testimonies for at least two reasons. First, testimonies should be considered for their potential contribution to the production of knowledge about gender, development, and globalization. Second, testimonies may present a venue for women, who are politically/culturally/educationally/socially/economically marginalized, to have their voices heard in text-oriented societies.

Turning to various testimonies by Latin American women as illustration,[29] we can glean some insights into their potential knowledge creation about gender and global restructuring as well as their resistance to neoliberalism. Testimonies usually involve the account of a woman's life story from birth until the present. These accounts tend to be very rich and can help to contextualize, for instance, the gendered impact of neoliberal policies. Moreover, they also force us to adopt a long-term perspective on such questions as marginalization, which predate the onslaught of neoliberalism. For example, Elvia Alvarado's story reveals the profound impact of machismo on her life: not only did her father prevent her sisters from attending school, but her mother went to live with a man, leaving Elvia and her siblings behind; and, finally, her brother almost killed Elvia when she got pregnant.[30] Testimonies also nicely illustrate how women may become involved in popular movements. Rigoberta Menchú, for instance, explains how her process of politicization was incremental: "My dreams came true when we started organising. Children had to behave like grownups. We women had to play our part as women in the community, together with our parents, our brothers, our neighbours. We all had to unite, all of us together. We held meetings. We began asking for a community school. We didn't have a school. We collected signatures. I was involved in this.... At the end of 1977, I decided to join a more formal group – a group of peasants in Huehuetenango.... And yet, I still hadn't reached the rewarding stage of participating fully, as an Indian first, and then as a woman, a peasant, a Christian, in the struggle of all my people."[31]

Testimonies not only provide a contextualization of issues such as gender, development, neoliberalism, and globalization, but they also allow an insight into women's views on these issues. Strikingly, Elvia Alvarado, Rigoberta Menchú, and la señora Aurora[32] approach development questions from an integral perspective and emphasize their interconnectedness. Elvia Alvarado's testimony clearly illustrates this by linking such issues as economic growth; redistribution of land; women's concerns about domestic violence and alcoholism, reproductive rights, health, etc.; militarization; democratization; and the role of the United States in Honduras. In her account Elvia Alvarado also addresses the highly "gendered" nature of development.[33] This can be concluded from the following list of development objectives: "...we have to build a society where everyone has the right to live a decent life."[34] "But if we really want to build a new society, we have to change the bad habits of the past. We can't build a new society if we are drunks, womanizers, or corrupt."[35] For Elvia Alvarado, the "right to live a decent life" requires the elimination of machismo.

In contrast, Rigoberta Menchú's notion of development is inextricably linked to a politics of (ethnic) identity. Although she does not mention the term "development" in her testimony, she discusses Guatemala's poverty situation quite extensively. In Rigoberta Menchú's view, however, no development can take place without granting the Guatemalan indigenous population cultural autonomy: "That is my cause. As I've already said, it wasn't born out of something good, it was born out of wretchedness and bitterness. It has been radicalized by the poverty in which my people live. It has been radicalized by the malnutrition which I, as an Indian, have seen and experienced. And by the exploitation and discrimination which I've felt in the flesh. And by the oppression which prevents us [from] performing our ceremonies, and shows no respect for our way of life, the way we are."[36]

The life story of the Mexican señora Aurora provides an individualized account of development and the struggle for survival. Her testimony reveals that families in the squatter settlement Ajusco have had to fight and overcome such obstacles as the environment, landlords, local government, and project developers in order to build their homes. This could not have happened without some degree of neighborhood organizing in which women have played a key role. It is Aurora's view that women need to resist machismo in order to improve their neighborhoods' living conditions.[37] As I have concluded elsewhere,

> a quick perusal of these three testimonies reveals that they (and others) are a goldmine of information, ideas and knowledge about Gender and Development [and globalization] issues. For all three women, development means more than the improvement in material living conditions. Contextualizing Gender and Development issues, formulating a holistic approach to problems and accepting the personal character of development are major themes in these testimonies. They also reveal the struggles of poor women to overcome the discursive explanations of their lives as poor, helpless and ignorant, and the capacity of women, whatever their education/position to define their lives, albeit frequently in circumstances not of their own choosing.[38]

Conclusion

Toward a gendered conceptualization of resistance

In current discussions about the politics of resistance against globalization, various authors have recognized the contributions made by women's movements. Yet these accounts tend to treat women's movements in an instrumental way by emphasizing their mobilizational capacities and lobbying activities over the issues they address. In other words, form is being privileged over content.

As I have argued in this exploratory essay, the active involvement of many women in social movements (in some places as much as 70 to 80 percent) in general and the numerous women's groups, networks, and movements that have been organized to stem the tide of neoliberalism, warrant at least a look at the politics of resistance through a gender lens. The example of Latin American women's testimonies suggests the existence of gendered resistance practices. Not only are most oral testimonies given by women but, more importantly, these testimonies are directly related to the positionalities of these women in the global political economy. For women like Elvia Alvarado and Rigoberta Menchú, giving their testimony has become part of their struggle to resist and undermine the dominant orthodoxy of neoliberal policies. It has become a way to participate and to be heard/read in an increasingly textually oriented environment. In other words, giving oral testimony involves attempts to reframe the hegemonic neoliberal development discourse from a subaltern position, and to bring subjectivity back into discussions about globalization. Moreover, these testimonies show rather nicely that form cannot be divorced from content. The objectives of recovering silenced voices and engaging in knowledge production are intricately tied, for instance, to the holistic reformulation of development.

Obviously, testimonies are not the only (gendered) resistance practice. As I mentioned before, it is also important to explore the possibility of masculinist resistance practices or to look at the feminist transnational organizing, for instance around regional arrangements such as the European Union or the North American Free Trade Agreement. Bringing the "gender question" to current discussions about the politics of resistance to globalization requires a reconceptualization so that the concept of positionality can be included. Janine Brodie's[39] ideas about global restructuring are very useful in this respect. She conceptualizes global restructuring as the (re)negotiation of boundaries between the state and market, national and international as well as public and private. In so doing, she is much more explicit than Walker when he suggests that social movements are engaged in (re)negotiating the boundaries of the "modern political." Because globalization consists of a multidimensional, complex, and contingent set of processes, I would suggest that this complexity is also reflected in boundary (re)negotiations. Going beyond Brodie's original formulation, global restructuring would involve boundary (re)negotiation between the state and market, global and local, national and international, public/semipublic/private/semi-private spheres or, spaces.[40] This conceptualization allows us to formulate positionality in relation to these various spheres, for instance which ones are more accessible to men as opposed to women. Likewise, the politics of resistance can be conceptualized in relation to various ongoing boundary (re)negotiations, focusing in particular on contradictions, inconsistencies, and specific points of intervention to undermine the neoliberal project.

Notes

1 On environmental security, see, for instance, Gareth Porter and Janet Welsh Brown, *Global Environmental Politics*, 2d ed. (Boulder, CO: Westview Press, 1995); on human rights, see David P. Forsythe, *The Internationalization of Human Rights* (Lexington, MA, and Toronto: Lexington Books, 1991).

2 On the Third Debate, see Yosef Lapid, "The Third Debate: On the Prospects of International Theory in a Post-Positivist Era," *International Studies Quarterly* 33, 3 (1989): 235–54. For feminist contributions to the debate, see, for instance, Cynthia Enloe, *Bananas, Beaches and Bases: Making Feminist Sense of International Politics* (Berkeley, CA: University of California Press, 1990); Rebecca Grant and Kathleen Newland, eds, *Gender and International Relations* (Bloomington: University of Indiana Press, 1991); V. Spike Peterson, ed., *Gendered States: Feminist (Re)Visions of International Relations Theory* (Boulder, CO: Lynne Rienner, 1992); Ann J. Tickner, *Gender in International Relations: Feminist Perspectives on Achieving Global Security* (New York: Columbia University Press, 1992); V. Spike Peterson and Anne Sisson Runyan, *Global Gender Issues* (Boulder, CO: Westview Press, 1993); Christine Sylvester, *Feminist Theory and International Relations* (Cambridge: Cambridge University Press, 1994); Jan Jindy Pettman, *Worlding Women: A Feminist International Politics* (London: Routledge, 1996). For a short introduction into post-positivist approaches to IR, see Jim George, *Discourses of Global Politics: A Critical (Re)Introduction to International Relations* (Boulder, CO: Lynne Rienner, 1994). For neo-Gramscian approaches to IR, see Robert W. Cox, *Production, Power, and World Order* (New York: Columbia University Press, 1987); Stephen Gill, ed., *Gramsci, Historical Materialism, and International Relations* (Cambridge: Cambridge University Press, 1993).

3 See, for instance, the special issue "Social Movements and World Politics," *Millennium* 23, 3 (Winter 1994): 511–798; Martin Shaw, *Global Society and International Relations* (Cambridge: Polity Press, 1994). On globalization, see Cox, *Production, Power, and World Order;* Peter Dicken, *Global Shift: The Internationalization of Economic Activity,* 2d ed. (London: Paul Chapman Publishing, 1992); Malcolm Waters, *Globalization* (London: Routledge, 1995); Eleonore Kofman and Gillian Youngs, eds, *Globalization: Theory and Practice* (London: Pinter, 1996). As I have argued elsewhere, "the term globalisation should be put in inverted commas because it is a very imprecise term and used too much as a blanket statement." In my view it is better to use "the term global restructuring as it explicitly refers to a process of (partially) breaking down an old order and the attempted construction of a new one, regardless of who or what is involved and whether this 'new order' actually materializes. Note that this 'new order' is not necessarily superior to the old one and that it doesn't necessarily involve a concerted effort to design and give meaning to this 'new social construct(s).' In sum, global restructuring entails the contingent social, political, economic, and cultural transformation(s) of the old world order into a new one; this involves the increased functional integration of economic activities (including the integration of financial markets and the emergence of a neofordist mode of production) which has been enabled by new communication technologies, the internationalization of the state and the emergence of a global civil society, increased individualization as well as mass-mediated images and representations of the emergence of a global culture and a global village." Marianne H. Marchand, "Reconceptualising 'Gender and Development' in an Era of 'Globalisation', " *Millennium* 25, 3 (Winter 1996): 577.
4 Gita Sen, *Globalization in the 21st Century: Challenges for Civil Society* (Amsterdam: GOM/InDRA, 1997).
5 See on these shifts the works by authors such as Cox, *Production, Power, and World Order;* André C. Drainville, "International Political Economy in the Age of Open Marxism," *Review of International Political Economy* 1, 1 (Spring 1994): 105–32; Stephen Gill, "Globalisation, Market Civilisation, and Disciplinary Neoliberalism," *Millennium* 24, 3 (Winter 1995): 399–424.
6 Rob B. J. Walker, "Social Movements/World Politics," *Millennium* 23, 3 (Winter 1994): 669.
7 André C. Drainville, "International Political Economy," 105–32.
8 Walker, "Social Movements/World Politics," 669–70.
9 David Slater, ed., *New Social Movements and the State in Latin America* (Amsterdam and Dordrecht: Center for Documentation on Latin America [CEDLA]/Fortis Publications, 1985); Claus Offe, "Challenging the Boundaries of Institutional Politics: Social Movements since the 1960s," in *Changing Boundaries of the Political: Essays on the Evolving Balance between the State and Society, Public and Private in Europe,* ed. Charles S. Maier (Cambridge: Cambridge University Press, 1987), 63–106.
10 Rob B. J. Walker, *One World, Many Worlds: Struggles for a Just World Peace* (Boulder, CO: Lynne Rienner Publishers, 1984).
11 Susan Eckstein, "Power and Popular Protest in Latin America," in *Power and Popular Protest: Latin American Social Movements,* ed. Susan Eckstein (Berkeley, CA: University of California Press, 1989), 1–60; Joe Foweraker, "Popular Movements and Political Change in Mexico," in *Popular Movements and Political Change in Mexico,* ed. Foweraker and Ann L. Craig (Boulder, CO: Lynne Rienner Publishers, 1990), 3–22; Arturo Escobar and Sonia Alvarez, eds, *The Making of Social Movements in Latin America: Identity, Strategy, and Democracy* (Boulder, CO: Westview Press, 1992).
12 Maxine Molyneux, "Mobilization without Emancipation? Women's Interests, the State, and Revolution in Nicaragua," *Feminist Studies* 11, 2 (Summer 1985): 227–54; Caroline O. N. Moser, *Gender Planning and Development: Theory, Practice and Training* (London: Routledge, 1993). As I have argued elsewhere the distinctions between feminine-feminist and practical-strategic gender needs is highly problematic because it not only imposes an a priori distinction but also implies a hierarchy between the two: "...The feminist-feminine dichotomy reveals a dual hierarchized opposition, which structures the discourse about Latin American women's movements similarly to the discursive role played by the Mediterranean ethos in modernization theory; in other words, the feminist-feminine dichotomy amounts to an adaptation of feminist neo-colonial discourses to accommodate the occurrence of women's movements in Latin America. Relying on the feminist-feminine dichotomy, Western feminist scholars reify the superiority of Western feminism. They thus send an important message: only a very small percentage of Latin American women are 'real' feminists and can thus be considered modern women (like us!)." Marianne H. Marchand, "Latin American Women Speak on Development: Are We Listening Yet?" in *Feminism/Postmodernism /Development,* ed. Marianne H. Marchand and Jane L. Parpart (London: Routledge, 1995), 63. For another critique on the feminist-feminine dichotomy see Sallie Westwood and Sarah A. Radcliffe, "Gender, Racism and

the Politics of Identities in Latin America," in *Viva: Women and Popular Protest in Latin America*, ed. Radcliffe and Westwood (London: Routledge, 1993), 1–29.

13 Drainville, "International Political Economy."

14 Walker, "Social Movements/World Politics," 697.

15 Drainville, "International Political Economy."

16 L. Amoore, R. Dodgson, B. K. Gills, P. Langely, D. Marshall and I. Watson, "Overturning 'Globalisation': Resisting the Teleological, Reclaiming the Political," *New Political Economy* 2, 1 (Spring 1997): 190.

17 Walker, "Social Movements/World Politics," 700.

18 Ibid., 675.

19 Amoore et al., "Overturning 'Globalisation,'" 191.

20 See Marianne H. Marchand and Anne Sisson Runyan, "Introduction: Feminist Sightings of Globalization: Conceptualizations and Reconceptualizations," in *Gender and Global Restructuring: Sightings, Sites and Resistances*, ed. Marchand and Runyan (London: Routledge, 2000).

21 I prefer the term/concept positionality over position because it conveys a notion of "fluidity" (i.e., men's and women's positions can change over time and in different contexts). Moreover, the concept of positionality is not inscribed in the object-subject dichotomy of structure vs. agency since it also partially involves a process of self-positioning. The concept of position on the other hand reflects the objective (i.e., structure-related) classification of women and men in terms of their class, social status, etc.

22 See for a further development of this idea Marianne H. Marchand, "Gendered Representations of the 'Global': Reading/Writing Globalization," in *Political Economy and the Changing Global Order*, ed. Richard Stubbs and Geoffrey Underhill (Toronto: Oxford University Press, 1999), 225–35.

23 The next section is largely taken from my earlier discussions on testimonies: Marianne H. Marchand, "Latin American Voices of Resistance: Women's Movements and Development Debates," in *The Global Economy as Political Space*, ed. Stephen J. Rosow, Naeem Inayatullah, and Mark Rupert (Boulder, CO: Lynne Rienner Publishers, 1994), 127–44 (in particular, 138–41); Marchand, "Latin American Women Speak" (in particular, 64–70).

24 Marchand, "Latin American Voices of Resistance"; Marchand, "Latin American Women Speak."

25 John Beverley and Marc Zimmerman, *Literature and Politics in the Central American Revolutions* (Austin: University of Texas Press, 1990).

26 Domitila Barrios de Chungara, with M. Viezzer, *Let me Speak!* (New York: Monthly Review Press, 1978); Elizabeth Burgos-Debray, ed., *I...Rigoberta Menchú* (New York: Verso, 1984); Medea Benjamin, ed. and trans., *Don't Be Afraid Gringo* (New York: Harper and Row, 1989).

27 Burgos-Debray, *I...Rigoberta Menchú*, 247.

28 Daphne Patai, "Constructing a Self: A Brazilian Life Story," *Feminist Studies* 14, 1 (Spring 1988): 143–66; Ruth Behar, *Translated Woman: Crossing the Border with Esperanza's Story* (Boston, MA: Beacon Press, 1993).

29 Burgos-Debray, *I...Rigoberta Menchú*; Benjamin, *Don't Be Afraid Gringo*; Alejandra Massolo, *Por Amor y Coraje* (Mexico City: El Colegio de México, 1992).

30 Benjamin, *Don't Be Afraid Gringo*, 2–3.

31 Burgos-Debray, *I...Rigoberta Menchú*, 120.

32 Alejandra Massolo has interviewed la señora Aurora about her life in a squatter settlement in Mexico City. Her testimony and those of a few other women form the bulk of Massolo's book on women in urban movements.

33 This analysis is taken from Marchand, "Latin American Women Speak," 69.

34 Benjamin, *Don't Be Afraid Gringo*, 27.

35 Ibid., 55.

36 Burgos-Debray, *I...Rigoberta Menchú*, 247.

37 In her testimony la señora Aurora discusses the policy of another urban popular organization in Monterrey where the women will go with a group to a husband if he doesn't allow his wife to participate in the organization. Also, if a husband engages in wife beating, he will be publicly criticized and expelled from the organization himself. See Massolo, *Por Amor y Coraje*, 198.

38 Marchand, "Latin American Women Speak," 70.

39 Janine Brodie, "Shifting Boundaries: Gender and the Politics of Restructuring," in *The Strategic Silence: Gender and Economic Policy*, ed. Isabella Bakker (London: Zed Books, in association with the North-South Institute, Ottawa, 1994), 46–60.

40 Marianne H. Marchand, "Reconceptualising 'Gender and Development'." 577–603.

19 The politics of resistance

Women as nonstate, antistate, and transstate actors

V. Spike Peterson and Anne Sisson Runyan

Source: V. Spike Peterson and Anne Sisson Runyan (1993), *Global Gender Issues*, Boulder, CO: Westview Press, pp. 113–148

The gendered division of power and its subsets, the gendered divisions of violence, labor, and resources, severely restrict the effects that women can have on world politics. The few women who have made it into the corridors of power as state actors have done little to dispel prevailing gender ideologies and divisions. Typically, they have adopted masculine leadership styles for themselves without disrupting feminine stereotypes more generally. These "steel magnolias" simply combine and, thus, reinforce the gender divisions of masculine and feminine. They do not challenge them.

At the same time, there are other female political actors who *do* challenge gender dichotomies. Because they typically organize outside of state structures, these actors tend to be invisible through the conventional state-centric lens on world politics. Such women are found in women's, peace, socialist-revolutionary, economic welfare, and ecology movements. Their activities are concentrated below the level of the state and are often geared toward agitating against oppressive state structures and policies. Women also tend to be involved in issues and movements that cut across state boundaries, for example, global-environmental groups and feminist networks. This chapter focuses on women in their roles as nonstate, antistate, and transstate actors who, to varying degrees, do challenge the gendered divisions of power, violence, labor, and resources. We focus on the multiple political roles that women play as well as on the systemic effects of their political activities to shift attention away from "fitting women into" traditional IR frameworks and toward an understanding that accommodates and empowers women's struggles against the hierarchical consequences of practicing "world politics as usual." Yet as we document the liberating dimensions of these struggles, we are reminded that they can perpetuate at the same time that they challenge gender dichotomies.

Women's movements

No woman is born, and not all women become, feminist, but some women *and* men do. How one becomes a feminist varies with each individual, but the impetus for developing a feminist consciousness often arises when a person experiences a contradiction between who that person thinks she or he is and what society wants her or him to be. It may arise out of a contradiction in the opportunities a society says it offers to an individual and what that individual actually experiences. In advanced (post)industrial societies, women are typically told that, under the law, they have equal opportunities (in the liberal democratic sense) to compete for political and economic power. However, in fact, indirect or structural barriers to full political and economic participation reduce most women's rights and choices. In more-traditional societies, particularly those that experienced some kind of colonial or neocolonial rule, colonially imposed laws and certain cultural and religious traditions combine to deny equal opportunities to women, even under the law. The gendered division of power in both cases circumscribes women's choices to be and do things deemed outside of their assigned gender roles.

Throughout history women – individually, collectively, and sometimes with men – have struggled against direct and indirect barriers to their self-development and their full social, political, and economic participation. In the modern era, they have often done so through organizing women's movements that have addressed many issues and, thus, taken many forms. People associate women's movements with campaigns to gain equal rights for women under the law. But women have often sought more-transformative changes in social, political, and economic systems because prevailing masculinist systems undermine women's struggles for gender equality despite formal equal rights. As a result, it is sometimes difficult to separate women's movements from other political movements agitating for social, political, and economic transformation. In this text, we regard as feminist those political movements in which participants self-consciously and deliberately link gender inequality with other forms of social, political, economic, and/or ecological injustice.

[...]

Antiwar and peace movements

The discipline of international relations, which essentially began after World War I – the war that was supposed to end all wars – has been preoccupied with the question of how to prevent or stop war. With the rise of peace studies during the Vietnam era, IR has also began to ask what peace is because surely it must be more than simply the time between wars. Women have long been involved in analyzing how to stop war and how to create peace, though they have received no attention for these activities in past and most contemporary international relations literature. Instead, their peace efforts have been ignored or trivialized – largely by men who stereotype women as soft-headed, irrational pacifists. This characterization is political because it excludes women's perspectives from the study of war and peace. Instead, that subject is reserved for and addressed by "realists": ostensibly hard-headed, rational men, especially those with military experience.

In addition, the gendered division of violence positions women as life-givers, expected to mourn the toll of war quietly, pick up the pieces when it is over, and not undermine the war effort by asking, for whom? and for what? Women who do ask questions are seen as ungrateful for the protection courageously delivered by men and states through their military might and actions. In spite of this gendered state of affairs, women have protested loudly and often against war and for a more just and peaceful world.

Examples extend from the fifth century B. C. Athenian play *Lysistrata*, in which women refused to sleep with men who went to war, to the International Women's Gulf Peace Initiative in 1991 against hostilities in the Persian Gulf. However, it was not until the rise of the first wave of feminism, during the latter part of the nineteenth century, that the political linkage between peace and women's emancipation was made. This pre-World War I period is considered the golden age of peace movements in the West. Predominantly white, middle-class women formed a variety of peace societies (such as the Union Internationale des Femmes, the Ligue des Femmes pour Desarmament, the

Alliance des Femmes pour la Paix, and the Société d'Education Pacifique in France), which were used as models for women's peace societies elsewhere in Western Europe, the United States, and even Japan.[1] Liberal feminist peace activists made their presence known at major international peace conferences, including the first and second Hague conferences in 1899 and 1907.[2] Socialist feminists organized their own international conferences, such as the First and the Second International Conference of Socialist Women, held in 1907 and 1910 respectively, at which they endorsed resolutions against the militarism of imperialist powers.[3]

In 1915, predominantly white, middle-class feminists in the United States under the leadership of Jane Addams formed the U.S. Woman's Peace party (WPP). The WPP tapped both practical and strategic gender interests by calling for women's suffrage (the right to vote) and arguing that women's role as mothers gave them a special moral responsibility to oppose war. Not all suffragists supported a platform of peace, especially after World War I had broken out. But in 1915, 1,136 delegates from twelve countries made a dangerous wartime journey to The Hague to attend the International Congress of Women to protest against the war. The congress passed twenty resolutions on the destruction of humanity, the use of sons for cannon fodder, and the victimization of mothers/women that war inflicted.[4] The congress also founded the Women's International League for Peace and Freedom, which continues to exist, with headquarters in Geneva and thousands of chapters all over the world.

During the interwar years, white, middle-class women in large numbers joined organizations such as the British Peace Pledge Union and within these organizations formed their own women's committees and peace campaigns.[5] As World War II loomed, such organizations collapsed when both women and men were drawn into the war effort by their governments. Governments appealed to women's practical and strategic gender interests. They encouraged women to support their "boys" by mothering the nation through rationing, buying war bonds, and doing volunteer work for the duration. They also offered women jobs in wartime industries that had previously been closed to them.[6] Yet this combination was not in fact liberating. Even though women went out to work in large numbers, they were still expected to fulfill the maternal role for servicemen and the nation.[7]

As a result, when men came home from war, most women were laid off from higher-paying jobs in wartime industries and were expected to go back to being full-time homemakers. However, this was a "luxury" affordable only to white, upper-middle-class women: Actually, 84 percent of all U.S. women working during 1944–1945 were doing so out of economic necessity,[8] and only 600,000 women had left the paid work force by 1946.[9] Nevertheless, 58 percent of U.S. women in 1943 felt that they could "best help the war effort by staying at home."[10] The onerous task of combining work with family led many married women to leave their jobs readily, albeit under pressure from husbands, unions, and bosses who were hostile to their presence in the work force when the war ended. In this sense, the disruptions of World War II did not really challenge or undermine gender roles and dichotomies, which were ultimately deepened and reinforced.

At the same time, the fact that women – especially white, middle-class women – were encouraged to take their role as wives and mothers seriously during the 1950s led some of them into antimilitary movements from the 1960s through the 1980s. For example, the 1960s saw the rise of Women Strike for Peace in the United States and the Voice of Women in Canada, which organized to "End the Arms Race, Not the Human Race."[11] Women Strike for Peace organized a one-day strike on November 1, 1961, in which 50,000 women left their homes and workplaces to protest the arms race. So threatening was this action to cold war orthodoxy that in 1962 the House Committee on Un-American Activities accused leaders of this grass-roots women's movement of being Communists.[12]

During the 1980s, a host of women's antinuclear groups emerged in response to the post-detente resurgence of the arms race and the U.S. testing and deployment of, cruise missiles. These groups ranged from the Oxford Mothers for Nuclear Disarmament (UK), Women Opposed to Nuclear Technology (UK), and the Women's Pentagon Action (U.S.), to women's peace camps set up outside nuclear installations throughout Europe and North America. These women's peace encampments, including Greenham Common and "Molesworth in England, Comiso in Italy, Hunsruck in West Germany, Seneca and Puget Sound in the United States, Nanoose in Canada, Soesterburg in Holland, Pine Gap in Australia, and others"[13] attracted many thousands of women who insisted that life on the nuclear precipice was intolerable to them, their children, and their grandchildren. This perspective encouraged many women to demand an end to East-West hostilities by staging "peace walks" from Stockholm to Moscow and organizing international women's peace conferences like the one called "The Urgency for True Security: Women's Alternatives for Negotiating Peace" held in Halifax, Nova Scotia (Canada), in 1985 and the subsequent Women's "Peace Tent" experiment at the Non-Governmental Forum for the end of the UN Decade for Women Conference in Nairobi, also in 1985.[14]

At the same time, groups like the Mothers of the Plaza de Mayo in Argentina and Mothers of El Salvador organized to bear witness to brutal regimes that had made their children "disappear." Women in Northern Ireland, like Mairead Corrigan and Betty Williams, who won the Nobel Peace Prize in 1977, rallied to stop the bloodshed between Protestants and Catholics. The Mothers of the Heroes and Martyrs in Nicaragua cried out against the U.S.-sponsored contra war against the Sandinista government and its people; the Shibokusa women of Mount Fuji in Japan protested the expropriation of land by the U.S. and Japanese militaries; the Sri Lankan Voice of Women for Peace was calling for the end of the civil war between Sinhalese and Tamils; women of Fiji appealed to the French government to stop nuclear testing in the South Pacific; and black South African women continued their struggles against the violence of apartheid.[15]

The motivation of much of this past and contemporary peace organizing by women has been their identification with and assigned responsibility for mothering. Many of these women have been interested in protecting their children and future generations from the ravages of war and war preparation, whether nuclear or conventional. But they also have been calling attention to the fact that their reproductive work in terms of providing food and shelter for their families is being made much more difficult and even impossible by war machines that eat up people and resources. Thus, women's political action on behalf of peace often arises from "practical" gender interests that enhance women's assigned roles in the so-called private sphere.

On the face of it, these women's struggles for peace do little to disrupt gender dichotomies because they leave in place the image of men as aggressive and bellicose life-takers/killers in contrast to women as pacifist life-givers/reproducers/mothers. However, these struggles do call into question certain other aspects of gender hierarchy produced by the gendered division of violence. For example, by the very act of "leaving home" and taking on so-called public-sphere institutions and issues – often at the risk of death and imprisonment or, at the very least, censure by governments and mainstream societies – these women challenge the idea that women are weak, passive victims who can only mourn their fate on the home front. At the same time, such actions belie the idea that it is only men who die from the ravages of war and war preparation and that these deaths only occur on the battlefield. In fact, women's protests against war and all other kinds of state violence reveal generally hidden and unfamiliar costs of modern total warfare.

Moreover, the horrors that women identify completely undermine the notion that men are protectors and that women are protected. Because the male-dominated state security apparatus is the cause of their suffering and that of their children, many of these female peace activists ask, Who is going to protect us, or how are we going to protect ourselves, from the protectors? It is in the struggle to answer this question that many women have become "soldiers for peace," a contradiction itself that forces us to rethink gender categories, identities, and practices.

Within these movements as well are women struggling on behalf their strategic gender interests. Peace activists who identify themselves as feminists are less likely than those who do not so identify themselves to promote or celebrate motherhood as the basis for women's peace activism.[16] Feminists are aware that women's responsibility for mothering has often brought them into the struggle for peace, yet they warn us that until reproductive labor is no longer the sole or major responsibility of women, there will be no real change in the priorities of states, international organizations, and the mostly elite men who run them. Moreover, as long as women remain tied to the currently devalued "private sphere," their protests will be marginalized by those in power, who will continue to expect the women to "pick up the pieces" in the wake of continual destruction. Indeed, feminists ask whether there can be any peace worth having in the absence of gender, race, and class justice.

Finally, feminist peace activists argue that neither women nor mothers are innately peaceful (here they agree with postmodern feminists) or necessarily life-givers. On the contrary, women, like men, have always served militaries and supported wars – as spouses, workers, soldiers, government officials, and parents. When we dispel the notion that the struggle for peace is not some innate feminine attribute that is "soft" and available only to women, the way will be opened up for many more to join the struggle for peace *and* justice that will make world politics enhance, rather than undermine, the survival and equality of all.

Revolutionary movements

The fact that women take up arms in national liberation struggles contradicts the stereotype that women are naturally peaceful. Throughout recorded history we find stories of women fomenting and engaging in populist violence as leaders and followers. For every female revolutionary leader such as Joan of Arc, Olympes de Gouge, Rosa Luxemburg, Alexandra Kollantai, Dora Maria Tellez, and Winnie Mandela, there have been millions of women who have participated in countless uprisings, guerrilla movements, and revolutions – ranging from the French, American, Russian, and Chinese revolutions to more recent revolutionary struggles throughout Latin America, the Caribbean, Africa, and the Middle East.[17] Not all these women have taken up arms. More typically they have worked in underground movements to hide and heal guerrilla fighters, pass information and weapons, and organize communities in support of the revolution. Still, most revolutionary women have supported armed struggle as a necessary, although not the only, facet of revolutionary action.

Although often motivated by the same concerns as men – a desire to overthrow corrupt regimes, to fight colonialism and imperialism, and to build nationalism and a national economy not controlled and impoverished by foreign elites – women also join or are encouraged to join revolutionary struggles on behalf of their practical and strategic gender interests. In the testimonial literature that chronicles women's experiences in revolutionary struggles, we find examples of women revolutionaries who were drawn into the struggle both as mothers responsible for providing for their families and as women seeking greater equality with men, first on the battlefield and then in the government of the new state-to-be. Like the pattern with peace movements, women tend to become involved in revolutions initially because of their practical gender interests and then work for their strategic gender interests when they run up against sexism in revolutionary movements.

An example is the role of women and women's associations in the revolutionary struggle against the Somoza regime in Nicaragua. Gloria Carrion was active in the Association of Nicaraguan Women Confronting the Nation's Problems (AMPRONAC) and became the general coordinator of the Luisa Amanda Espinosa Nicaraguan Women's Association (AMNLAE) after the victory of the Sandinista National Liberation Front (FSLN). Lea Guido was also an organizer with AMPRONAC and later, the minister of public health in the National Reconstruction government. In interviews, both Carrion and Guido reported that women were drawn into the struggle on the basis of their family and maternal roles.

Carrion described women as "the centres of their families – emotionally, ideologically and economically" who do not see themselves " 'simply' as housewives" subordinated to husbands.[18] Guido told of a women's campaign around the slogan "Our Children Are Hungry, Bring Down the Cost of Living." She argued that the parties of the traditional Left had failed to mobilize women because they did not address women's practical gender interests. The women's campaign was successful "because we learned how to involve women in the national struggle while at the same time organizing around problems specific to women."[19]

AMPRONAC and, later, AMNLAE brought many women into nonviolent aspects of revolutionary struggle on the basis of their practical gender interests. Engaging in revolutionary violence generated particular problems for women. By becoming guerrilla fighters, women transgressed their traditional gender roles and were often seen as threatening to revolutionary men. Confronting the sexism of their comrades, many women were awakened to strategic gender interests. Monica Baltonado, a guerrilla commander of the Nicaraguan Revolution, pointed out that the extent of sexism among men of the FMLN varied:

> Some comrades were open to dealing with sexism while others remained closed. Some said women were no good in the mountains, that they were only good "for screwing," that they created conflicts – sexual conflicts. But there were also men with very good positions. Carlos Fonseca, for example, was a solid comrade on this issue. It's been a long struggle! We won those battles through discussions and by women comrades demonstrating their ability and their resistance.[20]

Women, who constituted over 30 percent of guerrilla combatants, did prove their mettle in the insurrections against Somoza's regime.[21] However, after the triumph, they made up only 6 percent of military officers in the Sandinista People's Army (EPS), which discouraged women's participation on the basis that women's first obligation is to motherhood.[22] After protests from AMNLAE, three women's *reserve* battalions were set up. The majority of women who wanted to defend the revolution were active in two organizations: the Sandinista Popular Militias (MPS), designed to defend farms and factories against sabotage by U.S.-supported contra forces, and the Sandinista Defense Committees (CDS), which organized neighborhoods to create better living conditions. The MPS and the CDS were viewed – by male leaders and often by women themselves – as more consistent with women's mothering roles and family responsibilities. Indeed, although AMNLAE's symbol was a picture of a young woman with a rifle on her back and a baby in her arms, in actuality most Nicaraguan women were encouraged to put down the gun and pick up their baby after the triumph.

That mothering was incompatible with violent revolutionary action was recognized by women fighting for the independence of Zimbabwe in the 1970s. One young female guerrilla reported that women were able to convince their male comrades to accept the use of contraceptives by arguing that "to be sent back to Mozambique for five months to have a baby was a setback to the war."[23] The women who made this "practical" argument, however, had undergone deeper transformations that tapped their strategic gender interests, especially in regard to reproductive rights: "Our attitudes to contraception and abortion changed during the years of struggle. The girls really adopted a new way of living after what they've seen in the bush, the contacts they've had with other people from European countries, from the books they've read."[24]

Revolutionary struggles, indeed, create "new women" who transgress proscribed gender roles, but these women remain disadvantaged in terms of the gendered division of power and resources when the revolution is over. A spokesperson for the Omani Women's Organization, which was active in the People's Front for the Liberation of Oman in the mid-1970s, put it this way: "Many men had received education and political experience...before they joined the Front, while women had their first education and political experience when as young girls they joined the Revolution."[25] Because women had less formal training than men before the revolution, they were again left out of the picture when military demobilization proceeded. In sum, women are more easily demobilized and sent back home, whereas men assume positions of power in new regimes when revolutions are successful.[26]

A "successful" revolution is, conventionally, one in which a dictator or ruling regime is toppled and a new regime is put in its place. Rarely is a positive change in the condition and status of women viewed as a key measure of a revolution's "success." Nevertheless, there have been instances where conditions that intersect with women's practical gender interests have improved. Not infrequently, successful revolutions bring improvements in meeting basic human needs. For example, delivery of improved health care reduces rates of infant mortality, the provision of education expands work opportunities, and better nutrition supports a generally healthier population. Such gains particularly benefit the large numbers of poor women who are finally provided some assistance in meeting their assigned responsibility for sustaining the family.

In the area of women's strategic gender interests, some revolutionary movements and later governments have instituted reforms intended to break down sexual stereotypes and inequalities. For instance, Cuba's revolutionary government wrote a new Family Code that afforded women equal rights in marriage and divorce and called for equal responsibilities in the household, including shared housework.[27] Nicaragua's Sandinista government passed similar legislation in 1981. Even prior to this measure, the Sandinistas responded to demands made by AMPRONAC by legislating a ban on the sexist use of women in advertising and by outlawing prostitution – in the hopes of integrating women into alternative employment.[28]

Unfortunately, these and other such measures, although progressive in comparison to measures in many other countries, were not motivated solely or primarily by feminist concerns. More typically, the governments wanted to get more women into the productive labor force to increase the country's gross domestic product (GDP), combat Western cultural imperialism in the form of pornography and sensationalist press, and inculcate revolutionary "morals," particularly in Catholic countries. Indeed, abortion remained illegal in Nicaragua throughout the revolutionary period despite the fact that thousands of women died or were maimed there by back-alley abortions every year and despite AMNLAE's demands, beginning in the mid-1980s, for legalized abortions.[29] Moreover, the shared-domestic-responsibility clauses in both the Cuban and Nicaraguan family codes were rarely enforced, and men in these societies for the most part fail to participate equally in household decision-making and continue to do little reproductive labor. These responsibilities still fall heavily on women's shoulders. Finally, the gains women made as a result of socialist revolutions – either of the practical or strategic variety – have been seriously eroded. This is a consequence of both internal and external dynamics: the economic, political, and social turmoil created by foreign military intervention and economic embargoes, civil wars, and the overthrow of socialist regimes in Eastern Europe, the Soviet Union, and Latin America.

The failure of socialist regimes and their "democratizing" successors to place women's strategic gender interests at the center of their concerns is related to what feminist analysts call gendered nationalism. On this view, nationalist struggles have been gendered because they involve the manipulation of gender identities and symbols and gendered divisions of power, labor, and resources.

Nationalist fervor has served as the driving and unifying force behind liberal, socialist, and, most recently, anti-Communist revolutions. Struggles for economic and political justice have typically been framed within the context of national self-determination and autonomy – concepts that have a decidedly masculinist cast and, up to the present period, have for the most part translated into self-determination and autonomy for men and, especially, male leaders. As we have seen, this lauded self-determination and autonomy has been made possible largely through women's undervalued and unheralded reproductive labor, which "frees" men for the seemingly greater heroics that shape *the* national identity. As Enloe observed, "The notion of what 'the nation' was at its finest hour – when it was most unified, most altruistic – will be a community in which women sacrificed their desires for the sake of the male-led collective."[30]

Under this construction of the nation, women's feminist aspirations are forced into conflict with their national allegiance, and revolutionary malerun governments are able to ignore and even vilify feminist demands. An extreme example of gendered nationalism infused the 1978 Iranian Revolution, in which large numbers of women contributed to the downfall of the shah only to become the primary targets of sexual "purification" campaigns to limit their autonomy under the right-wing Islamist regime of the Ayatollah Khomeini.[31] But the pattern of gendered nationalism is in fact widespread. Virtually without exception, women have been used – as symbols of national morality, as behind-the-scenes support workers, as guerrilla fighters – to win nationalist struggles. But with victory, the practical and strategic interests of women are subordinated to masculinist priorities.

Thus, women's struggles on behalf of revolutionary movements, whether as combatants or as less-violent resistance workers and populist protesters, have not brought them "liberation" from gender oppression. To the degree that revolutions improve general conditions for meeting basic human needs, women's practical gender interests have been served. However, despite the personal transformations experienced by female revolutionaries who stepped outside their traditional roles, structural or systemic transformations in line with women's strategic gender interests have not been a consequence of male-led revolutions.

One reason for this lies in the failure of revolutionary women's struggles to undermine fundamental gender dichotomies. No matter what women do in combat, they are still expected, after and even during revolutions, to give life. Their primary roles as reproducers and mothers remain unquestioned. Men are not expected to perform this dual role during revolutions or to cease being the protectors when it is over. Nowhere is there a poster with a revolutionary man shouldering a gun while holding a baby. And nowhere has he picked up the baby when the gun is no longer necessary.

Jean Bethke Elshtain pointed out a second reason that women revolutionaries fail to undermine gender dichotomies. Under the gendered division of violence, "female violence is what happens when politics breaks down into riots, revolutions, or anarchy: when things are out of control," whereas the violent revolutionary male "can restore order, including the order he violated."[32] In other words, women's violence is exceptional, but men's violence is an accepted component of men's role as consolidators and sustainers of the political order. Robin Morgan conveyed this point in her discussion of terrorism. She argued that the stateless male terrorists of today are simply the statesmen of tomorrow, who will – as statesmen – purvey state terrorism, as history has amply shown us. In contrast, female terrorists – especially the bomb-planting and bomb-throwing variety who are not portrayed safely with babies in their arms – continue to be unnerving figures that represent the worst kind of disorder. They symbolize what lies outside and even threatens the conventional image of the transfer of power from terrorist men of the state-that-is to their heirs apparent, terrorist men of the state-that-would-be.[33]

We cannot, however, undermine the gendered division of violence simply by becoming more comfortable with the image and reality of the female "terrorist." That image in fact perpetuates the gendered division of violence because women's revolutionary action undertaken in the context of the struggle between men of the state-that-is and men of the state-that-would-be reinforces that which produced this contest.

Contemporary revolutionary movements tend to take the state system for granted, their leaders typically seeking to form a new state or seize power in an existing state. As a consequence, women's activities in these struggles also remain state focused.[34] Women are crucial both to mobilizing mass support for revolutionary struggle and to achieving victory through homefront and battlefront activities. Yet to women the benefits of successful revolutions are always tempered by the retention of masculinist principles.

After revolutionary movements achieve the status of "new states," no one denies their international significance because states are central actors. To understand how the gender dynamics of revolutionary movements affects world politics, we need to appreciate the linkages between the personal (gender-differentiated experiences in revolutionary struggle), the political (gender-differentiated costs and benefits), and the global (gendered interstate and transstate institutions and movements).

What begins to emerge when we look at these events through a gender-sensitive lens? One point is that women are essential to the success of revolutionary struggles. To the extent that these struggles shape international relations, the presence of women and the power of gender should be analyzed as significant determinants of world politics. Another, and broader, point is that women (and men) who engage in revolutionary activities are, by definition, challenging the status quo. Put into question are gender stereotypes as well as oppressive conditions, corrupt regimes, and economic exploitation. In the process of struggle, participants presumably develop a clearer understanding of how societies function and how structural change can be promoted and/or resisted. As our examples illustrate, women consistently find their interests subordinated to or denied by masculinist nation-states. This raises – often explicitly – the following questions: What should the priorities of a society be? How do societies sustain themselves? Are state orders capable of instituting justice and equity? How are the costs and benefits of struggle divided? Who wins as long as the gendered division of violence remains intact? These questions increasingly appear on the agenda of nonstate, antistate, and transstate movements, and the debates and actions they fuel are increasingly a dimension of world politics.

Economic movements

Women's protests in regard to economic conditions are perhaps the most durable and pervasive example of their being political actors. As we have seen, women are at a disadvantage owing to the gendered division of labor within the home and family (the unpaid labor force), the gendered division of labor in the workplace (the paid labor force), and the gendered international division of labor (the global economy). These processes have relegated large numbers of women, especially those with children, to poverty and have given most women few options for earning a living wage or for moving up the economic ladder. The struggle to provide for themselves and their families on a day-to-day basis limits women's time and energy for political activism. But it has also served as a motivating force for even the poorest of women to leave their homes to protest the unfair economic straits in which they find themselves. These economic protests take many forms and sometimes bring women into related struggles, such as women's, peace, revolutionary, and ecological movements. Like their participation in other movements, women's participation in economic movements often emerges from practical gender interests.

The gendered division of labor within the home holds women primarily responsible for the well-being of the family. As a result, women are usually quick to challenge authorities when the mainstays of life are threatened. It is the gender stereotype of women as life giving and life sustaining that positions women as primary caretakers and makes them the first to protest when economic conditions keep them from providing that care.

There are many examples of women taking to the streets collectively – in "bread riots," seizures of grain or foods, protests against the sale of overpriced goods, and/or demands for a just price for market products.[35] For instance, in the Flour War of 1775 that precipitated the French Revolution, women "took positive and often violent action to rectify intolerable conditions – conditions threatening to family and community stability."[36] In 1929, women in Nigeria responded in force against colonial taxation and marketplace policies: "Tens of thousands of Igbo women marched, dressed in symbolic war attire, danced, chanted, sang, 'sat on' offending men, destroyed courts and prisons, freed prisoners, cut telegraph wires, set up their own courts and offices, closed down markets, collected money to sustain their actions, and set up or revived organizations for mutual support."[37]

Such actions are especially common in nonindustrialized contexts where the marketplace is dominated by women as producers, exchangers, and consumers of basic goods. There, traditional gender assignments make the provision of basic goods women's domain and serve to legitimize women's acting on behalf of family and community to protest against basic goods shortages. Also in these contexts traditional gender assumptions that women are vulnerable and in need of protection serve, to some degree, to inhibit violent reprisals directed by authorities against their unauthorized demonstrations. However, women's participation is no guarantee that officials will not act swiftly and violently against economic protests, as the killing of fifty women in the Igbo "women's war" makes clear.[38]

In industrialized contexts, where most poor, urban women cannot produce basic goods and are made dependent on state welfare systems, women's protests against the impoverishment of their families often take the form of welfare rights movements. For example, from 1966 to 1970, the Brooklyn Welfare Action Council (B-WAC) organized thousands of welfare recipients to fight for minimum welfare standards that would guarantee the right of every family to have the essentials for survival and modern life. B-WAC members staged a number of visible and theatrical protests outside welfare offices and inside shopping complexes. They demanded supplemental payments and department store credit for welfare recipients who could not live from check to check. For a brief period of time, B-WAC succeeded in getting more funds to welfare recipients to pay for such modern essentials as "costs of laundry; graduation; layettes; confirmation, camp, gym, and spring clothes; and washing machines."[39]

These cases and many more like them suggest that women's struggles against the consequences of the gendered division of labor in the home – women's practical gender interests – are primarily local and short-term engagements. Because women are acting in their traditional roles as family caretakers, they are focused upon their most immediate economic needs and usually seek only relief, not social transformation. As a result, their gains are typically temporary. The basis of their struggles does not challenge – but rather reinforces – their gender roles, leaving them still responsible for reproductive labor, even under the worst economic conditions. The point is that as long as reproductive labor is viewed as a private matter to which women are assigned, neither men as individuals nor the agencies of the state are under any obligation to do more than provide temporary – and usually insufficient – relief in response to women's economic protests.

In the face of meager and grudging assistance to women responsible for "unpaid" reproductive tasks, some women are challenging the notion that women's reproductive labor is just a private matter that does not even constitute "work." Some women's economic movements emphasize the fact that reproductive labor is the precondition of all other human activities: We cannot exist without the work women do in food production and preparation, emotional and physical caretaking, and maintaining the material and psychological dimensions of what we think of as home. Domestic work is essential, yet we deny its value to ourselves as individuals whose emotional and material "basic needs" must be met and to our societies, which would perish without this unpaid labor. Just how extensive and valuable is this labor? The United Nations estimated that "if unpaid housework were valued at the cost of purchasing comparable goods and services . . . the measured value of GDP in countries would increase by 25–30 percent."[40]

Denying the centrality and value of domestic labor has various consequences for women's and men's lives. The most basic reality is that women, who spend more time working than men, are accorded less status for what they do, and men increasingly accumulate control over cash resources. "Tilting first under rules that say women must do all domestic work, the scales are tipped further by men's greater opportunities to earn wages. Advantage builds on advantage until today they are tilted so steeply that almost all of the world's wealth is on man's side, while most of the world's work is on woman."[41]

Women have protested the devaluation of domestic work and men's increasing economic control in diverse ways. The risk of divorce, loss of economic support, and the threat of violence (against themselves and/or their children), makes going on strike in the home a risky option for women. But women do resist by following strategies of "refusing to cooperate." For example, men grow maize (corn) and women grow groundnut (peanuts) in Zambia. When maize profits soared, women did not shift production in their fields to the more lucrative maize "because they – and not their husbands – kept the money from sales of groundnut."[42] Women also challenge the devaluation of their domestic work by insisting that they be paid for it. In the past several decades, "wages for housework" campaigns have been a feature of feminist debate and political action, especially in Europe and North America.

In a parallel vein, feminists have recently challenged national and international (UN, World Bank, IMF) accounting methods that keep women's domestic work invisible by according it no value in estimating national productivity. Women's groups in Canada, Trinidad, Australia, New Zealand, Norway, and India are promoting national studies to assess women's economic contributions to national income.[43] As Carol Lees pointed out, the effects of national accounting are not gender neutral: "As a result of the exclusion of women's labor from information gathering we are denied proper access to programs and policy at every level of government in every country."[44]

These actions, because their goals are not only better conditions for women to perform reproductive labor but also equity in the cash resources available to women and men, extend beyond women's practical gender interests. By redefining women's reproductive labor as work on which the public sphere depends and by demanding payment for this work, women are attacking the ideological and structural barriers that impoverish them relative to men. However, revaluing domestic work does not necessarily challenge the stereotype that only women should do it, nor does it disrupt the idea that men are better suited for more highly paid jobs in the public sphere.

The gendered division of labor in the work force has stirred many women to join trade union movements in the hope of improving general working conditions and wages as well as receiving pay equity relative to men in the same or comparable jobs. Berenice Carroll reminded us that it was women who initiated the earliest industrial labor strikes during the first half of the nineteenth century and a strike by women was the first of the rebellious actions that culminated in the Russian Revolution.[45] From the 1912 Lawrence, Massachusetts, textile workers strike that inspired the formation of the International Ladies Garment Workers Union to the Women Workers Movement founded in 1984 in the Philippines to protest labor conditions for women in export-processing zones, women have been active organizers and their efforts have had international implications. However, as these examples suggest, women often have created their own trade unions because they were marginalized or silenced by male-dominated unions concentrated in heavy industries, where women workers are in the minority.

Because of most women's locations within the wage labor market – in low-wage, light-industry and service jobs as well as in the so-called informal labor force of street vendors and subsistence agricultural producers – their labor organizing is more difficult, but also more varied, than the typical workplace-centered organizing that goes on in male-dominated industries. For example, in India, women street vendors formed the Self-Employed Women's Association (SEWA) to demand better wages from commodity suppliers. Traditional trade unions do not organize such workers, but SEWA developed an imaginative strategy. Women street vendors organized other women street vendors by visiting them on the street and in their homes and providing literacy training so that they could participate more fully and equally in decision-making. The Honduran Federation of Peasant Women, another group that was overlooked by industry-based union movements, did not seek better wages from their employers (multinational, or transnational, corporations paying them the equivalent of U.S. $2.00 a day) but rather alternative income-generating opportunities that would release them from having to work for MNCs.[46]

These examples show women's labor organizing to be oriented toward increasing women's autonomy as workers. Women's preference for more-flexible, self-directed, and home-based work reflects their practical gender interests in having more time and energy to perform their reproductive labor. However, the strategies employed to achieve these ends often lead women to challenge a host of institutions and policies that traditional labor organizing fails to confront. For example, in order to promote safer worker conditions for women in the Philippines, the feminist organization Gabriela has supported women's demands for health care and immigration policies offering some protection from the effects of the presence of U.S. military bases and foreign servicemen.[47] Gabriela also promotes income-generating activities, community development, vocational-training and educational programs, and opportunities for feminist research. In this way, women's strategic gender interests are awakened and mobilized in the process of fighting for working conditions that better meet their practical gender interests.

These national and local women's struggles in the waged labor force are linked through transnational women's economic movements that challenge the international gendered division of labor that shores up the current capitalist global economy. Formed in 1974, the Women's International Information and Communication Service (ISIS/WICCE), at different times based in Switzerland, Uganda, Italy, Philippines, and Chile, has connected more than 10,000 women's groups in 130 countries. Among the many issues and strategies ISIS/WICCE deals with are the organizing of women's groups against economic development policies that marginalize and exploit women workers.[48] Since 1978, the American Friends Service Committee, through its Women and Global Corporations Project, has linked workers, activists, and researchers worldwide who are promoting legislation to stop TNC practices that are reducing jobs and wages for women workers in the North and exploiting women's cheap labor in the South.[49]

The debt crises and structural adjustment programs imposed by international lending institutions have had particularly negative consequences for women. Therefore, a variety of global and regional women's and development organizations have focused on combatting these gender-differentiated effects. These groups include DAWN (Development Alternatives with Women for a New Era), founded by Third World and First World women researchers and activists, which produced its first analysis of development strategies and their gendered consequences for the Nairobi meeting that concluded the UN Decade for Women.[50] More recently, DAWN's Latin American Region Research Group has connected Latin American women's groups developing alternative economic strategies with poor women and their local organizations. This networking includes "the Centro de Estudios de la Mujer in Chile and in Argentina; La Morada, also in Chile; Flora Tristan in Peru; CIPAF in the Dominican Republic; IDAC in Rio de Janeiro; the Rede Mulher in São Paulo, CEAAL throughout Latin America; the SOS Corpo in Recife and innumerable other groups."[51] DAWN is also working with WAND (Women and Development Unit) in the Caribbean, and AAWORD (African Association of Women for Research and Development) in West Africa "to evaluate standard macro- and micro-economic analyses, document their negative impact on women, and develop alternative frameworks."[52]

Women in many countries are engaging in an unprecedented global and regional organizing effort to confront a host of economic exploiters – from development agencies to multinational corporations to sex tourism operators. Women's nongovernmental organizations are committed to grass-roots organizing by poor and working-class women, whose struggles are backed up by research by, but not led by, more privileged academic women. Although the immediate goal of these struggles is to meet the practical gender interests articulated by poor and working-class women, the analysis that informs these struggles goes to the heart of every woman's strategic gender interests. That analysis exposes the gendered division of labor in all its forms and shows that this division keeps most women from having an equitable share of local, national, and global wealth, despite the fact that they are now the primary breadwinners the world over.

Ecology movements

Perhaps the newest form of women's political action is in the area of saving the environment. From the tree-hugging Chipko Movement in India to the tree-planting Greenbelt Movement in Kenya and the nature-worshiping ecofeminist movement in North America, women are on the move to stop the rape of Mother Earth. For Third World rural women, saving the environment is crucial to their economic survival. As the primary food, fuel, and water gatherers, these women have particularly strong interests in reversing deforestation, desertification, and water pollution. When these processes threaten women's abilities to draw upon natural resources for themselves and their families, the women act in the only way available to them – putting their bodies on the line:

> In 1974, village women of the Reni forests of the Chamoli district in Uttar Pradesh decided to act against a commercial enterprise about to fell some 2,500 trees. The women were alone; the menfolk had left home in search of work. When the contractors arrived, the women went into the forest, joined hands and encircled the trees ("Chipko" means to hug). The women told the cutters that to cut the trees, they would first have to cut off their heads. The contractors withdrew and the forest was saved.[53]

Like women's struggles against immediate economic threats posed by the gendered division of labor, creative responses to the gendered division of resources may be effective in the short term, but they fail to address long-term systemic issues. In the Chipko case, the responses did not undermine forces of global capitalism that are among the major causes of deforestation, nor did they challenge the idea that only women need be the stewards of the environment because they are closer to nature than men. These spontaneous strategies also fail to redistribute in favor of women the resources necessary for more effective long-term organizing.

The Greenbelt Movement in Kenya, formed by Wangari Maathai, of the National Council of Women, has begun a resource-generating process through which women can become more effective stewards of the environment. After instituting an effective national tree-planting campaign, the movement established a tree nursery. "Women are involved in rearing the seedlings, planting and marketing; in addition to becoming expert foresters, they also earn a cash income. The Greenbelt Movement is not only restoring the environment, but also enables women to benefit from environmental education, and to practice professional forestry techniques, while at the same time they are developing their status."[54] This kind of organizing not only meets women's practical gender interests but also creates conditions under which women can fight for their strategic gender interests.

This holistic strategy is also evident in such movements as the Calcutta Social Project, started by middle-class Indian women in the 1960s. The Calcutta Social Project was designed to change the lives of the poor who were forced to live on and around the city's massive waste dumps. "They began with literacy and recreational classes for young garbage pickers in an abandoned shed. Then vocational training in carpentry, masonry, and sewing were added. A primary health care clinic now flourishes."[55] Such projects not only reduce the misery experienced by people living in extreme poverty but also gives them the tools to change their landscape and their work. Once again, however, such projects do not directly counteract the economic, political, and social forces that construct and perpetuate a "throwaway" society.

For Western ecofeminists, the key to confronting systemic forces that despoil the environment is questioning the treatment of both women and nature as resources to be used and abused by men and industries. This orientation gained momentum following the Three Mile Island nuclear power plant accident in Pennsylvania. Shortly afterward, 600 women gathered for a weekend meeting on "Women and Life on Earth: A Conference on Eco-Feminism in the Eighties." Ecofeminist, Ynestra King, opened this conference, proclaiming: "We're here to say the word ECOLOGY and announce that for us as feminists it's a political word – that it stands against the economics of the destroyers and the pathology of racist hatred. It's a way of being, which understands that there are connections between all living things and that indeed women are the fact and flesh of connectedness."[56]

In 1980 this U.S. movement spawned a similar one in the UK, which became known as Women for Life on Earth. Ecofeminist activists on both sides of the Atlantic were prominent in the 1980 and 1981 Women's Pentagon Actions and the December 12, 1980, encirclement of the Greenham Common nuclear base. These actions were based on the premise that "we see the devastation of the earth and her beings by the corporate warriors and the threat of nuclear annihilation by the military warriors as feminist concerns."[57]

From this ecofeminist perspective, if patriarchy, capitalism, racism, industrial development, and militarism are the sources of environmental degradation, women are the solution to it. Rather than questioning the gender stereotypes that associate women with nature and stewardship, most ecofeminists insist that women are closer to nature because of the reproductive and productive work they do and, thus, are in the best position to care for the environment. Ecofeminists use this argument in an attempt to counter other gender stereotypes about women and nature as objectified and passive resources, which powerful men may manipulate for their own purposes.

This perspective predominated at the October 1990 four-day meeting of fifty leading environmentalist women from Latin America, Africa, Asia, Europe, and North America. Assembled at the UN Church Center, participants drafted an international plan of action for the next decade with the following major goals:

- Full participation by women in environment policy at all levels
- Freedom of choice in family planning
- Redefinition of development on the principle that investment must not destroy the environment
- Increased education and information on the environment and development
- Protection of natural resources
- Development of a code of earth ethics[58]

The plan of action was created and signed by women from all over the world: Vandana Shiva of India; Wangari Maathai of the Greenbelt Movement in Kenya; Canadian radiation and health specialist Rosalie Bertell; Bella Abzug of the U.S. Women's Foreign Policy Council; Chodchoy Sophonpanich, president of the Thai Environmental and Community Development Association; Maria Eugenia de Cotter, director of the Arias Foundation of Costa Rica; Tamar Eschel, former member of the Israeli parliament; Rosina Wiltshire of the Caribbean Conservation Association; Gertrude Mongella, a member of the Central Committee of Tanzania's governing party; and Bernadette Vallely of the Women's Environmentalist Network in Britain. It was brought forward to the International Women's Congress on the Environment in Miami in November 1991 and to the UN Conference on Environment and Development (UNCED) in Rio de Janeiro in June 1992.

Although this international plan of action is consistent with the positions of most environmentalist groups, particularly in the North, it is distinguished by its insistence that women can no longer be shut out of environmental policy-making. Rather, it argues that women bear the brunt of environmental degradation and are therefore most likely to seek solutions to it. In addition, the drafters of this document held accountable not just the North but also all the male-dominated power structures – local, national, and international – for the state of the Earth. Nevertheless, the plan of action falls short of more-radical ecofeminist and nonfeminist "deep ecology" positions that draw from Native American traditions and claim that nature, or the Earth, has intrinsic value. In this view, human beings should cease imposing their own values on the Earth and encroach upon natural processes as little as possible.

This "Earth as inviolate" position is problematic to the degree that it celebrates "the primitive" in a way that denies development not only to the South generally but also to women, who have the least access to land, technologies, and resources worldwide. The ecofeminist strategy that maintains the connection of women to nature in order to argue that women and nature should be equally inviolate – safe from rape, abuse, and use as cheap resources – is flawed. It makes women so coterminous with nature that it provides a rationale for continuing to keep them out of decision-making about the use of nature by humans. Here, women's strategic gender interests, which lead to calls for low-technology strategies to protect women and nature, conflict with their practical gender interests in gaining access to the resources necessary for meeting the basic needs of their families. Radical ecofeminist definitions of strategic gender interests also conflict with other strategic gender interests in participating as equals in modern, high-technology, presently male-dominated institutions that control or "manage" resources.

Finally, what is still unchallenged by all types of women's ecology movements is that women are the most "natural" stewards of the environment. Certainly not all women are environmentalists. Middle- and upper-class women in the North and South, by being major consumers, are particularly profligate destroyers of natural resources. Moreover, poor and working-class women often lack the tools and skills necessary to be effective stewards. These contradictions within women's ecology movements once again remind us that there is no simple formula for righting gender wrongs. Ending the gendered division of resources is contingent on ending the assumption that masculinism equals resource ownership and exploitation. It is dependent too on feminism's relinquishing the principle that stewardship is the property and responsibility of women only.

Conclusion

The pursuit of practical gender interests often leads activists to discover strategic gender interests, which, in turn, drive the participation of women (and men) in anti- and transstate social movements. The issues raised and actions undertaken have important implications for both how we understand world politics and how we choose to shape our future.

That women's political movements of all types are complicit, to a greater or lesser degree, in gendering processes leads us to some ruminations in our final chapter on what it will take to "ungender" world politics. There, we hope to integrate our findings and our arguments and leave the reader with some sense of the enormity, but also the necessity, of the transformational project to ungender world politics.

Notes

1 See Sandi E. Cooper, "Women's Participation in European Peace Movements: The Struggle to Prevent World War I," in *Women and Peace: Theoretical, Historical, and Practical Perspectives*, ed. Ruth Roach Pierson (London: Croom Helm, 1987), pp. 51–75.

2 Ibid., pp. 63–65.

3 Ursula Herrmann, "Social Democratic Women in Germany and the Struggle for Peace Before and During the First World War," in *Women and Peace*, ed. Pierson, pp. 91–92.

4 See Lela B. Costin, "Feminism, Pacifism, Internationalism and the 1915 International Congress of Women," in *Women and Men's Wars*, ed. Judith Stiehm (Oxford: Pergamon Press, 1983), pp. 301–316.

5 See Yvonne Aleksandra Bennett, "Vera Brittain and the Peace Pledge Union: Women and Peace," in *Women and Peace*, ed. Pierson (London: Croom Heln), pp. 192–213.

6 See Ruth Roach Pierson, *"They're Still Women After All": The Second World War and Canadian Womanhood* (Toronto: McClelland and Stewart, 1986); Maureen Honey, *Creating Rosie the Riveter: Class, Gender, and Propaganda During World War II* (Amherst: University of Massachusetts Press, 1984).

7 See D'Ann Campbell, *Women at War with America* (Cambridge, MA: Harvard University Press, 1985).

8 Karen Beck Skold, " 'The Job He Left Behind': American Women in the Shipyards During World War II," in *Women, War and Revolution*, ed. Carol R. Berkin and Clara M. Lovett (New York: Holmes and Meier Pub., 1980), p. 69.

9 James J. Kenneally, "Women in the United States and Trade Unionism," in *The World of Women's Trade Unionism*, ed. Norbert C. Soldon (Westport, CO: Greenwood Press, 1985), p. 80.

10 Campbell, *Women at War*, p. 216.

11 Carolyn Strange, "Mothers on the March: Maternalism in Women's Protest for Peace in North America and Western Europe, 1900–1985," in *Women and Social Protest*, ed. Guida West and Rhoda Lois Blumberg (New York: Oxford University Press, 1990), p. 215.

12 Ibid., p. 216.

13 Berenice Carroll, "Women Take Action! Women's Direct Action and Social Change," *Women's Studies International Forum* 12, 1 (1989): 17.

14 See Anne Sisson Runyan, "Feminism, Peace, and International Politics: An Examination of Women Organizing Internationally for Peace and Security," (Ph.D. Dissertation, American University, Washington, DC, 1988).

15 See ibid.

16 See, for example, Lynne Segal, *Is the Future Female?* (New York: Peter Bedwick Books, 1987); Jean Bethke Elshtain, *Women and War* (New York: Basic Books, 1987); Christine Sylvester, "Some Dangers in Merging Feminist and Peace Projects," *Alternatives* 12 (October 1987): 493–510.

17 See, for example, Berkin and Lovett, eds, *Women, War, and Revolution*; Miranda Davies, comp., *Third World – Second Sex: Women's Struggles and National Liberation* (London: Zed Books, 1983); and Linda Labao, "Women in Revolutionary Movements: Changing Patterns of Latin American Guerrilla Struggle," in *Women and Social Protest*, ed. West and Blumberg, pp. 180–204.

18 Margaret Randall, *Sandino's Daughters: Testimonies of Nicaraguan Women in the Struggle* (Vancouver/Toronto: New Star Books, 1981), p. 10.

19 Ibid., p. 16.

20 Ibid., p. 66.

21 Jane Deighton, Rossana Horsley, Sarah Stewart, and Cathy Cain, *Sweet Ramparts: Women in Revolutionary Nicaragua* (London: War on Want and the Nicaraguan Solidarity Campaign, 1983), p. 50.

22 Ibid., p. 55.

23 Davies, *Third World – Second Sex*, p. 105.

24 Ibid.

25 Ibid., p. 119.

26 Ibid.

27 See Margaret E. Leahy, *Development Strategies and the Status of Women: A Comparative Study of the United States, Mexico, the Soviet Union, and Cuba* (Boulder, CO: Lynne Rienner Publishers, 1986).

28 Deighton *et al.*, *Sweet Ramparts*, p. 45.

29 Ibid., p. 154.

30 Cynthia Enloe, *Bananas, Beaches and Bases* (Berkeley, CA: University of California Press, 1990), p. 63.

31 See, for example, Minoll Reeves, *Female Warriors of Allah: Women and the Islamic Revolution* (New York: E. P. Dutton, 1989).

32 Elshtain, *Women and War*, p. 170.

33 See Robin Morgan, *The Demon Lover: On the Sexuality of Terrorism* (New York: W. W. Norton, 1989).

34 This does not mean, however, that women in such struggles are unaware of the ways that they are marginalized and stereotyped in the nation- and state-building process. For example, see Suha Sabbagh and Ghada Talhami, *Images and Reality: Palestinian Women Under Occupation and in the Diaspora* (Washington, DC: Institute for Arab Women's Studies, 1990).

35 Cynthia A. Bouton, "Gendered Behavior in Subsistence Riots," *Journal of Social History* 23, 4 (Summer 1990); Carroll, "Women Take Action!" pp. 3–24.

36 Bouton, "Gendered Behavior," p. 743.

37 Carroll, "Women Take Action!," p. 8.

38 Ibid.

39 Jackie Pope, "Women in the Welfare Rights Struggle: The Brooklyn Welfare Action Council," in *Women and Social Protest*, ed. West and Blumberg, p. 66.

40 United Nations, *The World's Women: 1970–1990 Trends and Statistics* (New York: United Nations, 1991), p. 90.

41 Debbie Taylor, "Women: An Analysis," in *Women: A World Report* (New York: Oxford University Press, 1985), p. 81.

42 Ibid., p. 26.

43 Marilyn Waring, "A Woman's Reckoning: Update on Unwaged Labor," *Ms.*, July/August 1991, p. 15.

44 Quoted in ibid. [no citation for original Lees remarks included in Waring article].

45 Carroll, "Women Take Action!," p. 17.

46 Enloe, *Bananas, Beaches*, pp. 144–146.

47 Ibid., p. 39.

48 See ISIS: Women's International Information and Communication Service, *Women in Development* (Philadelphia, PA: New Society Publishers, 1984).

49 See Rachael Kamel, *The Global Factory: Analysis and Action for a New Economic Era* (Philadelphia, PA: American Friends Service Committee, 1990).

50 See Gita Sen and Caren Grown, *Development, Crises, and Alternative Visions: Third World Women's Perspectives* (New York: Monthly Review Press, 1987).

51 Jeanne Vickers, *Women and the World Economic Crisis* (London: Zed Books, 1991), p. 112.

52 Ibid.

53 Annabel Rodda, *Women and the Environment* (London: Zed Books, 1991), p. 110.

54 Ibid., p. 111.

55 Ibid., p. 116.

56 Quoted in Leonie Caldecott and Stephanie Leland, eds, *Reclaim the Earth: Women Speak Out for Life on Earth* (London: Women's Press, 1983), p. 6.

57 Ibid., p. 7.

58 Marvine Howe, "Women's Group Seeks Environmental Role," *New York Times*, October 28, 1990, p. 16.

20 Globalization, governance and gender

Rethinking the agenda for the twenty-first century

Janine Brodie

Introduction

This chapter examines some of the many and complex ways in which globalization, governance and gender interact in the contemporary era.[1] These three 'big G' words are pervasive forces in our daily lives, influencing our personal identities and our collective futures in ever more immediate and interrelated ways. Although there is considerable disagreement about what these concepts actually entail, it is increasingly apparent that advancements toward human equality and security in the early twenty-first century increasingly depend on how globalization and gender are linked in our governing practices and public policies. This chapter first discusses two component parts of globalization – globality and globalism. Next, neoliberal globalism is examined as a contemporary philosophy of governance that has generated a contradictory gender order and an unstable system of social reproduction. Finally, the chapter explores how the contemporary good governance agenda of international agencies responds to the most pressing challenges that confront both citizens and policy-makers in an era of intensifying globalization.

Globalization

Although a fairly recent addition to our collective vocabulary, globalization has quickly entered into the dubious realm of common sense, informing the way we make sense of our daily lives, national public policy and international relations (Smith, 2002). Yet, both the meaning and implications of globalization remain illusive and contested. Few people any longer dismiss globalization outright as 'more of the same' or as a fashionable 'buzzword'. Others define globalization quite narrowly in terms of the current mode of economic governance of the international political economy, that is, as the removal of barriers to free trade, the deregulation of financial capital and international investment and the integration of national economies into global production processes (Stiglitz, 2002). Increasingly, however, globalization is understood as the primary organizing principle in both the study and the practice of politics in the early twenty-first century.

At the very least, globalization can be understood as an ongoing historical drama involving a number of critical processes, some mutually reinforcing and others conflicting. Taken together, these processes:

- stretch social, political and economic activities across political frontiers and the formal boundaries of the national state;

- intensify interdependencies, as international flows of trade, finance, culture and people multiply;
- accelerate social interaction and exchange through new technologies of communication and transportation;
- erode boundaries between the domestic and the global (Held and McGrew, 1999: 484).

Although globalization is imagined in a variety of completing ways, there is general consensus that the cornerstones of modern governance, especially the symmetries forged in the past two centuries between national states, national territory and national citizenship rights have been progressively fractured by transnational networks, flows and identities. Globalization is commonly linked to the erosion of the capacity of national states to exercise sovereignty over domestic policy and territorial boundaries and to buffer its citizens from an increasing predatory and unpredictable international political economy. As these epochal shifts become inescapable facts in our daily calculations, it is imperative that activists and policy-makers unpack globalization, both conceptually and empirically, into its component parts because they often have very different political and policy implications. Beck's distinction between *globality* and *globalism* is particularly useful because it separates current transformations in social organization from the political regulation of these changes (2000). In other words, this conceptual distinction recognizes the profound social changes that define this globalizing era while leaving open to analysis and activism the question of how these changes are or should be governed. Some of the forces propelling contemporary political transformations may be irreversible but, contrary to the pronouncements of neoliberal economists, there is nothing inevitable either about the way these forces are regulated or the pattern of winners and losers that they have left in their wake (Folbre, 2001: xvi).

Globality refers to epochal transformations in social, political and economic organization that have fundamentally altered our shared experiences of time and space as well as of self and community. Globality focuses attention on new technologies, global interdependencies, social issues that transcend the territorial boundaries and capacities of national states, the emergence of the planet as a relevant space for political action and the necessity of thinking in terms of global public goods and bads (Kaul *et al.*, 1999). As Beck explains, 'globality is an unavoidable condition of human intercourse' in the contemporary era and implies that nothing that happens on our planet is an isolated event. 'All interventions, victories, and catastrophes affect the whole world', and thus we must reorient our actions and institutions along a 'local-global axis' (Beck, 2000: 11–15).

Globality challenges the pre-eminent modernist notion that society is a discrete and governable entity that is contained within the territorial boundaries of the national state. The very idea of society is now complicated by a complex of forces, identities, issues and movements that touch individuals and social groups in different ways and at different scales of social and political organization. In the process, social space is being reorganized into what Held *et al.* call 'overlapping communities of fate' (1999: 42). Strings of transactions and interests as well as non-territorial and pre- and post-national solidarities run up and down through the national social fabric such that citizens are often more directly linked to distant forces and actors than to their national state. Local events, in turn, are shaped in transnational spaces, thus depriving the national state of the illusion of control. The state's capacity to protect is citizens, moreover, is diminished by the growing saliency of global policy issues that are largely immune from the policy interventions of any single state. Global environmental degradation is an obvious example.

The idea of globality poses serious questions for contemporary good governance agendas that focus almost exclusively on the rehabilitation of the national states of developing and transitional societies. The growing importance of different scales of social and political interaction suggests that the national state is not the only, or even the most appropriate, space for effective policy interventions, especially with respect to redistribution and human well-being. Increasingly, 'the unity of the national state and national society has become unstuck' with new relations of power, conflict and cooperation taking shape between local and transnational actors, identities, social spaces, situations and processes (Beck, 2000: 21). Noted social theorist Zygmunt Bauman argues that such fluidity is rapidly forming new axes of social stratification and advantage on a global scale. While some people become fully global, others are fixed to local spaces, places that can be 'neither pleasurable nor endurable in a world in which the "globals" set the tone and compose the rules of the game' (1998: 2). The poor and marginalized are contained within urban slums everywhere while the populations of the South are increasingly tied to their country of origin by the immigration, passport and visa restrictions of the wealthy fortresses of the North.

While globality refers to ongoing epochal changes in the constitution of contemporary social and political forces, *globalism*, in contrast, refers to the transnational embrace of a common world-view and philosophy of governance. The most obvious example is neoliberal globalism, sometimes termed the Washington Consensus, which prioritizes economic growth and markets over all other goals and institutions of government. With varying degrees of coercion, neoliberal globalism enforces on all countries, privatization, fiscal austerity, the erosion of collective provision and trade and financial liberalization. Before elaborating on the neo-liberal globalist experiment, however, I will turn briefly to the concept of governance and the historical construction of gender orders.

Governance and gender

Governance, simply defined, refers to the way we organize our collective affairs but the term highlights more than a particular configuration of institutions or set of decision-making processes. Contemporary discourses that focus exclusively on the latter are invariably informed by liberal, if not, neoliberal assumptions about the terrain and goals of governance. All governing actions and inactions are framed within a particular philosophy of governance that rests on its own vocabulary, set of ethical principles, and consensus about the nature, spheres and scope of legitimate political action and collective authority (Brodie, 1997). 'To govern', as Rose explains, 'is to cut experience in certain ways, to distribute attractions and repulsions, passions and fears across it, to bring new facets and forces, new intensities and relations into being' (1999: 26). Historical shifts in philosophies of governance reorder social domains and political institutions as well as relationships among individuals, public authority, civil society and the economy. Not the least, all governing philosophies advance a particular configuration of the boundaries between the public and private *sector* (the state vs. the economy) and the public and private *sphere* (the state and economy vs. the family and the individual) (Clarke, 2004a). In other words, these philosophies advance authoritative claims about what problems are to be treated as collective responsibilities, the way they are to be solved, and by whom. Yet, it is important to remember that these are simply experiments in political organization that can achieve targeted objectives for a time or miss entirely, often with terrible consequences for the vulnerable.

Feminist social scientists also remind us that philosophies of governance, rather than biology or divine providence, have envisioned and constructed historically specific gender orders that attempt to integrate, in complementary and seemingly natural ways, processes of economic production and social reproduction. Gender, the final element in our triad, represents both cultural and symbolic inscriptions on the body as well as a more or less rigid division of labour, social roles and identities that are assigned by, among other things, the prevailing philosophy of governance. Every institution, including markets and the state, construct and reproduce various kinds of femininity and masculinity that underpin social organizations and the exercise of political power (Connell, 1987). Almost everywhere, women have and continue to assume inordinate responsibility for social reproduction. This latter term entails the daily and generational reproduction of commodity labour power as well as the social processes and human relations necessary for the creation and maintenance of the communities (Bakker and Gill, 2003).

The manner in which women have engaged with the dynamics of social reproduction has shifted along side of, and usually commensurate with, different modes of production, stages of capitalist development and national state forms. The earliest liberal regimes, for example, rested on the illusory claim that the public sector, the market, and the domestic sphere were distinct and autonomous spheres, each governed by different rules, hierarchies and responsibilities (Brodie, 1997). The domestic sphere was governed by a patriarchal doctrine that enforced a rigid sexual division of labour and assigned women a large measure of responsibility for the ongoing care of the family and the household. Patriarchy both privileged men in economic and political life and ensured an abundant and exclusive source of unpaid domestic labour and caring activities (Folbre, 2001: 20). State regulations and social norms effectively locked women into the domestic sphere while the gender order idealized and rewarded the altruistic and nurturing mother. This model of male rule and of the enforced separation of social reproduction and care from the wage economy or public provision was entirely commensurate with the prevailing governing philosophy of those years – laissez-faire liberalism.

The development of the welfare state in the middle of the twentieth century in industrialized countries was informed by a new philosophy of governance and a changed gender order that involved ever increasing involvement of the state in the domestic sphere and in processes of social production. The welfare state is generally understood as the mid-twentieth century settlement between capital and labour in the industrialized economies of the North. The welfare state advanced a new understanding about the role of governments in regulating the economy and about the primacy of the visible hand of the state over the invisible hand of the market. The welfare state also built upon a relatively underdeveloped terrain of liberal governance – the social. It contained an ever-expanding basket of public policies designed to stabilize the economy, to reduce the social consequences of market instabilities and failures, and to secure the social cohesion of increasingly modernized, diverse and democratized societies (Perez-Baltodano, 1999: 21). The social field of governance was subsequently expanded as ever more public solutions were devised for an ever-wider range of problems thrown up by advanced capitalism and modern social formations (Dean, 1999).

However, if welfare state policies emerged partly as a response to market failures, they also addressed what Folbre calls 'family failures' – situations where networks of family and kin proved inadequate to the task of underwriting social reproduction (2001: 91). The welfare state rested on a reconfigured gender order that assumed a stable working/middle class nuclear family supported by a male breadwinner, containing a dependent wife and children, and sustained by women's unpaid domestic labour. The state, in turn, guaranteed, through progressive taxation, the protection of collective bargaining, social security programs and welfare policies that there would be an adequate family wage that combined wage labour with state income supports and collective provision for, among other things, unemployment, misfortune, illness and old age. Although women benefited from public services and income transfers, they were largely tied to the family wage system because of explicit state discrimination against women workers, their marginalization in the 'pink ghettos' of labour markets and limited access to birth control and childcare. The feminist movement of the postwar period struggled to reverse gender-informed discrimination with varying degrees of success. By the 1980s, however, shifts in the international political economy, stagnating economic fortunes and the ascendancy of a neoliberalism began to erode this postwar gender order. It was replaced, as discussed below, by a highly contradictory, fragile and inadequate model of integration of the economic production and social reproduction.

Neoliberal globalism

Neoliberal globalism is an experiment in governance and a theory of economic growth that envisions and attempts to enforce, primarily through international financial institutions (IFIs), the principles and institutions of economic liberalism on a global scale. Its critical governing strategies include privatization, commodification, liberalization, decentralization and individualization (Brodie, 1997; Beck and Beck-Gernsheim, 2002). Although realized through different policy practices than the first great era of laissez-faire, this governing philosophy seeks to expand existing markets, to create new ones and to construct a globally integrated production process and the uninhibited and spontaneous flow of capital to every corner of the planet. Although the pedlars of neoliberalism globalism shroud themselves behind the self-evident truths of neo-classical economic theory (all other things being equal), it is a profoundly political project that supplants the very ideas of the public, the social and societal protection with markets logics and hierarchies.

   Neoliberal globalism is often equated with the package of governing instruments associated with deregulation and retrenchment policies in the North and Structural Adjustment Policies (SAPs) in the South but it is also much more than this. It has exacted critical transformations in the very form and logic of contemporary governance. Two of these shifts are especially germane to this inquiry into globalization, gender and governance. First, neoliberal globalism has shifted the scales of governance of national social formations in historically unprecedented ways. The economic is increasingly governed at the level of the transnational while governance of the social remains attached to a diminished national state with fraying ties to democratic electorates. Through membership in the World Trade Organization (WTO), as signatories of regional trade agreements such as NAFTA, or under the weight of international debt, SAPs and, most recently, Poverty Reduction Strategy Papers, national governments everywhere have acquiesced, in varying degrees, to internal governance structures and rules that are controlled by external (and democratically unaccountable) actors.

   As Sassen reminds us, deregulation denationalizes national territory (1998: xxiv). National governmental institutions become infused with the global as policy-makers are forced to anticipate and integrate the demands of the global system into national and local strategies of governance. In the process, a series of pivotal modernist oppositions, for example, between international and national, public and private and artificial (corporations) and actual (persons) citizens, become blurred. This denationalization of economic governance is simultaneously outside of the national state and yet embedded within national institutions (Sassen, 1996: 23). As important, the new post-Bretton Woods financial architecture not only dominates national economic policy, it also affects its own inequitable patterns of transnational redistribution and global provision.

Second, neoliberal globalism has delinked economic and social policy. Under the welfare state, economic and social policies were connected through demand management policies in a way that enhanced economic stability, individual welfare and social cohesion. The unfettered globalization of production and finance, however, now enables global capital to transcend national boundaries, shop among jurisdictions for the lowest taxation regimes or the best infrastructure and just as quickly abandon commitments to workers, citizens and the environment. The ability of transnational capital to move relatively unrestricted around the globe is also commonly understood to undermine citizenship rights, especially postwar social citizenship rights, as national states engage in a 'race to the bottom', cutting taxes and social programs in order to retain and attract capital investment. States find themselves locked into a permanent referendum – being continuously monitored by IFIs, transnational corporations and bond rating agencies as to their desirability as sites for investment (Pierson, 1998: 68). The protection and advancement of national citizenship rights are relatively insignificant factors in this global calculus.

Economic policy, moreover, is now structured by constitution-like agreements that trump the aspirations of democratic electorates, are binding into the indefinite future and are difficult to amend. As Gill explains, this new constitutionalism mandates the insulation of key aspects of the economy from the influence of politicians or citizens, providing new rights for capital whilst 'constraining the democratization process that has involved struggles for representation for hundreds of years' (1995: 411). National states are increasingly locked into constitution-like discourses and structures that limit their capacity either to rehabilitate failed markets, stabilize business cycles or protect its citizens from the worst abuses of capitalism. As important, marginalized groups are constrained in their struggles for security and equality. Although the regulation of capital, the public sector and social spending have been employed, in the past, to advance the human condition, each of these mechanisms is discouraged if not disallowed by logic and institutions of neoliberal globalism. As more countries democratize, policy sectors that are fundamental to the promotion of social and environmental protection are increasingly deemed immune from the language and logics of democracy. Regulation, decommodification and social spending, three governing instruments, which have proved critical to the advancement and well-being of marginalized groups, are effectively taken off of the political agenda.

In sum, neoliberal globalism is an anti-political and anti-social governing doctrine that attempts to obfuscate the fundamental structuring principle of liberal-democratic governance – the conceptual and institutional separation of politics and economics (Beck, 2000: 9). Market logics are elevated both over the state and inside the state. Public goods are privatized while the public sphere embraces, as a measure of its own performance, market discourses and rationales. In the process, accounting practices and narrow cost – benefit definitions of efficiency assume more weight in the policy process than moral objectives of governance such as human equality and democratic accountability. Indeed, in its most extreme form, neoliberalism seeks to relieve governments from their primary task of advancing collective well-being and security and to supplant public processes with market rationales and distributive mechanisms.

A quarter century has passed since neoliberal globalism was first infused into the assumptions and governing practices of advanced capitalist countries and, especially, developing countries through SAPs and then Poverty Reduction Strategy Papers. There is a growing consensus, however, that this experiment has failed either to sustain stable economic growth or to improve the condition of the vast majority of the world's population. The unleashing and empowerment of market forces on a global scale as well as the application of neoliberal governing instruments on local terrains and cultures have exacted a heavy toll on individuals, families and communities, intensifying the desperation of poverty, opening a yawning gulf between the rich and the poor, both within and between countries, and fueling political alienation, insecurity and violence everywhere. If neoliberal globalism has pulled the world together with respect to economic governance, it also has forceful counteracting tendencies that are pulling societies apart along fragile and complex fracture lines. Inequalities between the North and the South, for example, have widened at an accelerated pace and to an intolerable and unsustainable extent. The income gap between the fifth of the world's population living in the richest countries and the fifth living in the poorest is now more than 75:1 (UNDP, 1999: 3). The United States Development Report now characterizes worldwide levels of inequality as 'grotesque' (2002: 18).

Gendered contradictions

We also know that this systematic and calculated process of human impoverishment is decidedly gendered with women and children comprising the vast majority of the world's poor. Neoliberalism is silent about gender as well as other dimensions of structurally based inequality but it is, nonetheless, a profoundly gendered philosophy of governance that has significantly disrupted gender orders in the North and the South. Two axes of change are particularly significant: (1) the simultaneous erosion and intensification of gender and (2) individualization and responsibilization. Combined these contradictory tendencies betray neoliberalism as an unsustainable governing project, not the least because, as feminists have long argued, it fails to successfully anticipate the necessities of social reproduction in the contemporary era.

In a challenging essay, written in the 1990s, Haraway characterized the late twentieth century as being marked by the simultaneous erosion and intensification of gender, both literally and metaphorically (1991: 166). Twentieth century feminism contested and eroded many societal expectations about gender as well as state regulations and social institutions that previously kept women locked inside the home and unable to pursue individual talents and aspirations. Doors to education, politics and the workforce, previously closed to women, were opened and women flooded into the postwar workforce. In this sense, the defining force of gender as a status identity was eroded.

As important, since the 1980s, the ascendancy of neoliberalism has virtually erased gender from policy making and as a legitimate grounds for making claims on the state. This worldview constructs individuals as rational and self-sufficient market players in the pursuit of self-interest. Neoliberalism further erases reference to gender and the gender order by disregarding the unpaid work of reproduction as relevant in its calculations. Women's reproductive labour is bracketed out as having no market value or, at best, is treated as an externality. The erosion of gender as a homogeneous social category also is revealed in growing racial and class-based disparities among women themselves, enabling some women to buy and exploit the domestic services of other women, a phenomenon that increasingly has taken on global proportions. Domestic workers are a primary export from selected countries in the South to the wealthy countries of the North (Young, 2000).

At the same time, the imprint of gender has intensified in everyday life. Neoliberalism puts renewed emphasis on the so-called 'feminine sphere of the home' and the 'feminine' qualities of selflessness, nurturing and caregiving while paid work is said to be increasingly 'feminized', that is, part time, low-waged and precarious. One of the contemporary paradoxes of gender is that women everywhere increasingly reflect a male biography with respect to the worlds of employment and education yet characteristics of traditional feminine biographies also are intensifying. For example, more women are obtaining higher education but they continue to receive fewer financial rewards than men, more women are in paid employment but the quality of the jobs and the degree of protection and rights attached to employment has dropped precipitously, and more women are entering legislative assemblies while effective political power has moved elsewhere (UNIFEM, 2000: 82). Most critically, however, there has been a marked increase in the 'feminization of poverty'. Gender is the strongest predictor of poverty in both developed and developing countries.

The second axes of contradiction – individualization and responsibilization – affects both men and women, although differently. This double movement points to the progressive detachment of individuals from social networks and supports while, at the same time, responsibility for social reproduction is being downloaded onto the individual (Rose, 1999: 154–155). Beck refers to this process as individualization, which differs from individualism understood either as self-actualization or as self-seeking behaviour. Instead, in sharp contrast with the experience of previous generations, individualization places steeply rising demands on people to find personal causes and responses to social problems – what Beck describes as the contemporary compulsion to find 'biographic solutions to system contradictions' (Beck and Beck-Gernsheim, 2002, chapter 1). Poverty, for example, is conceptualized and deemed remedial at the level of the individual through various self-help strategies or skills enhancement. As Bauman also notes, common problems cease to be additive – they do not add up to a common cause (quoted in ibid, xi). The paradox is that the individualization and fragmentation of inequalities into separate and individual biographies *is* our collective experience. Social inequality is on the rise precisely because the demands of individualism feed myopic and often antagonistic conceptions of collective welfare and public provision (Beck and Beck-Gernsheim, 2002: 169).

The tension between individualization and responsibilization is especially germane with respect to gender and social reproduction. Women have been invited into the workforce, in effect, to become 'genderless' workers and rational economic actors precisely at the same time as the social supports for reproductive and caring work have been progressively dismantled (Bakker, 2003). Most women, although obviously in varying degrees, find themselves squeezed between growing demands for their paid labour in order to support households and growing calls on their unpaid domestic and caring work as government austerity programs dismantle various forms of collective support and provision. Domestic labour and caring work may be purchased on the market but these costs are prohibitively high for most families. More commonly, the decline of the family wage in the North and economic instability and pervasive poverty in the South have pressured women to undertake paid labour or to participate in shadow economies in order to contribute to the family income, no matter how poor the pay or degrading the activity (Singh and Zammut, 2000). Neoliberal governance has meant fewer state services, especially for the poor, while the burden of care has fallen to communities, households and, ultimately, women. And, as Abrahamsen notes, although this downloading of responsibility is often shrouded in the language of empowerment and decentralization, there is nothing particularly democratic or empowering about shifting the burden of social reproduction to inadequately resourced social actors (2000: 58).

Thus, after two decades of neoliberal governance, there is an ever-widening gap between its promises and its lived realities for the majority of the world's people. As this experiment in governance proves unable to contain the contradictions of its own making, debates about ameliorative measures and alternate models of governance have gained momentum among both global policy elites and the anti-globalization movement. Since the Asian financial crisis of the late 1990s, in particular, there has been a pronounced shift in the policy concerns of IFIs away from a celebration of the miracles of the market to a critical examination of the very sustainability of neoliberal globalism. There are well-grounded arguments that this governing regime is incapable of reproducing itself, not the least because of recurrent financial crises, stark disparities between the North and the South, unemployment, fragile employment, jobless growth, inequality, poverty, social exclusion and environmental degradation (Beck, 2002).

We could add to this list growing frictions between neoliberal growth strategies and the requisites of social reproduction. Neoliberalism's penchant for privatizing public goods and services and renewed austerity programs have downloaded the costs of social reproduction onto civil society, households and individual women, assuming that these entities have the capacity, independent from the state, to fill the void or take up the slack. However, this vision of a restructured gender order has resisted institutionalization precisely because it rests on ill-conceived and unsustainable foundations. Prevailing discourses of gender neutrality and formal equality as well as the state's abdication from the social field did not make inequality and social needs disappear but, instead, aggravated them. Old social problems have become more severe as new ones have arisen. Under the current governing regime, most women face unsustainable pressures to be both full-time (nominally) genderless workers in the paid labour force and gendered domestic workers and caregivers in the unpaid domestic sphere. Neoliberalism's gender order is implicitly premised on the assumption that women's labour is infinitely elastic but daily experience demonstrates that there are limits and, for many women, these limits have been surpassed (Bakker, 2003).

The good governance agenda

As neoliberalism's mounting list of failures opens new spaces to rethink the objects and instruments of governance under conditions of globality, it is incumbent on citizens and policy-makers alike to exercise a cautious activism when presented with new blueprints for governance. In recent years, IFIs, especially the World Bank, the International Monetary Fund (IMF), and the United Nations have grasp upon the idea of good governance as the 'missing link' in their neoliberal policy agenda. In fact, UN Secretary-General, Kofi Annan, has identified good governance as 'the single most important factor in eradicating poverty and promoting development' (UNDP, 2002: 51). The World Bank first introduced the concept in 1989, arguing that poverty and uneven development in Africa were attributable, at least in part, to a lack of good governance. In the 1990s, both the World Bank and IMF embraced the idea that, if their market-oriented policies were to succeed, they needed to be underpinned by accountable, transparent and effective governance at the national level. Indeed, their 'new and improved' SAPs, called Poverty Reduction Strategy Papers, require that poor countries develop good governance practices in order to receive international loans and other financial aid (Taylor, 2004: 342–343).

These attempts to build a Post-Washington Consensus (PWC) that is sensitive to accountability, participation and transparency are to be applauded as a first step in long and necessarily conflictual process of rethinking how we organize our common affairs in an era of intensifying globalization. However, as Rist explains in his forceful analysis of politics of development theory, the strength of development discourse comes from its power 'to seduce, to charm, to please, to fascinate, to set dreaming, but also to abuse, to turn away from the truth, to deceive' (1997: 1). All governing strategies, in a sense, offer solutions to selected problems and ignore or deny others. Before being completely charmed, then, perhaps we should interrogate claims to 'good governance' by asking whether development strategy adequately addresses the issues of sustainable social reproduction, poverty and gender inequalities.

The good governance agenda now advanced by various international organizations and by advocates of a PWC has been critiqued on a number of fronts, not the least because of its treatment of governance as politically neutral and largely procedural, its managerialist approach to public administration, and its idealized understanding of civil society. The latter is said to be both too optimistic, underestimating the sources of conflict and oppression in civil society and too functional, representing civil society as a partner in governance rather than as a site of resistance (see Abrahamson, 2000; Phillips and Higgott, 1999). Two related issues, however, have particular relevance to the questions of gender inequality and poverty in the current era. The first is the almost exclusive emphasis of the good governance agenda on formal political rather than substantive social rights. The second relates to this strategy's sole preoccupation with the national state both as the site of democratization and of remedial action.

The good governance agenda links development and development aid by requiring poor countries to embrace the same liberal democratic institutions and processes that evolved in advanced capitalist countries over the course of two centuries of political struggle. Few would argue against democratization and the institutionalization of fair, transparent and accountable government. At the same time, linking development to the institutions of liberal democracy may detract us from more fundamental issues and from asking the right questions. First, there is an implicit assumption that countries that already have these institutions (the North) are, by definition, democratic, accountable and equitable. Growing evidence of public apathy, widespread distrust of government and crony capitalism in the North would seem to contradict this assumption. As important, the good governance agenda, by focusing on the recipient countries, implies that the established liberal democracies of the North are not implicated in the poverty or political and economic instabilities that plague many countries in the South. Centuries of imperial interventions in the domestic politics of countries of the South betray this assumption. Obviously, denial of responsibility and victim-blaming are evident in contemporary good governance discourse.

Good governance discourse also constructs democracy as being relevant only to public institutions and only within countries, thereby shielding international organizations such as the IMF and the World Bank, which are affecting global income redistribution from the South to the North, from democratic scrutiny and, ultimately, legitimizing these undemocratic instruments of global governance (Phillips and Higgott, 1999). Finally, the good governance agenda emphasizes formal democratic rights to the exclusion of social needs. Although this emphasis may be commensurate with the goal of fiscal austerity, democratic rights have little meaning for people hobbled by the indignities and insecurities of poverty. As Abrahamsen notes, for majority of people, democracy is valued not only because it offers the right to vote but also because it opens up political space for demanding social and economic rights (2000: 84). The contemporary implementation of good governance, however, constrains the range of policy options that poor governments can pursue, particularly those involving public ownership and universality.

Globalism and globality pose more fundamental challenges to contemporary notions of good governance – notably whether an exclusive focus on the national state is any longer an adequate or, indeed, an appropriate frame of reference for the reduction of poverty and social exclusion. As already discussed, economic governance is increasingly transnational, rules-based and binding, often prohibiting national governments from employing the public sector or regulation to advance social well being. Furthermore, the global deregulation of capital means that national states, especially those of developing countries, find themselves locked into a seemingly permanent referendum, conducted among IFIs, transnational corporations and bond rating agencies, on whether they have got the 'fundamentals' right.

The fundamentals are a metaphor for a host of potentially 'anti-social' policies, including fiscal austerity, off-loading, low tax regimes and minimum regulation of health, labour and environmental standards. As a result, all national states, although in varying degrees, find themselves caught up in a paradox of the social. Neoliberal globalism simultaneously minimizes spaces and strategies for social intervention and maximizes the need for it (Brodie, 2003). The almost singular focus of the good governance agenda with the formal institutions of liberal democracy and with efficient and transparent government fails to grapple with this fundamental obstacle in the pursuit of human security and social equality in a globalizing era. The glaring absence in this new formulation of governance is the spectre of the institutions of neoliberal globalism and of unregulated global capital that loom above and constrain national policy terrains.

Conclusion

One of the ultimate measures of good governance is and must be the creation and maintenance of healthy communities that are capable of providing their members with security, dignity and equity. As this chapter discusses, neoliberal globalism has disrupted previously established interconnections between economic and social governance and downloaded the weight of responsibility for social reproduction onto the shoulders of families and, especially, women. From the outset, feminists anticipated many of the gendered outcomes of neoliberal governance, such as the growth and intensification of the feminization of poverty, especially among single mothers, the elderly and racial minorities. More generally, issues of time, health and quality of life are rapidly becoming the new feminine mystique – 'the problem with no name'.

Neoliberal globalism is less a coherent ideology, however, than an amalgam of anti-social and contradictory governing strategies that invite both resistance and reformulations of the very idea of good governance in the contemporary era. In her 1984 book, *The Idea of Poverty*, social conservative Gertrude Himmelfarb describes how the social problems generated by the industrial revolution gave rise to concepts such as poverty and unemployment, to the generation of collective strategies to deal with these problems, and, most important, to a change in the 'moral imagination' of modernizing societies and their governments. The contemporary period obviously invites a revival of our moral imagination, one that demands that the goals of governance stretch beyond short-term calculations of economic efficiencies to address the grotesque income inequalities and mounting insecurities of the early twenty-first century. Good governance agendas, which promote formal democratic processes in combination with neoliberal economic strategies, do little to address the fundamental needs of social reproduction or pervasive gender inequalities. Indeed, national governments are increasingly prevented from developing social policy instruments that rely on public provision or ownership. Such governing formulae are neither democratic nor sustainable.

Previous formulations of social governance have been almost exclusively cast within the conceptual parameters of national territories and governments. Globalization does not lessen the necessity for sustained political activism aimed at maintaining and building the capacities of national governments everywhere to build secure and equitable communities. Unlike previous eras, however, a revived moral imagination and alternative strategies of social governance may very well demand that the solutions to persistent social problems of poverty and inequality be explored beyond the boundaries of national states and that the processes of economic production and social reproduction be reintegrated in entirely new ways. Globalization, in all its complexities, invites political activism and strategies of resistance that reach beyond the national state to transnational spaces. The World Social Forum (WSF), for example, constitutes a new public space, one that is 'placed but transnational', where other worlds and new visions of global citizenship are being imagined, contested and refined (Conway, 2004). This and other manifestations of global civil society, moreover, have been more self-consciously inclusive, not only of women, but a vast array of marginalized and previously excluded peoples.

Transnational civil society organizations as well as selected international governmental organizations (e.g. the United Nations Development Program) have documented the intensified exploitation of women both within countries and between the countries of the North and the South. Indeed, domestic and caring work increasingly has assumed a global form. The 'chains of care' that link women migrants to domestic and care work in the North also feed a growing crisis of care giving in the South (Clarke, 2004b: 78). From the perspective of many prominent observers, this crisis only promises to intensify in coming decades as families are fractured by the demands of new labour markets, populations migrate and age, and the spread of HIV/AIDS takes on horrific proportions (Daly and Standing, 2001: 4-6). These growing stresses on daily as well as generational reproduction weave through local social fabrics as well as across national borders in increasingly interrelated ways. As such, any meaningful interpretation of good governance in the contemporary era will require redistribution both, horizontally, through borders and across geographic and cultural expanses and, vertically, from those who have benefited disproportionately from neoliberal globalism to those it has forgotten.

Note

1 An earlier version of this chapter was presented at the Inaugural Panel at the Central American and Caribbean Regional Conference: Poverty Reduction, Good Governance, and Gender Equality. Managua, Nicaragua, 28–30 August 2002. Thanks to Malinda Smith and Louise Amoore for their helpful suggestions for revision.

References

Abrahamsen, R. (2000), *Disciplining Democracy: Development Discourse and Good Governance in Africa*, London: Zed Books.

Bakker, I. (2003), 'Neo-liberal Governance and the Reprivatization of Social Reproduction: Social Provisioning and Shifting Gender Orders', in Bakker, I. and Gill, S. (eds), *Power, Production, and Social Reproduction*, London: Macmillan Palgrave.

Bakker, I. and Gill, S. (2003), 'Global Political Economy and Social Reproduction', in Bakker, I. and Gill, S. (eds), *Power, Production, and Social Reproduction*, London: Macmillan Palgrave.

Bauman, Z. (1998), *Globalization: The Human Consequences*, New York: Columbia University Press.

Beck, U. (2000), *What is Globalization?* Translated by Patrick Camiller, London: Polity Press.

Beck, U. (2002), 'Redefining Power in a Global Economy', www.globaldimesions.net/articles/Beck/Beck.html. Downloaded March 2002.

Beck, U. and Beck-Gernsheim, E. (2002), *Individualization*, London: Sage.

Brodie, J. (1997), 'Meso Discourses, State Forms and the Gingering of Liberal-Democratic Citizenship', *Citizenship Studies*, 2:1.

Brodie, J. (2003), 'Globalization, In/security and the Paradoxes of the Social', in Bakker, I. and Gill, S. (eds), *Power, Production, and Social Reproduction*, London: Macmillan Palgrave.

Clarke, J. (2004a), 'Dissolving the Public Realm? The Logic and Limits of Neoliberalism', *International Journal of Social Policy*, 33:1.

Clarke, J. (2004b), *Changing Welfare Changing States: New Directions in Welfare Policy*, London: Sage.

Connell, R. W. (1987), *Gender and Power*, Cambridge, UK: Polity Press.

Conway, J. (2004), 'Citizenship in a Time of Empire: The World Social Forum as a New Public Space', *Citizenship Studies*, 8:4.

Daly, M. and Standing, G. (2001), 'Introduction', in Daly, M. (ed.), *Care Work: The Quest for Security*, Geneva: International Labour Organization.

Dean, M. (1999), *Governmentality: Power and Rule in Modern Society*, London: Sage.

Folbre, N. (2001), *The Invisible Heart: Economics and Family Values*, New York: The New Press.

Gill, S. (1995), 'Globalization, Market Civilization, and Disciplinary Neoliberalism', *Millennium: Journal of International Studies*, 24:3.

Haraway, D. (1991), *Simians, Cyborgs and Societies*, Oxford: Open University Press.

Held, D. and McGrew, A. (1999), 'Globalization', *Global Governance*, 5:4.

Held, D., McGrew, A., Goldblatt, D. and Perraton, J. (1999), *Global Transformations: Politics, Economics and Culture*, Stanford, CA: Standard University Press.

Himmelfarb, G. (1984), *The Idea of Poverty: England in an Industrial Age*, New York: Alfred A. Knopf.

Kaul, I., Grunberg, I. and Stern, M. (1999), *Global Public Goods*, New York: Oxford University Press.

Perez-Baltodano, A. (1999), 'Social Policy and Social Order in Transitional Societies', in Morales-Gomez, D. (ed.), *Transnational Social Policies: The New Development Challenges of Globalization*, London: Earthscan Publications.

Phillips, N. and Higgott, R. (1999), 'Global Governance and the Public Domain: Collective Goods in a Post Washington Consensus Era', CSGR Working Paper, No. 47/99, http://www.csgr.org. Downloaded June 2002.

Pierson, C. (1998), *Beyond the Welfare State: The New Political Economy of Welfare*, University Park, PA: The Pennsylvania State University Press.

Rist, G. (1997), *The History of Development: From Western Origin to Global Faith*, London: Zed Books.

Rose, N. (1999), *Powers of Freedom: Reframing Political Thought*, Cambridge, UK: Cambridge University Press.

Sassen, S. (1996), *Losing Control? Sovereignty in an Age of Globalization*, New York: Columbia University Press.

Sassen, S. (1998), *Globalization and its Discontents*, New York: The New Press.

Singh, A. and Zammut, A. (2000), 'International Capital Flows: Identifying the Gender Dimensions', *World Development*, 28:7.

Smith, M. (2002), 'Globalization, Postmodernity, and International Relations Theory', in Brodie, J. (ed.), *Critical Concepts: An Introduction to Politics*, 2nd edn, Toronto: Prentice-Hall.

Stiglitz, J. (2002), *Globalization and Its Discontents*, New York: W.W. Norton and Company.

Taylor, M. (2004), 'Good Governance in a Globalizing Era', in Brodie, J. and Rein, S. (eds), *Critical Concepts: An Introduction to Politics*, 3rd edn, Toronto: Pearson Prentice-Hall.

UNDP (1999, 2002), *Human Development Report*, New York: Oxford University Press.

UNIFEM (2000), *Progress of the World's Women: A Biannual Report*, New York: UNIFEM.

Young, B. (2000), 'The Mistress and the Maid in the Globalized Economy', in Panitch, L. and Leys, C. (eds), *Socialist Register 2001*, London: Merlin Press.

21 Toward an international social-movement unionism

Kim Moody

Source: Kim Moody (1997), *Workers in a Lean World*, London: Verso, pp. 269–292

By the late 1990s, the structure of world capitalism had become clear. Capitalism was now global, but the world economy it produced was fragmented and highly uneven. The old North–South divide had widened in terms of the incomes of the majority. The South was locked into the role of low-wage provider for corporations based in the North. Corporate-dominated systems of production crossed this North–South boundary, producing primarily for the markets of the North. The North itself was now divided into a Triad of major economic regions, which in turn crossed the North–South divide. Astride this divided world were the TNCs operating in each Triad region and beyond. The multilateral agreements and institutions that were said to regulate this process had been rigged to discipline governments and encourage centrifugal market forces. Together, these structures and forces sponsored a virtual race to the economic and social bottom for the workers of the world.

As the twenty-first century approached, however, a rebellion against capitalist globalization, its structures, and its effects had begun. The rebellion took shape on both sides of the North–South economic divide and, in varying degrees, within all three of the major Triad regions. It confronted the most basic effects of the process of globalization at the workplace level as conditions became intolerable. It confronted the conservative neoliberal agenda at the national level and, no matter how indirectly, the plans of capital's rickety multilateral regime at the international level. Its explosive force in some places surprised friends and foes alike. At the center of the rebellion were the working class and its most basic organization, the trade union.

This very class was in the midst of change: its composition was becoming more diverse in most places, as women and immigrants composed a larger proportion of the workforce, and its organizations were in flux – somewhere still declining, somewhere growing, everywhere changing. The rebellion was international in scope, but it was taking place mostly on national terrain. The need to create unity in action across racial, ethnic, and gender lines within the nation and across borders and seas was more apparent than ever. The difficulty of doing so was still daunting.

The rebellion had seemed unlikely because so many of its official leaders were reluctant warriors. The Brazilians, South Africans, Argentines, Venezuelans, Colombians, Ecuadoreans, and South Koreans might want to pick a fight with global capital or its local neoliberal representatives, but what about the "social partners" in Europe, the enterprise unionists in Japan, and the business unionists in North America? The change from paralysis to resistance could be explained by the specifics of each nation, but something lay beneath these specifics that drove labor in so many places toward confrontation.

The turn taken in so many countries in so short a period of time is all the harder to explain in the developed industrial nations because, with notable exceptions, many top trade union leaders had embraced a new "realism" that said competitive business considerations must be adhered to, cooperation with management was the means to that end, and partnership with national or regional capital was the road to employment stabilization. *Business Week* identified a new generation of European labor leaders willing to "deliver on needed cuts in pay and benefits." Among these were Nicole Notat of France's CFDT, John Monks of Britain's TUC, Humbertus Schmoldt of Germany's IG Chemie (chemical workers' union), Sergio Cofferati of Italy's formerly Communist CGIL, and Antonio Gutiérrez of Spain's similarly ex-Communist Comisiones Obreras. What they had in common was a commitment to "flexibility" in the workplace and the labor market.[1] Many more high-ranking names could be added to this roll of dishonor.

It is not so different in North America. The United Auto Workers' new president, Steve Yokich, could approve a dozen or so local strikes against GM, but still permit even more flexibility in the national contracts negotiated in 1996. The new president of the AFL–CIO could call for more militancy in organizing, but call on business leaders to engage in partnership. In Canada, reluctant leaders from the Canadian divisions of the American-dominated international unions resisted the Days of Action behind the scenes, but were forced to go along in the end. Even within some of the newer labor movements of the Third World, voices of moderation and "partnership" could be heard. Yet, the strikes continued.

The reason for this lay partly in the very nature of trade unions. They are ambiguous organizations. On the one hand, they are poised to fight capital in defense of labor. On the other hand, at the top level, they attempt to hold the lines of defense through long-term stable bargaining relations, a rudimentary type of social partnership. The step to a more ideological or even institutional "partnership" between the labor bureaucracy and capital's bureaucracy is not always a big one. But then the winds of economic change and competition come along and the house of cards collapses.

The lines of defense can no longer be held through the routine exercise of the bargaining relationship. A fight is called for and sometimes waged by these same leaders. Typically, it is waged in the name of the old stable relationship. For the top leaders there is no contradiction. There is, however, an underlying contradiction between the new demands of capital and the union's old line of defense. Stability is gone, but the paradise lost of stability and normal bargaining continues to inform the actions of the leaders even when they are confrontational. Their actions sometimes push forward even though their eyes are focused clearly on the past. That this contradiction is likely to limit the effectiveness of the unions is obvious, but it does not preclude such action.

This new generation of top labor leaders took office in a moment of transition across much of the developed industrial world. Most of them built their upward-bound careers during the long period of paralysis and restructuring of the 1980s. They tended to embrace the cooperation agenda of those years as something appropriate to the new global era. Expedience often took on a more ideological shape as the new leaders saw themselves as exponents of a "new realism" or "industrial democracy." They did so without strong opposition from a membership still in shock from the enormous changes. The activists in the workplace might be more suspicious of the new ambience of cooperation that inevitably pushed for more work and longer hours, on the one hand, and destroyed good jobs, on the other. But for most of this period they could not move their rank-and-file to action. The activists were themselves divided over what to do.

But the pressures of lean production, neoliberal austerity, and international competition bore down on more and more sectors of the working classes of more and more nations. The mass strikes of 1994–97 did not come out of nowhere. In most countries where these occurred there was already a pre-history of resistance in specific workplaces. Strikes in France's public-sector industries, such as Air France, France Télécom, the national railroad, and Paris transit began in 1992 or 1993. In fact, they began even earlier among rail workers and nurses in 1987, led by the rank-and-file "coordinations." Spain saw a long string of strikes in important industries as well as earlier mass strikes in 1993 and 1994. Italy had seen strikes called by unofficial "Cobas" among public-sector workers. In the US strikes returned in both the public and private sectors in the early 1990s.[2]

By the time the new leaders took office in the 1990s the mood of the ranks and of the activists was already beginning to change – or become more torn between fear and action. While fear of job loss remained a powerful force among the ranks and activists, it had become impossible to believe the promises of human resources management (HRM), team concept, total quality, or whatever name the new ways of working were known by. The new workplace, whether in the private or public sector, was worse, not better, in most cases. Job loss continued through downsizing and re-engineering. And national social safety nets were being cut back or even dismantled – threatening public employment, on the one hand, and the quality of life for more and more workers, on the other.

The return to action in the 1990s differed from the industrial upheaval of 1967–75 in a number of ways. While it was not on the scale of the 1960s, not yet an upheaval, it was more general – affecting not only more developed nations, but also many of the industrializing nations of the Third World. Like the processes that pushed more groups of workers into action, the rebellion itself was more truly global than any in the past. It pointed to one of the more suggestive strategic ideas of the period: the potential for joint action between the old unions in the North, which were beginning to change, and the new social movement unions in the most industrial nations of the South, which provided a model suited to the new era.

To a greater extent than the 1967–75 upheaval or that of the 1930s or 1940s, this was a rebellion led by public-sector workers.[3] While it was often the more "blue-collar" workers who initiated these events, this wave of mass strikes saw health-care workers, teachers, and others play an important role almost everywhere. Indeed, the more heavily female public-sector occupations swelled the ranks of these mass strikes from the beginning in many countries, reflecting the new role of women in both the workforce and the unions.

Looked at both nationally and internationally, the strikes and struggles that emerged in the mid-1990s reflected many of the changes in the workforce that were supposed to represent fragmentation. In the heat of mass action, however, international differences, ethnic and gender diversity, and old sectoral divisions, for example between public- and private-sector unions, appeared as strengths among both the strikers and the working-class public that expressed almost universal support for these movements. The 1996 strike by Oregon state workers might seem less spectacular than France's 1995 public-sector general strike, but it mobilized the same diversity of manual, service, and professional men and women workers of many races. Similarly, Ontario's one-day general strikes might appear almost tame compared with the struggles in South Korea or France, but this same mixture, in which women play a much larger role and racial and occupational diversity are taken as the norm, was apparent.

The new leaders who came to head many unions and federations in this changing context reflected the past in both ideology and, with some notable exceptions, ethnic or gender composition. Whether or not they were popular, they would certainly linger on for some time as the hesitant generals in a fight they never chose. While debate was growing and in some places oppositional movements forming, the ability of top leaders to hold on is one of the great problems of most trade-union structures. The lack of democracy and leadership accountability was a basic flaw and, under the new circumstances, a serious weakness for unions pushed into a fight. So, the fight for union democracy would have to become part of the agenda for change, if unions were to play an effective role.

Nowhere was the need for political change more apparent than in the area of internationalism. The top leaders who assumed office in the 1990s were certainly more aware of the international dimensions of collective bargaining than those they replaced. Indeed, global competitiveness routinely provided the argument for making concessions and taking retreats in stride. As globally minded as they might be in this sense, however, they still saw the unions and federations they governed in national and nationalist terms, as Dan Gallin pointed out.[4] Writing in *Labor Notes* after reading AFL-CIO president John Sweeney's book, *America Needs a Raise*, one German shop steward said, "I was shocked about the extreme nationalist viewpoint of Brother Sweeney."[5] But, in truth, much the same could be said of the leaders of most national labor federations in the industrial countries. Indeed, that is precisely what acceptance of the corporate competitiveness agenda means – a commitment to a specious "job security" at the national level by supporting the globally active employers of that country.

So, while the contours and vulnerabilities of international production chains may be well enough known in labor circles, very few unions actually acted on this basis. There were important exceptions, such as the UE's new plan to build cross-border networks on an industrial or corporate basis, FLOC's alliance with SNTOAC, Comisiones Obreras' attempts to build alliances with related unions in North Africa, or the CAW-Teamster-TGWU alliance at Air Canada, or the Canadian Auto Workers' work with unions in Mexico. Yet, while most union leaders across the industrial world were quick to send messages or even delegations of solidarity to South Korea or South Africa, or to attend the consensus or ceremonial meetings that pass for official labor internationalism, the more difficult work of building cross-border industrial alliances and networks remained a low priority. The International Trade Secretariats could have played a bigger role in this, but were limited by the nationalism of the affiliates that tend to dominate them.

The problem is not simply that today's leaders for the most part don't do enough on the international level. Most of the struggle against the structures and effects of globalization necessarily occurs on a national plane. That, after all, is where workers live, work, and fight. That also is the lesson of the first round of mass strikes and even the more localized struggles against the global regime of capital. The most basic feature of an effective internationalism for this period is the ability of the working class to mount opposition to the entire agenda of transnational capital and its politicians in their own "back yard." For this agenda, too, is ultimately carried out at the national level. It is the caution in the occasional battle and the open embrace of the enemy in the daily relationship of labor bureaucracy to corporate bureaucracy that is the fundamental problem. It is the ideology of partnership held by so many union leaders and institutionalized in the publications, educational programs, and official positions of the unions and federations that is a barrier to a clear course of action.

The often reluctant leadership is, nevertheless, engaging in battles with capital and the state at the national level. This new level of struggle, in turn, has a transformative power. It is in these kinds of struggle that people and their consciousness change. The inactive or fearful rank and file become the heroes of the street, whether it is in a mass demonstration or a more limited fight around workplace issues. Perceptions of what is possible change as new forces come into the struggle and the power of the class, long denied and hidden, becomes visible. Yesterday's competing ethnic or gender group is today's ally. The activists who have agitated for this fight now have a base; the conservatives in the union are, for the moment, isolated.

It is not possible to predict whether we are entering a period of intensified class struggle or whether the actions of recent years will fade as rapidly as they appeared. The political and economic pressures that produced these strikes and movements, however, will not go away. Neither lean production nor the rule of the market has alleviated the crisis of profitability. Indeed, the storms of international competition are, if anything, more destructive today. If history is any guide, the current period of renewed class conflict is likely to continue for at least a few years, perhaps a decade. These are the kinds of period in which bigger changes in the organization of the class become possible. This, in turn, alters what is possible in the realm of politics.

It is in such periods that the working class can glimpse the possibilities of social change or even revolution. It is in this kind of milieu of struggle and mass motion that answers to Margaret Thatcher's question about free market capitalism, "What is the alternative?", become more apparent. It is also in such periods that certain demands and changes in working-class organization come to the fore: the demand for the eight-hour day in the 1880s; workplace organization and shop stewards in 1914–21; industrial unionism in the 1930s; the forty-hour work week in the 1930s. These ideas motivated millions across the world in earlier times and gave focus to the strike movements, political fights, and new organizations that arose in those times.

The vision appropriate to the era of globalization is social-movement unionism. It has already been born in South Africa, Brazil, South Korea, and elsewhere in the more industrialized parts of the Third World. Within the industrial North it is implied in many of the ideas put forth by oppositional groups within unions, national cross-union networks of union activists, international solidarity networks and committees, official and unofficial cross-border networks, and the only global grassroots industrially based network, TIE. These forces are small, even marginal in some cases, but they speak with a clear voice and offer ideas pertinent to the epoch of capitalist globalization.

Social-movement unionism and union democracy

Social-movement unionism isn't about jurisdiction or structure, as is craft or industrial unionism. As Sam Gindin writes in his history of the Canadian Auto Workers, it is about "orientation." He writes:

> It means making the union into a vehicle through which its members can not only address their bargaining demands but actively lead the fight for everything that affects working people in their communities and the country. Movement unionism includes the shape of bargaining demands, the scope of union activities, the approach to issues of change, and above all, that sense of commitment to a larger movement that might suffer defeats, but can't be destroyed.[6]

This isn't just a warmed-over version of "political unionism," once common in Latin America and Europe, in which unions support one or another party of the left. Nor is it the same as the liberal or social-democratic "coalitionism" that sees unions and social movements as elements in an electoral coalition. In both of these versions of organized labor's role, the unions and their members are essentially passive troops in an orderly parade to the polls.

In social-movement unionism neither the unions nor their members are passive in any sense. Unions take an active lead in the streets, as well as in politics. They ally with other social movements, but provide a class vision and content that make for a stronger glue than that which usually holds electoral or temporary coalitions together. That content is not simply the demands of the movements, but the activation of the mass of union members as the leaders of the charge – those who in most cases have the greatest social and economic leverage in capitalist society. Social-movement unionism implies an active strategic orientation that uses the strongest of society's oppressed and exploited, generally organized workers, to mobilize those who are less able to sustain self-mobilization: the poor, the unemployed, the casualized workers, the neighborhood organizations.

The current debate in the US labor movement is often organized around the counterposition of the old business-union "service model" versus the newer "mobilizing" or "organizing" models. While the organizing or mobilizing concepts are obviously an improvement on the passive-service model, most versions of this counterposition narrow the debate in at least two ways. First, they leave the question of union hierarchy, the lack of membership control or leadership accountability, out of the debate. This is usually intentional, since much of this debate goes on among labor professionals and staff organizers who are employed by the hierarchy.[7]

As union organizer Michael Eisenscher argues, however, democracy is closely related to a union's ability effectively to mobilize and act. In a vein similar to what was said by the KCTU leader who linked democracy, solidarity, and mobilization, he writes:

> In confronting more powerful economic and social forces, democracy is an instrument for building solidarity, for establishing accountability, and for determining appropriate strategies – all of which are critical for sustaining and advancing worker and union interests. Union democracy is not synonymous with either union activism or militancy. Members can be mobilized for activities over which they have little or no control, for objectives determined for them rather than by them. Given that unions are institutions for the exercise of workers' power, their responsiveness to membership aspirations and needs is determined, in part, by the extent to which members can and do assert effective control over their political objectives, bargaining strategies, disposition of resources, accountability of staff and officers, and innumerable other aspects of organizational performance.[8]

Second, casting the debate as simply one between the "organizing" and "service" models also narrows the discussion by focusing exclusively on the union as an institution – its growth through organizing or its effectiveness in bargaining through occasional membership mobilization from above. But the idea of social-movement unionism is a labor movement "whose constituencies spread far beyond the factory gates and whose demands include broad social and economic change," as one study of the South African and Brazilian labor movements put it.[9] It is a movement in which unions provide much of the economic leverage and organizational resources, while social-movement organizations, like the popular urban movements in Latin America, provide greater numbers and a connection to the less well organized or positioned sections of the working class.

The activation of union members in order to reach and mobilize these broader constituencies is interwoven with the question of union democracy and leadership accountability. The members must have a hand in shaping the union's agenda at both the bargaining and the broad social level if they are going to invest the time and energy demanded by this kind of unionism. To look at it from another angle, as a leader of the opposition in the Transport Workers' Union in New York City put it, "democracy is power."[10]

It is typical of social-movement unions like those in Brazil, South Africa, and Canada that open debates on tough issues take place regularly. To be sure, these unions, too, face a tendency toward bureaucratization. But the members have enough experience in union affairs to resist this trend. In America's bureaucratic business unions or Europe's top-down political unions, the opening of debate is something new and very incomplete. It often has to be forced by grassroots-based opposition movement from within.

Members' involvement in union affairs and power over their leaders are also key to new organizing and recruitment if unions are to become powerful once again. Experience shows that active union members are better recruiters than paid organizers. A recent study done in the United States showed that unions won 73% of representation elections when members did the organizing, compared with 27% when it was done by professional organizers.[11] A passive membership is not likely to devote the time it takes to organize other workers, and passivity is largely a product of bureaucracy.

The fight for union democracy does not come out of nowhere. It is usually a function of conflict within the unions – differences over direction. It is typically the "dissidents" fighting from the ranks or the activist layer for some sort of alternative program of action who demand greater democracy. This process is visible not only in the US, where challenges and "reform" movements have become widespread, but across many of the older unions in the developed industrial nations.

Harmonizing collective bargaining and class interests

The demands put forth by unions are another key to social-movement unionism. In many countries unions are seen as, or cast by the experts as, the organizations of a privileged minority, a sort of "labor aristocracy." Overcoming this is not simply a matter of the union raising some broad political demands. Most unions, even very conservative ones, do that already. It is, rather, a matter of shaping even the union's bargaining demands in a way that has a positive impact on other working-class people, harmonizing the demands of the union with the broader needs of the class.

A good example of shaping bargaining demands in a broader social direction was the Canadian Auto Workers' (CAW) 1996 collective-bargaining program at the major auto companies. Unlike the United Auto Workers in the US that year, the CAW put forth an aggressive bargaining program that would increase employment in the industry and the country. Shorter work time, restrictions on outsourcing, and guaranteed job levels for the communities in which each plant was located was the heart of the bargaining program. With a bargaining program aimed at protecting and even increasing employment opportunities in the affected communities, it was easy to rally support from the working class of the region.

The CAW reached agreement with Ford and Chrysler, but General Motors (GM) was intent on increasing its level of outsourced production and balked. The CAW struck at GM for twenty-one days, but the turning point came when union members seized a plant from which GM was attempting to remove dies in order to resume production elsewhere. Far from alienating the public, the CAW's dramatic action and subsequent victory were widely supported. As the CAW's Dave Robertson told an audience of US auto workers:

> We also saw solidarity in how the community responded. We were not seen as an isolated aristocracy of labor, but as a social movement that was fighting to preserve communities. And that has to do with how we defined the union.[12]

It is not only the mass political strikes that have been perceived as having broader social implications. Struggles at the workplace or employer level that create jobs or preserve important public services are increasingly seen in this light as well. The various strikes at GM plants in the US, the 1996 CAW contract fight at GM, the French truckers' strike of 1996, the week-long strike by Oregon public workers, and many others were seen by much of the working-class public as a defense of jobs and/or public services that affected much of the working class of the area. In some cases social goals can be both political and bargaining demands. After a California ballot initiative for patient rights failed in 1996, the militant socially minded California Nurses' Association incorporated these rights into their 1997 collective-bargaining program.[13]

In countries where mass political strikes are unlikely in the foreseeable future, this harmonization of the interests of the workers covered in collective bargaining and the broader working-class public can begin to move unions toward a broader social agenda. Harmonization can touch on many of the issues of the crisis of working-class life. For example, when local unions win additional jobs, they also alleviate the health-and-safety or stress epidemic within the plants, taking some pressure off family life as well as improving workplace conditions. Contract demands for child care, pay equity (equal pay for comparable work), immigrant rights on the job, and affirmative action (positive discrimination in the UK) in hiring and promotions to reduce racial and gender inequalities at work can provide bridges across racial, national, and gender lines. White and/or male workers are much less likely to see such demands as threatening if the unions are fighting for and winning more jobs, relief from workplace stress, and growing incomes.

Most of the rebellion against capitalist globalization and its impact occurs on national terrain or even at the level of the workplace. Mass political strikes are, after all, directed at national or local states, which are still the mediators of the international regime. But even these strikes cannot be sustained or repeated regularly. Furthermore, the power and durability of the movement will depend on the strength of organization at the industry and workplace levels. Among other things this means there can not be a trade-off between organizing and recruitment, on the one hand, and strong democratic workplace organization, on the other.

The Teamsters Union in the US is a positive example of deepening democracy and extending recruitment by involving the rank and file. The holding of more democratic elections in 1991, the deepening reform process, which included eliminating one level of bureaucracy and opening more local unions to democratic control, and the successful effort to mobilize members as organizers at Overnite Transportation and elsewhere, have served as a model of how democracy and mobilization go hand in hand.

Internationalizing union practice

To say that most struggle is ultimately national or even local is not to say that international links, coordination, organization, and action are not critical to the success of social-movement unionism in today's globalizing international economy. Internationalism must be part of the perspective and practice of union leaders, activists, and members if global capital is to be contained at all.

The analysis presented earlier points toward the centrality of international production chains in developing a multi-layered strategy for dealing with TNCs. While only a minority of workers are employed directly by TNCs, their potential impact at the heart of the world economy gives these workers a uniquely strategic position. Clearly, the TNCs dominate many nominally independent employers, set the world-wide trends in working conditions, and preserve the unequal wage levels that perpetuate competition among workers even in the same TNC. These giant corporations have deep pockets to resist strikes or other forms of action, but they are also vulnerable at many points of their cross-border production chains.

The strong tendency of cross-border production systems to be located within one or another of the Triad regions gives unions in that region the more manageable task of making the links, exchanging information on company tactics or conditions, and eventually coordinating actions with specific goals and demands on a regional basis. The similar tendency of many industries to be geographically concentrated within each nation also lessens some of the difficulties in organizing and coordinating actions that one would find in a truly global production system. Mapping the course of production and ownership and its weak points is by now a fairly well known science.

Simply drawing up abstract plans for crippling internationalized production will be an exercise in futility, however, if the unions involved are too bureaucratic to mobilize their members for the fight and the leaders are committed to partnership and the nationalist thinking it implies. The International Trade Secretariats, which would be a logical forum for international coordination, tend to be dominated by partnership-minded union leaders from the US, Japan, Germany, and Britain. It should be obvious that the real difficulties and conflicts of interest between groups of workers in different countries are daunting enough. Union leaders who are ideologically and institutionally committed to the "competitiveness" of TNCs based in their own country through some kind of partnership program are unlikely to have the vision to overcome these very real stumbling blocks.

Much the same can be said of regionally based cross-border alliances. Simple alliances between leaders, like that between the leaders of the CWA, STRM, and CEP in the NAFTA region, will not be sufficient. At best, they will conduct worthwhile pressure campaigns such as the Sprint 'Conexión Familiar' campaign. At worst, such an alliance will only reflect the existing caution of the union bureaucracy. This could be the fate of the cross-border contacts provided by the European Works Councils as well, if they are not based on workplace representation. Just as national leaders often need to be pushed into bolder actions from below, so cross-border alliances of these same leaders will need to be pressured from the ranks, and local unions to turn these top-down connections into action and grapple with the workplace crisis facing most workers.

The importance of official efforts like the UE–FAT alliance has been their willingness to involve workplace-level activists and leaders. The UE proposal to bring together local unions within the same company across borders will be one of the first official experiments in North America to attempt such grassroots linkages. So far, however, it is the exception.

The unofficial transnational worker networks, like those organized through TIE or the UAW Local 879-Ford Workers' Democratic Movement pact, have an important transformative role to play as more unions experiment with different types of cross-border activities. By themselves, they lack the power and resources of the unions, but they have roots in the workplaces of the industries where they exist. Their role in the overall process of union transformation, of creating an international social-movement unionism, is not primarily as a pressure group. Rather it is to set examples and to act as ginger groups that set people in motion. Right now it is difficult for them to do more than provide information and an overview, but in doing so they contribute to the growth of a current working to change their unions and to a deepening of the international outlook of workplace activists.

All this occurs in a context where enormous economic and social pressures are pushing workers and their unions to act, where action is transforming more and more people and widening their perspectives, and where the old unions have increasingly become the sites of internal challenges and debates over direction. In this situation, the transnational worker networks should serve not as internal opposition groups, but as daily educators on the importance of international work, and the cultural and political tools needed to carry it out. The conferences, meetings, and tours conducted by these networks have an important role in broadening the outlook of the activist layer in particular. Such actions as the networks can mount also play a worker-to-worker educational role, just as local and national actions do.

Local strikes in key locations can be part of this strategy where they can close down international production systems in whole or part. Thus, in situations where a workplace union is part of the transnational worker network, they can go beyond education and symbolic actions actually to influence management decisions, whether this is in defense of victimized workers at home or abroad, or in a fight for common demands in the interests of the workers in all the affected countries. Common cross-border actions by local unions in different countries can cripple even the largest TNCs in their major markets. As the perception of this possibility becomes more widely recognized, the rules of the game will change.

[...]

Against neoliberalism: a labor politics for the moment

"Trade unions may be characterized as oppositions that never become governments," writes Dutch sociologist Jelle Visser. Today, labor movements in a growing number of countries have embraced this role with surprising enthusiasm. They have risen to this task in the realization that their power depends to a significant extent not only on their place in production, but on the social safety net they have won over the years. Capital and its neoliberal allies seek to dismantle this state-sponsored safety net from much the same understanding – that the welfare state supports the ability of workers and their unions to hold on through tough times.

As "oppositions that never become governments," unions must fight from the outside. Indeed, in today's world, workers and their unions are more and more cast as outsiders when they refuse or resist the corporate competitiveness agenda and the race to the bottom it implies. The alternative on offer is the paralysis of partnership. Many union leaders hope to have it both ways, but capital's contemporary agenda and the very goals the unions are fighting for, when they fight, are too much at odds. In taking to the streets in opposition to government austerity plans and cut-backs, the unions have found different allies across the working class. Top leaders will continue, to waver between these alternatives, at times undermining the struggle, but the direction of this struggle seems clear.

In the realm of politics, it is largely a defensive direction for the moment. The defense of welfare measures, pensions, health-care provision, unemployment benefits, and existing public services has been the motivation for most of the mass and general strikes of the past few of years. It has also become necessary to defend social gains of specific groups, such as affirmative action or immigrant rights, where they exist. Occasionally, in the area of collective bargaining, unions make some advances, as with the French truckers or the fight for the shorter work week in Germany, but mostly it is inherent in the period that most struggles will be defensive until labor builds and expands its power nationally and internationally.

There is a tendency on the political left and among supporters of organized labor to see defensive struggles as somehow bad or inadequate. Yet, almost all labor upheavals and advances in history have originated in defensive struggles – when employers and/or governments attempt to take back something previously won or simply make matters worse.

In this process, the defensive struggles provide the time and context in which labor recruits and builds or rebuilds its organizations. The siren voices of "partnership," however, advise that defensive struggles are: (a) hopeless in this global economy, or (b) conservative and backward-looking. They propose instead various forms of broader social partnership that are supposed to mend the economy, providing, of course, that unions abandon their hopeless fight for material improvements on the job, in incomes, or in broader social provisions. These various forms of social partnership or social contract are meant as alternatives to struggle – an easy road to renewed prosperity.

A version of this is the liberal-populist view expressed by writers such as Jeremy Rifkin in the US and Will Hutton in the UK that advocates a sort of "stakeholder" capitalism, in which the various organizations of "civil society" act as a counterweight to, or attempt to take on some institutional role within, major corporations, banks, and other financial institutions that can influence the direction of major business decisions.[14] They emphasize the idea of a "social contract" between capital and "civil society" or "Third Sector" of non-governmental organizations and volunteers that would create a more kind and gentle capitalism. Others call for the use of pension funds as a means of influencing the direction of investments.[15]

All of these schemes share an unspoken view of today's TNCs as passive institutions making bad decisions on the basis of short-sighted views of profitability. There is also an assumption in most cases that these global actors can be controlled at the national level through increased representation by "stakeholders" (like unions or various community organizations) or actual stockholders working through pension funds. In this version, big figures are thrown around to show the potential power of pension funds, should they ever come under democratic control. For example, in the US, pension funds control 25% of all stocks. What is not mentioned is that the other 75% of stocks are safely in the hands of the nation's wealthiest 10% of families (25% of all stocks) and the financial institutions (50%) that these same families disproportionately influence or own.

The usual argument for pension-fund capitalism is that this is a way democratically to affect society's investment priorities. In fact, in the US, one of the few countries, along with the UK, where pension funds have any importance, stocks have not been a source of investment funds for decades. Capital expenditures come almost entirely from internally generated profits. From the early 1950s, internal funds covered 95% of capital expenditures, and since 1990, 109%. Since the early 1980s, more stock has "disappeared" than been issued. The reason is that stocks have become one of capital's more recent competitive weapons in the war for market share, the merger and acquisition boom of the 1980s and 1990s – $1.5 trillion in mergers and acquisitions and $500 billion in buybacks.[16] This is a game pension funds cannot play.

These various stakeholder and stockholder proposals always rest on an analysis that dissolves real power relations. The capitalist corporation becomes just one more porous institution with neutral goals and various "stakeholders" whose interests can be harmonized with one another and with society as a whole. As one group of British researchers said in reference to Will Hutton's rendition, "the vision rests on a political fantasy about general benefits for all stakeholders and their economic analysis does not confront the structural reality of redistributive conflict between stakeholders."[17] The most obvious conflict is that between the workers and the real owners, but there are others as well, such as that between business customers and households in setting prices or rates.

In other versions, ownership becomes "social" simply because the capitalist class shares ownership through stocks, bonds, mutual funds, and other claims on wealth. As the Austrian Marxist Rudolph Hilferding pointed out in 1910, however, stock ownership was actually a way of centralizing capital. It allowed the biggest capitalists to expand their business by using the capital of many small stockholders; it didn't decrease their control or power, but enhanced it.[18] The modern mergers and acquisitions are just the contemporary form of this reality. Indeed, the biggest buyers of stocks in recent years have been corporations engaged in mergers and acquisitions. Since the early 1980s, fully $1.4 trillion in stock has been gobbled up in mergers and acquisitions, while another $500 billion has gone to corporate buybacks of stock – all enhancing the power of those at the center of control.[19]

Even more remarkable than the attempt to turn stock ownership into some form of social democracy is the assessment of the capitalist state on which Rifkin's vision of a "Third Sector" rests heavily. Knowing that the NGOs and volunteer organizations that compose this "Third Sector" are themselves financially strapped, he proposed a number of government funding programs. In order to make this sound realistic, he argues that government is becoming "less tied to the interests of the commercial economy and more aligned with the interests of the social economy."[20] It is hard to imagine just which contemporary government he could possibly be talking about.

The problems with all these alternatives to struggle is that today's corporations, led by the TNCs, are clearly predators waging class war to expand their world-wide empires and restore the legendary profit rates of decades ago. Governments are following their lead, coming more and more under the influence of "the commercial economy," not less. Under these circumstances something more than an amorphous "civil society" is needed as a counterweight, and that is the organized working class and its allies. Finally, of course, there is nothing in these proposals that guarantees real job creation, since the basic mechanisms of investment and internal profitability are left untouched.

The current emphasis on social safety-net issues and increased equality within the class, material issues from which working-class people can gain and strengthen their position, offers the best way to gather in broader forces and increase the power of the working class. All the various schemes for representation in the institutions of capital end up as versions of partnership in which unions or other members of "civil society" are dragged into the war that is real capitalist competition, which is more likely to destroy jobs than create them. Labor cannot advance through such competition. Its historic role is to limit and eventually suppress this destructive force. Social safety-net demands are one more way in which unions and their working-class allies can "take labor out of competition."

The fight for shorter work time, labor's major offensive issue, can and should also become a political fight as it did in the nineteenth century and the 1930s. The struggle to preserve publicly funded pensions, Social Security in the US, is a part of this fight to reduce total work time. But a national standard of thirty-five hours a week or less (with no pay reductions and no strings) implemented through legislation would contribute immediately to employment growth, strengthening the position of the working class. It is obvious that in most countries the old political parties of the left and the working class are unwilling, perhaps unable, to wage such a fight. It falls once again to the "oppositions that never become governments."

In the realm of international policy, renegotiating trade agreements would be part of a long-range program. But in terms of the politics of the moment, there is one goal that would do more to bring about "upward leveling" across the world than any other – cancellation of the Third World debt. For the Third World, debt to the banks of the North has been like a mortgage that never ends. As of 1994, according to the World Bank, this debt stood at 2.5 trillion, compared with $906 billion in 1980, about the time the Third World debt crisis surfaced.[21] This is an increase of over 250% in spite of the fact that almost all new Third World borrowing has been to pay off the initial debt, which in effect has been paid off many times over.

The cancellation of this debt or even its progressive reduction would free billions of dollars in interest paid annually to banks or bond-holders in the North by governments of the South. Where unions and other organizations were able to fight for the proper distribution of the new resources this would free up, social programs that provide the necessary safety net for so many in the Third World could be restored or even expanded. The parameters of struggle would be altered across the Third World. Obviously, a constructive redistribution of this potential wealth would require strong labor movements in both North and South. But it is a common goal that could do much to bind the movements in these two parts of the world that capital has sought to play against one another.

Toward a world-wide social-movement union current

The pressures of globalization and lean production, the transforming powers of renewed struggle, and the fresh forces that have come to the working class in recent decades are all pushing the working class and its organizations in a more aggressive and confrontational direction. Because so many top leaders still think and act in terms of the corporate competitiveness/partnership agenda, this process often begins with or includes internal union conflict. Debate and challenges are more common within unions and there are new social-movement unions in parts of the economic South to provide "role models" for activists in the North. Yet, there is nothing inevitable about the outcomes of these debates or challenges.

As noted earlier, the newest generation of top leaders in much of the North are the products of the 1980s, deeply committed to one or another form of partnership with capital. In fact, the end of the Cold War and the gathering in of more federations and unions in the ICFTU and the ITSs, on the one hand, and the rise in influence of the US, German, Japanese, and British leaders in these bodies, on the other, mean that the partnership advocates have a wider audience than in the past. They have behind them a seductive chorus of social-democratic politicians, and threats and promises from many of the TNCs themselves.

The context for a debate over the direction of world labor may be more favorable, but a fight is required. An international current is needed to promote the ideas and practices of social-movement unionism. The material for such a current is already at hand in unions such as those in South Korea, South Africa, Brazil, and other newer unions in Asia; in major tendencies within changing Latin American unions; in a few unions in the North, like the Canadian Auto Workers, the United Electrical Workers in the US, and SUD in France, among others; in oppositional or reform groups within unions; in the national networks of activists around publications such as *Labor Notes*; those in the international solidarity networks such as APWSL, CJM, US–GLEP, and the Maquiladora Workers' Support Committee; and the industrial networks of TIE.

Obviously, this is a diverse current and not an ideologically defined, left political tendency. It includes people from a variety of tendencies and even more of those with no left background. It contains organizations as different as unions and oppositional networks. It is world-wide, cutting across the North–South divide and spanning the three Triad regions.

What this current shares is not a single organization or a central leadership, but a view of what unionism can be in today's globalizing world. Central to this view of social-movement unionism are union democracy and leadership accountability, membership activation and involvement, a commitment to union growth and recruitment, a vision and practice that reach beyond even an expanding union membership to other sectors and organizations of the working class. This view sees unions as taking an active, leading role in the struggles against international and domestic capital and their neoliberal political allies.

Social-movement unionism is an orientation guided by these ideas and visions. It is not an attempt to reshape national labor-relations systems or make all unions have the same structure. While an industrial strategic approach is important, social-movement unionism can guide the actions of today's typical, merged general unions, as the case of the CAW indicates. It can be the practice and outlook of a single occupational union such as the California Nurses' Association, or of a government department or agency-based union such as SUD in France's telecom and postal systems. It can be a region of a national labor federation, such as the Catalan CCOO. What matters most is that its practice is a rank-and-file practice and not simply a matter of the progressive politics of a small group of leaders.

Above all, social-movement unionism is a perspective to be fought for on an international scale. The recognition of a common perspective by activists in different countries will both facilitate an internationalist practice and reinforce the struggle for this orientation at every level of existing working-class organization. It is a perspective that can maximize working-class power by drawing together the different sectors within the class around those organizations with the greatest existing and potential power at this juncture, the unions. It is a perspective that embraces the diversity of the working class in order to overcome its fragmentation. While it is not about "reforming" the old mass parties of the left, it is far more likely to move them off center than any amount of lobbying or conventional "boring within." It is, above all, a means, a rehearsal, for self-emancipation from below.

Conclusion

The reorganization of the world economy through the process of capitalist globalization paralysed much of the working class of the North for almost two decades. In many industrial nations, unions have declined as a proportion of the workforce, while the changing organization of work has appeared to fragment the class and its organizations permanently. The same process produced new labor movements in some parts of the South, while reviving older unions in other Third World areas. International labor appeared to be marching out of step.

By the mid-1990s, rebellion and militancy were sweeping through large parts of both the North and the South. The pressures associated with capitalist globalization pushed more working people into action. Furthermore, the shape and consequences of unregulated international economic integration became more apparent. The impersonal forces of the world market took on the faces of the neoliberal politicians charged with removing the final barriers to market control. Yesterday's invisible hand became highly visible, the process, in effect, politicized. The state had not disappeared so much as changed direction. States make good targets for mass discontent and the unions in many countries finally stepped into the vacuum left by the retreating parties that they had once supported – or even still did. Not surprisingly, public-sector unions led this rebellion. For the first time in decades, international labor was once again marching in step.

Beneath the surface, workplace rebellion also returned, particularly where the new ways of working had been in place for a while. The pressures on the workforce that Stephen Roach had spoken of had begun to produce the "worker backlash" he had warned of. Most of it was workplace guerrilla warfare, jostling over just how lean and mean conditions would be. But now and then it broke out as a militant action by the whole workforce. Increasingly, it took the form of new groups of workers organizing or joining unions. They spaned all countries and sectors: public and private, industry and service. While unions in some industrial countries had seriously declined, there was more hope of a reversal in fortunes. Globally, independent unionism now embraced more of working humanity than at any time in history.

The merging of workplace struggles with bigger political fights by labor across international lines offers a unique opportunity to revitalize unions and draw on the strengths and numbers of other working-class organizations and communities. The biggest as well as the most basic fights still occur at the national level, but the opportunity and necessity to reach across borders are greater than ever. The contours of globalizing capitalism are now apparent, as are its weak points. If a small group of English dock workers can reach across the planet and pull off a world-wide action, imagine what unions and international labor bodies with a clear purpose and the democratic organization to activate their members could do.

For this to happen, a new leadership more in tune with the times will have to arise from an angry and activated rank and file – not above them, but with them. Social-movement unionism, by whatever name, can be the democratic vision and the practice around which such a new leadership can rally and reach out across the many lines capitalism draws between people. If the struggles against the effects of globalization continue, as they most likely will, and more people are drawn into action, the leaders among them will be better able to look around and see that, as one African-American labor educator likes to say: "We are the leaders we've been looking for."[22]

Notes

1 *Business Week*, December 16, 1996, pp. 61–65.
2 Edwards, P. K., Hyman, R. (1994) "Strikes and industrial conflict: peace in europe?" in Hyman, R., Ferner, A., *New Frontiers in European Industrial Relations*, Cambridge: Cambridge University press, pp. 250–280; Bensaid, D. (1996) "Neo-liberal reform and popular rebellion," *New Left Review* 215, January/February; interviews with CGT officials, Air France, September 1994; Moody, K. (1995) "NAFTA and the corporate redesign of North America," *Latin American Perspectives*, 22:1, pp. 81–91.
3 For a detailed view of the upheaval of 1967–75 in various US industries see, Perusek, G. and Worcester, K., *Trade Union Politics*, New Jersey: Humanities press.
4 Gallin, D. (1994) "Inside the new world order," *New Politics*, 5:1, pp. 127–128.
5 *Labor notes*: Number 214, January 1997.
6 Gindin, S. (1997) "Rising from the ashes: labor in the age of global capitalism," *Monthly Review*, 49:3, p. 268.
7 See, for example, Lerner, S. (1996) "Reviving unions: a call to action," *Boston Review*, 21:3/4, pp. 1–5.
8 Eisenscher, M. (1996) "Critical Juncture: Unionism at the Crossroads," Center for Labor Research, University of Massachesetts-Boston, May 2, p. 3.
9 Seidman, G. (1994) *Manufacturing Militance: Workers' Movements in Brazil and South Africa, 1970–1985*, Berkeley: University of California press.
10 Schermerhorn, T. (1997) New Directions Cacus, Transport Workers' Union Local 100, Labor Notes Discussion, January 1997.
11 *Business Week*, February 17, 1997, p. 57.
12 *The Voice of New Directions*, February 1997.
13 California Nurses Association local official at new Directions Solidarity School, February 8, 1997.
14 Rifkin, J. (1995) *The End of Work: The Decline of the Global Labour Force and the Dawn of the Post-Market Era*, New York: Putnam's Sons, pp. 236–293; Hutton, W. (1995) *The State We're In*, London: Jonathan Cape.
15 Pollin, R. (1995) "Financial structures and egalitarian economic policy," *New Left Review* 214, pp. 26–61.
16 *Left Business Observer* 76, February 18, 1997.

17 Froud, J., Haslam, C., Johal, S., Shaoul, J., Williams, K. (1996) "Stakeholder Economy: From Utility Privatization to New Labour," Capital and Class 60, pp. 119–134.

18 Brewer, A. (1990) *Marxist Theories of Imperialism*, London: Routledge, pp. 89–91.

19 *Left Business Observer* 76, February 18, 1997.

20 Rifkin, pp. 236–274.

21 World Bank (1996) *World Development Report*, New York: Oxford University Press.

22 Bryant, E. (1993) closing speech, 1993 Labor Notes Conference, Detroit, April 1993.

22 Workers North and South

Beverly J. Silver and Giovanni Arrighi

Source: Beverly J. Silver and Giovanni Arrighi (2001) 'Workers North and South', *Socialist Register 2001*, pp. 53–76

One of the most puzzling developments of the closing decades of the twentieth century has been the precipitous decline of working-class consciousness and organization at a time of great numerical expansion of the world proletariat. What is most puzzling about this development is that it occurred in the wake of a deep crisis of global capitalism. It was not unreasonable to expect that the capitalist crisis of the 1970s would enhance rather than dampen the class consciousness of the expanding world proletariat. In the 1980s and 1990s, the crisis of capital turned instead into a crisis of labour, resulting in the destruction or fundamental restructuring of all the working-class organizations that had formed and consolidated over the preceding century.

The purpose of this paper is to highlight the relationship between the unevenness of capitalist development on a world scale and processes of working-class formation both before and during the current crisis. Our main argument is that, contrary to widespread opinion, the so-called North–South divide continues to constitute (as it has throughout the twentieth century) the main obstacle to the formation of a homogeneous world proletarian condition. In spite of the relocation of industrial activities from North to South typical of the current crisis, conditions of working-class formation remain thoroughly dependent on the huge and still widening gap that separates the wealth, status and power of a relatively small number of Western countries from those of the countries that contain the vast majority of the world's population. Any meaningful attempt to reconstruct socialist politics must put the overcoming of this gap at the centre of its theoretical and practical concerns.

[…]

Globalization, labour rights and development

Three years before the unravelling of the Soviet-centred Second World, Nigel Harris announced that the emergence of 'a global manufacturing system' was making the very notion of a Third World hopelessly obsolete.

> The conception of an interdependent, interacting, global manufacturing system cuts across the old view of a world consisting of nation-states as well as one of groups of countries, more or less developed and centrally planned – the First, the Third and the Second Worlds. Those notions bore some relationship to an older economy, one marked by the exchange of raw materials for manufacturing goods. But the new world that has superseded it is far more complex and does not lend itself to the simple identification of First and Third, haves and have-nots, rich and poor, industrialized and non-industrialized.[1]

Harris' contention that the spatial restructuring of industrial activities constitutes a fundamental departure from the real or imagined polarized structure of the world into 'First and Third, haves and have-nots, rich and poor, industrialized and non-industrialized' has gained credence, in one variant or another, among some of the best-informed observers of globalization.[2] According to this view, polarizing tendencies are still at work but *within* rather than between North and South, First and Third Worlds. 'Core-periphery' – in Ankie Hoogvelt's words – 'is becoming a social relationship, and no longer a geographical one.'[3]

We are not sure exactly what this means, since 'core-periphery', as we understand it, is always a social relationship. It is a relationship between groups that nominally belong to the same social class (most notably, a world bourgeoisie or a world proletariat) but substantively are separated from one another by a radically unequal command over resources. The fact that, historically, political geography has been a major determinant of position in the core-periphery hierarchy does not mean that such a hierarchy was any less 'social'. It simply means that political geography (as summed up in such categories as First, Second and Third Worlds, North and South, East and West, etc.) constituted an essential dimension of class politics on a world scale. From this standpoint, Hoogvelt's (and Harris') contention can only be interpreted as claiming that class politics has now emancipated itself from all (or most) previous geopolitical constraints and determinations.

The political significance of this contention is vividly illustrated by the disputes and conflicts that culminated in the 'Battle of Seattle' and the World Trade Organization (WTO) débâcle. An editorial of *The Nation* hailed Seattle as 'a milestone for a new kind of politics' – the politics of 'the fabled red-green alliance' that had become quite prominent in Europe but had until now remained 'a leftist fantasy' in the United States.

> Splits between labour and environmentalists, young and old, were not merely forgotten. They were actively overcome. Ageing boomers marvelled at the intelligence, discipline and imagination of a generation they had written off as slackers. Labour shed its nationalism for a new rhetoric of internationalism and solidarity.[4]

The greatest achievement of this new kind of politics was its contribution to the last-minute implosion of the WTO talks:

> many dissident trade ministers, seeing the eroding support for the US agenda on Clinton's own streets, felt less compelled to comply with US unilateralism in the convention halls. (Other factors range from resentment over US anti-dumping laws to Clinton's call, quickly muted, to include labour rights in the agreement – which alienated many delegates from the Third World, where elites routinely exploit workers and ravage the environment.)[5]

This reading of the Seattle events implicitly concurs with the Harris/Hoogvelt contention that the North–South dimension of class struggle on a world-scale has for all practical purposes become irrelevant. From this point of view, Third World elites and multinational corporations are seen as close allies in the exploitation of workers and the ravaging of environments. At the same time, the WTO is seen as a key instrument of this alliance through its role in intensifying the worldwide competition that undergirds the heightened exploitation of workers and ravaging of environments. It follows from this imagery that the struggle of the new-born US red-green alliance against the WTO is an act of internationalist solidarity with Third World workers.

Yet this is not the only possible interpretation of the Seattle events and WTO débâcle. Indeed, much of the evidence supports the radically different view that the débâcle was primarily the result of a growing North–South split over the modalities of further trade liberalization. According to this view, the seeds of the débâcle were sown in Geneva in the weeks before Seattle.

> Developing countries voiced disappointment that five years after the WTO's creation they had not seen promised benefits. They put forward dozens of proposals, including changing some of the rules. Most of their demands were dismissed. The major economies pushed instead their own proposals to further empower the WTO by introducing new areas such as investment, competition, government procurement, and labour and environmental standards. Developing countries in general opposed these new issues, which would open up their markets more widely to the rich nations' big companies or would give these rich states new protectionist tools.[6]

These frustrations were heightened in Seattle when Third World delegates were excluded from key meetings held privately by rich countries. As William Finnegan put it: 'The leaders of the poorer countries, though often depicted as pawns of the major powers, content to offer their countries' workers to the world market at the lowest possible wages – and to pollute the air and water and strip-mine their natural resources in exchange for their own commissions on the innumerable deals that come with corporate globalizations – in reality, have to answer, in many cases, to complex constituencies at home, many of whom are alarmed about their own economic recolonization.'[7] For Finnegan, the revolt of the delegates from poorer countries 'echoed the fundamental questions being asked in the streets about the mandate of the WTO.'[8]

Nevertheless, Seattle also revealed a fundamental divide. Underneath the internationalist rhetoric of the protesters Third World delegates saw a national-protectionist agenda that US negotiators were ready to exploit in their attempts to extract more concessions from poor countries. Indeed, 'President Clinton had hoped that vigorous protests in Seattle – he had urged people to "get it all out of their system" – would move trade ministers to include concerns about the environment, labour and human rights.'[9] The fact that just a month before the big November 30 demonstration AFL-CIO President John Sweeney joined a group of business leaders in signing a letter endorsing the Clinton Administration's trade agenda for the WTO negotiations[10] provided additional evidence in support of this interpretation.

In sum, the forces that brought about the WTO débâcle had two radically different images of the confrontation. On the one hand, the loose alliance of labour and environmental groups that demonstrated in the streets saw themselves struggling against an alliance of multinational corporations and Third World elites aimed at using the WTO as an instrument for increasing profits through the worldwide intensification of workers' exploitation and environmental destruction. In the words of Jay Mazur, Chair of the AFL-CIO International Affairs Committee: 'The divide is not between North and South, it is between workers everywhere and the great concentrations of capital and governments they dominate.'[11] On the other hand, the Third World delegates who torpedoed US attempts to launch a new round of trade liberalizing negotiations saw themselves as struggling against, among other things, an alliance of the US government and US labour and environmental groups aimed at using – in David Sanger's words – 'higher labour and environmental standards to keep out their products, or at least to level the playing field by raising the costs of production in developing countries.'[12]

Taking issue with this characterization of poor countries as being fundamentally opposed to higher labour and environmental standards, William Greider has criticized the media for neglecting to mention that

> the AFL-CIO collected endorsements for its demands from more than one hundred labour federations from around the world, including struggling independent union movements in the poorest places, where labour is often brutally suppressed by force. They know they're on a hopeless treadmill without international protection, because their wages and working conditions will be undercut by the next poor country below them on the food chain, bidding for industrial jobs by sacrificing workers.[13]

This, of course, is a reiteration of the Harris/Hoogvelt contention that the North–South conflict has been superseded by a fundamental unity of the class interests of Northern and Southern workers. Moreover, on the other side of the barricade, Greider sees a fundamental unity of interests between Northern capital and Southern elites. In line with this contention, he goes on to criticize the media for ignoring also that

> India, Brazil and Pakistan could not prevail alone but were joined in opposition by the largest multinationals. Does Boeing support the idea of independent trade unions in China, where its workers are supervised and disciplined by CP cadres?...No, of course not. In China, Mexico and many other low-wage production platforms, factory wages are effectively set by the government itself, not by free-market competition or collective bargaining. The companies like it that way. So, of course, do those governments.[14]

While reiterating the view of the 'Battle of Seattle' as the struggle of a potentially and embryonically united world working class against the alliance of multinational corporations and Third World elites, these passages highlight two closely related issues that constituted the subtext of the battle. The first is the issue of what mechanisms are most likely to ensure the universal protection of the rights of labour. And the second is the issue of what mechanisms are most likely to ensure a minimally equitable distribution of the costs and benefits of world trade and production. Let us briefly examine each issue in turn.

Labour rights and the race to the bottom: myths and reality

As Greider puts it in the passages quoted above, the US red-green alliance's case for enshrining higher labour standards for poor countries in the WTO agreements rests on two main assumptions. The first is that, without international protection, Southern workers are 'on a hopeless treadmill...because their wages and working conditions will be undercut by the next poor country below them on the food chain, bidding for industrial jobs by sacrificing workers.' The second assumption is that Southern governments set wages and working conditions at lower levels than free-market competition or collective bargaining would.

There is undoubtedly some truth in both assumptions. Nevertheless, both assumptions ignore important tendencies of labour–capital relations on a world-scale before and during so-called 'globalization'. First, the relocation of industrial activities from richer to poorer countries has often led to the emergence of strong new labour movements in the low-wage sites of investment, rather than an unambiguous 'race to the bottom'. Although corporations were initially attracted to particular Third World sites because they appeared to offer cheap and docile workers (e.g., Brazil, South Africa, South Korea), the subsequent expansion of capital-intensive mass-production industries created new and militant working classes with significant disruptive power.[15] This tendency is particularly evident if we focus on the leading industries of so-called Fordism such as the automobile industry,[16] but can be seen also in less propitious environments such as electronics.[17]

These labour movements not only succeeded in raising wages, improving working conditions, and strengthening workers' rights, they also often played a leading role in democracy movements.[18] Moreover, labour militancy pushed on to the agenda social transformations that went well beyond those envisioned by pro-democracy elites. Thus, a recurrent pattern is visible: while labour-repressive regimes have created the conditions for rapid industrialization and proletarianization ('economic miracles'), industrialization and proletarianization themselves unleashed processes that eventually undermined these same regimes.[19] In many of these cases international solidarity was non-existent. Liberation from labour-repressive regimes was generally brought about by workers' struggles on the ground. And even where vigorous solidarity movements existed (e.g., for South Africa), grass-roots militancy at home, rather than international solidarity, played the decisive role in the transformation.

This does not mean that all is well for the workers of the world. Far from it. Apart from the fact that the process of 'strengthening through industrialization' has affected only a small percentage of the Southern proletariat, the greater freedoms that have accrued to labour through the liquidation of labour repressive regimes have not always translated into greater welfare. For the latest spread of democracy has gone hand-in-hand with the liquidation of the development-friendly regime and the resurgence of a labour-*unfriendly* international regime. Under these circumstances, democratic governments are forced to make key economic and social policy decisions affecting living standards with 'an eye at least as much on pleasing the International Monetary Fund as appealing to an electorate.'[20]

As for the position of Northern workers, while it is unclear whether or not they have *on the whole* experienced a significant *absolute* worsening of their working and living conditions, the gap between rich and poor has widened rapidly, while conditions for those at the bottom of the wealth and income hierarchy have stagnated or declined. In Western Europe, massive unemployment (especially among youth) has been the main (but not only) form that the deterioration in conditions has taken since the 1980s. In the US, the portion of national income going to profits (rather than labour) has grown over the course of the past twenty years, erasing all of labour's gains from the 1960s and 1970s. And despite the long economic boom of the late 1990s, average real wages remain lower than they were thirty years ago.[21]

Thus, while all is far from well for the workers of the world, any observable *worsening* in their working and living conditions over the last 20–30 years *cannot* be attributed primarily (if at all) to either repressive Third World elites or the relocation of industrial activities from North to South. On the one hand, this period has been characterized by successive waves of democratization at the national level in the context of an increasingly labour-unfriendly international environment. On the other hand, had relocation been the main thrust of the ongoing restructuring of world capitalism, we would have most likely witnessed a general structural strengthening of labour, and it is unlikely that we would be speaking of a crisis of world labour today.[22] If we are speaking of such a crisis, it is because the spatial relocation of industrial activities to lower income countries – even the faster relocation made possible by the latest technological developments – is not the most fundamental aspect of the capitalist restructuring of the last 20–30 years.

As argued at length elsewhere,[23] the primary aspect of this restructuring is a change in the processes of capital accumulation on a world scale from material to financial expansion.

This change is not an aberration but a normal development of the capitalist accumulation of capital. From its earliest beginnings 600 years ago down to the present, the capitalist world economy has always expanded through two alternating phases: a phase of material expansion – in the course of which a growing mass of money capital was channelled into trade and production – and a phase of financial expansion, in the course of which a growing mass of capital reverted to its money form and went into lending, borrowing and speculation. As Fernand Braudel remarked in pointing out the recurrence of this pattern in the sixteenth, eighteenth and nineteenth centuries, 'every capitalist development of this order seems, by reaching the stage of financial expansion, to have in some sense announced its maturity: it was a sign of autumn.'[24]

As Braudel was writing, the great expansion of world trade and production of the 1950s and 1960s began announcing its own maturity by turning into the financial expansion of the 1970s and 1980s. In the 1970s, the expansion of financial activities was associated with, and in many ways contributed to, an expansion of capital flows from high- to lower-income countries. In the 1980s, cross-border borrowing and lending continued to grow exponentially – the stock of international bank lending rising from 4 percent of the total GDP of all OECD countries in 1980 to 44 percent in 1991.[25] But capital flows from high to lower income countries contracted sharply in the 1980s, from a net inflow of almost US $40 billion in 1981 to a net *outflow* of almost $40 billion in 1988.[26] In other words, the ultimate and privileged destination of the capital withdrawn from trade and production in core locations has not been lower income countries; rather it has been the locales and networks of financial speculation that connect high income countries to one another. It was this withdrawal, rather than the relocation of production, that in the 1980s precipitated the crisis of world labour.

It cannot be emphasized too strongly that this crisis and the underlying tendency towards the so-called financialization of capital were only in part due to a spontaneous capitalist reaction to the crisis of over-accumulation that resulted from the rapid expansion of world trade and production in the 1950s and 1960s. Equally essential was the change in government policies – a drastic contraction in money supply, higher interest rates, lower taxes for the wealthy and virtually unrestricted freedom of action for capitalist enterprise – through which between 1979 and 1982 the United States began to compete aggressively for capital worldwide. This change initiated and has kept alive the intense inter-state competition for mobile capital that has created the demand conditions for the great relocation of capital of the 1980s and 1990s from trade and production to financial intermediation and speculation.[27]

This relocation, rather than the incomparably smaller relocation of industrial activities from North to South, has been the main cause of whatever worsening of working and living conditions Northern and Southern workers have been experiencing over the past twenty years. More important, the world-wide relocation of capital to financial activities has benefited the North and South very unequally. What is forgotten by those who base their analysis on the North–South relocation of industrial activities is that the main direction of capital flows in the 1980s and 1990s has not been from North to South but from South to North (or wholly internal to the North). Crucial in this respect has been the transformation of the United States from being the main source of world liquidity and foreign investment – as it was through the 1950s and 1960s – to being the main debtor nation and largest recipient of foreign investment of the 1980s and 1990s.

This transformation radically changed the global context not just of labour–capital relations, North and South, but also and especially of Southern attempts to catch up with Northern standards of wealth. Contrary to Harris' and Hoogvelt's contention, the geographical dimension of core-periphery relations has become more rather than less marked, fully retaining its constraining and disposing influence on world-scale labour–capital relations. This brings us to the second issue raised by Greider in the passages quoted earlier on the issue of the inter-state distribution of the costs and benefits of world trade and production.

The strange death of the Third World

We have no dispute with Harris', Hoogvelt's and Greider's explicit or implicit contention that the Third World, as a political-ideological force, collapsed in the 1980s. But we question whether this has been accompanied by any levelling of economic opportunities. For the process of dispersal of industrial capacity that Harris and many others take at face value as 'development' has in fact been associated with a widening of the income gap that separates the vast majority of the population of the Third World from that of the First. The Third World has collapsed, along with the Second World, precisely because of a generalized failure to translate rapid industrial expansion into an advance up the value-added hierarchy of the world economy.

What is 'strange' about this collapse is that it occurred abruptly when Third World states were not just industrializing rapidly but were also wielding unprecedented power and influence in world politics. The Third World was primarily a political and ideological formation. Born out of the struggle for national self-determination of the peoples of Asia and Africa and of the parallel struggle for world hegemony between the US and the USSR, the 'Third World' experienced growing power and influence throughout the Vietnam War and its aftermath. Partly related to the US military effort in Vietnam, the economic conjuncture at this time also seemed to favour Third World countries. Their natural resources were in great demand, as was their abundant and cheap capital. Agents of First World bankers were queuing up in the antechambers of Third (and Second) World governments offering at bargain prices the over-abundant capital that could not find profitable investment in their home countries. Terms of trade had turned sharply against First World countries, and the income gap between the latter and Third World countries seemed to be narrowing.

Shortly after the oil shock of 1979, however, it became clear that any hope (or fear) of an imminent equalization of the economic opportunities of the peoples of the world was, to say the least, premature. US competition for mobile capital in world money markets to finance both a new escalation in the Cold War and the 'buying' of electoral votes at home through tax cuts, suddenly dried up the supply of funds to Third and Second World countries and triggered a major contraction in world purchasing power. Terms of trade swung back in favour of First World countries as fast and sharply as they had swung against them in the 1970s, and the income gap between the First World and the rest of the world became wider than ever. From 1982 onwards, it would no longer be First-World bankers begging Third World states to borrow their over-abundant capital; it would be Third World states begging First-World governments and bankers to grant them the credit needed to stay afloat in an increasingly integrated and competitive global economy. To make things worse for Third World states, they were soon joined in their cut-throat competition for mobile capital by Second-World states.

High finance is the arena where Third World solidarity, such as it was, was dissolved into cut-throat competition for mobile capital. This is the true significance of the Thatcher–Reagan counter-revolution. By shifting the terrain of the struggle to the arena of financial speculation, the counter-revolution threw the Third (and Second) Worlds into complete disarray and revived the fortunes of the First World, the United States in particular. This was not the only shift that enabled the First World to regain the upper hand. Militarily, for example, the Falkland/Malvinas War shifted the confrontation from the terrain of labour-intensive warfare to that of capital-intensive warfare, showing that, if Third World states could be drawn to fight on the latter terrain, all the disadvantages that had led to the defeat of the US in Vietnam would vanish. The validity of the lesson was confirmed most spectacularly by the Gulf War and again, though less spectacularly, in the 1999 war against Yugoslavia. But the most decisive weapon wielded by First World states under Anglo-American leadership in the destruction of the Second and Third Worlds was economic-financial rather than military-industrial. Third World states simply proved incapable of translating political-ideological power into economic-financial power.

This incapability had little, if anything, to do with deficiencies peculiar to Third World states. Rather, it had to do with law-like tendencies of the global capitalist system that buttress the existing hierarchy of wealth among countries. The durability of the global strat-ification of wealth has been documented for the 1938–1997 period in a series of studies.[28] Three findings deserve special attention. First, world population classified by the log of GNP per capita has tended to cluster into three strata (low-, middle-, and high-income) separated from one another by two low-frequency gaps. Second, while upward mobility of states across the two low-frequency gaps that separate the three strata occurred in the short run (one or two decades), it was rare for a country to be able to sustain an upward move in the long run (three or four decades) – a finding later replicated from a different perspective by Easterly *et al.*[29] As a result, only a few states have succeeded in consolidating their upward mobility from the low- to the middle-income stratum (Taiwan and South Korea) or from the middle- to the high-income stratum (Japan, Italy and, more recently, Singapore and Hong Kong as well). Moreover, owing to the faster demographic growth of the states in the lower-income strata, the relative demographic sizes of the three strata have remained roughly constant, in spite of these individual cases of upward mobility. Finally, starting in the 1960s, the difference in degree of industrialization between states in the high-income stratum and states in the other two strata (especially in the middle-income stratum) has decreased significantly. But whereas in the 1970s this tendency was associated with a narrowing of the income gap between the upper and the lower strata, in the 1980s and 1990s the continued narrowing of the industrialization gap was associated with a major widening of the income gap. In 1997, the average per capita GNP for countries in the middle-income stratum was only $2,465 or 12.5% of the average per capita GNP for countries in the high-income stratum; while the average per capita GNP of low-income countries was only $466 or 2.4% of the high-income countries.[30]

The image of development that emerges from the identification of these tendencies is one of a race in which low- and middle-income states attempted to move up in the value-added hierarchy of the world economy by internalizing within their domains one aspect or another of the 'modernity' of the wealthy countries (most notably, industrialization). As these attempts became general, however, they tended to defeat their purpose by activating interstate competition over resources that were made ever more scarce by the generalization of modernizing efforts – a competition, what's more, in which states in the high-income stratum were generally better positioned than states in the lower strata to come out on top. The idea that all states could catch up with the standards of national wealth of the high-income countries by internalizing the latter's modernity thus turned out to be an illusion. The spread of industrialization efforts, in other words, resulted more in the downgrading of industrial activities in the value-added hierarchy of the world-economy than in the upgrading of the low- and middle-income economies that were becoming more industrial.[31]

This stability of world income inequalities can be conceptualized in terms of Roy Harrod's and Fred Hirsch's notion of 'oligarchic wealth'[32] – a kind of long-term income that bears no relation to the intensity and efficiency of the efforts of its recipients and is never available to all no matter how intense and efficient their efforts are. Much of the political turbulence of the 1980s, and the related crisis of all variants of developmentalist efforts, can be traced to a situation in which a generalized attempt to attain oligarchic wealth through modernization left low- and middle-income states stranded with most of the costs and few of the benefits of industrialization.[33]

From this perspective, the 'retreat' of core capital into financial intermediation and speculation was a reaction to the intensification of competitive pressure in industrial activities as well as to the demands of both Northern workers and Third (and Second) World countries for a greater share of the pie. As previously noted, this retreat was not the outcome of spontaneous market forces acting on their own. Rather, both were the outcome of market forces acting under the direction and with the support of the US government. The simultaneous liquidation of the ideology and practice of the welfare and developmentalist states transformed the crisis of capital of the 1970s into the crisis of labour and of the Third (and Second) Worlds in the 1980s and 1990s.

Third World elites were not the passive victims of the US liquidation of the development project. At least some fractions of such elites were among the strongest supporters of the new Washington Consensus through which the liquidation was accomplished.[34] To the extent that this has been the case, Third World elites have been among the social forces that have promoted the liberalization of trade and capital movements.

But the same can be said of Northern workers' role in the liquidation of the welfare state. After all, it was a big swing in the US working-class vote (the so-called Reagan Democrats) that empowered the Republican Party to reverse New Deal policies in the United States and to escalate inter-state competition for mobile capital worldwide. And as the competition escalated, organized labour in Northern countries (the US in particular) generally supported their governments' efforts to out-compete one another (and especially poor countries) in attracting capital, thereby shifting competitive pressures onto workers elsewhere. While such efforts at 'self-protection' are hardly surprising, they do nothing to enhance the 'internationalist' credentials of Northern workers.

To be sure, such 'self-protection' efforts are not limited to Northern workers.[35] Nevertheless, it is difficult to place a significant share of the responsibility for the collapse of the developmental or welfare states on Southern workers. Indeed, if anything, the widespread and massive wave of anti-International Monetary Fund (IMF) protests carried out by Southern workers in the 1980s[36] slowed the transformation, well before the 'backlash' hit Paris in 1995[37] or Seattle in 1999.

In sum, it is plausible to conclude that both Third World elites and Northern workers have played some part in the success of the Reagan-Thatcher counter-revolution. The counter-revolution succeeded primarily because the welfare and developmental states had reached their limits in delivering on the promises of the global New Deal. But it also succeeded because the ruling groups of the United States managed to persuade Northern workers and Third World elites that, in order to break out of these limits, it was necessary to liquidate rather than preserve these two kinds of state.

The significance of Seattle is that Northern workers and Southern elites seem to have simultaneously realized that the dismantling of the welfare and developmental states benefited primarily Northern capital and did little or nothing in delivering on the unkept promises of the global New Deal. The positive outcome of this simultaneous realization has been to dramatize some of the limits and contradictions of the seemingly irresistible rise of US unilateralism in defining the rules of global competition. At the same time, however, this achievement was neither based upon, nor did it lead to the emergence of, a vision of labour–capital and core-periphery relations capable of constituting a more equitable alternative to US-sponsored globalization. On the contrary, Northern workers and Southern elites have so far seemed more inclined to pursue their own particularistic interests within the existing world order in opposition to one another, rather than join forces to figure out what alternative world order would make their interests converge.

The China syndrome

The issue of the universal protection of the rights of capital and the issue of the distribution of the costs/benefits of globalization between North and South were not the only issues that constituted the subtext of the Battle of Seattle. There was a third issue that, in a sense, encompassed the previous two. This is the issue of China's entry into the WTO. Although it was not even on the agenda of the WTO meeting, by most accounts this was the single most important issue in the back of many demonstrators' minds.

> 'China, we're coming atcha' yells Mike Dolan, the Nader group's organizer in Seattle, as he discusses the next item of business. 'There's no question about it. The next item of business is China.' Jeff Faux, director of the AFL-CIO-backed Economic Policy Institute, tells reporters that with China in the WTO it will be impossible to get labour and environmental standards installed, because China's too big...'The China vote is going to become proxy for all our concerns about globalization' says Denise Mitchell of the AFL-CIO.[38]

While conceding that 'there are Chinese elites oppressing Chinese masses inflicting dreadful working conditions and pay scales', Alexander Cockburn confesses that the sight of Western progressives execrating China makes him uncomfortable. It reminds him of how the century began – with 'the troops of the Western powers [breaking] the Boxer siege of the embassies in Peking, [looting] the Empress Dowager's summer palace and thus [destroying] for a time the valiant nationalist effort to halt colonial exploitation of China.' In the intervening hundred years China experienced a series of revolutions – part of the broader revolt against the West by the impoverished countries of Asia and Africa. Land and wealth were redistributed and an industrial base built in an attempt to foster internal demand and get a fair price for the commodities poor countries needed to sell abroad.

> The Western powers didn't care for that, any more than they liked the Boxers...They never relented, never forgave. Some revolutions struggled on for several decades, in varying states of siege, boycotts, embargoes, economic sabotage...The progressive intellectuals from the Economic Policy Institute who denounce China's 'state-controlled economic system' as 'market-distorting'...aren't so far removed from those who have administered the siege of Cuba all these years. Many liberal NGO types are interventionist by disposition. The Somalia debacle, and to some extent the Kosovo nightmare, were their shows...We don't need...at the end of this imperial century to be signing on to a Yellow Peril campaign.[39]

The imperialist record of Western powers in dealing with China over the last 150 years is undoubtedly a good enough reason for feeling uncomfortable with Western progressives execrating China. There are nonetheless two further reasons that bear directly on the issues of 'universal labour rights' and 'greater distributional justice' discussed earlier. One concerns the position of the Chinese working class in the world labour movement, and the other concerns the position of China in the global economy.

The historical record of the labour movement in China and in the North/West in the twentieth century lends no support to the Seattle demonstrators' claim that Northern pressures on the Chinese ruling elites are an essential condition for the emancipation of the Chinese working class from oppression and exploitation. On the one hand, the record shows that the militancy of the Chinese working class can be and has been second to none. The explosion of labour unrest in China of the 1920s was probably the greatest such explosion of the century in any country at China's level of proletarianization.[40] The explosion was drowned in blood by the Western-backed Guomindang regime. But the experience initiated that fundamental reorganization and reorientation of the policies of the Chinese Communist Party that eventually led to the establishment of a regime that by all available indicators did more for the improvement of the condition of the working class in China than any previous regime.[41]

On the other hand, organized labour in the North/West in general (and in the US in particular) did little or nothing to support the struggles of the Chinese working class. While Western support for the Guomindang repression of the Chinese workers' movement of the 1920s went largely unchallenged, the US-led siege, boycotts, and embargoes of Communist China enjoyed the full support of the AFL-CIO. Nor should we forget that some of the biggest US strikes of the late nineteenth and early twentieth century had among their targets the exclusion of Chinese workers from the US labour market, while the American Federation of Labour actively fanned the flames of anti-Chinese sentiment. In a 1905 speech Samuel Gompers assured his (presumably Caucasian) audience that 'Caucasians are not going to let their standard of living be destroyed by Negroes, Chinamen, Japs, or others.'[42] Indeed, according to Alexander Saxton:

> Throughout the nineties and on into the twentieth century, the Federation [AFL] kept up a barrage, in openly racist terms, against the Chinese and other Orientals. Thus, [in 1893], the AFL convention resolved that Chinese brought with them 'nothing but filth, vice and disease'; that 'all efforts to elevate them to a higher standard have proven futile'; and that the Chinese were to blame for degrading 'a part of our people on the Pacific Coast to such a degree that could it be published in detail the American people would in their just and righteous anger sweep them from the face of the earth.'[43]

In light of all this, only a complete amnesia of the most basic facts of twentieth-century Chinese and world-labour history can give any credence to the claim that US labour's advocacy of the exclusion of China from the WTO is primarily, if at all, motivated by international workers' solidarity. Throughout the century – from the Boxer Rebellion, through the great strike wave of the 1920s and the Revolution of 1949 – the Chinese working class had to rely primarily on domestic alliances to emancipate itself from poverty, insecurity, and oppression. Why, all of a sudden, should it have become so incapable of taking care of its own further emancipation as to require the assistance of Northern organizations that throughout the century have been part of its problem rather than of the solution? It is, of course, possible that the kinds of concessions that the United States has already extracted from China as a condition for its admittance to the WTO make exclusion rather than inclusion more beneficial for Chinese workers. But even if that were the case, on what grounds should Chinese workers interpret US labour advocacy of Chinese exclusion as an act of international solidarity? Have they not many more grounds for detecting some fundamental continuity between US labour action at the beginning of the twentieth century aimed at excluding Chinese immigrant labour, and US labour action at the end of the century aimed at excluding the products of Chinese labour?

The fact that the AFL-CIO, while formally endorsing the April 2000 anti-IMF/World Bank demonstrations in Washington, chose to concentrate its political energies for the season on a separate campaign to block normal trade relations between the United States and China[44] is the latest reason to suspect the depth and sincerity of US labour's new internationalism. Arguably, IMF structural adjustment and debt policies have had a far greater negative impact on the world's workers (including their indirect impact on workers in the North through intensification of labour market competition) than Chinese exports; yet the obsession with China is paramount.

This brings us to the second issue, that is, of global distributional justice. With this issue in mind, it is especially disturbing to note that the execration of China by Western progressives comes at a time when China appears to be emerging as the only poor country that has any chance in the foreseeable future of subverting the Western-dominated global hierarchy of wealth. China is not the only poor country that has escaped the ravages brought upon the Third and Second Worlds by the neoliberal counter-revolution of the 1980s. Several other states did much better than China, most notably South Korea, Taiwan, Hong Kong and Singapore. Nevertheless, these are small states, jointly accounting for an insignificant fraction of world population, whose upward mobility in the global hierarchy of wealth left the hierarchy itself as entrenched as ever. The far more limited economic advance of China, in contrast, involving as it does about one-fifth of the world population and more than one-third of the total population of low-income countries, threatens to subvert the pyramidal structure of the global hierarchy of wealth itself, and not just statistically, but economically, politically and culturally as well.

There is no denying that China's rapid growth raises in a particularly acute form the problem of absolute and relative scarcity of natural resources – a problem that the post-war world of oligarchic wealth accommodated through the exclusion of the majority of the world population from the mass consumption standards of the West. A new model of development that is less wasteful than the US-sponsored mass consumption model will be needed in a world of greater distributional justice. Unfortunately, there are few signs that China's ruling elites – any more than those of the West – are aware of the need to devise such an alternative model.

Granted this, directly or indirectly sabotaging China's further economic advance, as some Western progressives advocate, is not only morally untenable; it is in all likelihood a false solution of the problem. It is morally untenable because wealthy Western countries in general, and the United States in particular, have been and continue to be the world's leading polluters and destroyers of natural resources, both at home and abroad. And it is likely to be a false solution because the huge and growing disparities between the living standards of poor and wealthy countries are the single most important force that drives the elites of low- and middle-income countries into the adoption of the consumption norms and ecologically destructive practices of the wealthy countries.

For all the challenges it poses and continues to pose in this century, China's economic advance should be welcomed rather than feared and sabotaged by Western progressives, for two main reasons. One is that the advance is the most hopeful sign that the extreme global inequalities created under European colonial imperialism, and consolidated under US hegemony, will eventually give way to a more just and equal world. And the other is that its continuation is the best guarantee that a strong labour movement will emerge in China, capable of carrying one step further the 'long march' of the Chinese working classes towards their self-emancipation. Indeed, signs of such an emergent labour movement have grown together with China's industrialization/proletarianization.[45] Given the size and growing centrality of the Chinese working classes in world society, a strong Chinese labour movement would have a major invigorating impact on the world labour movement as a whole.

Conclusions

In a contribution to a forum on the 'Problems and Prospects of a Global Labour Movement', Dan Clawson chides left-academics for dismissing the protectionist strategy of 'most workers and many unions' as politically retrograde.[46] While acknowledging the potential affinity of protectionist strategies with racism and xenophobia (and hence its serious dangers), Clawson argues that 'workers also hold an important truth, and we need to take it seriously.'

> As an attempt to limit the impact of capital's internationalism, protectionism has almost invariably involved racist (e.g., anti-Japanese) and anti-immigrant stances ('they' are taking 'our' jobs; we need to keep 'them' out). But it is also an assertion that the economy should not be driven by an unfettered market, that limits need to be imposed on the drive for profits, and that some means must be found to protect workers and the environment in order to put human needs above cost-benefit analysis.[47]

Clawson goes on to argue that we need a general theory of international labour solidarity that 'recognizes the need for local community built on planning and some degree of protection from the unfettered market', at the same time as it embraces international labour solidarity and rejects racism and xenophobia. How is such a balance to be struck?

In this essay we have argued that the crisis of labour was brought on by the massive shift of capital from investment in production and trade to finance and speculation, rather than by industrial relocation or most other phenomena associated with 'globalization'. We also argued that the current financialization of capital is not unprecedented, and that the last analogous period at the end of the nineteenth and beginning of the twentieth centuries led to two world wars, imperialism and fascism. Both financial expansions – past and present – have been associated with a tremendous polarization of wealth within and between countries, and with rapid transformations that unsettled established ways of life and livelihood. National-protectionist reactions have been strong, with racist and xenophobic overtones.[48]

Labour movements, as we know, played at best an ambiguous role in the rise of national-protectionism and imperialism. As E. H. Carr noted in discussing the collapse of the Second International on the eve of the First World War:

> In the nineteenth century, when the nation belonged to the middle class and the worker had no fatherland, socialism had been international. The crisis of 1914 showed in a flash that, except for backward Russia, this attitude was everywhere obsolete. The mass of workers knew instinctively on which side their bread was buttered...International socialism ignominiously collapsed.[49]

To the extent that core labour movements once again decide that their 'bread is buttered' on the side of national-protectionism – that is, standing behind the power of their states to buttress global inequalities and divide the world's workers – our risk of descending into another lengthy period of systemic chaos and 'tribalism' is dramatically increased.

While the motivation for national-protectionism (and any attendant racism) may be rooted in the real insecurities experienced by workers, we should not repeat the mistake of pandering to working-class racism made by socialists in the late nineteenth and early twentieth centuries. Indeed, as Alexander Saxton points out: while it was socialists alone among labour activists who mounted any criticism of the anti-Chinese crusade of the late-nineteenth century, even they made a tactical decision to 'sail under the flag' of 'anti-coolieism' as 'a means of uniting and educating the working class.' Yet 'tactics... have a way of becoming habits', and when the socialists sought 'to haul down the tactical flag' and raise instead the 'strategic flag of working-class unity', they were no longer able to affect the course of events. Moreover, by allowing anti-Chinese rhetoric to go unchallenged they helped pave the way not only for the exclusion of the Chinese and other immigrants, but for a general turn to an openly racist labour-movement policy towards blacks.[50]

While standing firm against racism, we also need to push for a new labour-friendly international regime in order to provide a climate in which, in Clawson's words, local communities can make plans, workers' livelihoods are protected from an unfettered market, and human needs are put above cost-benefit analysis. As we have argued here, the financial expansion is the result of conscious profit strategies of firms and conscious power strategies of core states, especially the United States. Therefore, 'there is an alternative.' Labour activists should be struggling against policies at the national and international level that 'boost' the speculative bubble as well as in favour of policies that 'burst' it. From this point of view, the speech by the president of COSATU (South Africa's trade union federation) at a recent mass rally in Johannesburg is to be applauded. He called for an end to the private sector's 'investment strike' and demanded that capital invest in jobs rather than stock exchanges.[51]

But the solution ultimately must include a transformation at the international level. The vicious circle of domestic and international conflict was brought to an end in the mid-twentieth century only with the establishment of the labour-friendly and development-friendly international regime under US hegemony that, at least in part, addressed the demands explicitly and implicitly being thrown up by the movements from below. Nevertheless, the solution cannot be a simple return to the main elements of that regime. For in promising to meet the aspirations of the mass movements, the US-sponsored regime fudged several issues. In particular, the ideology of unlimited growth ignored both the capitalist limits and environmental limits to the promise that all could and would enter the Age of High Mass Consumption.

Contrary to its promises, the American Century has resulted in a consolidation of world inequalities in income and resource use/abuse. Moreover, the overlap between the racial and wealth divides on a world-scale has been consolidated, while environmental degradation has proceeded at a pace and scale that is unprecedented in human history. Indeed, to the extent the 'strike of productive capital' comes to an end, the environmental limits of universalized, rapid growth will come to the fore, bringing with it renewed impulses to exclude some large percentage of the world's population from the enjoyment of those resources. Here, ultimately, lies the great challenge that will face workers North and South in the twenty-first century: that is, the challenge to struggle, not just against exploitation and exclusion, but for consumption norms and secure livelihood standards that can be generalized to all and for policies that actually promote this generalization.

Notes

1 Nigel Harris, *The End of the Third World: Newly Industrializing Countries and the Decline of an Ideology*, Harmondsworth, Middlesex: Penguin Books, 1987, pp. 200–2.

2 For recent examples see Ankie Hoogvelt, *Globalization and the Postcolonial World: The New Political Economy of Development*, Baltimore, MD: Johns Hopkins University Press, 1997, pp. xii, 145; David Held, Anthony McGrew, David Goldblatt and Jonathan Perraton, *Global Transformations. Politics, Economics and Culture*, Stanford, CA: Stanford University Press, 1999, pp. 8, 177, 186–7.

3 Hoogvelt, *Globalization and the Postcolonial World*, p. 145.

4 'Democracy Bites the WTO' (Editorial), *The Nation*, 27 December 1999, p. 3.

5 'Democracy Bites the WTO', p. 4.

6 Martin Khor, 'Take Care, the WTO Majority Is Tired of Being Manipulated', *International Herald Tribune*, 21 December 1999, p. 4.

7 William Finnegan, 'After Seattle: Anarchists Get Organized', *The New Yorker*, 17 April 2000, p. 46.

8 Finnegan, 'After Seattle', p. 47.

9 Timothy Egan, 'New World Disorder: Free Trade Takes On Free Speech', *New York Times*, 5 December 1999, pp. iv, 5.

10 Kim Moody, 'On the Eve of Seattle Trade Protests, Sweeney Endorses Clinton's Trade Agenda', *Labour Notes* (Detroit), no. 249, December 1999, p. 1.

11 Jay Mazur, 'Labour's New Internationalism', *Foreign Affairs*, January/February 2000, p. 92.

12 David E. Sanger, 'The Shipwreck in Seattle', *New York Times*, 5 December 1999, p. 14.

13 William Greider, 'The Battle Beyond Seattle', *The Nation*, 27 December 1999, p. 5.

14 Greider, 'The Battle Beyond Seattle', p. 5.

15 Silver, 'World-Scale Patterns', p. 182.

16 Beverly J. Silver, 'Turning Points of Workers' Militancy in the World Automobile Industry, 1930s–1990s', *Research in the Sociology of Work*, vol. 6, 1997, pp. 43–71.

17 Jefferson Cowie, *Capital Moves: RCA's Seventy-Year Search for Cheap Labour*, Ithaca, NY: Cornell University Press, 1999.

18 Ruth Berins Collier, *Paths Toward Democracy: The Working Class and Elites in Western Europe and South America*, Cambridge: Cambridge University Press, 1999, ch. 4; Gay Seidman, *Manufacturing Militance: Workers' Movements in Brazil and South Africa, 1970–1985*, Berkeley: University of California Press, 1995.

19 See also Beverly J. Silver, 'The Contradictions of Semiperipheral Success: The Case of Israel', in W. G. Martin, ed., *Semiperipheral States in the World-Economy*, New York: Greenwood, 1990; Beverly J. Silver, *Labour Unrest and Capital Accumulation on a World Scale*, PhD Dissertation, Binghamton, NY: SUNY (Ann Arbor: University Microfilms International), 1992.

20 John Markoff, *Waves of Democracy: Social Movements and Political Change*, Thousand Oaks, CA: Pine Forge Press, 1996, pp. 132–5.

21 Robert Pollin, 'Globalization, Inequality and Financial Instability: Confronting the Marx, Keynes and Polanyi Problems in the Advanced Capitalist Economies', paper presented at the conference on 'Globalization and Ethics', Yale University, 31 March–2 April 2000, table 5; Louis Uchitelle, 'As Class Struggle Subsides, Less Pie for the Workers', *New York Times*, 5 December 1999, Business Section, p. 4.

22 See the conclusions of Arrighi and Silver, 'Labour Movements and Capital Migration'.

23 Giovanni Arrighi, *The Long Twentieth Century: Money, Power and the Origins of Our Times*, London: Verso, 1994; Arrighi and Silver *et al.*, 'Chaos and Governance'.

24 Fernand Braudel, *Civilization and Capitalism, Fifteenth–Eighteenth Century, volume 3. The Perspective of the World*, New York: Harper and Row, 1984, p. 246.

25 The Economist, 'World Economic Survey', *The Economist*, 19 September 1992.

26 UNDP, *Human Development Report 1992*, New York: Oxford University Press, 1992.

27 Arrighi and Silver, 'Global Inequalities'.

28 Giovanni Arrighi and Jessica Drangel, 'The Stratification of the World-Economy: An Exploration of the Semiperipheral Zone', *Review* (Fernand Braudel Centre), X, 1, Summer 1986, pp. 9–74; Roberto P. Korzeniewicz and William Martin, 'The Global Distribution of Commodity Chains', in G. Gereffi and M. Korzeniewicz, eds, *Commodity Chains and Global Capitalism*: Westport, CT: Praeger, 1994, pp. 67–91; Arrighi and Silver, 'Global Inequalities'.

29 William Easterly, Michael Kremer, Lant Pritchett, and Lawrence H. Summers, 'Good Policy or Good Luck? Country Growth Performance and Temporary Shocks', *Journal of Monetary Economics*, 32, 1993.

30 Arrighi and Silver, 'Global Inequalities', based on World Bank data.

31 Arrighi and Drangel, 'The Stratification of the World-Economy'; Arrighi and Silver, 'Global Inequalities'.

32 Roy Harrod, 'The Possibility of Economic Satiety – Use of Economic Growth for Improving the Quality of Education and Leisure', in *Problems of United States Economic Development*, 1, New York: Committee for Economic Development, 1958, pp. 207–13; Fred Hirsch, *Social Limits to Growth*, Cambridge, Mass.: Harvard University Press, 1976.

33 Giovanni Arrighi, 'The Developmentalist Illusion: A Reconceptualization of the Semiperiphery', in W. G. Martin, ed., *Semiperipheral States in the World-Economy*, New York: Greenwood Press, 1990, pp. 11–42; Giovanni Arrighi, 'World Income Inequality and the Future of Socialism', *New Left Review* 189, 1991, pp. 39–64; Silver, 'The Contradictions of Semiperipheral Success'.

34 Lance Taylor, 'The Revival of the Liberal Creed – the IMF and the World Bank in a Globalized Economy', *World Development*, vol. 25, no. 2, 1997, pp. 145–52.

35 See the discussion of the South African textile unions' protectionist stance *vis-à-vis* Zimbabwean imports in Patrick Bond, Darlene Miller and Greg Ruiters, 'The Southern African Working Class: Production, Reproduction and Politics', in this volume.

36 John Walton and Charles Ragin, 'Global and National Sources of Political Protest: Third World Responses' to the Debt Crisis', *American Sociological Review*, vol. 55, December 1990, pp. 876–7, 888.

37 R. Krishnan, 'December 1995: The First Revolt Against Globalization', *Monthly Review*, vol. 48, no. 1, May 1996, pp. 1–22.

38 Alexander Cockburn, 'Short History of the Twentieth Century', *The Nation*, 3 January 2000, p. 9.

39 Cockburn, 'Short History', p. 9.

40 Beverly J. Silver, Giovanni Arrighi and Melvyn Dubofsky, eds, 'Labour Unrest in the World Economy, 1870–1990', a special issue of *Review* (Fernand Braudel Centre), vol. 18, no. 1, Winter 1995, pp. 1–206; Mark Selden, 'Labour Unrest in China, 1831–1990', *Review* (Fernand Braudel Centre), vol. 18, no. 1, Winter 1995, pp. 69–86.

41 Selden, 'Labour Unrest in China'; Mark Selden, 'Yan'an Communism Reconsidered', *Modern China* 21, 1, pp. 8–44.

42 Quoted in Alexander Saxton, *The Indispensable Enemy: Labour and the Anti-Chinese Movement in California*, Berkeley: University of California Press, 1971, p. 273.

43 Saxton, 'The Indispensable Enemy', p. 271.

44 Finnegan, 'After Seattle', p. 49.

45 See for example, James Kynge, 'Riots in Chinese Mining Towns', *Financial Times*, 3 April 2000; Dorothy Solinger, *Contesting Citizenship in Urban China*, Berkeley: University of California Press, 1999, pp. 284–6.

46 Dan Clawson, 'Contradictions of Labour Solidarity', *Journal of World System Research*, vol. 4, no. 1, Winter 1998, pp. 7–8 [http://csf.colorado.edu/wsystems/jwsr.html].

47 Clawson, 'Contradictions of Labour Solidarity', p. 8.

48 Silver and Slater, 'The Social Origins of World Hegemonies'; cf. Karl Polanyi, *The Great Transformation*, Boston: Beacon, 1957.

49 Edward H. Carr, *Nationalism and After*, London: Macmillan, 1945, pp. 20–1.

50 Saxton, 'The Indispensable Enemy', pp. 266–7.

51 Eddie Jayiya, 'Mass Action Brings Jo'Burg to Standstill', *The Independent*, 13 April 2000.

23 Globalizing sex workers' rights

Kamala Kempadoo

Source: Kamala Kempadoo and Jo Doezema (eds) (1998), *Global Sex Workers: Rights, Resistance, and Redefinition*, London: Routledge, pp. 1–28

When I first heard about prostitutes organizing for their rights in Suriname in 1993, I was both excited and puzzled by the news. Was it a singular incident spurred by an outsider, or did it reflect a local movement? I wanted to know. Also, in this part of the world, were women serious about staying in the sex industry or anxious to have prostitution abolished? What were the aims of such an organization, and who were the activists? Was this an isolated group, and what was the response to this initiative from the rest of the women's movement in this corner of South America? Questions outweighed any answer I could find in libraries or books – I decided to travel to Suriname to find out more.

Curiosity opened my world to a movement not just in Suriname, but in other parts of the "Third World." I realized that sex workers' movements were no longer exclusive to the United States or Western Europe. Prostitutes and other sex workers were fighting to keep brothels open, challenging the various stigmas about prostitution, and exposing corruption within sex industries in many different countries – yet very few people had heard about these courageous steps. The voices and activities of sex workers outside the industrialized North went unheard, nearly invisible to all but those in the immediate surroundings. As someone trained to think that a documentation of social history is absolutely vital for the construction of knowledge, I believed the one thing I could do was to facilitate the recording of this new international movement.

[. . .]

Sex worker, prostitute or whore?

Identity, rights, working conditions, decriminalization, and legitimacy have been central issues collectively addressed by prostitutes for many years. Through these struggles the notion of the sex worker has emerged as a counter-point to traditionally derogatory names, under the broad banner of a prostitutes' rights movement, with some parts recovering and valorizing the name and identity of "whore." In this book we have chosen the term "sex worker" to reflect the current use throughout the world, although in many of the essays "sex worker" and "prostitute" are used interchangeably. It is a term that suggests we view prostitution not as an identity – a social or a psychological characteristic of women, often indicated by "whore" – but as an income-generating activity or form of labor for women and men. The definition stresses the social location of those engaged in sex industries as working people.

The idea of the sex worker is inextricably related to struggles for the recognition of women's work, for basic human rights and for decent working conditions. The definition emphasizes flexibility and variability of sexual labor as well as its similarities with other dimensions of working people's lives. In particular, the writings here illustrate the ways in which sex work is experienced as an integral part of many women's and men's lives around the world, and not necessarily as the sole defining activity around which their sense of self or identity is shaped. Moreover, commercial sex work in these accounts is not always a steady activity, but may occur simultaneously with other forms of income-generating work such as domestic service, informal commercial trading, market-vending, shoeshining or office work. Sex work can also be quite short-lived or be a part of an annual cycle of work – in few cases are women and men engaged full-time or as professionals. Consequently, in one person's lifetime, sex work is commonly just one of the multiple activities employed for generating income, and very few stay in prostitution for their entire adulthood. In most cases, sex work is not for individual wealth but for family well-being or survival; for working class women to clothe, feed and educate their children; and for young women and men to sustain themselves when the family income is inadequate. For many, sex work means migration away from their hometown or country. For others, it is associated with drug use, indentureship or debt-bondage. For the majority, participation in sex work entails a life in the margins.

The concept of sex work emerged in the 1970s through the prostitutes' rights movement in the United States and Western Europe and has been discussed in various publications.[1] Than-Dam Troung's study of prostitution and tourism in Southeast Asia produced one of the first extensive theoretical elaborations on the subject (1989). Defining human activity or work as the way in which basic needs are met and human life produced and reproduced, she argues that activities involving purely sexual elements of the body and sexual energy should also be considered vital to the fulfillment of basic human needs: for both procreation and bodily pleasure. Troung thus introduces the concept of sexual labor to capture the notion of the utilization of sexual elements of the body and as a way of understanding a productive life force that is employed by women and men. In this respect she proposes that sexual labor be considered similar to other forms of labor that humankind performs to sustain itself – such as mental and manual labor, all of which involve specific parts of the body and particular types of energy and skills. Furthermore, she points out, the social organization of sexual labor has taken a variety of forms in different historical contexts and political economies, whereby there is no universal form or appearance of either prostitution or sex work. Instead, she proposes, analyses of prostitution need to address and take into account the specific ways in which sexual subjectivity, sexual needs and desires are constructed in specific contexts. Wet-nursing, temple prostitution, "breeding" under slavery, surrogate child-bearing, donor sex, commercial sex and biological reproduction can thus be seen as illustrations of historical and contemporary ways in which sexual labor has been organized for the re-creation and replenishment of human and social life.

[. . .]

Transnational sex work and the global economy

Sex work across national boundaries is not new to the world. Donna Guy observes that "foreign prostitutes and pimps were already ensconced in Buenos Aires (Argentina) by 1860" and that between 1889 and 1901, seventy-five percent of the registered working women hailed from Europe and Russia (1990: 14–16). Between 1865 and 1885, around one quarter of the registered prostitutes in Bologna, Italy, were migrants, and during the 1880s young British women worked in Belgium and other parts of Europe (Gibson 1986, Walkowitz 1980). In India, a number of European women worked as prostitutes in the latter part of the nineteenth century, the majority of whom originated from Central and Eastern Europe, but also among them were English women (Levine 1994). In Russia, in the late 1880s, "non-Russian and foreign prostitutes" comprised around one-sixth of the registered prostitute population (Bernstein 1995: 97). During World War II, "haole" (white) women were the majority in brothels in Hawaii. Korean and Thai women were forced to "comfort" the Japanese military, and Cuban and Venezuelan women serviced the Dutch and American navies in Curacao (Bailey and Farber 1992, Hicks 1994, Kempadoo 1994). Specific political, economic and social events shaped the women's involvement in the sex trade at different times, in different places, within the context of a globalizing capitalist system, colonialism and masculinist hegemony.

In the late 1980s, Licia Brussa estimated that between thirty and sixty percent of the prostitutes in the Netherlands were from Third World countries, particularly Latin America and Asia (1989). Today, the migrant sex working population has been joined by women from Eastern Europe and West Africa. In 1991, around seventy percent of the sex workers in Japan were reported to be Filipino, and young Afghan and Bangladeshi women worked in prostitution in Pakistan (Korvinus 1992). In the same period, the red-light district in Bombay, India, relied predominantly upon migrant female labor, much of which originated in Nepal. By the mid-1990s, Eastern European, Russian and Vietnamese prostitutes were reported to be working in China while Russian women appeared in the Egyptian sex industry, and Mexican women moved into sex work in Japan (*BBC World Service*, April 28, 1994, *New York Times*, June 9, 1995, Azize *et al.* 1996). [. . .]

Indeed, transnational sex work has continued over the past hundred years, but the question arises about whether it has intensified, as many will argue, during the twentieth century and particularly over the last two decades. Given the lack of figures and documentation of what in most countries is an outlawed and underground activity, and the multiplicity of activities worldwide that constitute "sex work," it is virtually impossible to state with certainty that numbers have increased. Also, as with any activity in the informal sector, information on populations involved, income, types of activities, and international migration or trafficking routes is imprecise. A glaringly obvious example of the inaccuracies that exist is related to the number of prostitutes in Asia. Figures for the city of Bombay in India range from 100,000 (*Asia Watch* 1993) to 600,000 (Barry 1995) – a difference of half a million. In the case of Thailand, figures for "child prostitutes" range between 2,500 and 800,000, with the age range being equally as imprecise (Black 1995). To any conscientious social scientist, such discrepancies should be cause for extreme suspicion of the reliability of the research, yet when it comes to sex work and prostitution, few eyebrows are raised and the figures are easily bandied about without question.[2]

Nonetheless, since the 1970s a global restructuring of capitalist production and investment has taken place and this can be seen to have wide-scale gendered implications and, by association, an impact on sex industries and sex work internationally. New corporate strategies to increase profit have developed, involving the movement of capital from industrial centers to countries with cheap labor, the circumvention of unionized labor, and so-called flexible employment policies. Unemployment and temporary work plagues the industrialized centers as well as "developing" countries. The ILO estimated that in January 1994, around thirty percent of the world's labor force was unemployed and unable to sustain a minimum standard of living (Chomsky 1994: 188). The power and influence of transnational institutions such as the World Trade Organization, the World Bank and various corporations has superseded that of national governments and national businesses.[3] Measures imposed by the International Monetary Fund (IMF) for national debt-repayment, such as Structural

Adjustment programs, and international trade agreements, such as the North American Free Trade Agreement (NAFTA) and the General Agreement on Tariffs and Trade (GATT) squeeze national economies, creating displacement from rural agricultural communities, rising unemployment in urban centers, drops in real wages, and increasing poverty. Free Trade and Special Economic Zones for export-oriented production, cuts by governments in national expenditures in the social sector and the removal of trade restrictions, local food subsidies and price controls accompany these measures and agreements and impose even further hardships on working people.[4] The corporate drive to increase consumption, and hence profit margins, has also led to a proliferation of new products, goods and services and the cultivation of new desires and needs. Alongside apparel, automobile, electronic, computer and luxury goods industries, sex industries have grown since the mid-1970s to fully encompass live sex shows, sex shops, massage parlors, escort services, phone sex, sex tours, image clubs, and exotic dancing, and to creating, as Edward Herman states, "one of the booming markets in the New World Order – a multi-billion dollar industry with finders, brokers, syndicate operations and pimp 'managers' at the scene of action" (1995: 5). Sex tourism has become a new industry. Recruitment agencies and impresarios link the local sites and sex industries in various parts of the world, indicating a parallel with transnational corporations in the formal global economy. "The 'success' of the sex industry," write James Petras and Tienchai Wongchaisuwan about Thailand, "is based on a 'special relation' of shared interests among a complex network of military leaders, police officials, business tourist promoters, godfathers and pimps. At the international level, airline and hotel chains have worked closely with the local business-military elite to promote the sex tourist industry. The World Bank's support for the open economy and export oriented development strategy results in financial support of tourism" (1993: 36). In Thailand, the authors estimate, direct and indirect earnings from sex enterprises is about $5 billion a year. Elsewhere, as in Cuba and the Dominican Republic, the specter of sex tourism has become embedded in the economy. The sexual labor of young brown women in these playgrounds of the West has become increasingly important to the national economies, while prostitution remains condemned as degrading and destructive. In Cuba's case, it is viewed as a counterrevolutionary engagement. Nevertheless, State support or tolerance of this form of tourism is evident. Sex work fills the coffers of countries whose economic survival is increasingly dependent on global corporate capitalist interests.

The emerging global economic order has already wreaked havoc on women's lives. Recent studies document an increasing need of women to contribute to the household economy through waged labor, yet having to deal with declining real wages, lower wage structures than men and longer working hours.[5] Seasonal or flexible employment is the norm for women all over the world. Skilled and unskilled female workers constitute the main labor force in the new export-oriented industries – for shoe, toy, textile and garment production, in agribusinesses and electronic factories – where they are faced with poor working conditions, are continually threatened with unemployment due to automation and experience mass dismissals due to relocations of whole sectors of the industry. In many instances, minimum wage, health and safety laws are overridden by the transnational corporations in these new production zones, leaving women workers in particularly hazardous situations. Furthermore, with disruptions to traditional household and family structures, women are increasingly becoming heads of households, providing and nurturing the family. With dwindling family resources and the western emphasis on the independent nuclear family, women must also increasingly rely on the state for provisions such as maternity leave and child-care, yet fewer funds are allocated by governments for social welfare and programs.[6] Informal sector work and "moonlighting" is growing and engagement in the booming sex industries fills a gap created by globalization.

Migration is a road many take to seek other opportunities and to break away from oppressive local conditions caused by globalization. A 1996 ILO report describes the "feminization" of international labor migration as "one of the most striking economic and social phenomena of recent times" (1). This "phenomenon" according to the authors of the report, is most pronounced in Asian countries where women are migrating as "autonomous, economic agents" in their own right, "trying to seize economic opportunities overseas" (1). The Philippines has put more women onto the overseas labor market than any other country in the world (Rosca 1995). Within all this dislocation and movement, some migrant women become involved in sex work. However, laws prohibiting or regulating prostitution and migration, particularly from the South, combine to create highly complex and oppressive situations for women if they become involved in sex work once abroad. The illegal movement of persons for work elsewhere, commonly known as "trafficking" also becomes a very real issue for those who are being squeezed on all sides and have few options other than work in underground and informal sectors. Traffickers take advantage of the illegality of commercial sex work and migration, and are able to exert an undue amount of power and control over those seeking political or economic refuge or security. In such cases, it is the laws that prevent legal commercial sex work and immigration that form the major obstacles.

A related dimension to globalization with the expansion of sex industries, a heightened necessity for transnational migration for work, and increasing immiseration of women worldwide, is the spread of AIDS. Paul Farmer links the pandemic in sub-Saharan Africa to the social realities of the migrant labor system, rapid urbanization, high levels of war with military mobilization, landlessness and poverty that have been exacerbated by an economic crises caused by "poor terms of trade, the contradictions of post-colonial economies which generate class disparities and burdensome debt service" since the mid 1970s (1996: 71). These factors, he contends, are intricately intertwined with pervasive gender inequality and specific socially constructed meanings of gender and sex, creating a very complex situation regarding the epidemiology and, consequently, the prevention of AIDS. Around eighty-two percent of AIDS cases worldwide in 1996, he points out, were found in Africa, with women and children bearing the brunt of the epidemic. A similarly complex interrelationship between changing agriculture systems to meet New World Order demands, fueled by gendered traditions and inequalities, inadequate subsistence, a felt lack of desired consumption, goods, tourism and the drug trade enables the spread of AIDS in Asia (Farmer 1996: 82–88). For the Americas, Bond *et al.* note that labor migration between the Caribbean and the United States has been an important factor in the spread of HIV and AIDS, and that "the development of tourist industries, frequently based on U.S. capital as a replacement for the decline in profits from older colonially established sources such as sugar cane, has also traced the routes for HIV to follow" (1997: 7). With only an estimated four percent of the world's AIDS cases being registered in North America and Western Europe, it is particularly evident that it is the rest of the world that is at greatest risk (Farmer 1997).

This relatively new sexually transmitted disease and identification by world health authorities of a concentration of the epidemic in developing countries has led to government interventions. The attention has produced contradictions for sex workers around the world. As in the past, with state concern for public health matters, prostitutes are placed under scrutiny, subject to intense campaigning and roped into projects that define them as the vectors and transmitters of disease (Zalduondo 1991, Murray and Robinson 1996). Sex workers are continually blamed for the spread of the disease, with Eurocentric racist notions of cultural difference compounding the effect for Third World populations. Consequently, inappropriate methods of intervention have been introduced and sex workers burdened with having to take responsibility for the prevention and control of the disease. Farmer points out that "...while public health campaigns target sex workers, many African women take a different view of AIDS epidemiology and prevention. In their view, the epidemiology of HIV and Africa's economic crises suggest that HIV spreads not because of the 'exotic sexual practices' of Africans but because of the daily life within which women struggle to survive" (1996: 74). Bond *et al.*, in their studies of AIDS in Africa and the Caribbean apply a similar analysis. Arguing that there is "more to AIDS than 'truck drivers' and 'prostitutes'" the authors consider it of vital importance to examine relations of political and economic power in relationship to the spread of AIDS, with specific attention to the disempowered such as women and children (1997: xi). Placing the focus and blame on sex workers does not necessarily address the root of the problem, but serves to push them further into marginality and social isolation. On the other hand, some AIDS-prevention work has contributed to the formation, of new sex worker organizations, inadvertently empowering sex workers in other areas than just in health matters.

The global movement

Since the 1970s sex work has been an organizing basis for women, men, and transgenders in different parts of the world. But while the emergence of prostitutes' rights groups and organizations in Western Europe and North America up to the early 1990s has been well documented, there is little written on the global movement. Over the past ten years, the main recorders of the prostitutes' rights movement, Frederique Delacoste and Priscilla Alexander (1987), Laurie Bell (1987), Gail Pheterson (1989), Nicky Roberts (1992), Valerie Jenness (1993), Shannon Bell (1994), Wendy Chapkis (1997) and Jill Nagle (1997), describe the beginning of a self-identified prostitutes movement with the establishment of the prostitute organization, (COYOTE) Call Off Your Old Tired Ethics, in San Francisco in 1973 and sister or similar kinds of groups in various part of the United States around the same time. They locate the emergence of a highly politicized prostitute rights advocacy movement in Europe, starting with the strike by French prostitutes in 1975 which led to the creation of the French Collective of Prostitutes and which in turn inspired the formation of such groups as the English Collective of Prostitutes in England (1975), the New York Prostitutes Collective (1979), that later became USPROS, the Australian Prostitutes Collective (1981), which is now known as the Prostitutes Collective of Victoria (PCV) and the Italian Committee for the Civil Rights of Prostitutes (1982). CORP – the Canadian Organization for the Rights of Prostitutes – the Dutch Red Thread and HYDRA in Germany also assume a significant place in the history of the sex workers rights movement as chronicled by these authors. The writings also signal the formation of the International Committee for Prostitutes Rights (ICPR) in 1985, the two World Whores Congresses held respectively in Amsterdam, the Netherlands in 1985 and Brussels, Belgium in 1986, and the creation of the World Charter of Prostitutes Rights through these two congresses, as epitomizing a worldwide prostitutes' rights movement and politics. Nonetheless, the international character of the movement has been more wishful thinking than political reality. As Pheterson, rapporteur on the two congresses and co-director of ICPR, notes about the first congress. Third World sex workers did not formally participate and prostitute advocates represented sex workers for three countries, Singapore, Thailand and Vietnam (1989). At the second congress, a similar dominance of the West was evident. Pheterson further points out in her reflection on the ICPR's work at the end of the 1980s, "the numerous nationalities not represented point to work yet to be done in building a truly world movement of whores." Thus, much of what was laid out in the Charter and discussed at the congresses was defined by (white) western sex workers and advocates. Third World prostitutes' rights organizations, such as the Ecuadorian Association of Autonomous Women Workers, established in 1982, or the Uruguayan, Association of Public Prostitutes (AMEPU), founded in 1985, were at this point not an integral part of the "international" movement, although Pheterson attempted to correct this omission by including "new voices" in her report on the prostitutes' rights movement (1989). And despite Pheterson's awareness of the problem and her insistence that the movement needed to truly "internationalize," many writings in the 1990s have continued to reproduce a skewed representation of the prostitutes rights movement and to ignore sex workers' rights groups in developing countries.

Despite this lack of recognition, sex workers in Third World and other non-western countries have been busy, taking action, demonstrating against injustices they face, and demanding human, civil, political and social rights. Thus not only was an Ecuadorian association formed in 1982, but they held a sex workers' strike in 1988. In Brazil, a national prostitutes conference took place in 1987, giving rise to the establishment of the National Network of Prostitutes, Da Vida. In Montevideo, Uruguay, AMEPU inaugurated its childcare center and new headquarters after making its first public appearance in the annual May Day march in 1988. The Network of Sex Work Projects, founded in 1991, began to make links with sex workers' rights and health care projects in the Asian and Pacific region, slowly creating a truly international network that today includes at least forty different projects and groups in as many different countries around the world. 1992 witnessed the founding of the Venezuelan Association of Women for Welfare and Mutual Support (AMBAR), with the Chilean group Association for the Rights of Women, "Angela Lina" (APRODEM) and the Mexican Unión Única following suit in 1993. Two national congresses were held by the Ecuadorian sex workers' rights association in 1993 and 1994. The Maxi Linder Association in Suri-name, the Indian Mahila Samanwaya Committee, and the Colombian Association of Women (Cormujer), were also all established by 1994. In the same year, around 400 prostitutes staged a protest against the closing of a brothel in Lima, Peru, with the slogan "We Want to Work, We Want to Work" and in Paramaribo, Suriname, sex workers made a first mass public appearance on AIDS Day, marching through the city with the banner "No Condom, No Pussy," drawing attention to their demands for safe sex. Also, 1994 witnessed the founding of The Sex Worker Education and Advocacy Taskforce (SWEAT) in South Africa. In 1996, groups in Japan and the Dominican Republic – Sex Workers! Encourage, Empower, Trust and Love Yourselves! (SWEETLY) and Movement of United Women (MODEMU) – were formed, and in the same year the Indian organization held its first congress in Calcutta, as well as organizing several protests and demonstrations against harassment and brutality. In 1997, with the help of AMBAR in Venezuela, the Association for Women in Solidarity (AMAS) became the first Nicaraguan group, comprised mainly of street workers. Other sex worker organizations have been reported to exist in Indonesia, Tasmania, Taiwan, and Turkey. Several of these hitherto unrecognized or new groups and activities are described in this volume, through the eyes and words of the leading activists.

While this list of organizations is not exhaustive, and keeps growing, we must keep in mind that each group has a history that pre-dates its formal founding date. Sex workers as individuals and in informal groups have battled against stigmas and discriminatory laws, denounced social and political injustices, and fought for their basic human' rights in non-western settings for many years and there are often several years of organized activity before a formal organization appears on the map. Furthermore, in some instances the seeds of a contemporary organization are much older. The present Uruguayan organization, for example, claims a history lodged in the struggle of Polish sex workers during the nineteenth century in that country. Everyday resistances have also been documented for the mid-nineteenth century in Lucknow, India (Oldenburg 1990) and Guatemala (McCreery 1986), and in colonial Kenya in the 1920s–30s (White 1990). Sex workers' struggles are thus neither a creation of a western prostitutes' rights movement or the privilege of the past three decades.

The lack of Third World sex worker representation in the international arena began to be redressed in the 1990s, as the international AIDS conferences provided a new opportunity for sex workers to get together. Jo Doezema writes, "AIDS was an issue that gave new impetus to the flagging international movement by providing an issue around which to organize much needed funds and new alliances with gay organizations. Under-funded sex worker organizations in both the First and Third Worlds who would have been hard pressed to persuade their funders of the necessity of sending a representative to a 'whores conference' found it easier to get money when public health was, supposedly, at stake."[7] Thus, the AIDS conferences provided a platform for a revitalization of the international movement, and, for the first time, signaled the presence of Third World sex workers as equal participants on the international scene. A notable instance, as Doezema further notes, was the AIDS Conference in Yokohama, Japan, in 1994, when the Network of Sex work Projects organized its first Asia-Pacific regional conference, parallel to the AIDS Conference. Sex worker delegates from around the world put together an action plan for activism during the AIDS Conference itself and beyond. During the Conference, delegates were addressed by a panel of sex workers from countries including Brazil, Mexico and Malaysia, who presented their own analysis and strategies of AIDS prevention in the context of sex workers rights. The United Nations Fourth World Conference on Women in Beijing, China, in 1995 also drew various international sex workers' rights activists – many of whom formed a united delegation, spearheaded by the NWSP.[8]

In 1997, an international prostitution conference took place in California, U.S., divided into a sex worker-only pre-conference organized by NWSP and COYOTE and a conference for sex workers, academics, activists and others working with or for sex workers, organized by COYOTE and the University of California at Northridge. Sex workers representing organizations from countries including Mexico, Guatemala, Venezuela, Brazil, Nicaragua, India, Thailand, Japan, and Malaysia helped insure that the pre-conference worked to an agenda that reflected a truly international perspective.

New directions

Building upon the definition of sex work, prostitutes in the state of New South Wales in Australia became the first to gain acceptance as an official sex workers' union in 1996, under the umbrella of the Australian Liquor, Hospitality and Miscellaneous Workers' Union. Exotic dancers working at the "Lust Lady" in San Francisco in the United States followed suit. In April 1997, they entered into an agreement with the management of the theater and labor union. Local 790, the Service Employees International Union of the AFL-CIO which includes provisions on discrimination, sexual harassment, family and personal leave, pay, job evaluation, breaks and lunches, and dismissals. The notion of "sex worker" has then enabled prostitutes and others in the sex trade to not only articulate their needs as working peoples, but has brought a legitimacy hitherto unknown, and these examples may provide models for other groups in the future.

And while participation by Third World sex workers in the international movement is on the rise generally, not all regions participate equally. Central and South American, and increasingly, Asian sex workers' organizations are becoming a major voice in the international movement. In the former Soviet Union, Eastern Europe, Africa, and in the majority of Asian countries, however, independent organizing by sex workers is not yet visible. Here, as elsewhere, the AIDS pandemic has meant an upsurge in interest in sex workers as vectors of disease. While this has led, in some cases, to repressive measures against sex workers, it has also provided an opportunity for possible sex worker organizing. The projects such as Bliss without Risk in the Czech Republic, SYNVEV in Senegal. EMPOWER in Thailand, ZiTeng in Hong Kong, and others included in this volume, while not run by sex workers, are committed to the empowerment of sex workers. It is from groups such as these that autonomous sex worker organizations have begun. Continued AIDS prevention work of the type described here could thus lead to a strengthening of the movement, and to many more sex workers' rights groups worldwide.

Finally, in the global movement, struggles against western imperialism and racism within prostitutes' rights activism continues. The 1997 international conference provides a example of this struggle. Early Internet discussions between sex workers about the conference planning was dominated by those with access in the U.S., and focused almost exclusively on western, especially United States issues. This focus was later challenged by other sex workers, and resulted in fierce debate on the nature of an international conference.[9] Sex workers from Chile also frustratedly pointed out prior to the conference, that the organizers claim to internationalism was empty, given that there was an absence of travel funds and facilities for translation to enable Third World sex workers to participate in the conference. From Australia, Alison Murray withdrew from the conference, noting, among other things, that the conference was overly "North America centered."[10] The main conference reflected deep-seated ignorance of the importance, and even the existence, of sex worker organizations outside the United States and Europe. Third World and non-western sex workers felt marginalized, hurt and angry as promised interpretation facilities never materialized and as sessions highlighting the activities and issues of importance to Third World sex workers were relegated to difficult time-slots or even canceled when, due to scheduling problems, they threatened to conflict with "more important" sessions. This led to a storming of the podium during the final plenary session by Central and South American sex worker delegates, who, with full support from other sex workers and activists, denounced the academic organizers for the ill treatment they received. The conference thus ended in a strong anti-imperialist, anti-racist demonstration with the uproar forcing western sex workers to recognize and deal with these dimensions of power and inequality. Such consciousness within the movement can only continue to grow.

Notes

1 See Frederique Delacoste and Priscilla Alexander, *Sex Work: Writings by Women in the Sex Industry* (Pittsburgh, PA: Cleis Press, 1987); Laurie Bell, ed., *Good Girls: Feminist and Sex Trade Workers Face to Face* (Toronto, ON: The Women's Press, 1987); Gail Pheterson, ed., *A Vindication of the Rights of Whores* (Washington: Seal Press, 1989); Nickie Roberts, *Whores in History: Prostitution in Western Society* (London: Harper Collins, 1992); Valerie Jenness, *Making It Work: The Prostitutes' Rights Movement in Perspective* (Hawthorne, NY: Aldine de Gruyter, 1993); Anne McClintock, "Sex Workers and Sex Work: Introduction," *Social Text*, vol. 37 (Winter 1993) 1–10; Shannon Bell, *Reading, Writing and Rewriting the Prostitute Body*, (Bloomington, IN: Indiana University Press, 1994); Wendy Chapkis, *Live*

Sex Acts: Women Performing Erotic Labor (New York: Routledge, 1997); Jill Nagle, ed., *Whores and Other Feminists* (New York: Routledge, 1997).

2 As an example of this careless use, see Robert I. Friedman, "India's Shame," *The Nation* (April 8, 1996) 11–20.

3 See Sarah Anderson and John Cavanagh, *The Top 200: The Rise of Global Corporate Power* (Washington, DC: Institute for Policy Studies, 1996). In this survey of the world's largest corporations, Anderson and Cavanagh, found that "of the top 100 largest economies in the world, 51 are now global corporations, only 49 are countries" with Wal-Mart, bigger than 161 countries, Mitsubishi "larger than the fourth most populous nation on earth: Indonesia" and Ford's economy larger than that of South Africa.

4 See Noam Chomsky, *World Orders Old and New* (New York: Columbia University Press, 1994); Jeremy Brecher and Tim Costello, *Global Village or Global Pillagea; Economic Reconstruction, From the Bottom Up* (Boston, MA: South End Press, 1994); see also, Kevin Danaher, ed., *Fifty Years is Enough: The Case Against the World Bank and the International Monetary Fund* (Boston, MA: South End Press, 1994).

5 For details on gender inequalities worldwide see the United Nation publications: *Human Development Report 1995* and *The World's Women 1995: Trends and Statistics.*

6 Among the many who have written specifically on women in the New World Order, see Carmen Diana Deer, *et al.*, *In the Shadows of the Sun: Caribbean Development Alternatives and U.S. Policy* (Boulder, CO: Westview, 1990); Sheila Rowbotham and Swasti Mitter, eds., *Dignity and Daily Bread: New Forms of Economic Organizing Among Poor Women in the Third World and The First* (London: Routledge, 1994); M. Jaqui Alexander and Chandra Talpade Mohanty, eds., *Feminist Geneologies, Colonial Legacies. Democratic Futures* (New York: Routledge, 1997); Edna Bonachich, *et al.*, eds., *Global Production: The Apparel Industry in the Pacific Rim* (Philadelphia, PA: Temple University Press, 1994); and Annie Phizacklea and Carol Wolkowitz, *Homeworking Women: Gender, Racism and Class at Work* (London: Sage Publications, 1995).

7 Doezema, E-mail correspondence, July 25, 1997.

8 Ibid.

9 Ibid.

10 In an E-mail correspondence sent in January 1997 to James Elias, co-organizer of the conference.

24 Culture, economics, and politics in Latin American social movements: theory and research

Arturo Escobar

Source: Arturo Escobar and Sonia Alvarez (eds) (1992), *The Making of Social Movements in Latin America*, Boulder: Westview Press, pp. 62–85

[...]

This chapter looks at some of the most salient aspects of contemporary social movements theory and research. Rather than pretending to survey the landscape of theories, it focuses on the epistemological and political context within which theory is being produced, especially in Latin America. One essential aspect of this context is the crisis of development and its models for it is largely in response to the failure of development that social movements emerge. Here, it is crucial that development not be seen solely as an economic and political project but as an overarching cultural discourse that has had a profound impact on the fabric of the Third World. Moreover, the crisis of development must be assessed in terms of the broader crisis of the civilizational project of modernity. Once we situate social movements within a reinterpreted context of the crisis of development and modernity, it becomes impossible to see them only in economic or political terms. Indeed, their fundamental cultural character has to be recognized and subjected to theoretical analysis. Most of this chapter is devoted to this endeavor, that is, to developing a framework for understanding Latin American social movements as economic, political, *and* cultural struggles.

[...]

The crisis of development and modernity in Latin America

It is no secret that Latin America is going through its worst crisis in history. For some, the 1980s amounted to a "reversal of development" (Portes and Kincaid 1989; Dietz and James, eds., 1990), particularly through the transfer of capital from Latin America to Center countries through debt service "obligations." Persistent violence, growing political instability, falling standards of living, and aggravated social and economic conditions are the most dramatic manifestations of the crisis. Given the current restructuring of capital at the global level (Castells 1986; Harvey 1989; Amin 1990), most authors predict not an improvement but a worsening of conditions.

Much talk about the crisis, however, is imprecise at best, and it tends to focus exclusively on economic conditions, the need for the right "adjustment" packages, and the renewal of development. This is quite understandable, given the precariousness of living conditions and the magnitude of macroeconomic dislocations. But if forty years of "development" – always interspersed with adjustment and stabilization periods, at least since the early 1950s – have not produced stability and sustained economic improvements, it would seem unlikely that "more of the same" will yield different results. To the extent that Latin America continues to be seen in terms of the need for "development" based on capital, technology, insertion into the international division of labor, and so forth, the crisis will only continue to deepen, new forms of colonialism and dependence will be introduced, and social fragmentation and violence will become more virulent. Perhaps because it is becoming more and more evident that "development" has dug its own grave, a significant rethinking of the whole strategy has become a real possibility and is, indeed, in order.

To understand development in a radically new manner, we must first distance ourselves from prevalent forms of understanding it. Since its inception in the early post-World War II period, it has become customary to see development either as a series of strategies intended to bring about "progress" or, in the opposing view, as a form of neocolonialism and dependency, that is, an instrument of control over the Third World. What advocates and foes alike share is the assumption that some form of "development" must take place, even if they dispute the character and rationality of the necessary interventions. That the development process implies the destruction of traditions, the normalization of living conditions along Western criteria, and the restructuring of entire societies does not seem to concern those who advocate "progress" and the modernization of national societies.

The history of development is relatively recent and even precarious. It dates back to the early post-World War II period when the scientific gaze of the West focused on Asia, Africa, and Latin America in a new manner. It was during this period (roughly from 1945 to 1960) that the institutional apparatus for producing knowledge and forms of intervention in and about the Third World (the World Bank, the United Nations, bilateral development agencies, planning offices in the Third World, development organizations on the local level) was actually created. The terms *Third World, underdeveloped areas, development,* and the like were inventions of this period, integral components in a new system for producing truth about those parts of the world. During those years, Third World countries witnessed a steady influx of experts in all fields – economics, industrialization, agriculture, nutrition, family planning, education, health, the military – each of them measuring and observing a small part of their reality, each of them measuring and observing a small part of their reality, each of them addressing a "problem" to be corrected by the appropriate development intervention. Like the orientalist discourses addressed by Edward Said (1979), development discourses have functioned as powerful instruments for shaping and managing the Third World.[1]

The discourse of development portrayed Third World societies as imperfect, abnormal, or diseased entities in relation to the "developed" societies; the cure for this condition would be, of course, the development prescriptions handed down by Western experts and very often willingly adopted by Third World elites. The development discourse undoubtedly brought about a new hegemonic formation that has since significantly defined what can be thought and done – or even imagined – when dealing with the economies and societies of Asia, Africa, and Latin America. This hegemonic discourse transformed the system through which identities were defined. What we now have is a vast landscape of identities – the "illiterate," the "landless peasants," "women bypassed by development," the "hungry and malnourished," "those belonging to the informal sector," "urban marginals," and so forth – all of them created by the development discourse and cataloged among the many abnormalities that development would treat and reform through appropriate "interventions" (for instance, literacy campaigns, the Green revolution, birth control, basic needs programs, and integrated rural development projects). As I will show, this fragmentation of identities is essential for understanding contemporary movements. After all, is this not the cast of characters that are now becoming social actors in their own right?

[. . .]

The nature of culture in social movements research

It is essential to recognize the importance of economic factors and their structural determinants. But just as crucial as the reconstruction of economies – and indelibly linked to it – is the reconstitution of meanings at all levels, from everyday life to national development. Social movements must be seen equally and inseparably as struggles over meanings as well as material conditions, that is, as cultural struggles. Are economies not cultural forms, anyway? Do they not entail profound cultural choices, as the anthropology of modernity demonstrates? Certainly, Homo oeconomicus is not a culturally neutral subject. "Material needs" and "technologies" are permeated by cultural contents. Every new technology inaugurates a ritual – a way of doing things, of seeing the world, and of organizing the social field. How, then, could we brush aside the consideration of the cultural content of "economies"?

Thus, there is a cultural politics that must be brought to light in examining the politics of social movements. This cultural politics is rarely visible through conventional forms of analysis, although we already have some clues to help us in this task. The first is found in the importance granted by some authors to the terrain of everyday life – which, as anthropologists would have it, is fundamentally shaped by culture. Another guiding source originates in a number of concepts generated from within social movements theory itself, particularly Alain Touraine's notion of historicity, Alberto Melucci's proposition that social movements find their reason for being in submerged frameworks of meaning and in the daily practice of cultural innovation, and Ernesto Laclau and Chantal Mouffe's complex argument of politics as a discursive articulatory process. Contemporary theories of popular culture, especially those that highlight the role of the subalterns themselves in shaping the world in which they live, contribute an additional set of insights. These guideposts are briefly described in the rest of this chapter in an attempt to develop a coherent, albeit rudimentary and provisional, account of the cultural politics of social movements in Latin America and a cultural theory of social movements.

Social movements and the practice of everyday life

Not until recently has the domain of everyday life been given critical attention by scholars.[2] Yet, an adequate theorization of *the practice* of everyday life (especially collective practice) has proven elusive. Social movements research involves situations in which the interrelations between daily life, political practice, and social relations can be fruitfully investigated. This possibility has been best expressed by Elizabeth Jelin:

> If we study the meaning of political practice in daily life, the construction of identities and discourses, we do not do it assuming that these are determinant – or necessary – of practices at the institutional level. Neither do we assume the autonomy of democracy in relation to people's quotidian practices. The relationship between one and the other level are complex, mediated. Our intention is to point to *a field of construction of democracy* that, in the first place, is important in itself, that of the social relations of daily life. ... We believe that *daily life and social movements are privileged spaces in which to study these processes of mediation*, since social movements are situated, at least in theory, in the intermediate space between individualized, familiar, habitual, micro-climactic daily life, and socio-political processes writ large, of the State and the institutions, solemn and superior.[3]
>
> (1987b: 11, emphases added)

This is perhaps demonstrated most clearly when we look at women's movements, as Jelin concluded in her study of Latin American women's mobilizations. The fact that these movements seem to arise "naturally" out of daily life does not imply that their action is less important or restricted. What it means, actually, is that "the type of action in which women engage does not restrict itself to the traditional rules of politics but attempts to give a new meaning to politics" (Jelin, ed., 1990: 204). This conception is a far cry from older models of political practice that focused on the visible, macro aspects of protest and on empirically observable results (such as, in the classical model, the capture of the state). Said succinctly, the personal is political and cultural. To live differently, to assert one's difference, is to practice cultural innovation and to engage in some sort of political practice (even if not necessarily progressive, as the 1980s have shown in many parts of the world).

The centrality of daily life for social movements is difficult to perceive; like the self-understanding of the people, daily life has been rendered invisible or secondary by conventional social sciences, especially the positivist ones. The prevailing static understanding of culture as something embedded in a set of canonical texts, beliefs, and artifacts and characterized by a certain abstract universality for those who share it has contributed to this state of affairs. Culture is not something that exists in the abstract; it is embedded in practices, in the everyday life of people. Culture *is* (made of) people's practices. Encounters with others who are different from us intensify the awareness of our own culture and make us realize how we think and feel in some ways rather than others, that is, that we have "a culture."

When people "practice" their everyday lives, they are thus reproducing or creating culture. "We are all cultural producers in some way and of some kind in our everyday life," insisted a contemporary theorist of popular culture (Willis 1990: 128). Symbolic creativity in everyday life is vibrant, if somewhat invisible; it involves language, the body, performative rituals, work, and both individual and collective identities. It is essential for social movements research to tap into this level of popular practice. Everyday life involves a collective act of creation, a collective signification, a culture. It is out of this reservoir of meanings (that is, a "tradition") that people actually give shape to their struggle. Put in a more abstract and general manner, daily life is located at the intersection of processes of articulating meaning through practices, on the one hand, and macro processes of domination, on the other. Struggles over meanings at the level of daily life – as feminists and others do not cease to remind us – are the basis of contemporary social movements. The implications of this realization for theory and methodology are enormous, as we are just beginning to appreciate.

Historicity and the symbolic challenge of social movements

There is, then, the need to rethink the relationships between everyday life, culture, and politics. A series of notions produced by some prominent social movements theorists are helpful to our efforts to do this in the context of social movements. Let us start with Alain Touraine's notion of historicity. Touraine's central insight is that, for the first time, (post-industrial) society is the result of a complex set of actions that society performs on itself (1977, 1981, 1988a). No longer can social action be seen as the result of some metasocial principle – such as Tradition, God, Reason, the Economy, or the State; society itself is the result of a set of systems of action involving actors who may have conflictual interests but who share certain cultural orientations. Social movements, therefore, are not "dramatic events" but rather "the work that society performs upon itself" (Touraine 1981: 29). The goal of this action is the control of *historicity*, which is defined as "the set of cultural models that rule social practices" (Touraine 1988a: 8) and is embodied in knowledge, economic, and ethical models. What then is a social movement? "A social movement is the action, both culturally oriented and socially conflictual, of a class defined by its position of domination or dependency in the mode of appropriation of historicity, of the cultural models of investment, knowledge and morality towards which the social movement itself is oriented" (Touraine 1988a: 68).

The essential feature of this definition is that actors recognize the stakes in terms of a cultural project; in other words, what is at stake for social movements is historicity itself, not merely organizational forms, services, means of production, and the like. Moreover, only societies that have reached "the highest level of historicity" (that of self-production) – namely, postindustrial or "programmed" societies – can be said to be characterized by social movements of this kind. By the same token, Touraine concluded that most forms of collective mobilization in Latin America are not social movements proper but rather struggles for the control of the process of historical change and development. Given the reality of dependency, modernization, and the state, together with the state's intervention in all aspects of life, the stake for social actors is not historicity but greater participation in the political system. Latin America would be in the process of acceding to a higher level of historicity – that is, becoming a truly modern society – through industrialization and development (Touraine 1987).

Touraine's insistence on the cultural stakes of collective action is of utmost importance, even if many questions remain to be answered. For instance, what are the processes through which historicity is produced and contested, including the dynamic interaction of tradition and modernity, domination and resistance? How are long-standing, implicit cultural contents increasingly undermined and appropriated by "modern" scientific discourses, and to what extent is this process contested by social actors? What is the relation between political action and cultural forms? By highlighting action, Touraine's sociology affords many important elements for reinterpreting the nature of social movements. Yet, as Melucci (1988a), for instance, has pointed out, Touraine and others do not explain the process by which actors build a collective identity through interactions, negotiations, and relationships with the environment. For these authors, identity appears as an already accomplished fact, the essence of the movement. But, Melucci insisted, rather than assuming the existence of a relatively unified collective actor, the researcher must precisely explain how collective action is formed and maintained. This demands that the researcher provide a view of how actors construct common actions, explain how different elements are brought together, and describe the concrete processes through which individuals become involved in action.

The social construction of collective action and identity, according to Melucci, involves complex interactions along three axes: ends, means, and relationships with the environment. For the researchers, this entails making sense of the plurality of meanings and analytical levels and processes that define those axes – if they hope to account for the apparently unified empirical behavior of collective actors, which is actually the result of a process of construction. Melucci's "constructivist" view, in contrast to structural models or those based on individual motivations, focuses on collective action and identity as a process, not as a fact or an event. As he pointed out, concepts proposed by resource mobilization theory (such as "structure of opportunities," "discretional resources," and the like) are not really "objective" realities; they "imply the capacity of the actors to perceive, evaluate and determine the possibilities and limits afforded by the environment" (Melucci 1988a: 342). These prior operations are what have to be brought to light in the research process; they are what constructing an action system is all about, which Melucci referred to as "collective identity":

> Collective identity is an interactive and shared definition produced by several individuals and concerned with the orientations of action and the fields of opportunities and constraints in which the action takes place: by "interactive and shared" I mean a definition that must be conceived as a process, because it is constructed and negotiated through a repeated activation of the relationships that link individuals. The process of identity construction, adaptation and maintenance always has two aspects: the internal complexity of an actor (the plurality of orientations which characterizes him), and the actor's relationship with the environment (other actors, opportunities and constraints).
>
> (Melucci 1988a: 342)

The question of identity construction is crucial even in terms of thinking about strategy, as other theorists contend. Gerardo Munck's statement that "only on the basis of a constructed identity does it make sense to talk of strategies" (1990: 25) left no doubt in this regard. "Only by drawing upon the... 'new social movements' approach,'" he continued, "can we hope to explain how strategic calculations are made" (G. Munck 1990: 25). Melucci pointed to yet another level of analysis that most theorists of social movements overlook. Because these theorists concentrate on collective action as a fact, not a process, they make analytically invisible a crucial network of relationships that underlie collective action before, during, and after the events. The exclusion of this level from the field of analysis is of paramount importance because it is at this level that the creation of cultural models and symbolic challenges by the movements actually occurs. Melucci referred to this level as a "submerged reality" that constitutes both the condition of possibility and the very stuff of social action. Contemporary collective action, in his words,

> assumes the form of networks submerged in everyday life. Within these networks there is an experimentation with and direct practice of alternative frameworks of meaning, as a result of a personal commitment which is submerged and almost invisible. ... The "movements" emerge only in limited areas, for limited phases and by means of moments of mobilization which are the other, complementary phase of the submerged networks. ... What nourishes [collective action] is the daily production of alternative frameworks of meaning, on which the networks themselves are founded and live from day to day. ... This is because conflict takes place principally on symbolic grounds, by challenging and upsetting the dominant codes upon which social relationships are founded in high density informational systems. The mere existence of a symbolic challenge is in itself a method of unmasking the dominant codes, a different way of perceiving and naming the world.[4]
>
> (Melucci 1988b: 248)

Social movements, in this way, cannot be understood independently from the "submerged" social and cultural background from which they emerge. This might be described as the latent aspect of the movements, no less real because it is less readily observed empirically. A corollary of this notion is that it is more appropriate to speak of "movement networks" or "movement areas," rather than "movements"; the network would include both the movements and the "users" of the cultural products produced by the movements (that is, both latent and visible components). "The normal situation of today's 'movements,'" Melucci concluded (1985: 800), "is a network of small groups submerged in everyday life which requires a personal involvement in experiencing and practicing cultural innovation."

Social movements thus bring about social practices that operate, in part, through the creation of spaces for the production of meanings. But how does this "daily production of alternative frameworks of meaning," this "practice of cultural innovation," actually take place? Recent studies of popular culture and resistance, of growing importance in Latin America as well, shed some additional light on these questions.

Social movements and popular culture and resistance

As mentioned before, the relationships between the practice of everyday life, collective action, and politics is not yet well understood. Does cultural resistance in daily life, for instance, amount to anything politically? Can it foster more "visible" forms of protest? How are researchers to study "oppositional" or "alternative" meanings produced at the micro level of daily life by subaltern groups, as well as their relation to politics? Moreover, is it possible to study social movements without relying on existing models of political practice, such as those couched in terms of parties, organizations, resources, and so forth? In other words, can we place popular practice and culture at the center of social movements inquiry? And if we can, how do we do this?

It is true that most models of social production and action have largely focused on the macro aspects of these processes, especially on the structures and mechanisms of domination. In recent years, however, investigators have begun to give attention to the other side of the coin – namely, the subordinate – and not as a massive datum ("the masses") but as something characterized by complex, fluid, and heterogeneous elements and processes. A type of microsociology and ethnography of popular resistance is emerging. The work of Michel de Certeau has been quite important in this regard. If domination proceeds through *strategies* (economic, political, technological, institutional) that organize the world in ways that lead to the colonization of physical, social, and cultural environments, de Certeau argued, the "marginal majority" (that is, all those who have to exist within structures of domination) are nevertheless not merely passive receivers of these conditions. As "users" of them, people effect multiple and infinitesimal transformations of the dominant forms under which they inevitably have to live and operate in order to adapt them to their own interests and, to the extent possible, to subject them to their own rules. Users "reappropriate the space organized by socio-cultural production" (de Certeau 1984: xiv), thus effecting a veritable cultural production in their own right.

Unlike the strategies of domination, which structure the world into "readable spaces" (de Certeau 1984: 36) that dominant institutions can understand and control, popular production operates through *tactics*, small procedures and ruses in the realm of everyday life. Strategies and tactics are two different ways of knowing, of practicing life and organizing the social space. Strategies seek to discipline and manage people and institutions, whereas tactics constitute a sort of "antidiscipline," an "art of making" that proceeds by manipulating imposed knowledge and symbols at propitious moments. Tactics are "weapons of the weak," to use James Scott's catchy label (1985); they introduce a certain play into the system of power. Given the expansion of technocratic rationality in postindustrial societies, neither strategies nor tactics are any longer regulated by local communities. Strategies are produced by largely impersonal mechanisms (science, media, transnational economic forces, anonymous institutions); but tactics, too, are increasingly "cut loose from the traditional mechanisms that circumscribed their functioning" (de Certeau 1984: xx, 40). The universalization of the commodity form and the increased autonomy of the culture industries entail that "there is a loss of the fundament of culture in the local enactments of the speaking subjects," which undermines "the core activity that produces meaning" (Angus 1989: 345) – specifically, the link to community.

In Latin America, the breakdown of the local systems for the production of meaning is not as extended as it is in the postindustrial world. But the fact that the Latin American population is already 70 percent urban and very exposed to modern informational systems cannot be underestimated. Nevertheless, this fact must be considered together with the recognition that there still exist *socially significant* groups that represent alternative cultural possibilities. For instance, local tactics – some bound to community, some not – allowed peasants and indigenous groups to maintain an important degree of control over their environment and worldview. In sum, even if it is increasingly reinscribed into the market system, the production of meaning in Latin America retains a certain "hybrid" character, partly linked to the market and the transnational cultural system but also partly arising out of embodied communal systems and "the local enactments of the speaking subjects."

This conceptualization of popular resistance, although helpful, does not yet enable us to construct a direct link with social movements research. With this goal in mind, what else can we say about the nature of "popular cultural production"? In postindustrial societies, it is said, "people make popular culture at the interface between everyday life and the consumption of the products of the culture industry" (Fiske 1989b: 6). The aim of this productivity is to create meanings that are relevant to everyday experience. Part of this process takes the form of a sort of "semiotic resistance," which originates in "the desire of the subordinate to exert control over the meanings of their lives, a control that is typically denied them in the material social, conditions" (Fiske 1989b: 10). Those who focus merely on the "escapism" of the popular classes as they consume the products of the culture industries (TV, music videos and video games, school, shopping centers, romance novels, fashion, and so on) overlook the vibrant symbolic creativity that goes on in the daily encounter with those products.

This form of "semiotic power" is a type of social power, and hence it is actually or potentially political:

> Those who dominate social relations also dominate the production of the meanings that underpin them: Social power and semiotic power are different sides of the same coin. Challenging meanings and the social group with the right to make them is thus no act of escape. ...Semiotic power is not a mere symbol of, or licensed substitute for, "real" power. Its uses are not confined to the construction of resistant subjectivities but extend also to the construction of relevances, of ways of negotiating this interface between the products of the culture industries and the experience of everyday life.
>
> (Fiske 1989b: 132)

Beyond that, "resistances at the micro-level are necessary to produce social conditions for political action at the macro-level" (Fiske 1989a: 172). I will come back to this point when I discuss the concept of articulation. For now, it is important to emphasize that it is in the terrain of everyday life that the interests of the dominant culture are negotiated and contested: "speaking our meanings with their language," as Fiske (1989a: 36) summarized this dynamic. Popular culture involves the recognition of social difference and the affirmation of the culture's rights and identity. Difference is a social need and a social practice. This is true in the Third World as well, although the dynamics of cultural production are somewhat different. Cultural politics in Latin America cannot be reduced to the "uses" of dominant products or texts; this is doubly so given the state's acute limitations in providing services for large segments of the population, so that not infrequently people have to provide for their own. In

Latin America, the production and circulation of meanings are not so overdetermined by the commercial forms of Western capitalism. There still exist practices, "residual" and "emerging" (Williams 1980), that have a decisive collective character, and these provide a different basis for resistance and collective action.

Finally, how are people's production and negotiation of meanings going to be studied? If this production is at the basis of cultural politics, whether in the form of social movements or in "minor" forms of resistance, how is it going to be made visible? Generally speaking, one needs to understand how meanings are made (for example, through "development," mass media, or seemingly trivial daily acts of creation and resistance) and how they relate to social experience (that is, how they allow people to create elements or engage in practices that are relevant to them, particularly in terms of their struggles against specific forms of power). Theorists of popular culture advocate a type of ethnographic approach that moves from dominant "text" (cultural form or product) to its concrete appropriations by the people (its "users"). This "ethnosemiotic approach" highlights the role of the people as "agent[s] of culture in process" and as "structured instances of culture in practice" (Fiske 1990: 86). Here, we are speaking of a type of cultural analysis that requires a close reading and inter-pretation of popular experiences, including, but not restricted to, class, gender, ethnic, and politico-economic aspects. "Ethnography," Fiske summarized (1990: 98), "is concerned to trace the specifics of the uses of a system, the ways that the various formations of the people have evolved of making do with the resources it provides. Ethnosemiotics is concerned with interpreting these uses and their politics and in tracing in them instances of the larger system through which culture (meanings) and politics (action) intersect."

This approach has important methodological consequences for social movements research. It requires a close relationship between investigator and people and a significant engagement in concrete situations. Ethnographic techniques, critical inquiry, and textual analysis are all involved. One possible and provisional way of imagining the research process from an ethnosemiotic perspective is in terms of the following processes. First, the popular practice/"text" (produced either through more or less autonomous creation or through the consumption of a dominant product/text) and its context have to be generated for analysis, always in terms of "peoples' own practices, meanings and usages of them, as gathered through our direct fieldwork methods" (Willis 1990: 7). Second, this "re-generated" text, along with the processes by which it was produced, must be interpreted; this interpretation has to start with the self-understanding of the agents and move beyond it, toward an expla-nation couched in terms that make the practice in question clearer to both agents and researchers (and, hopefully, permit a more effective or clairvoyant practice by the agents, as Taylor (1985) would have it). Third, the practice/text's relation to a politics, that is, to the redistribution of social power, has to be ascertained. Finally – and of particular importance in the case of social movements research – the extent to which this cultural politics fosters alternative political cultures must also be examined.

All of these steps involve complex theoretical and methodological questions that I will not attempt to analyze here. The end result of the process should be a more intimate and complex account of the movement and of those who make it, not merely an overview of its organizational structure, its relation to parties, and the like. As in the case of the life history of individuals, this research approach requires that we see the social actor "as engaged in the meaningful creation of a life world":

> Rather than looking at social and cultural systems solely as they impinge on a life, and turn it into an object, a life history should allow one to see how an actor makes culturally

meaningful history, how history is produced in action and on the actor's retrospective reflections on that action. A life history narrative should allow one to see the subjective mapping of experience, the working out of a culture and a social system that is often obscured in a typified account.

(Behar 1990: 225)

Behar's complex life history of a poor Mexican woman suggests that there are possibilities for seeing Latin American women in terms different from those already fixed in much academic and political discourse (mothers, wives, activists, "beasts of burden," and so forth). "It suggests that, if looked at from a cultural perspective, Latin American women can emerge as thinkers, cosmologists, creators of worlds" (Behar 1990: 230). So it would be with contemporary movements and those enagaged in them. They would appear as engaged in the self-production of their reality in multifaceted and complex ways, including their responses to harsh social and economic conditions.

[...]

Conclusion

A point stressed throughout the chapter is that contemporary social movements in Latin America have a multiple character, as economic, social, political, and cultural struggles. The boundaries and dependencies among these domains are blurred, in some cases indistinguishable. In particular, it is important to be open to the deeply cultural character of these struggles. This realization is crucial even in terms of the economy; as Stuart Hall pointedly stated (1991: 64), "Everybody, including people in poor societies whom we in the West frequently speak about as if they inhabit a world *outside* of culture, know that today's 'goods' double up as social signs and produce meanings as well as energy." Social movements are about the transformation of many of the practices of development and modernity, about the envisioning and reconstruction of social orders, perhaps alternative modernities or different modes of historicity.

To understand these processes, I have argued, one must look at the micro level of everyday practices and their imbrication with larger processes of development, patriarchy, capital, and the state. How these forces find their way into people's lives, their effects on people's identity and social relations, and people's responses and "uses" of them have to be examined through a close engagement and reading of popular actions. It is also true that the system that accounted for and stabilized identities has changed dramatically. Even up to the 1960s, identities were, in a sense, clearly defined and unproblematic. One knew who was who, so to speak, and how he or she was defined as a member of a group. One also knew what to do and how to do it (Development or Revolution, depending on one's perspective). But this is no longer true. Theorists refer to this change as the proliferation of identities and cite the fact that identities are constructed and that this construction takes place through processes of articulation. In the interface of identity and articulation one finds the manifold political strategies and tactics that more clearly account for a "movement." It is at this level that the various "paradigms" of social movements research cohere. Questions of strategy and questions of identity are inextricably linked, and the links can be most fruitfully investigated at the level of the cultural politics of the movements.

This also means that the nature and impact of social movements is not restricted to their most visible manifestations. Even when the state, becoming conscious of a new challenge in the form of a movement, tries to co-opt it or repress it, it is possible that the movement has already spread thin throughout a vast social domain. In other words, social movements are somewhat exterior to the state, and if it is true that the state is a key interlocutor for the movements, these latter cannot be reduced to the logic of the state.[5] The state, to be sure, is too powerful a social force to be left to the politicians and economic elites; it is still particularly important in relation to the provision of basic needs. Yet, at least in part, the social reconfiguration that social movements are bringing about has to be found in a different space, in whatever way we may be able to think of it (for instance, social relations of daily life, transformed cultural understandings, new political cultures, new public domains, and the like). Beyond the borders of the region, Latin American social movements are nourishing a crop of meanings that in some ways are freer of modern forms of rationality and control and that could foster a renewal not only of the awareness of suffering but also of the awareness of forms of freedom and of life as a collective process. And this might have unique importance in today's world.

In her study of "the alchemy of race and rights" in the system of North American law, Patricia Williams spoke thus of the reality of "unowned" or emancipated slaves after the Civil War:

> After the Civil War, when slaves were unowned – I hesitate to use the word emancipated even yet – they were also disowned: They were thrust out of the market and into a nowhere land that was not quite the mainstream labor market, and very much outside the marketplace of rights. They were placed beyond the bounds of valuation, in much the same way that the homeless are or that nomads and gypsies are, or tribal people who refuse to ascribe to the notion of private space and who refuse or are refused traditional jobs or stationary employment; they became like all those who cannot express themselves in the language of power and assertion and staked claims – all those who are nevertheless deserving of the dignity of social valuation, yet those who are so often denied survival itself.
>
> (1991: 21)

One is tempted to think similarly of many people in the Third World today, the vast numbers of people placed under conditions of marginality or in the space of the informal economy, "not quite the mainstream labor market" – which, as we know, shrank significantly in the 1980s – "and very much outside the marketplace of rights" because the language of rights and the language of justice also seemed to fade away from public discourse in the wake of the worst-ever IMF-imposed "austerity" and "stabilization" programs. But perhaps the same people are learning how to negotiate more explicitly their participation in the transnational markets of commodities and meanings that characterize Latin America today; perhaps they are coming to reject more efficiently the "bounds of valuation" within which they can only be seen as second-class, "underdeveloped" subjects; perhaps they are coming to assert themselves in a language of power that they have crafted through forms of collective action such as those discussed [here].

Notes

1 For a more exhaustive discussion of the origins and modes of operation of the discourse of development, see A. Escobar 1984, 1988.

2 The work of the Annales School, Norbert Elias (1978), and Foucault, as well as feminist theory and ecology, are among the most important factors behind the increasing interest in everyday life.

3 This and all other translations from the Spanish are my own.

4 This English translation from the Italian original was slightly modified by me based on the Spanish translation in Calderon, ed., 1988.
5 The hypothesis of the exteriority of social movements in relation to the state originated in the work of Deleuze and Guattari (1987). See also A. Escobar, in press.

Selected references

Angus, I. (1989) 'Circumscribing Postmodern Culture', in Ian Angus and Sut Jhally (eds) *Cultural Politics in Contemporary America*, New York: Routledge.
Amin, S. (1990) *Maldevelopment*, London: Zed Books.
Behar, R. (1990) 'Rage and Redemption: Reading the Life Story of a Mexican Marketing Woman', *Feminist Studies*, 16(2), 223–258.
Castells, M. (1986) 'High Technology, World Development, and Structural Transformation: The Trends and the Debate', *Alternatives*, 11(3), 297–344.
de Certeau, M. (1984) *The Practice of Everyday Life*, Berkeley, CA: University of California Press.
Deleuze, G. and Guattari, F. (1987) *A Thousand Pateaus: Capitalism and Schizophrenia*, Minneapolis, MN: University of Minnesota Press.
Dietz, J. and James, D. (eds) (1990) *Progress Toward Development in Latin America*, Boulder: Lynne Rienner.
Elizabeth, J. (1987) *Ciudadania e Identidad: Las Mujeres en los Movimentos Sociales Latino-Americanos*, Geneva: United Nations.
Elias, N. (1978) *What is Sociology?*, New York: Columbia University Press.
Escobar, S. (1988) 'The Possibility for Democracy', *The Other Side of Mexico*, 6, August 15.
Fiske, J. (1989a) *Understanding Popular Culture*, Boston, MA: Unwin Hyman.
Fiske, J. (1989b) *Reading the Popular*, Boston, MA: Unwin Hyman.
Fiske, J. (1990) *Introduction to Communication Studies*, London: Routledge.
Foucault, M. (1977) *Discipline and Punish*, New York: Vintage Books.
Foucault, M. (1980) *Power/Knowledge*, New York: Pantheon Books.
Hall, S. (1991) 'The Local and the Global: Globalization and Ethnicity', in A.D. King (ed.) *Culture, Globalization and the World-System*, London: Macmillan.
Harvey, D. (1989) *The Condition of Postmodernity*, Oxford: Basil Blackwell.
Jelin, E. (1990) (ed.) *Women and Social Change in Latin America*, London: Zed Books.
Melucci, A. (1985) 'The symbolic challenge of contemporary movements', *Social research*, 52(4), 789–816.
Melucci, A. (1988a) *Nomads of the Present: Social Movements and Individual Needs in Contemporary Society*, Philadelphia: Temple University Press.
Melucci, A. (1988b) 'Social Movements and the Democratization of Everyday Life', in Deane, J. (ed.) *Civil Society and the State: New European Perspectives*, London: Verso.
Mouffe, C. (1988) 'Radical Democracy: Modern or Postmodern', in Ross, A. (ed.) *Universal Abandon? The Politics of Postmodernism*, Minneapolis, MN: University of Minnesota Press.
Munck, G. (1990) 'Identity and Ambiguity in Democratic Struggles', in Foweraker, J. and Craig, A. (eds) *Popular Movements and Political Change in Mexico*, Boulder: Lynne Rienner.
Portes, A. and Kincaid, D. (1989) 'Sociology and Development in the 1990's: Critical Challenges and Empirical Trends', *Sociological Forum*, 4(4), 479–503.
Scott, J. (1985) *Weapons of the Weak: Everyday Forms of Peasant Resistance*, New Haven: Yale University Press.
Taylor, C. (1985) *Philosophy and the Human Sciences*, Cambridge: Cambridge University Press.
Touraine A. (1981) *The Voice and the Eye: An analysis of social movements*, Cambridge: Cambridge University Press.
Touraine, A. (1987) *The Return of the Actor*, Minneapolis, MN: University of Minnesota Press.
Touraine, A. (1988) *The Return of the Actor*, Minneapolis: University of Minnesota Press.
Williams, P. (1991) *The Alchemy of Race and Rights*, Cambridge: Harvard University Press.
Williams, R. (1980) 'Base and Superstructure in Marxist Cultural Theory', in Williams, R. (ed.) *Problems in Materialism and Culture*, London: NLB.
Willis, P (1990) *Common Culture*, Boulder: Westview.

25 The economic bondage of debt – and the birth of a new movement

Ann Pettifor

Source: Ann Pettifor (1998) 'The Economic Bondage of Debt – and the Birth of a New Movement', *New Left Review* 230, pp. 115–122

On 16 May 1998, the Jubilee 2000 Coalition drew a crowd of more than 70,000 people in Birmingham, meeting place of this year's G8 summit, to form Britain's first-ever mass protest in the form of a Human Chain. The crowd came together to demand that the leaders of the rich countries 'break the chains of debt' imposed on more than fifty of the world's poorest countries. These countries are held in bondage by a G8-dominated institution that acts as the agent for all international creditors (public and private): the IMF. The Human Chain was to be the central event of a range of meetings held over several days under the banner of 'The People's Summit', organized and led by the New Economics Foundation and the Jubilee 2000 Coalition. The Chain itself was routed to surround Birmingham's International Conference Centre, the focal point for the Summit meetings.

The decision to form a human chain had been taken for two reasons. First, the symbolism of chains is central to the Coalition's definition of debt as a form of human bondage, or slavery; yet chains can also symbolize constructive links between people, and the power of such bonds to break bondage. Second, the organizers believed that a human chain would be an innovative way of altering the dynamics between a large protest group and the authorities.

The campaign had an effect upon the G8 Summit even before the day's protests had begun. When the Summit agenda was first drawn up, the subject of debt was absent. But pressure from the Coalition caused the British hosts to include the subject in pre-Summit meetings with 'sherpas'. In fact, debt was not only on the agenda but was to dominate the day's proceedings.

As tens of thousands of demonstrators began making their way to Birmingham (from all parts of Britain, and many parts of the globe), news broke that the G8 were decamping to a stately home, Weston Park, well outside the city and beyond the reach of any protest. Undeterred, the Coalition's supporters continued on their way to Birmingham and its Conference Centre where much of the world's press were assembled.

By rickshaw and coracle

Hundreds of protesters arrived on foot, embarking on pilgrimages from different points around Britain in the weeks before, and stopping off to give talks and slide shows to church groups and other community organizations. Some protesters came by bike, others in a flotilla of barges on Birmingham's many canals. One even came in a coracle, another by rickshaw. Some had hoped to arrive by balloon, but this idea was vetoed by Clinton's security team. Most came by coach or train. The largest number came from the north of England

and from Scotland. Jubilee 2000 supporters also came from the US and Canada, Germany and Italy – all of which have formally established coalitions (the organization is conspicuously weak in France and Japan). Coachloads came from Norway, Sweden and Finland, and there were delegations from Spain, Holland, Belgium, Portugal, and Austria. Most of these countries provide generous aid to indebted countries, a large proportion of which is returned as debt service to the World Bank, the IMF or other creditor governments. Christian Aid, one of the main forces behind the UK Coalition, had brought together a group from the Poor Eight (P8) to represent the most indebted nations – Jamaica, Bolivia, Nicaragua, Bangladesh, Tanzania, Malawi, Mozambique and Ethiopia.

Jubilee 2000's main venue was St. Martin's in the Bullring, a church in the heart of the city, surrounded by Birmingham's largest market place. The church could seat 800 people, but by mid-morning a crowd of more than 2,000 people had spilled out into the surrounding gardens. Soon they were filling the different levels of a nearby car park, leaning over its balconies, straining to catch speeches broadcast by a public address system.

The speakers included Martin Dent and Bill Peters, the first in Britain to propose that the celebration of the new Millennium should be linked to the Jubilee concept and the urgent need for debt relief. (The idea originated with the Pope in his 1986 encyclical for the new Millennium – Tertio Millennio Adveniente.) Rodney Bickerstaffe, general secretary of the public sector trade union UNISON, also addressed the packed church; as did Shirley Williams representing the Liberal Democrats; Kofi Mawuli Klu representing the African Liberation Support Campaign; Sheelu Francis, a community activist from Tamil Nadu who had led a long march of Indian supporters through her home state in support of the Coalition's aims; Johnny Hansen, a representative of the Ghanaian Jubilee 2000 campaign; Laurie Green, the Anglican bishop of Bradwell; Bernie Grant MP, who has strong links to highly indebted Caribbean countries; Doug Balfour, director of the evangelical aid agency, Tearfund; Daleep Mukerjee, the newly appointed director of Christian Aid; Barry Coates, director of the World Development Movement; Clare Short, Secretary of State for International Development; and Ed Mayo, director of the New Economics Foundation.

Halfway through the morning's speeches, the protesters received some important news. The Prime Minister's office had called to say that Blair had decided to return early from Weston Park, and was requesting an urgent meeting with the Coalition's director and three of her nominees that evening at Summit headquarters. The protest was having further impact on the G8 leaders.

Following this, the estimated 70,000 strong crowd began to assemble. All those who had registered were sent to different sectors on the nine-kilometre route. One of the organizers, Nick Buxton, ran along the chain for two miles to deliver banners in different languages to its international section. 'I passed gospel choirs, doctors dressed in surgeons' outfits, students dressed as bankers whipping scantily dressed slaves, dreadlocked crusties and church congregations. There were masses of banners, painted faces, samba drums.' At 3 p.m. a wall of sound erupted along the chain. Bishop John Davies gave this report of his experience: 'I got caught up with a group of about sixteen bishops... we walked around about half the chain ending up at St. Phillips Cathedral, where Clare Short received boxes of petitions from many different countries. This procession was an extraordinary experience. As we walked we were greeted all along with deafening cheering, whistles, drums, rattles, as if we were a winning football team... and as if we were somehow responsible. At Birmingham thousands of people had caught a straight simple enthusiasm for a straight simple idea: whatever the complications and difficulties, it is intolerable to allow the present arrangements of unpayable debt to continue.'

The Jubilee idea

The call for Jubilee in the year 2000 is a call to lift the yoke of economic degradation from those enslaved by economic forces, in particular by high levels of international debt. For the Israelites whose story is told in Leviticus, debt was a form of slavery. The Lord's speech in Leviticus uses imagery derived from the experience of a slave community, degraded by debt. Deprived of wealth, alienated from the land, from their own labour and from each other, the call is for the return 'of every man unto his possession...and unto his family'.

The Jubilee 2000 Coalition grew out of an alliance of aid agencies, the Debt Crisis Network, led by the New Economics Foundation, Christian Aid and the World Development Movement. Agencies had been working since the Mexican debt crisis in 1982 on the complex issues it raised for international finance. Increasingly they were lobbied by project coordinators in the South to increase advocacy for debt relief. For every $1 of aid sent to developing countries in 1996, $11 was returned in the form of debt service. The, in any case diminishing, trickle of aid to Africa was negligible compared to the vast outflow of funds necessary to service and repay debt.

Aid agency lobbying has had a considerable impact on officials in the World Bank and IMF, so much so that in October 1996 these twin sisters of international financial relations proposed a package of debt relief for the poorest countries – the Heavily Indebted Poor Country (HIPC) initiative. But such lobbying was not enough. Creditor governments dragged their heels in negotiations. Debt relief took the form of (relatively) tiny shavings and reschedulings from a backlog of unpayable debts. The very process of agreeing debt relief – agreement by the creditors – blocked further progress. It was necessary that the issue be brought to the attention of the broader public, who would have to grapple with its complexities, so that they could place pressure on elected representatives in creditor nations.

It was decided to broaden the educational work of the Debt Crisis Network. This decision coincided with an approach by Martin Dent and Bill Peters, who had long been advocating the need to link the Biblical concept of Jubilee with the Millennium and with the urgent need to cancel the poorest countries' international debt. Bill Peters, a retired diplomat, had, early in his career, advised a poor country to take out a loan – one of many they now find unpayable. Martin Dent, as well as being an academic at Keele University, had close links with Nigeria where he had once served as a district official.

Most of the secular aid agencies were not persuaded. But the three Christian agencies, Christian Aid, CAFOD and Tearfund cautiously explored the possibilities of a broad campaign. The lobbyist for the Debt Crisis Network, a non-Christian, was charged with taking the concept forward. In April 1996, with the committed support of a Tearfund employee, Isabel Carter, and the financial backing of a retired banker, Will Reid, a small office was set up in a shed on the roof of Christian Aid's building in Waterloo. In October 1997, at the behest of Michael Taylor, director of Christian Aid and previously chair of the Anti-Apartheid coalition of churches and aid agencies, a formal Coalition of more than seventy organizations was established, including many secular groups. The Jubilee 2000 Coalition was launched in the Grand Committee room of the House of Commons on 13 October 1997 (the Jubilee room having proved too small for the large numbers of MPs, Peers and supporters wishing to attend).

Today, two years later, Jubilee 2000 has a wide public base of support, not just in Britain but in countries around the world. There are offices, staff and a Jubilee 2000 organization in five of the G7 countries. There are informal coalitions in forty countries in Europe,

Africa, Latin America, South Asia and Australia. The Jubilee 2000 Petition has been circulated globally, and is being signed in 69 countries.

The composition of the coalition

The UK Coalition is now an extraordinary alliance of secular and religious organizations. The breadth of ecumenical cooperation within the Coalition is astonishing, given the divergent constituencies of Catholic and evangelical denominations. The Pope, the Archbishop of Canterbury, and the leaders of all the free churches including the Baptists, the Methodists and the Church of Scotland, all give support and encouragement to the Coalition, and actively promote its aims. This has enabled the Coalition to quickly spread world-wide through missionary organizations. In addition, the Coalition has support from the Jewish Reform Synagogues, a leading British Buddhist group and influential Muslim organizations.

The trades union movement is represented by the British TUC and the International Confederation of Free Trades Unions, with Britain's white collar union UNISON playing a major role, both in the UK and internationally through Public Services International. International aid agencies are the next largest constituency and include CAFOD, Christian Aid, Action Aid, Tools for Self-Reliance, Tearfund and the World Development Movement. Leading figures within the Coalition come from British black refugee and community groups (led by the African Liberation Support Campaign and the 1990 Trust), who in turn have links to newly established Jubilee 2000 groups in Africa and the Caribbean. A large constituency consists of women's organizations with links to groups in the South, including the YWCA, the Mothers' Union and Britain's National Federation of Women's Institutes. The medical profession is very active because of concern at how debt service payments in poor countries crowd out spending on health, clean water and sanitation. The profession is represented by international physicians' organizations (the IPPNW and MEDACT), as well as the British Medical Association. Celebrities, comics and stars welcome the Coalition's work as more fundamental than the 'band aids' of small well-meaning projects, and as more meaningful than most millennial projects. They are represented by Comic Relief and the musicians organization, War Child.

The only British political party formally affiliated is the Green Party, but the Coalition receives active support from a wide range of MPs in all three major parties. The all-party Jubilee 2000 group is co-chaired by Bill Cash MP (Conservative) and Frank Cook MP (Labour). A recent report of the Parliamentary Select Committee for International Development, chaired by Bowen Wells MP (Conservative) gave a substantial boost to the demand that deeper and speedier debt relief be offered to the poorest countries by the year 2000.

The coalition's principles

The Coalition does not use the phrase 'debt forgiveness' in its campaigning. This would imply that the 'sin' of falling into debt was committed solely by elites in debtor countries. Rather, the elites of the more powerful nations are considered co-responsible. Ninety-five per cent of the debts owed to the UK are held by the Export Credit Guarantee Dept (ECGD) of the Department of Trade and Industry, and most credits are aggressively promoted to encourage poor countries to buy British goods – particularly arms. Increasingly, creditor nations use this hidden subsidy to exporters to compete against other OECD exports, and to improve their competitive edge in international markets. At the same time, there is a strong incentive for elites in borrowing nations to take out loans since the repayment terms often extend well beyond their own stewardship of the economy.

The Coalition asserts the differences between popular understandings of personal and company debts, and the debts of sovereign nations. In most cases of domestic indebtedness, it is possible to draw a line under debts and bring them to an end. That line is called bankruptcy which, combined with the concept of limited liability, protects debtors, their families and succeeding generations from hostile creditors. No such line can be drawn in international law. Governments, it is often asserted, cannot become bankrupt. In fact they do, and countries like Liberia, Burundi, Rwanda, Mozambique and Nicaragua spiral deeper into the abyss of debt, while creditors, represented by the IMF and World Bank, offer new loans to help pay off old ones. International financial relations are dominated at all stages by creditors who decide on the conditions for repayment, closely monitor the implementation of conditions, and determine whether to offer rescheduling, or write off of loans. Creditors act as plaintiff, judge and jury in their relations with debtors – with the IMF, as the agent of all creditors, playing the lead role. There is no independent assessor, arbitrator or 'receiver'. For many of the poorest countries, debts represent an unpayable burden. According to the World Bank, actual debt service payments are roughly half of those scheduled. In any normal creditor–debtor relationship these bad debts would be written off. Not so with sovereign debt.

The Southeast Asian crisis is essentially a crisis of reckless over-lending. The IMF's approach is to protect creditors by transferring risks and losses to taxpayers – both in OECD countries and in Southeast Asia. These actions have angered the US Congress which is refusing to allot funds to help out the IMF. Republicans and Democrats alike accuse the IMF of offering 'welfare to bankers'. In the words of one commentator, it has been a case of 'socialism for bankers, and capitalism for debtors'. It was ever thus for developing countries.

In Africa, IMF and World Bank lending policies have exacerbated the debt problem. The IMF expects to have received at least $600 million more from Africa than it put in during 1997. Under such high levels of indebtedness and dependency, many countries have ceased to function as sovereign states. Some, like the new Democratic Republic of the Congo, Sierra Leone and Liberia, have become subsistence economies, and are ravaged by unchecked disease and civil war. The need to raise hard currency to repay debts has forced indebted states to skew their economies in favour of exports. So African countries grow carnations, coffee and cocoa, using a large proportion of their export revenues to repay debts. At the same time, a substantial share of their tax revenues are diverted to the same purpose. This distortion of the economy means that people have insufficient food, shelter and clothing, and that cuts are made in spending on education, health and sanitation.

High levels of debt undermine any attempt to build democratic institutions. This is because indebted countries are bound to their Western creditors who make concerted efforts to govern their economic regimes through the IMF. In Africa for example, elites are forced to seek election on the basis of economic policies considered unacceptable in Western Europe, Japan or the US. While Helmut Kohl will not campaign in the coming German general election for the removal of EU subsidies from German farmers, his representative on the Board of the IMF insists on the removal of subsidies from farmers in indebted countries, as part of IMF-imposed 'structural adjustment' policies. While Newt Gingrich in his Contract with America never contemplated removing farm subsidies, or the removal of protectionist barriers from US industries, the US representative on the Board of the IMF insists that a poor country like Rwanda must remove subsidies and protectionist barriers before being given any form of support or debt relief by international creditors. While Bill Clinton is keen to promote a bill through Congress calling for free trade with Africa, cotton industry lobbyists worked hard to insert clauses which would discourage the imports of African cotton and textiles.[1] A case of free trade for the single-commodity economies of Africa, and protectionism for that industrial giant of the world economy, the US. While Western leaders actively promote privatization of economies in developing countries, and encourage their own industrial giants to cherry-pick assets in these IMF-dominated states, they force indebted countries like Thailand to nationalize highly indebted banks, so transferring losses to taxpayers.

These double standards in the world economy, coupled with the imposition of economic policies by the IMF, limits action by elected politicians, and causes disillusionment in the democratic process. Increasingly, African leaders implementing IMF programmes resort to the rigging of elections, and are, in effect, supported in this by their creditors.

Debt slavery

There are striking parallels between the twentieth-century millstone of debt and the practice of slavery in preceding centuries. One of the most important is that the trade in debt is accepted by public opinion as an unpleasant but necessary by-product of an economic system from which the North benefits. In just the same way, the eighteenth-century trade in slaves was tolerated. Christian campaigners against slavery were deeply embarrassed by the Christian organizations which supported it. Their task was difficult: to challenge the dominant ethic which led to the Church's tolerance of slavery as a necessary evil.

Today Jubilee 2000 supporters around the world are similarly challenging the new dominant ethic: acceptance of a trade in debt which removes choice from the governments of developing nations and denies people in these countries control over their own destinies. The Club of OECD creditors has this in common with the alliance of slave-holding nations of the eighteenth century. It is an overwhelmingly white, European-led group, whose actions and decisions result in an equivalent form of oppression of formerly colonial nations.

The Jubilee 2000 Coalition does not seek to write off every penny owing on 31 December 1999. Rather it seeks to have the inert, unpayable backlog of debt written off, and debts reduced to a level which will permit sustainable human, environmental and economic development. As with the campaign to abolish slavery, so the campaign for the remission of debt will be fought across several continents. As with the campaign to abolish slavery, so a successful conclusion will require a massive shift in the popular consensus. It will require the introduction of a fair, independent legal framework to govern relations between international creditor and debtor. As with the campaign against slavery, religious and secular organizations are challenging the new bondage, and calling for drastic and urgent debt relief. They are calling for no less than a new economic order. This will require a new beginning – a jubilee year – in which those in bondage will be granted economic redemption, through debt remission, and be returned to their own possessions.

If the cancer of slavery could be removed from the global economic order by citizens around the world determined to achieve justice, then it should be possible for citizens to remove the cancer of debt, too. That was why 70,000 people gathered in Birmingham. The G8's response was disappointing, the communiqué bleak. Behind the scenes, the G8 leaders were deeply split, with Germany blocking more generous, speedier debt relief. Jubilee 2000's attention is now turned to Germany where Helmut Kohl is to stand for election on his record as a 'world statesman', and where every effort will be made to document this record in relation to the poorest countries. Germans will be reminded of the extraordinarily generous treatment they were given by Allies through the London Accord of 1953, when a large proportion of Germany's debts were written off.[2] Next year's G8 Summit is to be held in Cologne in June. G8 leaders can be in no doubt of the determination of this international movement: to sound the trumpet of Jubilee and 'proclaim liberty throughout all the land'.[3]

Notes

1 HR 1432, 105th Congress, p. 9. An Act to authorize a new trade and investment policy for sub-Saharan Africa.

2 Joe Hanlon, ' "We've been here before" – debt, default and relief in the past – and how we are demanding that the poor pay more this time', Jubilee 2000 Coalition, April 1998.

3 These words from Leviticus 25 are engraved on the Liberty Bell in Philadelphia, and served as an inspirational text for the American Revolution.

26 Globalization and local resistance

The case of Shell versus the Ogoni

Cyril I. Obi

Source: Barry K. Gills (ed.) (2000), *Globalization and the Politics of Resistance*, Basingstoke: Macmillan, pp. 280–294

Introduction

The extractive and polluting activities of Shell, the Anglo-Dutch global oil giant which produces slightly over half of Nigeria's oil, has spawned alienation, protests and resistance across the local host communities of the oil-rich Niger delta region in the past two decades. These took a turn for the worse from the mid-1980s in the wake of a deepening economic crisis, the throes of structural adjustment and a political transition. The Movement for the Survival of Ogoni People (MOSOP) was driven by the quest for self-determination; their aim was to force Shell and the Nigerian state to accept their right to control their own land, and the proceeds therefrom.

To stem the further 'production of environmental degradation' and the expropriation of the oil-rich Ogoni ecology, MOSOP waged a popular-based campaign against Shell and the state in Nigeria, locally and globally. The Nigerian state remains a significant factor in the local–global nexus. Entirely dependent on externally realized oil rents for its reproduction, this state is an expression of a fragile yet strong power bloc seeking to impose its hegemony and legitimacy on the Nigerian 'nation', while guaranteeing the local conditions for unimpeded global accumulation in Nigeria. The case of the Ogoni reflects how the balance of social forces influences outcomes locally. The environment becomes a contested terrain reflecting social and political relations of power over production, distribution and access.

The dialectics of globalization and local resistance

The politics of local resistance is a collective action directed at blocking further alienation, expropriation and environmental degradation. It represents a mass project of restitution and self-determination. To grasp the dialectics of globalization and local resistance in the context of the Ogoni struggle, we should situate our analysis in the structure of the on-going project of globalization. This avoids the limitations of state-centric approaches and the tendency for mainstream international relations theory to inadequately address the politics of global environmental change (Williams, 1996: 42). In considering the global logic of capital and its connections with environmental degradation and local resistance, attention will be paid to the 'national' context of the struggle, the social and political forces locked in the conflict, and their position in the global accumulation of capital at the local level.

Globalization, Shell and local resistance

Shell's interaction with the Ogoni environment is at the root of the conflict. The Ogoni – the indigenous landowners – have been increasingly alienated from the products of their land. Shell has polluted the ecosystem and damaged the livelihood of the local Ogoni peasantry without paying sufficient heed to initially peaceful demands for restitution.

To get at the root of Ogoni resistance, one needs to 'focus on the underlying structural conditions that give rise to expropriation and environmental degradation at the local level (Woodhouse, 1992), and its connection with global accumulation. Conceptually, one cannot separate the environmental crisis in Ogoni land from the process of globalization. What then is Shell's role in the process of globalization?

A lot has been written about the immense power, political clout, wealth and global spread of the seven leading oil multinationals (Sampson, 1973). What is important is the strategic link between the oil giants and the energy needs of the industrial powers, particularly the G-7 countries. Oil is strategic as the most viable source of energy for transforming nature into commodities, which are exchanged to realize surplus. Thus, control of oil is directly linked to the reproduction and expansion of capital on a global scale.

Shell[1] is located in 'a global structure of material accumulation which simultaneously concentrates wealth and energy both in certain locales and at certain social levels of extracting and dispossessing from other locales and social levels' (Saurin, 1996: 87). In the Ogoni context, Shell need not 'attend to either (local) labour needs or local ecological propriety'. As Saurin argues (*ibid.*: 88):

> the destruction of Ogoni lands in Southern Nigeria by oil companies including allegedly Royal Dutch Shell satisfies the covetous and distanced shareholders who derive huge financial benefit from these lands and people. At the same time, the Ogoni pay the permanent costs of ecological degradation and repression, whilst relinquishing their control over what happens to their land, to the oil, or the product of their labour.

As observed by MOSOP, Ogoni indigenous people were not employed by Shell, their locality lacks basic infrastructure, and pollution has destroyed the local economy: farming, fishing, hunting and petty trading. What was at stake was the very existence of the Ogoni – the right to be. It is this struggle for achieving control of the land, and re-imposing environmentally sustainable local economic practices, that pitched the Ogoni against the further penetration of global capital.

Shell versus the Ogoni: from the local to the global

Having been marked out and given to Shell since 1938 (Soremekun and Obi, 1993a) Ogoni land was integrated into 'globalized capitalist relations' (Giddens, 1990: 18). The specificities of the Ogoni struggle for self-determination have been variously treated. Apart from the writings, interviews and speeches of its prominent spokesperson and leader of MOSOP, the late Ken Saro-Wiwa,[2] other writers have treated it in terms of a struggle against 'internal colonization' (Naanen, 1995), ethnic minority elite agitation (Osaghae, 1995) or the unresolved minority nationality question in Nigeria's federalism (Ngemutu-Roberts, 1994). Welch presents the Ogoni struggle within the context of the risks involved in the quest for social justice and self-determination in sub-Saharan Africa (Welch, 1995). A common thread linking these works is the broadly state-centric descriptive approach, which pays inadequate attention to the critical nexus between local resistance and the contradictions arising from the global social relations of production. Steeped in positivist social science, this approach glosses over the economic and political impact of Shell's interventionism on the Ogoni ecosystem, while treating the social forces in conflict as undifferentiated ethnic 'wholes' without considering the differences in their location on the 'basis of the power relations between dominant classes among interacting ethnic groups' (Syahuka-Muhindo, 1995). The vital trans- and inter-class coalitions which cut across ethnic and national lines, and the ways these reflect the balance of social forces and power are therefore lost. The important question is not the identification of the ethnic appearance of 'minority group resistance', but how the transnational class coalition subverts the ranks of the social and political forces which resist global accumulation in their locality.

This approach enables us to transcend analysis which queries the Ogoni struggle on the grounds that they were not the only marginalized ethnic minority group in Nigeria, or others that catalogue how the 'majority ethnic groups'[3] controlled the oil wealth to the exclusion of the Ogoni. The transnational class, made up of factions of the dominant class at the global, national and local levels, benefits from the expropriation and degradation of the oil-rich Ogoni ecology. It is also necessary to examine the role of the state, and its structural inability to resist globalization.

Shell and the state in Nigeria: the unequal partnership

The state in Nigeria is the product of colonialism. Its early form was clearly interventionist, directed at the forceful integration of Nigeria into the global capitalist system: as a source of supply for cheap raw materials, and a ready market for finished products from the global centres of industrial capital. The task of integration and the process of defining the territoriality of the colonial state involved the process of forcefully bringing together people of diverse nationalities and pre-capitalist modes of production (Soremekun and Obi, 1993b, 1995). The centralized nature of colonial patrimonialism gave factions of certain numerically superior ethnic groups a head start in the sharing of spoils within the colonial state. This in turn gave them effective control over cash-crop based accumulation and a role in exercising power at the regional level (Obi, 1995). The consequence of this was that the dominant factions found in ethnicity a ready tool for access to resources and power. In the equation of colonial patrimonialism, the ethnic minorities often lost out. Their response was one of using ethnicity to push for self-determination – usually expressed in the form of demands for exclusive space, or state creation, which would give them room to exercise autonomy over resources, and protection from having resources taken away by factions from the majority ethnic groups.

As far back as 1889, 1907 and 1914, the colonial state had legislated the monopoly of oil concessions in Nigeria to 'British or British-allied capital' (Lolomari, 1976: 14; Soremekun and Obi, 1993a: 8). Under the 1914 law, Shell in 1938 (and later Shell-BP) was granted an oil exploration licence covering the entire mainland of Nigeria, an area of 367,000 square miles (Shatzl, 1968: 24–6). Shell's monopoly was exercised without local participation. Shell exercised this monopoly over Nigeria's oil until 1959 – one year prior to independence in 1960 – when it reduced its acreage to 16,000 square miles. Between 1938 and 1956, when it first struck oil in commercial quantity at Oloibiri, and the commencement of oil exports in 1958, Shell was able to establish control over the most promising oil acreage and reserves, and concretized its head start over the other oil majors.[4] The wider implications of Shell's advantaged position, and the global control of Nigeria's oil *vis-à-vis* the role of the state, did not become obvious until the collapse of the cash crop economic base in the mid-1960s.

Thus, from the 1970s onwards, oil became the fiscal basis of the Nigerian state, accounting for over 80 per cent of national revenue and 95 per cent of foreign exchange earnings (Soremekun and Obi, 1993b: 209). Due to the social relations spawned by global oil, Nigerians were excluded from production, while the local dominant class factions engaged in a zero-sum contest for niches in the distribution of oil surplus, mediated by the state's formal authority over the collection (and allocation) of oil rents.[5]

It is important to note the shift by the state from non-participation to participation in the oil industry. This cemented the ties between national and global capital. From being content to be a mere collector of taxes or rents, starting with the 1959 Petroleum Profits tax, the state began to acquire participation rights in the operating companies mining oil in Nigeria. This also provided a cloak of legitimacy, via economic nationalism, for the state, and increased its access to oil rents.

The 1969 Decree No. 51, which abrogated the 1914 Petroleum Act, theoretically transferred the control of oil from the oil giants operating in Nigeria to the state. It also vested all oil revenues -- on-shore and off-shore -- in the state. The state also took up equity interest in the joint ventures it had with the oil companies. The state took up equity in Shell–NNPC joint ventures to the tune of 60 per cent then 80 per cent (with the nationalization of BP assets in Nigeria in 1979). By the late 1990s it was about 55 per cent to the Nigerian National Petroleum Company (NNPC), 10 per cent to Elf and 5 per cent to Agip, while Shell owned 30 per cent equity participation. Shell remains Nigeria's largest operator and the state's interest in oil surplus is mostly represented in its joint venture with Shell and its critical role in Nigeria's Liquefied Natural Gas Project. Thus, the state and Shell have a common stake in the creation of oil surplus, and global oil-based accumulation (Shell, 1993). In the mid 1990s, Shell derived 14 per cent of all its oil from Nigeria (Greenpeace, 1995), while the oil-dependent state of Nigeria relied on Shell to produce 51 per cent of 'its' oil.

Due to the dependence of the Nigerian state on oil surplus it is integrated into the global relations of production which expropriates the oil resources of its own territory and people. Its role of mediation reflects the divisions within the ranks of the domestic ruling class and the balance of forces in society. Indeed, the ruling coalition has remained riven by 'regional political and ruling structures that have overlapped with historical patterns of economic and educational opportunity to create distinct regional fractions of the bourgeoisie that are hegemonic in their respective sectors' (Lubeck and Watts, 1994: 210). It is this ruling coalition and its global partners who have 'privatized' the state. At the local level, the oil minorities faction have found themselves playing a marginal role, often co-opted by the dominant groups but left out of the 'commanding heights' of the power bloc. Therefore, control over oil, being the key to Nigeria's participation in global accumulation, is a contested terrain by all social groups, while the state, as the sum total of relations arising from the global character of oil production, is a site of constant struggles for access to power and accumulation. The state's existence and that of the ruling coalition depends on the global oil giants which produce the oil, particularly Shell.

Apart from its role in defining the parameters of Nigeria's oil for the global market, Shell's status as a power house of global capital renders the state in Nigeria a weak partner. Providing a picture of Shell's might, Miller (1995: 35) notes that:

> Shell Oil's 1990 gross national income was more than the combined GNPs of Tanzania, Ethiopia, Nepal, Bangladesh, Zaire, Uganda, Nigeria, Kenya and Pakistan – countries that represent almost one-tenth of the world's population.

Shell runs fully integrated oil operations in over one hundred countries and has substantial interests in gas, chemicals, mining and real estate (Obi, 1997). Its joint venture partner (and competitor), the NNPC, is no match for Shell.

Thus, Shell's position in Nigeria's political economy and its role as the cutting edge of the global control of Nigeria's oil, offers its 'unequal' partner – the state - little autonomy *vis-à-vis* the imperatives of globalization. Thus the state in Nigeria defends its partner from contending social and political forces, repressing local opposition to Shell. By reinforcing its control over the political, the state protects global accumulation and the interests of the transnational class, while still projecting itself as the protector of the national interest in order to retain its legitimacy. The objective role of the state and the interests of the ruling coalition perceive the Ogoni resistance as subversion, an act obstructive of the expansion of global oil capital in a period of crisis.

The Ogoni versus global oil

The Ogoni struggle against Shell goes back to 1958. It had its background in the forceful integration of Ogoni into the global oil economy. As oil capital penetrated deeper into the Ogoni ecosystem, it spawned relations of production which alienated the landowners and producers from the products of their land, while degrading the environment and destroying the basis of livelihood in the agro-based peasant economy. This led to the clash between Shell and the Ogoni people.

Several developments acted as catalysts in the escalation of this clash of opposing forces: the Nigerian civil war, the impact of structural adjustment on social and power relations, and changes in global politics in the post-cold war era.

The Nigerian civil war led to some shifts in the balance of social and political forces in Nigeria. At the onset of the war, the four regions were split into twelve states,[6] satisfying to some extent the age-old quest of ethnic minorities for self-determination. With respect to the ethnic minorities of the Niger delta, they soon found out that what they gained within the twelve state-federal structure was lost in terms of non-access to oil revenue. What this implied politically was that the regionally defined factions of the dominant class, particularly those which had defeated Biafran claims to the oil fields of the Niger delta, were now in control of the distribution of oil-rents, while the oil minorities faction found itself marginalized.

A new struggle was defined within the dominant class, in which oil minorities factions were variously either co-opted or sacrificed. In the struggle between the dominant class and the oil minorities faction, the latter mobilized popular forces against the former on the grounds of the solidarity of the oppressed, the quest for justice and self-determination, and the need to resist further marginalization.

The response of the oil minorities faction immediately after the war was largely one of disappointment that its tactical support for the federalist dominant class did not translate into compensation in the form of access to oil surplus. Rather, it led to the blockage of access (Saro-Wiwa, 1984, 1995). The oil minorities factions were basically united by the quest for more access to oil surplus, increased autonomy and power at the local level, and restitution for ecological damage by oil companies. Internal debate between those who believed in limited protest, and full co-optation into the hegemonic agenda of the transnational class, and an opposing faction which believed in confronting the transnational coalition with evidence of its atrocities and using popular power to wrest restitution, increased autonomy and power at the local level.

Ogoni resistance can also be linked to the high concentration of global capital in its region. As Claude Welch (1995: 636) puts it:

> the Ogoni live atop some of the richest real estate in Africa yet few Ogoni benefit from jobs, developments or amenities in the oil industry. Instead, they suffer serious environmental degradation that has polluted streams and fresh water sources, poisoned land through spills and blowouts, and created an atmosphere fouled by decades of flaring natural gas.

Within an area of 404 square miles, Ogoni is host to six oil fields with numerous pipes crossing overland, connecting various oil installations, two refineries, a huge fertilizer plant, petrochemical plants and an ocean port (Naanen, 1995). Ogoni represents the paradox of capitalist accumulation – as the poorest and yet most industrialized enclave in Nigeria (Naanen, 1995). At the heart of this contradiction lies the roots of the Ogoni revolution. It pitched the global against the local; accumulation against resistance. The immersion of Nigeria in economic crisis, and its socially harsh programme of economic adjustments in the midst of a political transition, sharpened these contradictions, leading to open confrontation between the opposing forces.

The politics of adjustments in Nigeria has received academic attention (Olukoshi, 1993). Its immediate impact was the deepening of the social and economic crisis. This took place within a political context marked by authoritarianism and the shrinking of political space to exclude all those opposed to the military wing of the power bloc (*ibid.*). Thus the initially peaceful protests of the social movements of the Niger delta assumed more frequency as the harsh effects of adjustment sank deeper. The situation was worsened by the deregulation of the oil industry, which underscored the desperation of the state to get more oil rents to service its huge external debt (Obi, 1994).

For global oil, it was an equally period with the competing oil giants keen to build up their reserves and expand the process of capital accumulation. The deregulation of the oil industry in Nigeria gave the oil companies better leverage to expand investments. The consequence of the foregoing was the deepening of contradictions between the transnational coalition and the people of the Niger delta. It was the balance of power between the feuding oil minorities' factions *vis-à-vis* the transnational coalition and the coercive apparatus of the state that eventually defined the outcome of the struggle.

Under structural adjustments, the state reinforced its political functions, and remained central to the process of oil-based accumulation. The radicalization of the Ogoni struggle which had become evident in the demands listed in the 1990 Ogoni Bill of Rights, gave notice to the state that the struggle was directed against oil-based accumulation – the very basis of state power, dominant class hegemony, Shell and Nigeria's place in the global capitalist system:

> Justifying Ogoni resistance, Ken Saro-Wiwa stressed its moral advantage...Over the past thirty years, Ogoni has given Nigeria an estimated US thirty billion dollars and received NOTHING in return, except a blighted countryside, an atmosphere full of carbon dioxide, carbon monoxide and hydrocarbons, a land in which wildlife is unknown, a land of polluted streams and creeks, of rivers without fish, a land which was in every sense of the term an ecological disaster.
>
> (Saro-Wiwa, 1995: 74)

The formation of the Movement for the survival of Ogoni people (MOSOP) in 1991, under the leadership of a broad coalition of the Ogoni faction of the Oil Minorities took the struggle to a higher level. It was in the thick of this struggle that the cracks within the Ogoni widened, and the radical and more militant faction of MOSOP assumed ascendancy to the desperation of the more conservative elements and their transnational allies. The basic issues on which the MOSOP-led resistance against shell and the state were based included the following: the need for social justice for minorities, equity in power sharing in Nigeria, compensation for environmental devastation and the restoration of the environment, payment of economic rents to oil-producing areas, human dignity and self-actualization (Saro-Wiwa, 1994: 17). There is no doubt that these considerations ran against the logic of the expansion of global capital and domestic accumulation in Nigeria. By 1993, MOSOP decided to apply more pressure. According to Saro-Wiwa, MOSOP decided to apply more pressure. According to Saro-Wiwa, MOSOP had the moral advantage, and 'time and world opinion was on the side of the Ogoni struggle'.

From 1991 onwards, MOSOP internationalized its struggle, taking its case to Amnesty International, Greenpeace and the Geneva-based organization – the Unrepresented Nations and peoples Organization (UNPO), the London Rainforest Action Group and eventually, the United Nations (Saro-Wiwa, 1995; Greenpeace, 1994, 1995; Rowell, 1994). It wages its campaign through lecture tours, newspaper articles, and documentary films showing the atrocities being committed against the Ogoni by shell and the state in Nigeria. This way the dimensions of the ecological disaster and denial of rights which the Ogoni suffered from shell and the state was used in shocking the global community into putting pressure on the 'unequal partnership' to respect the rights of the Ogoni to self-determination.

The Ogoni strategy of internationalizing its struggle was partly based on its reading of certain developments at the global level: 'the end of the cold war, increasing attention being paid to the global environment, and the insistence of the European Community that minority rights be respected in the USSR successor states and in Yugoslavia' (Saro-Wiwa, 1992: 7). By 1993, MOSOP had been transformed by the dialectics of the struggle into a popular social movement. The conservative leadership was pushed aside by the more militant cadres in the National Youth Council for the Survival of Ogoni People (NYCOP) and the Federation of Ogoni Women's Associations (FOWA). NYCOP and FOWA were able to mobilize the Ogoni masses under the leadership of MOSOP. As tensions rose, they became more militant. The final split in MOSOP took place when the conservative faction lost a crucial vote to prevent the Ogoni from boycotting the 12 June 1993 presidential elections. The radicals, who had demonstrated their strength earlier in the year when they successfully organized a huge peaceful rally marking Ogoni day, purged the leadership of MOSOP of the conservatives, and voted Ken Saro-Wiwa as the leader. Under his leadership, the radi-calization of the social movement grew very fast and before long the people had been able to block access to oil wells in Ogoni, forcing Shell to stop operations and costing the Shell-state partnership an estimated daily loss of N9.9 million from May 1993 (Izeze, 1994: 1). Equally significant was that some oil communities, following the MOSOP example, drew up Charters of Demands and raised pressure on Shell and the state (Obi, 1995). The developments of 1993 and 1994 clearly convinced the transnational alliance that the danger they faced was the possible subversion of oil-based accumulation in Nigeria. To the domestic dominant class, the revolutionary activities of MOSOP were a direct threat to its hegemony, as well as the legitimacy of the oil minorities faction aligned to the dominant class.

Neither Shell nor the state acceded to the demands of MOSOP. Shell's strategy was to deny responsibility, insisting that MOSOP was making unreasonable demands, sabotaging oil instal-lations and exaggerating the extent of ecological damage in Ogoni (Shell, 1994, 1995; Achebe, 1996). The state on its part viewed MOSOP activities as subversion and economic sabotage.

Consequently, the struggle became militarized with the state mobilizing armed troops to force through the continued global project of controlling the Ogoni environment. These troops occupied Ogoni villages and unleashed a reign of terror against suspected MOSOP cadres and the peasantry who sympathized with the MOSOP cause. Entire villages were sacked, people lost their lives, and many took to hiding in the bush. Nothing was spared in crushing the MOSOP revolution. At the same time, the conflict between the radicals and the conservatives raged within the Ogoni elite. The local conservatives, backed by global and state forces, became the target of MOSOP militant cadres, and were increasingly despised by the social and political forces ranged against the transnational coalition. It was during one such incident that four leading members of the Ogoni political class suspected of being 'counter revolutionaries' were murdered by a mob in Ogoni land. The state moved in, and in November 1995, nine leaders of MOSOP, including Ken Saro-Wiwa were hanged on the orders of a tribunal, after being convicted on counts of inciting a mob to murder the four Ogoni chiefs.

After the conviction and hangings the Ogoni struggle went into retreat locally, while the international campaign was sustained by Ogoni activists in exile (Owens Wiwa, 1996). The international campaign sought to mobilize support for the imposition of sanctions on Nigeria, and 'calling Shell to order' (Ake, 1996), and the release of MOSOP activists (Sakaar, 1996).

Outcomes and lessons

It is difficult to predict the eventual outcome of local resistance of the Ogoni against Shell and the state. However, at the conjuncture of the aftermath of Ken Saro Wiwa's execution, it spelt tragedy for local resistance. Nevertheless, the domestic ruling coalition suffered from internal contradictions and a crisis of governance. Tensions ran high just below the surface. Violent unrest burst out into the open again in the Niger delta in the autumn of 1998, revealing the continued possibility of the rise of local resistance. The recent return to democracy in Nigeria may offer possibilities for dialogue not possible previously.

The primary lesson of the reversal of the Ogoni revolution is the danger in underestimating the capacity of global capital and the local state to defend oil-based accumulation in Nigeria. The Ogoni resistance failed partly because it took place ahead of its time, and partly because MOSOP did not work hard enough to build solid tactics and local or regional alliances. Indeed the revolution hardly spread beyond Ogoni land. Without strong linkages to neighboring oil communities or movements outside the Niger delta, it was easy for the state to isolate the Ogoni locally and stifle their protest.

Equally important is the overestimation of the pressure that the global civil society could bring to bear on Shell and the state in Nigeria, not knowing the extent to which organizations such as Amnesty, Greenpeace and UNPO could go in actually stopping the ecological devastation of Ogoni, and the limitations they faced if they attempted to block Shell and the vital interests of the G-7 countries.

It is not clear if MOSOP had an advanced ideological clarity about the ramifications of its struggle. A lot rested on the moral advantage and the justness of its cause. Anger, bitterness and personality differences played a major role in sowing discord in the ranks of Ogoni leadership. The infiltration of the movement by 'counter revolutionary forces' of the transnational coalition paved the way for its subversion from within.

The remnants of MOSOP's cadres in Ogoni continue to carry on the struggle. The lesson of the Ogoni tragedy for other social movements seeking to make a revolution at the dawn of the twenty-first century is that the task is much more difficult, and requires rigorous preparation based on the correct reading of the balance of social and political forces and their position in the globalized empire of capital.

Notes

1 Shell Petroleum Development Company (Nigeria) Limited is a local subsidiary of Shell International Petroleum Company.
2 Ken Saro-Wiwa and eight of his MOSOP colleagues were hanged in a Port Harcourt Prison on 10 November 1995.
3 The three dominant ethnic groups in Nigeria are the Hausa-Fulani, Ibo and the Yoruba.
4 The oil companies included Mobil, Gulf (now Chevron), Agip, Safrap (now Elf), Tenneco and Amoseas (Texaco/Chevron).
5 Formal state control was enshrined in Decree 51 of November 1969 which vested in the state entire ownership and control of oil. While Decree 38 of 1971 extended the limits of Nigeria's territorial waters, and gave the Commissioner of Mines and Power (later Petroleum Resources) the power to grant oil exploration, oil mining and oil production licences.
6 From the initial number of twelve states, the number has now risen to thirty-six.

References

Achebe, Emeka (1996), 'Shell and the Truth', *The Guardian*, 25 January.

Ake, Claude (1996), 'Shelling Nigeria Ablaze', *Tell*, Vol. 129 (January).

Giddens, A. (1990), *The Consequences of Modernity* (Cambridge University Press).

Greenpeace (1994, 1995), *Shell (Nigeria) Campaign*.

Izeze, Ifeanyi (1994), 'Nigeria Loses N2.732 billion to Ogoni Crisis', *Daily Sunray*, 3 February.

Lolomari, Odoliyi (1976), 'The Evolution of Nigeria's Oil Policy', in *Edited Proceedings of the 1976 Annual Conference of the Nigerian Economic Society* (Nigerian Economic Society).

Lubeck, Paul and Watts, Michael (1994), 'An Alliance of Oil and Maize': The Response of Indigenous and State Capital to Structural Adjustment in Nigeria', in Bruce Berman and Colin Leys (eds), *African Capitalists in African Development* (Lynne Rienner).

Miller, Marian (1995), *The Third World in Global Environmental Politics* (Lynne Rienner).

Naanen, Ben (1995), 'Oil-producing Minorities and the Restructuring of Nigerian Federalism: The Case of the Ogoni People', *Journal of Commonwealth and Comparative Studies*, Vol. 32, No. 1.

Ngemutu-Roberts, F. O. (1994), 'Federalism, Minorities and Political Contestation in Nigeria: From Henry Willink to the MOSOP Phenomenon'. Paper presented to the 20th Nigeria Political Science Association Conference, Ile-Ife, 28 February to 2 March.

Obi, Cyril (1994), *Structural Adjustment, Oil and Popular Struggles: The Deepening Crisis of State Legitimacy and Governance in Nigeria*. Research Report submitted to CODESRIA, Dakar.

Obi, Cyril (1995), 'Oil Minority Rights versus the Nigerian State: Environmental Conflict, Its Implications and Transcendence'. Paper presented to CODESRIA's 8th General Assembly and Conference, Dakar, 26 June to 2 July.

Obi, Cyril (1997), *Oil, Environmental Conflict and National Security in Nigeria: Ramifications of the Ecology-Security Nexus for Sub-Regional Peace* (ACDIS Occasional Paper).

Obi, Cyril and Soremekun, Kayode (1995), 'Oil and the Nigerian State: An Overview', in Kayode Soremekun (ed.) *Perspectives on the Nigeria Oil Industry* (Amkra).

Olukoshi, Adebayo (ed.) (1993), *The Politics of Structural Adjustment in Nigeria* (James Currey).

Osaghae, Eghosa (1995), 'The Ogoni Uprising: Oil Politics, Minority Agitation and the Future of the Nigerian State', *Africa Affairs*, Vol. 94, No. 376.

Rowell, A. (1994), *Shell-Shocked: The Environmental and Social Costs of Living with Shell in Nigeria* (Greenpeace).

Sakaar, Dornu (1996), '19 More Ogoni's for the Justice Auta Special Military Tribunal'. MOSOP Crisis Management Committee Press Release.

Sampson, Anthony (1973), *The Seven Sisters: The Great Oil Companies and the World They Shaped* (Viking Press).

Saro-Wiwa, Ken (1984), *On a Darkling Plain* (Saros).

Saro-Wiwa, Ken (1992), *Genocide in Nigeria: The Ogoni Tragedy* (Saros).

Saro-Wiwa, Ken (1994), 'Oil and the Basic Issues at Stake', *Guardian*, 1 April.

Saro-Wiwa, Ken (1995), *A Month and a Day: A Detention Diary* (Penguin).

Saurin, Julian (1996), 'International Relations, Social Ecology and the Globalization of Environmental Change', in John Vogler and Mark F. Imber (eds) *The Environment and International Relations* (Routledge).

Shatzl, Ludwig (1968), *Petroleum in Nigeria* (Oxford University Press).

Shell Petroleum Development Corporation (1993), *Nigeria and Shell: Partners in Progress* (Shell).

Shell International Petroleum Corporation (1994), 'Shell Briefing Note' (Press Release).

Shell International Petroleum Corporation (1995), 'Clear Thinking in Troubled Times' (Press Release).

Soremekun, Kayode and Obi, Cyril (1993a), 'The Changing Pattern of Private Foreign Investments in the Nigerian Oil Industry', *Africa Development*, Vol. 18, No. 3.

Soremekun, Kayode and Obi, Cyril (1993b), 'Oil and the National Question', in *Edited Proceedings of the Nigeria Economic Society 1993 Annual Conference* (Nigerian Economic Society).

Syahuka-Muhindo, A. (1995), 'The Rwenzururu Movement and the Democratic Struggle', in Mahmood Mamdani and Ernest Wamba-dia-Wamba (eds) *African Studies in Social Movements and Democracy* (CODESRIA).

Welch, Claude (1995), 'The Ogoni and Self-determination: Increasing Violence in Nigeria', *Journal of Modern African Studies*, Vol. 33, No. 4.

Williams, Marc (1996), 'International Political Economy and Global Environmental Change', in John Vogler and Mark Imber (eds) *The Environment and International Relations* (Routledge).

Wiwa, Owens (1996), 'The Agony of the Ogoni', *Africa Notes* (March).

Woodhouse, P. (1992), 'Environmental Degradation and Sustainability', in T. Allen and A. Thomas (eds) *Poverty and Development in the 1990s* (Oxford University Press).

27 Power politics

Arundhati Roy

Source: Arundhati Roy (2002), *The Algebra of Infinite Justice*,
London: HarperCollins, pp. 129–163

The reincarnation of Rumpelstiltskin

Remember him? The gnome who could turn straw into gold? Well he's back now, but you wouldn't recognize him. To begin with, he's not an individual gnome anymore. I'm not sure how best to describe him. Let's just say he's metamorphosed into an accretion, a cabal, an assemblage, a malevolent, incorporeal, transnational multignome. Rumpelstiltskin is a notion (gnotion), a piece of deviant, insidious, white logic that will eventually self-annihilate. But for now he's more than okay. He's cock of the walk. King of All That Really Counts (Cash). He's decimated the competition, killed all the other kings, the other kinds of kings. He's persuaded us that he's all we have left. Our only salvation.

What king or potentate is Rumpelstiltskin? Powerful, pitiless and armed to the teeth. He's the kind of king the world has never known before. His realm is raw capital, his conquests emerging markets, his prayers profits, his borders limitless, his weapons nuclear. To even try and imagine him, to hold the whole of him in your field of vision, is to situate yourself at the very edge of sanity, to offer yourself up for ridicule. King Rumpel reveals only part of himself at a time. He has a bank account heart. He has television eyes and a newspaper nose in which you see only what he wants you to see and read only what he wants you to read. (See what I mean about the edge of sanity?) There's more: a Surround Sound stereo mouth which amplifies his voice and filters out the sound of the rest of the world, so that you can't hear it even when it's shouting (or starving or dying) and King Rumpel is only whispering, rolling his r's in his North American way.

Listen carefully. This is most of the rest of his story. (It hasn't ended yet, but it will. It must.) It ranges across seas and continents, sometimes majestic and universal, sometimes confining and local. Now and then I'll peg it down with disparate bits of history and geography that could mar the gentle art of storytelling. So, please bear with me.

In March 2000, the President of the US (H.E. the most exalted plenipotentiary of Rumpeldom) visited India. He brought his own bed, the feather pillow he hugs at night, and a merry band of businessmen. He was courted and fawned over by the genuflecting representatives of this ancient civilization with a fervour that can only be described as indecent. Whole cities were superficially spruced up. The poor were herded away, hidden from the presidential gaze. Streets were soaped and scrubbed and festooned with balloons and welcome banners.

In Delhi's dirty sky, vindicated nuclear hawks banked and whistled: *Dekho ji dekho!* Bill is here because we have the Bomb!

Those Indian citizens with even a modicum of self-respect were so ashamed they stayed in bed for days. Some of us had puzzled furrows on our brows. Since everybody behaved like a craven, happy slave when Master visited, we wondered why we hadn't gone the whole distance. Why hadn't we crawled under Master's nuclear umbrella in the first place? Then we could spend our pocket money on other things (instead of bombs) and still be all safe and slavey. No?

Just before The Visit, the Government of India lifted import restrictions on 1,400 commodities including milk, grain, sugar and cotton (even though there was a glut of sugar and cotton in the market, even though forty-two million tonnes of grain was rotting in government storehouses).[1] During The Visit, contracts worth about three (some say four) billion dollars were signed.[2]

For reasons of my own, I was particularly interested in a Memorandum of Intent signed between the Ogden Energy Group, a company that specializes in operating garbage incinerators in the United States, and the S. Kumars, an Indian textile company that manufactures what it calls 'suiting blends'.[3] Now what might garbage incineration and suiting blends possibly have in common? Suit incineration? Guess again. Garbage-blends? Nope.

A big hydroelectric dam on the river Narmada in central India. Neither Ogden nor the S. Kumars has ever built or operated a large dam before.

The 400-megawatt Shri Maheshwar Hydel Project being promoted by the S. Kumars is part of the Narmada Valley Development Project, which boasts of being the most ambitious river valley project in the world. It envisages building 3,200 dams (thirty big dams, 135 medium dams, and the rest small) that will reconstitute the Narmada and her forty-one tributaries into a series of stepped reservoirs.[4]

The dams that have been built on the river so far are all government projects. The Maheshwar dam is slated to be India's first major private hydro-electric power project.

What is interesting about this is not only that it's part of the most bitterly opposed river valley project in India, but also that it is a strand in the skein of a mammoth global enterprise. Understanding what is happening in Maheshwar, decoding the nature of the deals that are being struck between two of the world's great democracies, will go a long way towards gaining a rudimentary grasp of what is being done to us, while we, poor fools, stand by and clap and cheer and hasten things along. (When I say 'us', I mean people, human beings. Not countries, not governments.)

Personally, I took the first step towards this understanding when, over a few days in March 2000, I lived through a writer's bad dream. I witnessed the ritualistic slaughter of language as I know and understand it. Let me explain.

On the very days that President Clinton was in India, in far-away Holland, the World Water Forum was convened.[5] Three thousand five hundred bankers, businessmen, government ministers, policy writers, engineers, economists (and – in order to pretend that the 'other side' was also represented – a handful of activists, indigenous dance troupes, impoverished street theatre groups, and half a dozen young girls dressed as inflatable silver faucets) gathered at the Hague to discuss the future of the world's water. Every speech was percussive with phrases like 'women's empowerment', 'people's participation' and 'deepening democracy'. Yet it turned out that the whole purpose of the forum was to press for the privatization of the world's water. There was righteous talk of making access to drinking water a Basic Human Right. How would this be implemented, you might ask. Simple. By putting a market value on water. By selling it at its 'true' price. (It's common knowledge that water is becoming a scarce resource. As we know, about a billion people in the world have no access to safe drinking water.)[6] The 'market' decrees that the scarcer something is, the more expensive it becomes. But there is a difference between valuing water and putting a market value on water. No one values water more than a village woman who has to walk miles to fetch it. No one values it less than urban folk who pay for it to flow endlessly at the turn of a tap.

So the talk of connecting human rights to a 'true price' was more than a little baffling. At first I didn't quite get their drift – did they believe in human rights for the rich, that only the rich are human, or that all humans are rich? But I see it now. A shiny, climate-controlled human rights supermarket with a clearance sale on Christmas Day.

One marrowy American panellist put it rather nicely – 'God gave us the rivers,' he drawled, 'but he didn't put in the delivery systems. That's why we need private enterprise.' No doubt with a little Structural Adjustment to the rest of the things God gave us, we could all live in a simpler world. (If all the seas were one sea, what a big sea it would be...) Evian could own the water, Rand the earth, Enron the air. Old Rumpelstiltskin could be the handsomely paid supreme CEO.

When all the rivers and valleys and forests and hills of the world have been priced, packaged, bar-coded and stacked in the local supermarket, when all the hay and coal and earth and wood and water has been turned to gold, what then shall we do with all the gold? Make nuclear bombs to obliterate what's left of the ravaged landscapes and the notional nations in our ruined world?

As a writer, one spends a lifetime journeying into the heart of language, trying to minimize, if not eliminate, the distance between language and thought. 'Language is the skin on my thought,' I remember saying to someone who once asked what language meant to me. At The Hague I stumbled on a denomination, a sub-world, whose life's endeavour was to mask intent. They earn their abundant livings by converting bar graphs that plot their companies' profits into consummately written, politically exemplary, socially just policy documents that are impossible to implement and designed to remain forever on paper, secret even (especially) from the people they're written for. They breed and prosper in the space that lies between what they say and what they sell. What they're lobbying for is not simply the privatization of natural resources and essential infrastructure, but the privatization of policy making itself.

Dam builders want to control public water policies. Power utility companies want to supervise government disinvestments.

Let's begin at the beginning. What does privatization really mean? Essentially, it is the transfer of productive public assets from the state to private companies. Productive assets include natural resources. Earth, forest, water, air. These are assets that the state holds in trust for the people. In a country like India, seventy per cent of the population lives in rural areas. That's seven hundred million people.[7] Their lives depend directly on access to natural resources. To snatch these away and sell them as stock to private companies is a process of barbaric dispossession on a scale that has no parallel in history.

What happens when you 'privatize' something as essential to human survival as water? What happens when you commodify water and say that only those who can come up with the cash to pay the 'market price' can have it? In 1999, the Government of Bolivia privatized the public water supply system in the city of Cochabamba, and signed a forty-year lease with Bechtel, a giant US engineering firm. The first thing Bechtel did was to triple the price of water. Hundreds of thousands of people simply couldn't afford it any more. Citizens took to the streets in protest. A transport strike brought the entire city to a standstill. Hugo Banzer, the former Bolivian dictator (now the president), ordered the police to fire at the crowds. Six people were killed, 175 injured and two children blinded. The protest continued because people had no option – what's the option to thirst? In April 2000, Banzer declared martial law. The protest continued. Eventually Bechtel was forced to flee its offices.[8] Now it's trying to extort a $12 million exit payment from the Bolivian government.

Cochabamba has a population of half a million people. Think of what would happen in an Indian city. Even a small one.

Rumpelstiltskin thinks big. Today he's stalking megagame: dams, mines, armaments, power plants, public water supply, telecommunication, the management and dissemination of knowledge, biodiversity, seeds (he wants to own life and the very process of reproduction), and the industrial infrastructure that supports all this. His minions arrive in Third World countries masquerading as missionaries come to redeem the wretched. They have a completely different dossier in their briefcases. To understand what they're really saying (selling), you have to teach yourself to unscramble their vernacular.

Recently, Jack Welch, then CEO of General Electric (GE), visited India and was on national news.[9] 'I beg and pray to the Indian government to improve infrastructure,' he said, and added touchingly, 'Don't do it for GE's sake, do it for yourselves.' He went on to say that privatizing the power sector was the only way to bring India's one billion people into the digital network. 'You can talk about information and intellectual capital, but without the power to drive it, you will miss the next revolution.'

What he meant, of course, was: 'You are a market of one billion customers. If you don't buy our equipment, *we* will miss the next revolution.'

The story behind the story is as follows: there are four corporations that dominate the production of power generation equipment in the world. GE is one of them. Together, each year they manufacture (and therefore need to sell) equipment that can generate 20,000 megawatts of power.[10] For a variety of reasons, there is little (read almost zero) additional demand for power equipment in the First World. This leaves these mammoth multinationals with a redundant capacity that they desperately need to offload. India and China are their big target markets because between these two countries the demand for power-generating equipment is 10,000 megawatts per year.[11]

The First World needs to sell, the Third World needs to buy – it ought to be a reasonable business proposition. But it isn't. For many years, India has been more or less self-sufficient in power equipment. The Indian public sector company, Bharat Heavy Electricals (BHEL), manufactured and even exported world-class power equipment. All that's changed now. Over the years, our own government has starved it of orders, cut off funds for research and development, and more or less edged it out of a dignified existence. Today BHEL is no more than a sweatshop. It is being forced into 'joint ventures' (one with GE and one with Siemens) in which its only role is to provide cheap labour while they provide the equipment and the technology.[12]

Why? Why does more expensive, imported foreign equipment suit our bureaucrats and politicians better? We all know why. Because graft is factored into the deal. Buying equipment from your local store is just not the same thing. It's not surprising that almost half the officials named in the major corruption scandal that came to be known as the Jain Hawala case were officials from the power sector involved with the selection and purchase of power equipment.[13]

The privatization of power (felicitous phrase!) is at the top of the Indian government's agenda. The United States is the single largest foreign investor in the power sector (which, to some extent, explains The Visit).[14] The argument being advanced (both by the government and by the private sector) in favour of privatization is that over the last fifty years the government has bungled its brief. It has failed to deliver. The State Electricity Boards

(SEBs) are insolvent. Inefficiency, corruption, theft and heavy subsidies have run them into the ground.

[…]

Now, coming back to the story of the Maheshwar Dam…

What the Maheshwar experience illustrates, in relentless detail, is that in a private project, the only thing that's more efficient and better managed is the corruption, the lies, and the swiftness and brutality of repression. And, of course, the escalating costs.

In 1994, the project cost of the Maheshwar dam was estimated at Rs 465 crore.[15] In 1996, following the contract with the S. Kumars, it rose to Rs 1,569 crore. Today it stands at Rs 2,200 crore. Initially, eighty per cent of this money was to be raised from foreign investors. There has been a procession of them – Pacgen of the United States, Bayernwerk, VEW, Siemens, and the Hypovereinsbank of Germany. And now, the latest in the line of ardent suitors, Ogden of the US.

According to the NBA's calculations, the cost of the electricity at the factory gate will be Rs 6.55 per unit, which is twenty-six times more expensive than existing hydel power in the state, five and a half times more expensive than thermal power, and four times more expensive than power from the central grid. (It's worth mentioning here that Madhya Pradesh today generates 1,500 megawatts more power than it can transmit and distribute.)

Though the installed capacity of the Maheshwar project is supposed to be 480 megawatts, studies using twenty-eight years of actual river flow data show that eighty per cent of the electricity will be generated only during the monsoon months, when the river is full. What this means is that most of the supply will be generated when it's least needed.[16]

The S. Kumars have no worries on this count. They have Enron as a precedent. They have an escrow clause in their contract, which guarantees them first call on government funds. This means that however much (or however little) electricity they produce, whether anybody buys it or not, for the next thirty-five years they are guaranteed a minimum payment from the government of approximately Rs 600 crore a year. This money will be paid to them even before the employees of the bankrupt State Electricity Board get their salaries.

What did the S. Kumars do to deserve this largesse? It isn't hard to guess.

So who's actually paying for this dam that nobody needs?

According to government surveys, the reservoir of the Maheshwar dam will submerge sixty-one villages. Thirteen, they say, will be wholly submerged, the rest will lose their farmlands.[17] (The agency in charge of the survey is the same one that was in charge of the surveys for the Bargi reservoir. We know what happened there.) As usual, the villagers were not informed about the dam or their impending eviction. Of course, if they go to court now they'll be told it's too late since construction has already begun. The first surveys were done under a ruse that a railway line was being constructed. It was only in 1997, when blasting began at the dam site, that realization dawned on people, and the NBA became active in Maheshwar.

People in the submergence zone of the Maheshwar dam say that the surveys are completely wrong. Some villages marked for submergence are at a higher level than villages that are not counted as Project Affected. Since the Maheshwar dam is located in the broad plains of Nimad, even a small miscalculation in the surveys will lead to huge discrepancies between what is marked for submergence and what is actually submerged. The consequences of these errors will be far worse than what happened at Bargi.

There are other egregious assumptions in the 'survey'. Annexure Six of the resettlement plan states that there are thirty-eight wells and 176 trees in all the affected sixty-one villages combined. The villagers point out that in just a single village – Pathrad – there are forty wells and more than 4,000 trees.

As with trees and wells, so with people. There is no accurate estimate of how many people will be affected by the dam. Even the project authorities admit that new surveys must be done. So far, they've managed to survey only one out of the sixty-one villages. The number of affected households rose from 190 (in the preliminary survey) to 300 (in the new one).

In circumstances like these, it's impossible for even the NBA to have an accurate idea of the numbers of Project Affected people. Their rough guess is about 50,000. More than half of them are Dalits, Kevats and Kahars – ancient communities of ferrymen, fisherfolk, sand quarriers and cultivators of the river bed. Most of them own no land, but the river sustains them and means more to them than anyone else. If the dam is built, thousands of them will lose their only source of livelihood. Yet simply because they are landless, they do not qualify as Project Affected and will not be eligible for rehabilitation.

Jalud is the first of the sixty-one villages slated for submergence in the reservoir of the dam.[18] As early as 1985, twelve families, mostly Dalit, who had small holdings near the dam site had their land acquired. When they protested, cement was poured into their water pipes, their standing crops were bulldozed, and the police occupied their land by force. All twelve families are now landless and work as wage labourers. The new 'private' initiative has made no effort to help them.

According to the environmental clearance from the Central government, the people affected by the project ought to have been resettled in 1997. To date, the S. Kumars haven't even managed to produce a list of Project Affected people, let alone land on which they are to be resettled. Yet construction continues. The S. Kumars are so well entrenched with the state government that they don't even need to pretend to cover their tracks.

The Rajputs of Jalud are slated to be moved to a new village – a 'model resettlement village' – a few kilometres inland, away from the river, adjoining a predominantly Dalit and Adivasi precinct in a village called Samraj. A huge tract of land has been marked off for them. It's a hard, stony hillock with stubbly grass and scrub, on which truckloads of silt have been unloaded and spread out in a thin layer to make it look like rich, black humus.

On behalf of the S. Kumars, the District Magistrate acquired the hillock, which was actually village common grazing land that belonged to the people of Samraj. In addition to this, the land of thirty-four Dalit and Adivasi villagers was acquired. No compensation was paid.

The villagers, whose main source of income was their livestock, had to sell their goats and buffaloes because they no longer had anywhere to graze them. Their only remaining source of income lies (lay) on the banks of a small pond on the edge of the village. In summer, when the water level recedes, it leaves a shallow ring of rich silt on which the villagers grow (grew) rice and melons and cucumber. The S. Kumars excavated this silt to cosmetically cover the stony grazing ground (that the Rajputs of Jalud don't want). The banks of the pond are now steep and uncultivable.

The already impoverished people of Samraj have been left to starve, while this photo opportunity is being readied for German and Swiss funders, Indian courts and anybody else who cares to pass that way.

This is the legacy that the Ogden Energy Group of the US was so keen to inherit. What it didn't realize is that the fight is on. Over the last three years, the struggle against the Maheshwar dam has grown into a veritable civil disobedience movement, though you wouldn't know it if you read the papers. (The S. Kumars sponsor massive advertisements for their blended suitings. After their James Bond campaign with Pierce Brosnan, they've signed India's biggest film star – Hrithik Roshan – as their star campaigner.[19] It's extraordinary how much silent admiration and support a hunk in a blended suit can evoke.)

Over the years, tens of thousands of villagers have captured the dam site several times and halted construction work.[20] Protests in the region forced two companies, Bayernwerk and VEW of Germany, to withdraw from the project.[21] The German company Siemens remained in the fray (angling for an export credit guarantee from Hermes, the German ECA). In the summer of 2000, the German Ministry of Economic Cooperation and Development sent in a team of experts headed by Richard Bissell (former chairman of the Inspection Panel of the World Bank) to do an independent review of the Resettlement and Rehabilitation aspects of the project. The report, published on 15 June 2000, was unambiguous that resettlement and rehabilitation of people displaced by the Maheshwar dam was simply not possible.[22]

At the end of August, Siemens withdrew its application for a Hermes guarantee.[23]

The people of the valley don't get much time to recover between bouts of fighting. In September 2000, the S. Kumars were part of the Indian Prime Minister's business entourage when he visited the US.[24] Desperate to find a replacement for Siemens, they were hoping to convert their Memorandum of Understanding with Ogden into a final contract. That, fortunately (for Ogden as much as the people of Maheshwar), hasn't happened yet.

The only time I have ever felt anything close to national pride was when I walked one night with 4,000 people towards the Maheshwar dam site, where we knew hundreds of armed policemen were waiting for us. From the previous evening, people from all over the valley had begun to gather in a village called Sulgaon. They came in tractors, in bullock carts, and on foot. They came prepared to be beaten, humiliated and taken to prison.

We set out at three in the morning. We walked for three hours – farmers, fisherfolk, sand-miners, writers, painters, film-makers, lawyers, journalists. All of India was represented. Urban, rural, touchable, untouchable. This alliance is what gives the movement its raw power, its intellectual rigour and its phenomenal tenacity. As we crossed fields and forded streams, I remember thinking – this is my land, this is the dream to which the whole of me belongs, this is worth more to me than anything else in the world. We were not just fighting against a dam. We were fighting for a philosophy. For a world view.

We walked in utter silence. Not a throat was cleared. Not a beedi lit. We arrived at the dam site at dawn. Though the police were expecting us, they didn't know exactly where we would come from. We captured the dam site. People were beaten, humiliated and arrested.

I was arrested and pushed into a private car that belonged to the S. Kumars. I remember feeling a hot stab of shame – as quick and sharp as my earlier sense of pride. This was my land too. My feudal land. Where even the police have been privatized. (On the way to the police station, they complained that the S. Kumars had given them nothing to eat all day.) That evening, there were so many arrests, the jail could not contain the people. The administration broke down and abandoned the jail. The people locked themselves in and demanded answers to their questions. So far, none have been forthcoming.

A Dutch documentary film-maker recently asked me a very simple question: What can India teach the world?

A documentary film-maker needs to see to understand. I thought of three places I could take him to.

First, to a 'Call Centre College' in Gurgaon on the outskirts of Delhi. I thought it would be interesting for a film-maker to see how easily an ancient civilization can be humiliated and made to abase itself completely. In a Call Centre College, hundreds of young English-speaking Indians are being groomed to man the backroom operations of giant transnational companies.[25] They are trained to answer telephone queries from the US and the UK (on subjects ranging from a credit card enquiry to advice about a malfunctioning washing machine or the availability of cinema tickets). On no account must the caller know that his or her enquiry is being attended to by an Indian, sitting at a desk on the outskirts of Delhi.

The Call Centre Colleges train their students to speak in American and British accents. They have to read foreign papers so they can chitchat about the news or the weather. On duty they have to change their given names. Sushma becomes Susie, Govind becomes Jerry, Advani becomes Andy. (Hi! I'm Andy. Gee, hot day, innit? Shoot, how can I help ya?) Actually it's worse: Sushma becomes Mary. Govind becomes David. Perhaps Advani becomes Ulysses.

Call Centre workers are paid exactly one-tenth of the salaries of their counterparts abroad. From all accounts, Call Centres in India are billed to become a multi-million dollar industry.[26] Imagine that – a multi-million dollar industry built on a bedrock of lies, false identities and racism.

Recently the giant Tata industrial group announced their plans to redeploy 20,000 of their retrenched workers in Call Centres after a brief 'period of training' for the business, such as 'picking up the American accent and slang'.[27] The news report said that the older employees may find it difficult to work at night – a requirement for US-based companies, given the time difference between India and the US.

The second place I thought I'd take the film-maker to is another kind of training centre: a Rashtriya Swayam Sewak (RSS) *shakha*, where the terrible backlash to this enforced abasement is being nurtured and groomed. Where ordinary people march around in khaki shorts and learn that amassing nuclear weapons, religious bigotry, misogyny, homophobia, book burning and outright hatred are the ways in which to retrieve a nation's lost dignity. Here he might see for himself how the two arms of government work in synergy. How they have evolved and pretty near perfected an extraordinary pincer action – while one arm is busy selling the nation off in chunks, the other, to divert attention, is orchestrating a baying, howling, deranged chorus of cultural chauvinism. It would be fascinating to actually see how the inexorable ruthlessness of one process results in the naked, vulgar terrorism perpetrated by the other. They're Siamese twins – Advani and Andy. They share organs. They have the ability to say two entirely contradictory things simultaneously, to hold all positions at all times. There's no separating them.

The third place I thought I'd take him to is the Narmada valley. To witness the ferocious, magical, magnificent, tenacious and above all non-violent resistance that has grown on the banks of that beautiful river.

What is happening to our world is almost too colossal for human comprehension to contain. But it is a terrible, terrible thing. To contemplate its girth and circumference, to attempt to define it, to try and fight it all at once, is impossible. The only way to combat it is by fighting specific wars in specific ways. A good place to begin would be the Narmada valley.

The borders are open. Come on in. Let's bury Rumpelstiltskin.

Notes

1 'US–India Agreement', *New York Times*, 11 January 2000, p. 4.
2 'US, India Announce Deals of Dollars 4bn', *Financial Times*, 25 March 2000, p. 10.
3 A Memorandum of Intent signed by the Ogden Energy Group and S. Kumars: Peter Popham, 'Clinton's Visit Seals Future for Controversial Indian Dam', *The Independent*, 28 March 2000, p. 16; and 'S. Kumars Ties Up with Ogden for MP Project', *Economic Times of India*, 14 December 1999.
4 See WCD Report, p. 117; Steven A. Brandt and Fekri Hassan, 'Dams and Cultural Heritage Management: Final Report – August 2000', WCD Working Paper (online at http://www.dams.org/docs/html/contrib/soc212.htm); and WCD, 'Flooded Fortunes: Dams and Cultural Heritage Management', Press Release, 26 September 2000 (online at http://www.dams.org/press/pressrelease_61.htm). See also 'Do or Die: The People Versus Development in the Narmada Valley', *New Internationalist*, 336 (July 2001) (online at

http://www.oneworld.org/ni/issue336/title336.htm) and documentation Friends of the River Narmada (online at http://www.narmada.org/nvdp.dams/).

5 Second World Water Forum: From Vision to Action, 17–22 March 2000, The Hague. See online report at http://www.worldwaterforum.net/

6 UNDP, *Human Development Report 2000: Human Rights and Human Development*, Oxford University Press, New York, 2000, p. 4.

7 UNDP, *Human Development Report* (Note 6 above), p. 225.

8 See 'Bolivian Water Plan Dropped After Protests Turn Into Melees', *New York Times*, 11 April 2000.

9 'Develop Infrastructure to Cope With Digital Revolution: Jack Welch', *The Hindu*, 17 September 2000; and 'Welch Makes a Power Point', *The Economic Times of India*, 17 September 2000. Webcast of Jack Welch's 16 September 2000 speech online at http://www.ge.com/in/webcast.html

10 Peter Marsh, 'Big Four Lead the Field in Power Stakes: The Main Players', *Financial Times*, 4 June 2001, p. 2.

11 US Department of Energy, Energy Information Administration, *International Energy Outlook 1998*, Electricity Report (DOE/EIA-0484 [98]). Online at http://www.eia.doe.gov/oiaf/archive/ieo98/elec.html

12 See 'India: Bharat Heavy Electricals–GE's Refurbishment Centre', *The Hindu*, 17 March 2001; and 'BHEL Net Rises 10% to Rs 599 Crore', *The Economic Times of India*, 30 September 2000.

13 Abhay Mehta, *Power Play: A study of the Enron Project*, Orient Longman, Hyderabad, 2000, p. 15; Irfan Aziz, 'The Supreme Court Upheld the Ruling that the Jain Diary Constituted Insufficient: Evidence', Rediff.com, 22 July 2000 (online at http://www.rediff.com/news/2000/jul/22spec.htm); and Ritu Sarin, 'Ex-CBI Official Accuses Vijaya Rama Rao', *Financial Express*, 11 May 1997.

14 See. figures on 'Clinton's India Sojourn: Industry Hopes Doubling of FDI, Better Access to US Markets', 27 March 2000, DHAN.com News Track (online: at http://www.india-world.co.in/home/dhan/news/y2k0327-news.html); and George Pickart, 'Address to the Network of South Asian Professional', Washington, DC, 9 August 1997 (online at http://www.indiainc.org.in/h0809971.htm).

15 See 'The Maheshwar Dam: A Brief Introduction' and related links online at http://www.narmada.org/maheshwar.html; Meena Menon, 'Damned by the People: The Maheshwar Hydro-Electricity Project in Madhya Pradesh', *Business Line*, 15 June 1998; Sanjay Sangvai, *The River and Life. People's Struggle in the Narmada Valley*, Earthcare Books, Mumbai, 2000, pp. 81–4; and Richard E. Bissell, Shekhar Singh and Hermann Warth, *Maheshwar Hydroelectric Project: Resettlement and Rehabilitation: An Independent Review Conducted for the Ministry of Economic Cooperation and Development (BMZ), Government of Germany*, 15 June 2000 (online at http://www.brnz.de/medien/misc/maheshwar_report.pdf).

16 See 'Mardana Resolution' online at http://www.narmada.org/maheshwar/mardana.declaration.html; NBA Press Note, 'Hundreds of Maheshwar Dam Affected People Demonstrate at IFCI, Delhi', 16 November 2000 (online at http://www.narmada.org/nba-press-releases/november-2000/ifci.demo.html); and Sangvai, *The River and Life* (Note 33 above), Annexure 4. pp. 194–7 and Annexure 6, pp. 200–201.

17 See Heffa Schucking, 'The Maheshwar Dam in India', March 1999 (online-at http://www.narmada.org/urg990421.3.html).

18 See Meena Menon, 'Damned by the People' (Note 15 above).

19 See 'S. Kumars Forays into Ready-to-Wear Apparel', *India Info*, 10 December 2000; and 'S. Kumars Ups Ads-Spend by 66% with Kapil Dev on Board', *The Indian Express*, 8 July 1999.

20 See Meena Menon, 'Damned by the People' (Note 15 above).

21 See 'German Firms Pull Out of MP Dam Project', *The States-man*, 21 April 1999. See also Desikan Thirunarayanapuram, 'Siemens Role in Dam Project Doubtful', *The Statesman*, 30 June 2000.

22 See Bissell *et al.*, *Maheshwar Hydroelectric Project* (Note 15 above).

23 See 'Leaked Letter Shows German Company Quits Bid for Dam Credit', *Deuische Presse-Agentur*. 25 August 2000; and 'US Firm Pulls Out of Narmada Hydel Project', *The Statesman*. 13 December 2000.

24 'PM's is Going to Be a "Power Trip" ', *The Indian Express*, 4 September 2000.

25 See Mark Landler, 'Hi, I'm in Bangalore (But I Can't Say So)', *New York Times*, 21 March 2001, p. A1.

26 See David Gardiner, 'Impossible India's Improbable Chance', *The World in 2001*, *The Economist*, London, 2000, p. 46.

27 See Prabhakar Sinha, 'Tatas Plan Foray Into Call Centre Business', *The Times of India*, 7 October 2000.

28 Environmental regeneration

Paul Ekins

Source: Paul Ekins (1992), *A New World Order: Grassroots Movements for Global Change*, London: Routledge, pp. 139–165

The earlier analysis of the environmental crisis revealed two principal causes of the destruction of the environment:

1   Wasteful, polluting, resource-intensive consumption patterns of the rich;
2   Environmentally destructive practices of the very poor.

Between these two causes there is a third that partakes of both: a 'development' pattern that takes natural resources away from the poor, who were using them sustainably, and gives them to the relatively rich, who exploit them unsustainably. Where poor people are subject to displacement onto marginal or unsuitable forest land, whether by cash-cropping (e.g. plantations, ranches) or government policy (e.g. Indonesian transmigration programme), their struggle for survival will obviously impact negatively on the environment. Moreover, the use by subsistence-based people of forest resources for their survival is often in conflict with these resources' use for industrial or cash-crop purposes, as countless conflicts from Brazil (e.g. the assassination of Chico Mendes) to Sarawak (e.g. the logging blockades by the Penan people), India (e.g. social forestry in Karnataka, see EDF (1987), and the Narmada Valley Project, and Thailand, demonstrate.

The cash crops versus food crops issue is described thus in Timberlake (1985):

> The widespread planting of cash crops can also cause desertification. First, in situations where croppers are borrowing temperate agricultural practices for large cash-crop monocultures – without making due allowance for the realities of Africa's soil and climate – then the schemes themselves can overburden the land. Second, planting the best land in cash crops, which almost invariably use less labour than food crops, can push large numbers of subsistence farmers and herders onto more marginal land, resulting in desertification.
>
> (p. 69)

Norman Myers perceives the small-scale farmer to be responsible for more deforestation than commercial loggers and cattle ranchers combined, while being the least to blame.

> In his main manifestation as the shifted (displaced) cultivator, the small scale farmer is subject to a host of forces – population pressures, pervasive poverty, maldistribution of traditional farmlands, inequitable land tenure systems, inadequate attention to subsistence

agriculture, adverse trade and aid patterns, and international debt – that he is little able to comprehend let alone to control. Thus he reflects a failure of development strategies overall, and his problem can be confronted only by a major restructuring of policies on the part of governments and international agencies concerned.

(Myers 1989)

Myers' analysis is essentially confirmed by the World Resources Institute, one of the original framers of the Tropical Forestry Action Plan (see pp. 149ff.), who acknowledge that the causes of deforestation include not only population pressure for agricultural land and the demand for firewood and fodder but also:

> skewed land distribution and insecure tenure ... unsustainable exploitation of forests for industrial timber production and export, and inappropriate government policies regarding land tenure, economic incentives, forest settlement and other population issues.... Commercial exploitation is a major cause of deforestation.... Large-scale development projects in agriculture and other sectors, including projects funded by international development assistance agencies are major factors as well. As these and other forces reduce the amount of available forest and arable land, poor farmers are forced to move into fragile upland forest areas and marginal lowlands that cannot support large numbers of people practising subsistence agriculture.... To hold the poor responsible for this worsening situation is factually and morally wrong.
>
> (WRI 1987 p. 10, cited in Colchester and Lohmann 1990 p. 6)

Lohmann (1990a) gives a practical example of just this sort of situation from Thailand:

> The proponents of large-scale afforestation schemes in Thailand are using environmental concerns as a smokescreen for the commercialisation of common lands and the destruction of the rural subsistence economy. Hundreds of thousands of local people will be thrown off their lands, many with little option but to encroach on the country's remaining forests thus exacerbating the deforestation crisis. Rural activists are fighting for their livelihoods against multinationals, aid agencies and the Thai business elite who are vigorously promoting the plantations.
>
> (p. 9)

Thus a variety of power realities in many developing countries and internationally result in the forcible dispossession or marginalisation of subsistence farmers as more powerful social groups seek to benefit from their resources. Resource degradation is a frequent result. So there is a third significant engine of unsustainability: transfer of resources from the poor, who were using them sustainably, to the relatively rich who do not do so.

The three root causes of environmental destruction can thus be seen not to be very complex conceptually. Similarly their solutions are easily described:

1 *Development and deployment of resource-efficient, less polluting technologies* which enable relatively high standards of living to be sustained at a fraction of current environmental impacts, combined with a willingness on behalf of consumers to forgo consumption that is not environmentally sustainable.

2 *A reorientation of investment* away from resource-exploitation to a massive programme involving the sustainable production of biomass. This is the solution advocated

by Agarwal (1985):

> The answer to India's immediate problem of poverty, therefore, lies in increasing the biomass available in nature, and moreover, increasing it in such a manner that access to it is ensured on an equitable basis.
>
> (p. 23)

3   *A reversal of policies of dispossession* to those of granting to the poor access to resources, especially land, with incentives for them to be used sustainably.

While these solutions are unproblematic on paper, and there is no doubt that the world community has ample resources to implement them, unfortunately each one is opposed by formidable vested interests which have so far thwarted the sort of response the environmental crisis demands. One example of this is given in Lovins (1989) with regard to the deployment of new energy technologies which could stop the greenhouse effect more or less dead in its tracks:

> The good news is that if we simply pursue the narrowest of economic interests, the energy problem has already been solved by new technologies.... The bad news is that most governments and many private sector actors are less committed to market-outcomes in energy policy than to corporate socialism – to bailing out their favourite technologies, many of which are now dying from an incurable attack of market forces. So long as this ideology continues to dominate public policy and the private investments which that policy influences, energy will continue to impose intractable economic, environmental and security constraints on even the type and degree of global development that is vital for basic decency.
>
> (pp. 1–2)

This issue is explored in more detail later in this chapter. Other examples of policies that go against both economic efficiency and sustainability are given in the series of recent publications from the World Resources Institute in Washington DC with titles like *The Forest for the Trees? Government Policies and the Misuse of Forest Resources, Paying the Price: Pesticide Subsidies in Developing Countries* and *Money to Burn: the High Cost of Energy Subsidies*.

The following examples of concrete attempts to address the environmental crisis all illustrate one of the three simple solutions cited. They provide ample evidence of the crisis' essentially institutional and political, rather than technical, nature. They have been grouped under the headings damage limitation; regeneration; and reforming consumption.

Damage limitation

Chipko Movement (India)

The forests of India are a critical resource for the subsistence of rural peoples throughout the country, but especially in hill and mountain areas, both because of their direct provision of food, fuel and fodder and because of their role in stabilising soil and water resources. As these forests have been increasingly felled for commerce and industry, Indian villagers, mainly women, have sought to protect their livelihoods through the Gandhian method of *satyagraha* – non-violent resistance. In the 1970s and 1980s this resistance to the destruction of forests spread throughout India and became organised and known as the Chipko Movement.

The first Chipko action took place spontaneously in Uttar Pradesh in April 1973 and over the next five years spread to many other districts of the Himalayas. The name of the movement comes from a word meaning 'embrace': the villagers, mainly women, hug the trees, saving them by interposing their bodies between them and the contractors' axes. The Chipko protests in Uttar Pradesh achieved a major victory in 1980 with a fifteen-year ban on green felling in the Himalayan forests of that state by order of India's then Prime Minister, Indira Gandhi. Since then the movement has spread to Himachal Pradesh in the North, Karnataka in the South, Rajasthan in the West, Bihar in the East and to the Vindhyas in Central India. In addition to the fifteen-year ban in Uttar Pradesh, the movement has stopped clear felling in the Western Ghats and the Vindhyas and generated pressure for a natural resource policy which is more sensitive to people's needs and ecological requirements.

The Chipko Movement is the result of hundreds of decentralised and locally autonomous initiatives. Its leaders and activists are primarily village women, acting to save their means of subsistence and their communities. Men are involved too, however, and some of these have given wider leadership to the movement. One of these is Sunderlal Bahuguna, a Gandhian activist and philosopher, whose appeal to Mrs Gandhi resulted in the green-felling ban and whose 5,000 kilometre trans-Himalaya footmarch in 1981–3 was crucial in spreading the Chipko message. Bahuguna coined the Chipko slogan: 'Ecology is permanent economy'.

A feature published by the United Nations Environment Programme reported the Chipko movement thus: 'In effect the Chipko people are working a socio-economic revolution by winning control of their forest resources from the hands of a distant bureaucracy which is concerned with selling the forest for making urban-oriented products' (Lamb 1981, p. 4).

[...]

Regeneration

Green Belt Movement (Kenya)

The principal promoter of the Green Belt Movement has been Professor Wangari Maathai, who was born in Kenya in 1940 and received her doctorate in 1971. She became head of veterinary anatomy and Associate Professor of Anatomy at Nairobi University in 1976 and 1977 respectively.

Maathai has also long been active in the National Council of Women of Kenya, of which she has been Chair since 1980, and it was in the National Council of Women that the idea of the Green Belt Movement, a broad-based, grassroots tree-planting activity was born. Its first trees were planted on 5 June, World Environment Day, 1977.

The Green Belt Movement grew very fast. By the mid-1980s Maathai estimated that it had about 600 tree-nurseries, involving and earning income for 2,000–3,000 women; had planted about 2,000 green belts of at least 1,000 trees each, involving about half a million schoolchildren; and had assisted some 15,000 farmers to plant private green belts. Maathai is currently taking forward a proposal with the United Nations Environment Programme for a Pan-African Green Belt Movement, to spread the successful Kenyan experience to twelve other African countries.

Through the planting of Green Belts, the Movement seeks to achieve many different objectives including: avoiding desertification; promoting the ideas and creating public awareness of environment and development; providing fuelwood for energy; promoting a variety of trees for human and animal use; encouraging soil conservation and land rehabilitation; creating jobs in the rural areas especially for the handicapped and rural poor; creating self-employment opportunities for young people in agriculture; giving women the positive image appropriate to their leading role in development processes; promoting sound nutrition based on traditional foodstuffs; carrying out research in conjunction with academic institutions; developing a replicable methodology for rural development. In its first ten years all of these objectives were realised by the Movement to some degree.

In 1989 Maathai's position and that of the whole Green Belt Movement in Kenya was threatened by her opposition to a plan to build a world media centre, including the highest projected building in Africa, on Nairobi's principal inner-city park which was much enjoyed by the city's poor and children. The new centre was a joint project between the Government of Kenya and one of Robert Maxwell's companies and was to feature a more than lifesize statue of President Arap Moi. As Maathai mobilised her contacts against the project and international pressure especially mounted, she was vilified and placed under virtual house arrest. When the Norwegian ambassador, whose country had significantly backed the Green Belt Movement, protested he was summarily sent back to Norway and pressure was exerted on the Movement itself. In November 1990 Maathai herself was prevented from returning to Kenya after a trip to the US. The whole story is a classic example of the connection between human rights abuse, 'prestige project' development and unsustainability.

[…]

Reforming Consumption

[…]

Almost all industrial countries have seen a significant spread in recent years among consumers of the awareness of the ability of their purchasing power to support environmentally sound products and business practices. The UK has been especially significant since *The Green Consumer Guide* (Elkington and Hailes 1988) was published in September 1988 and sold 300,000 copies within a year. Enormous activity on the producer side followed, with high level oversubscribed conferences on how to attract the green consumer and numerous 'green product' innovations. Detergents, batteries, motor cars, supermarkets – all these industries made significant green pitches during 1989–90. Mainstream business and marketing magazines kept up the steady exhortation to business to respond to this new consumer pressure as a business opportunity. Even the government felt moved to respond to the new mood and the Department of the Environment (DOE) introduced a discussion paper on the theme of ecolabelling (DOE 1989) as well as commissioning a wide ranging report on the economy and the environment (Pearce *et al.* 1989). In Europe ecolabelling was first introduced by West Germany with its Blue Angel Scheme, and it may be that that country is Europe's most environmentally aware nation. If so, it is largely due to the energy and activities of such people as Dr Maximilian Gege.

Maximilian Gege (Germany)

Maximilian Gege was born in 1945 and was the director of management planning and environment for a Hamburg business. In the late 1970s he became increasingly aware of environmental problems which led to activism in citizens' groups for clean air, against roads, etc. In 1983 he invented the concept of 'environmental advisers' and in 1984 set up

AUGE (Action Association for Environment, Health and Food) to promote this:

> Environmental advisers attempt to realize the following main objectives:
>
> - To awaken in people a greater environmental awareness and motivate them towards a less environmentally harmful consumer behaviour;
> - To increase the demand for environmentally sound products with low emissions;
> - To further the development of environmentally sound products by talking with manufacturers;
> - To implement behavioural changes that help to reduce environmental pollution;
> - To make cost-saving suggestions for households (up to 2,500 DM/year) and for communities, which also reduce environmental burdens (i.e. reduction of solid and liquid wastes, lower costs through reduction of water and energy consumption, etc.);
> - To show how a better environmental policy not only helps to solve current environmental problems, but to improve the community image.
>
> (AUGE 1986, p. 7)

From the start Gege conceived the environmental adviser as a new professional. The first three were employed in Hamburg in collaboration with a conservation group. In co-operation with AUGE, a Swiss firm was brought in to give training advice and unemployed scientists started to be retrained as environmental advisers. Extensive networking and promotional work – including publication of a book *Öko-Sparbuch für Haushalt und Familie* (Ecology Savings Book for Household and Family) (Gege *et al.* 1986) which sold 50,000 copies, royalties to AUGE – meant that by 1987 nearly eighty environmental advisers were employed in the FRG.

The success of the environmental adviser concept in West Germany meant that Gege won a commission in 1986 from the European Commission to study its feasibility in England, Spain and France as well, where fifty environmental advisers are now working. The concept has also spread to Luxembourg, Austria, Denmark, the Netherlands and Switzerland, with contacts in Hungary, Canada and other countries. By 1991 about 1,000 environmental advisers were working in Germany and about 500 in other countries, only four years after Gege invented the concept. Courses of study for these posts have been set up at universities and other institutions, and Gege has also developed a large-scale course of self-study to qualify as an environmental adviser which already has about 500 students.

In Germany AUGE's activities were further developed with a massive water-saving programme for Hamburg; an environmental computer program that helps households save money; collaboration with a large mail-order firm Otto Versand to develop an environmentally-sound catalogue; and a nationwide competition, in search of the environmentally soundest household for 1988–9.

This competition was a most ambitious and successful affair. Twenty-three million brochures were distributed to German households, with the declared goal of promoting ecological behaviour by every citizen, resulting in the return of 350,000 questionnaires. This makes it probably the largest mass ecological conscientisation initiative ever undertaken. Winning households from different parts of West Germany were presented with DM20,000 cheques, normally by the State Environmental Minister, with great attendant publicity. All the recipients were women – financial recognition at last for good housekeeping.

To promote the environmentally-minded enterprise, Gege and Georg Winter founded in 1985, BAUM (Bundesdeutschen Arbeitskreis fur umweltbewusstes Management e.v. – German Association for Environmentalist Management) of which Gege became Executive

Director in 1989. BAUM is an initiative for the business community trying to promote a holistic concept of environmental awareness in corporate management. Gege also worked with Georg Winter on a book in this field, entitled *Das Umweltbewusste Management* (Business and the Environment) (Winter 1988, also translated into French and Spanish). At present, BAUM has nearly 300 members, most of which are small and medium-sized companies, but there are also some large companies operating on a global scale.

In just a few years, BAUM made itself a name in the Federal Republic of Germany as a multi-sector, non-profit and non-party organisation that has played a decisive role in establishing a movement for environmental management. Since then, major steps have been taken both in the private and in the public sector for reorientation of thinking and action.

There is an increasing number of companies which are gaining market success by changing over to environmentally sounder products and reducing their costs by programmes to save energy, water and raw materials. Waste disposal costs and risks are increasingly being reduced by modern waste avoidance strategies and recycling. Staff are showing increased motivation and initiative. The attitude of the general public, formerly very critical of industry, has become more positive.

The activities of BAUM are based on the 'Integrated System of Environmental Management' which has been developed, tested and successfully used in medium-sized companies. The management model is based on the need to fulfil the economic and ecological requirements simultaneously in all functional areas and at all levels of the company. Another book, which Gege co-authored with K. Apitz and published in November 1990, is entitled *What Managers Could Learn from a Greenfly* (Apitz and Gege 1990) and stresses the need for the human economy to take sustainability lessons from nature.

BAUM has a major role in the research project 'Environmental Business Management' of the German Ministry of the Environment and the German Environmental Agency. BAUM has developed environmental guidelines for the Environment Department of one of the German Länder, to be applicable for all public procurement activities of that Land.

All the projects conducted by BAUM so far with private- and public-sector organisations have shown that ecological measures also give economic benefits. They improve the cost-effectiveness of the company, or show the company new products and new markets.

Yet another initiative of Gege's launched in 1990 is the AUGE Children's Environmental Club, a systematic multi-media attempt to raise children's consciousness of environmental issues. It comprises a magazine, videos, environmental holidays, an environmental protection board game, teaching materials and a touring 'Enviromobile'. Gege is concerned to improve the quality of what is available to and marketed for children and young people, especially with regard to food, school facilities and free time and is setting up discussions with industry to achieve this. Characteristically ambitious, Gege hopes that by post-1992 the Children's Club will have become a European affair, and is establishing a European network to this end.

From these organisations emerges the 'grand plan' behind Gege's activities: he is seeking systematically to conscientise, inform and persuade people about environment protection at each of the most critical human/environment interfaces: childhood and youth (Children's Club); consumers/households (AUGE); business (BAUM); government (environmental advisers). Gege's business skills seem to have ensured that each of these dimensions has been most professionally approached and his effectiveness has been recognised by several environmental awards. It is an impressive record that could well serve as a model for other countries.

[...]

Conclusion

Of course the initiatives and projects which have been described here represent a tiny fraction of the popular action which is being mobilised around the world by increasingly serious and widespread environmental concern. In its report to the Brundtland Commission, the Environment Liaison Centre in Nairobi reported that

> The NGO response to the growing challenge of sustainable development, though hindered in recent years by a deterioration in the wider institutional context, has been decisive. NGOs have swung into action in increasing numbers and at all levels from the local to the global, taking up a lengthening list of environment-development issues; developing innovative forms of cooperation between organisations and undertaking a broad range of tasks from advocacy to the initiation of pioneering projects.
>
> (ELC 1986, p. 4)

These popular initiatives badly need to be combined with firm governmental and intergovernmental action across the whole range of issues with implications for environmental sustainability. The earlier analysis permits the outline of a possible scenario incorporating such actions.

First, the North accepts its essential responsibility for the environmental crisis and institutes a massive programme of conservation, resource-efficiency and pollution control in its own countries, perhaps through the imposition of annually increasing environmental taxes. This would certainly result in major lifestyle changes, such as a fall in the use of the private motor-car.

The North also recognises the constraints on sustainable development in the South caused by the world economic system, and undertakes its systematic reform involving debt cancellation and fairer trading relationships (involving issues such as commodity prices, protectionism against Southern manufacturers, corporate codes of conduct, exploitation of the global commons). It also agrees to the concessional transfer of clean, efficient technologies for appropriate Southern industrialisation, and of resources for Southern environmental regeneration.

However, this programme of reform has fundamental conditions for Southern elites, expressed by the words justice, democracy and sustainability. Justice demands the return of illegal flight capital from Northern banks to its countries of origin to fulfil the development tasks for which it was intended. It also demands a recognition of peasant and indigenous land rights through comprehensive and effective programmes of land reform. Democracy demands that people become the controllers of their development rather than its passive instruments or, worse, its victims. This involves the option of rejecting certain development patterns as well as full participation in those chosen. Sustainability involves absolute respect for and conservation of critical global resources such as rainforests as well as rigorously sustainable use of all renewable resources and strict adherence to internationally agreed emission quotas.

Such a programme would cost the North large sums of money which could probably only be found by plundering arms budgets. It would also include lifestyle shifts and a drop in Northern incomes. It would cost the Southern elites their autocratic power and many of their Northern lifestyle trappings. It would give new life and hope to the rural poor worldwide. It would also give the human race a secure future. It remains to be seen whether this final benefit can muster the political will to overthrow the vested interests that currently stand between this scenario and reality.

So far, as has been seen, the political will has been notably absent. There can be few greater examples of lack of vision in world 'leaders' than that, despite their access to the very latest scientific evidence, they have trailed far behind their peoples in recognition of the environmental crisis, which is likely to be the most important political and human issue of the 1990s. It is only a few years since President Reagan was blaming pollution on trees and the UK Environment Secretary Nicholas Ridley called the ecological critique 'intellectually bankrupt'. Once again it has been ordinary people working through largely voluntary organisations who have acted decisively for human wellbeing, while the established power structures were either blind to the perils or actively promoting them.

Selected references

Agarwal, M. (1985) *India and the World Economy*, Princeton NJ: PUP.

EDF (Environmental Defense Fund) (1987) 'The Failure of Social Forests in Karnataka', *The Ecologist*, 17, 4, pp. 151–4.

Lohmann, L. (1990) 'Commercial Tree Plantations in Thailand: Deforestation by Another Name', *The Ecologist*, 20, 1, pp. 61–6.

Myers, N. (1989) *Deforestation Rates in Tropical Forests and their Climatic Implications*, London: friends of the earth.

Timberlake, L. (1985) *Africa in Crisis*, London: Earthscan.

WRI (World Resources Institute) (1987) *The Tropical Forestry Action Plan*, Washington DC: WRI.

29 Environmental activism and world civic politics

Paul Wapner

Source: Paul Wapner (1996), *Environmental Activism and World Civic Politics*,
Albany, NY: State University of New York Press, pp. 152–164

> Rarer by far than originality in science or art is originality in political action. And rarer still is
> original political action that enlarges, rather than blights or destroys, human possibilities.
>
> (Jonathan Schell)

Nation-states are so important in world affairs that we tend to associate their activities with the meaning of world politics itself. States enjoy the ability to reach into and influence the lives of their citizens, and thus it makes sense to see them as fundamental to international political life. Nonetheless, as this study of transnational environmental activist groups demonstrates, states do not monopolize world political activity. They share the international stage with other actors. While not as powerful as states, transnational environmental groups significantly shape widespread behavior as it relates to environmental issues. They play an important role in contemporary world environmental politics.

For most people, this is no surprise. Transnational groups such as Greenpeace – with an operating budget of over $100 million, 6 million members and offices worldwide – *must* play a part in shaping the way people interact with the natural environment; they must change the way people act toward the environment. Problems arise, however, when one seeks to understand exactly *how* activists effect change. The conventional understanding is that environmental activists are politically effective when they influence state behavior. That is, they bring about change by lobbying states to enact environmental policies. According to this view, widespread human behavior shifts because of states. They are the political agents; activists serve only as pressure groups that shape governmental policy.

A central aim of this book has been to show that this view is not so much wrong as incomplete. Transnational environmental groups not only lobby states but also directly shape the activities of other institutions, collectivities, and individuals. They do so by manipulating mechanisms of power that exist outside the realm of state-to-state relations. These include economic, social, and cultural practices that traverse countries and have an impact on public life. To use the conceptual language that is at the core of this book, Greenpeace, Friends of the Earth, and World Wildlife Fund politicize global civil society and thus engage in world civic politics.

The practice of world civic politics represents a distinct approach to global environmental governance. Most people look to states and the regimes states create to address environmental issues. They recognize that states are the primary actors in world affairs and count on them to pursue actions that advance environmental well-being. In earlier chapters I referred to this perspective as *statism* because it sees environmental governance strictly as a matter of state action. While statism has many advocates, it is not the only form or scenario of global environmental governance. For some thinkers, statism possesses inherent problems that compromise its ability to address appropriately environmental issues. For these thinkers, effective environmental governance necessitates moving political authority beyond the level of the state and shifting it upward or downward, as it were, to protect the earth's ecosystem. The two most important schools of thought along these lines are supra-statism and sub-statism, with the first calling for some form of world government and the second arguing for decentralizing governmental power.

For transnational environmental activists, statism, supra-statism, and sub-statism represent, at best, partial approaches to global environmental governance. Each perspective sees the state as playing a central role – as either the answer to environmental problems or the foil against which alternative responses must be explored. Each reifies the governmental dimension of politics and sees it as the overriding focus of a sound environmental strategy. This is unfortunate because such a view bleaches out the potential of other forms of world political activity that can be and are being enlisted in the service of environmental protection. World civic politics, which takes place in global civil society, has its own role to play and has already brought about changes with regard to environmental issues that are outside the capacity of nation-states. World civic politics, then, is a parallel type of activity. It does not replace statism nor categorically dismiss supra-statism and sub-statism. Rather, it represents a qualitatively different approach to global environmental governance.

[. . .]

Non state-oriented world political activity

One alternative conceptualization to the state system as a mechanism for solving global problems is supra-statism. This scheme seeks to create some sort of world government. It suggests an institutional presence at the global level that will determine worldwide environmental policy and enforce it through law backed by force. The central notion is that the present world of sovereign states is too fragmented and competitive to address global ecological problems successfully and thus some meta-institutional presence is necessary to do the job.

Earlier I contrasted this with the work of Greenpeace. Greenpeace pitches its efforts toward the global arena, although its orientation is not to create an institutional presence. Rather, it tries to change consciousness. Its work is process rather than institutionally oriented. It seeks to alter people's minds and actions throughout the world by disseminating an ecological sensibility. For Greenpeace, consciousness itself can be a form of governance. It can modify human practices and thus represents an important avenue for creating conditions that will direct the behavior of others. Greenpeace targets this dimension of collective life. To highlight the distinction between Greenpeace's work and the supra-statist approach, I suggested we think of Greenpeace's politics as a form of globalism rather than supra-statism.

The same contrast exists between sub-statism and the political efficacy of World Wildlife Fund. Sub-statists feel the problem with the present state system is that the nation-state is too big to address environmental dangers successfully. It is too insensitive to the local dynamics of environmental harm and thus unable to achieve genuine environmental protection. Instead, sub-statists prescribe breaking it into smaller units within which people can be more aware of and responsive to the environmental consequences of their actions. In one formulation, sub-statists call for establishing bioregions that forge communities around ecological rather than formally governmental boundaries.

World Wildlife Fund also works at the local level insofar as it undertakes many of its projects within Third World villages but pursues a fundamentally different strategy than sub-statism. WWF is not concerned with constructing an institutional, administrative presence at the local level that would replace the nation-state or even refashion communities in a way that would necessarily shift citizen's loyalty. Rather, it seeks to carry out ecological work at this level with the hope of empowering local people to protect their own environments and, in turn, to exert pressure upward through the international system for more ecologically sound practices worldwide. The emphasis is on just that, *practices*, not institutional arrangements. Like Greenpeace, WWF is committed to a process approach to ecological restoration and protection, not an institutional one. To accentuate the difference between the work of WWF and sub-statist approaches, I referred to WWF's efforts as a form of localism versus sub-statism.

Finally, the same sort of contrast exists between statism and the orientation of Friends of the Earth. Statism assumes that because states are the main actors in world affairs, they themselves will undertake or at least orchestrate all significant political activity directed at environmental protection. Domestically, states will pass legislation and work nationally for environmental well-being; transnationally and globally, they will create regimes to coordinate international environmental efforts. Statism, in other words, sees state action as central to environmental protection and trusts that states will effectively respond to environmental challenges.

FOE works at the level of states, as it were, but is less confident about states' ability to address environmental problems on their own. While it understands that states can do much to protect the environment, it nevertheless feels that such effort can go only so far. Operating within a self-help, relatively competitive system, states have difficulty fashioning long-term, promising responses to environmental issues. According to FOE, states must be forced, from the outside, to undertake environmental protection. This involves, to be sure, lobbying – that is, directly pressuring governments to adopt environmentalist objectives – and FOE, like other transnational groups, engages in such effort. Additionally, however, because of limitations associated with lobbying, FOE also mobilizes other pressures on states. Foremost, it turns the interdependencies of world affairs into mechanisms that promote environmental protection. As state activity intersects with these interdependencies, states are forced, often unwittingly, to pursue environmentally sound practices. The difference between statism and FOE's orientation, then, turns on where political activity is located. Statism places it in the state; world politics is about interstate relations and thus focusing on the institution of the nation-state is the key to environmental protection. Alternatively, FOE locates it outside the state, at the intersections of transnational economic, social, and cultural activities. It understands that the processes of world collective life are themselves forms of governance and can be enlisted in the service of environmental protection. To highlight this approach, I called it *internationalism* to distinguish it from *statism*.

What is important to recognize in all these transnational, process-oriented efforts is that the mechanisms environmental groups activate are forms of governance. They have control over people's lives. Put differently, they represent ways of ordering widespread human action. For this reason, it is important to see the work of transnational groups as genuinely political even though their efforts do not emanate from a state or take on the coercive character of its policies and instrumentalities.

World civic politics

In his book, *Green Political Thought*, Andrew Dobson outlines the degrees to which activists engage in what he calls *extra-parliamentary* activities. In doing so, he points out how the situations of their political work and modes of expression are often outside formal channels of state power.[1] While Dobson refers predominantly to domestic activists, his insight is helpful for understanding the politics of transnational environmental groups.

Greenpeace's most significant form of political activity is disseminating an ecological sensibility. It works to spread an appreciation for the dangers of ecological destruction to communities throughout the world and to inspire as many people as possible to adopt practices that are "kind" to the planet. Its target, then, is the thin but increasingly emerging global cultural sphere. Through presenting alternative images of the environment, bearing witness, criticizing predominant modes of conduct, and exposing ecological atrocities, Greenpeace tries to express itself through communication technologies to joggle the minds of the world. It literally speaks through the air waves spanning the globe. Satellite dishes, fax machines, video cameras, and electronic mail services are the tools of Greenpeace's political action. And these are, essentially, entry ways into the world media network. Global communication systems are the sites for disseminating an ecological sensibility.

World Wildlife Fund targets particular spaces for its activities. WWF applies itself, in many of its projects, to villages in the Third World. These can be thought of as the capillaries of anti-ecological practices; they sit at the most local of levels of ecological destruction. WWF focuses on this level because even though the actions of villagers reflect a response to global pressures to exploit the environment, power relations in these local circumstances are much different than at the heights of global political, economic, and social structures; these areas represent the extremities of global power relations and as such are more fragile and thus amenable to alternative practices. Third World, local situations represent the arena of WWF's politics.

Friends of the Earth also targets a particular site for its activities. It focuses on the intersections of collective life. Local, national, and international processes represent different spheres of political experience; likewise corporate, social, and governmental arenas represent different areas of collective activity. In between these spheres there are "switching points." These are places where one type of social life interacts with another. When a company sells a product, for example, it does so in numerous settings that span municipal, regional, and at times international jurisdictions. Similarly, when a multilateral bank loans money abroad it works through different state and corporate agencies in a number of countries. At each step a type of translation takes place where one discourse meets another, where different sets of rules apply. At these intersections there is an "opening" for political manipulation and expression. To be sure, Friends of the Earth focuses on these with the aim of cornering states, but the quality and location of the site is outside, as it were, the state system per se.

The predominant aspect of all these sites is that they sit outside the formal control of states. They are far from the halls of parliaments, offices of congresspeople, residences of world leaders. To be sure, states compete for control of these arenas. They have not yet, and seemingly cannot, however, monopolize the dynamics of these regions. These arenas are, then, semiautonomous. They represent domains that can be co-opted or colonized by different actors. Transnational ecological groups work to win control of these openings.

In addition to extra-parliamentary sites of activity, transnational groups use modes of effectiveness that are not informed by the predominant type of power exercised by the state. The main efficacy of state power emanates from its ability to set-up laws and ensure compliance through force. Activists use a different type of power. When Greenpeace disseminates an ecological sensibility, WWF empowers local residents, and Friends of the Earth entangles states in interdependencies, they enlist the instrumentalities of information, image-making, exposés, hands-on ecological restoration and protection, and corporate education. These aim to change consciousness, empower local residents, and create mechanisms of accountability. What is important to notice is that these actions have their own "pull" on people. They involve channeling human behavior in significant ways.

An important characteristic of these forms of power is that they do not work against the will of others but rather in tandem with it. Another way of saying this is that they work through persuasion rather than coercion; they enlist subjects in their own subjectification rather than bringing physical force to bear on them. This form of power will be familiar to readers acquainted with the thought of people such as Russell, Foucault, or Lukes.[2] These authors emphasize the constitutive character of dominant discourses, norms, moral codes, and knowledge. These conditions exert pressure on people and, by instilling certain understandings, determine human practices. Transnational ecological groups implicitly recognize the dynamics of these forms of power and devise strategies for enlisting them.

When one discusses extra-parliamentary sites and modes of political activity, one implicitly suggests that there is an arena of collective life that sits outside of state constraints yet that plays a part in political affairs. In domestic regimes this is increasingly recognized as the sphere of civil society. Civil society is that slice of collective life that takes place above the individual yet below the state. It is the sphere of economic, cultural, and social interaction as opposed to state activity. Contemporary usage stems in large part from Hegel insofar as he defined civil society in contrast to the state.[3] For Hegel, civil society is an arena wherein people pursue their particular private interests in common independent from, and in fact prior to, the state.[4] Many contemporary theorists also understand civil society in contrast to the state and identify it with forms of collective interaction that are voluntary, spontaneous, customary, and nonlegalistic in nature. The state, on the other hand, is a complex network of governmental institutions that operate formally and legalistically.

This distinction, while overly formulaic, is helpful for conceptualizing a politically relevant sphere of collective life that is separate from the state. When transnational groups manipulate cultural symbols to disseminate an ecological sensibility, or work with and empower local inhabitants, or carry out protests, boycotts, and educational campaigns at the intersections of collective life, they undertake activities outside of formal statist structures. At these times they operate in the sphere of customary, spontaneous, and voluntary collective life and not within the governmental, legalistic one. In fact, it is only because such activities can be undertaken in this sphere that environmental groups even have a chance to utilize them. They are forms of activity that are not already monopolized by the state. (To be sure, states engage in similar activities and thus vie for control of civil society. Short of totalitarian regimes, however, they have been unsuccessful at capturing all the dynamics of civil life.)[5]

When environmental activist groups work in this realm they are deliberately politicizing the social, economic, and cultural spheres of transnational life. They are constituting global civil society in a way that makes it an explicit arena of political activity. The idea is to discover unconventional levers of power and employ nontraditional modes of action that can affect, if only unevenly and imperfectly, the global community. This involves teasing out and utilizing nonformal channels and mechanisms of political engagement or, put differently, manipulating forms of power that are generally considered ineffectual in the larger context of so-called genuine politics.

One of the best articulations of this form of politics comes out of the theoretical work on new social movements. In the early 1980s, German sociologists coined the phrase, *Neue soziale Bewegungen*, to describe the activities of contemporary human rights, peace, feminist, and environmental activist groups operating in Western democracies. They claimed that these organizations represented qualitatively new forms of political activity and therefore needed to be distinguished from interest groups, political parties, and traditional labor movements.[6]

The literature is heterogeneous on what exactly constitutes the novelty of these movements. Some theorists suggest that new movements are ideologically distinct from their predecessors. New movements are preoccupied less with issues of economic growth, distribution of resources, and security, and more with "quality of life" concerns.[7] Others identify the novelty in the organizational structure of activist groups. They point out that many groups stress participatory decision making, a decentralized structure and opposition to bureaucratic procedures.[8] Still others contend that new movements are qualitatively distinct because they arise in response to fundamentally new challenges facing postindustrial societies. Contradictions in the welfare state, extensive colonization of the "life world" by governments, and global threats such as large-scale ecological collapse are overwhelming governmental capabilities and therefore give way to social movement activity.[9]

In addition to these insights, a number of theorists point to the tactics new movements use to induce change as the distinguishing characteristic of new social movements. Instead of merely lobbying government officials, participating in governmental commissions and supporting candidates for office, new movements employ a wide repertoire of actions. These include activities such as nature walks, film showings, conferences, and citizen tribunals.[10] The important aspect of these types of activities is their unofficial, extra-parliamentary character. It is this last characteristic of new movements that signals the civil dimension of their politics.

To date, most of the literature on new social movements focuses on domestic politics. It examines the politicization of civil society within, for example, Germany, France, Poland, or the United States.[11] In my view, it is possible to witness and theorize about *world* civic politics. In fact, this is exactly the kind of activity transnational ecological groups undertake. Greenpeace, World Wildlife Fund, and Friends of the Earth have offices in more than one country and pursue actions across state boundaries. They work literally worldwide. In addition to lobbying diverse governments, they work through global civil society to shape widespread practices. Activists see the political world as an expansive field of activity populated by a host of potential and actual mechanisms able to change human behavior. The state system is only one among many of such mechanisms.

Transnational environmental groups and world politics

Throughout this book I have been emphasizing how scholars privilege the state in their analysis of world political events. This is particularly true of political realists but is also the case with other intellectual traditions within international relations. I am obviously not the first to question such an approach to world politics. As mentioned in the Introduction, in the 1970s numerous scholars in the field did so. My work differs significantly, however, from this earlier critique. The key argument of people like Keohane, Nye, Mansbach, Ferguson, Lampert, Vernon, and Feld was that nonstate actors were growing in number and importance and that some of their actions were having an equal or larger impact on world affairs than nation-states. At a minimum, they claimed that transnational relations play into the calculations of states and force them to change their politics. At the extreme, they argued that NGOs, such as multinational corporations, would eventually eclipse the state as the preeminent political force in the world.[12]

In my view, this early work got off to a good start. One of its most significant contributions was to raise the issue of the meaning of politics itself. In their edited volume, *Transnational Relations and World Politics*, Keohane and Nye offer the following definition of politics, which reflects their sensitivity to transnational actors. Politics "refers to relationships in which at least one actor consciously employs resources, both material and symbolic, including the threat or exercise of punishment, to induce other actors to behave differently than they would otherwise behave."[13] They go on to emphasize that such actors need not be states.[14] While this is significant and commendable in that it raises the issue of politics itself, Keohane and Nye quickly skirt a frontal attack on the predominant view in the way they formulate the importance of this notion of politics. In the introductory essay, Keohane and Nye pose themes for the entire volume. The first and most important one is to assess the net effect of transnational relations on the ability of governments to operate. That is, transnationalism must be understood in terms of its effects on state behavior. Like much of the early transnational work, then, Keohane and Nye raise the minimalist position, viz., transnationalism is meaningful to the degree it plays into the calculations of states and induces them to modify policy. Furthermore, their second thematic question has to do with the influence of transnationalism for the study of international relations. Keohane and Nye want to know if an increase in transnational activity calls sufficient attention away from the state as the primary unit of analysis. Should scholars shift from a focus on states to multinational corporations, the Catholic Church, and so forth? Here the problem is less one of privileging the state so much as willing to set up the debate in either/or terms: either the state is the primary mover and shaker of world affairs or not.[15] This reflects the maximalist position, viz., that NGOs have replaced the state as the most important actor in world affairs.

By raising the issue of transnationalism in terms of minimalist and maximalist positions, scholars in general, and Keohane and Nye in particular, unnecessarily restrict their understanding of politics. In the first instance, they treat the state as a giant cash register: everything that happens politically must be paid for in its terms. Consequently, all other activities that could be politically relevant, although not having to do with the state per se, get bleached out of observation and analysis. In the second instance, setting up the debate in terms of the unit of analysis issue is problematic because it fashioned the controversy in a way that the transnationalist critique could be easily beaten back by state-centric thinkers. Indeed, people only had to prove the superior efficacy of the state to dismiss the transnationalist challenge. As I mentioned in the first chapter, this is exactly what happened. Gilpin, Waltz, Sullivan, and others argued successfully that the state was not going away as the central unit of analysis and still very much dictates world politics. This took a tremendous amount of wind out of the transnationalists' sails.

My own work uses the transnationalist critique as a point of departure but asks a different set of questions about world politics. Instead of getting into a debate about relative impact, I essentially bracket the role of states in world politics and examine nonstatist activities for their own richness and effectiveness. In 1970, commenting on recent scholarship on transnationalism, Peter Evans claimed that, "It is not interesting to exclude traditional state behavior and then study the residual only."[16] I disagree. I think it is extremely interesting to put questions of state activity in parentheses and explore the actual work of nonstate actors to appreciate the full spectrum of world politically relevant activity. Otherwise, all activity becomes obscured in the shadow of the state. This is important not to "knock off" the primary unit of analysis but to allow for fuller accounts of world political events and to introduce people to alternative forms of political activity that will expand and deepen the repertoire of responses to global problems. In short, while I appreciate the transnationalist critique and use it as a springboard for inquiry, I assume a different orientation. I utilize it to give voice to nonstatist forms of world politics and to emphasize their efficacy. I use it to illuminate world civic politics.

My hope is that an appreciation for this dimension of global experience will sensitize people to the limitations of the traditional understanding of *world politics*. First, it should cast into doubt the equation of *world* with *state system*. The world, in a political context, is more than the existence of nation-states. States represent only the most obvious components. Indeed, understanding *world* simply as a configuration of states is like believing a university is made up solely of students and professors. Such an understanding may reveal much about a university; it certainly will not provide a full or even accurate account of the dynamics at work or the institution's overall character. Emphasizing world civic politics, then, highlights the importance of nonstate actors and thus complicates the view that the word *world*, in the phrase *world politics*, refers simply to states or, as it is traditionally understood, international.

Second, an appreciation for nonstate forces adds depth to the notion of *politics*. Traditionally, politics is associated with the governing capabilities of government. Insofar as governments are those institutions endowed with the authority to make binding decisions applicable to the whole community, politics – as the use of power in a public context – is understood as the way governments implement such decisions. This view is problematic insofar as it equates authority with a particular notion of governance, viz., law backed by force. Governance entails more than this. As Lukes, Foucault, and others remind us, there are forms of power associated with norms, rules, and discourses that actually shape people's desires, conceptions, understandings of the self, and, ultimately, behavior without recourse to law or the threat of physical coercion. My emphasis on nonstate forces in world affairs borrows from these conceptions of power and extends them to the realm of world collective life. These more subtle forms of power have political consequences, and we should take them seriously if for no other reason than they can and are being used to create conditions that order the actions of people within a world context. Thus, it is imperative to expand our notion of politics itself (in the phrase *world politics*) to include nonstatist modes of governance.

The field of international relations is not blind to the importance of redefining world politics. An appreciation for the host of nonstate activities has led to a spate of formulations that try to capture such a sensitivity. Rosenau suggests referring to the field as *post-international relations*; Ashley offers the term *post-modern world politics*; Richard Falk talks, at times, of *post-realism*. I support these efforts. My own contribution to them is in putting the processes and activities involved in world civic politics into sharp relief. I give voice to a politics that is relevant in a world context but that takes place outside the grasp of states.

Conclusion

Expanding the concept of world politics is important for scholarly inquiry. I wish I could say, however, that the stakes involved were of such limited scope. Unfortunately, the problems of the globe do not turn merely on academic debate or the refinement of intellectual categories. The world faces dangers that threaten all living beings on earth. The greenhouse effect, ozone depletion, species extinction, and so forth are threats to the very infrastructure that supports life on earth. Addressing them properly is one of the most considerable responsibilities currently facing human beings. The task at hand involves changing widespread behavior. It is a first order challenge of politics.

By expanding the notion of world politics through an appreciation of its civil dimension, my hope is that I have not only provided an accurate understanding of transnational environmental activism but have also offered intellectual support for further fashioning global civil society into an arena within which people can advance the project of environmental protection. In many ways, transnational environmental groups work in global civil society without really knowing it. (One is reminded of Molière's remark that for forty years he did not know that he was speaking in prose.) They engage in world civic politics often unaware of the dynamics involved or the promise of more sustained effort directed immediately at global civil society. My work tries to provide some insight along these lines. It delineates the quality of agency at work and reflects upon the practice of world civic politics as an approach to global environmental governance. It suggests that, in addition to existing efforts, the dynamics of global civil society can be further explored and engaged to address environmental dangers. The instruments of power available in this realm can operate in places where states cannot go, and the quality of governance thus enlisted can shape widespread behavior in a different mode than the instrumentalities of states. To be sure, in itself, world civic politics is not an answer to environmental issues – there is no single answer. It represents, however, a significant contribution to environmental protection efforts. It can work at the local, international, and global levels of collective life to steer humanity toward more ecologically sensitive ways of living with, enjoying, and sustaining our blue-green planet.

Notes

1 Andrew Dobson, *Green Political Thought* (London: Unwin Hyman, 1990), 139ff.

2 For example, Bertrand Russell, *Power: A New Social Analysis* (New York: W. W. Norton, 1938); Michel Foucault, *Power/Knowledge: Selected Interviews and Other Writings, 1972–1977*, ed., Colin Gordon (New York: Pantheon, 1980); Steven Lukes, *Power: A Radical View* (London: Macmillan, 1974).

3 There are, of course, traditions that use the term *civil society* in ways that differ from Hegel's understanding. Hobbes, Locke, Kant, and Mill put forth various conceptions that suggest alternative types of formulations. See John Keane, *Democracy and Civil Society* (London: Verso, 1988), 35–64.

4 T. M. Knox, trans., *Hegel's Philosophy of Right* (London: Oxford University Press, 1967).

5 Gramsci, at times, disagrees with this. In fact, often he understands civil society itself as an array of religious, educational, and associational institutions that ensure the domination of the ruling class. In particular, it serves to guarantee the ideological hegemony of that class's interest. At other times, however, Gramsci sees strands of civil society able to be enlisted in a counter-hegemonic effort that can lead ultimately to capturing state control. See Antonio Gramsci, *The Prison Notebooks* (New York: International Publishers, 1985), 210–275. This latter emphasis by Gramsci, which he ascribes to certain societies at particular historical moments, is closer to my own understanding of civil society.

6 Russell Dalton, Manfred Kuechler, and Wilhelm Burklin, "The Challenge of New Movements," in Russell Dalton and Manfred Kuechler, eds, *Challenging the Political Order: New Social and Political Movements in Western Democracies* (New York: Oxford University Press, 1990), 4.

7 Ronald Inglehart, "Values, Ideology, and Cognitive Mobilization in New Social Movements," in Dalton and Kuechler, *Challenging the Political Order*; Alberto Mellucci, "The Symbolic Challenge of Contemporary Movements," *Social Research* 52, no. 4 (1985).

8 Claus Offe, "New Social Movements: Challenging the Boundaries of Institutional Politics," *Social Research* 52, no. 4 (1985); Fritjof Capra Charlene Spretnak and Wulf-Rudiger Lutz, *Green Politics* (New York: Dutton, 1984); Leslie Paul Thiele, "Social Movements and the Interface of Domestic and International Politics: A Study of Peace Activism," Paper presented at the annual meeting of the American Political Science Association, San Francisco, CA, 1990.

9 Jurgen Habermas, "What Does a Crisis Mean Today? Legitimation Problems in Late Capitalism," in Steven Seidman, ed., *Jurgen Habermas on Society and Politics* (Boston: Beacon Press, 1989); Andrew Buchwalter, "Translator's Introduction," in Jurgen Habermas, ed., *Observations on "The Spiritual Situation of the Age,": Contemporary German Perspectives* (Cambridge, MA: MIT Press, 1985).

10 Dorothy Nelkin and Michael Pollak, *The Atom Besieged. Extra-parliamentary Dissent in France and Germany* (Cambridge, MA: MIT Press, 1981); Thomas Rochor *Mobilizing for Peace: Antinuclear Movements in Western Europe* (Princeton, NJ: Princeton University Press, 1988); Dieter Rucht, "The Strategies and Action Repertoires of New Movements," in Dalton and Kuechler, *Challenging the Political Order*.

11 See Alain Touraine, *Anti-Nuclear Protest: The Opposition to Nuclear Energy in France* (New York: Cambridge University Press, 1983); Adam Michnik, *Letters From Prison and Other Essays*, trans. Maya Latynski, (Berkeley: University of California Press, 1987); Harry Boyte, *The Backyard Revolution: Understanding the New Citizen Movement* (Philadelphia: Temple University Press, 1980); Claus Offe, "Challenging the Boundaries of Institutional Politics: Social Movements Since the 1960s," in Charles Maier, ed., *Changing Boundaries of the Political* (Cambridge: Cambridge University Press, 1987).

12 For an extensive discussion of this literature, see chapter 1.

13 Robert Keohane and Joseph Nye, "Transnational Relations and World Politics: An Introduction," *Transnational Relations and World Politics* (Cambridge, MA: Harvard University Press, 1972), xxiv.

14 Ibid., xxv.

15 To be sure, Keohane and Nye had changed their focus by the time they wrote *Power and Interdependence*, but, by this time, their attention had shifted from NGOs to international regimes.

16 Quoted in Keohane and Nye, "Transnational Relations and World Politics," xxiv.

Part 4

Cultures of resistance

Technologies, tactics, tensions

Introduction

The chapter in this *Reader* have explored how we have come to understand resistance, and in what ways processes of globalization have challenged our assumptions about the politics of resistance. Central to the contemporary debates about transnational struggles has been a 'cultural turn', a revived interest in the construction, mediation and contestation of meaning in social life. After all, can we know what is 'resisted', or why, unless we consider the concrete experiences that give meaning to particular practices of resistance? Instead of treating resistance as a given response to an act (or acts) of domination, a reflection on culture reveals the ways in which resistances are constituted through the routines of everyday life. The chapters in Part 4 have been selected so as to explore the ways in which resistances are constituted, mediated and expressed.

Monbiot's chapter on the anti-war movement explicitly acknowledges the role of the news media in amplifying or silencing acts of resistance. As Monbiot suggests, 'September 11 muffled the protests for a while', with much of the media in the United Kingdom and the United States making 'anti-globalization' a taboo. Monbiot's comment on the media is 'that we no longer need them'. 'We have our own channels of communication', he writes, 'our own websites and pamphlets and magazines'. A first key theme in the chapters in Part 4, then, is the technologies that provide a communications infrastructure for contemporary social movements.

In the chapters by Castells and Sassen we find discussion of the political potential that may be offered by technological modes of communication. As Castells explains, 'people are finding ways to be together with much more diversity and importance than has been the experience before in history: chat groups, multidimensional communication, cultural expressions of all kind, people building their own websites'. Sassen similarly notes that 'the Net has emerged as a powerful medium for non-elites to communicate, support each other's struggles'. Yet, despite the non-hierarchical, network-like quality of these technologies, as described in these chapters, each of the texts also points to an inherent contradiction. The 'space of flows' is simultaneously a space of domination – a vehicle for transnational finance and production, for example, or a private digital network (Sassen) – and a potential space of resistance. As Castells puts it, 'the attempt by capital, media, and power to escape into the abstraction of the space of flows...is being challenged from many sources by the grass-rooting of the space of flows'.

The chapters suggest that perhaps we cannot take electronic spaces to be open and unenclosed realms in which movements can freely communicate and organize. As Balliger argues, recalling Williams, 'technology is not a predetermined instrument of domination or liberation, but a "moment of choice" '. Sassen emphasizes the inequalities that continue to characterize the use of the Internet, with the effect that 'power, contestation, inequality, in brief, hierarchy, inscribe electronic space' (Sassen). The communication of resistances along electronic lines, then, is subject to the very power relations and exclusions that we would expect to find in other social spaces.

A second major theme of the chapters in Part 4, recalling Scott and Foucault from Part 1, is that of discursive resistance and the expression of resistance through the routine gestures of everyday life. In her study of the artistic and carnivalesque practices that contribute to a politics of resistance of global finance, Marieke de Goede reminds us that 'these cultural practices are ways in which people cope with the seemingly overwhelming power of finance in everyday life'. De Goede offers a number of rich examples of the reappropriation and politicization of money through laughter and jokes on an everyday level. She points out that the artists and groups she discusses 'neither can nor wish to overthrow global capital', yet they can 'disturb the assumed unity of capital, question its rationality, and reappropriate its language'. This politics of transgression – identified also by Bleiker in the Berg poetry, and by Scott among the Sedaka peasants – stands in stark contrast to Monbiot's claim that movements must 'move on from the playing of games and the staging of parties'. Instead, playful resistances and celebratory festivals become a potential means to temporarily interrupt the pressures of everyday life and to suggest alternative ways of life. Perhaps playful or theatrical gestures, festivals and carnivals can be understood as sites of resistance, then, in the sense that they escape the confines of conventional politics and intervene with the unexpected.

A number of the chapters in Part 4 refer to a third central theme – 'subcultures of resistance' – denoting practices as diverse as the setting up of websites and petty thefts. The chapters by Bleiker, Balliger and Klein have been selected for their explicit focus on the subcultures of resistance found in poetry, music and art. Bleiker's account of the Bohemian artistic and literary scene in East Berlin observes 'how dissent functions in more mundane daily contexts'. For Bleiker, poetry has the potential to protest against established systems of exclusion by forcing 'the reader to confront what s/he has habitually refused to confront'. The underground poetry of a diverse social group is understood by Bleiker to represent an act of dissent in that it offered new perspectives on the reality of life in Communist Germany. Bleiker reveals also the tensions embodied by the poetic resistances. Some of the poets became paid informants of the Stasi and, indeed, most of the poetry refused to 'engage direct political issues'. Rather than locating resistances in direct political slogans or anthemic verses, Bleiker observes a dissent that 'works slowly, by changing the way we speak and think about ourselves and the world we live in'.

Balliger's chapter offers further insight into the controversy opened up by Bleiker. Just as the Berg poetry could not entirely escape the network of power which it sought to oppose, so 'music and noise', as part of the making of meaning in social life, are 'an important site of control and resisatnce'. On the one hand, music has been subject to 'multinational capitalism's relentless search for markets'. Yet, on the other, Balliger finds that 'music inhabits a site where hegemonic processes are contested'. For excluded peoples such as slaves, migrants or colonized societies, for example, music offers 'a central site for the intervention in dominant discourses' and for 'creating forms of expression that are culturally affirming'. In a similar way to Bleiker's poetic dissent, Balliger envisages a potential for music to puncture the illusions of particular systems – whether capitalism, colonialism or slavery, and so on – and to open up a 'temporary autonomous zone' in which dominant meanings can be contested. Again, we find a politics of resistance that may not be directly expressed through the text or verse of a song, but which is articulated more broadly in terms of 'a total transformation of values and lived behaviour'.

Klein's chapter on the practice of 'culture jamming' provides a further example of the intersection between the processes of corporate commodification and the potential for resistances. Discussing the performance art witnessed on billboards across North America, Klein suggests that this practice should not be understood merely as conveying a political message or slogan, but rather as an attempt to direct the viewer to 'a consideration of the original corporate strategy'. Attention is thus drawn to the privatization of public space that takes place as aggressive advertising campaigns colonize streets, shopping malls, even schools and our homes. As with Bleiker's poetic resistances, the purpose is to encourage people to confront and reflect on the things they see habitually on a daily basis. 'The most sophisticated culture jams', writes Klein, 'are not stand-alone ad parodies but interceptions – countermessages that hack into a corporation's own method of communication'. By tapping into the medium and aesthetic used by the corporate advertisers themselves, of course, the culture jammers encounter a further tension in their practices of resistance. As Klein notes, 'the ad industry is proving that it is capable of cutting off the culture jammers at the pass'. Her examples of Nike and Diesel jeans campaigns illustrate how the language of the dissenters can be re-appropriated by the corporations. Perhaps this suggests that we should confront the possibility that resistances, particularly so-called 'subcultures' of resistance, are not themselves immune to processes of commodification and re-branding. Following the targeting of shop windows in the Seattle protests, for example, a number of high street stores used graffiti-style slogans in their shop fronts for the following season's collection. The chapters presented here reveal the ongoing mediation and contestation that characterizes cultures of resistance, challenging the view that resistance politics can be delineated in clear opposition to the forces of global capitalism.

30 Stronger than ever

Far from fizzling out, the global justice movement is growing in numbers and maturity

George Monbiot

Source: *The Guardian*, January 28, 2003

Mr Bush and Mr Blair might have a tougher fight than they anticipated. Not from Saddam Hussein perhaps – although it is still not obvious that they can capture and hold Iraq's cities without major losses – but from an anti-war movement that is beginning to look like nothing the world has seen before.

It's not just that people have begun to gather in great numbers even before a shot has been fired. It's not just that they are doing so without the inducement of conscription or any other direct threat to their welfare. It's not just that there have already been meetings or demonstrations in almost every nation on Earth. It's also that the campaign is being coordinated globally with an unprecedented precision. And the people partly responsible for this are the members of a movement which, even within the past few weeks, the mainstream media has pronounced extinct.

Last year, 40,000 members of the global justice movement gathered at the World Social Forum in Porto Alegre, Brazil. This year, more than 100,000, from 150 nations, have come – for a meeting! The world has seldom seen such political assemblies since Daniel O'Connell's "monster meetings" in the 1840s.

Far from dying away, our movement has grown bigger than most of us could have guessed. September 11 muffled the protests for a while, but since then they have returned with greater vehemence, everywhere except the US. The last major global demonstration it convened was the rally at the European summit in Barcelona. Some 350,000 activists rose from the dead. They came despite the terrifying response to the marches in June 2001 in Genoa, where the police burst into protesters' dormitories and beat them with truncheons as they lay in their sleeping bags, tortured others in the cells and shot one man dead.

But neither the violent response, nor September 11, nor the indifference of the media have quelled this rising. Ever ready to believe their own story, the newsrooms have interpreted the absence of coverage (by the newsrooms) as an absence of activity. One of our recent discoveries is that we no longer need them. We have our own channels of communication, our own websites and pamphlets and magazines, and those who wish to find us can do so without their help. They can pronounce us dead as often as they like, and we shall, as many times, be resurrected.

The media can be forgiven for expecting us to disappear. In the past, it was hard to sustain global movements of this kind. The socialist international, for example, was famously interrupted by nationalism. When the nations to which the comrades belonged went to war, they forgot their common struggle and took to arms against each other. But now, thanks to the globalisation some members of the movement contest, nationalism is a far weaker force.

American citizens are meeting and debating with Iraqis, even as their countries prepare to go to war. We can no longer be called to heel. Our loyalty is to the principles we defend and to those who share them, irrespective of where they come from.

One of the reasons why the movement appears destined only to grow is that it provides the only major channel through which we can engage with the most critical issues. Climate change, international debt, poverty, the hegemony of the G8 nations, the IMF and the World Bank, the depletion of natural resources, nuclear proliferation and low-level conflict are major themes in the lives of most of the world's people, but minor themes in almost all mainstream political discourse. We are told that the mind-rotting drivel which now fills the pages of the newspapers is a necessary commercial response to the demands of younger readers. This may, to some extent, be true. But here are tens of thousands of young people who have less interest in celebrity culture than George Bush has in Wittgenstein. They have evolved their own scale of values, and re-enfranchised themselves by pursuing what they know to be important. For the great majority of activists – those who live in the poor world – the movement offers the only effective means of reaching people in the richer nations.

We have often been told that the reason we're dead is that we have been overtaken by and subsumed within the anti-war campaign. It would be more accurate to say that the anti-war campaign has, in large part, grown out of the global justice movement. This movement has never recognised a distinction between the power of the rich world's governments and their appointed institutions (the IMF, the World Bank, the World Trade Organisation) to wage economic warfare and the power of the same governments, working through different institutions (the UN security council, NATO) to send in the bombers. Far from competing with our concerns, the impending war has reinforced our determination to tackle the grotesque maldistribution of power which permits a few national governments to assert a global mandate. When the activists leave Porto Alegre tomorrow, they will take home to their 150 nations a new resolve to turn the struggle against the war with Iraq into a contest over the future of the world.

While younger activists are eager to absorb the experience of people like Noam Chomsky, Tariq Ali, Lula, Victor Chavez, Michael Albert and Arundhati Roy, all of whom are speaking in Porto Alegre, our movement is, as yet, more eager than wise, fired by passions we have yet to master. We have yet to understand, despite the police response in Genoa, the mechanical determination of our opponents.

We are still rather too prepared to believe that spectacular marches can change the world. While the splits between the movement's marxists, anarchists and liberals are well-rehearsed, our real division – between the diversalists and the universalists – has, so far, scarcely been explored. Most of the movement believes that the best means of regaining control over political life is through local community action. A smaller faction (to which I belong) believes that this response is insufficient, and that we must seek to create democratically accountable global institutions. The debates have, so far, been muted. But when they emerge, they will be fierce.

For all that, I think most of us have noticed that something has changed, that we are beginning to move on from the playing of games and the staging of parties, that we are coming to develop a more mature analysis, a better grasp of tactics, an understanding of the need for policy. We are, in other words, beginning for the first time to look like a revolutionary movement. We are finding, too, among some of the indebted states of the poor world, a new preparedness to engage with us. In doing so, they speed our maturation: the more we are taken seriously, the more seriously we take ourselves.

Whether we are noticed or not is no longer relevant. We know that, with or without the media's help, we are a gathering force which might one day prove unstoppable.

31 Grassrooting the space of flows

Manuel Castells

Source: Manuel Castells (1999), 'Grassrooting the Space of Flows',
Urban Geography, 20: 4, pp. 294–302

Our historic time is defined fundamentally by the transformation of our geographic space. This is a key dimension of the multilayered social and technological transformation that ushers in the so-called "Information Age." Ten years ago, I proposed the concept of space of flows in order to understand such a spatial transformation. At that time, the aim was to acknowledge the reality and the significance of the transformation without yielding to the simplistic notions of futurologists announcing the death of distance and the end of cities.

Empirical evidence continues to show that new information and communication technologies fit into the pattern of flexible production and network organization – permitting the simultaneous centralization and decentralization of activities and population settlements – because different locations can be reunited in their functioning and interaction by means of the new technological system. This system is created from telecommunications, computers, and fast reliable transportation systems, as well as dispatching centers, nodes, and hubs. Therefore, new communication technologies allow for the centralization of corporate activities in a given space, precisely because they can reach the whole world from the City of London and from Manhattan without losing the dense network of localized, ancillary firms as well as the opportunities of face-to-face interaction created by territorial agglomeration.

At the same time, back offices can decentralize into the suburbs, in newly developed metropolitan areas, or in some other country and be part of the same system. New business centers can be created around the country and around the world that always follow the logic of clustering and decentralizing at the same type and of concentrating and networking, thus creating a selective world wide web of business services. The new industrial space is characterized also by its similar pattern of spatial dispersion of activities, concentration of innovation, and strategic decision-making – around what Peter Hall and I propose to label as "milieux of innovation," following the evidence gathered by a series of studies undertaken in the 1980s at Berkeley by the Institute of Urban and Regional Development. The new media also have become built around the double process of globalization of capital and customization/networking of information and images that respond to the localization of markets and segmentation of audiences. In territorial terms, the age of information is not just the age of spatial dispersal, it is the age of generalized urbanization. In the next decade, it is likely that most people of the world will be living in the cities for the first time. Yet cities are, and will be, of very different kinds depending on cultures, institutions, histories, and economies, but they will continue to share a spatial logic that is specific to the Information Age. This logic is characterized by the combination of territorial sprawl and locational concentration. Thus, intrametropolitan, interregional, and international networks connect with global networks in a structure of variable geometry that is enacted and modified by flows of information and electronic circuits and fast, information-based, transportation systems. In the last decade, studies by Peter Hall, Peter Daniels, AnnaLee Saxenian, Michael Batty, Jim Wheeler, Barry Wellman, Jeff Henderson, Roberto Camagni, Stephen Graham, Marvin Simon, Amy Glasmeier, and so many other scholars have substantiated, empirically the emergence of a new spatial structure. This structure is defined by articulated territorial concentration and decentralization in which the unit is the network. This particular model of spatial organization, which seems to be characteristic of the Information Age, is the model that I tried to conceptualize 10 years ago as the space of flows.

The space of flows

As I understand it, "space of flows" means that the material arrangements allow for simultaneity of social practices without territorial contiguity. It is not a purely electronic space nor what Batty has called a "cyberspace," although cyberspace is a component of the space of flows. First, it is made up of a technological infrastructure of information systems, telecommunications, and transportation lines. The capacity and characteristics of this infrastructure and the location of its elements determine the functions of the space of flows, and its relationship to other spatial forms and processes. The space of flows is also made of networks of interaction, and the goals and task of each network configurate a different space of flows. Thus, financial markets, high-technology manufacturing, business services, entertainment, media news, drug traffic, science and technology, fashion design, art, sports, or religion constitute a specific network with a specific technological system and various territorial profiles. So they all operate on the logic of the space of flows but they specify this logic.

Second, the space of flows is made up of nodes and hubs. These nodes and hubs structure the connections, and the key activities in a given locale or locales. For instance, Wall Street or Ginza are such nodes, as well as Cali and Tijuana in their specific trade, or Berkeley, Stanford, and MIT in computer sciences. Hubs are communication sites (e.g., airports, harbors, trains, or bus stations) that organize exchanges of all kinds, as they increasingly are interconnected and spatially related. However, what characterizes the new role of these hubs and nodes is that they are dependent on the network, that their logic depends on their place in the network, and that they are sites to process signals that do not originate from any specific place but from endless recurrent interactions in the network.

Third, the space of flows is also made of habitats for the social actors that operate the networks, be it residential spaces adjacent to the nodes, protected and secluded spaces of consumption, or global corridors of social segregation separating these corridors from the surrounding places around the globe (e.g., VIP lounges, the virtual office, computing on the run, standardized international hotels).

Fourth, the space of flows comprises electronic spaces such as websites, spaces of interaction, as well as spaces of one-directional communication, be it interactive or not, such as information systems. A growing proportion of activity is from the web and the visual design of websites, as well as the structure of an operation of their content is becoming a fundamental frame for decision making, information making, and communication.

Space of places

I have described the new spatial structure of the Information Age, the space of flows. But we really need to know that not all the space is organized around the space of flows. As was the case in the whole history of humankind, most people live, work, and construct their meaning around places. I define a place as the locale whose form, function, and meaning are self-contained within the boundaries of territorial contiguity. People tend to construct their life in reference to places, such as their home, neighborhood, city, region, or country. This is not to say that the local community is thriving. In fact, all over the world, research shows that there has been a process of individualization and atomization of place-based relationships. The loss of community is the founding theme of urban sociology, since the Chicago School. Yet you may have no community, but still refer to your place as your main source of experience. Social organization and political representation also are predominately place based. And cultural identity is often built on the basis of sharing historical experience in a given territory.

When analyzing spatial transformation in the Information Age and showing the emergence of a new spatial form (i.e., the space of flows), I emphasized the persistence of the space of places, as the most usual form of spatial existence for humankind. I also observed that, while most dominant activities were constructed around the space of flows, most experience and social interaction was and still is organized around places. When using the term "dominant activities," I am referring to (1) financial flows, (2) management of major corporations in services and manufacturing, (3) ancillary networks of firms for major corporations, and (4) media, entertainment, professional sports, science and technology, institutionalized religion, military power, and global criminal economy. Thus, I added that the constitution of the space of flows was in itself a form of domination, since the space of flows, even in its diversity, is interrelated and can escape the control of any locale, while the space of places is fragmented, localized, and thus increasingly powerless vis à vis the versatility of the space of flows. The only chance of resistance for localities is to refuse landing rights for overwhelming flows – only to see that they land in the locale nearby, therefore inducing the bypassing and marginalization of rebellious communities.

This was my analysis some time ago, which has been presented in various publications during the last decade. I still sustain most of this analysis, and I think it can be backed up empirically. However, an analysis of transformation of space in a given historical moment – that is, the moment of the dawn of the Information Age – should not be cast in stone as an iron rule of spatial development. Yes, there are two different forms of space, flows and places. Yes, the space of flows is historically new in its overwhelming prevalence because it can deploy its logic through a new technological medium. Yes, dominant activities in our society are organized around the logic of the space of flows, while most, and the most powerful forms of autonomous construction of meaning, and social and political resistance to the powers that be are being constructed, currently are around places. But, two major qualifications may be introduced:

(1) The space of flows includes some places. Indeed, the space of flows is not simply an electronic space. Electronic spaces – such as the internet or global communication media – are but one dimension, however important of the space of flows.

(2) Both electronic spaces, and the space of flows at large, are not organized exclusively around and by social/economic/cultural domination. Societies are not closed systems, they are always open processes, characterized by conflict. History, in fact, is a very tiresome experience. It never ends, against the claims of the neoliberal illusion. Wherever there is domination, there is resistance to domination. Wherever there is imposition of meaning, there are projects of construction of alternative meaning. And the realms of this resistance, and this autonomous meaning are ubiquitous. Which means, concretely, that while the space of flows has been produced by and around dominant activities and social groups, it can be penetrated by resistance, and diversified in its meaning. The grassroots of societies do not cease to exist in the Information Age. And after an initial moment of exclusion and confusion,

people and values of all kinds are now penetrating and using the space of flows, the internet and beyond, in the same way that the Parisian Champs Elysees dreamed by Hausman to escape the populace of the rive gauche, have become, in the 1990s, the hang out place for the festive, and multiethnic young lot of the Paris banlieues. While the space of flows remains the space in which dominant activities are spatially operated, it is experiencing at the same time, the growing influence and pressure of the grassroots, and the insertion of personal meaning by social actors, in a process that may alter the cultural and political dynamics of our societies and, ultimately, may alter the space of flows itself. So let me review the main dimensions of this grassrooting of the space of flows.

The space of flows and the grassroots

First, I will refer to a series of dimensions of autonomous expression of social meaning in the space of flows, with emphasis in electronic spaces, but in interaction with the space of places. First is personal interaction, people using the net for themselves and electronic mail as recuperating letter writing as a form of communication. And people are finding ways to be together with much more diversity and importance than has been the experience before in history: chat groups, multidimensional communication, cultural expressions of all kind, people building their websites. People build their fantasies, but they also experience their needs and exchange their information. They are inhabiting the space of flows and thus transforming it. Am I talking maybe about a small global elite? Well not so small, and not so elite.

A second dimension for autonomous expression is represented by purposive, horizontal communication, not just personal feelings of casual communication. Horizontal communication occurs among people and across countries, and establishes information systems that are alternative to the media. They are in fact doubling the media. There is, indeed, much gossip and irresponsible information. As you know, the news that triggered one of the latest scandals relating to President Clinton was first sent from the internet through a news bulletin, which is a one-man operation out of his home office in Los Angeles, while Newsweek was weighing the opportunity of the publication. There are people and institutions very concerned about the lack of control of information in the net. Everywhere, many governments are terrified of losing control of information, a fundamental source of power throughout history. They usually argue in terms of controlling child pornography. I think child pornography is terrible, but what happens in countries like France or Spain for instance is that it is perfectly legal to sell child pornography. It is not legal to produce the images nor to hire or kidnap the children to do it, but selling it is not a problem. But you cannot do it on the internet. Why? Because the internet is a mass media, or so the statist argument goes. The fact is that horizontal communication in the internet by bypassing both the media and governmental controls is becoming a most fundamental political issue, which ultimately reflects who we are collectively, as a society. And if some of us are enjoying child pornography, if we are this kind of monster, this appears reflected in the internet. The internet brings us face to face with the mirror of who we actually are. So I would rather work on ourselves rather than close down the net. The fight is against the self not against the net.

Third, there is a fast growth of networks of solidarity and cooperation in the internet, with people bringing together their resources, to live and to survive. To give an example, the senior net in the United States not only brings information (e.g., medical information to counter the monopoly of medical information by doctors) and resources together; it also develops solidarity ties between senior people, thus reinforcing the group to which all of us belong, or will belong, if we are lucky. Thus, at the time the welfare state, at least as constructed in the last half century, is being challenged economically and politically, people are reconstructing networks of solidarity and reflecting/debating about them at the same time.

The fourth dimension is social movements. The net is used increasingly by social movements, of all kinds, as their organizing ground and as their privileged means to break their isolation. The greatest example here and one that has become classic is the Zapatistas in Chiapas, Mexico. Without fully presenting the case, on which I have written in my latest book, let me remind you of some interesting facts on this social movement. Zapatistas organized solidarity groups around the world on the internet. And they very effectively used the internet to diffuse their information and to obtain interactive communication between their different solidarity groups. They also have used the internet in a protective way to fight repression when, in February 1995, there was a major military offensive that forced them to escape to the forest. They sent a message over the internet asking everybody to flood the White House with messages because at that point the White House had put our money into the Mexican bailout. A major crisis in Mexico would jeopardize the entire stability of the region, ultimately wasting United States taxpayers' money. So, in one day, over 30 thousand messages came to the White House. That does not mean that street demonstrations in front of the White House are not important, but you cannot organize them in 24 hours; and in this particular case, it was a matter of life and death in these 24 hours. This ability of the Zapatistas to work on the net does not come from Marcos as people would say, even if he was a communications professor or from the Indian communities. It came from women's groups in Mexico. In 1993, women's groups organized an internet network in Mexico to support women's solidarity funded by the Catholic church and organized instrumentally by the Institute of Global Communication in San Francisco, a group of progressive computer people out of Silicon Valley. The global communications institute and women's groups sent several people to Chiapas, where they organized an extension of the women's network that was called La Neta. La Neta is an interesting expression because, on the one hand, it is the Spanish feminine term for the net; but also in Mexican slang it means the truth. So this La Neta network branched out in Chiapas and trained a number of people in Chiapas that human rights groups were the ones who were able to link up with the Zapatistas and provide both the technological and knowledge support for their internet operations.

However, not only progressive movements are on the internet. Everybody is on the internet and our societies are on the internet. The internet has played a major role in the development of American militia groups. The internet is as real as life itself. Increasingly, global movements of solidarity, environmentalists, human rights, and women's groups are organized on the internet again on the basis of local/global connection. One of the greatest and latest examples in the United States was the Fall 1997 One Million Women March organized by two Black women in Philadelphia. There was practically no organization, no sponsorship, and yet a small group of women in Philadelphia went on the net and called a demonstration, obtaining an extraordinary level of support and mobilization. But going to a place, I think is the most interesting thing. The space of flows is not just being in the net. It is to organize in the net to be in Philadelphia on a given day – that is, using the net to control space.

Fifth, linkages are a development that we have to pay close attention to, increasing linkages between people and institutions in an interactive process. The creation of what some people call virtual cities are renewing local governments and citizen democracy. We have some relatively old experiments, such as in 1986, Santa Monica's PEN program allowing public debate between citizens – including debates on major issues such as homelessness in

Santa Monica, with the homeless themselves being able to get into the debate. European cities are organizing participation in information systems. Graham and Aurigi have studied these experiments and say that they usually are one-directional information systems. So still it is not a full-fledged participatory democracy; it is more information than participation and democracy, but they are still evolving and changing.

And there is potential for much more. I am personally struck by the experience of Amsterdam's Digital City, an autonomous group originally supported by the municipality of Amsterdam. It is a private foundation that has organized a system of citizen participation and citizen interaction. You have to register to take part, anyone can visit the site, but to really participate and go into houses, you have to be registered. By 1998, they had 80,000 fully registered, participating "residents." They have activities organized around different squares: larger squares and micro-squares. Each square relates to different activities (e.g., cultural politics, sports, business, homes). People build houses, sometimes also marry, initiate recall elections, certainly become involved in debates, and from time to time link these activities to real life in a very close interaction. So the digital-city experience has shown the possibility of mobilizing the population at dramatically different levels from the most political activist to chat groups. What strikes me too is how much the group is connected to the local, political, and spatial experience in Amsterdam. On the one hand, this is a movement that grew out of the squatters movement in Amsterdam. Caroline Nevejan and Marlene Strikker, the two women who lead the movement and who lead this program, were members of this squatters movement and, in their own view, they have not changed their values much. They have continued their ability to mobilize people and change society through the new medium without abandoning the idea of the city as a place.

Even symbolically the city has ceded them as their headquarters place one of the most historic buildings in Amsterdam, the Waag, the building that in the 16th century used to close the canals for trade when ships were arriving in Amsterdam. This building also housed the School of Medicine where illegal autopsies were being performed because of the church's repression. In that building, there is a room where Rembrandt painted his famous "Lesson of Anatomy." It is in that very room where the server of the digital city is located. I think this kind of historical continuity and this linkage between history and information flows, place and electronic networks, is representative of something new happening in the space of flows.

Another example of this linkage between institutions, civil society, grassroots groups, something that is less known because it is only in the project stage, is the Barcelona Internet Citizen Project. This project is being sponsored by the city of Barcelona and linked to a mega-project that they called Forum 2004. It is in fact a good example of connecting the global to the local, internet to grassroots. Remember that the 1992 Olympic games created a great transformation in Barcelona. Among other things, Barcelona opened up to the sea by building a whole new neighborhood, connecting seaside promenade and beaches to the harbor. Now a group of local leaders, with the support of the municipality, have conceived a new project, an Olympics of sort: the Forum 2004, with the sponsorship of UNESCO and the pope. Over the course of six months in 2004, the project will plan to bring in half-a-million young people from all over the world into Barcelona in 2004 to discuss what to do with the world in the 21st century. And of course they need to build a city to organize this project, therefore another 20 km of seaside development.

Furthermore, the project includes the idea of linking up the world to those thousands of youths, sharing the debate on the net. For the Barcelona citizens to be apt to the task, there is a project to set up an internet Citizen center to train and diffuse the uses of the internet to people at large. Most people in Barcelona are unaware of the potential uses of the internet, so that a literacy campaigning directly linked to an event and with the purpose of participating in a global debate could just be a key trigger in bringing Barcelona as a whole into the Information Age.

As you can see, there is a gradual opening up of the Information of Age to different avenues. So through a blossoming of initiatives, people are taking on the net without uprooting themselves from their places. And through this practice, they transform both forms of the space. However, are we talking only about a small elite? Are people not being in fact massively excluded from the net? Well first of all, the recent data show there is a large number of elites, about 128 million users in 1998. Yes, data are shaky, but the same shaky data were indicating about 30 million users in 1995/1996. What seems to be a little more solid is the rate of diffusion among users, which seems to be nearly doubling every year. By the end of 2000, we should be approaching 500 million internet users. Serious experts in the communication business predict about 1 billion users by the middle of the first decade of the 21st century, considering a slow down in the rate of diffusion when less-advanced countries and less-educated and less-affluent groups become the new frontier of expansion. The computer capacity and the telecommunications capacity is already there, the issue is how to bring people into the net. And for what?

Yet there is certainly a social bias in terms of who uses the internet. There is a gender bias, with the proportion of men to women being three to one. There is also an ethnic bias, with ethnic minorities having much lower rates of the internet use, although in the case of Hispanics in the United States, the rates of incorporation are extremely high. There is a country bias too. In fact, Scandinavia is advancing over everybody else. Finland has decided to become the first Information Society in the world. Projections are that by the year 2000 there will be more websites in Finland than Finnish people. Still, in absolute terms, there is a dominance of the internet by American users.

However, more importantly, the bias is not only in terms of use, but use for what, that is the level of education required to look for and retrieve information. I have proposed a notion that we are living in a world that is made of the interactive and the interacted. We interact but many people are just interacted. For many people, the net may become an extension of a multimedia-based, one-directional system, so that they may receive some basic information to which they just have to react, as in some marketing device. However, if we look historically into the diffusion of information and to the diffusion of technology and to the ability to upgrade the level of consciousness and the level of information, there has always been a connection between open-minded, educated social groups and the uneducated masses that through this connection become educated. As in the historic example of the development of the labor movement, printing workers were critical in that they knew how to read, where most workers did not know how to read or what to read. Printing workers were the ones that in many countries created the basis for self-training, self-development, and self-organization of these uneducated masses. And this is happening now in many countries. Low-income communities are being brought into the internet in different ways by local community groups.

I also personally know some important experiences that are highly developed as in the working-class periphery of Barcelona, an area called the lower Llobregat, in which the unions and the municipalities decided that they have to move into the Information Age and develop social struggles and social consciousness. They have created a cultural organization, and a network of internet-based, publicized activities, around a journal titled "La Factoria," which you can access on the net. Thus, they have started a process of mass education of social debate, mixing the print, the net, the city, the factory, and ultimately grassrooting the net.

Finally, even if there is still a minority of users (but a minority that is going to be numbered in the hundreds of millions), their eruption in the net, with the creative cacophony of their social diversity, with the plurality of their values and interests, and given the linkage between places and information flows, transforms the logic of the space of flows, making it a contested space. And a plural and diversified space.

Conclusion

So, whither the theory of the space of flows? Not necessarily, because this theory was always based on analyzing the linkage between electronic space and places through networks of flows. This is indeed, increasingly, the space in which most important activities operate in our societies. There is interaction, there is connection. Moreover, it remains true, I think, and can be empirically sustained that strategically dominant activities are operated essentially through the space of flows, and that global elites ensure their domination in this process, bypassing segmented, isolated localities. And trenches of resistance to the domination of flows of capital and information are being built primarily around places.

However, new dynamics are operating, dynamics of interpenetration of uniformity and autonomy, of domination and resistance, and of instrumentality and experience, within the space of flows. So, historically produced forms of space, even as complex and new, such as the space of flows, by their very existence are transformed through the process of their enactment. They become contested spaces as well, freedom is carved in their hallways, and cultural identity is built, and affirmed, in the net. So, the geography of the new history will not be made, after all, of the separation between places and flows, but out of the interface between places and flows and between cultures and social interests, both in the space of flows and in the space of places. The attempt by capital, media, and power to escape into the abstraction of the space of flows, bypassing democracy and experience by confining them in the space of places, is being challenged from many sources by the grassrooting of the space of flows.

32 Digital networks and the state

Some governance questions

Saskia Sassen

Source: Saskia Sassen (2000), 'Digital Networks and the State – Some Governance Questions', *Theory, Culture and Society*, 17: 4, pp. 19–33

The rapid proliferation of digital networks and the growing digitization of a broad array of economic activities have raised a number of questions about the state's capacity to regulate this domain and about the latter's potential for undermining sovereignty. Most of the focus has been on the Internet.[1] The major lines of the debate in general commentaries are increasingly polarized among those who believe that the Internet undermines, or at the least weakens, state authority and those who believe that it strengthens liberal democracy and thereby the liberal state. Not unrelated to these two positions is the more technical debate between those who find that the notion of governments regulating the Internet does not carry much meaning (Post, 1995; Mueller, 1998) and those who maintain that there are various legal instruments and technical standards through which states can directly or indirectly regulate the Internet (Lessig, 1999; Reidenberg, 1998).

My concern here is with the broader theoretical and political implications of the characterization of the two fundamental concepts in the debate. Among the issues I want to focus on concerning the Internet are (a) the confusion between privately owned digital networks and digital space available to 'the public' even if for a fee, specifically the Internet, and (b) the possibilities for regulating the Internet (see also Perritt, 1999).

Very briefly, my argument will be that it is the enormous growth of private digital networks – especially the case of the global financial markets – rather than the Internet, which is having the greater impact on national sovereignty and indeed transforming particular features of it. More generally, economic globalization and technology have brought with them significant transformations in the authority of national states. Especially important here is the growth of new non-state-centered governance mechanisms which have transformed the meaning of national territorial sovereignty independently from whatever impact the Internet has so far had. Second, there are features of the Internet today which suggest that regulation is possible. But it is a radically different version of regulation from that we have associated with the modern state over the last half century.

Economic power and state power in the Internet

The condition of the Internet as a decentralized network of networks has contributed to strong notions about its built-in autonomy from state power and its capacity to enhance democracy from the bottom up via a strengthening of both market dynamics and access by civil society.[2] Yet, while in principle many of the key features of the Internet do indeed have this capacity to enhance democracy, its openness and its technology also contain possibilities for significant control and the imposition of limitations on access. Here I want to discuss briefly three aspects of this contrarian argument.

In my own research I have come to regard the Internet as a space produced and marked through the software that gives it its features and the particular aspects of the hardware mobilized by the software.[3] There are significant implications attached to the fact that the leading Internet software design focus in the last few years has been on firewalled intranets for firms and firewalled tunnels for firm-to-firm transactions.[4] Both of these represent, in some sense, private appropriations of a 'public' space.[5] Further, the growing interest in e-commerce has stimulated the development of software linked to identity verification, trademarks protection, billing. The rapid growth of this type of software and its use in the Internet does not necessarily strengthen the public-ness of the Net. This is especially significant if there is less production of software aimed at strengthening the openness and decentralization of the Net as was the case in the earlier phases of the Internet. Further, this newer type of software also sets up the conditions for copyrighting, including the possibility of charging for what can be set up as copyrighted use/access, including per use charge. In my reading, far from strengthening the Internet's democratic potential as many liberal and neoliberal commentators maintain, this type of commercialization can threaten it.

Along these same lines of analysis – though with another type of norm in mind – Lessig (1999), for instance, has pointed out that since 1995/6 the work of political entities and technicians has brought about what may be interpreted as an increase in controls. Prior to 1995 the architecture of the Internet inhibited 'zoning' – any technique that facilitates discrimination in access to or distribution of some good or service.[6] Users could more easily maintain their anonymity while online and it was difficult to verify user identity, thereby ensuring better privacy protection. Since then, with the drive to facilitate e-commerce, this has changed: the architecture of the Internet now facilitates zoning.[7]

Coming from a different angle but based upon a similar understanding, Boyle (1997) has examined how the built-in set of standards that constitute the Internet undermines claims that the state cannot regulate the Internet. Indeed, he argues that the state's regulatory agenda is already partially contained in the design of the technologies. Thus the state can regulate in this case even though it is not via sanctions. Boyle in fact alerts us to the fact that privatized and technologically based rule enforcement would take policing away from the scrutiny of public law, freeing states from some of the constitutional and other constraints restricting their options. This can be problematic even in the case of states that operate under the rule of law, as examples of abuse of power by various government agencies in the US make clear.

These three analyses, different as they are in the origins and end results of the argumentation, do intersect on one point: that simply leaving the Internet to its own evolution is not necessarily going to strengthen the forces of democracy. The differential economic power of different types of users is shaping the development of privatizing dynamics that remain unaccountable, and the indirect incorporation of state powers in the design of technical standards is creating a domain for state power that falls outside the public sphere where state action can be subjected to public accountability. All three views would seem to suggest that it is misguided to think that leaving this evolution to the market is somehow going to ensure freedom and democracy.

Although the Net as a space of distributed power can thrive even against growing commercialization, and today's non-commercial uses still dominate the Internet, the race is on. Considerable resources are being allocated to invent ways of expanding electronic commerce, ensuring safety of payment transactions and implementing copyright. These are not easy tasks. At the 1997 Aspen Roundtable on Electronic Commerce, an annual event that brings together the CEOs of the main software and hardware firms as well as the key venture capitalists in the sector, it was once again established by these insiders that there are limits to the medium as a venue for commerce and that it will probably tend to cater to particular niche markets, with a few possible exceptions. In this regard, the reawakened recognition among non-commercial digital organizations and digital activists of the viability of open-source systems is worth noting, as is the commercial interest in Linux, one of the hottest open-source systems at this time. We are seeing the rapid growth of a new generation of alternative organizations and of individuals knowledgeable about digital technologies who are working on the public dimensions and free access questions.[8] This signals that the Internet may continue to be a space for de facto (i.e. not necessarily self-conscious) democratic practices. But it will be so partly as a form of resistance against overarching powers of the economy and of the state, rather than the space of unlimited freedom which is still part of its representation today in many milieux.[9]

One aspect important to the positive democracy effect of the Net is that there has been a proliferation of non-commercial uses and users. From struggles around human rights, the environment and workers' strikes around the world, to genuinely trivial pursuits, the Net has emerged as a powerful medium for non-elites to communicate, support each other's struggles and create the equivalent of insider groups at scales going from the local to the global. The political and civic potential of these trends is enormous. It offers the possibility for interested citizens to act in concert.[10] The possibility of doing so transnationally at a time when a growing set of issues is seen as escaping the bounds of national states makes this even more significant. We are also seeing a greater variety of subcultures on the Net in the last decade after it having been dominated, at first, by young white men, especially from the US. Finally, insofar as the growth of global corporate actors has pressured governments to support the interests of global capital, it has become even more important to use the Internet as a force through which a multiplicity of public interests can raise critical issues and demand accountability (Perritt, 1999).

[...]

Distinguishing private and public digital space

Many assertions about digital dynamics and potentials are actually about processes happening in private digital space and have little to do with the Internet. I consider this a serious, though fairly common, confusion. Most financial activity and other significant digital economic activities take place in private digital networks.[11]

Private digital networks make possible forms of power other than the distributed power we associate with public access digital networks. The financial markets illustrate this well. The three properties of electronic networks – speed, simultaneity and interconnectivity – have produced orders of magnitude far surpassing anything we had ever seen in financial markets. In 1999 the worldwide value of traded derivatives reached over US$65 trillion – a figure that dwarfs the value of cross-border trade and investment. The consequence has been that the global capital market now has the power to discipline national governments, as became evident with the 1994–5 Mexico 'crisis' and the 1997–8 Asian 'crisis', when investors were capable of leaving *en masse* taking out well over US $100 billion over a short period of time. The foreign currency markets had the orders of magnitude to alter exchange rates radically for some of these currencies and overwhelm each and all of the central banks involved and their futile attempt to defend their currencies against the onslaught.

The global capital market: power and norm-making

What I want to emphasize here is that the formation of a global capital market represents a concentration of power that is capable of influencing national government economic policy and, by extension, other policies. A key issue here has to do with questions of normativity – the fact that the global financial markets are not only capable of deploying raw power but have also produced a logic that is now seen as setting the criteria for 'proper' economic policy. IMF conditionality has some of these features.[12] These markets can now exercise the accountability functions associated with citizenship: they can vote governments' economic policies down or in; they can force governments to take certain measures and not others.

The deregulation of domestic financial markets, the liberalization of international capital flows, computers and telecommunications, have all contributed to an explosive growth in financial markets. Since 1980, the total stock of financial assets has increased two and a half times faster than the aggregate GDP of all the rich industrial economies. And the volume of trading in currencies, bonds and equities has increased about five times faster. The global capital market makes it possible for money to flow anywhere regardless of national origin and boundaries. There are some countries that are, of course, not integrated.

The foreign exchange market was the first one to globalize, in the mid-1970s. Today it is the biggest and in many ways the only truly global market. It has gone from a daily turnover rate of about US$15 billion in the 1970s, to US$60 billion in the early 1980s, and an estimated US$1.3 trillion in 1999. In contrast, the total foreign currency reserves of the rich industrial countries amounted to under US$1 trillion. Just to make it more concrete, foreign exchange transactions were ten times as large as world trade in 1983; only ten years later, in 1992, they were 60 times larger and by 1999, 70 times larger. And world trade has itself grown sharply over this period.

According to some estimates, we have reached only the mid-point of a 50-year process in terms of the full integration of these markets. The financial markets are expected to expand even further in relation to the size of the real economy. It is estimated that the total stock of financial assets traded in the global capital markets is equivalent to twice the GDP of OECD countries – that is, the 23 richest industrial countries in the world. The forecast is that this value will rise to US$83 trillion by the year 2000 to represent three times the aggregate OECD's GDP. Much more integration and power may lie ahead for capital markets.[13] What really counts is how much capital can be moved across borders in how short a period of time. It is clearly an immense amount.

How does this massive growth of financial flows and assets, and the fact of an integrated global capital market, affect states in their economic policy making? Conceivably a global capital market could just be a vast pool of money for investors to shop in without conferring power over governments. The fact that it can discipline governments' economic policy making is a distinct power, one that is not ipso facto inherent in the existence of a large global capital market.

There are important differences between today's global capital market and the period of the gold standard before the First World War. Let me just emphasize one for the purposes of this article: the difference that digital networks bring to the financial markets is instantaneous transmission, interconnectivity and speed. Gross volumes have increased enormously even when relative net flows between countries are not higher. And the speed of transactions has brought its own consequences. Trading in currencies and securities is instant thanks to vast computer networks. And the high degree of interconnectivity in combination with instantaneous transmission signals the potential for exponential growth (I discuss other differences in Sassen, 2000a: ch. 4).

Does this concentration of capital in unregulated markets affect national economies and government policies? Does it alter the functioning of democratic governments? Does this kind of concentration of capital reshape the accountability relation between governments and their people which have operated through electoral politics? In brief, does it affect national sovereignty? It does. Elsewhere (1996: ch. 2) I have examined the mechanisms through which the global capital market actually exercises its disciplining function on national governments and pressures them to become accountable to the logic of these markets.

Here I want to make just two observations. One is that national states have participated in its formation and implementation – a subject I have addressed elsewhere (Sassen, 1999a). There is a consensus among states to further the interests of this type of economic globalization (see Mittelman, 1996; Panitch, 1996). Second, there are what have been called the implicit ground rules of our legal system – matter which has not been formalized into rules of prohibition or permission, and constitutes a de facto set of rules of permission.[14] The ground rules on which economic globalization is proceeding contain far more permissions than have been formalized in explicit rules of permission and prohibition. Private firms in international finance, accounting and law, the new private standards for international accounting and financial reporting, and supra-national organizations such as the WTO, all play strategic non-government-centered governance functions.

The embeddedness of digital networks

It is significant that, although in some ways the power of these financial digital networks rests on a kind of distributed power, i.e. millions of investors and their millions of decisions, it ends up as concentrated power. The trajectory followed by what begins as a form of distributed power may assume many forms, in this case one radically different from that of the Internet. It signals the possibility that digital network power is not inherently distributive. Intervening mechanisms can reshape its organization. To keep it as a form of distributed power requires that it be embedded in a particular kind of structure.

In addition to being embedded in some of the technical features and standards of the hardware and software, digital space, whether private or public, is partly embedded in actual societal structures and power dynamics. Its topography weaves in and out of non-electronic space. In the case of private digital space, this feature carries enormous implications for theory, for the results of the digitalization of economic activity and for the conditions in which governments and citizens can act on this new electronic world of the economy and power. The embeddedness of private economic electronic space entails the formation of massive concentrations of infrastructure, not only worldwide dispersal, and a complex interaction between conventional communications infrastructure and digitalization. The notion of 'global cities' captures this particular embeddedness of global finance in actual financial centers.[15]

There is no purely digital economy and no completely virtual corporation. This means that power, contestation, inequality, in brief, hierarchy, inscribe electronic space. And although the digitalized portions of these industries, particularly finance, have the capacity to subvert the established hierarchies, new hierarchies are being formed, born out of the existing material conditions underlying power and the new conditions created by digital space.

Conclusion

The Internet is only one portion of the vast new world of digital space. If we are going to consider issues of sovereignty and democracy, then we must ask a critical question about what actors are gaining influence under conditions of digitization and whose claims are gaining legitimacy. For instance, it could be argued (and it is my argument) that private digital space has had a far sharper impact on questions of sovereignty than the Internet. The globalization and digitization of financial markets have made these markets a powerful presence. Indeed, the logic of the global capital markets is today not merely a condition of raw power but one with normative potential. The logic of these markets has contributed to the elaboration of a set of criteria for what is proper government conduct on the economy. This new power of the financial markets is partly a consequence of the orders of magnitude they have reached, in good part through their digitalization and the fact that they are globally integrated, two conditions that are mutually reinforcing. The capacity of these markets to affect existing meanings of sovereignty is considerable and, in my view, thus far has been greater than that of the Internet.

When it comes to the Internet's capacity to undermine state authority and the state's capacity to regulate the Internet, two issues stand out in my reading. One is that the state has instruments through which it can exercise a certain kind of authority, especially through the venue of technical standards in the hardware and software, through the protection of property rights and, quite likely, through some of the features of the Internet addressing system and domain registry. The second is that much of the work of developing the instruments through which the state can exercise this authority is dominated by a limited number of countries, and, in some aspects, largely by the US, certainly until recently. This leaves most states in the world in the position of having to implement and enforce standards and property rights developed elsewhere if various digital networks in their countries are going to be connected to the Internet, which they mostly are already today.

The greatest challenge comes from the lack of accountability built into many of the capabilities that can be deployed by powerful actors, be they private or governmental, in the pursuit of their interests. This gives such unaccountable actors the power to shape potentially key features of Internet use and access. In the case of private actors, this brings up the question of which actors can claim legitimacy for their interests (e.g. in 'cybersquatting'), and in the case of governments, it raises the issue of ensuring public scrutiny of government actions. There are strong parallels here with some of the challenges for accountability raised by the growth of economic globalization and the ascendance of the so-called competitive state.

Notes

This is based on a larger project on 'Governance and Accountability in a Global Economy' (Department of Sociology, University of Chicago, on file with author).

1   A good example in the legal scholarship is the recent special issue of the *Indiana Journal for Global Legal Studies*.
2   The Internet is a dynamic condition subject to a variety of pressures. In earlier articles I have discussed how, notwithstanding its brief history, the Internet can already be thought of as having had three phases (Sassen, 1999c, 2000b). To this I would add that it is now entering a fourth phase, characterized by the privatizing of much of the backbone and a development of software aimed at protecting private property, including intellectual, rights and verification and billing. In the same articles I also discussed the different types of interpretation of the Internet and its positive and negative potentials, e.g. utopian and dystopian perspectives.

3 There are capabilities in the hardware that are not utilized by the software that is being designed. In that regard, the software is truly the domain for examining use and applications. A broader concept is that of the architecture of the Internet, which includes all the protocols and other features that make the system work. But these are embedded in the software as well. Operationally, when researching the changes one might detect in the features of the Internet, I use the types of software being produced as an indicator of these changes.

4 This saves companies the cost of private computer networks, with the requisite staffing and servicing, and the cost of frame relay connections or the costs of using intermediaries for firm-to-firm transactions.

5 An additional issue, one which I am not referring to here, is the privatization of infrastructure that has also taken place over the last two years (see Sassen, 1998a: ch. 9). Since the mid-1990s the backbone has been privatized where before it was financed by the US government, that is to say, taxpayers. This in turn changes the discussion of cyberspace as a public space, but only partly: it can remain public even if there is a fee to be paid for access. For a resource to be public it need not necessarily be free.

6 Lessig labels the architecture of the Internet 'code' and he means by this the software and hardware that constitutes it and determines how people interact or exist in this space.

7 Elsewhere I have made a similar argument using the notion of the emergence of cybersegmentations (see e.g. Sassen, 1999c, 2000b).

8 See for instance the March 1999 Next Five Minutes meetings in Amsterdam and Rotterdam, especially the technical workshops, and the Wizards of OS meeting in Berlin (July 1999). For reports on these and other such initiatives see Nettime (continuous online reporting) and ADILKNO (1998).

9 For an elaboration of this issue of representation and a new literature that addresses it see Sassen (1999c, 2000b).

10 Several authors have examined the possibility of enhancing democratic practices through the formation of communities on the Net and the possible role of governments in supporting them (Nettime, 1997; ADILKNO, 1998; Calabrese and Borchert, 1996; Calabrese and Burgelman, 1999). See also my review of various web sites of this type in *Artforum* (Sassen, 1998b: 30).

11 The growing sector of direct online investment often uses the Internet. It is mostly retail and represents a minor share of the overall global financial market. Even factoring in its expected tripling in value over the next three or four years will not give it the type of power of the global financial market I am discussing here.

12 There is an emerging literature on this. I have discussed this issue and some of the literature in Sassen (1996: ch. 2).

13 For instance figures show that countries with high savings have high domestic investment. Most savings are still invested in the domestic economy. Only 10 percent of the assets of the world's 500 largest institutional portfolios are invested in foreign assets. Some argue that a more integrated capital market would raise this level significantly and hence raise the vulnerability to and dependence on the capital markets. It should be noted that extrapolating the potential for growth from the current level of 10 percent may be somewhat dubious; it may not reflect the potential for capital mobility across borders or a variety of other factors which may be keeping managers from using the option of cross-border investments. This may well be an under-used option and it may remain that way, no matter what the actual cross-border capacities in the system.

14 See Duncan Kennedy (1993); cf. the argument that these ground rules in the case of the US contain rules of permission that strengthen the power of employers over workers, or that allow for a level in the concentration of wealth under the aegis of the protection of property rights that is not necessary to that extent in order to ensure the protection of property rights.

15 I examine some of these issues in 'Global Financial Centers' (Sassen, 1999b). The growth of electronic trading and electronic network alliances between major financial centers is allowing us to see the particular way in which digitalized markets are partly embedded in these vast concentrations of material resources and human talents which financial centers are (see also Sassen, 2000a).

References

ADILKNO (1998) *The Media Archive. World Edition.* New York: Autonomedia, and Amsterdam: ADILKNO.

Aspen Institute (1998) *The Global Advance of Electronic Commerce: Reinventing Markets, Management and National Sovereignty*, Report of the Sixth Annual Aspen Institute Roundtable on Information Technology, Aspen, CO, 21–3 August 1997, David Bollier Rapporteur. Washington, DC: Aspen Institute, Communications and Society Program.

Boyle, James (1997) *Foucault in Cyberspace: Surveillance, Sovereignty, and Hard-Wired Censors*. Washington: College of Law, American University [http://www.wcl.american.edu/pub/faculty/boyle/foucault.htm].

Calabrese, Andrew and Mark Borchert (1996) 'Prospects for Electronic Democracy in the United States: Rethinking Communication and Social Policy', *Media, Culture & Society* 18: 249–68.

Calabrese, Andrew and Jean-Claude Burgelman (eds) (1999) *Communication, Citizenship and Social Policy*. New York: Rowman and Littlefield.

Indiana Journal of Global Legal Studies (1999) Special Issue: *The Internet and Sovereignty* Spring.

Kennedy, Duncan (1993) 'The Stakes of Law, or Hale and Foucault', pp. 83–125 in *Sexy Dressing Etc.: Essays on the Power and Politics of Cultural Identity*. Cambridge, MA: Harvard University Press.

Lessig, Lawrence (1999) *Code and Other Laws of Cyberspace*. New York: Basic Books.

Mittelman, James (ed.) (1996) *Globalization: Critical Reflections. Yearbook of International Political Economy*, vol. 9. Boulder, CO: Lynne Rienner Publishers.

Mueller, Milton (1998) 'The "Governance" Debacle: How the Ideal of Internet-working Got Buried by Politics', paper presented at INET 98, Geneva, Switzerland [http://www.isoc.org/inet98/proceedings/a/5a_l.html].

Nettime (1997) *Net Critique*, compiled by Geert Lovink and Pit Schultz. Berlin: Edition ID-ARchiv [http://mediafilter.org/nettime].

Panitch, Leo (1996) 'Rethinking the Role of the State in an Era of Globalization', in James Mittelman (ed.) *Globalization: Critical Reflections. Yearbook of International Political Economy*, vol. 9. Boulder, CO: Lynne Rienner Publishers.

Perritt, Jr, Henry H. (1999) 'International Administrative Law for the Internet: Mechanisms of Accountability', *Administrative Law Review* 51(3): 871–900.

Post, David G. (1995) 'Anarchy, State, and the Internet: An Essay on Law-Making in Cyberspace', *Journal of Online Law* [http://www.cli.org/Dpost/X0023_ANARCHY.html].

Reidenberg, Joel R. (1998) 'Lex Informatica: The Formulation of Information Policy Rules Through Technology', *Texas Law Review* 76(553) [http://www.epic.org/misc/gulc/materials/reidenberg2. html].

Sassen, Saskia (1996) *Losing Control? Sovereignty in an Age of Globalization*, the 1995 Columbia University Leonard Hastings Schoff Memorial Lectures. New York: Columbia University Press.

Sassen, Saskia (1998a) *Globalization and Its Discontents*. New York: New Press.

Sassen, Saskia (1998b) *Artforum* Nov.: 30.

Sassen, Saskia (1999a) 'Embedding the Global in the National: Implications for the Role of the State', in David Smith, D. Solinger and S. Topik (eds) *States and Sovereignty in the Global Economy*. London: Routledge.

Sassen, Saskia (1999b) 'Global Financial Centers', *Foreign Affairs* 78(1): 75–87.

Sassen, Saskia (1999c) 'Digital Networks and Power', pp. 49–63 in M. Featherstone and S. Lash (eds) *Spaces of Culture: City, Nation, World*. London: Sage.

Sassen, Saskia (2000a) *The Global City: New York, London, Tokyo* (new fully updated edition). Princeton, NJ: Princeton University Press.

Sassen, Saskia (2000b) 'Spatialities and Temporalities of the Global: Elements for a Theorization', *Public Culture* 12(1).

33 Carnival of money

Politics of dissent in an era of globalizing finance

Marieke de Goede

Introduction: ethical inconsistency

In the recent Radcliffe Harvard Lecture, Zadie Smith (2003: 2) celebrates the work of E. M. Forster as a novelist whose 'deliberate rejection of controlled style reflects the messy complexities of the human heart'. Smith holds up Forster as an author whose muddled stories and inconsistent characters are not literarily flawed but closer to the bewildering realities of life while opening up an ethical space. Forster's style has been often criticized and ridiculed, but why, argues Smith, do we value consistency and rationality so much? Clarity and consistency in literary characters and plots are not just *unreal* – does everyday life ever adhere to such structure? – but can also be morally problematic: '[t]he lesson of the comic novel', Smith (2003: 3) writes, 'is that our moral enthusiasms make us inflexible, one-dimensional, flat... [W]e lose a vital dimension when we embrace the *esprit des serieux*'. Indeed, Smith (2003: 4) argues, 'there might be some ethical advantage in not always pursuing a perfect and unyielding rationality'. Smith's analysis emphasizes the ethical and political dimensions of comedy and ambiguity: instead of moral certainty and consistency, a comic literary muddle opens up an ethical space in which we as readers 'find ourselves caring about people who are various, muddled, uncertain and not quite like us' (Smith 2003: 4).

This chapter theorizes the politics of dissent and resistance in an era of globalizing finance, when nothing short of broad-based and internally consistent global movements seem to be able to challenge the power of financial institutions. Smith's suggestion that there might be ethical advantage in not always pursuing an unyielding rationality is relevant in light of the increasing call for global resistance movements to develop coherent, rational programmes for reform in order to be taken seriously. This call comes from those unsympathetic to global dissent movements, but increasingly also from within the movements themselves. British journalist and activist George Monbiot, for example, has recently launched a comprehensive proposal for global governance, seeking consensus and unity. 'For until we have a programme behind which we can unite', Monbiot (2003) writes, 'we will neither present a viable threat to the current rulers of the world, nor seize the revolutionary moment which their miscalculation affords us'. Monbiot sees political divergence as a weakness to be conquered on the road to a revolution in global governance, the proper endgoal of protests like those in Seattle (cf. Cox, 1999; Gill, 2000; Kaldor, 2000; Scholte, 2002).

I will argue that understanding global resistance in terms of a coherent programme entails a limited definition of contemporary political possibilities of dissent. By defining and delineating not just the new global movements but also their goals and ideals, some authors tend to read each dissenting voice in the context of a larger global purpose, while devaluing those, often complex and contradictory, political practices of festivals, laughter and everyday coping strategies that cannot be seen to contribute to this purpose. Here, I build on existing critiques of global civil society in order to offer a reading of the multiple possibilities of the politics of dissent in an era of globalizing finance which do not aspire to culminate in a new world order, but which *do* transform people's everyday experiences of money and finance in important ways. Carnival and laughter play a special role in the examples offered here: I argue that laughing about financial practices is more than a help-less gesture in the face of financial power, but has the potential to challenge its rationality and expose its contingency. These cultural practices are ways in which people cope with the seemingly overwhelming power of finance in everyday life, and create space for imagining financial alternatives.

The politics of 'making strange'

In their drive to detect a common programme behind the many possible acts and move-ments of resistance, theorists of civil society may erase the ambiguities and contradictions inherent in the contemporary politics of dissent. It is easily assumed, for example, that the manifold movements protesting at Seattle have a commonality. 'Look a little closer', writes Naomi Klein for example, 'and it's clear that these smaller targeted movements are indeed battling the same forces' (quoted in Amoore and Langley 2004: 107–108). In their article 'Ambiguities of Global Civil Society', Amoore and Langley (2004: 107) argue that civil society theory 'celebrates diversity and difference within settled, defined and clearly delimited boundaries'. Amoore and Langley instead emphasize the conceptual and political ambiguity of civil society, and encourage thinking about the contradictions within the global political economy. 'Within existing conceptions of [Global Civil Society]', Amoore and Langley (2004: 106) ask,

> do we have ways of thinking about the individual who is a member of Amnesty International while simultaneously holding portfolio investments in a number of large multination corporations; the Visa holder who joins Reclaim the Streets?; or the report from the Seattle protests that asked: 'did the protester who was filmed kicking lumps off the Nike sign while wearing Nike shoes see the irony?' For it is in such contradictory relationships with the global political economy that we all find ourselves.

Dissolving the contradictions and ambiguities of global protest is not just a conceptual weakness of civil society theory, but it is politically problematic. Mostly, finding commonal-ities in diverse movements and practices of opposition is held out as the road to political strength (Cox, 1999; Monbiot, 2003). However, eliminating ambiguity in favour of unity can also be interpreted as a political weakness. First, reducing the multiplicity of possible refusals and resistances to a single force or movement can be seen as an exclusionary politi-cal project in itself. Civil society organizations, Scholte (2002: 28) notes rightly, are not always democratic organizations themselves, and they 'may purport to speak on behalf of certain constituencies without adequately consulting them'. Put differently, global protest move-ments may be dominated by elite participants who have access to networks of communica-tion and travel but who nonetheless claim to speak for a disenfranchised mass. The danger becomes, according to Pasha and Blaney (1998: 435) that 'the vision of Global Civil Society itself...appears as a hegemonic project; as the imposition of a particular norm of civility in the name of global values and democracy'. Without outrightly rejecting existing proposals for reform, these criticisms suggest that it may not always be desirable to transform a plurality of protest into a unity of programme.

Second, ambiguity, laughter and *making strange* can be important political practices *in their own right*, which may not add up to a revolutionary politics of global change, but which may constitute important transformations of people's experiences of money and finance. According to Bleiker (2000: 256), dissent is too often understood 'in romantic and masculine terms, as heroic rebellions against authority, exemplified by demonstrating masses, striking workers, brick-throwing students and fasting dissidents'. For Bleiker however, dissent can work more slowly, more insidiously but also ambiguously, for example, through poetry and other practices of discursive dissent. In the place of the heroic act or singular programme against domination, it is possible to observe manifold discursive practices that transform and challenge dominant discourses and create space for alternative imaginations.

The practice of criticism, according to Michel Foucault, begins by denaturalizing, or *making strange*, political practices that appear as natural or common sense. Criticism, writes Foucault (1988: 154), 'is a matter of pointing out on what kinds of assumptions, what kinds of familiar, unchallenged, unconsidered modes of thought the practices that we accept rest'. It is in this way that space for transformation and the imagination of alternatives is opened, according to Foucault. '[A]s soon as one can no longer think things as one formerly thought them, transformation becomes both very urgent, very difficult and quite possible', Foucault (1988: 155) continues, '[i]t not therefore a question of there being a time for criticism and a time for transformation'. In other words, social transformation does not need necessarily critique *first*, and the development of effective political programmes second, but requires 'a *permanent* criticism' or making strange (Foucault 1988: 155, emphasis added).

Comedy and carnival can be important ways of practicing *financial* criticism precisely because the authority and legitimacy of financial practices is underpinned by their rationality and differentiation from emotion. When in the eighteenth and nineteenth centuries the emerging *Bourses* were accused of being little more than gambling houses, and thus morally and socially corrupt, defenders of the *Bourses* argued that the new credit practices provided security in the face of the uncertain business future through the rational calculation and hedging of future scenarios (de Goede, 2004). Graphical and statistical methods, borrowed from physics, contributed to the image of scientific objectivity of financial practices and rendered possible their legal and moral – albeit unstable – separation from gambling (cf. Poovey, 1998; Preda, 2001). In this sense, financial discourse is profoundly *modern*, influenced by an Enlightenment thinking which sought to effect 'the disenchantment of the world; the dissolution of myths and the substitution of knowledge for fancy' (Adorno and Horkheimer quoted in Odysseos, 2001: 709). The comical narrative lost its political function and educative role in Enlightenment society, and, according to Bakhtin (1968: 67), joking became relegated to the private sphere because '[t]hat which is important and essential cannot be comical'.

Because the calculative rationality of finance is not a logical corollary of its practices, but a conscious political move to foster its moral legitimacy, the disturbance of this rationality, through jokes or gambling, can form a threat to its existence. Indeed, precisely *because* in the modern worldview the important cannot be comical, it became crucial for financial institutions – attacked in pamphlets, poems and plays – to assert their seriousness with the help of the scientific method. Laughter, then, is more than a superficial attack or helpless gesture in the face of the power of financial institutions: it has a potential to shake the discursive foundations of modern financial rationality. '[C]omedy', Odysseos (2001: 730) writes, 'highlights the limits of rational discourse.... [I]t allows critical reflection to render the commonplace strange'. Comedy and carnival – by virtue of being both emotive and populist – have the potential to 'make strange' the unquestioned rationality of money and finance.

Carnival is characterized by a reversal of the 'normal' social order and an atmosphere of licentiousness during which prohibitions are challenged. 'What is most interesting about carnival', writes Scott (1990: 173), 'is the way it allows certain things to be said, certain forms of social power to be exercised that are muted or suppressed outside this social sphere'. Carnival moreover involves the appropriation of, for example, symbols, clothes and language by those to whom these practices are normally barred – cross-dressing and the adornments of Prince Carnival being traditional examples. But these festive appropriations of the symbols and practices of power can have important political meanings. According to Scott (1990: 168), they 'play an important imaginative function...They...create an imaginative breathing space in which the normal categories of order and hierarchy seem less than completely inevitable'.

According to Appadurai (2002: 43) moreover, festive appropriations of dominant practices can contribute to more democratic and inclusive forms of dissent than what he calls 'the politics of charity, training and projectization'. Appadurai (2002: 37) discusses the housing and toilet festivals organized by a slum dweller's coalition in Mumbai (Bombay) as both a 'creative hijacking of an upper-class form' and as a way in which slum dwellers' own knowledge and expertise to build 'adequate housing out of the flimsiest of materials and in the most insecure of circumstances' became visible. The slum dwellers alliance theorized by Appadurai (2002: 28) has an explicitly 'populist and anti-expert...strategy and flavour' and is committed to building on 'what poor persons already know and understand'. Anti-expert dissent is of crucial importance to financial politics, where non-experts are easily disqualified, while experts tend to share similar assumptions about the nature of the financial system (even if they do not always agree on policy proposals) (de Goede, forthcoming 2005, chapter 1). In financial politics, the Jubilee 2000 coalition campaigning for debt relief has most notably called for a popularization of financial knowledge. Jubilee's policies were anti-expert and according to campaign President Ann Pettifor '*all* can understand and grapple with supposedly complex financial matters' (Barrett, 2000, emphasis added).

Through carnivalesque dissent, the contingency and vulnerability of financial power may be exposed – in contrast to the serious and expert demeanour which underpins financial exclusion. Such dissent moreover enables a different conception of *agency* than prevalent in calls for programmatic resistance. In Monbiot's world order, for example, one *either* belongs to the elite *or* the disenfranchised, one either governs from the institutions of global capitalism or articulates alternative – but consistent – programmes, one either profits from capital's power or is swallowed up by it. There is little space, as Amoore and Langley (2004) point out, to consider the many contradictions of the global political economy within which we all find ourselves. In carnivalesque politics, the figure of Capital itself – and the divisions it gives rise to – appears much less stable and secure: its rationality is laughed at, its power is disturbed and the contradictions within the global political economy become apparent (cf. Gibson-Graham, 1996). In the examples that follow, we encounter a financial advisor who jokes with investment practice; a group of artists who appropriate financial discourse; a rural carnival that laughs at its money but still uses it. These agents neither *can* nor *wish* to overthrow global Capital; however, they disturb the assumed unity of capital, question its rationality, and reappropriate its language.

Appropriating the images and rituals of money

There are numerous examples of the appropriation of money and financial symbols in art and carnival: Agnew (1986: 35), for example, documents that medieval carnival was a marketplace festival in which 'mock coinage passed from hand to hand'. Money itself provides a rich canvas for political dissent, precisely because of the icons of state, religion and authority that are portrayed on paper money (Goux, 1999). On the one hand, the images of authority and national greatness which, at least since the nineteenth century, circulate on paper money are a way of educating the masses in the national history and, according to one nineteenth-century US government official, 'imbuing them with a National feeling' (quoted in Helleiner 2003: 106). On the other hand, these images of authority are precisely the way in which the value and reliability of the note are communicated and even generated (Goggin, 2003; Shell, 1999). Thus, the imagery on paper money can be understood as not just an adornment of pre-existing value, but the *very way* in which modern monetary value emerges. The iconography of paper money, according to Goggin (2003: 273), is 'universally recognised yet overlooked' in everyday life.

Precisely because the functioning of paper money in everyday life depends upon a forgetting of its contestability, the iconography of paper money is an important site for financial dissent. As lawyer Stapel (1995) argues in her examination of the legal conflict between US counterfeiting law and the First Amendment, the 'tremendous symbolic value' of the image of money in general and the American dollar bill in particular makes it 'a rich symbol in the vocabulary of those seeking to express thoughts lying at the heart of the First Amendment's protection'. That making fun of money and the appropriation of its iconography and rituals are important sites of financial dissent is underlined by the monetary authorities' often harsh reactions to money art, as for instance in their persecution of nineteenth-century *trompe d'oeil* painters who worked with images of money (Wenschler, 1999: 85–91). Stapel (1995: 13) concludes that US counterfeiting law is used regularly for pursuing those whose money paintings do *not* have the intention to defraud. Thus counterfeiting law can be seen as having less to do with the state's desire to maintain the currency's buying power, and more with its desire to maintain 'control over the currency's image'.

It is the very the *circulation* of currency that gives defacing or reappropriating money its political potential, according to Wambui Mwangi's study of the iconography of East African colonial money. This iconography included a depiction of a lion in an empty, wild African landscape, until – to the horror of the British rulers – a five shilling note was signalled with the words 'Mau Mau Very Good' scrawled upon it. According to Mwangi (2002: 49), the anxiety of the British was less to do with the question whether banks would still accept the note – as was argued by one British official – and more to do with fear that 'this five-shilling note, and possibly countless others like it, all inscribed with "Mau Mau" propaganda, were circulating freely among the Africans'. The Mau Mau insurrection in Kenya appropriated not just the colonial currency to spread its political message, but also translated Christian songs and parables in ways that gave them new, subversive meanings, which, according to one British official, were nonetheless 'so cleverly worded that it would be impossible to prove in a court of law that this was their meaning used' (Mwangi 2002: 51). In the case of the symbols on paper money, Mwangi (2002: 49) concludes, '[t]he Mau Mau had put Africans back into the empty landscape'. The reappropriation of the (cultural) symbols of power is a carnivalesque form of dissent – not just because it can be funny, but also because it is based on a 'ritual of reversal' in which subordinate groups use the language, symbols and songs that *are not theirs to use* (Scott, 1990).

A recent example of the reappropriation of money – which straddles the divide between dissent and counterfeiting – is a $200 bill featuring a smiling President Bush which was successfully used to pay for groceries in Kentucky in January 2001.[1] This 'Moral Reserve Note' (instead of Federal Reserve Note) has replaced the seal of the Federal Reserve System with the words 'The Right to Bear Arms', and depicts a number of protest signs on the White House lawn, including an image of an oil crane and the slogan 'No More Scandals'. Another sign on the lawn reads 'We like Broccoli', apparently a reference to George Bush Sr'.s profound dislike of the vegetable (BBC, 2001). The combination of amusing alternative symbols on the note can be read as a political commentary on the Bush government's close connections to the oil industry and the arms lobby. The note draws the image of money into the moral domain, and provides a funny but ambiguous voice of dissent. The bill moreover managed to skirt the counterfeiting issue in a comical way. 'Because there is no $200 bill', a Kentucky police detective told the BBC (2001), 'the perpetrator is likely to face a charge of theft by deception, but not counterfeiting'.

An artist who has not only redesigned money for more than 20 years, but whose performances open questions of value and faith in paper money on an every day level is JSG Boggs. Boggs never sells his painted banknotes to collectors, but spends them in 'proper' economic transactions, where he asks people – waiters, hotel managers, shop assistants – to accept his art notes instead of banknotes and to give him the correct change and receipts for the transactions. By doing so, Boggs provokes a moment of thought in naturalized economic practices: according to journalist Wenschler (1999: 49), he 'is engaged in philosophical disruptions, in provoking brief, momentary tears in the ordinarily seamless fabric of taken-for-granted mundanity'. One of Boggs's most striking recent bills is the 1999 Josie bill. On it, the traditional monetary iconography of a figure of authority – usually a (male) head of state or a (male) nationally renowned artist – has been replaced by the portrait of a young girl. If the portrait of the elder statesmen can be seen as a way of infusing the bill with authority and projecting its reliability, the Josie bill effects a complete reversal of the masculine discourse of value and authority. Boggs has furthermore replaced the words on the 'Federal Reserve Bank of America' seal with the words 'Fedreal Reverse Kunstbank' and he reverses the ownership of the note's iconography by replacing the words 'this note is legal tender' with the words 'this note is legal art so keep your sticky fingers off!' The latter is important in the context of Boggs' ongoing legal battles with the Federal Reserve, which in 1992 confiscated a number of his works on charges of counterfeiting.

Appropriating the images and rituals of money in a way that causes both questions and laughter on an everyday level, is also at the heart of the work of British-based art group *foreign investment*. The performances of *foreign investment* play with the corporate language, image and dress code, partly in order to challenge the commercialization of the art world which transforms the art object and the image of the individual artist into investment tools. *Foreign investment*, according to its press release, 'devises and sets up performances in public places which involve the passer-by in familiar, unfamiliar and almost familiar exchange'. The performances of *foreign investment* include carefully staged rituals, which accord new value to everyday objects – eggs, nuts, objects that visitors find in their pockets – by submitting them to the capitalist practices of measuring, weighing, registering, transcribing and, in one show, gilding. These performances on the one hand make visible and demystify the capitalist rituals, but on the other hand seek to accord value to things that are not generally valued in late-modern capitalist practices. 'It's not adding value, but it's making visible an inherent value of these things', one *foreign investment* member explains of a show involving the re-importation of Brazil nuts (packaged in the West) into Brazil and their weighing, measuring and gilding.[2] *Foreign investment's* business-like objectives, such as the realization of the 'eggsess dividend' in the Breeding show, and the slogans in its *operational review* ('providing tomorrow's solutions today' and 'spontaneity cannot be underestimated. It is a vital part of our work and therefore executed with meticulous care') moreover ridicule the corporate language, while making us think twice about its actual content. As one *foreign investment* member explains: 'it's a kind of interference, like almost sending another wavelength into a certain jargon. ...Appropriation is always getting hold of something which is threatening to get hold of you'.[3]

One performance by *foreign investment* which is of particular relevance to the argument developed here is its 1998 *Laughing Stock Exchange*. This performance incorporates the elements of appropriating and ridiculing financial language and rituals, while according new value to the ephemeral object of jokes. 'Your joke and your laughter are an important contribution to the archive of laughter and jokes for the generations of the coming millennium', a flyer for the *laughing stock exchange* reads, 'visit us at the laughing stock exchange and trade in your laughter/all you need is a joke'. The show invited people to tell their jokes or listen to pre-recorded jokes, while members of *foreign investment* recorded both jokes and laughter. The staging of the show was very formal, offering a ritual involving headphones, a choice of languages, recording equipment and transcription of the jokes, which turned the joke into a commercialized product. Thus, the laughing stock exchange played with the way in which abstract notions of value and security (in the form of stocks, options, futures) are turned into objects to be traded on financial exchanges. As one member of *foreign investment* explained:

> It was yet another quasi-ephemeral product we were using .... [J]okes and laughter are a kind of currency that passes around people, and somehow don't belong to anyone. They are being retold, and appear throughout different languages, and there's no-one who actually made them. The interesting thing is, can you *tell* them well, at this moment in time? Can you remember them and tell them well?[4]

The idea of jokes and laughter being a precious resource for the future which needs to be carefully collected, taped and stored, however, is the anathema of the logic of financial exchange, whose risk-trading, I argued, *depends upon* its differentiation from irrationality and comedy. The particular setting of the *laughing stock exchange*, which invited people off the streets of Berlin and Liverpool to participate, moreover confronted an unsuspecting public with questions of ownership and exchange. *Foreign investment*, in its name, shows and products makes fun of the seriousness of the actual exchanges. More generally, all examples discussed here involve the appropriation of images and discourses of money that are, normally, not for the wider public to use, and the authority of which depends precisely on its possession by experts.

Carnival and April fool's

On 1 April 2000, the respected Dutch investment website iex.nl announced: 'F/Rite Air IPO [Initial Public Offering] Will Be Big Hit'. The press release announced the stock offering of the Californian biotech company F/Rite Air, which had registered patents for the 'ionization' of normal air with a positive effect on the human nervous system, leading to 'increased physical resistance, stress resistance, and ability to concentrate'. It was further reported that this product was used in secret by fighter pilots of the Israeli army and 'Top Gun squadrons', and that Pfizer could be behind the development of these patents. The report announced that F/Rite Air would be noted on the exchanges with the ticker symbol FRYD, that the share price of the IPO would be $26–28, and that George Soros and Bill Gates had already invested (Kraland, 2000a). Within hours, iex.nl received pledges of 15 million Dutch guilders (around €7 million) from interested investors, so eager to grab the chance to invest in F/Rite Air that none of them asked for a company brochure. Later the same day, iex.nl released the message 'Fried Air Offering is Cancelled', explaining:

> We have good and bad news for our dear readers. The bad news is that the April 1 offering of F/Rite Air (pronounced Fried Air), the wondercompany that ionises

microwaves, with a euphoric effect surpassing Prozac and Viagra, is cancelled. The reason is that the company does not exist. The good news is that we have collected 15 million guilders in a few hours.

(Kraland, 2000b)

Fried Air – *gebakken lucht* – is Dutch for hot air, and the F/Rite Air April fool's joke provided a sharp and comical critique of the investment climate during the so-called dotcom boom. 'The joke was so obvious, it's unbelievable that people actually went for it', says F/Rite Air inventor and investment manager Michael Kraland, 'it showed how gullible people are. Fear and greed are the driving forces on the exchanges'. According to Kraland, there is not enough fun and laughter on the exchanges and this demeanour of seriousness underlies people's credulity because, wrapped in numbers and statistics, nonsense stories will be believed. 'Only laughter is not yet taxed', concludes Kraland jokingly, 'it has an anti-oxydating effect and is one of the few pleasures that does not make you fat or is bad for the environment'.[5] Although the joke elicited some angry responses from iex.nl readers, it received wide international media attention as a warning against investor optimism during the dotcom boom.

It was no coincidence, then, that F/Rite Air was a Californian-based biotech company, designing products similar to Prozac and Viagra: the story was carefully designed to include the buzz words of the new economy. A second parody of the new economy is the website iTulip.com, launched in 1998 and dedicated to nothing but selling its own stock certificates for US$10 each. iTulip.com defines itself as

> a corporation that relies on the Internet to deliver products or services to its customers at a loss; a. requires private or public capital to maintain unprofitable operations indefinitely; b. raises capital through the public markets to achieve an historically unprecedented market capitalization induced by the stock performance of similar companies, none of which are profitable.[6]

The site named itself after the famous Dutch seventeenth-century tulip bubble, and provides accounts of past financial crises juxtaposed with recent quotes of business and government leaders heralding a new age of unprecedented wealth and profit. 'Now you too can enjoy the thrill of owning an uneconomical Internet company's stock certificate without fear of losing all your money', the site announces, 'Buy an iTulip.com Stock Certificate. Not only does iTulip.com not have any assets, revenues or profits, *it doesn't even exist*. Of course, some Internet companies won't exist either after the Internet stock speculative mania ends'.[7]

These new economy jokes – F/Rite Air and iTulip.com – play with what have been identified as the most important aspects of the new economy, namely the 'extension of the financial audience', through romanticized tales of limitless profit-opportunities and a culture of entrepreneurialism (Thrift 2001: 422). The extension of the financial audience was bound up with an explosion of financial media – magazines, websites, special news-channels – where the new economy story was told by financial analysts and business gurus and affirmed by political leaders. 'Running the new economy story through this financial machine had enormous benefits for a number of actors', writes Thrift (2001: 425), 'it added value to particular shares…it proved analysts' worth and made media stars of some of them, it demonstrated the worth of the system as a whole and so on'. It is precisely this connection between the media, the extension of the financial audience and the very real effects on financial entitlements that is subject of the F/Rite Air and the iTulip satires. Both jokes provide sharp commentary on the eagerness and greed of investors; both spoof the culture of financial media and expertise by offering a product for sale that follows the logic of the new economy to absurdity. And just as the dotcom boom has permanently transformed financial practices and entitlements (Feng *et al.*, 2001; Thrift, 2001), these jokes maintain their satirical – albeit ambiguous – political message, even though now the bubble is pronounced burst.

Carnivalesque dissent cannot be observed just within the channels of the new economy itself (the internet), but also in the more traditional space of the carnival. In the Wasungen carnival in former East Germany in February 2003, for example, the new European currency proved a rich topic for satire. The introduction of the Euro in European states in 2000 had been preceded by protracted, complex and mystifying negotiations at EU level, largely invisible to the European populations. Two years after its introduction, the Euro has come under increasing popular criticism, especially for having made daily life more expensive. Participants in the Wasungen carnival turned the Euro into a comic monster, through images of hell and vultures. 'Zum Teufel mit dem T€uro' ('To hell with the expensive Euro'), one float with a massive papier-mâché devil read (Figure 33.1). The Euro-demon was

Figure 33.1 Euro-devil at Wasungen carnival, Germany, 2003. Photo by author.

Figure 33.2 Euro-vulture at Wasungen carnival, Germany, 2003. Photo courtesy of Lorenz Grimm.

surrounded by small torches, a pitchfork and people in costumes with the sun on one side and rain on the other – a comment on the instability of the economic climate. One of the other Euro floats was a massive vulture, surrounded by people in shiny costumes of old German pennies, with the comment 'The €uro trick: our pennies are being destroyed by the vulture' (Figure 33.2). 'We express what everybody is thinking', says Heiner Kämpf, one of the makers of the Euro-floats, 'the Euro makes the poor poorer within the EU, and other values, like ecological values, are forgotten about. We use a kind of black humour to get people to think about these things'.[8]

The significance of Medieval laughter, according to Bakhtin (1968: 91) lies in its 'victory over fear': 'We always find [in Medieval comic images] the defeat of fear presented in a droll and monstrous form, the symbols of power and violence turned inside out.... All that was terrifying becomes grotesque.... The people play with terror and laugh at it; *the awesome becomes a comic monster*' (emphasis added). The Wasungen carnival provides examples of how the serious but mystifying power of finance is turned into a comic monster. Images of hell, demons and death in carnival rituals, for Bakhtin, were precisely the means through which fear and intimidation could be overcome. The set of hell, which was a traditional part of the Medieval carnival, 'was solemnly burned at the peak of the festivities' (Bakhtin, 1968: 91). In financial discourse, the association between money and the devil moreover is a historically important one, from medieval prohibitions on usury – making interest and speculation the work of the devil – to the way in which critics made sense of 'devilish' credit money

(Shell, 1995: 63–72). The incomprehensible and at times unreliable magic of credit-creation gave rise to a whole series of money-devils which were used to make sense of, for example, the tulip bubble in Holland and the 1720 Mississippi bubble in France. The Euro devil of the Wasungen carnival then, has a long historical lineage while providing a rare popular and comical comment on the highly technical and depoliticized Euro debate. This carnivalesque critique of the new European currency provokes thought on an everyday level, and opens space for alternative imaginations.

Conclusions: carnival through the year

Clearly, neither laughter nor irony are inherent forces for good. Bakhtin's enthusiasms for 'images of the material bodily lower stratum', Bleiker (2000: 205) points out, 'never touches upon the issue of gender relations and related systems of exclusion. He never asks *who laughs at whom* in Rabelais' world' (emphasis added). Still, I argue that joking, laughter and carnival *can be* important politics of dissent in an era when the political legitimacy of financial practices depends upon their rationality and coherence. It is often argued that laughter is either a superficial and helpless gesture in the face of power, or, worse, a safety-valve which allows power to operate by providing insignificant spaces of relief which distract from planning 'real' resistance. 'Bakhtin himself could imply that things were not so bad so long as people laughed and swore, mocked and refused to take things seriously' Hirschkop (1999: 291) writes for example, 'but...laughter and festivity in themselves do not make for fearless people'.

Scott (1990: 168), however, strongly opposes the reading of carnival as a practice which 'harmlessly drains away social tensions that might otherwise become dangerous to the existing social order'. First, Scott argues, it is possible to find ample historical evidence that authorities tried to regulate or suppress carnivalesque practices. 'Why have there been such strenuous attempts to abolish Carnival', Jackson (1988: 222) argues similarly in his examination of the Notting Hill carnival in London, 'if it is...no more than harmless release of energy?' Second, it is important to see how carnival creates spaces for alternative imaginations and, in the words of *foreign investment*, *interferes* with the dominant discourse – disturbs it and makes it less intimidating. This practice of criticism or making strange questions existing power relationships, and, in Scott's words (1990: 168) make the 'normal categories of order and hierarchy' appear '*less than completely inevitable*' (emphasis added). Or, as one member of *foreign investment* describes her experience of the Rio carnival, 'when you have seen the carnival once, you are able to see it throughout the year in everyday life'.

Practices of joking, carnival and refusing to take seriously are not at all incompatible with a larger scale protest, and mass protests such as in Seattle are often accompanied by a carnival atmosphere and artists' challenges of the dominant discourse. For example, the Stop the War campaign's demonstration against the UK visit of President Bush in November 2003, included besides its main mass demonstration an alternative state procession with a mock queen and a mock president, and an invitation to the public to 'attire themselves in colourful raiment in the manner and style of our Royal Person, our Most Loyal Consort the Duke of Edinburgh, members of Our Government'.[9] However, I argue that current calls for coherent resistance and programmatic reform tend to devalue the politics of making strange, which, according to Foucault, are indispensable to criticism and transformation. Highlighting the plurality and ambiguity of dissent can contribute to overcoming the 'fear and hopelessness generated by monolithic accounts of the "neoliberal project,"' in which only broad-based counter-hegemonic challenges are considered purposeful (Larner 2003: 512). The political practices of dissent discussed here may not form a consistent counter-hegemonic programme, but they do transform people's experiences of monetary instruments and financial discourses in important ways. They challenge the unity, seriousness and reach of contemporary financial practices and open space for alternative imaginations.

Acknowledgements

The author wishes to thank *foreign investment*, Johannes Artus, Heiner Kämpf and Michael Kraland. For comments on earlier versions of this essay, many thanks to Louise Amoore, Martin Coward, Gunther Irmer, Paul Langley, Kees van der Pijl, Erna Rijsdijk, my 'NGO' colleagues, and participants in the Research-in-Progress seminar at the University of Sussex in November 2003.

Notes

1 An image of the bill can be found at http://www.thesmokinggun.com/archive/bushbill1.html
2 Interview *foreign investment*, Newcastle upon Tyne, 15 September 2003.
3 Interview *foreign investment*, Newcastle upon Tyne, 15 September 2003.
4 Interview *foreign investment*, Newcastle upon Tyne, 15 September 2003.
5 Michael Kraland, personal correspondence and telephone interview, Amsterdam, 7 October 2003.
6 http://www.itulip.com
7 http://www.itulip.com/productsnew.htm
8 Heiner Kämpf, interview, Wasungen, Germany, 29 December 2003.
9 http://www.stopwar.org.uk/Resources/altstateproc.pdf

References

All URLs, also those noted in the footnotes, were accessible in June 2004.

Agnew, J.-C. (1986), *Worlds Apart: the Market and the Theatre in Anglo-American Thought*, 1550–1750. Cambridge: Cambridge University Press.

Amoore, L. and Langley, P. (2004) 'Ambiguities of Global Civil Society', *Review of International Studies*, 30(1): 89–110.

Appadurai, A. (2002), 'Deep Democracy: Urban Governmentality and the Horizon of Politics', *Public Culture*, 14(1): 21–47.

Bakhtin, M. (1968), *Rabelais and His World*, translated by Helene Iswolsky, Bloomington: Indiana University Press.

Barrett, M. (ed.) (2000), *The World Will Never Be the Same Again*, Jubilee 2000 Coalition, December. http://www.jubilee2000uk.org/analysis/reports/world_never_same_again/contents.htm

BBC (2001), 'Funny Money in Kentucky', January 31. http://news.bbc.co.uk/1/hi/world/americas/1147246.stm

Bleiker, R. (2000), *Popular Dissent, Human Agency and Global Politics*. Cambridge: Cambridge University Press.

Cox, R. W. (1999), 'Civil Society at the Turn of the Millennium: Prospects for an Alternative World Order', *Review of International Studies*, 25(1): 3–28.

de Goede, M. (2004) 'Repoliticizing Financial Risk', *Economy and Society*, 33(2): 197–217.

de Goede, M. (2005), *Virtue, Fortune and Faith: a Genealogy of Finance*. Minneapolis: University of Minnesota Press.

Feng, H., Froud, J., Johal, S., Haslam, C. and Williams, K. (2001), 'A New Business Model? The Capital Market and the New Economy', *Economy & Society*, 30(4): 467–503.

Foucault, M. (1988) [1981], 'Practicing Criticism', in Kritzman, L. D. (ed.) *Michel Foucault: Politics, Philosophy, Culture, Interviews and Other Writings 1977–1984*, New York: Routledge.

Gibson-Graham, J. K., (1996), *The End of Capitalism (As We Knew It)*, Oxford: Blackwell.

Gill, S. (2000), 'Toward a Postmodern Prince? The Battle of Seattle as a Moment in the New Politics of Globalisation', *Millennium*, 29(1): 131–140.

Goggin, J. (2003), 'Images of Nationhood: Currency Art', in Nancy Pedri (ed.), *Travelling Concepts III: Memory, Narrative, Image*, Amsterdam: ASCA Press.

Goux, J.-J. (1999), 'Cash, Check, or Charge?', in Osteen, M. and Woodmansee, M. (eds), *The New Economic Criticism: Studies at the Intersection of Literature and Economics*, London: Routledge.

Helleiner, E. (2003), *The Making of National Money: Territorial Currencies in National Perspective*, Ithaca: Cornell University Press.

Hirschkop, K. (1999), *Mikhail Bakhtin: an Aesthetic for Democracy*, Oxford University Press.

Jackson, P. (1988), 'Street Life: the Politics of Carnival', *Environment and Planning D: Society and Space*, 6: 213–227.

Kaldor, M. (2000), 'Civilising Globalisation? The Implications of the Battle of Seattle', *Millennium*, 29(1): 105–114.

Kraland, M. (2000a), 'F.Rite Air IPO wordt knaller' ('F/Rite Air IPO will be Big Hit'), http://iex.nl/columns/columns_artikel.asp?colid = 852.

Kraland, M. (2000b), 'Gebakken Lucht Emissie gaat niet Door' ('Hot Air Offering is Cancelled'), http://iex.nl/columns/columns_artikel.asp?colid = 853%20.

Larner, W. (2003), 'Neoliberalism?', *Environment and Planning D: Society and Space*, 21(5): 509–512.

Monbiot, G. (2003), 'Seize the Day', *The Guardian*, June 17, http://www.monbiot.com/archives/2003/06/17/seize-the-day/

Mwangi, W. (2002), 'The Lion, the Native and the Coffee Plant: Political Imagery and the Ambiguous Art of Currency Design in Colonial Kenya', *Geopolitics*, 7(1): 31–62.

Odysseos, L. (2001), 'Laughing Matters: Peace, Democracy and the Challenge of the Comic Narrative', *Millennium*, 30(3): 709–732.

Pasha, M. K. and Blaney, D. L. (1998), 'Elusive Paradise? The Promise and Peril of Global Civil Society', Alternatives, 23: 417–450.

Poovey, M. (1998), *A History of the Modern Fact: Problems of Knowledge in the Sciences of Wealth and Society*, Chicago: University of Chicago Press.

Preda, A. (2001), 'The Rise of the Popular Investor: Financial Knowledge and Investing in England and France, 1840–1880', *The Sociological Quarterly*, 42(2): 205–232.

Scholte, J.-A. (2002), 'Civil Society and the Governance of Global Finance', in Scholte, J.-A. and Schnabel, A. (eds), *Civil Society and Global Finance*, London: Routledge.

Scott, J. (1990), *Domination and the Arts of Resistance: Hidden Transcripts*. New Haven: Yale University Press.

Shell, M. (1995), *Art & Money*. Chicago: University of Chicago Press.

Smith, Z. (2003), 'Love, Actually', *Guardian Book Review*, November 1, pp. 2–4.

Stapel, J. K. (1995), 'Money Talks: the First Amendment Implications for Counterfeiting Law', *Indiana Law Journal*, 71(1).

Thrift, N. (2001), 'It's the Romance, not the Finance, that Makes the Business Worth Pursuing', *Economy and Society*, 30(4): 412–432.

Wenschler, L. (1999), *Boggs: A Comedy of Values*, Chicago: University of Chicago Press.

34 Beyond the war of words

Cautious resistance and calculated conformity

James C. Scott

Source: James C. Scott (1985), *Weapons of the Weak: Everyday Forms of Peasant Resistance*, New Haven: Yale University Press, pp. 241–303

Whatever happens Schweik mustn't turn into a cunning, underhanded Saboteur, he is merely an opportunist exploiting the tiny openings left him.

(Bertolt Brecht, *Journal*, May 27, 1943)

The damned impertinence of these politicians, priests, literary men, and what-not who lecture the working class socialist for his "materialism"! All that the working man demands is what these others would consider the undispensable minimum without which human life cannot be lived at all.... How right the working classes are in their "materialism"! How right they are to realize that the belly comes before the soul, not in the scale of values but in point of time.

(George Orwell, "Looking Back on the Spanish War", 1943)

From the account thus far, one might justifiably assume that the struggle between rich and poor was largely confined to a war of words. That assumption would not be entirely wrong, but it would be misleading. For the poor and wealthy peasants of Sedaka are not merely having an *argument*; they are also having a fight. Under the circumstances, the fight is less a pitched battle than a low-grade, hit-and-run, guerrilla action. The kind of "fight" to be described and analyzed in this chapter is, I believe, the typical, "garden variety" resistance that characterizes much of the peasantry and other subordinate classes through much of their unfortunate history. More specifically, however, we are dealing here with the undramatic but ubiquitous struggle against the effects of state-fostered capitalist development in the countryside: the loss of access to the means of production (proletarianization), the loss of work (marginalization) and income, and the loss of what little status and few claims the poor could assert before double-cropping. Most readings of the history of capitalist development, or simply a glance at the current odds in this context, would conclude that this struggle is a lost cause. It may well be just that. If so, the poor peasantry of Sedaka finds itself in distinguished and numerous historical company.

After considering the major reasons why open collective protest is rare, I examine the actual patterns of resistance to changes in production relations: arson, sabotage, boycotts, disguised strikes, theft, and imposed mutuality among the poor. I then assess the role of coercion – of what might be called "everyday forms of repression" – in producing such disguised forms of struggle amidst overt compliance. Finally, I take a step backward to explore, in more general terms, the definition of resistance and the reasons why many of the actions considered here might justifiably be termed resistance.

Obstacles to open, collective resistance

An observer need not look long and hard to find examples of further resistance in Sedaka. In fact, they abound. They are, however, forms of resistance that reflect the conditions and constraints under which they are generated. If they are open, they are rarely collective, and, if they are collective, they are rarely open. The encounters seldom amount to more than "incidents," the results are usually inconclusive, and the perpetrators move under cover of darkness or anonymity, melting back into the "civilian" population for protective cover.

To appreciate why resistance should assume such guises, it is helpful to pause briefly to consider a few of the major "givens" that determine the range of available options.

Perhaps the most important "given" that structures the options open to Sedaka's poor is simply the nature of the changes they have experienced. Some varieties of change, other things equal, are more explosive than others – more likely to provoke open, collective defiance. In this category I might place those massive and sudden changes that decisively destroy nearly all the routines of daily life and, at the same time, threaten the livelihood of much of the population. Here in Sedaka, however, the changes that constitute the green revolution have been experienced as a series of piecemeal shifts in tenure and technique. As painful as the changes were, they tended to come gradually and to affect only a small minority of villagers at any one time. The shift from rents collected after the harvest (*sewa padi*) to fixed rents paid before planting (*sewa tunai*), for example, affected only tenants and was pushed through over several seasons, so that only a few tenants found themselves simultaneously in jeopardy. Furthermore, most of them were able to hang on to their tenancy even if it meant an additional burden of debt. If we could imagine a single, large landlord insisting on *sewa tunai* from all the village tenants in the same season, the response might have been very different. The loss of tenancies that resulted when landlords decided to resume cultivation themselves or to lease (*pajak*) their land to wealthy commercial operators followed a similar pattern. Much the same can be said for the raising of rents and for the substitution of broadcasting for transplanting. The screws were turned piecemeal and at varying speeds, so that the victims were never more than a handful at a time. In this case as in others, each landlord or farmer insisting on the change represented a *particular* situation confronting one or, at most, a few individuals.

The only exception to this pattern was the introduction of combine-harvesting and, as we shall see, it provoked the nearest thing to open, collective defiance. Even in this case, however, the impact was not instantaneous, nor was it without a certain ambiguity for many in the village. For the first two or three seasons the economic impact on the poor was noticeable but not devastating. Middle peasants were genuinely torn between the advantage of getting their crop in quickly and the loss of wage earning for themselves or their children. A few of the smallest farmers, as I have noted, succumbed to the temptation to use the combine in order to hasten their exit for contract labor in the city. At no single moment did combine-harvesting represent a collective threat to the livelihood of a solid majority of villagers.

Another striking characteristic of the agricultural transformation in Kedah – one that serves very powerfully to defuse class conflict – is the fact that it removes the poor from the productive process rather than directly exploits them. One after another, the large farmers and landlords in the Muda Scheme have *eliminated* terrains of potential struggle over the distribution of the harvest and profits from paddy growing. In place of the struggle over piece-rates for cutting and threshing, there is now only a single payment to the machine broker. In place of negotiations over transplanting costs, there is the option of broadcasting the seed and avoiding the conflict altogether. In place of tense and contentious disputes over the timing and level of rents, there is the alternative of hiring the machines and farming oneself or leasing to an outsider for a lump sum. Even the shift to *sewa tunai* eliminates the tales of woe and ruin that previously dominated the post-harvest claims for rent adjustment. The changes themselves, of course – dismissing a tenant, switching to the machines, moving to fixed rents before planting – are not so simple to put across. But once they have been put across, the ex-tenant or ex-wage laborer simply ceases to be relevant; there is no further season-by-season struggle. Once the connection and the struggle in the realm of production have been severed, it is a simple matter also to sever the connection – and the struggle – in the realm of ritual, charity, and even sociability. This aspect of the green revolution, by itself, goes a long way toward accounting for the relative absence, here and elsewhere, of mass violence. If the profits of the green revolution had depended on squeezing more from the tenants, rather than dismissing them, or extracting more work for less pay from laborers, the consequences for class conflict would surely have been far more dramatic. As it is, the profits from double-cropping depend much less on exploiting the poor directly than on ignoring and replacing them.[1] Class conflict, like any conflict, is played out on a site – the threshing floor, the assembly line, the place where piece-rates or rents are settled – where vital interests are at stake. What double-cropping in Muda has achieved is a gradual bulldozing of the sites where class conflict has historically occurred.

A second obstacle to open protest is already implicit in the piecemeal impact of double-cropping. The impact of each of the changes we have discussed is mediated by the very complex and overlapping class structure of Sedaka. There are well-off tenants and very poor tenants; there are landlords who are (or whose children are) also tenants and laborers; there are smallholders who need wage work to survive but also hire the combines. Thus each of the important shifts in tenure and production creates not only victims and beneficiaries but also a substantial strata whose interests are not so easily discerned. Sedaka is not Morelos, where a poor and largely undifferentiated peasantry confronted a common enemy in the sugar plantation. It is in fact only in comparatively rare circumstances that the class structure of the countryside was such as to produce either a decisive single cleavage or a nearly uniform response to external pressure. The very complexity of the class structure in Sedaka militates against collective opinion and, hence, collective action on most issues.

The obstacles to collective action presented by the local class structure are compounded by other cleavages and alliances that cut across class. These are the familiar links of kinship, friendship, faction, patronage, and ritual ties that muddy the "class waters" in virtually *any* small community. Nearly without exception, they operate to the advantage of the richer farmers by creating a relationship of dependence that restrains the prudent poor man or woman from acting in class terms. Thus Mansur, a poor landless laborer, is related to Shamsul, one of the richest men in the village, and can expect occasional free meals at his house as well as casual work now and then. While this does not prevent Mansur from privately complaining about the loss of work and the tightfisted rich in general, it does help explain his UMNO membership and his deferential profile in village politics. Mat "halus" is extremely poor, rather outspoken privately on class issues, and a member of PAS. But he rents a single relong from his father-in-law, Abdul Rahman, a fairly wealthy UMNO landowner, and takes care not to embarrass him by making trouble in the village. Other examples might be cited, but the point is clear. A small minority of the village poor are hedged in by links of kinship and/or petty economic dependencies they are reluctant to jeopardize. If they disagree with their relative, landlord, or employer, they are likely to do so with circumspection. It would be a mistake to overemphasize such ties, for they are certainly rarer and more fragile than they once were, and many of the poor are not constrained in this way at all. They do, nevertheless, neutralize a fraction of the poor.[2]

A third obstacle to open resistance is, perhaps, not so much an obstacle as a viable alternative. As Moore reminds us in quite another context, "throughout the centuries one of the common man's most frequent and effective responses to oppression [has been] *flight*."[3] Nowhere has this option been more historically significant than in Southeast Asia in general and Malaya in particular. So long as there was a land frontier and so long as control over manpower rather than land was the basis of surplus extraction, the possibility of what one writer has awkwardly called "avoidance protest" has *always* proved more attractive than the risk of open confrontation.[4] Much to the consternation of their indigenous leaders as well as their colonial rulers, the rural Malay population has always been exceptionally mobile – moving to another petty chiefdom, leaving one plot of land to make a new clearing and homestead in the forest, switching crops and often occupations in the process – and has classically "voted with its feet." Because of its particular demography and social organization, it would not be an exaggeration to say that "exit" rather than "voice" had come to characterize the traditional and preferred response to oppression in Malay society.[5] Fortunately for the contemporary losers in the green revolution, this traditional option is still available to many.

For half a century at the very least, a substantial portion of the population increase in Kedah's rice bowl has been moving away. They have contributed, as pioneers, to the opening up of new paddy areas in Perak, Perlis, Pahang, Johor, and the inland districts of Kedah itself. Virtually every poor family in the village has, at one time or another, applied for acceptance to government-sponsored settlement schemes (*ranchangan*), where incomes from rubber and especially oil palm are routinely more than can be wrested from even a substantial paddy farm. Only a few have been selected, and they are typically not from among the poorest villagers. Still, the slim chance of becoming a sponsored settler (*peneroka*) is a factor in preventing more open expressions of local conflict. For the children of modest and poor villagers, the option of factory work and domestic service (for women) and full-time urban contract labor (for men) are available. For the poor families who largely choose to remain, short-term contract labor in the cities offers a means to a viable, if unsatisfactory, livelihood. This last, and most common, resort not only reduces the economic pressure on poor families but also removes the head of household from active participation in village affairs for much of the year. Such semiproletarians still reside largely in the village and may even farm a small plot of paddy land, but they play an increasingly marginal role in the local issues that might provoke class conflict. A major slump in off-farm employment would, of course, change this picture dramatically by making local work and access to land that much more salient.[6] For the time being, however, the ability to raid the cash economy to make good the local subsistence deficit continues to provide a less risky alternative to local conflict.

[...]

The fifth and final obstacle to open resistance makes sense only against a background of expected repression. This obstacle is simply the day-to-day imperative of earning a living – of household survival – which Marx appropriately termed "the dull compulsion of economic relations."[7] Lacking any realistic possibility, for the time being, of directly and collectively redressing their situation, the village poor have little choice but to adjust, as best they can, to the circumstances they confront daily. Tenants may bitterly resent the rent they must pay for their small plot, but they must pay it or lose the land; the near landless may deplore the loss of wage work, but they must scramble for the few opportunities available; they may harbor deep animosities toward the clique that dominates village politics, but they must act with circumspection if they wish to benefit from any of the small advantages that clique can confer.

At least two aspects of this grudging, pragmatic adaptation to the realities merit emphasis. The first is that it does not rule but certain forms of resistance, although it surely sets limits that only the foolhardy would transgress. The second is that it is above all pragmatic; it does not imply normative consent to those realities. To understand this is simply to grasp what is, in all likelihood, the situation for most subordinate classes historically. They struggle under conditions that are largely not of their own making, and their pressing material needs necessitate something of a daily accommodation to those conditions. Dissident intellectuals from the middle or upper classes may occasionally have the luxury of focusing exclusively on the prospects for long-term structural change, but the peasantry or the working class are granted no holiday from the mundane pressures of making a living. If we observe, as we shall, a good deal of "conforming" behavior in daily social life in Sedaka, we have no reason to assume that it derives from some symbolic hegemony or normative consensus engineered by elites or by the state. The duress of the quotidian is quite sufficient. Durkheim and Weber recognized, as did Marx, "that human beings are forced to behave in certain directions regardless of their own preferences and inclinations."[8] Durkheim's view of the daily constraints on the industrial working class could be applied with even greater emphasis to the peasantry:

> This tension in social relations is due, in part, to the fact that the working classes are not really satisfied with the conditions under which they live, but very often accept them only as constrained and forced, since they have not the means to change them.[9]

In the long run, and in certain circumstances, the peasantry and the working class *do* have "the means to change" fundamentally their situation. But in the short run – today, tomorrow, and the day after – they face a situation that very sharply restricts their real options.[10] The few opportunities for land and work remaining to Sedaka's poor depend today, as always, on the sufferance of the wealthy. If much of the day-to-day public behavior of the poor reflects that fact, it can be explained by nothing more than a healthy and expedient regard for survival. "Going for broke" can have little appeal in a context in which the final word of this expression must be taken quite literally.

The effort to stop the combine-harvester

The introduction of combine-harvesting, as the most sudden and devastating of the changes associated with double-cropping, also stirred the most active resistance. This resistance went well beyond the arguments about its efficiency, the complaints over lost wages, and the slander directed against those who hired it, which I have already described. Throughout the rice bowl of Kedah there were efforts physically to obstruct its entry into the fields, incidents of arson and sabotage, and widespread attempts to organize "strikes" of transplanters against those who first hired the machine. All of these actions ultimately failed to prevent the mechanization of the paddy harvest, although they undoubtedly delayed it somewhat. A close examination of the forms of resistance and the responses of large farmers can teach us a great deal about both the possibilities and limits that help structure this resistance.

[...]

I made no effort to assemble a complete inventory of reported incidents, although it was a rare peasant who could not recall one or two. No one, however, could recall any such incident in Sedaka itself. This may merely reflect an understandable reluctance to call attention to themselves. And at no time did the overall volume of sabotage reach anything like the level of machine breaking that accompanied the introduction of mechanical threshers into England in the 1830s.[11]

At the same time that individuals and small groups of men were attacking the machines, there were the beginnings of a quiet but more collective effort by women to bring pressure to bear on the farmers who hired the machines. Men and women – often from the same family – had, of course, each lost work to the combine, but it was only the women who still had any real bargaining power. They were, for the time being, still in control of transplanting.[12] The group of women (*kumpulan share*, from the English) who reaped a farmer's land were typically the same group that had earlier transplanted the same field. They were losing roughly half their seasonal earnings, and they understandably resented transplanting a crop for a farmer who would use the combine at harvest time. Thus, in Sedaka and, it appears, throughout much of the Muda region, such women resolved to organize a boycott (*boikot*) that would deny transplanting services to their employers who hired the combine.

Three of the five "share groups" in Sedaka evidently made some attempts to enforce such a boycott. Those groups of anywhere from six to nine women were led by Rosni (a widow), Rokiah (the wife of Mat Buyong), and Miriam (the wife of Mat Isa). The remaining two groups, led by the wives of Tajuddin and Ariffin, appear not to have been involved, but neither group would agree to plant paddy for a farmer who was being boycotted by one of the other three gangs. Why the groups of Rosni, Rokiah, and Miriam took the initiative is not entirely clear. They are composed of women from families that are, on average, slightly poorer than those in the remaining two groups, but only slightly. The first two are, as well, largely from PAS households, but this may be as much due to kinship and neighborhood as to factionalism per se, and in any case they were frequently boycotting farmers from their own political faction. If we rely on local explanations for the pattern of resistance, the consensus is that Rosni and Rokiah depend heavily on wage labor to support their families and are at the same time "courageous" (*berani*).[13]

The forms the boycott took were very much in keeping with the kinds of cautious resistance I have so far described. At no time was there ever an open confrontation between a farmer who used the combine and his transplanters. Instead, the anonymous and indirect approach of *cara sembunyi tau* with which we are familiar was employed. The women "let it be known" through intermediaries that the group was dissatisfied (*tak puas hati*) with the loss of harvest work and would be reluctant (*segan*) to transplant the fields of those who had hired the combine the previous season. They also let it be known that, when and if a combine broke down in the course of the harvest, a farmer who wanted then to get his crop in by hand could not count on his old workers to bail him out.

When it came time at the beginning of the irrigated season of 1977 to make good on this threat, circumspection again prevailed. None of the three groups refused outright to transplant paddy for those who had harvested with the combine in the previous season. Rather, they delayed; the head of the share group would tell the offending farmer that they were busy and could not get to his land just yet. Only a dozen or so farmers had used the combine the previous season, so the share groups had a good deal of work to occupy them just transplanting the crops of those who had not mechanized.[14] The transplanters thus kept their options open; they avoided a direct refusal to transplant, which would have provoked an open break. Fully abreast of the rumors of a boycott, the farmers who had been put off became increasingly anxious as their nursery paddy was passing its prime and as they feared their crop might not be fully mature before the scheduled date for shutting off the supply of water. Their state of mind was not improved by the sight of their neighbors' newly transplanted fields next to their own vacant plots.

After more than two weeks of this war of nerves – the seeming boycott that never fully announced itself – six farmers "let it be known" that they were arranging for outside laborers to come and transplant their crops. By most accounts, these six were Haji Kadir, Haji Salim, Tok Kasim, Lazim, Kamil, and Cik Mah, who between them cultivate nearly 100 relong. They claimed in their defense that they had pressed for a firm commitment for a transplanting date from their local share group and, only after being put off again, had they moved. At this point, the boycott collapsed. Each of the three share groups was faced with defections, as women feared that the transplanting work would be permanently lost to outsiders. They hastily sent word that they would begin transplanting the land in question within the next few days. Three of the six farmers canceled their arrangements with the outside gangs, while the other three went ahead either, because they felt it was too late to cancel or because they wished to teach the women a lesson. Transplanters came from the town of Yan (just outside the irrigation scheme) and from Singkir and Merbuk, farther away. Haji Salim, using his considerable political influence, arranged with MADA to bring in a gang of Thai transplanters – a practice he has continued and for which he is bitterly resented.

The brief and abortive attempt to stop the combine by collective action was the subject of demoralized or self-satisfied postmortems, depending on which side of the fence one happened to be. Aside from the pleasure or disappointment expressed, the postmortems, for once, converged on the inevitability of the outcome. Those with most to lose from mechanization realized that the women could not really move beyond talk and threats. Thus, Wahid said that the rumored boycott was "just talk and they planted anyway." "What could they do?" he asked, throwing up his hands. Tok Mahmud echoed this assessment: "Other people took the work; once the work is gone they couldn't do anything." "People are clever," Sukur added, "If you don't want to transplant, they'll take the work and money." It is for this reason, Samad claimed, that the women were careful not to burn their bridges and only talked of a boycott well out of earshot (*kot jauh saja*) of large farmers. Finally, in the same vein, Hamzah summed up the long odds against the women:

> Whether you complain or don't complain, it's no use. You can't do anything; you can't win. If you say anything, they won't hire you to plant even. The women will even have to cut paddy for a farmer if the combine breaks down. If you're hard up, you have to take the work. If you refuse (*tolak*), if you don't do it, others will. Only those who are well-off (*senang*) can refuse.

We could ask for no clearer exposition of the "dull compulsion of economic relations." The well-to-do were not only aware of this "dull compulsion" but were counting on it. As Mat Isa noted, "They didn't *do* anything; it was only idle talk (*mulut saja*)."[15] Tok Kasim, whose stake in mechanization was higher because he was a machine broker as well as a farmer, realized the boycott would never be carried out, since "the poor have to work anyway; they can't hold out (*tahan*)." And Lebai Hussein said that, although they were "angry," the women could only talk about (*sembang-sembang saja*) a boycott, since they needed the money. He concluded with a Malay saying that precisely captured the difficulties the women faced: "Angry with their rice, they throw it out for the chickens to eat."[16] The closest English equivalent is "cutting off your nose to spite your face."

If we step back a few paces from our single village perspective, a wider and more melancholy pattern appears. The share groups of women in Sedaka were, in this same period, occasionally hired to transplant paddy fields as much as thirty miles away. Rosni told me that once a woman from Setiti Batu, where their share groups was planting, had told her that the farmer for whom they were working had not been able to recruit local transplanters because he had harvested last season with the combine. When she learned this, Rosni told the woman that she was "sick at heart" (*sakit hati*) but that the work was nearly finished anyway.[17] It is only too likely that there were similar cases as well. Thus, from this wider perspective, the poorer women of Sedaka were inadvertently serving as "strike-breakers" in other Muda villages. And women from these villages, or others like them, were undoubtedly coming to break the boycott in Sedaka. What we have here is a nearly classic example of the crippling effect of class action by peasants when it is confined, as it typically is, to one or a few villages in a much wider labor market.[18]

[…]

When the would-be boycotters and machine breakers of Sedaka spoke about their own experience or about the relative success of others, what one heard was not just a litany of discouragement and despair. There was also more than just a glimmer of what might have been (or might be) if the poor had acted with more unity and force. Thus Samad saw Permatang Buluh as something of an inspiration: "If we had done the same thing here, the machines wouldn't have come. It would have been good (*bagus*) if we had, but we weren't organized (*tak teratur*)."[19] Rokiah herself spoke with disdain of the share groups in Sedaka compared with Permatang Buluh: "Here they didn't want [to carry it through]." "If they had all agreed, if they had struck, [the machines] would not have been brave enough to come in."[20] Mansur, one of the few pure landless laborers in the village, echoed these sentiments precisely. "People here weren't unified; they were afraid and only followed [the rich]; if they were stronger, then they could lift themselves up." The same assessment of present disunity together with a faint promise of greater solidarity is evident when talk turned to the possibility that there will one day be transplanting machines that will replace the women. Bakri bin Haji Wahab said that if such machines came the women would then charge a dollar for uprooting each small bundle (*cap*) of seedlings from the nursery bed. "It could become a war," he added.[21] Then Ishak more realistically pointed out that if the women charged M$1 for each bundle then others would agree to do it for 90 cents, others for 80 cents or 70 cents and that "would be the end of it."

As the large farmers see it, the attempted boycott was "all talk" – virtually a "nonevent." There is something to this view, inasmuch as the boycott was never openly declared and collapsed without fanfare. The use of delays and barely plausible excuses meant that the intention to boycott itself could be disavowed. As the losers see it, however, it was an effort in the right direction that fell short. They are under no illusions about their own weak position or the obstacles in their path, but they do look to the modest successes elsewhere as something of a goad and inspiration.

"Routine" resistance

The attempt to halt combine-harvesting, while hardly the stuff of high drama, was at least out of the ordinary – a new, if largely futile, initiative. It took place against a rarely noticed background of routine resistance over wages, tenancy, rents, and the distribution of paddy that is a permanent feature of life in Sedaka and in any stratified agrarian setting. A close examination of this realm of struggle exposes an implicit form of local trade unionism that is reinforced both by mutuality among the poor and by a considerable amount of theft and violence against property. Very little of this activity, as we shall see, poses a fundamental threat to the basic structure of agrarian inequalities, either materially or symbolically. What it does represent, however, is a constant process of testing and renegotiation of production relations between classes. On both sides – landlord-tenant, farmer–wage laborer – there is a never-ending attempt to seize each small advantage and press it home, to probe the limits of the existing relationships, to see precisely what can be gotten away with at the margin, and to include this margin as a part of an accepted, or at least tolerated, territorial claim. Over the past decade the flow of this frontier battle has, of course, rather consistently favored the fortunes of the large farmers and landlords. They have not only swallowed large pieces of the territory defended by wage workers and tenants, but in doing so they have thereby reduced (through marginalization) the perimeter along which the struggle continues. Even along this reduced perimeter, however, there is constant pressure exerted by those who hope to regain at least a small patch of what they have grudgingly lost. The resisters require little explicit coordination to conduct this struggle, for the simple imperative of making a tolerable living is enough to make them dig in their heels.

My goal here is only to convey something of the dimensions and conduct of this routine resistance, not its full extent, for that could fill a volume in itself. Inasmuch as a great deal of this resistance concerns the disposition of the proceeds of paddy farming, the best place to begin is in the paddy field itself, with threshing.

Trade unionism without trade unions

Threshers, unlike reapers, are hired and paid by the farmer as individuals. They work in pairs at a single threshing tub and then divide the piece-rate earnings at the end of the day. In 1979, the average piece-rate per gunny sack was M$2. The piece-work organization of the work produces a conflict of interest between the thresher and the farmer whose paddy is being threshed. The farmer naturally wants *all* the rice from his field and, for that reason, prefers to have the threshers beat each bundle of cut paddy until virtually all the grains are in the tub. The thresher, in contrast, is interested in the cash he can earn for a day's work.[22] Depending on the ripeness of the paddy, roughly 80–90 percent of the grains are dislodged in the first two or three strokes. To dislodge most of the remaining paddy may require as many as six or seven strokes. The tub fills up faster, and the thresher earns more for the day's work, if he beats each sheaf only two or three times and moves quickly to the next sheaf.[23] If he were to work in this fashion, he might thresh as many as ten gunny sacks (M$20) in a day, compared with, say, M$10 or M$12 if he were to thresh each sheaf thoroughly. The difference is vital when one recalls that, for poor men, threshing is the best-paid work of the season, and there is a premium on making the most of it while it lasts. Nor does the conflict of interest between the thresher's wages and the farmer's paddy end here. A thresher can, in fact, recover the paddy he has left on the stalks if there is someone in his family who gleans. The more paddy poor men leave lying beside the threshing tubs, the more paddy the women in their household can collect once the harvest is over. This provides them with a further incentive to leave some behind.

[...]

Imposed mutuality

It would be apparent that even the modest forms of resistance mounted in Sedaka depend for their effect upon a certain degree of mutuality among the poor. That is, the first, and minimal, requirement of class solidarity is a negative one: that the poor at least refrain from undercutting one another and thereby further magnifying the considerable economic power of their employers and landlords. "Otherwise," as Marx notes, "they are on hostile terms with each other as competitors"[24] – surviving at one another's expense. The mutuality that exists can be seen in the refusal of other share groups or threshers to act as strikebreakers in the village. It exists, as we shall see, in the vital realm of tenancy, where those seeking land are unwilling to undercut their own neighbors. No extravagant claims can be made for this sanctioned self-restraint, inasmuch as it operates only within the confines of the village itself, and even in this context its operation is narrowly circumscribed.[25] It does, however, prevent the most damaging excesses of competition between the poor for the few opportunities available.[26]

Such minimal solidarity depends, here as elsewhere, not just on a seemly regard for one's fellows, but on the sanctions that the poor can bring to bear to keep one another in line. Since the temptation to break ranks is always alluring to members of a class that has chronic difficulty making ends meet, these sanctions must be powerful enough to prevent an ever immanent Hobbesian struggle among the poor. The modest level of restraint that has been achieved makes ample use of social sanctions such as gossip, character assassination, and public shunning. There is no surer way for poor men or women to call scorn upon themselves than to work at a lower wage than the prevailing rate or to take a job that "belongs" by custom to others. Nor is it merely a question of reputation, for the offender will find that he or she is shunned in labor exchange (*derau*), not included in share groups, not told about possibilities of finding work, denied the petty jobs that the poor can occasionally offer, and not invited to join "rotating credit associations" (*kut*) in their neighborhood. Each of these material sanctions, taken separately, is fairly trivial, but collectively they represent a potential loss of some magnitude. Nor is the threat of violence entirely absent from these sanctions, as we shall see. Thus, the poor man who is tempted to break ranks must measure very carefully his short-term gain against the losses his angry neighbors may be able to impose. By their opinion and by their sanctions, the poor have erected a set of customary prohibitions that symbolize the acceptable limits of self-seeking.

[...]

Self-help and/or enforcement

Thus far I have dealt largely with attempts at collective action – with "sanctions" that the poor bring to bear on their landlords and employers, as well as on themselves, to prevent a "dog-eat-dog" competition. There is, however, another realm of resistance that is more shadowy and individual; it includes a large variety of thefts and the murder of livestock. Inquiry into this realm is a necessarily delicate affair, inasmuch as the silence of most of the participants is compounded by an understandable desire on the part of the inquirer to avoid danger. Without ever pursuing this matter actively, a pattern of facts nevertheless emerged from casual listening over two years which suggested that such activities had implications for class relations and resistance.

Rural theft by itself is unremarkable; it is a nearly permanent feature of agrarian life whenever and wherever the state and its agents are insufficient to control it. When such theft takes on the dimensions of a struggle in which property rights are contested, however, it becomes essential to any careful analysis of class relations. Such was certainly the case for parts of England, where poaching was the most common – and the most popular – crime for at least two centuries, and in France, where Zola claimed without undue exaggeration that "Every peasant had a poacher hidden inside him."[27] Here the political and class meaning of poaching was perfectly evident, since the peasantry had never fully accepted the property rights of those who claimed ownership of the forests, streams, "wastes," and commons that had previously been the joint property of the community. Poaching was not simply a necessary subsistence option but an enactment of what was seen to be a natural right.[28]

Theft was far more common in Kedah before 1950 than it is today. Older residents of Sedaka can recall a time not so very long ago when the rustling of water buffalo was such a common occurrence that every man slept with a rope tied to his wrist that led through the floor to his water buffalo's nose beneath to alert him in case rustlers approached. They can also remember the names and exploits of the most famous rural bandits, such as Awang Poh, Saleh Tui, and Nayan, who acquired reputations as "social bandits," robbing from the rich and giving to the poor.[29] At that time, settlements were smaller and more scattered, and much uncleared brush and forest remained. This frontier quality of many Kedah districts, the weakness of rural police units, and the poverty and mobility of the peasantry all provided a hospitable environment for banditry and rustling.

Today neither the physical terrain nor the freedom from pursuit provide anything like a favorable setting for bandits with any large ambitions. All the land around Sedaka is flat and cultivated and the police in Kepala Batas and in Yan are far more numerous, mobile, and well armed. Nor is there the class provocation of a mere one or two huge landowners, who have monopolized virtually all of the land, facing a uniformly poor and united peasantry. The sort of theft one finds now in Sedaka reflects all these conditions; it is carried out anonymously under cover of darkness; it appears to be the work of individuals or, at most, pairs; it is what the police records would call "petty larceny."

All kinds of things disappear regularly in Sedaka. Fruit regularly disappears from trees and around the houses of wealthier farmers, and few expect to harvest more than half of their small crop of mangoes, papayas, fallen coconuts, or bananas. Those who have the palms whose leaves are required for making mats, baskets, or the traditional attap roofing regularly complain that fronds frequently disappear. Those who keep small livestock, such as chickens, ducks, or geese, complain that both the eggs and the fowl themselves are regularly pilfered. During the dry season, when drinking water is sporadically delivered in government tank trucks, the villagers must leave their plastic or metal water cans (*tong ayer*) near the main road to take advantage of unpredictable delivery. These containers, typically worth roughly M$5, are often stolen. On a somewhat larger scale there are occasional thefts of bicycles, water buffalo, and even motorcycles (three thefts in the last two years).

These petty, and not so petty, thefts have a pattern that is inscribed in the very social structure of the village. The targets are, with the possible exception of bicycles, the wealthier inhabitants of Sedaka. This is hardly surprising in view of the fact that it is the relatively well-to-do who are most likely to have the large house lot with fruit trees and palms, who have the largest number of water containers, who have the feed for small livestock, who are most likely to own a water buffalo or a motorcycle. The perpetrators, it is generally agreed, are to be found among Sedaka's poorer inhabitants. This pattern is not in itself proof that such thefts are conceived by the poor as a means of resistance or some form of "social banditry." Evidence on this score was simply unobtainable. What is significant, however, is that the class character of theft is built into the very property relations prevailing in Sedaka. The rich, by and large, possess what is worth taking, while the poor have the greatest incentive to take it. One is reminded of the reply of the American bank robber, "Slick" Willie Sutton, when he was asked why he robbed banks: "Because that's where the money is."

Apart from the disappearance of water buffalo and motorcycles, the other forms of pilfering we have encountered are deplored by well-off villagers, but they are more of a nuisance than a serious threat. Their concern is focused on the main product of this single-crop economy: paddy. For the would-be thief the advantages of stealing paddy are self-evident. It is all about him, it is easily taken in small quantities, and, once taken, it is virtually untraceable.

[...]

There is one final dimension to what may be termed clandestine and anonymous resistance in Sedaka. It finds expression in the killing of small and, more rarely, large livestock by the poor. Most of the village's ragtag collection of chickens, ducks, geese, goats, water buffalo, and three beef cattle are owned by well-to-do households. They pose a considerable nuisance to the poor in many ways. Although barriers and chicken wire are often used to bar them, they frequently forage into the nursery beds, paddy fields, and small gardens of the poor, doing considerable damage. The poor are, of course, not the only ones affected (the livestock have, as yet, no class loyalties themselves), but they are the ones most deeply angered. Their anger does not merely stem from the fact that they can least afford the loss; it grows from something that might be called a "moral economy of diet." What is at stake can be captured from Hamzah's complaints about Haji Kadir's chickens next door, which he frequently finds in his kitchen pecking rice through the small holes in the bags of rice stacked there. As Hamzah puts it, "His meat is eating my rice." Once we recall that Hamzah's family and many other poor families eat meat only when they are invited to a *kenduri*, the injustice is palpable. After a warning or two the recourse of the poor man is to kill the animal, as happens with some regularity. The fact that the animal is killed, not stolen, is an indication that this is a protest and not a theft.[30] Two of Haji Kadir's goats broke down the fence around Rokiah's small vegetable garden on the canal bund behind her house and ate everything except the watermelon. Her anger was put in nearly the same terms as Hamzah's: "Pak Haji's meat is eating my vegetables." One or two goats and quite a few chickens (more rarely ducks and geese) are found slashed or beaten to death annually.[31] Six years ago, Tok Long's water buffalo was found slashed with a *parang* and dying in a poor man's paddy field after having broken its tether. The "murderer" was never identified, but that particular water buffalo had been infamous for breaking loose and grazing in the ripening paddy. Double-cropping has, in this context, made matters appreciably worse by eliminating the long, dry off-season when livestock could roam the stubble without fear of damage. The fairly regular killing of livestock is, like the theft of grain, a petty affair that hardly touches the overall structure of property relations and power. But both of these acts of token resistance are among the few, relatively safe, methods of resistance open to peasants seeking to protect their hold on the means of subsistence.[32]

Prototype resistance

My concern with the forms of resistance available to the poor has excluded any consideration of a host of conflicts and strategies that have little or no direct bearing on local class relations. Thus, for example, I have not dealt with the many disputes over water rights or with the ways in which land may be appropriated by moving boundary markers or by gradually shifting the bunds in one's field to add another row of paddy at the neighbor's expense. Nor have I examined the resistance of the village as a whole to the Islamic tithe or to other government initiatives affecting all paddy farmers. The resistance of the rich would itself make for a fascinating inquiry that could fill volumes. While I have described some aspects of their resistance as it relates to wages, employment, and tenure, it takes many other forms that contribute to their domination of both local institutions and the local economy.[33] Whatever place resistance in this larger sense might justifiably occupy in a full account of social relations in Sedaka, it is marginal to my main objective.

The diverse forms of resistance by the poor that I have examined bear certain distinguishing marks. Whether it is a matter of resistance to combine-harvesting, wage negotiations, the effort to prevent ruinous competition among the poor, theft, or the murder of livestock, the relative absence of any open confrontation between classes is striking. Where resistance is collective, it is carefully circumspect; where it is an individual or small group attack on property, it is anonymous and usually nocturnal.[34] By its calculated prudence and secrecy it preserves, for the most part, the onstage theater of power that dominates public life in Sedaka. Any intention to storm the stage can be disavowed and options are consciously kept open. Deference and conformity, though rarely cringing, continue to be the public posture of the poor. For all that, however, one can clearly make out backstage a continuous testing of limits. At the very least, one can say that there is much more here than simply consent, resignation, and deference.

Resistance in Sedaka has virtually nothing that one expects to find in the typical history of rural conflict. There are no riots, no demonstrations, no arson, no organized social banditry, no open violence. The resistance I have discovered is not linked to any larger outside political movements, ideologies, or revolutionary cadres, although it is clear that similar struggles have been occurring in virtually every village in the region. The sorts of activities found here require little coordination, let alone political organization, though they might benefit from it. They are, in short, forms of struggle that are almost entirely indigenous to the village sphere. Providing that we are careful about the use of the term, these activities might appropriately be called *primitive* resistance, or perhaps *ur* resistance. The use of *primitive* does not imply, as Hobsbawm does, that they are somehow backward and destined to give way to more sophisticated ideologies and tactics.[35] It implies only that such forms of resistance are the nearly permanent, continuous, daily strategies of subordinate rural classes under difficult conditions. At times of crisis or momentous political change, they may be complemented by other forms of struggle that are more opportune. They are unlikely, however, to disappear altogether so long as the rural social structure remains exploitive and inequitable. They are the stubborn bedrock upon which other forms of resistance may grow, and they are likely to persist after such other forms have failed or produced, in turn, a new pattern of inequity.

[…]

Routine compliance and resistance that covers its tracks

[…]

In this respect, there is a striking analogy between routine compliance and routine resistance. If routine compliance is conducted with a calculating eye to the structure of power and rewards in the village, so is routine resistance. If routine compliance avoids unnecessary risks, so does routine resistance. Nearly all the resistance we have encountered in Sedaka is the kind of resistance that rather effectively "covers its own tracks." A snub on the village path can be excused later by haste or inattention. What appears to be a boycott of transplanting can be rationalized as a delay or difficulties in assembling the work force. And, of course, acts of theft, sabotage, and vandalism have no authors at all. Thus, while there is a fair amount of resistance in Sedaka, there are virtually no publicly announced resisters or troublemakers.

Even the more purely symbolic resistance – malicious gossip, character assassination, nicknames, rumors – we have examined follows the same pattern.[36] Gossip, after all, is almost by definition a story told about an absent third party; once launched, it becomes an anonymous tale with no author but many retailers. Although it is by no means a respecter of persons, malicious gossip *is* a respecter of the larger normative order within which it operates. Behind every piece of gossip that is not merely news is an implicit statement of a rule or norm that has been broken. It is in fact only the violation of expected behavior that makes an event worth gossiping about. The rule or norm in question is often only formulated or brought to consciousness by the violation itself. Deviance, in this sense, defines what is normal. Thus, no one may pay attention to the prevailing code of dress until it is breached and thereby provokes a statement of what is proper.[37] Rules of grammar, only implicitly known, pass unnoticed until a speaker or writer makes an obvious misstep. Much of the gossip and character assassination that are relevant to class relations in Sedaka are an appeal by the poor to norms of tenancy, generosity, charity, employment, and feasts that were taken for granted before double-cropping. At the same time that a reputation is slandered by gossip, a rule that was once generally accepted is being affirmed and promoted. Gossip is never "disinterested"; it is a partisan effort (by class, faction, family) to advance its claims and interests against those of others. But this manipulation of the rules can only be successful to the extent that an appeal is made to standards of conduct that are generally accepted. Gossip thus accomplishes its malicious work as an admittedly weak social sanction by remaining more or less *within* the established normative framework. In this respect the use of gossip by the poor also manifests a kind of prudence and respect, however manipulative, of its own.

As a form of resistance, then, gossip is a kind of democratic "voice" in conditions where power and possible repression make open acts of disrespect dangerous. The rich, of course, are far freer to show openly their contempt for the "undeserving poor." For the poor, however, gossip achieves the expression of opinion, of contempt, of disapproval while minimizing the risks of identification and reprisal. Malicious gossip symbolically chips away at the reputations of the rich in Sedaka in the same fashion that anonymous thefts in the night materially chip away at the property of the rich. The overall impact on the structure of power of this nibbling away is not very appreciable. But it is one of the few means available to a subordinate class to clothe the practice of resistance with the safe disguise of outward compliance.

[...]

What is resistance?

We have encountered a bewildering array of resistance and compliance within Sedaka. It is no simple matter to determine just where compliance ends and resistance begins, as the circumstances lead many of the poor to clothe their resistance in the public language of conformity. If one takes the dictionary definition of the verb *to resist* – "to exert oneself so as to withstand or counteract the force or effect of..." – how is one to categorize the subtle mixture of outward compliance and tentative resistance involved in the attempted boycott of combine-using farmers? So far as the public record is concerned, it never happened and yet, at another level, it was a labor strike, albeit one that failed. There are still other problems. Can individual acts such as theft or the murder of livestock be considered resistance even though they involve no collective action and do not openly challenge the basic structure of property and domination? Can largely symbolic acts such as boycotting feasts or defaming reputations be called resistance, although they appear to make little or no dent in the distribution of resources? Behind each of these queries is the prior question, "What is resistance?" More accurately stated – since definitions are analytical tools and not ends in themselves – what, for my purposes, can usefully be considered acts of resistance?

At a first approximation, I might claim that class resistance includes *any* act(s) by member(s) of a subordinate class that is or are *intended* either to mitigate or deny claims (for example, rents, taxes, prestige) made on that class by superordinate classes (for example, landlords, large farmers, the state) or to advance its own claims (for example, work, land, charity, respect) vis-à-vis those super-ordinate classes. While this definition, as we shall see, is not without problems, it does have several advantages. It focuses on the material basis of class relations and class struggle. It allows for both individual and collective acts of resistance. It does not exclude those forms of ideological resistance that challenge the dominant definition of the situation and assert different standards, of justice and equity. Finally, it focuses on intentions rather than consequences, recognizing that many acts of resistance may fail to achieve their intended result.

Where there is strong evidence for the intention behind the act, the case for resistance is correspondingly strengthened. Thus it is reasonably clear that the women in the share groups intended to deny machine users transplanting services and thereby force them to revert to hand harvesting. The mutuality among the poor that prevents them competing for tenancies is also clearly intended to prevent a scramble that would eventually harm all tenants. In each case, the intentions are not inferred directly from the action but rather from the explanations the participants give for their behavior. For "speech acts," such as character assassination or malicious gossip directed against wealthy villagers, the act and the intention are fused into one whole; the condemnations of the stingy rich have inscribed within them the intention to recall them to a different standard of conduct or, failing that, to destroy their social standing and influence.

The insistence that acts of resistance must be *shown* to be intended, however, creates enormous difficulties for a whole realm of peasant activity which, in Sedaka and elsewhere, has often been considered resistance. Take, for example, the question of theft or pilferage. What are we to call the poor man in Sedaka who "appropriates" a gunny sack of paddy from a rich man's field: a thief, *tout court*, or a resister as well? What are we to call the act of a thresher who takes care to leave plenty of paddy on the stalks for his wife and children who will glean tomorrow: an act of petty pilfering or an act of resistance? There are two problems here. The first is the practical problem of obtaining evidence of the intentions behind the act, of what it means for the actor. The very nature of the enterprise is such that the actor is unlikely to admit to the action itself, let alone explain what he had in mind. That some poor men in Sedaka considered such thefts to be a kind of self-help *zakat* gift may count as circumstantial evidence that such thieves see themselves as taking what is theirs by right, but it is hardly decisive. Thus, while it may be possible to uncover a set of beliefs shared by a class that legitimize theft or pilfering, it will rarely be possible to uncover the beliefs of the actor in question. The "transcript" of petty thieves, especially those not yet apprehended, is notoriously hard to come by.

The second problem concerns broader issues of definition and analysis. We tend to think of resistance as actions that involve at least some short-run individual or collective sacrifice in order to bring about a longer-range, beneficial goal. The immediate losses of a strike, a boycott, or even the refusal to compete with other members of one's class for land or work are obvious cases in point. When it comes to acts like theft, however, we encounter a combination of immediate individual gain and what *may* be resistance. How are we to judge which of the two purposes is uppermost or decisive? What is at stake is not a petty definitional matter but rather the interpretation of a whole range of actions that seem to me to lie historically at the core of everyday class relations.

[...]

If we were to confine our search for peasant resistance to formally organized activity, we would search largely in vain, for in Malaysia as in many other Third World countries, such organizations are either absent or the creations of officials and rural elites. We would simply miss much of what is happening. The history of Malay peasant resistance to the state, for example, has yet to be written. When, and if, it is written, however, it will not be a history in which open rebellion or formal organizations play a significant role. The account of resistance in the precolonial era would perhaps be dominated by flight and avoidance of corvée labor and a host of tolls and taxes. Resistance to colonial rule was marked far less by open confrontations than by willful and massive noncompliance with its most threatening aspects, for example, the persistent underreporting of land-holdings and crop yields to minimize taxes, the relentless disregard for all regulations designed to restrict smallholders' rubber planting and marketing, the unabated pioneer settlement of new land despite a host of laws forbidding it. Much of this continues today. There is ample evidence for this resistance in the archives,[38] but, inasmuch as its goal was to evade the state and the legal order, not to attack them, it has received far less historical attention than the quite rare and small revolts that had far less impact on the course of colonial rule. Even in advanced capitalist nations, the "movements" of the poor take place largely outside the sphere of formal political activity.[39] It follows that, if a persuasive case can be made for such forms of political activity among the poor in highly industrialized, urban economies with high rates of literacy and a relatively open political system, the case would be far stronger for the peasantry in agrarian economy where open political activity is sharply restricted. Formal political activity may be the norm for the elites, the intelligentsia, and the middle classes which, in the Third World as well as in the West, have a near monopoly of institutional skills and access. But it would be naive to expect that peasant resistance can or will normally take the same form.

Notes

1 As a recently sacked factory worker once remarked ruefully to me, "The only thing worse than being exploited is *not* being exploited."

2 It goes virtually without saying that the meager possibilities for joint action among the village poor all but evaporate once we leave the community. Even the values that the poor use to justify their claim to work, land, and charity are meant to apply largely within the village itself. While kinship links join most of the poor to relatives elsewhere, these are links of family and not of class. If there were a national or even regional political vehicle that gave effective voice to the class interests of the poor on such issues as land reform, mechanization, and employment, it would undoubtedly find a large following. But Partai Islam (PAS) is not that vehicle, dominated as it is by large landowners, and the socialist party (Partai Rakyat), for reasons of repression and communalism, has never established a real foothold in Kedah.

3 Barrington Moore, Jr., *Injustice: The Social Bases of Obedience and Revolt* (White Plains: M. E. Sharpe, 1978), 125.

4 For an illuminating discussion of this pattern in the region generally, see Michael Adas, "From Avoidance to Confrontation: Peasant Protest in Precolonial and Colonial Southeast Asia," *Comparative Studies in Society and History* 23, no. 2 (April 1981): 217–47.

5 The terms "exit" and "voice" are taken from the analysis in Albert O. Hirschman, *Exit, Voice, and Loyalty: Responses to Decline in Firms, Organizations and States* (Cambridge, Mass.: Harvard Univ. Press, 1970).

6 Malaysia's strong foreign-exchange position and its diversified exports make it less vulnerable than many other Third World economies, but it is nevertheless vulnerable to any deep and prolonged slump. Shortfalls in private investment and in export earnings and the resulting need to trim public spending over the past two years (1981–82) have made this vulnerability increasingly apparent.

7 Karl Marx, *Capital*, vol. 1 (Harmondsworth: Penguin, 1970): 737.

8 Nicholas Abercrombie, Stephen Hill, and Bryan S. Turner, *The Dominant Ideology Thesis* (London: Allen & Unwin, 1980), 46. In their analysis of feudalism, early capitalism, and late capitalism these three authors present a persuasive case that the concept of "the dominant ideology" or "hegemony," as expounded by such well-known contemporary Marxist scholars as Althusser, Poulantzas, Miliband, and Habermas, are neither logically convincing nor empirically persuasive. I will return to the issue of "hegemony" and "false-consciousness" in the next chapter.

9 Emile Durkheim, *The Division of Labour in Society* (New York: Free Press, 1964), 356, quoted in Abercrombie *et al.*, *Dominant Ideology Thesis*, 43.

10 For two studies which, in different contexts, emphasize both repression and "the compulsion of economic relations," see Juan Martinez Alier, *Labourers and Landowners in Southern Spain*, St. Anthony's College, Oxford, Publications, No. 4 (London: Allen & Unwin, 1971), and John Gaventa, *Power and Powerlessness: Quiescence and Rebellion in an Appalachian Valley* (Urbana: Univ. of Illinois Press, 1980).

11 For the now classic study of this movement, see E. J. Hobsbawn and George Rude, *Captain Swing* (New York: Pantheon, 1968). Without attempting an inevitably strained comparison, I note that the rural Luddites of the early nineteenth century had several advantages over the peasantry of Kedah when it came to mobilizing against threshing machines. They were far more fully proletarianized and dependent on wage labor; they could look to a set of traditional legal protections that reinforced their claim to a living wage; and they faced a repressive apparatus that was less firmly planted in the countryside. They too, of course, were overcome, but only by a military force that by the standards of the time was unprecedented. The resistance in Kedah was much more sporadic and abbreviated, although the saboteurs shared with their English counterparts a preference for the anonymity that acting under cover of darkness provided. By 1979, public warnings by officials and more rigorous guarding of the machines themselves had reduced the incidence of this form of resistance to negligible proportions.

12 Broadcasting (*tabor kering*) only began to pose a serious threat to hand transplanting by 1979 or 1980.

13 Rosni, as we have noted, is a widow, while Rokiah's husband is considered rather weak-minded, so that Rokiah is normally seen as the head of her household, making all the basic decisions. Such women, especially if they are past child-bearing age, are treated virtually as "honorary" males and are exempt from many of the customary requirements of modesty and deference expected of women in Malay society.

14 Not all farmers in Sedaka that season could be neatly classified either as combine hirers or share-group hirers, since at least four farmers had used the combine for one plot and hand labor for another. In two cases, these were decisions based on the ripeness of the crops in each field when the combine was available or the inability of the machine to harvest a given plot (because it was on soft, waterlogged land or because it was surrounded by plots or unripe paddy). In the remaining two cases, the decision was almost certainly an attempt by the farmer to hedge his bets and avoid the threatened boycott.

15 He then concluded by saying *padi tumpah*, which, literally, means "spilled paddy," but its idiomatic sense would perhaps best be expressed by the English "just chaff" (as opposed to wheat).

16 *Marah sama nasi, tauk, bagi ayam makan.*

17 The fact that the paddy field they were planting belonged to the brother of one of the women in the share group further complicated matters.

18 This serves as a salutary reminder of the limitations of local or village studies that treat only local fragments of class which stretch over wider areas and whose members are unknown personally to

one another. A more accurate view of class would in fact include not only a spatial dimension but a temporal one as well, as the class of tenants as a concept must include those who have ever had this status in the past as well as those who are tenants today. The spatial dimension of class by itself may, in this context, seem to argue for the role of an elite or intelligentsia to coordinate and unify its fragmented action. As we shall see later, this conclusion is not necessarily warranted.

19 *Teratur* might in this context be translated also as "disciplined."

20 *Kalau berpakat, kalau mogok, tak berani masuk.* The term *mogok* is the standard Malay word for "strike."

21 *Boleh jadi perang.*

22 This is especially the case if the season is a busy one and other threshing jobs are available when the current one is finished. Frequently threshing work is in fact morning work rather than day-long work, since the job is so physically demanding that the day begins at dawn and ends early in the afternoon. If the moon is bright, threshing is occasionally done in the evening to take advantage of the cool temperatures.

23 There is also, to be sure, an element of competition among the threshers as well if we see each pair competing to thresh as much as possible of the paddy in a given field.

24 Karl Marx, *Pre-Capitalist Economic Formations*, trans. Jack Cohen, with an Introduction by E. J. Hobsbawm (London: London & Wishart, 1964), 133.

25 Thus, for example, while a share group will not agree to replace its "striking" colleagues, it will accept work the following season from a large farmer who wishes to hire a new group to replace those who gave him trouble the previous season.

26 What prevails in Sedaka is a variant of what Alier has called "union" in Southern Spain. As he describes it, "Labourers use the word *union* when trying to explain the existence of norms which make obligatory – or at least commendable – ways of behaving which aim at maintaining or increasing wages, or at reducing unemployment. These ways of behaving are, on many occasions opposed to the individual workers interest, and they may even entail some risk or sacrifice." While such norms are occasionally violated, they appear to work best in small villages. Thus a laborer told Alier, "It is very rare to work for less than the prevailing wage, in this village, because it is small and people know each other. They do not do it; they would be badly looked upon." Alier, *Labourers and Landowners in Southern Spain*, 122, 136.

27 Emile Zola, *The Earth*, trans. Douglas Parmee (Harmondsworth: Penguin, 1980), 317. For additional literary evidence from rural France, see Honoré de Balzac, *Les Paysans* (Paris: Pleiades, 1949). For English material, see Douglas Hay, "Poaching and the Game Laws on Cannock Chase," in *Albion's Fatal Tree: Crime and Society in Eighteenth-Century England*, by Douglas Hay, Peter Linebaugh, John G. Rule, E. P. Thompson, and Cal Winslow (New York: Pantheon, 1975), 189–253.

28 Marx is said to have told Engels that "it was the study of the law on the theft of wood and the situation of the Mosell peasantry that led him to pass from a purely political viewpoint to the study of economy and from that to socialism." Peter Linebaugh, "Karl Marx, The Theft of Wood, and Working Class Composition: A Contribution to the Current Debate," *Crime and Social Justice* 6 (Fall–Winter, 1976): 5–16.

29 See Cheah Boon Kheng's excellent account of Nayan and Saleh Tui in "Social Banditry and Rural Crime in Kedah, 1910–1929: Historical and Folk Perceptions" (Paper presented to Conference of International Association of Historians of Asia, Kuala Lumpur, 1980).

30 Chickens are stolen as well but not in cases like this. When they are stolen they must be sold, for the smell of chicken cooking in a poor man's compound would be a dead giveaway.

31 Not having been slaughtered by bleeding (*sembelih*) in the proper way, such animals cannot be eaten by Muslims even if they are discovered immediately after death.

32 For a fascinating analysis of rural crime and disorder on a much larger, but still uncoordinated, scale, see Neil B. Weissman, "Rural Crime in Tsarist Russia: The Question of Hooliganism, 1905–1914," *Slavic Review* 37, no. 2 (1978): 228–40.

33 The way in which the rich farmers are able to turn government policies and programs – loan programs, the state fertilizer subsidy, development subsidies, school admissions, settlement scheme applications, small-business subsidies, licenses for rice mills and taxis, government employment – to their advantage would constitute the core of any such analysis.

34 For some interesting parallels, see Thompson, "The Crime of Anonymity," in *Albion's Fatal Tree*, by Hay *et al.*, 255–344.

35 See E. J. Hobsbawm's *Primitive Rebels: Studies in Archaic Forms of Social Movement in the 19th and 20th Centuries* (New York: Norton, 1965). Hobsbawm's otherwise illuminating account is, I believe,

burdened unduly with a unilinear theory of lower-class history which anticipates that every primitive form of resistance will in due course be superseded by a more progressive form until a mature
Marxist–Leninist vision is reached.

36 I am indebted here to the discussion of gossip in John Beard Haviland, *Gossip, Reputation, and
Knowledge in Zinacantan* (Chicago: Univ. of Chicago Press, 1977).

37 Ibid., 160.

38 Tax evasion is evident from the steady reports of land tax arrears from Kedah and from indica-
tions of systematic misreporting of yields. Thus, Unfederated Malay States, *Annual Report of the
Advisor to the Kedah Government, 1921* (Alor Setar: Government Printer, 1922), 38, notes, "The padi
planter regards with suspicion the collection of statistics as a possible basis for further taxation and
minimizes his harvest." The *Report* for May 1930 to May 1931 puts the underreporting between 15
and 18 percent (p. 8), in some districts at nearly 50 percent (p. 55). For evasion of the rubber restriction schemes from 1913 until World War II, see Lim Teck Ghee, *Peasants and Their Agricultural
Economy in Colonial Malaya, 1874–1941* (Kuala Lumpur: Oxford Univ. Press, 1977), and Donald M.
Nonini, Paul Diener, and Eugene E. Robkin, "Ecology and Evolution: Population, Primitive
Accumulation, and the Malay Peasantry" (Typescript, 1979).

39 "Whatever the intellectual sources of error, the effect of equating movements with movement
organizations – and thus requiring that protests have a leader, a constitution, a legislative program,
or at least a banner before they are recognized as such – is to divert attention from many forms of
political unrest and to consign them by definition to the more shadowy realms of social problems
and deviant behavior. As a result such events as massive school truancy or rising worker absen-
teeism or mounting applications for public welfare or spreading rent defaults rarely attract the
attention of political analysts. Having decided by definitional fiat that nothing political has
occurred, nothing has to be explained, at least not in terms of political protest." Frances Fox Piven
and Richard A. Cloward, *Poor People's Movements: Why They Succeed, How They Fail* (New York:
Vintage, 1977), 5.

35 Political boundaries, poetic transgressions

Roland Bleiker

Source: Roland Bleiker (2000), *Popular Dissent, Human Agency and Global Politics*, Cambridge: Cambridge University Press, pp. 244–272

[. . .] Poetry is unique, and offers valuable insight, insofar as it engages the relationship between language and socio-political reality in a highly self-conscious manner. This is why it is worthwhile to preoccupy oneself with a form of speaking and writing whose impact remains confined, in most cases, to a small literary audience. What one can learn from observing poetic subversions of linguistically entrenched forms of domination can facilitate understanding, at least to some extent, of how dissent functions in more mundane daily contexts, which, by definition, mostly elude the eyes and ears of intellectual observers.

This chapter illustrates the potential and limits of poetic dissent by engaging in one more rereading of the events that led to the collapse of the Berlin Wall. The focus now lies with a young generation of poets that emerged in the late 1970s and flourished, mostly underground, until the communist regime began to disintegrate in late 1989. Epitomising the activities of this generation is the area around Prenzlauer Berg, a run-down workers' quarter in East Berlin which, during the 1980s, turned into a Bohemian artist and literary scene. Out of it emerged a counter-culture, a kind of ersatz public sphere that opened up possibilities for poetry readings, art exhibitions, film showings and the publication of various unofficial magazines. Handwritten at times, they were produced in only small editions; copies were passed on directly from person to person.

Vibrant and symbolic as the Bohemian underground scene at Prenzlauer Berg was, it soon came to stand as a metaphor to capture the spirit of an entire generation of East German writers. It must be noted, however, that underground scenes developed in other cities too, in Dresden and Leipzig, for instance. The poets of the 1980s were a heterogeneous group of individuals, whose visions and forms of expression cannot be lumped together into a common movement, or even be captured with the term 'generation'. They ranged from urban punks to rural housewives, from poets who were able to publish their texts in an officially sanctioned form (in the East or West) to those many more who were driven out of the public sphere.

The spirit of the young poets revolved, by and large, around an intensive engagement with the spatial and linguistic constitution of the society they lived in. The contention of boundaries became, as Karen Leeder emphasises, the central theme of Prenzlauer Berg poetry. This ubiquitous theme not only expresses an awareness of boundaries, namely 'encroaching political and geographical horizons, walls, barriers, frontiers, perimeters, barbed wire, stone – but also a yearning for the open spaces beyond'.[1]

It is this *Entgrenzung*, this breaking out of boundaries, this yearning for a world beyond the spatial givenness of Cold War politics, that rendered Prenzlauer Berg poetry inherently transversal. The poets of the 1980s shaped and were shaped by various cross-territorial struggles. Many of their texts were influenced by images projected through Western mass media, by recent trends in French literary theory, or by a range of other discursive aspects that transgressed the Iron Curtain and penetrated East German society despite the government's attempt to shield its population from such subversive influences. The work of the poets, in turn, generated similar crossterritorial dynamics. It led to various reactions from the outside world that put pressure back on the East German government.

The poems written at Prenzlauer Berg are forms of transversal dissent, for they not only traverse boundaries but, to borrow from David Campbell, they also 'are about those boundaries, their erasure or inscription, and the identity formations to which they give rise'.[2] This discursive subversion of political boundaries seems, at first sight, void of direct political significance. Dissent, for most of the Prenzlauer Berg poets, was apolitical. As opposed to previous generations of dissident writers, they did not directly engage the authoritarian regime. The purpose was, rather, to elude its political and linguistic spell altogether. Instead of getting entangled in the agitation that permeates heated political manoeuvrings, dissent was supposed to engage the forces that had already framed the issue, circumvented the range of discussions and thus pre-empted fundamental political debates. Dissent thus dealt with language, with the discursive construction and objectification of Cold War political realities.

Some authors advance rather bold claims on behalf of the Prenzlauer Berg poets. David Bathrick, for instance, believes that they succeeded in creating a counter-public sphere that challenged the one-dimensionality of the official political discourse. They were part of a literary intelligentsia whose activities, he stresses, 'contributed to the process of peaceful social change, even "revolution" in [East Germany]'.[3] Although Bathrick's arguments are compelling, it is too early to suggest, in a definitive manner and backed up with concrete evidence, that the poets of the 1980s have directly contributed to the fall of the Berlin Wall. Too diffused are the links between cause and effect to endow an underground and thus relatively marginal literary movement with such revolutionary credentials. But this is not to say that poetic forms of dissent were ineffective. The literary scene of the 1980s undoubtedly exerted a transversal form of human agency. The challenge now consists of recognising the complexities through which these poetic activities have possibly shaped socio-political dynamics. Needless to say, such a momentous task cannot possibly be laid to rest in a chapter-length inquiry.

The purpose of this chapter is thus limited to a micro-level study that illustrates, through a few selective examples, how a group of poets struggled with the discursive boundaries of the society they lived in; how this struggle took on transversal dimensions; and how these dimensions challenged the spatial constitution of Cold War politics. The analysis begins by introducing the context within which the East German poetry scene of the 1980s emerged. By closely reading and examining passages of several poems, I then demonstrate how a deliberate stretching, even violating, of linguistic conventions can open up spaces to think and act. The limits of this process will be outlined in relation to damaging revelations that document how the Prenzlauer Berg subculture had, after all, been penetrated by the *Staatssicherheit*, the state's notorious security service.

The politics of living in a socio-linguistic order

Most observers of Cold War politics stress that East Germany was characterised by an unusual absence of prominent dissident intellectuals. The communist regime in Berlin never had to deal with critics as outspoken as, say, Alexander Solzhenitsyn, Vaclav Havel or Adam

Michnik.[4] The absence of radical dissidents is said to have multiple reasons. Among the older generation of East German writers the regime enjoyed a certain level of legitimacy because several of its leaders, including Erich Honecker, had stood at the forefront of the fight against fascism. Many intellectuals also shared the desire to find a societal order more just and egalitarian than capitalism. The dissidents that did exist were therefore often not radicals – they wanted to reform the communist system, rather than destroy it altogether. Some poets, playwrights and novelists took a more confrontational line during the 1960s and 1970s. But most of them ended up, for one reason or another, in West Germany – a country that could provide them not only with political, but also with linguistic asylum. A case in point is the forceful expatriation, in 1976, of the prominent satirist and songwriter Wolf Biermann.[5]

The writings of the subsequent generation of East German authors emerged in response to a new set of issues. Those who were active in the poetry scene of the 1980s differed sharply from previous East German intellectuals, in part because they had actually been born into an already existing socialist edifice; that is, as opposed to their fathers and mothers, the writers of Prenzlauer Berg did not witness the spread of fascism, the end of the war and the division of their country into two separate states. They were born in the 1950s and 1960s, long after the post-war redrawing of geopolitical maps. Theirs was a struggle for meaning, a desire to think and live outside the prescribed boundaries of political and social acceptability. Uwe Kolbe, one of the most active poets at Prenzlauer Berg, explains in his much cited 'Born into it':

Tall wide green land,
Fence-scattered plain.
Red
Sun-tree at the horizon.
The wind is mine
And mine the birds.

Small green land narrow,
Barbed-wire-landscape.
Black
Tree besides me.
Harsh wind.
Strange birds.[6]

There is disillusionment in these lines, an unresolved tension between youthful dreams and the realities in which they have failed to materialise. There is a clear recognition of boundaries, and the painful impositions they have imposed on people's lives. One can hear the frustrated voice of an individual who simply wanted to live his life. Nothing more. Nothing less.

Born into the political boundaries of an already existing socialist order meant a variety of things: born into a country that built walls to keep its citizens from voting with their feet; born into a bi-polar vision of global politics; born into a dichotomy of barbed-wirelandscapes on the inside and a vast, mostly unseen world on the outside; born into a political idea at a time when its contradictions became increasingly visible; born into a society that had, despite its crumbling foundations, allegedly solved all major social problems and arrived, so to speak, at the end of history. There was nothing left to deal with, except the immobility of daily routines. Kurt Drawert, trying to figure out how to live a historical moment that was not his:

What was it worth, my
presence in an already thought through world,

ordered, in definitions, tables,
headlines delivered?
Ready-made-conditions and ready-made-judgements.
History was over. The present

was over, the future, the revolution,
the answers were over.[7]

Drawert, like many of his fellow poets, searched for an 'I' in a void, for a purpose in a world where the individual had no more historical task to fulfil. The frustration of feeling homeless at home was only amplified by a perceived lack of alternatives. It was this loss of meaning and the attempt at working through it, futile as it may have seemed at times, that provided the younger writers with a poetic raison d'être.

One could say that the dilemmas they dealt with arose from being born into a language whose boundaries had already circumscribed the range of their possible experiences. The language they had was simply not adequate to express their agonies, frustrations and confusions, in short, the world they lived in. Neither did it permit the development of a critical attitude towards either domestic or international politics.

The existing language had thrown sheet after sheet of silence over a generation of writers long before even one of its members could have raised her voice in protest. 'People are formed by language – if one has devoured the language, then one has eaten the order as well', says the poet Stefan Dörig.[8] Uwe Kolbe goes even further. The frustration of being sucked into the political vortex of an existing language led him to believe that there had never been an authentic opposition in East Germany. This, he claimed, was true of prominent dissident writers like Christa Wolf, Heiner Müller, Rudolf Bahro and Wolf Biermann. Although some of them were imprisoned and suffered extensively as a result of their opposition to the authoritarian regime, they cannot be considered genuine opposition because they articulated their critique from within the dominant world-view, and especially from within the dominant Marxist language.[9] Kolbe may have somewhat overstated the case, but he was certainly not the only one who struggled with the inadequacy of the language the younger generation had inherited. Two poetic examples. Kurt Drawert:

> I did not want to speak like my father (or grandfather, for instance)...to use this language would have been a form of subjugation...I felt that whenever father (or grandfather, for instance) spoke, it was not really father (or, for instance, grandfather) who spoke, but something distant, strange, external, something that merely used his (or her) voice...I had no choice but to speak and thus to be forced into misunderstandings or lies, to feel observed, influenced and dominated by something distant, strange and external.[10]

Jayne-Ann (formerly Bernt) Igel uses a more lyrical form to emphasise the silences that are imposed by the inadequacies of existing speech forms. S/he was among those who not only struggled for voice, but also voiced the very process of this struggle. 'The Pupil':

> was i caught forever, as i learned their language, my
> voice a bird-squeak, keeping me under their spell; they held
> me near the house like a vine, whose shoots they clip
> ped, so that they do not darken the rooms

and close to the wall of the house i played, under the light
of drying sheets, the fingers pierced through the plaster, i
did not want to miss the personified sound of my name, which
smelled like urine; those who carried my name in their mouth,
held me by the neck with their teeth[11]

Igel refuses to close a question ('was I caught forever, as I learned their language') with an appropriate question mark. One is inevitably thrown into a continuous questioning mood that lasts until the end of the poem. The sense of suspense is further accentuated by the fact that Igel merges sentences with commas, semi-colons or a simple 'and' where they normally would be terminated with a full stop. Indeed, the suspense of the initial question even continues beyond the end of the poem, for Igel refuses to close it with any sort of punctuation. The desperate scream 'was i caught forever, as i learned their language' echoes long after the last word is read.

Needed: a radical critique of language that could pierce through the plaster of existing speech, break its spell, slip away from the linguistic teeth drilled into one's neck. Needed: language that is not a vine, confined to the wall of the house and constantly trimmed, but a freestanding and freely growing tree, pushing its branches up into the open sky.

Transgressing the boundaries of normalised thought

The younger generation of East German poets stretched the boundaries of language with a high degree of self-awareness. They assumed that language had to be critiqued before one could even begin to critique the social and political structures of domestic or international politics. This is why the notion of *Sprachkritik*, presented in the previous chapter, became the key feature around which the literary scene at Prenzlauer Berg revolved.[12]

Poetry is critique of language *par excellence*. A poem is a conscious transgression of existing linguistic conventions, a protest against an established language game and the systems of exclusion that are embedded in it. In this sense poetry sets itself apart from prose because it negates, not by chance or as a side effect, but because it cannot do otherwise, because this is what poetry is all about.[13] A poet renders strange that which is familiar and thus forces the reader to confront what s/he habitually has refused to confront. For Julia Kristeva, poetic language disturbs, transgresses rules, fractures meaning. In doing so it 'breaks up the inertia of language habits' and 'liberates the subject from a number of linguistic, psychic, and social networks'.[14] Nicole Brossard argues likewise that poetic practices, such as shaking the syntax, breaking grammatical rules, disrespecting punctuation and using blank space, have a profound effect on readers. They offer new perspectives on reality and make room for alternative ways of perceiving life and its meanings.[15]

By trying to break through the existing web of language and power, the young East German poets of the 1980s purposely wrote in ways that violated both poetological traditions and guidelines of ideological correctness. They tried to 'formulate what language does not yet contain'.[16] They searched for ways of expression that go 'beyond the vocabulary of power and assimilation'.[17] In some sense these experiments with language were simply meant to shock, to serve as an avant-gardist confrontation with the establishment. But many of the poems undoubtedly did more than just provoke. They sought to articulate a different form of dissent.

The poetic and political purpose of the Prenzlauer Berg writers was no longer to critique the existing system in order to replace it with something else, a superior ideology or a more adequate way of advancing the old one. The writer was no longer supposed to confront the system, as most previous dissidents had seen their vocation, but to refuse it, to step outside of it altogether. Years of dialogue had led nowhere. Resistance was now perceived to be a matter of eluding the system altogether, of breaking the old dichotomy of dissident/collaborator. Elke Erb, the co-editor of an influential early anthology of works by the young authors of the 1980s, characterises the transgression of linguistic conventions that mark their work as the result of 'an exit from the authoritarian system, a liberation from the tutelage of predetermined meanings'.[18] The textual landscape of the poet thus looked somewhat like a caravan of refugees, trying to leave behind a world whose main premises ceased to offer hope long ago. The poems written in the 1980s were traces of flight that featured strikingly little direct criticism of politics and ideology. There were hardly any references to historical struggles and class conflict. Critique became a process of forgetting, as in eluding the spell of the old world by not even naming it. But this apoliticality rendered the ensuing poetic forms of dissent all the more political.

Most striking, from both a political and a poetological point of view, is the persistent use of spatial metaphors. They signify the transversal aspirations of the Prenzlauer Berg scene, the willingness to transgress and challenge the constitution of Cold War international politics. Constantly recurring tropes like 'horizon', 'wall', 'border', 'narrow land', and 'barbed-wire landscapes' suggest a strong desire to break out of an entire way of living and thinking. Bert Papenfuß-Gorek, one of the more radical poets of the 1980s, destroyed linguistic conventions in an attempt to envisage what may lie beyond the horizon:

> scream against the wall
> scribble it at the wall
> stroll through the wall
>
> varieti not simpliciti
> & you sighter of varieti
> are not simpliciti but
> stand and stem of varieti[19]

Papenfuß-Gorek's poetry is characterised by a disregard for existing orthographic conventions. At times he ventures into a nearly incomprehensible (and untranslatable) private language. He breaks up words into their components or experiments with grammar, syntax and style. There are moments, however, where his misspelled adventures and his play with words and double-meanings manage astonishingly well to open up dialogical spaces by transgressing linguistically fixed modes of thinking.

Papenfuß-Gorek's desire to 'stroll through the wall', to leave the old world behind without the least trait of melancholy, did, indeed, anticipate the explosions and implosions that were to take place in November 1989, the moment when, after months of sustained mass demonstrations, hundreds of thousands of East Germans literally strolled through the Berlin Wall to take their first glimpse of the West. The image of the disintegrating Wall remains deeply engraved in our collective memories of late twentieth-century global politics. It must be remembered, though, that at the time the Prenzlauer Berg poets wrote, in the early and mid 1980s, there was little hope for such a spectacular turnaround. Hardly anybody in the East or West, neither international relations scholars nor Cold War politicians, had expected the foundations of the Soviet alliance system to crumble like a house of cards. Papenfuß-Gorek's transversal persistence is thus all the more astonishing. Nineteen-eighty-four, from the 'underground' in East Berlin:

> pOwer will fall
> down, i.e. over
> thrown until stum-
> bling, ignored it will
> turn into motherearth[20]

Various modernist and postmodernist themes resonate in the approach to language that became central to the work of Papenfuß-Gorek and other Prenzlauer Berg poets. Indeed, Sascha Anderson, one of the key figures of the underground literary scene, emphasises the strong influence that writers such as Foucault, Baudrillard and Barthes exerted on him and fellow writers.[21] The prevalence of these themes testify to the regime's inability to shield its population from 'subversive' outside influences. The transversal nature of contemporary cultural and political struggles rendered the Iron Curtain porous, to the extent that the formation of domestic opinion has become intrinsically linked to the cross-territorial flow of ideas.

As a result of these transversal dynamics, the discursive dimension of power, particularly its link with the production and diffusion of knowledge, is an ever-present theme in Prenzlauer Berg poetry. And so is the challenge of any truth claims. The poets of the 1980s relied on what could be called a later Wittgensteinean view of language and politics. Words were no longer perceived as representations of an externally existing reality. Rather, language was seen as an activity in itself – an activity that already contained, by definition, various political dimension. Rainer Schedlinski, one of Prenzlauer Berg's most articulate theorists, speaks of the 'resistance of forms', of a protest culture that attacks the sign itself, rather than merely the meaning that it arbitrarily imposed on us (or, more precisely, on other signs).[22]

For many observers, though, this transversally inspired avantgardist move was everything but dissent. Its so-called postmodern aesthetic was said to lack both moral integrity and the power to oppose a very real political force, the authoritarian East German government. Clearly, the Prenzlauer Berg writers were not dissidents in the normal sense, nor did they want to be seen as such. But dissent has, as argued throughout this book, too often been understood only in romantic and masculine terms, as heroic rebellions against authority, exemplified by demonstrating masses, striking workers, brickthrowing students and fasting dissidents. Dissent is often a far more intricate and far more mundane phenomenon.

If poets, as those at Prenzlauer Berg, explore their own poetic world, then this is not necessarily to search for a perfect language or to ignore the multiple realities of social and political life. If a poem speaks only in its own matter it draws attention to the fact that words are arbitrary signs. By refusing to go beyond the poem, the poet subverts the often unquestioned link between the sign and the referent, the non-linguistic reality that the sign designates. The previous chapter has already debated the relative merits and problems of such a non-referential view of language, and later sections of the present chapter will do so again. At this point, however, it is more important to keep in mind that when pursuing their form of subversive writing, the poets of the 1980s considered language itself as a site where important political and social struggles take place. Schedlinski:

```
        ...covered
    black                                    you see
            snow                                          the
                    on the
                            sides
    are gratings                                 the lines
            of humanity
                            language
    prison                                       an open
            where
                    there is
                        no
                            outside²³
```

This poem does not only speak of spatial and linguistic prisons, but actually visualises them through its appearance on the page. The text is like a grating. Confinement, however, is only one aspect that is evoked by this particular spatial arrangement of words. One discovers, at the same time, an array of escape routes. Because the poem can be read in a variety of ways – horizontally, vertically, diagonally – it offers an alternative to the monological thought form that dominated much of the political rhetoric in East Germany. Prison and polyphony at once, Schedlinski's poetic grating accepts the limits of language but urges us to search for the multitude of voices that can be heard and explored within these limits. In this sense, the poem resembles what Gilles Deleuze and Félix Guattari called a rhizome: a multiplicity that has no coherent and bounded whole, no beginning or end, only a middle from where it expands and overspills. Any point of the rhizome is connected to any other. It has no fixed points to anchor thought, only lines, magnitudes, dimensions, plateaus, and they are always in motion.²⁴

[...]

Poetic dissent and the limits of aesthetic autonomy

[...]

The archives of the disintegrated old regime have revealed that various poets were paid informants of the *Staatssicherheit or Stasi*, the notorious state security service. Anderson and Schedlinski were the most prominent among them. Anderson's role was particularly damaging. As opposed to his more elusive poetry, his Stasi reports, filed over a period of twenty years, were precisely articulated and contained incriminating evidence against his fellow writers who often took great personal risks in articulating their avant-garde poetry. Intensive and emotional debates emerged in Germany. The Stasi affair not only questioned how successful the younger generation of writers were in breaking out of boundaries, but also shattered the cliché of the Bohemian underground poet. Of course, virtually all oppositional activities were infiltrated by the Stasi. But Prenzlauer Berg poets were supposed to be different. The whole premise of their activities was based on refusal and flight, on stepping altogether outside the system and its realm of influence. This strategy had contributed to the high level of integrity that the Prenzlauer Berg poets enjoyed during the 1980s, particularly in the West. They stood for 'a seemingly intact critical identity'.²⁵ They appeared 'to have successfully stepped free of the burden of complicity with which older writers had to come to terms after 1989'.[26] The fall from grace was thus all the harder when the Stasi revelations gradually emerged in November 1991.

Many writers from the previous generation were particularly harsh in their judgements of the Prenzlauer Berg scene. There was talk of hypocrisy and betrayal. Wolf Biermann, who dismissed the Prenzlauer Berg poets as 'late-dadaistic garden gnomes with pencil and brush',[27] was the most outspoken, but certainly not the only hostile voice. He and others spoke of lacking responsibility, of a generation that had abandoned the commitment of revolutionary poetry for a naive and impotent avant-gardism. The fact that Anderson and Schedlinski put some of their fellow writers at risk signified for many the moral bankruptcy of the postmodernism that drove the writings of the 1980s. The autonomy of the aesthetic sucked back from its theoretical loftiness to the sump-hole of dirty politics?

[. . .]

The accusations against Anderson and Schedlinski, and their selfserving theoretical defence, go to the core of the problem of language and human agency. Can poetry that refuses to engage direct political issues have any validity as a practice of dissent? Is the amoral poetcollaborator a necessary consequence of an approach that assumes language has to be critiqued before a fundamental political critique becomes even possible? More generally, can a position that rejects any objective truth claims still retain an ethics of responsibility in a destitute time?

These are difficult questions and, as such, beg for difficult answers. They certainly cannot be put to rest by a stereotypical lashing out against something called postmodernism. Such a polemic is unable to understand not only the complexities of the theoretical issues at stake, but also the contradictions that characterised the lives of a generation that was born into an existing socialist state. It trivialises the centrality of political boundaries and the attempts that were undertaken to transgress them. Most of the Prenzlauer Berg poets had, in fact, never claimed to be conventional dissidents. And to dismiss an entire generation of writers by the behaviour of two of its members is a highly problematic exercise, especially if done from a comfortable position of hindsight. A personal act of an author, no matter how ethically questionable, does not provide sufficient ground to dismiss everything s/he has ever said or written, yet alone everything an entire tradition of thought has ever produced.[28]

The writers of the 1980s were not the uniform generation of poets that some of their critics want them to be. There were always tensions and disagreements, even within Prenzlauer Berg. Jan Faktor, for instance, left the scene in disgust over its lack of political commitment, its 'panic fear to produce texts in which anything could be fixed clearly and definitely'.[29] And even those who stayed had strong reservations about the actions of Anderson and Schedlinski. Hardly any fellow poet thought that 'it was all the same', or accepted as normal the paralysing atmosphere of mistrust that resulted from the constant Stasi-threat.[30] Perhaps it is simply too early to evaluate the contribution of the Prenzlauer Berg poets. Too close and emotionally laden are the grim wastelands of East German communism and the turbulent events of 1989 to allow for even remotely detached judgements about these writers and the difficult situation they faced. What is needed, however, is a commitment towards a continuous and differentiated inquiry into the multiple and transversal dimensions that makes up the complex relationship between language and politics.

[. . .]

Linguistic dissent works slowly, by changing the way we speak and think about ourselves and the world we live in. The young poets of the 1980s were part of this constant process of reframing meaning. They may not have been the heroic freedom fighters they were sometimes taken to be, but their works and lives can shed light on the complexities that make up the increasingly cross-territorial interaction between domination and resistance. Some of their poetic engagements with daily life in East Germany will remain important, if only because they captured a certain zeitgeist, the spirit of a decaying regime. And, for better or for worse, the Prenzlauer Berg writers have triggered a series of controversies that led to considerable public debate. The best we can hope for, in a sense, is that the ensuing issues, difficult as they are, remain debated in a serious and sustained manner. It is through the creation of such a debate that the Prenzlauer Berg writers have transcended their immediate sphere of activity. By embarking on a self-conscious exploration of form, the poets of the 1980s have opened up opportunities to rethink the crucial relationship between language and politics in spaces that lie far beyond the gradually fading memory of East German wastelands.

Summary

This chapter was the last step in a journey that theorised human agency through an examination of various transversal practices of dissent. The chosen route has led away from great revolutionary acts towards an appreciation of less spectacular but equally effective daily practices of resistance. Their potential to engender transformation comes into view as soon as one conceptualises global politics not only in terms of interactions among sovereign states, but also, and primarily, as a complex and discursively conditioned site of transversal struggles.

Poetry is one of the dissident practices that become visible through this reframing of global politics. Poetic engagements with the linguistic constitution of political practices testify to the transversal and transformative potential that is contained in everyday forms of resistance. But poetry is, of course, only one of many linguistic and discursive sites of dissent. At a time when the local and the global become ever-more intertwined, a great variety of activities, often of a daily and mundane nature, have the potential to acquire significant transversal dimensions. An analysis of poetic dissent provides insight into the processes through which these sites of struggle operate. In doing so, poetry draws attention to a multitude of increasingly important transversal spheres that have all too often been ignored by international relations scholars, whose purview has tended to be confined to the domain of high politics.

The poetic imagination not only illustrates why global politics cannot be separated from the manner in which it has been constituted and objectified, but also reveals how linguistic interferences with these objectifications can exert human agency and engender processes of social change. Rather than attacking direct manifestations of power, poetic dissent seeks to undermine the linguistic and discursive foundations that have already normalised political practices. The potential of such interferences can only be unleashed through a long process. This is true of critique of language in general, whatever form it takes. There are no quick and miraculous forms of resistance to discursive domination. Dissent works by digging, slowly, underneath the foundations of authority. It unfolds its power through a gradual and largely inaudible transversal transformation of values.

But how can something as inaudible as transversal poetic dissent possibly be evaluated? How can a form of resistance that engages linguistic and discursive practices be judged, or merely be understood, by the very nexus of power and knowledge it seeks to distance itself from? These difficult questions beg for complex answers. I do not claim to have solved them here, nor do I believe that they can actually be solved, at least not in an absolute and definitive way. The impact of discursive dissent on transversal social and political dynamics is mediated through tactical and temporal processes. A poem, for instance, does not directly cause particular events, it does not visualise an opponent in space and time. A linguistic expression of dissent works by insinuating itself into its target – the population at large – without taking it over, but also without being separated from it. Even the agent becomes gradually blurred. The effect of a poem cannot be reduced to its author or even to the poem itself. Those who have read it may have passed altered knowledge on to other people, and thus influenced the transversal constitution of societal values.

Discursive forms of transversal dissent will always remain elusive. But this does not render their effects any less potent or real. Neither does this recognition invalidate efforts to assess the role of language in interfering with the constitution of global politics. It does, however, call for a more sensitive and modest approach to the question of evidence and human agency.

The East German poetry scene at Prenzlauer Berg, particularly its attempt to challenge the political, spatial and linguistic constitution of Cold War international politics, has served to illustrate the complexities that are entailed in transversal struggles. In some ways the young writers of the 1980s have shown that poetic dissent can be politically relevant even though, or, rather, precisely because it refuses to be drawn into narrow political debates. Their works were transgressions, attempts to stretch language such that a more critical view of daily life in East Germany could be expressed. While having succeeded in subverting various linguistic aspects of the existing order, the poetry scene at Prenzlauer Berg also epitomises some of the difficulties that are entailed in discursive forms of transversal dissent. The fact that the underground poetry scene was penetrated by the State Security Service has challenged both the credibility of the poets and their attempt to carve out an autonomous aesthetic space. But rather than undermining the validity of their activities altogether, the Stasi revelations highlight the need to come to terms with the complex and transversal elements that are entailed in breaking out of existing webs of power and discourse. It is in this sense that the Prenzlauer Berg poetry scene – precisely because of its mixed success, precisely because of its controversies and failures – has contributed a great deal to our understanding of the transversal struggles that make up contemporary global politics.

Notes

1 Karen Leeder, *Breaking Boundaries: A New Generation of Poets in the GDR* (Oxford: Clarendon Press, 1996), p. 55.
2 David Campbell, 'Political Prosaics, Transversal Politics, and the Anarchical World', in Michael J. and Hayward R. Alker (eds), *Challenging Boundaries: Global Flows, Territorial Identities* (Minneapolis: University of Minnesota Press, 1996), p. 23.
3 David Bathrick, *The Powers of Speech: The Politics of Culture in the GDR* (Lincoln: University of Nebraska Press, 1995), pp. 2, 240.
4 See, in particular, Christian Joppke, *East German Dissidents and the Revolution of 1989* (London: Macmillan, 1995).
5 See Bathrick, *The Powers of Speech*, esp. pp. 70–7.
6 Uwe Kolbe, 'Hineingeboren', in *Hineingeboren: Gedichte 1975–1979* (Berlin and Weimar: Aufbau, 1980), p. 47. 'Hohes weites grünes Land,/zaundurchsetzte Ebene./Roter/Sonnenbaum am Horizont./Der Wind ist mein/und mein die Vögel.//Kleines grünes Land enges,/Stacheldrahtlandschaft./Schwarzer/Baum neben mir./Harter Wind/Fremde Vögel.'
7 Kurt Drawert, 'Zweite Inventur', in *Zweite Inventur* (Berlin und Weimar: Aufbau, 1987), p. 12. 'Was war sie wert, meine/Anwesenheit in einer Welt die dekliniert war,//geordnet, in Definitionen, Tabellen,/Schlagzeilen gebracht?/Fertigbedingungen und Fertiggerichte./Die Geschichte war fertig. Die Gegenwart//war fertig, die Zukunft, die Revolution,/die Antworten waren fertig.'
8 Dörig, translated by Bathrick in *The Powers of Speech*, p. 239. For a detailed discussion see Leeder, *Breaking Boundaries*, pp. 19–76.
9 Kolbe, 'Die Heimat der Dissidenten: Nachbemerkungen zum Phantom der DDR-Opposition', in K. Deiritz and H. Krauss (eds), *Der deutsch-deutsche Literaturstreit oder 'Freunde es spricht sich schlecht mit gebundener Zunge* (Frankfurt: Luchterhand, 1991), pp. 33–9.

10 Kurt Drawert, *Spiegelland: Ein deutscher Monolog* (Frankfurt: Suhrkamp, 1992), pp. 25–7. 'aber wie mein Vater (or Großvater, beispielsweise) wollte ich nicht sprechen…diese Sprache zu benutzen ware zugleich eine Form der Unterwerfung gewesen…Ich spürte, sobald Vater (oder Großvater, beispielsweise) sprach, daß nicht tatsächlich Vater (oder beispielswise Großvater) sprach, sondern dass etwas Fernes, Fremdes, Äusseres gesprochen hatte, etwas, das sich lediglich seiner (oder ihrer) Stimme bediente…Also blieb nur, zu sprechen und damit dem Mißverstandnis oder der Lüge zu verfallen und im Sprechen sich beobachtet, beeinflußt und beherrscht zu wissen von etwas Fernem, Fremden und Äusseren…'.

11 Jayne-Ann Igel, 'Der Zogling', in T. Elm, *Kristallisationen: Deutsche Gedichte der achtziger Jahre* (Stuttgart: Reclam, 1992), p. 158. 'war ich endültig gefangen, als ich ihre sprache lernte, meine/ stimme ein vogellaut, der mich ihnen bewahrte; sie hielten/mich am hause gleich dem rebstock, dessen triebe sie be/schnitten, dass er die zimmer nicht verdunkele//und dicht bei der mauer des hauses spielte ich, unterm lichte/trocknender laken, die finger durchlocherten den putz, nicht/missen mochte ich den leibhaftigen klang meines names, der/nach urin roch; die meinen namen in ihrem munde führten,/hielten mich mit den zähnen fest am genick.'

12 Michael Thulin, 'Sprache und Sprachkritik: Die Literatur des Prenzlauer Bergs in Berlin/DDR', in H. L. Arnold (ed.), *Die andere Sprache: Neue DDR Literatur der 80er Jahre* (Munich: Text and Kritik, 1990), pp. 234–42.

13 Ulrich Schodlbauer, 'Die Modernitätsfalle der Lyrik', in *Merkur*, No. 551, vol. 49, No. 2, Feb 1995, p. 174.

14 Julia Kristeva, *Recherches pour une sémanalyze* (Paris: Seuil, 1969), pp. 178–9, tr. L. S. Roudiez in the introduction to Kristeva's *Revolution in Poetic Language* (New York: Columbia University Press, 1984), p. 2.

15 Nicole Brossard, Poetic 'Politics', in C. Bernstein (ed.), *The Politics of Poetic Form: Poetry and Public Policy* (New York: ROOF, 1990), p. 79.

16 *ariadnefabrik*, IV/1987, cited in Olaf Nicolai, 'die fäden der ariadne,' in Arnold, *Die Andere Sprache*, p. 91.

17 Editorial of *Mikado*, cited in K. Michael and T. Wohlfahrt (eds), *Vogel oder Käfig sein: Kunst und Literatur aus unabhängigen Zeitschriften der DRR 1979–1989* (Berlin: Galrev, 1991), p. 348.

18 Elke Erb, 'Vorwort' to E. Erb and S. Anderson, *Berührung ist nur eine Randerscheinung: Neue Literatur as der DDR* (Cologn: Kiepenheuer & Witsch, 1985), p. 15.

19 Bert Papenfuß-Gorek, 'SOndern,' in S. Anderson and E. Erb (eds), *Berührung ist nur eine Randerscheinung*, p. 162. 'schrei gegen die wand/schreib es an die wand/schreite durch die wand//fielfalt anstatt einfalt/& du einsteller der fielfalt/bistnicht einfalt sondern/baustein & bein der fielfalt'.

20 Papenfuß-Gorek, *vorwärts im zorn &sw. gedichte*, cited in Jürgen Zenke, 'Vom Regen und von den Traufen. Bert Papenfuß-Gorek: die lichtscheuen scheiche versunkener reiche', in W. Hinck (ed.), *Gedichte und Interpretationen*, vol. VII (Stuttgart, Philipp Reclam, 1997), p. 146. 'die mAcht wir runter-/ kommen, d.h. gestürzt/werden bis sie stol-/pert, liegengelassen/wird sie zu muttererde'.

21 Sascha Anderson, interviewed in Robert von Hallberg, *Literary Intellectuals and the Dissolution of the State: Professionalism and Conformity in the GDR* (Chicago: University of Chicago Press, 1996), p. 263.

22 Rainer Schedlinski. 'Die Unzuständigkeit der Macht', *neue deutsche literatur*, 40, 474, June 1992, 97.

23 Rainer Schedlinski, 'die unvordenkliche lichtung der worte', *die rationen des ja und des nein: Gedichte* (Berlin und Weimar: Aufbau, 1988), cited in Leeder, *Breaking Boundaries*, p. 67. 'verdeckt/schwarzen siehst du/schnee den/auf den/seiten/sind gitter die zeilen/des menschen/sprache/gefängnis ein offenes/dort/gibt es/kein/draussen.'

24 Gilles Deleuze and Félix Guattari, *A Thousand Plateaus: Capitalism & Schizophrenia* tr. B. Massumi (London: The Athlone Press, 1996/1980), pp. 3–25, 377.

25 Peter Böthig and Klaus Michael, 'Der 'Zweite Text,' in their *MachtSpiele*, p. 12.

26 Robert von Hallberg, 'Introduction' to *Literary Intellectuals and the Dissolution of the State*, p. 24.

27 Biermann, cited by Alison Lewis, 'Power, Opposition and Subcultures: The Prenzlauer Berg "Scene" in East Berlin and the Stasi', *UTS Review*, 3, 2, November 1997, 139.

28 Parallels exist here with how Paul de Man's sympathies for the regime have been employed to discredit not only all of his remaining work, but also the entire literature on deconstruction. For an analysis that engages this difficult theoretical and ethical issue in more complex terms see Campbell, 'Political Prosaics, Transversal Politics, and the Anarchical World', pp. 14–16.

29 Jan Faktor, "Sechzehn Punkte zur Prenzlauer-Berg-Szeme', in Böthig and Michael, MachtSpiele, p. 98.

30 See, for instance, Drawert, 'Sie schweigen. Oder sie lügen', in Bötig and Michael MachtSpiele, pp. 74–82; and Kolbe, Die Situation (Göttingen: Wallstein Verlag, 1994), p. 23; 'Offener Brief an Sascha Anderson', in MachtSpiele, pp. 318–20.

36 Sounds of resistance

Robin Balliger

Source: Ron Sakolsky and Fred Wei-han Ho (eds) (1995), *Sounding Off: Music as Subversion/Resistance/Revolution*, New York: Autonomedia, pp. 13–26

Music...site of oral history; sounds of war; social gathering for dancing, pleasure, fun, sex; emotional, spiritual, rapturous like Jimi Hendrix and Mozart's "Requiem"; career stardom, commodification, cultural imperialism; state censorship; protest songs, punk, nueva cancion, and Fela's "Zombie"; vibration and breath; the reason people go to political rallies!; slave trade and musical codes indomitable as heartbeats; noise, sound soundtrack; immaterial and uncontrollable; music institutions, discipline and disciplines...

How has music gone from its "old role" as an organizing practice of social groups, to being entertaining fluff or employed for emotional effect in nationalist causes? How can the "political correctness" of music be determined through an "objective" reading of lyrics? Why is it even possible to dissect a song and consider the music itself to be without meaning? These questions point to how music is represented in our society, representations which are not the revelation of some timeless Truth, but constructed by specific societal interests: In the following pages, I develop an understanding of music and noise as social forces, fully involved in the "dialogic process" of social life and as such, an important site of control – and resistance.

Political music or the politics of music

As a practice, music is situated in particular social relationships and locations that are a product of complex intersections of culture, class, gender, etc., in lived experience. Music and representations of music are contextualized activities that have social and political meaning. This view shifts us away from asking: "which music is political?" to "what is the particular politics of a music and how is it political?" What is considered to be music itself is controversial and linked to large-scale ideological formations invested in defining "music" apart from non-music.

This operation is an effect of power, one that functions through discursive strategies that construct "music" as an aspect of civilization, while sound and noise are linked to the uncivilized. In Hieronymus Bosch's famous painting, "Garden of Earthly Delights" (early 16th century), hell is rendered through the din and chaos created by creatures playing fantastic musical instruments which swallow-up and torture the bodies of the dammed. Epitomized by the Enlightenment and 18th century classical music, societal sound began to be brought under control through dominant representations linking "music" to order/civilization/mind, and "noise" to chaos/the primitive/body. In *Noise: The Political Economy of Music* (1985), Attali argue that a central controlling mechanism of the State is the monopolization of noise emitted in society. "…Music and noises in general, are stakes in games of power. Their forms, sources, and roles have changed along with and by means of the changes in systems of power." Through mechanical reproduction in the 20th century, sound has also been controlled through its incitement. Repressing rhythm and noise has become more selective, while its management has been enabled through the wallpaper-like proliferation and commodification of music.

The dominant constructions of music as non-referential and non-ideological (Western classical music) or as marginalized and primitive (popular and ethnic musics) are implicated in strategies of control that make legitimate music into something transcendental that exists apart from practice. This shields music from being implicated in relations of power and at the same time inhibits understanding about performative practices because it is difficult to conceive of performance or participation as a total experience. The closest we come to conceptualizing a performance that at once mobilizes music/dance/thought/history/play/ spirituality etc., is the idea of ritual, but this word is problematic as it still marks off and compartmentalizes human activity. Music is neither transcendental nor trivial, but inhabits a site where hegemonic processes are contested. Placing music back in the world does not reduce music, but gives it social force.

In the following discussion of music and resistance, my purpose, in part, is to explode reified representations of "political music." Discussions of popular music have often suffered from a kind of reductionism by certain Left and reactionary positions, which sense the power of music but are uneasy about its inaccessibility to rational critique and control. I explore how popular music becomes a site of resistance through four lines of investigation: textual analysis focusing on the lyrics of songs; subaltern cultural production; music as performance and its relation to autonomy; and music as a sonic activity or tactic. I argue that oppositional music practices not only act as a form of resistance against domination, but generate social relationships and experience which can form the basis of a new cultural sensibility and, in fact, are involved in the struggle for a new culture.

Textual analysis or, Bow wow wow yippee yo yippee yay, bow wow yippee yo yippee yay! (George Clinton "Atomic Dog")

Textual analyses focus on the lyrics in music as the primary or only site of meaning. The words in music have been particularly important as a medium of communication in cultures and historical periods where there are no written texts, texts are only available to a privileged group, or to deliberately subvert the power of the written word. Beyond the notion of "protest songs," lyrics are multivalent, employing discursive strategies which form a poetics of resistance. I will also discuss the limitations of these text-based analyses, particularly with regard to meaning reception, the elision of social context and issues of cultural production, and most obviously, the inability to consider meaning in instrumental music.

Recent literary criticism emphasizes the importance of "Voice" in cultural resistance. For oppressed peoples under slavery, in colonial contexts and the underclasses of global capitalism, music has often been a central site for the intervention in dominant discourses and for creating forms of expression that are culturally affirming. Because of the dominance of metropolitan languages, illiteracy or lack of access to print mediums, orality has played a major role in contesting the universalizing discourses of empire. Locating a position of vocality and self-representation is central to creating a counter-narrative, positing a counter-essence and in critically attacking the legitimacy of "objective" knowledge and truth.

Popular forms of music have become an effective site of enunciation and people involved in indigenous struggles have mixed traditional elements of music with rock to reach a mass audience through the circulation of world music. Essays in *Rockin' the Boat: Mass Music and Mass Movements* detail such political music from Hawaii and Australia. In Australia, Aboriginal musicians blend indigenous forms with rock to preserve traditional values, represent their own history and protest oppression. Contemporary Aboriginal music was first influenced by the guitar style and personal song genre of American country-western musicians and in the 1970s became highly influenced by the message of black liberation and reggae music of Bob Marley. Aboriginal Australians are using music as a "political weapon in the long-term struggle of Aboriginal people for dignity respect, and land rights claims" (Breen). The song lyrics by musician Archie Roach and bands, No Fixed Address and Us Mob, are direct social commentaries, convey the Aboriginal experience in Australia, or are programmatic like a song such as "AIDS, It's a Killer." Breen largely lets the lyrics speak for themselves in his analysis of the music's politics.

In analyzing calypso lyrics of the 1930s and 40s, which are usually thought of as topical social commentary, the lyrics employ various discursive strategies beyond the surface "meaning." Together these devices form a poetics of protest which in some cases utilize techniques of reappropriation usually associated with postmodernism. Three of these discursive strategies are, first, that calypso were a form of "autoethnography," through which a colonized people could represent themselves and retell history with their image and voice fully included. Second, through irreverence and parody, the calypsonians punctured the screen of colonial superiority by revealing scandals in the British ruling class and challenged the civilizing mission by contrasting it to the actions of the colonizer. Third, calypsos created a counter-narrative to official accounts of events.

As an example, I discuss a song written in the context of colonial rule, global economic depression and socialist organizing of the 1930s. In 1937, a black labor activist named "Buzz" Butler led a wildcat strike of Trinidadian oil workers which resulted in rioting and an extreme use of force by the government. Butler was jailed, but anger over police violence intensified when an official report whitewashing the incident was later released. Below are the last two stanzas of Atilla's calypso, "Commission's Report":

> They said through the evidence they had
> That the riot started at Fyzabad
> By the hooligan element under their leader
> A fanatic Negro called Butler
> Who uttered speeches inflammatory
> And caused disorders in this colony
> The only time they found the police was wrong
> Was when they stayed too long to shoot people down.
> A peculiar thing of this Commission
> In their ninety-two lines of dissertation
> Is there no talk of exploitation
> Of the worker or his tragic condition
> Read through the pages there is no mention
> Of capitalistic oppression
> Which leads one to entertain a thought
> And wonder if it's a one-sided report.

Atilla's song thoroughly indicts the official story through mimicking the jargon of the report itself and unmasking media representations. He links the words "commission" and "dissertation" with "exploitation" and "tragic condition," syntactically showing their real connection. Atilla attacks the scapegoating of Butler by reappropriating the language of the media and defusing the "moral panic" induced by such buzz-words as "hooligan," "fanatic," and "inflammatory speeches." In this song, he also brings together the rioting and capitalist oppression, which challenges the controlling mechanism of representing these issues separately; rioting portrayed as unconscious acts of violence, while oppressive economic and social conditions are channeled into "appropriate" avenues of reform.

However, political communication in music has traditionally been analyzed only in terms of the "self-evident" meaning of song lyrics. Examples of this programmatic approach to political music are common among the organized Left (and in nationalist causes) and are found in Pring-Mill's article, "Revolutionary Song in Nicaragua" (1987). These "didactic songs" include inspirational anthems and historical accounts, as well as songs which are educational, from the learning of multiplication tables to a song that replaces a written manual for the stripping down and reassembly of the "Carabina M-1" (by Luis Enrique Mejia Godoy) Pring-Mill's insights into the emotional meaning and educational uses of these songs are largely gleaned through analyzing a letter by one of the revolutionary leaders, Carlos Nunez Tellez, in which he praises the musical group Pancasán. His article gives little sense of the meaning of these songs in a broader context and, again, the lyrics are considered the only political component. In fact, Pring-Mill states:

> What may strike one as most surprising about that letter is its total silence regarding the music of such songs, which is simply taken for granted: their didactic and emotive functions, while reinforced by the music, clearly centre on the lyrics. Yet all the most successful songs owe much of their persuasive power to setting and performance – although the contribution of the musical element to the total "meaning" of a song is something much harder to analyze than that of its text.

This quote speaks to the paradox of constructing political communication only in terms of the text. Whereas the meaning of these songs is only represented as a function of the lyrics, the music is critical to conveying the message. But what is the message of the music? Reading didactic lyrics as literal and complete in the communication of meaning ignores the many subtexts and levels of meaning occurring in the production and performance of music.

Within an analysis of political content based on lyrics, there are problems raised by semiotics such as the unpredictability of sign activity, reception and how meaning is context bound and multiple. In understanding the meaning of songs, musical experience and cultural background are significant factors. In addition, one empirical study suggests only ten to thirty percent of high school and college students "correctly identified the 'intended messages' in songs." In a recent article, Angelica Madeira raises these issues to further ask: "wherein lies popular music's political power?" She doesn't fully address the question, but points in a direction forged by Bakhtin (a Soviet philosopher and literary critic), centering on the "indestructible character and universality of popular culture." She argues that "music is empowering not only because of the explicit political ends it is able to serve, but also because it formulates yearnings and values for an entire generation." While I find the direction of her argument salutary, she neglects to contextualize Bakhtin's writings and how emphasizing nonconformity, irreverence, festivity and pleasure in Stalinist Russia, requires a completely different analysis when applied to the contemporary United States. This highlights the necessity to locate resistance in relation to specific strategies of control and domination.

Understanding the politics of music from a text-based analysis is particularly problematic with forms of music that are heavily coded (possibly to avoid censure), or where the lyrics are of secondary importance or even misleading. And what might "protest lyrics" be in social contexts where the very language of struggle has been co-opted? In an interesting article, Rey Chow analyzes Chinese popular music and how it creates a discourse of resistance in a context where the rhetoric of class struggle has become part of the dominant discourse. In this situation, lightheartedness, emotion and physicality are the central trans-linguistic themes. Chow suggests that meaning is created in the clash of words (often from Chinese history) and rock music, a meaning which becomes audible through "striking notes of difference" from the single voice of official culture. Instead of emphasizing "voice" or "who speaks," Chow suggests we ask "what plays?" and "who listens" She concludes with the critical distinction between passivity and "silent sabotage," through a literal and metaphorical discussion of the cassette Walkman creating a kind of sonic barrier. These examples show how music is a form of resistance beyond an objectified reading of political lyrics through emphasizing the structure of listening, in which meaning is mutually produced in different contexts.

Cultural production or, "Classical music, jazz... those are categories of things you buy, that's not music." (Yo Yo Ma, cellist)

In "The Work of Art in the Age of Mechanical Reproduction," Walter Benjamin argues that technologies of artistic reproduction that originated in the early 20th century began to create an undifferentiated visual or musical terrain that separated the artist or author from his/her work. Since this time, critical theory has emphasized the mediation inherent in all mass produced cultural products and two primary positions have developed about mass culture. The first equates economic domination with cultural domination and implicates mass culture in the reproduction of hegemony. The second view argues that mass culture is a site of contestation and that popular music is not a completely controlled and manufactured product of the West. Electric guitars and synthesizers shape the sound of a transnational technoculture which reflects a process of urbanization, not Westernization, as musicians constantly create new sounds for their own purposes. In this section, I detail these arguments, along with ways in which decreasing costs of music technology have facilitated subaltern cultural production and have effectively challenged the hegemony of mass cultural products and ideologies.

Adorno's writings on music represent one extreme in arguments over the role and influence of cultural production in society. For Adorno, the centralized production of popular music is part of a system of control aimed at the creation of mechanized individuals whose habits and desires comply with the needs of capitalism and the State. While his position is understandable, having witnessed the power of music and the "loudspeaker" as employed by the Nazis, Adorno makes the mistake of equating all forms of popular, rhythmic music with sounds that serve dominant interests. His view of popular music and serious music (Western classical) is manichean, and the role of popular music in society is to create escape or distraction, and as a social cement in which the rhythms of popular dance music and jazz produce a standardized individual.

A central problem with Adorno's argument is the positing of a subject as pure receptor. In his work on rock and roll, Grossberg cites communication theories that ascribe a more active role to the audience in the construction of meaning and ideology.

> . . . it is the audience that interprets the text, defines its message, "decodes" it by bringing it into its own already constituted realities, or "uses" it to satisfy already present needs. In either case, the audience make the text fit into its experiences.

While I agree with Grossberg's contextualizing and creating a dynamic of interaction between mass cultural products and audience, there is a danger of creating a subject in the Americanized sense of individual free will and choice. I am suspicious of theories based on boundaries and difference without thoroughly addressing how the production of difference often conceals a broader conformity that is not only little threat to capitalism but is vital to it.

In addition to the problem of Adorno's subject, his blatant Eurocentrism and dismissal of black cultural forms and their meaning in the context of racial oppression in the United States is, frankly, abhorrent. In a scathing indictment of Horkheimer and Adorno, who were writing in Los Angeles during WWII, Mike Davis states:

> They described the Culture Industry not merely as political economy, but as a specific spatiality that vitiated the classical proportions of European urbanity, expelling from the stage both the "masses" (in their heroic, history-changing incarnation) and the critical intelligentsia. Exhibiting no apparent interest in the wartime turmoil in the local aircraft plants nor inclined to appreciate the vigorous nightlife of Los Angeles's Central Avenue ghetto, Horkheimer and Adorno focused instead on the little single-family boxes that seemed to absorb the world-historic mission of the proletariat into family centered consumerism under the direction of radio jingles and *Life* magazine ads.

Before dismissing the "Culture Industry," it is important to consider the global stratification of the record industry and its economic and cultural influence, in addition to ways in which cultural products are interpreted and appropriated in local contexts. Wallis and Mailm provide comprehensive data on the global production and media activity (such as radio airplay) of music and argue that corporate activity in the music industry duplicates large-scale patterns of economic change and distributions of wealth worldwide. Currently, five major record labels "dominate the greater part of the global production and distribution of recorded music. The smaller independents take the risks in the local market, and achieve a high degree of local competence developing artists and repertoire talent which the majors can occasionally exploit internationally." In addition to changes in recording technology, the organization of the music industry, issues of control, authorship, copyright, studio budgets, recording contracts, manufacturing budgets, distribution and payola are major factors in the global flow of mass music products. Through the forces of competition, Simon Frith argues that the industry is intensely conservative, protecting certain styles and their profitability rather than taking risks on new sounds and artists. He concludes that the prevalence of cassette piracy (which is estimated at 66 percent in some markets), and other structural changes in the industry and technology will provide new opportunities for the independents and make cultural production more in tune with the "sounds of the street" and "music as a human activity."

In *Cassette Culture*, Peter Manuel argues that the accessibility of music technology since the mid-1980s has decentered control in the music industry, creating a surge in local music production and the democratization of expression. Manuel sees technology itself as the major determinant of change in musical and political expression away from monopoly and towards pluralism in cultural production, particularly in "developing nations." His study of popular music in India shows an explosion of locally recorded, produced and manufactured cassettes, some of which sell only a few copies, but others become widely popular in ways that could not have occurred with earlier forms of music production and industry control. He argues that this change liberates public expression from the homogenizing and "deculturating" effects of mass media products; preserves folk genres that might otherwise become extinct, as well as fueling "proletarian hybrid genres"; and promotes local and regional identity. While Manuel clearly espouses the revolutionary potential of cassette technology against foreign cultural domination, he admits that the localized quality of cassettes "culture" reinforces and may even intensify pre-existing social divisions. Through recorded music and speeches, cassettes have been highly effective in political organizing, a "new media" for grassroots organizing and lowerclass empowerment. But cassettes have been utilized by "every major socio-political campaign," including political and religious causes far removed from the "leftist mobilization and subaltern empowerment" envisioned by some.

Developments in music technology and mass communications have created avenues of expression for previously silenced groups, facilitated networks of alternative music like rap and punk and create the potential for a transnational oppositional culture. By suggesting this potentiality, I do not argue that resistance to either economic or "cultural" imperialism is predicated on new technologies or that a single meaning can be gleaned from these developments. Reformulations of identity through the circulation of popular music products simply raises the possibility of new kinds of organization and community. At the same time, multinational capitalism's "restless search for markets" has meant the increased commodification and consumption of global cultural products, but the social meaning of this marketing and how musicians and cultural producers negotiate this terrain must be addressed in its particularities. Raymond Williams argues that technology is not a predetermined instrument of domination or liberation but "a moment of choice," and instead emphasizes "the intense vitality of some kinds of popular music, always being reached for by the market and often grasped and tamed, but repeatedly renewing its impulses in new and vigorous forms." The next section addresses how popular music production in recorded and live forms interacts with the politics of location.

Performance and the temporary autonomous zone or, "Space is the Place" (SunRa)

The practice of oppressed groups in society trying to achieve "relative autonomy" is historically inseparable from domination itself. Critical studies that go beyond analyzing text and cultural production suggest a linkage between music practices and social formations that seek autonomy from the effects of power in the broadest sense. In developing a complex description of music activity as resistance in such situations, I explore three themes in this section: performance as social organization and cultural empowerment of oppressed groups; music as pleasure, use-value and threat to the necessary commodification of desire under capitalism; music as site of Refusal and the "temporary autonomous zone."

The performance of music is enigmatic from a Western/capitalist perspective because it is often unproductive (materially) and yet it produces (socially). Popular music is a social activity, a site of interaction and ideology, a temporary community that usually includes some type of movement or physical expression that is pleasurable. While music performance is an "extreme occasion" because it is temporal and not repeatable, musicologist John Shepherd states that "all music should be understood within the context of the politics of the everyday." He argues that the activity of music, through its complex system of signification, has the ability to shape awareness, individual subjectivity, and social formations. It is only in the industrialized world that music has become constructed as privileged property, leisure activity or mass distraction. Through its ability to mediate the social – temporally, spatially and bodily – music is a powerful site of struggle in the organization of meaning and lived experience. "Music can at the same time 'territorialize' and 'deterritorialize' the everyday, evoking and transcending its terrains, spaces, and temporalities as these are visually and linguistically mediated."

Beyond music as a site of critique of dominant ideologies, cultural critics have stressed the importance of cultural solidarity that occurs through performance. For the African diaspora and other groups oppressed by colonialism and repressive regimes, cultural expressions of music and dance have been a source of strength and identity formation critical to liberation struggles. Gilroy states that "Black expressive cultures affirm while they protest." This is well demonstrated in the calypso music of Trinidad, which is historically linked to both emancipation and decolonization. The French Catholic tradition of carnival began to be celebrated in Trinidad in the early 19th century and for the next hundred years, carnival, freedom, rioting and music were all linked in various ways. The "yard" was a space of relative autonomy for slaves and through elaborate secret societies and coded forms of communication resistance to slavery was built. By the 1830s, an extensive network of information had evolved as slaves were overheard singing a song in Patois about a successful slave revolt in Haiti. After emancipation, plantation owners replaced slave labor with indentured East Indian immigrants, driving many blacks into urban centers and continued poverty. The tradition of music and expression continued in the urban yard and in the early 20th century carnival music began to be performed in performance "tents." The calypso tents effectively merged a music born in resistance and a broad-based audience into a regularized social gathering through which a counter-narrative to colonial discourse and an emergent cultural identity were shaped. As the songs were performed in front of an audience they were immediately validated or repudiated by the public, and the wit and creativity of the calypsonians were a source of cultural empowerment for all.

Another example of the interlocution of cultural affirmation and political resistance is elaborated by Fairley's discussion of the Chilean group Karaxú!, which was formed shortly after the U.S.-backed coup in 1973. Fairley argues that:

> . . . musical meaning is negotiated between elements of performance and between performers and audience. It is inextricably tied to lived experience, political praxis, feelings and beliefs. It is rooted in social and political life . . . The creation and performance of this music is part of the process of learning to live with, and making sense of, experience – of re-integrating the dis-integrated.

Fairley describes Karaxú!'s performances as important "ritual occasions" to emphasize both the complexity of meaning and inclusion of the audience as integral to the event. Their performances are an active, if symbolically rendered, reminder of historical events and political mobilization in which cultural expression and political commitment survive together in exile.

Second, I address music as pleasure, the politics of forms of pleasure that exist as "use value" and how this is a threat to the capitalist commodification of desire. With few exceptions, political theory and activity in the West has been constructed as a totally serious and difficult practice. While I would certainly agree with most political activists that the global history of genocidal campaigns, ongoing struggles against oppression and even the smallest acts of social and physical domination evoke both rage and the necessity of political organization and action, I also argue that political ideology and strategies need to be continually reformulated. In this period, which might be thought of as the historic defeat of the Left, questions have been raised about paradigms of political theory and praxis, particularly with regard to the thinking behind slogans like "the road is hard but the future is bright." Constructing politics and pleasure as incommensurable spheres has been a major problem, creating both a denigration of the body (which has been implicated in forms of political tyranny), and it also has difficulty explaining both the attraction and persistence of forms of "entertainment" and "spirituality."

Some theorists are beginning to recognize the need to reintegrate these spheres and develop more complicated notions of resistance distinct from the purely politically instrumental. McClary and Walser critique the traditional Left and musicology for their positivist, Enlightenment-derived approach to meaning in music, and implicate both in systems designed to reinforce norms rather than liberate.

Part of the problem is one that chronically plagues the Left: a desire to find explicit political agendas and intellectual complexity in the art it wants to claim and a distrust of those dimensions of art that appeal to the senses, to physical pleasure. Yet pleasure frequently is the politics of music – pleasure as interference, the pleasure of marginalized people that has evaded channelization. Rock is a discourse that has frequently been at its most effective politically when its producers and consumers are least aware of any political or intellectual dimensions....

In a unique approach, Attali (1985) theorizes historical change in society through a semiotic reading of sound. He maps the global spread of capitalism through the control of societal sound and the "deritualizing" of music's "old code" – locus of social organization, mythology and healing. Attali articulates the difference between music produced by an industry and music as unproductive, an end in itself with the capacity to create its own code. Music is a threat to hegemonic forms of discourse and social relations because it offers the greatest potential to create new forms of communication and create "pleasure in being instead of having." Attali's construction of music as resistance follows from both Marx's theory of commodity fetishism and Foucault's theory of power as the saturation of discourse, social relations and bodies.

> In the seventeenth and eighteenth centuries a form of power comes into being that begins to exercise itself through social production and social service. It becomes a matter of obtaining productive service from individuals in their concrete lives. And in consequence, a real and effective "incorporation" of power was necessary, in the sense that power had to be able to gain access to the bodies of individuals, to their acts, attitudes and modes of everyday behavior (Foucault 1980).

Are there not ways in which music is a constant reminder of the existence of pleasure as use-value and as such poses a threat to a system that necessarily seeks out and exploits all forms of pleasure and energy for productive use?

My third point addresses Attali's notion of music as a site of "reality under construction." This idea is echoed by cultural critics who write on subcultures, black expressive culture and by theorists who articulate resistance in the broadest possible sense – beyond political ideology to a total transformation of values and lived behavior. I suggest thinking about these ideas through a more mobile category that conceives of forms of collective, cultural resistance as the situated practices of specific groups. The "Temporary Autonomous Zone," or TAZ, is useful in articulating this concept and I apply it to music in specific situations. Hakim Bey's theory of TAZ begins with a critique of revolution from two main positions. He argues that the current period is one in which a "vast undertaking would be futile martyrdom" and, coming from an anarchist tradition, he distrusts revolution because of its historical tendency to reinstitute authoritarianism in a different guise. He contrasts revolution with uprising, focusing on this activity as a kind of "free enclave," as festival, and a temporary or limited Refusal in which to "withdraw from the area of simulation." Bey views the TAZ as both a strategy and "condition for life." He states,

> The TAZ is thus a perfect tactic for an era in which the State is omnipresent and all-powerful and yet simultaneously riddled with cracks and vacancies. And because the TAZ is a microcosm of that 'anarchist dream' of a free culture, I can think of no better tactic by which to work toward that goal while at the same time experiencing some of its benefits here and now.

Ultimately the TAZ is a space beyond the gaze of power and the State. Bey draws inspiration from the spirit of the Paris Commune and the maroon communities of Jamaica and Suriname.

While Bey briefly mentions "music as an organizational principle," Hebdige and Gilroy link African music to a kind of oppositional, utopian space. While both tend to essentialize African music in a way I find problematic, the substance of their discussion of subcultures and black performance traditions speaks to this idea of temporary autonomy. Hebdige stresses the ideological character of everyday activities and how subcultural style in Britain is a symbolic form of struggle against the social order, or "a practice of resistance through style." In describing punk, Hebdige argues that music and dance formed a central site in which to perform revolt that "undermined every relevant discourse" and created an "alternative value system." "Conventional ideas of prettiness were jettisoned... fragments of school uniforms were symbolically defiled... punk dances like the pogo upset traditional courtship patterns... overt displays of heterosexual interest were generally regarded with contempt and suspicion... frontal attacks (on) the bourgeois notion of entertainment or the classical concept of 'high art'..." Hebdige's account resonates with my own involvement with punk in San Francisco in the late 1970s and early 80s. What I found most significant about this scene was that it fostered an ethos of "direct action" through which behavior and ideologies (mostly reactionary positions and some aspects of leftist politics) were overtly challenged and in some cases transformed. This sense of engagement had a significant impact on gender roles as many women were not content to be fans or only singers, but began playing instruments in bands and expressing themselves in numbers that were virtually unprecedented in Western popular music.

Paul Gilroy discusses British punk and its links with reggae through the "two-tone" movement and youth organization, Rock Against Racism, but focuses primarily on black expressive culture as a site of "collective memory, perception and experience in the present... the construction of community by symbolic and ritual means..." Writing on rap, funk and reggae, he argues that the public spaces in which dances occur "are transformed by the power of these musics to disperse and suspend the temporal and spatial order of the dominant culture." In Rastafarianism, "Babylon system" symbolizes the total rejection of "mental slavery," racism and exploitative economic conditions under capitalism; it is "a critique of the economy of time and space which is identified with the world of work and wages from which blacks are excluded and from which they, as a result, announce and celebrate their exclusion." In Gilroy's recent work he also stresses the need to distinguish the "political aesthetics" of different music groups within black popular culture.

My last example centers on an article by Pablo Vila, "*Rock Nacional* and Dictatorship in Argentina" (1992), in which he argues that concerts created a space in which a "we" was constructed that formed a cultural challenge to the ideology of the dictatorship. As the military regime took power in 1976 and sought to disperse all collectivities and suppress traditional political formations, rock concerts became a site of heavily coded oppositional activity. Vila refers to these sites as autonomous spaces of interaction "for broad sections of youth, a refuge, a sphere of resistance, and a channel for participation in the context of a closed and authoritarian society in crisis." The common experience of youth rebellion and its form, the rock concert, became highly politicized in the context of the military dictatorship and the censure of political and cultural expression.

Vila states that the message was in the activity as the music fostered a culture which demanded incorruptibility against *transar* (interactions with the system) and for *zafar* (escape from the system by all possible means). He cites the importance of the *rock nacional* movement for Argentinian youth as "salvaging the meaning of life in a context of lies and terror, consolidating a collective actor as a means of counteracting an individualistic model of life, counterposing a supportive community of actions and interests to the primacy of the market."

In this section I have shown ways in which music as a popular performance medium which engages the body and mind in a collective expression, has the power to transform values, ideology and lived behavior through generating a "temporary autonomous zone." Music is hardly just sound that is passively listened to, but a sonic force that acts on bodies and minds and creates its own life rhythms; rhythms that power recognizes and tries to monopolize through a relentless domination of societal noise. But, because of its unique properties music can be employed as a powerful counter-hegemonic device that goes beyond thought to being. Music as socially organized use-value is a threat to the individuated, consumption-oriented desiring machine of advanced capitalism. As a pleasurable collective expression the practice of music provides important clues to what Foucault describes as the "art of living counter to all forms of fascism" through constantly creating "de-individualization" and how it is "the connection of desire to reality (and not its retreat into the forms of representation) that possesses revolutionary force" (1992).

Sonic squatting

In this final section I show how subordinate groups have used music as a weapon which is able to penetrate walls and minds. In addition to the fact that drumming can reproduce language, territorialization through sound marks off areas of political or cultural significance and has played a major role in human activities such as religion and war. From kettledrums to bagpipes, sound exhorted troops, relayed commands, and was used to terrify enemies. Sound has remained a potent weapon, a force that disturbs through the fact that it is unhinged from the visual or the knowable and symbolically acts on the imagination, infiltrating and destabilizing power.

In Arguedas' novel, *Yawar Fiesta*, about indigenous struggles in the highlands of Peru, the *wakawak'ras*, or "trumpets of the earth," are a very disturbing sound for the local authorities. The trumpets announce the Yawar Fiesta, an indigenous form of bullfighting that articulates conflict in the novel. While the town of Puquio is geographically divided by class and ethnicity, and controlled by the Civil Patrol, sound is not so easily contained, as the "voices" of the *wakawak'ras* well up "from below" and invade every house, every room, every person. Sound is not only a form of resistance, but an attack on domination materially represented in distinct forms of spatiality.

> From the four quarters, as the night began, the bullfight music would rise up to the Girón Bolívar. From the Chaupi square, straight up to Girón Bolívar, the *turupukllay* rose on the wind. In the shops, in the pool hall, in the notables' houses, the girls and the townsmen would hear it.
>
> "At night that music sounds like it's coming from the graveyard," they'd say.
>
> "Yeah, man. It troubles your mind…"
>
> "That *cholo* Maywa is the worst of all. His music goes right down to the depths of my soul."
>
> The sound of the *wakawak'ras* interrupted the mistis' conversation under the lamps on the corners of the Girón Bolívar; it disturbed the peace of the diners in the houses of the leading citizens. In the Indian neighborhoods, the boys would gather when Don Maywa played…
>
> Sometimes Don Maywa's trumpet was heard in the town when the Priest was saying the rosary in church with the ladies and girls of the town and with some of the women from the Indian neighborhoods. The bullfight music was dispiriting to those pious souls; the Priest, too, would pause for a moment when the melody came in to him. The girls and ladies would look at one another uneasily, as if the brindled or tawny bulls were bellowing from the church doorway.
>
> "Devil's music!" the Vicar would say.
>
> (Arguedas)

Beyond associations with the bullfight, the simple moaning of the *wakawak'ras* is complex in its signification, at once recalling the presence of the Indians and the threat posed by their historically incomplete domination by both church and state. The music is particularly powerful in its ability to conjure up unknown aspects of the Other, unleashing fear and anxiety that exists in the minds of the *mistis* (*ladinos*). In this regard it operates as a psychological/spatial tactic that is difficult to contain.

Sound or P.A. systems may create an internal spatiality or "temporary autonomous zone," but through them music can traverse and challenge spatially organized social divisions. In his work on the cultural character of ethnic and class divisions in Cartagena, Colombia, Joel Streicker describes the use of sound as resistance and a "non-spatial way to reclaim space." He historicizes the construction of urban space which has become increasingly divided by class and race to make certain areas "safe" for the "rich" and tourism. The spatial separation of rich and poor is culturally symbolized by the Independence Day Festival which once involved all social groups, but more recently local elites have shaped it into an event which excludes the poor (who are largely of African descent). Many lower class youths have reclaimed the Festival's dance through what Streicker describes as a "budding, racially conscious, popular class cultural movement centered on music and dance called *champeta*." In addition to constructing an alternative identity through African music as opposed to Latin music, the loud sound systems at these dances broadcast the music past the walls of the colonial city. "This music speaks of – and is – a presence that the rich cannot avoid, a nearly dusk-to-dawn siege reminding the wealthy of the popular class' Otherness… and a way for disenfranchised groups to exercise control over space..." Through broadcasting their own music directly into the site of official culture the champetudos create a struggle over class privilege and identity through sound.

Conclusion

In this chapter I have shown how popular music can be a site of counter-hegemonic activity. For explanatory purposes I have deconstructed music activities and forms in an artificial way. Performance and commodification of music products are not clearly bounded and how musicians and audiences negotiate these spheres varies in every situation. There is no correct strategy here. In fact, resistance is necessarily a creative, imaginative process and arguments that purport to have "the one answer" are increasingly suspect. Instead, I argue that music and resistance are shaped in the moment of their coming into being, a musical/political praxis that is negotiated by social actors in particular spatial and temporal locations. As fixity itself is increasingly recognized as a necessary condition for the deployment of power, performative practices like music and dance suggest forms of resistance that produce experience in ever changing forms.

It is important to remember that music is a universal activity that emerged with "culture" as a defining characteristic of human communities. I do not raise this point to suggest some essentialized meaning or origin of music, but to generate further thought about deep cultural assumptions in the West that are prevalent across the political spectrum. In an era when music and the arts are being eliminated from public schools in the United States through specific discourses about the "productive" individual and an emphasis on education that facilitates employment, I argue that these actions have more to do with a particular kind of social reproduction than simply balancing budgets. As music is a common practice of subordinate groups and its practice is a form of social organization, it is an important site of management by dominant forces in society. Finally, I suggest that music draws its power from the fact that it is both ordinary and mystical. Music is something pleasurable that everyone can participate in and create their own bit of magic outside the loop of production and consumption. This is why it is so dangerous.

Acknowledgments

I would like to thank the following people for their encouragement and input on earlier drafts of this paper: Paula Ebron, Sylvia Yanagisako, Mary Louise Pratt, Don Moore, Harumi Befu, Bill Maurer, Joel Streicker, Mat Callahan.

Bibliography

Adorno, Theodor. (1990). On Popular Music. In *On Record: Rock, Pop, and The Written Word*. Simon Frith and Andrew Goodwin, eds. pp.301–314. New York: Pantheon.
Arguedas, José María. (1985). *Yawar Fiesta*. Austin: University of Texas Press.
Attali, Jacques. (1985). *Noise: The Political Economy of Music*. Minneapolis: University of Minnesota Press.
Bey, Hakim. (1991). *T.A.Z.: The Temporary Autonomous Zone, Ontological Anarchy, Poetic Terrorism*. Brooklyn: Autonomedia. (anti-copyright)
Breen, Marcus. (1992). "Desert Dreams, Media, and Interventions in Reality: Australian Robin Balliger Aboriginal Music." In *Rockin' The Boat: Mass Music and Mass Movements*. Reebee Garofalo, ed. pp. 149–170. Boston: South End Press.

Chow, Rey. (1993). "Listening Otherwise, Music Miniaturized: A Different Type of Question about Revolution." In *The Cultural Studies Reader*. Simon During, ed. pp. 382–402. London: Routledge.

Davis, Mike. (1990). *City of Quartz: Excavating the Future in Los Angeles*. New York: Vintage.

Fairley, Jan. (1989). "Analysing Performance: Narrative and Ideology in Concerts by Karaxú!" In *Popular Music*. Vol. 8/1. pp. 1–30.

Foucault, Michel. (1980). *Power/Knowledge: Selected Interviews and Other Writings 1972–1977*. Colin Gordon, ed. New York: Pantheon.

Foucault, Michel. (1992). Preface. In *Anti-Oedipus: Capitalism and Schizophrenia*. Gilles Deleuze and Felix Guattari. Minneapolis: University of Minnesota Press.

Frith, Simon. (1987). "The Industrialization of Popular Music." In *Popular Music and Communication*. James Lull, ed. pp. 53–77. Newbury Park: Sage.

Frith, Simon. (1989). Introduction. In *World Music, Politics and Social Change*. Simon Frith, ed. pp. 1–6. Manchester: Manchester University Press.

Gilroy, Paul. (1991). *"There Ain't No Black in the Union Jack": The Cultural Politics of Race and Nation*. Chicago: University of Chicago Press.

Gilroy, Paul. (1993). *Small Acts: Thoughts On The Politics of Black Cultures*. London: Serpent's Tail.

Grossberg, Lawrence. (1987). "Rock and Roll in Search of an Audience." In *Popular Music and Communication*. James Lull, ed. pp. 175–197. Newbury Park: Sage.

Hebdige, Dick. (1991), *Subculture: The Meaning of Style*. London: Routledge.

McClary, Susan and Robert Walser. (1990). "Start Making Sense! Musicology Wrestles with Rock." In *On Record: Rock, Pop, and The Written Word*. Simon Frith and Andrew Goodwin, eds. pp. 227–292. New York: Pantheon.

Madeira, Angelica. (1993). "Popular Music: Resistance or Irreverence?" In *Semiotica* 94–1/2. pp. 157–168.

Manuel, Peter. (1993). *Cassette Culture: Popular Music and Technology in North India*. Chicago: The University of Chicago Press.

Pring-Mill, Robert. (1987). "The Roles of Revolutionary Song – A Nicaraguan Assessment." In *Popular Music*. Vol. 6/2. pp. 179–187.

Shepherd, John. (1993). "Popular Music Studies: Challenges to Musicology." In *Stanford Humanities Review*. Vol. 3 No. 2. pp. 17–36.

Streicker, Joel. (1994). *"Spatial Reconfigurations, Imagined Geographies, and Social Conflicts in Cartagena, Columbia."* (Unpublished manuscript, Stanford University).

Vila, Pablo. (1992). "Rock Nacional and Dictatorship in Argentina." In *Rockin' The Boat: Mass Music and Mass Movements*. Reebee Garofalo, ed. pp. 209–230. Boston: South End Press.

Wallis, Roger and Krister Malm. (1984). *Big Sounds from Small Peoples: The Music Industry in Small Countries*. London: Constable.

Wallis, Roger and Krister Malm. (1992). *Media Policy and Music Activity*. London: Routledge.

Williams, Raymond. (1989). *The Politics of Modernism*. London: Verso.

37 Culture jamming

Ads under attack

Naomi Klein

Source: Naomi Klein (2000), *No Logo*, London: Flamingo, pp. 279–309

> Advertising men are indeed very unhappy these days, very nervous, with a kind of apocalyptic expectancy. Often when I have lunched with an agency friend, a half dozen worried copy writers and art directors have accompanied us. Invariably they want to know when the revolution is coming, and where will they get off if it does come.
>
> (Ex-adman James Rorty, *Our Master's Voice*, 1934)

It's Sunday morning on the edge of New York's Alphabet City and Jorge Rodriguez de Gerada is perched at the top of a high ladder, ripping the paper off a cigarette billboard. Moments before, the billboard at the corner of Houston and Attorney sported a fun-loving Newport couple jostling over a pretzel. Now it showcases the haunting face of a child, which Rodriguez de Gerada has painted in rust. To finish it off, he pastes up a few hand-torn strips of the old Newport ad, which form a fluorescent green frame around the child's face.

When it's done, the installation looks as the thirty-one-year-old artist had intended: as if years of cigarette, beer and car ads had been scraped away to reveal the rusted backing of the billboard. Burned into the metal is the real commodity of the advertising transaction. "After the ads are taken down," he says, "what is left is the impact on the children in the area, staring at these images."[1]

Unlike some of the growing legion of New York guerrilla artists, Rodriguez de Gerada refuses to slink around at night like a vandal, choosing instead to make his statements in broad daylight. For that matter, he doesn't much like the phrase "guerrilla art," preferring "citizen art" instead. He wants the dialogue he has been having with the city's billboards for more than ten years to be seen as a normal mode of discourse in a democratic society – not as some edgy vanguard act. While he paints and pastes, he wants kids to stop and watch – as they do on this sunny day, just as an old man offers to help support the ladder.

Rodriguez de Gerada even claims to have talked cops out of arresting him on three different occasions. "I say, 'Look, look what's around here, look what's happening. Let me explain to you why I do it.'" He tells the police officer about how poor neighborhoods have a disproportionately high number of billboards selling tobacco and hard liquor products. He talks about how these ads always feature models sailing, skiing or playing golf, making the addictive products they promote particularly glamorous to kids stuck in the ghetto, longing for escape. Unlike the advertisers who pitch and run, he wants his work to be part of a community discussion about the politics of public space.

Rodriguez de Gerada is widely recognized as one of the most skilled and creative founders of culture jamming, the practice of parodying advertisements and hijacking billboards in order to drastically alter their messages. Streets are public spaces, adbusters argue, and since most residents can't afford to counter corporate messages by purchasing their own ads, they should have the right to talk back to images they never asked to see. In recent years, this argument has been bolstered by advertising's mounting aggressiveness in the public domain – the ads discussed in "No Space," painted and projected onto sidewalks; reaching around entire buildings and buses; into schools; onto basketball courts and on the Internet. At the same time, as discussed in "No Choice," the proliferation of the quasi-public "town squares" of malls and superstores has created more and more spaces where commercial messages are the only ones permitted. Adding even greater urgency to their cause is the belief among many jammers that concentration of media ownership has successfully devalued the right to free speech by severing it from the right to be heard.

All at once, these forces are coalescing to create a climate of semiotic Robin Hoodism. A growing number of activists believe the time has come for the public to stop asking that some space be left unsponsored, and to begin seizing it back. Culture jamming baldly rejects the idea that marketing – because it buys its way into our public spaces – must be passively accepted as a one-way information flow.

The most sophisticated culture jams are not stand-alone ad parodies but interceptions – counter-messages that hack into a corporation's own method of communication to send a message starkly at odds with the one that was intended. The process forces the company to foot the bill for its own subversion, either literally, because the company is the one that paid for the billboard, or figuratively, because anytime people mess with a logo, they are tapping into the vast resources spent to make that logo meaningful. Kalle Lasn, editor of Vancouver-based *Adbusters* magazine, uses the martial art of jujitsu as a precise metaphor to explain the mechanics of the jam. "In one simple deft move you slap the giant on its back. We use the momentum of the enemy." It's an image borrowed from Saul Alinsky who, in his activist bible, *Rules for Radicals*, defines "mass political jujitsu" as "utilizing the power of one part of the power structure against another part...the superior strength of the Haves become their own undoing."[2] So, by rappelling off the side of a thirty-by-ninety-foot Levi's billboard (the largest in San Francisco) and pasting the face of serial killer Charles Manson over the image, a group of jammers attempts to leave a disruptive message about the labor practices employed to make Levi's jeans. In the statement it left on the scene, the Billboard Liberation Front said they chose Manson's face because the jeans were "Assembled by prisoners in China, sold to penal institutions in the Americas."

The term "culture jamming" was coined in 1984 by the San Francisco audio-collage band Negativland. "The skillfully reworked billboard...directs the public viewer to a consideration of the original corporate strategy," a band member states on the album *Jamcon '84*. The jujitsu metaphor isn't as apt for jammers who insist that they aren't inverting ad messages but are rather improving, editing, augmenting or unmasking them. "This is extreme truth in advertising," one billboard artist tells me.[3] A good jam, in other words, is an X-ray of the subconscious of a campaign, uncovering not an opposite meaning but the deeper truth hiding beneath the layers of advertising euphemisms. So, according to these principles, with a slight turn of the imagery knob, the now-retired Joe Camel turns into Joe Chemo, hooked up to an IV machine. That's what's in his future, isn't it? Or Joe is shown about fifteen years younger than his usual swinger self. Like Baby Smurf, the "Cancer Kid" is cute and cuddly and playing with building blocks instead of sports cars and pool cues. And why not? Before R. J. Reynolds reached a $206 billion settlement with forty-six states, the American government accused the tobacco company of using the cartoon camel to entice children to start smoking – why not go further, the culture jammers ask, and reach out to even younger would-be smokers? Apple computers' "Think Different" campaign of famous figures both living and dead has been the subject of numerous simple hacks: a photograph of Stalin appears with the altered slogan "Think Really Different"; the caption for the ad featuring the Dalai Lama is changed to "Think Disillusioned" and the rainbow Apple logo is morphed into a skull. My favorite truth-inadvertising campaign is a simple jam on Exxon that appeared just after the 1989 Valdez spill: "Shit Happens. New Exxon," two towering billboards announced to millions of San Francisco commuters.

Attempting to pinpoint the roots of culture jamming is next to impossible, largely because the practice is itself a cutting and pasting of graffiti, modern art, do-it-yourself punk philosophy and age-old pranksterism. And using billboards as an activist canvas isn't a new revolutionary tactic either. San Francisco's Billboard Liberation Front (responsible for the Exxon and Levi's jams) has been altering ads for twenty years, while Australia's Billboard Utilizing Graffitists Against Unhealthy Promotions (BUG-UP) reached its peak in 1983, causing an unprecedented $1 million worth of damage to tobacco billboards in and around Sydney.

It was Guy Debord and the Situationists, the muses and theorists of the theatrical student uprising of Paris, May 1968, who first articulated the power of a simple *détournement*, defined as an image, message or artifact lifted out of its context to create a new meaning. But though culture jammers borrow liberally from the avant-garde art movements of the past – from Dada and Surrealism to Conceptualism and Situationism – the canvas these art revolutionaries were attacking tended to be the art world and its passive culture of spectatorship, as well as the anti-pleasure ethos of mainstream capitalist society. For many French students in the late sixties, the enemy was the rigidity and conformity of the Company Man; the company itself proved markedly less engaging. So where Situationist Asger Jorn hurled paint at pastoral paintings bought at flea markets, today's culture jammers prefer to hack into corporate advertising and other avenues of corporate speech. And if the culture jammers' messages are more pointedly political than their predecessors', that may be because what were indeed subversive messages in the sixties – "Never Work," "It Is Forbidden to Forbid," "Take Your Desires for Reality" – now sound more like Sprite or Nike slogans: Just Feel It. And the "situations" or "happenings" staged by the political pranksters in 1968, though genuinely shocking and disruptive at the time, are the Absolut Vodka ad of 1998 – the one featuring purple-clad art school students storming bars and restaurants banging on bottles.

In 1993, Mark Dery wrote "Culture Jamming: Hacking, Slashing and Sniping in the Empire of Signs," a booklet published by the Open Magazine Pamphlet Series. For Dery, jamming incorporates such eclectic combinations of theater and, activism as the Guerrilla Girls, who highlighted the art world's exclusion of female artists by holding demonstrations outside the Whitney Museum in gorilla masks; Joey Skagg, who has pulled off countless successful media hoaxes; and Artfux's execution-in-effigy of arch-Republican Jesse Helms on Capitol Hill. For Dery, culture jamming is anything, essentially, that mixes art, media, parody and the outsider stance. But within these subcultures, there has always been a tension between the forces of the merry prankster and the hard-core revolutionary. Nagging questions re-emerge: are play and pleasure themselves revolutionary acts, as the Situationists might argue? Is screwing up the culture's information flows inherently subversive, as Skagg would hold? Or is the mix of art and politics just a matter of making sure, to paraphrase Emma Goldman, that somebody has hooked up a good sound system at the revolution?

Though culture jamming is an undercurrent that never dries up entirely, there is no doubt that for the last five years it has been in the midst of a revival, and one focused more on politics than on pranksterism. For a growing number of young activists, adbusting has presented itself as the perfect tool with which to register disapproval of the multinational corporations that have so aggressively stalked them as shoppers, and so unceremoniously dumped them as workers. Influenced by media theorists such as Noam Chomsky, Edward Herman, Mark Crispin Miller, Robert McChesney and Ben Bagdikian, all of whom have explored ideas about corporate control over information flows, the adbusters are writing theory on the streets, literally deconstructing corporate culture with a waterproof magic marker and a bucket of wheatpaste.

Jammers span a significant range of backgrounds, from purer-than-thou Marxist-anarchists who refuse interviews with "the corporate press" to those like Rodriguez de Gerada who work in the advertising industry by day (his paying job, ironically, is putting up commercial signs and superstore window displays) and long to use their skills to send messages they consider constructive. Besides a fair bit of animosity between these camps, the only ideology bridging the spectrum of culture jamming is the belief that free speech is meaningless if the commercial cacophony has risen to the point that no one can hear you. "I think everyone should have their own billboard, but they don't," says Jack Napier (a pseudonym) of the Billboard Liberation Front.[4]

On the more radical end of the spectrum, a network of "media collectives" has emerged, decentralized and anarchic, that combine adbusting with zinc publishing, pirate radio, activist video, Internet development and community activism. Chapters of the collective have popped up in Tallahassee, Boston, Seattle, Montreal and Winnipeg – often splintering off into other organizations. In London, where adbusting is called "subvertising," a new group has been formed, called the UK Subs after the seventies punk group of the same name. And in the past two years, the real-world jammers have been joined by a global network of on-line "hacktivists" who carry out their raids on the Internet, mostly by breaking into corporate Web sites and leaving their own messages behind.

More mainstream groups have also been getting in on the action. The U.S. Teamsters have taken quite a shine to the ad jam, using it to build up support for striking workers in several recent labor disputes. For instance, Miller Brewing found itself on the receiving end of a similar jam when it laid off workers at a St. Louis plant. The Teamsters purchased a billboard that parodied a then current Miller campaign; as *Business Week* reported, "Instead of two bottles of beer in a snowbank with the tagline 'Two Cold', the ad showed two frozen workers in a snowbank labeled 'Too Cold: Miller canned 88 St. Louis workers.'"[5] As organizer Ron Carver says, "When you're doing this, you're threatening multimillion-dollar ad campaigns."[6]

One high-profile culture jam arrived in the fall of 1997 when the New York antitobacco lobby purchased hundreds of rooftop taxi ads to hawk "Virginia Slime" and "Cancer Country" brand cigarettes. All over Manhattan, as yellow cabs got stuck in gridlock, the jammed ads jostled with the real ones.

[...]

Listening to the marketer within

In a *New Yorker* article entitled "The Big Sellout," author John Seabrook discusses the phenomenon of "the marketer within." He argues persuasively that an emerging generation of artists will not concern themselves with old ethical dilemmas like "selling out" since they are a walking sales pitch for themselves already, intuitively understanding how to produce prepackaged art, to be their own brand. "The artists of the next generation will make their art with an internal marketing barometer already in place. The auteur as marketer, the artist in a suit of his own: the ultimate in vertical integration."[7]

Seabrook is right in his observation that the rhythm of the pitch is hardwired into the synapses of many young artists, but he is mistaken in assuming that the built-in marketing barometer will only be used to seek fame and fortune in the culture industries. As Carly Stasko points out, many people who grew up sold are so attuned to the tempo of marketing that as soon as they read or hear a new slogan, they begin to flip it and play with it in their minds, as she herself does. For Stasko, it is the adbuster that is within, and every ad campaign is a riddle just waiting for the right jam. So the skill Seabrook identifies, which allows artists to write the press bumf for their own gallery openings and musicians to churn out metaphor-filled bios for their liner notes, is the same quality that makes for a deadly clever culture jammer. The culture jammer is the activist artist as *antimarketer*, using a childhood filled with Trix commercials, and an adolescence spent spotting the product placement on *Seinfeld*, to mess with a system that once saw itself as a specialized science. Jamie Batsy, a Toronto-area "hacktivist," puts it like this: "Advertisers and other opinion makers are now in a position where they are up against a generation of activists that were watching television before they could walk. This generation wants their brains back and mass media is their home turf."[8]

Culture jammers are drawn to the world of marketing like moths to a flame, and the high-gloss sheen on their work is achieved precisely because they still feel an affection – however deeply ambivalent – for media spectacle and the mechanics of persuasion. "I think a lot of people who are really interested in subverting advertising or studying advertising probably, at one time, wanted to be ad people themselves," says Carrie McLaren, editor of the New York zine *Stay Free!*[9] You can see it in her own ad busts, which are painstakingly seamless in their design and savage in their content. In one issue, a full-page anti-ad shows a beat-up kid face down on the concrete with no shoes on. In the corner of the frame is a hand making away with his Nike sneakers. "Just do it"; the slogan says.

Nowhere is the adbuster's ear for the pitch used to fuller effect than in the promotion of adbusting itself, a fact that might explain why culture jamming's truest believers often sound like an odd cross between used-car salesmen and tenured semiotics professors. Second only to Internet hucksters and rappers, adbusters are susceptible to a spiraling bravado and to a level of self-promotion that can be just plain silly. There is much fondness for claiming to be Marshall McLuhan's son, daughter, grandchild or bastard progeny. There is a strong tendency to exaggerate the power of wheatpaste and a damn good joke. And to overstate their own power: one culture-jamming manifesto, far instance, explains that "the billboard artist's goal is to throw a well aimed spanner into the media's gears, bringing the image factory to a shuddering halt."[10]

Adbusters has taken this hard-sell approach to such an extreme that it has raised hackles among rival culture jammers. Particularly galling to its critics is the magazine's line of anti-consumer products that they say has made the magazine less a culture-jamming clearing-house than a home-shopping network for adbusting accessories. Culture-jammer "tool boxes" are listed for sale: posters, videos, stickers and postcards; most ironically, it used to sell calendars and T-shirts to coincide with Buy Nothing Day, though better sense eventually prevailed. "What comes out is no real alternative to our culture of consumption," Carrie McLaren writes. "Just a different brand." Fellow Vancouver jammers Guerrilla Media (GM) take a more vicious shot at *Adbusters* in the GM inaugural newsletter. "We promise there are no GM calendars, key chains or coffee mugs in the offing. We are, however, still working on those T-shirts that some of you ordered – we're just looking for that perfect sweatshop to produce them."[11]

Marketing the antimarketers

The attacks are much the same as those lobbed at every punk band that signs a record deal and every zine that goes glossy: *Adbusters* has simply become too popular to have much cachet for the radicals who once dusted it off in their local secondhand bookstore like a precious stone. But beyond the standard-issue purism, the question of how best to "market" an antimarketing movement is a uniquely thorny dilemma. There is a sense among some adbusters that culture jamming, like punk itself, must remain something of a porcupine; that to defy its own inevitable commodification, it must keep its protective quills sharp. After the great Alternative and Girl Power™ cashins, the very process of naming a trend, or coining a catchphrase, is regarded by some with deep suspicion. "*Adbusters* jumped on it and were ready to claim this movement before it ever really existed," says McLaren, who complains bitterly in her own writing about the "USA Today/MTV-ization" of *Adbusters*. "It's become an advertisement for anti-advertising."[12]

There is another fear underlying this debate, one more confusing for its proponents than the prospect of culture jamming "selling out" to the dictates of marketing. What if, despite all the rhetorical flair its adherents can muster, culture jamming doesn't actually matter? What if there is no jujitsu, only semiotic shadowboxing? Kalle Lasn insists that his magazine has the power :to "jolt postmodern society out of its media trance" and that his uncommercials threaten to shake network television to its core. "The television mindscape has been homogenized over the last 30 to 40 years. It's a space that is very safe for commercial messages. So, if you suddenly introduce a note of cognitive dissonance with a spot that says 'Don't buy a car', or in the middle of a fashion show somebody suddenly says 'What about anorexia?' there's a powerful moment of truth."[13] But the real truth is that, as a culture, we seem to be capable of absorbing limitless amounts of cognitive dissonance on our TV sets. We culture jam manually every time we channel surf – catapulting from the desperate fundraising pleas of the Foster Parent Plan to infomercials for Buns of Steel; from Jerry Springer to Jerry Falwell; from New Country to Marilyn Manson. In these information-numb times, we are beyond being abruptly awakened by a startling image, a sharp juxtaposition or even a fabulously clever détournement.

Jaggi Singh is one activist who has become disillusioned with the jujitsu theory. "When you're jamming, you're sort of playing their game, and I think ultimately that playing field is stacked against us because they can saturate…we don't have the resources to do all those billboards, we don't have the resources to buy up all that time, and in a sense, it almost becomes pretty scientific – who can afford these feeds?"

Logo overload

To add further evidence that culture jamming is more drop in the bucket than spanner in the works, marketers are increasingly deciding to join in the fun. When Kalle Lasn says culture jamming has the feeling of "a bit of a fad," he's not exaggerating.[14] It turns out that culture jamming – with its combination of hip-hop attitude, punk anti-authoritarianism and a well of visual gimmicks – has great sales potential.

Yahoo! already has an official culture jamming site on the Internet, filed under "alternative." At Soho Down & Under on West Broadway in New York, Camden Market in London or any other high street where alterno gear is for sale, you can load up on logo-jammed T-shirts, stickers and badges. Recurring détournements – to use a word that seems suddenly misplaced – include Kraft changed to "Krap," Tide changed to "Jive," Ford changed to "Fucked" and Goodyear changed to "Goodbeer." It's not exactly trenchant social commentary, particularly since the jammed logos appear to be interchangeable with the corporate kitsch of unaltered Dubble Bubble and Tide T-shirts. In the rave scene, logo play is all the rage – in clothing, temporary tattoos, body paint and even ecstasy pills. Ecstasy dealers have taken to branding their tablets with famous logos: there is Big Mac E, Purple Nike Swirl E, X-Files E, and a mixture of uppers and downers called a "Happy Meal." Musician Jeff Renton explains the drug culture's appropriation of corporate logos as a revolt against invasive marketing. "I think it's a matter of: 'You come into our lives with your million-dollar advertising campaigns putting logos in places that make us feel uncomfortable, so we're going to take your logo back and use it in places that make you feel uncomfortable,'" he says.[15]

But after a while, what began as a way to talk back to the ads starts to feel more like evidence of our total colonization by them, and especially because the ad industry is proving that it is capable of cutting off the culture jammers at the pass. Examples of pre-jammed ads include a 1997 Nike campaign that used the slogan "I am not/A target market/I am an athlete" and Sprite's "Image Is Nothing" campaign, featuring a young black man saying that all his life he has been bombarded with media lies telling him that soft drinks will make him a better athlete or more attractive, until he realized that "image is nothing." Diesel jeans, however, has gone furthest in incorporating the political content of adbusting's anticorporate attacks. One of the most popular ways for artists and activists to highlight the inequalities of freemarket globalization is by juxtaposing First World icons with Third World scenes: Marlboro Country in the war-torn rubble of Beirut; an obviously malnourished Haitian girl wearing Mickey Mouse glasses; *Dynasty* playing on a TV set in an African hut; Indonesian students rioting in front of McDonald's arches. The power of these visual critiques of happy one-worldism is precisely what the Diesel clothing company's "Brand O" ad campaign attempts to co-opt. The campaign features ads within ads: a series of billboards flogging a fictional Brand O line of products in a nameless North Korean city. In one, a glamorous skinny blonde is pictured on the side of a bus that is overflowing with frail-looking workers. The ad is selling "Brand O Diet – There's no limit to how thin you can get." Another shows an Asian man huddled under a piece of cardboard. Above him towers a Ken and Barbie Brand O billboard.

Perhaps the point of no return came in 1997 when Mark Hosler of Negativland received a call from the ultra-hip ad agency Wieden & Kennedy asking if the band that coined the term "culture jamming" would do the soundtrack for a new Miller Genuine Draft commercial. The decision to turn down the request and the money was simple enough, but it still sent him spinning. "They utterly failed to grasp that our entire work is essentially in opposition to everything that they are connected to, and it made me really depressed because I had thought that our esthetic couldn't be absorbed into marketing," Hosler says.[16] Another rude awakening came when Hosler first saw Sprite's "Obey Your Thirst" campaign. "That commercial was a hair's breadth away from a song on our [*Dispepsi*] record. It was surreal. It's not just the fringe that's getting absorbed now – that's always happened. What's getting absorbed now is the idea that there's no opposition left, that any resistance is futile."[17]

I'm not so sure. Yes, some marketers have found a way to distill culture jamming into a particularly edgy kind of nonlinear advertising, and there is no doubt that Madison Avenue's embrace of the techniques of adbusting has succeeded in moving product off the superstore shelves. Since Diesel began its aggressively ironic "Reasons for Living" and "Brand O" campaigns in the U.S., sales have gone from $2 million to $23 million in four years,[18] and the Sprite "Image Is Nothing" campaign is credited with a 35 percent rise in sales in just three years:[19] That said, the success of these individual campaigns has done nothing to disarm the antimarketing rage that fueled adbusting in the first place. In fact, it may be having the opposite effect.

Notes

1 Personal interview.
2 Saul D. Alinsky, *Rules for Radicals: A Pragmatic Primer for Realistic Radicals* (Random House: New York, 1971), 152.
3 Personal interview. Many adbusters I interviewed chose to remain anonymous.
4 Personal interview.
5 Mary Kuntz, "Is Nothing Sacred," *Business Week*, 18 May 1998, 130–37.
6 Ibid.
7 John Seabrook, "The Big Sellout," *New Yorker*, 20 & 27 October 1997, 182–95.
8 Bob Paquin, "E-Guerrillas in the Mist," *Ottawa Citizen*, 26 October 1998.
9 Personal interview.
10 Manifesto produced by Earth First! in Brighton, England.
11 *Guerrilla Shots* 1, no. 1.
12 Carrie McLaren, "Advertising the Uncommercial," *Escandola*, published by Matador Records, November 1995.
13 Jim Boothroyd, "ABC Opens the Door," *Adbusters*, Winter 1998, 53–54.
14 Personal interview.
15 Mitchel Raphael, "Corporate Perversion," *Toronto Star*, 7 February 1998, M1.
16 Doug Saunders, "One Person's Audio Debris Is Another's Musical Treasure," *Globe and Mail*, 25 September 1997, C5.
17 Barnaby Marshall, "Negativland: Mark Hosler on the Ad Assault," *Shift* on-line, 22.
18 *Time*, 17 November 1997.
19 *Advertising Age*, 18 November 1996.

Index

Lightning Source UK Ltd.
Milton Keynes UK
UKOW040656130112

185284UK00007B/19/P